Microeconomics for Managers

Microeconomics for Managers

Second Edition

David M. Kreps

Princeton University Press

Princeton and Oxford

Copyright © 2019 by Princeton University Press

Published by Princeton University Press
41 William Street, Princeton, New Jersey 08540
6 Oxford Street, Woodstock, Oxfordshire OX20 1TR

press.princeton.edu

LCCN: 2018957922
ISBN 978-0-691-18269-8

British Library Cataloging-in-Publication Data is available

Editorial: Joe Jackson and Samantha Nader
Production Editorial: Nathan Carr
Production: Erin Suydam
Publicity: Taylor Lord and Julia Hall
Copyeditor: Emily Shelton

This book has been composed in Plain TeX

The publisher would like to acknowledge the author of this volume for providing the camera-ready copy from which this book was printed.

Printed on acid-free paper. ∞

Printed in the United States of America

1 3 5 7 9 10 8 6 4 2

Contents

Preface to the Second Edition

Microeconomics for Managers is a textbook for an introductory microeconomics course, for MBA students. In U.S. terminology, this is an intermediate-level text, at the more sophisticated end of the spectrum of such books. But in terms of content, the book is distinguished from standard intermediate-micro texts in ways that increase its appeal to students of management:

- I emphasize applications of microeconomics to problems confronting managers and, in particular, general managers.

- In a number of places, I discuss the relationship between microeconomics and the functional fields of management: financial and managerial accounting, finance, marketing, operations, human resource management, and strategic management.

- I shift the topical emphasis away from classical topics such as the theory of the consumer and perfect competition (although they are not abandoned) and toward topics such as uncertainty, information, reciprocity, credibility, reputation, and transaction costs.

- Topics are covered in an order that is very atypical: The book begins with the economics of relationships, then discusses pricing decisions and constrained optimization, and only then moves to what economists will recognize as perfect competition and the picture of supply equals demand. (It ends with uncertainty, moral hazard and incentives, and adverse selection and signaling.) The purpose of this strange order is to begin and end with topics that more naturally resonate with MBA students, with the "painful" bits coming in the middle.

One of the important lessons of microeconomics is that the world is filled with trade-offs. In particular, a product or strategy well designed for one market or context is very likely to be ill suited for others. So let me be clear: this book is designed with MBA students in mind. In particular, it was crafted from a required course taught in the MBA program at Stanford University's Graduate School of Business. This specific group of students is fairly old (median age around 27) and experienced: Most students have three or more years of significant post-BA experience in the real world. The group is on average highly skilled analytically but with tremendous variation, ranging from PhDs in mathematical and scientific fields to those whose last organized math class was in high school. The students exhibit significant intellectual curiosity taken individually and in small groups, but in the larger "sections" of around 65 students in which the course is taught, the group ethic is that ideas that do not pay back in the first 5 months on the job are suspect and those that might not pay back in the first 5 years are a complete waste of time. Stanford MBA students tend to learn inductively and by analogy much more than deductively and by theory: The standard response after the course to the question *What do you know about implicit collusion with noisy observables?* is *Huh?* But if you ask them *What does the GE-Westinghouse case* (the classic Harvard Business School case on the topic) *have to say about this or that industry?* you often get a sophisticated and nuanced answer.

To match this audience, this book is strongly oriented toward people interested in and somewhat knowledgeable about general management. I assume a background knowledge about management and the functional tasks facing management. I use a modicum of calculus and some basic probability, but not a lot, and I generally take a lot of care to explain what the math means. I spend a lot of time justifying what I am doing, trying to convince the reader that the on-the-job payback is going to be relatively short, especially if the reader is willing to settle for a payback that takes the form of insight. While I present abstract ideas, I usually work in terms of examples first, and I believe the only place the word *theorem* appears is in a very loose and imprecise rendering of the folk theorem.

Because of the high average analytical skills of Stanford MBAs, I may have overreached for some MBA programs, but I hope this is not so: Owing to the enormous dispersion of those skills among the students at Stanford, I am quite deliberate throughout. Certainly, analytically adept Stanford students complain about the slow pace of the book, once we get (in Part II) to the taking of derivatives.

I use calculus, because calculus makes things a lot easier, and the level of calculus required is really quite minimal. An appendix (found not in the text itself but in the *Online Supplement*) reviews the little calculus that is needed.

The other mathematics requirements of the book are facility with basic graphs and, in particular, linear functions; the ability to solve simultaneous linear equations, especially two equations in two unknowns; moderate facility with spreadsheets, including the use of an optimizer add-in such as Solver for Microsoft Excel; and, near the end of the book, an understanding of basic probability theory. In a couple of places, I talk as if the student knows basic classical statistics to the level of one-equation, multiple (OLS) regression.

Especially in the asides that talk about the connections between microeconomics and the functions of management, I assume a general business background that students fresh from college may lack. For instance, I assume readers know a bit about income statements and balance sheets; that asset depreciation is a charge against current income and bad debts are generally written off quickly. I also assume that readers know about discounting. As for non-MBA audiences:

- Readers with a scientific or engineering background will find the math easy to swallow. The emphasis on micro applied to management is probably right for most scientists or engineers interested in economics, especially in professional MS programs at engineering schools.

- Undergraduates headed for professional schools may like the selection of topics, if they have the business background needed to cope. But the book has either light or nonexistent coverage of topics that are important for undergraduates headed for graduate study in economics, such as public-sector economics and the theory of the consumer (nothing on income and substitution effects; Engel curves; or luxury, inferior, and Giffen goods).

Accompanying this textbook is an *Online Supplement*, which provides solutions to the problems given in the book, a few longer caselike exercises, sets of review problems, and some supplementary material in a series of appendices. The URL for the *Online Supplement* is https://micro4managers.stanford.edu.

Microeconomics? For Managers?

Let me say a few words to students who are reading this preface, wondering what the subject is about and why they, as aspiring (or practicing) managers, should be interested.

A general and abstract definition of economics was offered by Paul A. Samuelson, one of the leading economists of the 20th century, in a textbook that revolutionized teaching of the subject:

> Economics is the study of how men and society *choose*, with or without the use of money, to employ *scarce* productive resources, which could have alternative uses, to produce various commodities over time and distribute them for consumption, now and in the future, among various people and groups in society. [1]

Within this general definition, *micro*economics is concerned with the behavior of individual consumers and individual firms, acting and interacting in markets and in industry groups. *Macro*economics, in contrast, is concerned with the workings of national and international economies.

Since Samuelson provided that general description, economics has evolved. His definition is still a good one, but nowadays economists increasingly emphasize "without money," nonmarket contexts, and decisions individuals make for reasons other than consumption. In other words, the domain of economics is expanding.

Samuelson's definition is directed at the contextual subject matter of economics. But economics is equally a way of thinking; it can be characterized

---

[1] Emphasis in the original, from P. A. Samuelson, *Economics: An Introductory Analysis*, 7th edition (New York: McGraw-Hill, 1955).

by answering the question, *How* does economics address its subject matter? A different definition that stresses means more than context is:

> Economics is concerned with modeling the behavior of individuals and organizations—for-profit firms, nonprofit organizations, government entities, and so on—in market and nonmarket settings. Its models almost always assume that behavior is *purposeful*—directed at some clear goal—and it usually studies how diverse behaviors that have conflicting objectives are brought into *equilibrium* by market and nonmarket institutions. This study is both *descriptive* (describing what happens) and *evaluative* (measuring what happens against some notion of an ideal outcome). After describing and evaluating particular institutions, economists often move on to policy *prescription*, considering how some objective might better be achieved if the institutions were modified.

That's quite a mouthful, so let's take it a piece at a time.

Purposeful Behavior

Economic models begin with entities that act purposefully. Purposeful behavior is modeled as striving to maximize some numerical measure of well-being, subject to constraints imposed by institutions and the actions of others. Among these entities can be individual consumers, firms, governments, political parties, and families, depending on the specific model and the purpose for which it is created.

Equilibrium

In most circumstances, the objectives of the different entities or actors come into conflict: Resources are scarce and more for one person means less for others. Economists model the balance that is achieved with the general notion of an *equilibrium*. Equilibria come in many different shapes and forms, which will be discussed later. For now you should understand that there is a lot more to equilibrium than "supply equals demand."

Equilibria take place within a model of an institutional setting. Most people associate economics with *market* institutions, but as already noted, economics is increasingly concerned with other institutional settings. Prominent in the list of other settings is the firm. This means that when economists model firms, the individual firm is sometimes a purposeful entity, while in other models it is the institutional setting within which diverse entities interact and come into equilibrium. Since this book is intended for managers, this duality is a major theme of the book.

Evaluation and Improvement of Outcomes

Once economists identify what they think will happen in a particular context, they often examine how good or bad the outcome is and what might be done to make things better. Policy instruments they consider range from taxes and subsidies to administered prices to changing features of the institutional setting, including the provision of information.

We do relatively little of this in this book. However, managers face the pressure of public opinion and government intervention, so they, and you, should know how policy questions of this sort are addressed. For this reason, we spend time contrasting the concepts of *equity*, about which economists rarely have much to say that is useful; and *efficiency*, which economists discuss incessantly.

Please note that policy debates rarely are resolved on purely economic grounds; the forces that affect managers in this realm are more often and more powerfully political than economic. To do justice to this topic in a managerially relevant way would take another book, one that addresses political forces as well as economic arguments. So I leave this to others.[2]

Models and Analysis

Go back to the second description of economics, which began, "Economics is concerned with *modeling* the behavior of individuals and organizations—firms, nonprofit organizations, and so on—in market and nonmarket settings. Its *models* almost always assume . . ." The words *modeling* and *model* are italicized to make the point that economists work largely with models.

A dictionary definition of *model* is "a hypothetical or stylized representation of something." In economics, models can represent how people or institutions act. For instance, *Firms maximize profits from a given set of feasible production plans* is a model. *The price of a good will rest at a point where supply equals demand* is another. In all cases, models in economics are *analytical* and *simplified* depictions of reality.

The need for simplification is obvious. Models are built to help us understand very complex realities by focusing attention on what is important, so we can understand the essence or gist of the phenomenon being modeled. A model as complex as the reality it depicts is useless. Of course, intuiting which features are important and should therefore be built into the model takes considerable skill, which is crucial in applications: A model focused on unimportant features can be badly misleading.

Models in economics are invariably analytical. A dictionary definition is this: A model is *analytical* if it takes a whole and examines it by considering the pieces separately and then reassembles the pieces.

Suppose, for instance, you run a large chemical facility, say, an oil refinery.

---

[2] If you are interested in such a book, I recommend David Baron, *Business and Its Environment*, 4th edition (Englewood Cliffs, NJ: Prentice-Hall, 2003).

You have on hand various raw materials, with shipments due on various days and with some ability to buy others. You can manufacture various products, some to fill commitments but others to sell on the spot market. You face various constraints on processes and on storage capacity. The question is, How much of the various products should you make? Suppose your objective is to maximize the facility's contributions to profit made from products sold on the spot market, subject to meeting long-run constraints.

This sort of problem can be very difficult to solve, because of the complex interrelationships among the variables. But often it can be modeled fairly accurately as a linear programming problem, a mathematical model that looks separately at pieces like process constraints, raw material availability, and so forth. If modeled in this fashion, the problem can be easily solved on the computer to find the profit-maximizing plan. Moreover, it is a model that, once built, can be used to test the sensitivity of the "answer" to various assumptions; for example, what will happen if the tanker currently at sea is 36 hours late? What will happen if the spot-market price of aviation fuel falls by 5%? Because this type of model is often a very good approximation to reality, and sensitivity analysis permits the model maker to identify crucial variables so that they can be subjected to intense scrutiny, the numbers that emerge can be and are taken very seriously.

Economics also uses models so highly simplified and stylized that the numbers that emerge are not taken at all seriously. Instead, the point of the model is to sharpen intuition qualitatively, to learn "what is important and why." This book is filled with this sort of model, so it is best to wait for a detailed example. But to give you a bit of a preview: In Chapter 3, we look at how large firms that compete can keep from competing so viciously that the competition drains away their profits. To understand the basics of this, we'll use a model of two individuals who play a simple game, the Prisoners' Dilemma, repeatedly. The model is a ridiculously simplified model of industrial competition. But the insights gained from the model go a very long way in understanding when and how restrained competition can be achieved.

What Sort of Insight?

You study microeconomics to gain insight into real-world phenomena. Some of the phenomena are "functional" in character: Microeconomic concepts and ideas are the bedrock on which most of finance, a large part of accounting, about half of marketing and strategic management, and at least a substantial fraction of operations and human resource management are constructed.

But, to pitch this a different way, here are a few "mysteries" that, after finishing this book, you will understand.

- Between 1973 and 1987, General Motors sold pickup trucks with gas tanks mounted outside the main structural firm of the truck. It was alleged that this design presented a fire hazard, and GM faced a number of class action suits by owners of the trucks, seeking compensation. To settle these suits, GM proposed to provide the owners of these trucks a coupon that would be worth $1000 off the price of a new GM light truck if used by the party to whom the coupon was issued (or members of their immediate family), and $500 off if the coupon was transferred to any third party. GM would issue 4.7 million of these coupons and, in press releases, stressed that this offer was costly—4.7 million times $500 is $2.35 billion—as well as generous, since these trucks had values in the range of $1500 to $8000. But the judge to whom this settlement was proposed rejected it on grounds that, despite the "generosity" of the offer, it would produce virtually no compensation for most (over 80%) of the old truck owners and would cost GM on the order of $200 million, not $2 billion. The judge was entirely correct. (This story reappears in Chapter 13.)

- In 1991, it was cheaper to fly first class from San Francisco to Tokyo to London and back to San Francisco than to fly business class from San Francisco to Tokyo and back. (See Chapter 8 for the explanation.)

- For many years, the Japanese government has resisted the free importation of rice into Japan from major rice producers, such as Thailand. The usual explanation is interest-group politics in Japan; rice farmers are an important and powerful political constituency. But it is worth noting that the impact of these restrictions probably means much *higher* profits for Thai rice producers as a class than they would have if free importation were allowed. In similar fashion, when Japanese car manufacturers entered into a program of voluntary export restraints into the United States, the net short-run result was a massive transfer of wealth from American consumers to Japanese car manufacturers, although in the longer-run, these restraints brought a large number of excellent blue-collar jobs to Americans living in southern states. (See Chapter 16.)

- When Xerox pioneered the technology for plain-paper copying, to maximize the profits they would earn, they leased their copiers to high-value users (such as law firms) rather than selling the copiers. (See Chapter 4.)

If understanding these stories is of interest to you—and if you plan a career in management, they should be of interest—learning microeconomics will give you the tools you need.

What Does It Take to Learn Microeconomics?

How can you learn microeconomics efficaciously? What will it take from you?

Consider as an analogy learning how to play tennis. Assume that your objective in learning to play tennis is not simply recreational; you hope to find yourself one day at Centre Court, Wimbledon. You certainly don't begin to learn the game at Wimbledon; you don't even begin in a local tournament. Instead, you might begin by reading some material that explains the rules of the game, basic tactics, and the mechanics of the different sorts of strokes. Then you hit the courts with an instructor, who begins teaching you the basic strokes. You might hit 50 backhands in succession and then 50 forehands. At some point, you begin to rally with your instructor who, if she is a good instructor, will hit to your backhand for a while, then to your forehand, and so forth. Slowly, the rallies will become more and more realistic. You begin to play some points and then games. Meanwhile, you begin playing others recreationally, and at some point, you start entering tournaments, with Wimbledon looming off in the distance.

Of course, it isn't so linear or cut and dried as this. After your first tournament, it may be back to the practice courts to rework your backhand. The point is that, between your first purchase of a racket and your confident stride onto Wimbledon Centre Court, you pass through a number of steps, increasing in complexity and similarity, to what you do when, eventually, you play for pay.

While the analogy is strained, learning to apply economics is similar. You begin with the basic concepts. Once you have the basics down, you can move to more complex problems and cases. Eventually, you apply what you learned in the real world, recognizing that even tennis pros sometimes return to the practice court and their teachers, going back to basics from time to time.

The basic concepts are often best learned by studying and analyzing ultra-simple models. To understand why airlines price tickets the way they do, we'll start with a model of a bakery on the California coast that wants to discriminate between locals and tourists, charging the tourists a higher price. In the model, the bakery will know how much it can sell at every price to each of the two groups, and it (that is, you) will find the "optimal" pricing scheme by taking the appropriate derivatives and setting them equal to zero. Students complain that, in the real world, no one—certainly not airlines—do it this way. And that's right. But the point of the bakery example is not that "this is how it is done in the real world." The point is for you to see in a stark setting what are the basic principles of price discrimination. Once you understand those basic principles, you can begin to appreciate why airlines do what they do, even if it will take more study to learn how they do it.

This book is largely about the basics. It shows you how to solve some very simple models and then asks you to solve some more. This is like a tennis instructor showing you how to hit a backhand in ideal conditions and then having you hit fifty or so backhands in a row, in as close to ideal conditions as the instructor can create. On the tennis court, you complement this type of training by playing games. To learn to use microeconomics, you should complement what this book can provide you by applying these concepts in situations closer to the real world, which ideally means a mixture of case-study analysis and, because cases too often come with the key questions and key information teed up for you, some out-of-the-classroom, into-the-field study.

Acknowledgements

My biggest debt of thanks is to the generations of Stanford GSB students who have taken this course from me. They contributed a lot to my understanding of economics and, even more, of how to teach them economics and convince them that this stuff is useful. My experiences with participants in the Stanford Executive Program leave me in their debt as well.

This book has been created from class notes that I've accumulated over many years of teaching microeconomics (and, before that, decision analysis) at Stanford. I had a succession of teaching assistants who have helped proofread these notes (and provided more general, valuable comments); I wish to acknowledge Dana Heller in this role, in particular.

I taught this course with a number of colleagues, many of whom have been gracious enough to use my notes and provide feedback. Two colleagues, Jeremy Bulow and Peter Reiss, have been particularly patient when I was obtuse and generous with ideas and specific materials. In particular, Bulow provided the wonderful GM truck coupon problem that serves as the lietmotif for the first half of the book, and Reiss, the Porsche story that appears in Chapter 6. Five others, Yossi Feinberg, Faruk Gul, Sven Rady, Andy Skrzypacz, and Dimitri Vayanos, also deserve specific mention for comments. While Eddie Lazear has his own way of teaching micro, very different from mine, I benefited from teaching with him. Jim Baron, with whom I taught and then wrote a book about human resource management, taught me a lot of economics, even though he thinks it is sociology and social psychology. And I received more specific assistance from David Baron, David Brady, Don Brown, Rick Lambert, John Roberts, Garth Saloner, Andrea Shepard, Itamar Simonson, and Mark Wolfson; I'm grateful to them all.

Jack Repcheck was the acquisition editor for the first edition of the book (at W. W. Norton). He was both champion and critic, as warranted by circumstances. The book is much better than it would otherwise have been because of his efforts. Jack's too-early passing is a loss to the literature of economics generally and to me specifically.

W. W. Norton decided not to proceed with a second edition, but were very kind in allowing the rights to revert to me. Princeton University Press then stepped forward to produce this second edition: I am grateful to Nathan Carr, Seth Ditchik, Peter Dougherty, Joe Jackson, and Emily Shelton, for their help in creating this book.

Figure 13.2 (page 299) is adapted from Jensen, Robert, "The Digital Provide: Information (Technology), Market Performance, and Welfare in the South Indian Fisheries Sector," *The Quarterly Journal of Economics*, Volume 122, Issue 3, 1

August 2007, pages 879–924, with permission from Copyright Clearance Center for Oxford University Press.

The economics in this book is neither original nor especially deep. But I hope it is pedagogically innovative and sound. If it is, this is due in large part to an extraordinary group of teachers who taught me both subject matter and, perhaps more important for current purposes, different ways to teach. I thought of dedicating this book to them as a group, but the list became too long, so I compromise as follows: The key, I believe, to first-rate management education is to combine rigorous disciplinary thought with a range of "applications," from models to real-world applications, that both motivate the student and show how the disciplinary thought can be used. Many of my senior colleagues at the GSB taught me to do this, but four had a particularly strong influence on my development as a teacher: Joel S. Demski, Charles A. Holloway, Charles T. Horngren, and Robert K. Jaedecke.

Part I
The Economics of Relationships

1. The Economics of Relationships (and Porter's Five Forces)

This first part of this book concerns the economics of relationships. In this chapter, we explain what this means and motivate what is to come by asking the question, What makes some industries more profitable than others?

Which industries are more profitable, and which are less? And why?

While there is no obvious measure of industry profitability, it is pretty clear that firms in some lines of business "do better" on average than do firms in other industries. For instance, Cynthia Montgomery[1] measures the average *return on equity* for firms in different industries over the period 1990 to 2010, finding the tobacco industry in first place with an ROE of over 30%, while pharmaceuticals averaged nearly 20%, automobile-industry firms averaged around 10%, and airlines averaged −9% or so. Michael Porter[2] provides average return on invested capital (earnings before interest and taxes divided by invested capital less excess cash) for the period 1992 to 2006, and while he doesn't supply numbers for the tobacco industry or the automobile industry, he has airlines at 5.9% and pharmaceuticals at 31.7%. (Mobile Homes recorded 15.0% and Tires, 19.5%.)

One can certainly argue with the specific measures these analyses employ.[3] But it can't be disputed that some industries are more profitable—whatever that vague term means—averaging over the firms in the industry, than others. *Why?*

Porter, in the classic business strategy textbook *Competitive Strategy*,[4] provides a framework for trying to answer this question, called the *Five Forces*. This framework takes the form of a checklist: *Here are the (five) categories of things to investigate concerning a specific industry, to understand how profitable are the firms in that industry.* The five categories, or forces, and the basic logic behind including them on this checklist, are:

---

[1] In Cynthia Montgomery, *The Strategist*, (New York: HarperCollins, 2012)

[2] In "The Five Competitive Forces that Shape Strategy," *Harvard Business Review*, January 2008, 78–93.

[3] In particular, if, say, the return on equity for firms in the tobacco industry is three times the ROE for firms in the automobile industry, why doesn't the market price of equity in the tobacco industry increase relative to the price of equity in automobiles? Readers who have studied finance can offer a variety of explanations, such as that future prospects for earnings versus current earnings are higher in automobiles than in tobacco; the price of equity concerns future prospects, which may not be perfectly correlated with current earnings. Note: this is a question about using the E part of ROE as a measure of profitability and not about the basic assertion that some industries are "more profitable" on average than others.

[4] Michael Porter, *Competitive Strategy*, (New York: Free Press, 1980)

- *Barriers to entry.* If firms within an industry are relatively profitable, the industry will attract new entrants, to the extent that there are no barriers in the way of those entrants. And those new entrants will tend to compete away the relatively good profits that drew their attention. So, high barriers to entry tend to go along with supernormal profitability. (And, for declining industries, *barriers to exit* will mean subnormal profits, insofar as firms in the industry find it hard to get out.)

- *Substitute and complementary products.* Firms inside an industry are more profitable the higher the prices they can charge their customers. Insofar as there are substitutes for what the firms are selling, they are limited in how high they can raise their prices. Hence, an industry whose products have a lot of good substitutes is likely to be less profitable on average than one whose products have few, bad, or no substitutes. On the other side, demand for an industry's products or services is higher—and they can charge higher prices, hence be more profitable—the more available and cheaper are goods that are complementary to what they sell. (Automobile manufacturers are more profitable, for instance, when the price of fuel is lower.)

- *Supplier power.* Suppose firms in an industry are making supernormal profits. Suppliers to the industry, *if they can,* will suck those profits upstream, lowering those profits. The key here is the italicized *if they can*: It is a matter of the relative bargaining strength of the suppliers to the industry vis-à-vis firms in the industry. If there are lots of potential suppliers who compete among themselves, firms in the industry needn't worry much about having their profits sucked upstream. If a critical input to the industry is supplied by a single and powerful supplier, firms in the industry must worry, and perhaps even resign themselves to not being hugely profitable.

- *Customer power.* The category of *substitutes* captures one aspect of the relationship between firms in the industry and their customers: Can customers find good alternatives to what the firms in the industry are selling? But even if there are no good substitutes, customers may be able to bargain for low prices. Suppose, for instance, that a large share of the retail market in a particular good is held by Walmart. Firms that manufacture this good probably don't get very high margins on what they sell to Walmart for resale.

- *Rivalry.* The fifth and final of Porter's forces is rivalry: How hard do firms within the industry compete with one another? If competition among firms in the industry is fierce, with price cutting and price wars the norm, profits will be relatively low. If firms in the industry compete in restrained fashion, profits are more likely to be relatively high.

Those are Porter's Five Forces.[5] We might consider adding a sixth to his list, namely the force of the legal, political, and social environments within which the industry operates. Legal forces certainly affect what firms can and cannot do—think of the impact of antitrust laws, or regulatory forces—and, perhaps more subtly, the political and social environments can be important as well. Some aspects of the legal, social, political, and social environments can be incorporated into Porter's original list of five. For instance, laws against explicit bargains between rivals can and should be considered under rivalry. One important factor of production in most industries is labor, and laws regarding the ability of employees to organize (form a union) and general societal norms about how unions, where they exist, interact with management, should certainly be part of your analysis of supplier power.

But some aspects of the legal, political, and social environments don't fit so neatly into one of Porter's five categories. Can firms within the industry rely on their lobbying power to gain favorable treatment by the government? Do social concerns about the industry's products (think, tobacco; power generation using fossil fuels; lumber and paper products) affect the taxes they face or just the hostility their products arouse in the general populace? Are firms affected, for good or for ill, by temporal shifts in social mores? When and if you conduct a Porter's Five Forces analysis of an industry, it is a good idea to make a special effort to think about these sorts of things, to be sure you don't miss important factors influencing the industry's firms.

1.1. The Economics of Relationships

In the world of Strategic Management, Porter's Five Forces is one of the pillars of analysis. Different strategy textbooks give variations on this specific theme, but in some form or another, the strategic analysis of an industry often starts with a filling-out of the specific details of these "forces."

But while it is one thing to say, "Think about rivalry in the industry," or "Gauge the relative bargaining positions of firms in the industry and their suppliers/customers," it is another thing to know *how* to do this. And while Porter provides some tendencies in how these factors affect profitability—for instance, weaker suppliers tend to enhance profitability—these are only tendencies. When we have a better, more nuanced understanding of how suppliers are connected to the industry in question, we might learn—in particular cases, we *will* learn—that stronger suppliers can sometimes be better for firms in the industry.

Ultimately, a lot of this comes down to the *relationships* the firms within the industry have with one another and with their various suppliers and customers:

---

[5] A more detailed description of the Five Forces can be found in the *Online Supplement*, which is available online at https//micro4managers.stanford.edu.

- This is perhaps most obvious when it comes to the relationships between firms and their customers, and between firms and their suppliers. One category of supplier, in particular, deserves emphasis: suppliers of labor inputs or, in other words, the employees of the firm. How a firm deals with its employees is all about relationships.

- And the importance of relationships to rivalry is obvious.

- Perhaps less obviously, relationships are important to entry barriers: A potential entrant to an industry must evaluate many things when contemplating entry, such as: How much of the market can I expect to capture?; how high will my fixed costs be—can I quickly gain enough share to achieve profitability?; do incumbent firms have a cost advantage, based on their experience and technological know-how? But other questions are: What is the relationship between firms already in the industry and suppliers of critical inputs to production? Do incumbent firms have critical suppliers locked up? What is the relationship between incumbent firms and customers? Will I be able to wean away enough customers to make this worth my while? If the good is retailed by others, will I be able to convince retailers to give my product shelf space? What are the relationships between the industry—and firms within the industry—and important legal and political entities that set the "rules" that the firms must follow? And, perhaps most important, what will be the reaction of incumbent firms if and when I enter? Will they "welcome me to the club" or "go to the mattresses" in an attempt to blockade my entry? In other words, what (can I anticipate) will be *my* relationship with them, if I enter?

- And the relationships between firms in the industry and legal, legislative, and administrative organs of government, as well as with the industry's relationships with the general society within which it is embedded, are all important.

Therefore, to carry out an intelligent analysis of the Five Forces, you need to understand the nature of economic relationships. But an understanding of the economic nature of relationships goes beyond industry analysis. For an individual firm (or other organization), the level of success it can achieve, both in absolute terms and relative to other firms with which it competes, is often hugely influenced by how well it manages its many relationships with other parties. So we begin this book with the economics of relationships.

1.2. Economics or Psychology?

Are relationships governed by economic forces or by psychology? The short answer is, Yes. Both economic and psychological considerations come into play. This fact has substantial consequences for what we do in this first part of the book. Most readers, I expect, have had previous exposure to textbook economics. Most readers will think of economics as being all about the famous picture and slogan: *Equilibrium price is where supply equals demand*. We get to this picture and slogan in Part IV, but if you remember that stuff and, even more, if you think that supply equals demand is what economics is about, stop thinking that way, at least for now. Supply equals demand is largely about situations in which relationships play no part: It is about the economics of large numbers of otherwise anonymous buyers and sellers. That's useful stuff in some contexts, but not when you are trying to understand the economic relationships that connect, say, United Airlines and Delta Airlines in their competition for passengers between Los Angeles and New York City, or between Toyota Motors and its network of suppliers, or between you and your next employer. In relationships, partners to the relationships are anything but anonymous. They have specific identities, known as such to one another. And how the parties act and react are influenced both by the economics of the situation and by its psychology.

In consequence, if you recall (fondly or not) the sharpness and precision of supply equals demand, where one price and only one price would clear markets, you must now be ready for a lot less sharpness and precision. And with that warning, let's get started by learning a language for modeling and analyzing relationships.

2. Noncooperative Game Theory

A key to understanding multiparty interactions, including all forms of relationships—whether you are an outsider trying to understand the interaction or you are a participant in it—is to understand the interaction from the perspective of each of the parties simultaneously. For an outside analyst, this is relatively natural. But for protagonists, understanding too often ends at "how things look to me," which can lead to a poor understanding of the situation. To model, analyze, and discuss multiparty interactions, economists use the language and concepts of *noncooperative game theory*. This chapter provides a primer on the subject:

- We discuss two ways to model multiparty interactions, strategic-form and extensive-form games.
- We show how to analyze these models using dominance analysis and Nash-equilibrium analysis.

Many of the examples used in this chapter are chosen to be simple—to expose basic concepts clearly—not to be managerially relevant. After we nail down basic ideas in this chapter, managerially relevant applications to the subject of relationships follow in Chapters 3, 4, and 5.

To keep things simple, we avoid formal definitions and "rules" as much as possible, relying instead on examples to illustrate how this theory works. If, after you finish this chapter, you want a more detailed and systematic treatment of the basics, you should consult one of the references given at the end of the chapter.

Most of what we discuss in this chapter can be illustrated by a simple story. Two friends, Sam (she) and Jan (he), must decide independently where to spend a Tuesday evening after work. The three possible choices are a bar named Old Pros, an art museum, and a coffee house named Cafeen. Sam and Jan have preferences over these three spots, but they also have a general desire to be together, rather than apart. More specifically,

- Sam's first choice is to be with Jan at Old Pros, second is to be with Jan at the art museum, third is to be alone at Old Pros, fourth is to be with Jan at Cafeen, fifth is to be at the art museum alone, and last is alone at Cafeen.

- Jan's ranking is, from best to worst, be with Sam at Cafeen, be with Sam at the art museum, be with Sam at Old Pros, be alone at the art museum, be alone at Cafeen, and be alone at Old Pros.

A model of this situation is shown in Figure 2.1. You see there a 3×3 table. The three rows give Sam's three choices; the three columns give Jan's.

In each of the nine cells in the table are two numbers. These numbers assign *utilities* or *payoffs* to the nine possible outcomes (where is Sam and where is Jan), corresponding to the preferences for the two just outlined: larger utilities or payoffs are more preferred outcomes for the individual. The first number in each cell is Sam's payoff, the second is Jan's. Please note that:

- In the rankings given previously, six and not nine outcomes are ranked. This is because of an implicit (now explicit) assumption that, if the other person is somewhere else, it does not matter to Sam or Jan where is that somewhere else. Therefore, if Sam is at Old Pros (row 1), Sam gets the same payoff (4) whether Jan is at the art museum or at Cafeen. Of course, Jan's payoff does depend on which of these prevails.

- The rankings are an *ordinal* ranking of the outcomes. The translation in Figure 2.1 into numerical utilities is consistent with those rankings, but the exact numbers are otherwise entirely arbitrary; I simply assigned 6 to the best option, 5 to the second best, and so forth.

| | | Jan's choice | | |
		Old Pros	Art Museum	Cafeen
	Old Pros	6,4	4,3	4,2
Sam's choice	Art Museum	2,1	5,5	2,2
	Cafeen	1,1	1,3	3,6

Figure 2.1. The situation facing Sam and Jan. As described in the text, Sam and Jan must decide independently whether to go to Old Pros, the art museum, or Cafeen. Sam's choice determines the row, and Jan's choice determines the column. The two numbers in the cell are Sam's payoff first and then Jan's.

Now for an assumption that is critical to the story: Sam and Jan must choose independently where to go, without knowing what the other party has done. Can they consult (say, by cell phone) before making their choices? I leave this question open for now.

Sam Is Not Going to Cafeen. Is Jan?

Can we say, based on what we have done so far, what will happen? Can we say where Jan or Sam will go? Can we say for sure what will *not* happen?

If—and this is a big *if* in applications of game theory—we have the payoffs of Sam right, we can be fairly sure that Sam is not going to Cafeen. No matter what Jan does, Sam is better off going to Old Pros than to Cafeen.

Can we say anything more? Suppose—and this is a big *suppose*—Jan is familiar enough with Sam to know Sam's payoffs for the nine outcomes. Then Jan should conclude, just as we did, that Sam is not going to Cafeen. Once there is no chance of this, Jan's payoffs—if we have them right—are such that he prefers the art museum with or without Sam to being at Cafeen without

Sam. So if (big *if*) we suppose that Jan comes to the conclusion of the previous paragraph, and if (another big *if*) we have Jan's payoffs right, we know Jan will not choose Cafeen.

Two objections typically emerge at this point. (1) Being at Cafeen with Sam is Jan's first choice. If Sam and Jan are friends, is there no chance that Sam will sacrifice her own interests to please Jan? (2) If the two friends get together frequently, might not Sam sacrifice her own interests on this one occasion, expecting that Jan would reciprocate in the future? In real life, the answer to both questions is, Yes, this is possible. But if these are possibilities, then: (1) We are unsure about Sam's payoffs. If she prefers to please Jan and sacrifice her own selfish interests, then the ranking we assumed for her is incorrect. (2) If the two friends face this sort of situation repeatedly, the "game" they play is a lot more complex than a one-shot choice of a place to go. Repeated play can change everything, as we see at length in Chapters 3 and 4.

Can We Go Further?

So, after ruling out these two objections, we are left with the conclusions that Sam will not choose Cafeen and, if Jan realizes this, neither will he. But this still leaves Sam and Jan each with a choice of either the art museum or Old Pros. Now we reach an impasse. If Jan could anticipate that Sam would go to the art museum, the art museum is his best response. If he anticipates that she would go to Old Pros, Old Pros is his best response. The same is true of Sam; her best choice is to match whatever she anticipates he would do. Logic alone does not seem to answer the question, Where will they wind up?

Students sometimes assert that logic dictates that Sam go to Old Pros and Jan to the art museum. Why? Sam, not knowing anything more, chooses Old Pros because this guarantees her a payoff of 4 or more. And Jan chooses the art museum, as this guarantees him at least 3. But is this logical? It cannot be entirely obvious that this would happen, because if it were entirely obvious, it would in particular be obvious to Sam. Then Sam, anticipating that Jan would choose the art museum, would choose the art museum also. I am not asserting that there is an obvious answer to the question, *Where will they wind up?* Rather, I am asserting that *if* that question has an obvious answer, the obvious answer cannot be Sam at Old Pros and Jan at the art museum. At least, that answer cannot be so obvious that both parties recognize it.

If we cannot say how Sam and Jan will coordinate their actions, can we at least predict that they will? That depends. If they could converse on the phone beforehand, it seems likely they will do so. If they have to guess at what each other will do, they might not.

Suppose Jan Moves First

All this analysis supposes that both Sam and Jan must choose where to go independently, without knowing what the other person is choosing. Suppose instead that Jan moves first. Specifically, Jan chooses a location, goes there, and phones Sam, saying reliably and credibly, "I'm at location X, and I'm not moving." Never mind the impoliteness of such an action; if we have the payoffs right, what do we predict?

Jan reasons as follows: "If I go to Old Pros, Sam will follow me there. If I go to the art museum, Sam will follow me there. If I go to Cafeen, Sam will go to Old Pros. So predicting Sam's responses, I'm best off going to the art museum."

Fitting the Example to the Rest of the Chapter

This example illustrates much—but not all—of the content of this chapter. When Sam and Jan move simultaneously, they engage in a game in which their *strategies* are simple actions and, therefore, Figure 2.1 represents their situation as a *strategic-form game*. When we rule out Sam going to Cafeen, we are applying a *dominance* argument. Jan's decision in consequence not to go to Cafeen is an application of *iterated dominance*. When we argue that it is not "the answer" for Sam to go to Old Pros and Jan to the art museum, it is because this *strategy profile* does not constitute a *Nash equilibrium*. This story gives us too little to conclude that the two wind up at an equilibrium, although the possibility of preplay communication (a phone call) makes it more likely that they reach one. And we have no basis on which to predict which equilibrium (both at Old Pros or both at the art museum) they would select, assuming they select one. If Jan gets to move first, though, and Sam, having learned Jan's choice, responds, then the game is converted to a simple *extensive-form game of complete and perfect information*, which is simple enough that we can apply *backward induction*, to conclude that Jan goes to the art museum and Sam follows. The point of this chapter is to flesh out those italicized terms, add a few more, and then discuss how economists use simple models to gain insight into complex economic interactions.

2.1. Modeling Situations as Games

A game-theoretic model has the following pieces:

- A list of individuals or parties involved, called the *players*.

- The *rules* of the game, which specify the options the players have, when they must make their various choices, and what information they will possess when they must choose.

- For every possible play of the game, a *payoff* for each player.

We always begin with a list of players. For instance, the game-theoretic model just constructed involves Sam and Jan. Next comes the rules of the game. These can be specified in either of two ways, as a *strategic-form* or an *extensive-form* game.

Strategic-Form Games

In a strategic-form game, we specify for each player a list of his/her/its *strategies*. A strategy is a complete plan for playing the game, for any one of the players. Depending on how complex the game is, strategies can be ferociously complex. But, in simple games, strategies are usually fairly simple. For instance:

- In the Sam and Jan game, Sam and Jan must make a single choice where to go, and they must choose independently. Hence, each has three strategies, namely (1) go to Old Pros, (2) go to the art museum, or (3) go to Cafeen.

- But suppose we change the way the game is played. Specifically, suppose Jan chooses where to go first, goes there, and then Sam, knowing Jan's choice, responds. Jan has a simple choice of Old Pros, the art museum, and Cafeen; Jan has three strategies. But Sam's strategies are more complex, because Sam has to plan what she will do contingent on what she learns about Jan's choice. One strategy for Sam is to go to Old Pros no matter what Jan does. A second is to go to Old Pros if Jan goes to Old Pros and to go to the art museum if Jan goes to either the art museum or to Cafeen. Since Sam has to choose one of three places to go and she must plan her choice in each of three "information states," Sam has $3 \times 3 \times 3 = 27$ strategies under these rules.

For even moderately complex games, the number of strategies a player possesses can be enormous. But, at least conceptually, we can imagine listing out all the player's strategies. This list (one for each player) is what gives a strategic-form game its name.

Given a list of strategies for each player, the term *strategy profile* is used for a vector of strategy choices, one for each player. In the Sam and Jan game where the two must choose simultaneously, and so each has three strategies, there are $3 \times 3 = 9$ strategy profiles. In the formulation where Jan chooses first where to go, Sam learns Jan's choice, and then Sam decides how to respond, Jan has three strategies and Sam has 27, so there are $3 \times 27 = 81$ strategy profiles.

The third and final piece of a strategic-form game is a specification of payoffs for the players, which is meant to reflect their relative preferences for the possible outcomes of the game. Formally, this is, for each strategy profile, a payoff (number) for each player.

- So, in the original formulation with nine strategy profiles, if Jan chooses to go to Old Pros and Sam chooses the Art Museum, the payoff to Jan is 1 and the payoff for Sam is 2.

- Or, in the formulation where Jan chooses first and Sam responds, suppose Jan's choice of strategy "go to the art museum" and Sam chooses the strategy "go to the Old Pros if Jan goes to Old Pros, go to the art museum if Jan goes to the art museum, go to Old Pros if Jan goes to Cafeen." Then the *outcome* under this particular strategy profile is that they both end up at the art museum, and so we assign payoffs of 5 to both Sam and Jan (consult Figure 2.1 and, in particular, the cell in the center of the table).

When the game has only two players, as in either version of the Sam and Jan game, all the data can be represented by the sort of table you see in Figure 2.1: The strategies of one player are rows of the table, and the strategies of the other player are columns. Inside the cells of the table, we record payoffs, where the convention is that the first number in a cell gives the payoff to the row-choosing player and the second number is the payoff to the column-choosing player.

Note, please, that Figure 2.1 depicts in this fashion the first formulation of the Sam and Jan game: three strategies for each, so three rows and three columns. If our model involved Jan going first and Sam, knowing what Jan selected, responding, we'd need a 27-row-by-3-column table: the table in Figure 2.2.

Sam's strategy: Where to go, given Jan's choice			Jan's strategy: Where to go		
If Jan chooses Old Pros, go to:	If Jan chooses Museum, go to:	If Jan chooses Cafeen, go to:	Old Pros	Art Museum	Cafeen
Old Pros	Old Pros	Old Pros	6,4	4,3	4,2
Old Pros	Old Pros	Art Museum	6,4	4,3	2,2
Old Pros	Old Pros	Cafeen	6,4	4,3	3,6
Old Pros	Art Museum	Old Pros	6,4	5,5	4,2
Old Pros	Art Museum	Art Museum	6,4	5,5	2,2
Old Pros	Art Museum	Cafeen	6,4	5,5	3,6
Old Pros	Cafeen	Old Pros	6,4	1,3	4,2
Old Pros	Cafeen	Art Museum	6,4	1,3	2,2
Old Pros	Cafeen	Cafeen	6,4	1,3	3,6
Art Museum	Old Pros	Old Pros	2,1	4,3	4,2
Art Museum	Old Pros	Art Museum	2,1	4,3	2,2
Art Museum	Old Pros	Cafeen	2,1	4,3	3,6
Art Museum	Art Museum	Old Pros	2,1	4,3	4,2
Art Museum	Art Museum	Art Museum	2,1	4,3	2,2
Art Museum	Art Museum	Cafeen	2,1	4,3	3,6
Art Museum	Cafeen	Old Pros	2,1	5,5	4,2
Art Museum	Cafeen	Art Museum	2,1	5,5	2,2
Art Museum	Cafeen	Cafeen	2,1	5,5	3,6
Cafeen	Old Pros	Old Pros	1,1	1,3	4,2
Cafeen	Old Pros	Art Museum	1,1	1,3	2,2
Cafeen	Old Pros	Cafeen	1,1	1,3	3,6
Cafeen	Art Museum	Old Pros	1,1	5,5	4,2
Cafeen	Art Museum	Art Museum	1,1	5,5	2,2
Cafeen	Art Museum	Cafeen	1,1	5,5	3,6
Cafeen	Cafeen	Old Pros	1,1	1,3	4,2
Cafeen	Cafeen	Art Museum	1,1	1,3	2,2
Cafeen	Cafeen	Cafeen	1,1	1,3	3,6

Figure 2.2. A strategic-form game depicting the situation where Jan chooses first, Sam learns where Jan went, and then Sam chooses. Now Sam has twenty-seven strategies, because for each of Jan's possible choices (three of them), Sam has three possible responses. Since Jan has three strategies, there are 81 *strategy profiles*, hence 81 cells in the table. And, in each cell, Sam's payoffs are listed first.

Tables of this sort are inadequate when there are more than two players, and other means are needed to present the data.

In some games, for every strategy profile, the sum of the payoffs to the players is constant. Such games are called *constant-sum* games. Old time game-theory books would take the constant to be zero and call them *zero-sum* games. Constant- (or zero-) sum games give rise to some interesting theoretical developments, but we don't explore them, because most interesting game-theoretic models of economic situations are not constant sum.

Extensive-Form Games

In extensive-form games, an alternative way to depict (model) a competitive situation, the emphasis is on the dynamic back-and-forth tactics of the players. The second version of the Sam and Jan game provides an ideal example.

In Figure 2.3, you see an extensive-form representation of the second Sam and Jan game. There are *nodes* (one open circle and some filled-in circles); *labels* on each node, where each node is labelled with the name of one of the players; *moves*, which are depicted by arrows leading from one node to another node, with labels on the arrows that give the name of the particular move; and, at the end of each sequence of moves (or each path from the open circle, which is where the game begins, to the "end" of the game), *payoffs* for the players.

The open circle is where the game begins: Jan moves first, so his name labels this node; he chooses what happens there. He has three choices, hence there are three arrows coming out of the this node; the labels are Old Pros, Art Museum, and Cafeen. Each of these arrows points to a (solid, hence not-initial) node labelled Sam. Sam, then, has a choice of Old Pros, Art Museum, or Cafeen, in each of three cases: after Jan has chosen Old Pros; after Jan has chosen Art Museum; and after Jan has chosen Cafeen. And that (Sam's choice in response) ends this game, so after each of the nine arrows representing possible choices-in-response by Sam, we have payoff vectors; in this diagram, Sam's payoff is given first and Jan's payoff is given second.

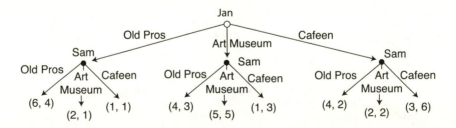

Figure 2.3. *An extensive-form representation of the variation on the Sam and Jan game, in which Jan moves first and Sam responds.* Sam's payoffs are listed first, then Jan's.

One important rule in depicting games in this fashion is that the diagram must never cycle back on itself: No path of arrows beginning at any node can point in a circle, back to where it started. Something happens, then something else, and so forth, so that the game takes the form of a stylized tree; for this reason, people refer to the structure as the *game tree*.

Information Sets

Can we model the original formulation of the Sam and Jan game, where the two must choose simultaneously, with an extensive-form game?

It seems impossible. If they move simultaneously, then neither goes first; so who should we record as going first? But simultaneity is not the important issue. Suppose, for the sake of argument, that Sam lives further from all three locales, so in terms of the timing of decision, Sam does choose before Jan. If we put Sam's choice first and Jan's second, Jan does not know, when it is his turn to choose, what Sam chose. Of course, this makes a difference. How do we record this difference?

The device used is called an *information set*. Follow along with Figure 2.4a. This gives the same "picture" as in Figure 2.3, except that we have joined the three nodes that belong to Sam (where she must choose) with a dashed line and we have put her name on the line rather than at each decision node.[1] This indicates that, when Sam must choose, she isn't provided with information about which of these three situations prevails. If she has a good guess what he will do, she might have a good guess where she is. But she isn't *told* (under the rules of the game) which choice Jan made. It is important that her choices at all three nodes in this information set are identical; if she had different sets of options from which to choose, that would tell them apart for her.

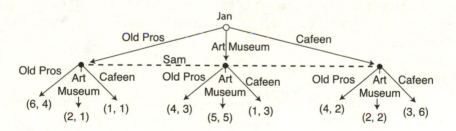

Figure 2.4a. An extensive-form representation of the original Sam-and-Jan game. In the original game, Sam had to choose without knowing Jan's choice. By joining Sam's three "Sam-moves-here" nodes with a dashed line, we indicate that Sam isn't informed at which of the three she is when she must choose. She may *suspect* or *guess* which of the three it is, based on her assessments of what Jan will do. But she isn't handed this information. Sam's payoffs are listed first.

Suppose the situation is that Jan chooses first and then, if Jan chooses Cafeen, Sam is informed of this. If Sam doesn't receive this information, she knows that

---

[1] In other books you may encounter, information sets are indicated not by this sort of dashed line but instead by a "cloud" that encompasses all the nodes in a given information set.

Jan didn't choose Cafeen, but she doesn't know whether Jan chose Old Pros or the art museum. How would we depict this? [Think about it before reading on.] The answer is, with Figure 2.4b. Sam has two information sets. One, depicted by the dashed line, consists of the two nodes following choices of Old Pros or the art museum by Jan. The second, which doesn't need a dashed line because it consists of a single node, is where Jan has chosen Cafeen.

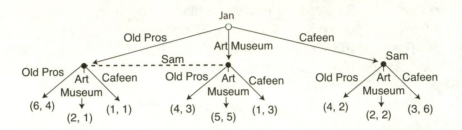

Figure 2.4b. An extensive-form representation of a third alternative Sam-and-Jan game. In this version, Jan goes first, and Sam is told whether or not Jan chose Cafeen.

There is an important but subtle point buried in the previous paragraph. In game-theoretic models, it is a maintained hypothesis that the players know "the rules." If, according to the rules, Sam will be informed if Jan chooses Cafeen, Sam knows that this is so, and Sam *therefore infers, if she didn't receive this information, that Jan chose either Old Pros or the art museum.* In real life, things can be more complex. Sam may not know that she will be told that Jan chose Cafeen if indeed he does, and so, absent such information, she may not know that Cafeen is ruled out. There are ways to use game-theoretic models to deal with this sort of complication, but we will not get to them here.[2]

Moves by Nature

As we turn our attention from Sam and Jan to more managerially relevant situations, another complication intrudes. In all sorts of competitive situations, pure chance can play a part. When a firm engages in speculative R&D, it is unclear whether the particular research will pan out. From the perspective of the firm considering whether to do the R&D, this is a random event and, unlike the actions of rivals and other players, it is a random event whose outcome is under no one's particular control. How do we model such things?

It is easiest to illustrate with an example. Imagine two firms, call them A and B, that are separately contemplating entering into the market for a brand new

---

[2] Readers who recall Sherlock Holmes and "the dog that didn't bark" will recognize the issue: Players in game-theoretic models of the sort we consider possess the perspicacity of Sherlock Holmes. Of course, this limits what you will be able to do with these models, absent some advanced techniques.

product. Each is concerned with two things: How expensive will the product be to produce? And will the other firm enter as well?

In terms of timing, suppose that Firm A must decide whether to enter in the next month, while Firm B has the luxury of waiting to see what Firm A does. (Is this a luxury?) Firm A, however, is able to decide right now whether to pursue some quick R&D that will tell it whether the production costs will be high or low. (Firm B cannot engage in this R&D.) That is, in the model we build, costs will be high or low, and doing the R&D will tell Firm A which it is. Firm A does not need to do this R&D; that is a choice it can make.

Follow along in Figure 2.5. Firm A has the first move (the open circle, in the middle left of the diagram); it decides whether to undertake the R&D or not. If it does not, then it has a second decision, whether to enter the market or not. On the other hand, if it does undertake the R&D, it learns whether the costs are high or low. Note carefully, we aren't saying that it can control these costs; this isn't making an investment that improves the odds of low costs. Instead, this is purely information gathering.

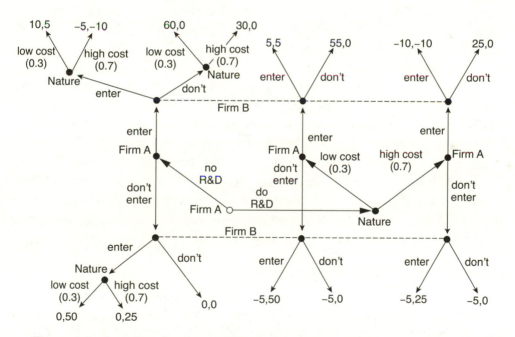

Figure 2.5. An extensive-form-game model of a two-firm entry story. Payoffs are listed in the order: Firm A's payoff first, and Firm B's second.

In this model, we are assuming that neither "player"—that is, neither firm—controls whether costs are high or low. That bit of uncertainty just ... happens. So in the model we are building, if Firm A decides to do the R&D, we next put in a node belonging to Nature, who (which?) "decides" whether costs are high or low. Presumably, there are odds that costs are high or low; we record those odds as probabilities on the branches; in this case, the diagram shows that the odds of high costs are 0.7, while the odds of low costs are 0.3.

And then, Firm A has to decide whether to enter the market or not. Since we are in the part of the game tree in which Firm A chose to do the R&D, it knows what Nature decided, and we have two different decision nodes for Firm A: one for each of Nature's two choices.

Now it is the turn of Firm B: Does it enter the market or not? Note the use of information sets here: Clearly, we are supposing that Firm B knows whether Firm A entered or not—Firm B's information sets don't include nodes both in the top, where Firm A chose to enter, and the bottom, where Firm A chose not to enter, at the same time. But what have we assumed about Firm B's knowledge of whether Firm A did the R&D? We could assume (if it were appropriate) that Firm B did see whether Firm A did the R&D, even if Firm B doesn't learn the results. And we could assume that Firm B only knows if Firm A entered or not. The diagram in Figure 2.5 models the situation where Firm B doesn't know whether Firm A undertook the R&D. (How would we depict the situation where we assume instead that Firm B had this information?)

We're almost, but not quite, done. We need to put into our model the payoffs to the two firms. Presumably, these depend on (a) which firms entered the market, (b) what are the production costs (high or low), and (c), for firm A, whether it undertook the R&D (since the R&D probably wasn't free). If we have all the numbers handy, we can supply those payoffs in the part of the tree where we know the production costs. But if Firm A did not undertake the R&D but did enter, or if A did not undertake the R&D and chose not to enter but Firm B did enter, we need to know what are those costs. So, in the part of the tree where A has chosen not to do the R&D—the left-hand side in Figure 2.5—and after A and B have made their entry choices, we need nodes for Nature's moves, determining the costs and, then, at the end of each complete path or branch, the payoffs. That gives us the game tree in Figure 2.5. (Do not worry about how the payoffs were determined: Just accept them for now.)

Strategies and the Strategic Form

A *strategy* within a extensive-form game model is a complete specification of what an individual player will do, as situations arise in which the player is called upon to move. So, for instance, for the game in Figure 2.5, here is a list of available strategies for Firm A.

- A1. Don't do the R&D. Enter the market.

- A2. Don't do the R&D. Don't enter the market.

- A3. Do the R&D. Enter the market regardless of what is learned about the costs.

- A4. Do the R&D. Enter the market if costs are low, but don't enter if they are high.

- A5. Do the R&D. Enter the market if costs are high, but don't enter if they low.

- A6. Do the R&D. Don't enter the market regardless of what is learned about the costs.

You may object to three of these as being silly: #3 involves doing the R&D but ignoring it. If you are going to enter regardless of what is learned, why bother to get the information? #6 suffers from a similar defect. And #5 involves going against what firm A learned. Why enter when costs are high but not when they are low? These are silly strategies, as we will see later. But, for now, as we make a list of all the strategies, we mean *all*, and they are possible strategies for Firm A.

And what are the strategies for Firm B?

- B1: Enter regardless of what Firm A does.

- B2: Enter if Firm A does enter. Do not enter if Firm A does not enter.

- B3: Don't enter if Firm A enters. Enter if Firm A does not enter.

- B4: Do not enter, regardless of what Firm A does.

These lists of strategies suggest that we can present the extensive-form game in Figure 2.5 as a strategic-form game, with a six-row- (six strategies for A) by-four-column (four strategies for B) table. And, indeed, we can do so, although we need to work out what are the payoffs in each cell. Here's an example how to do it:

Suppose we look at the situation where A chooses strategy A4 and B chooses B1. Then we wind up in one of two positions: If the market costs are low, A enters after doing the R&D and, per strategy B1, B enters. That branch in the tree (in Figure 2.5) gives payoffs of 5 to A and 5 to B. But if market costs are high, A does the R&D but chooses (subsequently) not to enter, while B enters. The payoffs to A and B if that happens (in Figure 2.5) are −5 and 25. We need to combine the two payoffs for A and the two for B, and the way this is done in game theory is to compute *expected payoffs*, or averages, averaging with the probabilities of nature's choice of cost. In Figure 2.5—in our model—it says that costs will be low with probability 0.3 and high with probabiity 0.7, so the payoffs for A and B, respectively, in the cell A4–B1 are

$$(0.3)(5) + (0.7)(-5) = -2 \text{ for A and } (0.3)(5) + (0.7)(25) = 19 \text{ for B.}$$

If you carry this out for each of the $6 \times 4 = 24$ cells, you get the strategic-form representation of the situation that is shown in Figure 2.6. (The entry for strategy profile A4-B1 that we just computed is highlighted.)

	Firm B's strategy			
Firm A's strategy	Enter regardless of what A does	Enter if A enters. Don't enter if A doesn't	Don't enter if A enters. Enter if A does not	Don't enter regardless of what A does
Don't do R&D, enter	−0.5, −5.5	−0.5, −5.5	39, 0	39, 0
Don't do R&D, don't enter	0, 32.5	0, 0	0, 32.5	0, 0
Do R&D, enter regardless of results	−5.5, −5.5	−5.5, −5.5	34, 0	34, 0
Do R&D, enter if costs low (only)	**−2, 19**	−2, 1.5	13, 17.5	13, 0
Do R&D, enter if costs high (only)	−8.5, 8	−8.5, −7	16, 15	16, 0
Do R&D, don't enter regardless	−5, 32.5	−5, 0	−5, 32.5	−5, 0

Figure 2.6. *A strategic-form representation of the extensive-form game in Figure 2.5.* Note the payoffs in the highlighted cell, which correspond to the computation done in the text.

Two points: (1) This use of "probability-weighted average payoffs" should be done using the probabilities that (you believe) firms A and B assess about whether costs will be high or low. If (you think) they have different assessments, you use A's assessment for A's average or expected payoff, and B's assessment for B's expected payoff.[3] And (2) we'll have more to say about the use of these expected payoffs in Chapter 18, when we discuss risk aversion and expected utility. For now, use the procedure just described—we'll discuss when and why this is appropriate later.

2.2. Dominance and Strategic-Form Games

Having modeled a particular situation with an extensive-form or strategic-form game, the next step is to analyze the model, to try to predict what will happen in the real-world situation of concern. This can be done to predict how actors behave, as descriptive economics, or to help a player–analyst decide how to act in a particular situation.

For games in strategic form, one form of analysis is directed at the question, Can we confidently predict that certain strategies will *not* be employed by the players involved? Affirmative answers to this questions involve *dominance* arguments.

Figure 2.7 shows a two-player game in strategic form. The two players are Alice and Bob, Alice's strategies are row 1 and row 2, and Bob's are columns 1, 2, and 3. Recall that we think of the players choosing strategies simultaneously and independently. Given this, can we rule out either strategy of Alice? Can we rule out any of Bob's three strategies?

---

[3] Well, it is more complicated than this: Why do they have different assessments? Do they know each other's assessment? If so, are they content to have a different assessment than does their rival? These get into some very deep questions in formal game theory that we will not discuss. If you are interested, look for *games of incomplete information, hierarchies of beliefs,* and *the common-prior assumption.*

| | | Bob chooses the column | | |
		column 1	column 2	column 3
Alice chooses the row	row 1	7, 3	3, 1	0, 5
	row 2	5, 1	5, 3	2, 2

Figure 2.7. A strategic form game solved by iterated dominance. In this game, column 3 dominates column 1, so we predict that column 1 will not be selected. And if Alice, who chooses a row, comes to this conclusion, row 2 dominates row 1—that is, row 2 iteratively dominates row 1—so iterative dominance leads to the prediction that row 1 will not be selected. Then, if Bob replicates this logic, he predicts that Alice will choose row 2, so by another round of iterated dominance, Bob chooses column 2.

- *Column 1 is dominated by column 3*: If Alice chooses row 1, then Bob is better off with column 3 than with column 1. And if Alice chooses row 2, then Bob is better off with column 3 than with column 1. We say, therefore, that column 3 dominates column 1, and we predict that Bob is not going to choose column 1.

  To be very clear about this, Bob is better off with column 1 if Alice picks row 1 than he is with column 3 if Alice picks row 2. If Bob's choice of column could influence Alice's choice of row, we could not rule out column 1. But if Alice and Bob choose strategies independently, Bob's choice of column cannot influence Alice's choice, and whichever row Alice selects, Bob is better off with column 3 than with column 1.

  Also, we *are not* asserting that Bob will choose column 3. He might decide to choose column 2. But, we assert, he *will not* choose column 1.

- *Row 1 is iteratively dominated by row 2*: Suppose that Alice is smart enough to replicate our argument that Bob will not choose column 1. Whether Bob chooses column 2 or column 3, Alice is better off with row 2 than with row 1. Therefore, row 2 *iteratively* dominates row 1, following the first dominance argument that eliminated column 1. Based on an argument of *iterated dominance*, the prediction is that Alice will not choose row 1.

  Again taking this very carefully, row 2 does not dominate row 1, as long as column 1 is viewed as a possible choice for Bob. But if we can confidently predict that column 1 will not be played, and if (a big *if*) we believe that Alice understands this, then we can eliminate row 1 from consideration.

- Having eliminated row 1 from consideration, *column 2 iteratively dominates column 3*. After removing column 1 and then row 1 from consideration, column 2 is Bob's clear best choice.

- Column 2 and row 2 are all that remain. *By iterated dominance, the prediction is that Alice chooses row 2 and Bob chooses column 2.*

Because the application of iterated dominance got us to a single strategy profile—

more properly said, because it eliminated all strategies but one for each of the players—we say this game is *dominance solvable*. Dominance solvability is not always available; if you go back to the Sam and Jan game in Figure 2.1, you'll see that we eliminated Sam going to Cafeen by dominance and then Jan going to Cafeen by iterated dominance. But that is as far as dominance or iterated dominance take us in that game.

Are the Predictions of (Iterated) Dominance Believable?

That is how dominance and iterated dominance work, mechanically. But should you believe in them? Is it really the case that no one would ever play a dominated strategy? How about a strategy that is eliminated by iterated dominance?

Words like *never* and *zero probability* simply do not belong in a discussion of real-life behavior. Suppose you invited a sequence of individuals into a room and gave them a choice: "On the table in front of you, you see a $20 bill and a $1 bill. Choose one and leave." Run this experiment enough times, and someone will inexplicably walk away with the $1 bill. So, when you read a phrase like *no one would ever play a dominated strategy*, you should immediately translate this to "almost no one would ever...."

That understood, the only way to answer the question posed is empirically. For instance, in preparing this book, I asked a collection of 330 or so individuals (first-year students in the Stanford MBA program) how they would play games like that depicted in Figure 2.7, translating the units of payoffs into money at some specified rate of exchange. In particular, for the game in Figure 2.7, I specified an exchange rate of $0.25 per one unit of utility, meaning that if one student, in the role of ROW, chose row 2, while the student in the role of COL chose column 2, ROW would be given $0.25 \times 5 = 1.25, while COL would get $0.25 \times 3 = 0.75. These questions were asked of students prior to a discussion of game theory or dominance, so they were somewhat neophyte subjects. Also, the questions were posed in a fashion that gave the students a (very small) incentive to take the questions seriously: Students were chosen at random and rewarded according to how they said they would play. For the game in Figure 2.7, 92% said that, if they were choosing a row, they would pick row 2, with 8% choosing row 1; while if they were choosing a column, 1% chose column 1, 36% chose column 2, and 63% chose column 3.

So dominance worked fairly well: A very small number of students (three out of 330) selected column 1. But iterated dominance fared a bit worse: 8% choose row 1. And iterated-twice dominance failed miserably: A majority chose column 3.

This should not surprise you. Dominance involves a single player and his or her own incentives. Iterated dominance, on the other hand, involves one player putting himself or herself in the shoes of the other player, deciding what the other player will do, which involves giving the other player credit for intelligence and responding according to one's own payoffs. And iterated-twice dominance involves a player putting himself or herself into the shoes of the second player and imagining the second player puts herself or himself in the shoes of the first player, giving the first player credit for enough intelligence to choose according to his or her best interests, then responding according to her or his own best interests, then responding to his or her best interests in what remains. (If you find the last sentence hard to parse, that is precisely the point.)

The conclusion, backed by a lot of empirical evidence, is that dominance typically works fairly well; dominated strategies are not played (but see the next section). The predictive power of iterated dominance is not so good, however, and it gets downright poor as you iterate a second time and beyond.

Payoffs Sometimes Reflect Things Other Than Money

In some cases, simple dominance fails empirically, providing the text for another lesson about using game theory to study the real world. Consider the game depicted in Figure 2.8, known as the *Prisoners' Dilemma*. For reasons to be given next chapter, this game is the basis for an enormous literature in game theory. The story that goes with this game is that two individuals commit a crime (a burglary, say) and are apprehended by the police, but only after they have hidden the loot. The police know these two committed the crime but have no evidence and, lacking a confession by either one, must let both go free. So the police separate the two and say to each individually:

> "We are willing to make a deal with you. Confess to the crime, implicating your partner. If you confess and he does not, we will give you a suspended sentence for cooperating with the authorities and lock your partner up for a long time. You will go free and enjoy all the loot. Of course, if you both confess, you both go to jail, but for a shorter time. And if you do not confess and your partner does, he gets the suspended sentence and the loot, and you get a long spell in jail."

Although it is not part of the speech, both individuals know that if each remains silent, both will be let go, and they will split the loot. Moreover, each understands that the same speech is being made to his partner. So they recognize that they are playing a simultaneous move, two-player, two-strategy-apiece game, in which the strategies are *confess* or *remain silent*.

		Prisoner 2	
		remain silent	confess
Prisoner 1	remain silent	5, 5	−3, 8
	confess	8, −3	0, 0

Figure 2.8. The Prisoners' Dilemma. Two individuals who jointly committed a crime are held by the police and individually given the option of remaining silent or confessing to the crime.

The payoffs in Figure 2.8 reflect the following ranking of outcomes. Best is to confess and inform on one's partner while he remains silent: this gives no jail time and all the loot. Second best is for neither to confess: no jail time and half the loot. Third is both confess: moderate jail sentences and, presumably, a split of the loot when both get out. Worst is to remain silent while your partner confesses, informing on you: this gives you a long jail sentence and no loot.

You might argue with this ranking of the outcomes. But, given this ranking, confess dominates remain silent for both players: if your partner confesses, you would rather confess than remain silent; if he remains silent, you would rather confess. Application of simple dominance, with no iterations, predicts that both confess.

I asked the 330 Stanford MBA students how they would play the game in Figure 2.8 for money, where the exchange rate was one unit of utility equals $0.50 and with a change in labels: the strategies labeled *confess* in Figure 2.8 were labeled *fink* for the MBA students, and the label *remain silent* was changed to *cooperate* (with each other, not with the authorities). Notwithstanding that confess (fink) dominates remain silent (cooperate)—so dominance suggests that players will choose it—74% of the MBA students said that if asked to play this game against a classmate, they would remain silent.

Why? Because money is not everything. Finking gives more money to player 1 than does cooperating, regardless of what player 2 does. But, for students playing this game in public, it might be worth $1.50 to establish a reputation as someone who does not fink, but instead tries to cooperate. The payoffs for a player who has these preferences are not what is written in Figure 21.5, and fink does not dominate cooperate according to what really motivates the players.[4] The point is that, when writing down a model of a situation as a game, you should not blithely assume that money equals payoffs for the players. It is not so, and if you assume it is, a game-theoretic analysis can sometimes lead you astray.

Weak Dominance

To finish the discussion of dominance, consider the game in Figure 2.9. In this game, row 1 *weakly dominates* row 2: Against column 2, row 1 does strictly better than row 2, while against column 1, row 1 does just as well as row 2. Can we therefore conclude that row 2, which is weakly dominated, will not be chosen? Can we iterate on this and say that, once the column-selecting player concludes that row 2 will not be chosen (hence row 1 must be), column 2 will be the choice of the column player? Certainly the logic is less compelling than when we have the type of dominance discussed before, where one row or column

---

[4] This is particularly true at Stanford, whose MBA students pride themselves on having a culture of cooperation. It would be interesting to see the percentage of finking that would prevail at other schools of management.

is strictly better than another for every choice the opponent might make. (To distinguish from weak dominance, the form of dominance where one strategy does strictly better than another for every choice by the opponents is sometimes called *strict dominance*.) Once again, the answer to this question must be settled empirically; without going into detail, I simply assert that weak dominance, at least in some games, does not do nearly as well as strict dominance, and iterated weak dominance can do quite poorly. Be wary of analyses you see that invoke weak dominance.

	column 1	column 2
row 1	3, 0	2, 1
row 2	3, 4	0, 0

Figure 2.9. Weak dominance. Row 1 weakly dominates Row 2. Having eliminated Row 2 by weak dominance, iterated dominance eliminates Column 1, yielding the prediction that the players would choose Row 1, Column 2.

2.3. Backward Induction in Simple Extensive-Form Games

Have a look at the game depicted in Figure 2.10. This is a four-player extensive-form game in which there are no information sets and no moves by nature. The lack of information sets is particularly relevant: This means that whenever a player is called upon to move, he or she knows precisely what happened in earlier moves and (so) precisely where in the game tree things stand.[5]

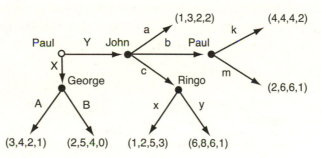

Figure 2.10. A simple extensive-form game. Payoffs are given in the order Paul's first, then John's, George's, and finally Ringo's. Because this game has no information sets (or moves by nature), we can use backward induction to get a game-theoretic prediction as to what will happen. See the text for details.

Suppose that Paul begins by choosing Y and John follows this with a choice of b. It is Paul's turn to move again: If Paul chooses k, Paul will get a payoff of 4, while choosing m will give Paul a payoff of 2. It makes sense, for this reason, to

---

[5] The technical term for extensive-form games of this type is *games of complete and perfect information*.

suppose that Paul, put in this position, will choose k. Similarly, if Paul chooses Y and John chooses c, Ringo has a choice of x, for a payoff to him (Ringo) of 3, or y, which brings him 1. So, the analysis goes, if Paul chooses Y, John reasons: "If I choose a, I will get 3. If I choose b, Paul will choose k and I'll get 4. If I choose c, Ringo will choose x as the better option for him, which gives me 2. So my best option is b."

And now Paul reasons: "If I choose Y, John will reason as above and choose b, and I will then choose k, and so I'll get 4. My other option is X. With this choice, George is given the move, and I anticipate that he'll choose B (4 for George), since A gives George only 2. So, if I choose Y, I anticipate getting 4. If I choose X, I anticipate getting 2. My best choice is Y."

And, as outsider looking at this game, *if we think that the players see the game as we do and reason in the manner just suggested*, we predict Paul will choose Y, John will choose b, and Paul will choose k.

This is *backward induction* applied to this simple game. We reason from the back or end of the game: First, at every move that is followed (only) by payoffs, we anticipate what the player will do, based on his or her (own) payoffs. Then, looking at a move that is followed either by payoffs or by nodes that were "resolved" in the previous step, we figure out what will happen there, and so on, back to the start of the game.

Here is another example: Figure 2.11 reproduces from Figure 2.3, the Sam-and-Jan game in which Jan moves first and then Sam responds. Since there are no information sets, we can apply backward induction. If Jan chooses Old Pros, Sam's best response is Old Pros, which gives Jan 4. If Jan chooses the art museum, Sam will go to the art museum, giving Jan 5. If Jan goes to Cafeen, Sam will go to Old Pros, giving Jan 2. So, per this analysis, Jan should go to the art museum, expecting Sam to follow him there.

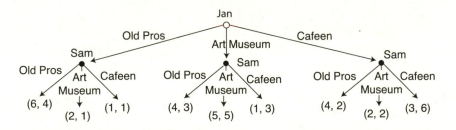

Figure 2.11. *Sam-and-Jan where Jan moves first: Backward induction and weak dominance.* Sam's payoffs are listed first.

Backward Induction Is Iterated Weak Dominance

(This subsection can be skipped on a first reading.) Backward induction in the extensive form is equivalent to the application of (iterated) weak dominance in the corresponding strategic form. Look back at Figure 2.2, which gives the

strategic-form version of the Jan-moves-first game. Compare row 1 with row 10 and row 19. In terms of what Sam is doing, we are comparing the strategies where her response to art museum is Old Pros and to Cafeen is Old Pros—this is the same in each of these three rows—but her response to Jan choosing Old Pros changes. We see that row 1 weakly dominates rows 10 and 19 for Sam—she gets 6 versus 2 versus 1 in the first column, 4 in the second column, and 4 in the third column. Similarly, row 2 weakly dominates rows 11 and 20, row 3 weakly dominates rows 12 and 21, and so forth. What we are seeing here is: If Sam holds fixed his response to Jan going to the art museum and Cafeen and asks, "What is best for me if Jan chooses Old Pros?," the answer is, follow Jan to Old Pros. Similarly, row 4 weakly dominates rows 1 and 7; row 5 weakly dominates rows 2 and 8, and row 6 weakly dominates rows 3 and 9: Looking only at those rows in which Sam follows Jan to Old Pros if Jan goes there, Sam's best response to Jan going to the art museum is to follow Jan to the art museum. And so forth.

Three Technical Points about Backward Induction

1. The key to applying backward induction is that there are no information sets (or, more precisely, every individual node in the game tree is its own information set). You can have moves by nature; when you come to a node which is nature's move, you simply average what you've computed will happen at each successor node, using the probabilities assigned to nature's choice of "action."

2. One problem you can encounter in applying backward induction is: What do you do if you reach a node where the player moving is indifferent between two or more options, but it matters to other players which choice is made? There are a variety of suggestions that game-theorists make about how to proceed at such a point; but since this won't happen in any game we'll encounter, I won't bother with this here.

3. Finally, this technique works as long as the game can consist of no more than some finite number of moves by players: You begin backwards iteration at a "last-move node"; that is, by a node that is followed (only) by payoffs. But what if there is no such node? You could take the position that no real-life game can continue forever, so there must be some last move.[6] But, as a modeling conceit, economists sometimes model real-life situations with lots of moves as games with no "last move." And I can't say we won't encounter such models, since the next chapter is full of them. You can (sometimes) apply advanced forms of backward induction to such games, but we won't do so: The bottom line here is that this technique only works (in a technical

---

[6] In fact, the issue isn't quite whether the game eventually ends, but whether there is a node followed only by payoffs. Next chapter we will look at games where, whenever a player has a choice, he or she isn't sure that this is the last move, even though eventually (because of moves by nature) the game will end. For such games, simple backward induction cannot be applied.

sense) for games where there are definite last moves.

Should You Believe the Predictions of Backward Induction?

Backward induction, like dominance and iterated dominance, is a technique for analyzing a game-theoretic model, to try to predict what will and will not happen. And, just as with dominance and iterated dominance, you should be wary of predictions made in this fashion.

- For one thing, the model you build may not capture the preferences of the players. An example of this is known as the ultimatum game. Here is a simple version: There are two players, A and B. A moves first and chooses to be either greedy or fair. If A is fair, each side gets $5. If A is greedy, B must accept A's greed, giving $9 to A and $1 to B, or reject A's offer, which gives $0 to both. (You should be able to draw the extensive-form representation of this game.) Backward induction applies: If B is asked to confirm A's offer of $1, where his other choice is to reject this and get $0, and *if money-earned are appropriate payoffs*, B will accept this offer. So A, faced with either being fair or greedy, is better off *in terms of money earned* by being greedy.

  As you can imagine, real people playing this game don't always conform to this prediction. In cases where A is greedy, B would rather have $0 and the satisfaction of denying anything to A than take $1 and reward A for her greed. Sometimes, A, anticipating this, takes the "safe" course of action and offers to be fair, splitting the money $5 apiece. In some cases, A puts enough value on being fair so that she wouldn't choose to take $9, even if she thought B would let her get away with it.

  If that makes sense to you, consider the following elaboration: The game begins as above. But if A makes the greedy offer of $9 for herself and $1 for B, B has a choice of accepting that offer or, instead, counteroffering either $4 apiece or $7 for B and $1 for A. If B offers $4 apiece, that happens. But if B offers $7 for B and $1 for A, A can either accept that offer or reject it, which ends the game with A and B both getting $0. What does backward induction predict? What do you predict would happen if two of your classmates, randomly selected, played this game?

- A second reason to doubt backward induction is that it does poorly when the number of nodes along branches through the tree gets very large. Chess is a good example. The rules of chess are such that the game must end in a finite number of moves; if 50 moves pass without a pawn being advanced or a piece taken, the game is a draw, unless a forced mate is in progress. In theory, we could take the extensive-form game that describes chess and work our way back through the tree, to see how it would be played by completely rational players. If this were so, watching a chess match between two completely rational players would be boring. They would know that it is either a forced win for white, or for black, or a forced draw, and to save time, they would simply announce the result, shake hands, and go home. But the game tree of chess is very large, and no one has ever worked out the rational way to play, nor is anyone likely to do so in the foreseeable future.

An example a bit more relevant to business applications is the centipede game. Here is one version. Two players are selected to play, designated as Players 1 and 2, and one dollar is put on the table. Player 1 has the first move; she can either take the dollar, leaving Player 2 with nothing, or say "I pass." If she passes, a second dollar is put on the table, and it is Player 2's turn to take the money, leaving Player 1 with nothing, or to say "I pass." If Player 2 passes, a third dollar is put on the table, and we go back to Player 1. And so on, and so on. This continues until either one of the players takes the money off the table, ending the game, or the amount of money on the table reaches $10. When $10 is reached, it is Player 2's turn: He can take the $10 or say "Not yet." If he says "Not yet," four five-dollar bills are added to the pot, for a total of $30, and Player 1 makes the final choice: She can say "I want it all" or she can say "$15 for each." And whatever she says is how the game ends.[7]

Backward induction says that Player 1 will take the $1 at the start of the game. (Work it out if this isn't obvious to you. Or read this footnote.[8] Is this what you predict would happen if two of your classmates, selected at random, played this game? Is this what you would do if you were Player 1, playing against one of your classmates?

What explains why backward induction fails in the centipede game? It involves many stages of backward induction but, unlike the case of chess, it is easy to carry out all those steps.

So is this a matter of "money isn't necessarily payoffs"? If you are Player 1 and we reach the stage where $30 is on the table, will you take all $30, or will you feel better if you settle for $15 and let Player 2 have $15? And if you are Player 2 and you've reached the stage where $10 is on the table, what do you anticipate Player 1 will do next turn if you say "Not yet"? If you are Player 1 and you've reached the stage where $9 is on the table, what does Player 2 anticipate you will do if you reach the final stage, and will your refusal to grab $9 affect what Player 2 anticipates? ... And, way back when there is, say, $2 on the table, should Player 2 take the $2—not a lot of money—or hand the move

---

[7] This probably doesn't sound as if it is relevant to business applications, but it captures some aspects of a situation in which two individuals or two firms begin a relationship by trusting one another, a little at first and then with more and more at stake, building to a day when one of them must either take advantage of the other or treat the other in an "equitable" manner.

[8] If money equals payoffs, on the final stage, Player 1 should take $30, leaving Player 2 with nothing. So one step earlier, Player 2 should grab the $10. So one step before that, Player 1 should grab $9. And so on, back to stage 1: Player 1 takes the $1, ending the game, in anticipation that Player 2 will take $2 next turn.

back to Player 1? If, at the very beginning, you are Player 1 and $1 is on the table, answering that question is key to whether you grab $1 or, at least, play for $3 or more.

The point is: *Even if* money is everything to the players with very high probability, a lot of stages in the game where the potential benefits to the players grow if they trust each other, combined with slight doubts about the other party's motivations, can overthrow the logic of backward induction. Backward induction is premised on every player knowing *for certain* what will happen for the rest of the game. That can be a fairly heroic premise.

2.4. Nash Equilibrium

Economists employ dominance and iterated dominance, both strict and weak, whenever they can. But, in many economic contexts, such as the original Sam and Jan game, this does not get all the way to a predicted outcome. And in extensive-form games, backward induction can be at least difficult and, in some cases, impossible to apply; information sets can intefere. In such cases, the analysis turns to Nash equilibria.

The definition is simple: *For a strategic-form game, a Nash equilibrium is a strategy profile (a specification of one strategy for each player from that player's list of strategies) such that no player, by changing his or her part of the strategy profile unilaterally, can improve his or her payoff.*

Look, for example, at the original Sam and Jan game, reproduced here as Figure 2.12.

- Suppose Sam chooses Old Pros. Jan's best response is Old Pros; this nets him 4, against 3 from going to the art museum and 2 from Cafeen. And if Jan chooses Old Pros, Old Pros is Sam's best response. Hence, *the strategy profile in which Sam chooses Old Pros and Jan chooses Old Pros is a Nash equilibrium. Each is playing a best response to what the other person is doing.*

		Old Pros	Jan's choice Art Museum	Cafeen
Sam's choice	Old Pros	6,4	4,3	4,2
	Art Museum	2,1	5,5	2,2
	Cafeen	1,1	1,3	3,6

Figure 2.12. The original Sam-and-Jan Game in strategic form..

- Suppose Sam chooses the art museum. Jan's best response is the art museum, to which Sam's best response is the art museum. *This is another Nash equilibrium.*

- And suppose Sam chooses Cafeen. Jan's best response is Cafeen. But Sam's best response to this is Old Pros. So Sam choosing Cafeen is not part of a

Nash equilibrium.

If we look for Nash equilibria by starting with Jan's choice first, we get the same pair of Nash equilibria. If Jan chooses Old Pros, Sam's best response is Old Pros, to which Jan's best response is Old Pros: *Nash equilibrium*. If Jan chooses art museum, Sam's best response is art museum, to which Jans best response is art museum: *Nash equilibrium*. If Jan chooses Cafeen, Sam's best response is Old Pros, to which Jan's best response is not Cafeen: Jan choosing Cafeen is NOT part of a Nash equilibrium.

What Does It Mean? Games with and without an "Obvious Way to Play"

The formal idea of a Nash equilibrium is remarkably simple. But what does it mean? What good is it? The answer to these questions is somewhat lengthy, so your patience is requested. Look at the four strategic-form games depicted in Figure 2.13. For each one, ask:

- How would you play the game, matched against a peer (a fellow student, if you are a student), where you assume the role of the player selecting the row or the column?

- Do you think you can predict with substantial confidence how a peer of yours, playing the game against you, would play?

- Suppose two individuals were selected from some population—say, if you are reading this book as part of a course, the population of your coursemates— at random and asked to play the game. Can you predict, with substantial confidence, what each would do? Do you think that they could predict, with substantial confidence, how each other would play?

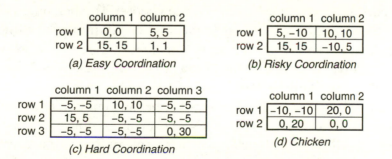

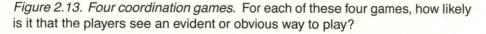

Figure 2.13. *Four coordination games.* For each of these four games, how likely is it that the players see an evident or obvious way to play?

These are variations on the general question, *Does the game have an obvious way to play?* The general question is meant to encompass the players themselves, first of all. Do they see the game, and the role of each player in playing the game, as obvious? Then, if you are studying the game as an outside analyst or observer, can you discern that obvious way to play?

For some games, the answer is No. For other games, the answer is Yes. For instance, I imagine that most people, looking at the game in Figure 2.13(a), called *Easy Coordination*, see row 2–column 1 as pretty obvious. You probably would play your part of this strategy profile if you were in the game and expect your rival (as long as he or she is relatively intelligent) to play the other part. As a third-party observer, you probably expect and predict row 2–column 1 to happen with high probability, and indeed it does. In my sample of MBA students, with payoff units of $0.25, less than 2% of the students indicated the intention of playing row 1 or column 2. Why? Because it is in the players' joint interest to coordinate their choices this way.

The game in Figure 2.13(b), called *Risky Coordination*, is less clear. The two players can coordinate their actions with row 2–column 1 or with row 1–column 2. Since row 2–column 1 does better for both than row 1–column 2, the same "logic" used in Easy Coordination to conclude that row 2–column 1 is obvious would seem to apply here. But in this case, additional benefits accrue from trying the other strategy: If Row picks row 1, she is guaranteed at least 5. And there are risks in going with row 2: If Col happens to go with the safer course of action for him, column 2, Row gets −10. Note that the logic of making the "safe" choice reinforces itself: Row is safer choosing row 1. Col is safer choosing column 2. And the risks of the unsafe choices grow the more each side thinks that the other side, thinking in this fashion, would choose to play safe.

The sample of MBAs, playing this game for units of $0.25, exhibited some of this behavior. Asked which row they intended to choose, 36% chose row 1 instead of row 2; and 32% said they intended to choose column 2.

The game in Figure 2.13(c), called *Harder Coordination*, presents three ways for the players to coordinate: row 1–column 2, row 2–column 1, and row 3–column 3. The players do not agree which to choose: The person picking the row prefers the second, and the person picking the column prefers the third. My experience has been that most people who believe that they know what to do and what to expect think that the "answer" is row 1–column 2, because it is the equitable thing to do; both sides benefit, more or less equally. But, while this logic is appealing to some folks, it is not appealing enough to describe row 1–column 2 as an obvious way to play the game; in my sample of MBA students only 44% said that they would pick row 1 in the role of Row (40%, row 2; 16%, row 3), while 60% expressed an intention to choose column 2 (28%, column 1; 12%, column 3). Based on these data, I do not think we can say that this game has an obvious way to play.

Finally we come to the game in Figure 2.13(d), called *Chicken*. American students and, I expect, others recognize the name and the game as describing the popular pastime of preadolescent bike riders, who ride straight at one another, trying to see who will veer off first and win the undesirable reputation of a chicken. Both get this reputation if both veer off. If neither one does, they both get a trip to the first-aid station. The players can coordinate their actions in two ways: fold–dare and dare–fold, which have dramatically different consequences for the two players. Unless the two players know each other and, based on previous interactions, know which side should defer to the other, it is a question of how aggressive each is. I can report that Stanford MBA students are somewhat aggressive: 60% opted to dare their opponent, while 40% said they intended to fold.

So, of the four games in Figure 2.13, at least *when played by randomly selected students from the Stanford MBA classroom, with no preplay communication*, only the first seems to have an obvious way to play. To explain the italicized caveats, if the two can communicate beforehand, the answer we give may change. For instance, a small amount of preplay communication in Risky Coordination normally suffices to get the two to row 2–column 1. Preplay communication also can be quite effective in Harder Coordination, at least in the sense that preplay communication increases the odds that the two parties involved figure out some way to coordinate. (If preplay communication were allowed and the players could redivide their winnings after the game is over, then one begins to expect that they would settle on row 3–column 3, since that maximizes the sum of their prizes, giving them the most to split between themselves afterward. But that changes the rules of the game quite dramatically.) And identity matters: Harder Coordination and Chicken, played by, say, a Japanese student and his or her undergraduate professor are very likely to result in the student deferring to the professor, and the professor anticipating this deference. Either game played by some (not all) married couples or by siblings who have an understanding of who defers to whom are likewise more likely to be obvious to the two parties, if not to a third-party observer.

At the risk of overdoing this, here are two further examples. The first is a game for any number of players. Each player must simultaneously and independently write down a number, either 5 or 3. The choices are revealed, and payoffs are made by this rule: Each player gets $5 if everyone picks 5; a player gets $3 regardless of what anyone else did if he or she chose 3; and a player who chose 5 gets −$4 if anyone else chose 3. With two players who know each other well, my experience has been that, a vast proportion of time, both pick 5, expecting that of each other. When the number of people playing the game gets up to four or five, it is no longer obvious how to play: Everyone would like to coordinate on all 5. But can everyone trust that, in a group of four or five, no one would play it safe with 3? So going from two players to, say, five, make is less obvious what you should do. But keep going: When we reach, say, twenty players, we once again reach a stage where nearly everyone understands that choosing 5 is too dangerous; the obvious way to play is to pick 3.

Now consider the following two-player game, based on the following list of 11 cities in the United States: Atlanta, Boston, Chicago, Denver, Los Angeles, New York, Philadelphia, Phoenix, San Francisco, San Diego, and Seattle. One player is told to put his name on a piece of paper and then list some of these cities. His list *must* include Boston. The other is told to put her name on a different piece of paper and list some of these cities; her list *must* include San Francisco. Each is free to list as many or as few other cities as he or she desires. The lists are compared, and each gets $0.50 for each city that appears on his or her list, but (in addition) loses $1.50 for every city on both lists. So, for instance, if she lists six other cities in addition to San Francisco, but two of her seven cities are on his list as well, she gets $7 \times \$0.50 - 2 \times \$1.50 = \$0.50$. To add social color to the situation, he is told to pretend he is an MBA student at Harvard Business School, and she is told to pretend she is an MBA student from Stanford. Finally, all the rules are explained to the two simultaneously, so each understands the rules and each understands that the other player understands the rules.

Before reading further, decide how you would play this game, against a randomly selected student from the Stanford MBA program. Assume you are given the role in which you must have Boston on your list. What other cities would you list, in addition to Boston? What cities would you expect your opponent to list? To be clear, what you want is to list any city you feel your rival is unlikely to list; specifically, to maximize your expected payoff, you should list cities for which you assess probability less than $\frac{1}{3}$ your rival will list.

This is a game with a lot of ways to coordinate. Perfect coordination, which you might think is impossible, involves each of the nine "free" cities found on one list or the other but not both; there are 512 ways to do this. Despite the huge number of ways to coordinate, my experience has been that, in a significant fraction of the time (around 50%), Stanford MBA students either coordinate or come very close. Moreover, they coordinate (or come close) in a very specific way. Something in the description of the game suggests to them that the Mississippi River is a good way to divide the cities, so the Boston player chooses Atlanta, Chicago, New York, and Philadelphia (sometimes omitting Chicago, since it is not on the East Coast), while the San Francisco player chooses Denver, Los Angeles, Phoenix, San Diego, and Seattle. If both players are U.S. nationals, and if both know that their rival is a U.S. National (and that both know that both know this), the odds of coordinating in this fashion rise. If I am nasty and substitute, say, Minneapolis for Atlanta, the odds of coordination decrease, not merely because Minneapolis is on the "border" but because its presence on the list suggests that dividing using the Mississippi River is not a good idea. The main point is that, in this very complex game, with a lot of ways to coordinate, we see something approximating an "obvious way to play" in a surprising number of cases.

These are just examples, but they suggest that some games, in some situations, can be assigned to the *clear-what-to-do-and-expect* category, while others cannot. What does it take for a particular game, played in particular conditions by particular players, to make it into this set? There are no exact answers, no test applies universally, but some obvious factors are the following:

- First, it is usually helpful, perhaps even essential, that all participants have a common understanding of the rules of the encounter, what options each has, and the like.

- Some games can be "solved" logically. Usually, logical solutions involve the application of dominance or a few rounds of iterated dominance: Player A would not choose her strategy X, and everyone realizes this. So Player B can safely eliminate his strategy Z from consideration. If Player A and Player B each have only two choices, that does it.

- Consultations before the players select their strategies normally help.

- When the participants have a long history of interacting with each other, especially in similar situations, and they know with whom they are inter- acting, predictability is usually enhanced. Think of two siblings, or two kids living on the same street, playing a round of Chicken. But repeated interactions can be tricky, as we see in Chapter 3.

- Small numbers of participants can be a plus if they know each other. But in some encounters, large numbers can be helpful, because large numbers and a good sense of how the population responds can be clarifying.

- Social conventions and norms that govern behavior in general can some- times be applied to the specific situation. For example, think of a Japanese student and professor playing Harder Coordination.

- Sometimes we can apply nebulous principles of common understanding, which in Economese are called *focal point arguments*. Examples include broad principles such as *go for the joint maximum* or *split gains equally* and the sort of implicit understanding that leads students, in the 11 cities game, to use the Mississippi River as a dividing line.

This list of factors is not complete, but it does cover a lot of the territory. It is probably worth adding, in conclusion, that in situations of interest to man- agers, the most relevant and powerful of these are social roles and conventions, including organizational and professional norms, direct communication, and direct experience.

Nash Equilibrium?

In the analysis of situations modeled as games, the concept of a Nash equilib- rium is used as follows: Having formulated the situation as a game, we ask, Is there any reason to believe that the participants to the game have a fairly good conception of how the game is played? Do they have experience with each other? Might they have consulted? Might they have gone through an elaborate ritual of signaling to each other their intentions? Can a social convention be applied? Can logic be applied? The answer to all these questions might be No. But when the answer is Yes to one or more, we expect to see them play some Nash equilibrium of the game. If each participant can predict what the others do, each would maximize for himself or herself given those predictions, always assuming that the payoffs capture what is important to the players. Since this is meant to be true about all the participants, the predicted way to play must be such that no single individual, knowing what the others do, wants to deviate. Which is, precisely, the statement that the predicted way to play constitutes a Nash equilibrium.

Note well that the previous sentence reads *a* Nash equilibrium. The indefinite article *a* refers to two things here. First, many games have multiple Nash equilibria (you already have seen a number of them), and an obvious way to play, when one exists, must be one of them. The implication runs in one direction only. Although contrived, so I do not bother to give details, one can manufacture games with a single Nash equilibrium but no obvious way to play, in which almost no one ever chooses his or her part of the Nash equilibrium profile. Second, the logic of the previous paragraph is about the perceptions of the players in the game. They must have a clear understanding of how to play. It is a bonus when, as a third-party observer, an analyst studying the situation shares that understanding. But if you think about the Sam and Jan game played under conditions where the two can engage in preplay communication, you see that there are cases in which we believe the players in a game have a clear conception of how to play, which means a Nash equilibrium, but as outsiders, we await the data to see which of the two equilibria they choose.

Moreover, and most importantly, all this is predicated on the existence of a clear, common conception of how to play, at least for the players. If that is lacking or if we are unsure whether it is there, the concept of a Nash equilibrium is of no value or use regarding the specific situation. Unless you can say, with reasonable confidence, that the participants in the situation being modeled have, for some reason or other, a clear, common conception of how each acts, there is no point in launching into a Nash equilibrium analysis.

Following this chapter, as we apply game theory to situations of interest to managers, we say that this or that is a Nash equilibrium for a given model of a real-life situation. Whenever, in this book or elsewhere, you hear that said— whenever someone announces that, "Aha, here is a Nash equilibrium in the model"—respond with some skepticism. Unless you are convinced that the parties involved in the interaction have a clear conception of how to play, the fact that this or that mode of behavior is a Nash equilibrium is of little value. In fact, ideally, the analysis should proceed along very different lines. First, after modeling the situation, an argument should be given that some particular mode of behavior is anticipated by everyone. Then, a test of the consistency of that claim is that the predicted mode of behavior should be a Nash equilibrium. Or, less definitive but sometimes still useful, if an argument can be mounted that the parties have a common understanding of the obvious way to play the game, the common understanding lies in the *set* of Nash equilibria.

Mixed Strategies and Games Where It Pays to Be Unpredictable

Most of the games studied so far have been games in which, at some level, the players involved want to coordinate their actions. They may disagree about which particular brand of coordination is best—Sam would like to meet at Old Pros, while Jan, knowing that he cannot have Cafeen because Sam is not going there, would prefer the art museum—but if they can sort that out, they still want to coordinate. A different way to say this is that, in most of the games so far, each player would like to change the rules so that he or she moves first and rivals respond to that choice.

But, in some competitive situations, moving first is something to avoid. When choosing strategies simultaneously, players do not wish to be predictable. A very simple, standard example is the children's game rock–paper–scissors, in which two players simultaneously signal with their hands *rock* (a closed fist), *paper* (flat hand), or *scissors* (fore and middle finger make a V). If they choose the same sign, it is a tie. Otherwise, rock versus paper is a win for paper, paper versus scissors is a win for scissors, and rock versus scissors is a win for rock. As anyone who has played this game can tell you, you do not want your rival to guess what you will do. You certainly do not want to move first.

To take a richer example, many readers have played poker and know about the phenomenon of bluffing: When you have good cards in your hand, you want to bet aggressively. But if you bid aggressively only when you hold good cards, your betting behavior reveals the quality of your hand, and you wind up seeing your rivals fold their hands when they have mediocre cards and you are betting. So poker players bluff: They sometimes bet aggressively when they hold poor cards, with two objectives—they wish to bluff rivals into folding, because the rivals see the aggressive betting as a sign that the party betting has a good hand. At the same time, by bluffing, a poker player confuses her rivals. When betting aggressively, she might be bluffing. So folding whenever she bets aggressively is a bad idea. Then the first player, holding a good hand, can bet somewhat aggressively and hope that her rivals do not fold, allowing her to win a fair amount of money from her good cards. In short, people bluff in poker to become unpredictable.

In business and managerial contexts, coordination and predictability are usually more important than unpredictability. But this is not always true. Consider, for instance, a situation in which one party seeks to check on the work done by a second party, but doesn't wish to check all the time. In such circumstances, the first party often wants to engage in "surprise inspections," inspections that the second party can't predict and so must be prepared for at all times.

With such applications in mind, we can ask whether the concept of Nash equilibria has anything to say about games where unpredictability is a virtue.

Such games pose a problem for Nash equilibrium; they seem to have none. Consider the game in Figure 2.14, played by Alice and Bob. In this game, if Alice chooses row 1, the Bob wants column 2. But, Alice's best response to column 2 is row 2, and Bob's best response to row 2 is column 1, to which Alice wishes row 1. No single strategy profile is a Nash equilibrium.

Bob chooses the column

column 1 column 2

	column 1	column 2
Alice chooses the row row 1	2, 1	0,4
row 2	0, 1	3,0

Figure 2.14. A 2×2 strategic-form game in which unpredictability is a virtue. This game has no pure-strategy Nash equilibria; from every cell, one player or the other wishes to deviate; both players prefer to be unpredictable.

In fact, a Nash equilibrium does exist if you are willing to extend the notion of a strategy for a player. So far a strategy is a definite choice of action, like scissors in rock–paper–scissors or row 1 in Figure 2.14. These are called *pure strategies*. Suppose we imagine that Alice chooses which row to play according to some probability distribution set in advance. For instance, in the game in Figure 2.14, she can decide to play row 1 with probability 1/3 and row 2 with probability 2/3. Such a strategy is called a *mixed strategy*, and a *mixed-strategy profile* is a set of (possibly) mixed strategies, one for each player.

To deal with mixed strategies, some immediate technical qualifications are needed. Suppose, in the game in Figure 2.14, Alice plays the mixed strategy in which she chooses row 1 with probability 1/3 and row 2 with probability 2/3. Is Bob better off with column 1 or column 2? Column 1 guarantees a payoff of 1, while column 1 gives payoff 4 with probability 1/3 and 0 with probability 2/3. Which is better? When practicing game theory, it is universally assumed that the players maximize the expected values of their payoffs. There are reasonably good reasons for this, but we don't discuss them until late in the book, so for now, just accept that this is so.

Now consider the mixed strategy profile in which Alice chooses row 1 with probability 1/4 and row 2 with probability 3/4, while Bob chooses column 1 with probability 3/5 and column 2 with probability 2/5. Against Alice's mixed strategy, you can compute that Bob's expected payoff from choosing column 1 is 1, and his expected payoff from choosing column 2 is 1. He is indifferent between the two. So, in particular, mixing between the two is a best response for him to what Alice is doing. And if Bob chooses column 1 with probability 2/5 and column 2 with probability 3/5, you can calculate that Alice has an expected payoff of 6/5 with row 1 and an expected payoff of 6/5 with row 2. So among her best responses is the mixed strategy where she chooses row 1 with probability 1/4. We have a Nash equilibrium.

Is this sort of Nash equilibrium completely crazy? Sophisticated poker players who play other sophisticated players recognize that it is not. Good poker players bluff to appear random to their rivals—if rivals know when a bluff is being run, the bluff accomplishes nothing—and they bluff just enough that, seeing them bet aggressively, rivals on average are unsure how to respond. In response, rivals call bluffs unpredictably, just enough so that their rivals are indifferent between bluffing and not. This, of course, describes the essence of a mixed-strategy Nash equilibrium. (If you play poker, since most rivals you face at the poker table are unlikely to be sophisticated poker players, take this with a grain of salt as practical advice.)

Do mixed strategies have any relevance for managers? Do we really expect a CEO to make an important decision based on a coin flip or the roll of a pair of dice? If she does, do we expect her to keep her job, if the decision turns out wrong? In situations where it pays to be unpredictable, the notion of a mixed strategy is relevant. But rarely is there a need for a manager—or a poker player—to decide what to do based on a coin flip or the roll of a pair of dice. The important thing is to act unpredictably from the perspective of one's rivals. And in most real-life applications, including poker, the player who seeks to be unpredictable has a lot of private information that, together with the actions of his or her rival, affects how well or poorly he or she does. As long as this information is private in the sense that rivals don't know the information, basing the decision on what to do on the precise "values" of the information makes the actions unpredictable.

It should be noted, finally, that mixed-strategy Nash equilibria can be found in games where it pays to be predictable, but they are rarely relevant there. For instance, in the Sam and Jan game of Figure 21.1, suppose Sam goes to Old Pros with probability 0.8 and to the art museum with probability 0.2, and Jan responds by going to Old Pros with probability 0.2 and to the art museum with probability 0.8. This is a mixed-strategy Nash equilibrium: In response to Sam's strategy, Jan's expected payoffs are 3.4, 3.4, and 2, from Old Pros, the art museum, and Cafeen, respectively; while Sam's expected payoffs in response to Jan's strategy are 4.4, 4.4, and 1, respectively. This mixed-strategy Nash equilibrium gives both players worse expected payoffs than if they manage to coordinate at either Old Pros or the art museum. Coordination-style games typically have mixed-strategy equilibria that are worse for both players than the game's pure-strategy equilibria. Therefore, it would be remarkable in the extreme if one of them turned out to be the obvious way to play.

We do not deal in mixed strategies any further in this book. If you want to learn more about them and their interpretation, almost any textbook devoted to game theory will pick up the story from here.

Nash Equilibrium and Dominance

We have now seen two methods or modes of analysis of strategic-form games: dominance, including weak dominance and iterated dominance, and Nash equilibrium. It is natural to ask, How are the two connected?

- A strategy that is eliminated by iterated strict dominance can never be part of a Nash equilibrium. If we can eliminate all the strategies but one for each player by iterated strict dominance, the strategy profile that remains is the unique Nash equilibrium of the game.

- If you eliminate some strategies by iterated dominance, where some of the steps may use weak dominance, there is a Nash equilibrium for the entire game among the strategies that are not eliminated. Therefore, if we can eliminate all the strategies but one for each player by iterated dominance, where some of the steps may invoke weak dominance, the strategy profile that remains is a Nash equilibrium for the entire game, but it may not be the only one.

Nash Equilibrium in General Extensive-Form Games

For extensive-form games, the only form of analysis we have is backward induction, and that works only for games without information sets. Is there anything more?

There is: Nash equilibrium. The concept of a strategy for an extensive-form game is clear (and we've discussed it, back on pages 18 and 19), so we can define for an extensive-form game a Nash equilibrium as a profile of strategies, one strategy for every player, where each player is choosing a strategy that is a best response (for the player) to the strategy choices of all other players. Sometimes it will be easiest, when looking for Nash equilibria of extensive-form games, to follow the path outlined on pages 18 through 20: Given an extensive-form game (e.g., as in Figure 2.5), list all the strategies for each player and then convert to a strategic-form representation, as in Figure 2.6. You should have no problem identifying the Nash equilibria in the game shown in Figure 2.6. But for other extensive-form games—and in particular game models of particular relevance to the economics of relationships—this path is practically useless. (We'll get back to this in the next chapter.)

Moreover, when you move from extensive-form games to their associated strategic forms, a lot of Nash equilibria can "turn up." For instance, in Figure 2.6, A1 vs. B3 is a Nash equilibrium, but so are A1 vs. B4 and A2 vs. B1. (If you haven't done so already, go back to Figure 2.6 and check that these are the only three Nash equilibria.) Figuring out which of these, *if any*, is the "obvious way to play the game" takes logic that will (typically) lead you back to thinking through the extensive-form model you have built. There are, in the more advanced literature of game theory, some formal criteria that can be employed—look (in a textbook on game theory) for terms like *refinements of Nash equilibrium, perfection,* and *forward induction*. But don't worry if you don't know these. In the end, the acid test is: Can we give good reasons why a particular strategy profile is the obvious way (obvious to the participants, at least) to play the game? If you can answer in the affirmative, (a) it will be a Nash equilibrium, and (b) it will almost undoubtedly pass all the formal tests we don't discuss here.

2.5. Is Game Theory a Theory?

Critics of game theory and its application to economics sometimes object that it is a bad theory because it is untestable. When the theory says, for the game depicted in Figure 2.8, the Prisoners' Dilemma, players will confess because confessing strictly dominates remaining silent, and when MBA students playing the game choose remain silent, game-theory enthusiasts will spin stories about how the theory is okay, but the model of what matters to the players—in other words, their payoffs—fails to capture reality. The critics hear this and conclude: "This theory can never be rejected."

And, speaking of game theory, they are right. The word *theory* has several meanings: A *scientific theory* is a coherent set of propositions about the real world, which one can test and, in principle, reject empirically. For instance, evolution is a theory. But a very different meaning of the term attaches to its use, for instance, in *number theory*: A theory in this sense is a system of deductively derived results, derived from some basic axioms or assumptions. Theories of this sort aren't in the least bit testable: As long as no logical errors were made, the theory is correct.

Game theory is very much the second sort of theory. And, as such, it holds little to no practical interest to practicing and aspiring managers. But the language and concepts of game theory can be used to frame theories of the first sort; for instance, we'll use game-theoretic models in the next chapter to develop theories of what is important for rival firms in an industry to restrain their competitive urges. That is a testable theory and is the way we employ game theory, to gain insight, sometimes normative and sometimes descriptive, into how the world works.

2.6. A Case-Let

We'll end with an extended exercise for you to study, which will illustrate how these sorts of models can be employed normatively (telling you what to do). (The analysis of this extended exercise can be found in the *Online Supplement*.)

Two firms, A and B, are considering whether to enter the market for a new product. The profits they will make depend on a variety of factors, such as the cost of producing the product, the size of the market, whether they will be alone in the market or have the other firm present and, if the other firm is present, whether they will be restrained in their competition or not.

Suppose Firm A has a choice whether to move first by plunging into the market or to wait to see what Firm B does and then decide. Which option is better?

There is no single and easy answer to this question, other than It depends. But suppose Firm A decides to try to model this situation as a game and, as a first step, looks at what will happen if it moves first. Specifically, Firm A decides before Firm B can do anything whether to enter or not, where choosing not to enter is final. (This is a simplification we'll want to examine later.)

And Firm A puts into its model an option for discovering whether the costs of manufacture will be high or low, prior to deciding whether to enter. But, for a first cut model, the model will not take into account uncertainty about market size.

The model will need some profit figures: The analysts at Firm A decide to begin with the following numbers.

- If we are alone in the market and costs are low, we'll make $60 (or $60 thousand or $60 million—choose whatever units you feel are realistic). If costs are high, this will cut our profits to $30.
- But if we have to share the market with Firm B, our profits will be $10 if costs are low, and we'll take a loss of $5 is costs are high.
- These figures are all gross of the costs of discovering whether costs are high or low: Finding this out costs us an additional $5.
- The probability of low costs is 0.3 and of high costs is 0.7.

What should we do?

Of course, this depends on what Firm A thinks Firm B will do. So the modeling exercise continues:

- Firm B has no access to information about whether costs will be high or low, and they assess the same 0.3 probability that we do that costs will be low.
- If they are alone in the market, they will make $50 if costs are low and $25 if costs are high.
- But if they share the market with us, they will make $5 if costs are low and lose $5 if costs are high.

What does Firm A learn from building and analyzing this model? [Hint: This presumably has something to do with Figures 2.5 and 2.6. But don't settle for a mechanical analysis of those figures. This is a model: What is the model telling us? How robust are those conclusions to changes we might make in the model?]

2.7. Books about Game Theory

As I stated at the outset, in this chapter I have not been formal about definitions or results. Rather, I've tried to give you enough of an introduction to noncooperative game theory so that we can discuss applications of the theory to microeconomics in subsequent chapters. There are many books that you can access for a more systematic treatment of the subject. Here are two written at the advanced undergraduate level that I recommend in particular:

Game Theory: An Introduction, by Steven Tadelis, Princeton University Press, 2013.

Strategy: An Introduction to Game Theory, by Joel Watson, W. W. Norton, 2013 (third edition).

A bit more technical, and probably intended more for professional economists, is *Game Theory for Applied Econommists*, by Robert S. Gibbons, Princeton University Press, 1992.

And if you want a book that discusses the strengths and weaknesses of game theory as a tool of economic analysis: *Game Theory and Economic Modelling*, by David M. Kreps, Oxford University Press, 1990.

Executive Summary

- When studying a competitive or cooperative situation or when engaged in one, whether as analyst or as participant, try to see the situation from the varying perspectives of all participants. We use noncooperative game theory to do this, modeling and analyzing situations in which various parties with conflicting interests interact.

- Noncooperative game theory uses two general sorts of models, strategic-form and extensive-form games, and employs two general sorts of analysis, dominance and Nash equilibrium analysis.

- A strategic-form game is specified by a list of players, for each player a list of strategies, and for each strategy profile (choice of a strategy for each player), a vector of payoffs obtained by the players.

- Extensive-form games give a dynamic picture of the game, with players moving and responding to one another's moves and to information they receive. In extensive-form games of complete and perfect information, players take turns moving; and at any point in the game, the player moving knows the choices made by those who moved earlier, as well as the information possessed by those who moved earlier. The notion of an information set can be used to study extensive-form games with simultaneous moves or where one player acts in ignorance of what other players know or have done previously.

- One strategy for a player dominates another if, no matter what strategies the player's opponents choose, the player does better with the dominating strategy than with the dominated strategy. We do not expect a player to use a dominated strategy.

- If the player does strictly better with the first strategy than with the second, for every set of strategy choices by the opponents, we say the first strategy strictly dominates the second. If there are ties for some strategy choices by the opponents, we have weak dominance.

- After eliminating from consideration some strategies for some players by the application of dominance, it may be possible to eliminate other strategies for other players using dominance in the "game that remains." This sort of procedure is known as iterated dominance.

- Predictions of the form *a player would not play a dominated strategy or one eliminated by the iterated application of dominance* do not always work empirically. For one thing, the payoffs in the model may not capture what really motivates the players. Beyond this, players sometimes play weakly dominated strategies, believing their rivals are sure to play a strategy selection that makes the weakly dominated strategy as good as the dominating strategy. As we iterate dominance, more and more assumptions about what each player is thinking about what others think and do are bundled in, making the conclusion less and less robust.

- To analyze extensive-form games of complete and perfect information, we use backward induction analysis: Work from the ends of an extensive-form game to figure out what each player would do given the backward-induction predictions of what his or her successors would do. Absent any ties in the backward-induction procedure, this gives a unique prediction of what happens if the game is played. This prediction is not always supported empirically, because both the payoffs in the model may not capture the players' true objectives and rolling back many times essentially involves each player piling on assumptions about how other players think and act.

- A Nash equilibrium is a strategy profile, one strategy selection for each player, such that no player can improve his or her payoff with a unilateral deviation. The force of this concept is that, *if* players have an "obvious way to play," in the sense that it is obvious to them, it is obvious to them that it is obvious to each other, and so forth, then that way to play must be a Nash equilibrium. A variety of reasons can be offered for why a game might possess an obvious way to play, including the application of logic by players, preplay communication and negotiation, specific experience with one another, general social experience in this sort of situation, and, most vague, a sense that this is what everyone would do, based on the notion of a focal point. When a game in a specific context and with specific players does not possess for those players an obvious way to play, then the concept of a Nash equilibrium is of little use or value.

- In some games, such as poker, players are better off if they are not predictable. Game theory uses the notions of a randomized strategy and Nash equilibria in randomized strategies in such cases.

- The connections between Nash equilibrium and dominance are that no strategy eliminated by the iterated application of strict dominance can be part of a Nash equilibrium. In a game that is strictly dominance solvable (where the application of iterated strict dominance eliminates all strategy profiles but one), the remaining strategy profile is the game's unique Nash equilibrium. If the application of iterated dominance, weak or strong, results in everything but a single strategy profile being eliminated, the remaining profile is a Nash equilibrium (but there may be others).

- The concept of a Nash equilibrium applies unchanged to extensive-form games. For games of complete and perfect information, backward induction yields a Nash equilibrium of the game, but there may be other Nash equilibria that involve threats that are not credible.

Problems

(Solutions to all the problems in this textbook can be found in the *Online Supplement*, which is available at https://micro4managers.stanford.edu.)

2.1 (a) In the game in Figure 2.15(a), is row 1–column 2 a Nash equilibrium? (In all the strategic form games in these problems, the payoff of the person selecting the row is given first.)

	column 1	column 2
row 1	0, 0	6, 6
row 2	2, 2	7, 0

(a)

	column 1	column 2	column 3
row 1	4, 1	3, 2	5, 1
row 2	5, 10	1, 7	6, 6
row 3	4, 4	2, 3	10, 5

(b)

Figure 2.15. Problem 2.1: Two strategic-form games.

(b) Find all the Nash equilibria in the game in Figure 2.15(b).

2.2 Find all the Nash equilibria in the game in Figure 2.16.

	column 1	column 2	column 3	column 4
row 1	1, 9	2, 9	2, 8	7, 3
row 2	3, 3	4, 4	1, 1	6, 3
row 3	0, 10	1, 7	2, 9	2, 1
row 4	2, 2	0, 0	3, 3	1, 0

Figure 2.16. Problem 2.2: A strategic-form game.

2.3 Apply iterated dominance to the game in Figure 2.17.

	column 1	column 2	column 3	column 4
row 1	6,1	2, 1	5, 2	2, 3
row 2	8,0	10, 1	4, 5	1, 2
row 3	4,4	10, 0	3, 0	1, 1

Figure 2.17. Problem 2.3: A strategic-form game.

2.4 Apply iterated dominance to the game in Figure 2.18.

	column 1	column 2	column 3	column 4
row 1	1, 9	2, 9	2, 8	7, 3
row 2	3, 3	4, 4	1, 1	6, 3
row 3	0, 10	1, 7	2, 9	2, 1
row 4	2, 2	0, 0	3, 3	1, 0

Figure 2.18. Problem 2.4: A strategic-form game.

2.5 A common procedure for selling a single indivisible object is a sealed-bid auction. In sealed-bid auctions, all prospective buyers are given the opportunity to examine the object, then each places a "bid" in a sealed envelope, which is given to the auctioneer. After all the bids are collected, they are opened and revealed. In the most common form of sealed-bid auction, the object is awarded to whoever bid the highest amount, in return for a payment equal to the amount this person bid. This is known as a *first-price* auction. In a less common form, the object is awarded to whoever bid the highest amount, but this person must pay only as much as the second highest bid. This is known as a *second-price* or *Vickrey* auction.

Imagine you are taking part in an auction, where the object being auctioned is a vacation trip. There are 15 other prospective buyers in addition to you. You have determined that the trip is worth $2000 to you: You would rather have the trip and pay some amount less than $2000 than to miss the trip (and pay nothing), but you would rather miss the trip (and pay nothing) than take the trip if it costs more than $2000. You are indifferent between missing the trip and paying nothing and going on the trip if it costs $2000. To be very specific, your payoff is 0 if you do not win the auction (and pay nothing) and it is $2000 - P$ if you win the trip and pay P.

You have very little idea how much the trip is worth to the other 15 bidders or how they bid.

(a) Suppose this is a first-price auction. Why does the strategy of bidding $1950 weakly dominate the strategy of bidding $2000 for you? Can you compare (using dominance) bidding $1950 or bidding $1960? Can you compare (using dominance) bidding $2000 and bidding an amount more than $2000?

(b) Suppose this is a second-price auction. Why does the strategy of bidding $2000 weakly dominate *every* other strategy for you?

2.6 Figure 2.19 shows two extensive-form games of complete and perfect information: the threat game in panel a, and the trust game in panel b. Solve each by backward induction. Then, do you think that your peers, playing the games in, say, units of $1 equals one unit of payoff, would follow the prediction of the Nash equilibrium analysis?

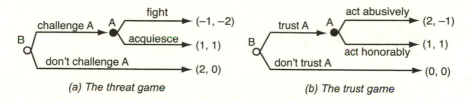

(a) The threat game   (b) The trust game

Figure 2.19. Two extensive-form games of complete and perfect information. A's payoff is listed first in each case.

2.7   Among the earliest application of game-theoretic ideas in economics was the investigation of equilibria in duopolies, by A. Cournot (in 1838), J. Bertrand (1883), and H. Von Stackelberg (1934). As the dates indicate, this all predates the formal development of game theory, which began with von Neumann and Morgenstern (1944). This problem takes you through the basic models of Cournot (part a), Bertrand (part b), and Von Stackelberg (part c and, at least in spirit, part d), for two firms whose products are somewhat differentiated. You should not attempt this problem unless you both are skilled in and enjoy algebraic manipulation. The solution, with very extensive commentary included, is found in Appendix 3 of the *Online Supplement.*

Imagine two firms, labeled A and B, producing products that are substitutes but not perfect substitutes. The inverse demand functions for their two goods are

$$p_A = a - x_A - bx_B, \quad \text{and} \quad p_B = a - x_B - bx_A$$

for a positive constant a and for $0 < b < 1$, with the same constants a and b appearing in both inverse demand functions. Each firm has a constant marginal cost of production c.

(a) Suppose the two firms must simultaneously and independently choose quantities to produce, each without knowing what the other has chosen. What are (or is) the Nash equilibria of this game?

(b) Suppose that the two firms must simultaneously and independently choose prices to charge, each without knowing what price the other has chosen. What are (or is) the Nash equilibria of this game?

(c) Suppose Firm A can choose its production quantity first. Firm B sees this choice, then chooses its production quantity. What do you predict would happen?

(d) Suppose Firm A can choose its price first. Firm B sees this choice, then B chooses its price. What do you predict would happen?

3. Reciprocity and Collusion

This chapter concerns reciprocity and cooperation in repeated interactions: How and when do repeated interactions allow essentially selfish parties to cooperate? After answering this question somewhat abstractly, we apply the answers to the subject of tacit and explicit collusion in oligopolies.

Large electric turbine generators are enormous, expensive pieces of capital equipment that turn mechanical energy into electricity. They are essential to the production of electricity by large electric utilities, in applications where fossil fuels are burned, where steam is produced by nuclear reactors, and in large hydroelectric facilities. In the late 1950s, large turbine generators for the U.S. market were produced by three large industrial firms: General Electric, Westinghouse, and Allis-Chalmers.[1]

A Porteresque five-forces analysis of this industry as of the 1950s and 1960s leads to the conclusion that, at least potentially, this could have been a very profitable industry. Entry barriers were absolutely formidable. Complements, notably fossil fuels, were cheap, and substitutes—essentially methods for generating electricity on a smaller scale—were not economical. Suppliers to the industry, with the possible exception of the Electrical Workers' Union, which organized the blue-collar workforce at the three firms, were relatively weak. Customers were relatively weak; the way most customers' (utilities') businesses were run, as regulated utilities, meant the customers were not very price sensitive and instead were under pressure to increase generating capacity to meet the peak-load demands they faced.

In the 1950s, the three firms reaped tremendous profits. But in the early 1960s, they were much less profitable. In fact, in the early 1960s, their levels of profit were so low that the smallest of the three, Allis-Chalmers, was driven out of the industry, leaving GE and Westinghouse to share very low levels of profit. Yet by 1970, GE and Westinghouse were once again earning enormous profits.

The wide swings in profitability were due to changes in the nature of rivalry in the industry. In the 1950s, GE, Westinghouse, and Allis-Chalmers found a very clever—and utterly illegal—way to coordinate their prices, leading to high profits. In this business, a customer (typically a large electric utility like Consolidated Edison of New York or Pacific Gas and Electric) in need of a turbine generator would make a formal announcement of this fact, complete with specifications to be met, asking for potential suppliers to submit bids. At

---

[1]   The story of the large turbine generator business related here is taken from "General Electric vs. Westinghouse in Large Turbine Generators (A, B, C)" (HBS9-380-128, 129, 130), which should be consulted for a lot of extraordinarily interesting detail.

the moment such a formal solicitation of bids was made, the three suppliers would consult a lunar calendar. On Days 1 through 17 of the lunar month, with the New Moon counting as Day 1, GE was understood by the three firms to "own" the contract; GE would make a bid at a relatively high price, and Westinghouse and Allis-Chalmers would put in bids at even higher prices. If the solicitation of bids occurred on Days 18 through 25 of the lunar month, Westinghouse was understood to "own" the contract. And if it occurred on Days 26 through 28, Allis-Chalmers was understood to "own" the contract.[2] This collusive scheme had been arranged by the three in secret negotiations conducted in a hotel room.

To be very clear, this was a price-fixing conspiracy, directly violating the Sherman Antitrust Act. It was so blatant a violation of U.S. antitrust law that, when the U.S. Department of Justice figured out the scheme, it pursued criminal charges against executives of the three firms and jail time was handed down. But, because the people at the Department of Justice did not think to consult a lunar calendar, they did not figure out how the three firms were coordinating their bids for quite some time, and until the DoJ figured it out, the three firms made sizeable profits.

In the early 1960s, after the DoJ put a stop to the phases-of-the-moon collusion, Allis-Chalmers dropped out and rivalry between GE and Westinghouse became intense. Then, in 1963, GE made a strategic move that permitted it and Westinghouse to return to relative benign rivalry, and profits shot up. In this chapter I do not discuss either the events of the early 1960s or GE's strategic move; I suggest in the strongest possible terms that, after you read this chapter, you study the GE–Westinghouse cases cited previously. Roughly, the A case explains why competition was so intense in the early 1960s, and the B case describes GE's 1963 opening gambit. The C case describes what happened over the following decade or so, up to the next move in the "game" by the U.S. antitrust authorities. Although the case is quite old, there is no better vehicle for understanding the concepts we discuss here. I do not want to spoil the story for you or your instructor, but I will say this: GE's actions in 1963 may have been in violation of the spirit or letter of antitrust law and for that reason may not be something to be admired generally. (To the best of my knowledge, the courts have come to no definitive ruling whether GE's actions were in violation of the law, so the *may have been* is accurate.) But, setting aside the legality of GE's actions and looking at them solely as an attempt to bend the rules of a "game" in a fashion favorable to the party doing the bending, this was simply magnificent, the Beethoven's *Ninth Symphony* of business strategy. The cases are fascinating.

---

[2] I am not certain about the precise apportioning of the lunar month, but this gives market shares of around 60% to GE, 30% to Westinghouse, and 10% to A-C, which is about the share that each had. If I am off, it is probably only by a day or so.

While we do not discuss the post-phases-of-the-moon period, I want to address the question, Why did the phases of the moon scheme work? Suppose it is Day 25 of the lunar month, and Con Ed of New York solicits bids for a generator. Westinghouse owns Day 25 according to the agreed-to scheme. So Westinghouse prepares a bid that leaves it with a substantial profit, expecting GE and A-C to make even higher bids. Imagine you are the CEO of Allis-Chalmers. Your market share is, on average, around 10%, because you own only 3 days out of 28. Moreover, the luck of the draw, combined with a slow market, may mean that you have not gotten an order for a year. Your skilled-labor force is mostly idle, draining cash from your firm. Why not defect from the agreement and steal this order from Westinghouse? After all, if Westinghouse's bid is going to leave it with a substantial profit, there is plenty of room for you to capture the order and still make a fair piece of change. You need not fear that Westinghouse will take you to court for breaking this agreement: Since the deal is illegal, it is not enforceable in court. Why do you adhere to the deal?

This main subject of this chapter is the answer to this question or, more precisely, the answer to the question, Under what conditions will parties to this sort of arrangement adhere to the deal they struck? The general topic is reciprocity in repeated interactions: How and when can we get cooperation from folks who are essentially selfish?

3.1. A Game-Theoretic Analysis of Reciprocity: The Folk Theorem

The story starts with the Prisoners' Dilemma game from last chapter. I reproduce the game in Figure 3.1, with the prisoners now named Alice and Bob. Let me remind you what we said about this game: Confessing is a dominant strategy for each side and, therefore, confess–confess is the only Nash equilibrium of the game. This isn't a very happy conclusion for Alice and Bob, because they wind up with 0 each, rather than the 5 apiece they would get if they could find a way to sustain the cooperative outcome where each remains silent. This is the prisoners' dilemma: How can the two attain this cooperative outcome, when the selfish interests of each leads each one to confess?

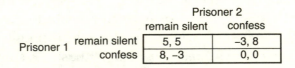

Figure 3.1. The Prisoners' Dilemma.

One way to escape the dilemma is to form a legally enforceable agreement to cooperate by remaining silent. In some contexts, this is possible. But, if this is not possible, another possibility arises if the two are involved in this situation repeatedly. Imagine, say, that Alice and Bob play the game once, with the results revealed at the end of play. Then some random event is conducted such that with probability 0.8, the two play a second time, while with probability 0.2, the encounter ends. After they play the second time, if they do, the results are again revealed, and another random event is conducted independently, so the probability of going on to a third round of play is 0.8, and so on. After each round of play, the chance of proceeding to another round is 0.8 and the chance that the encounter ends is 0.2, independent of what has happened in the past. Assume that payoffs for a string of plays for each player are just the sum of their payoffs in each round; and insofar as a player is uncertain what payoffs he or she will get, for instance, because of uncertainty concerning how long the game will last, the player seeks to maximize the *expected value* or probability-weighted average (mean) of his or her summed payoff.

This is a fairly complex extensive-form game. It isn't complex in terms of the rules, but drawing a game-tree representation is challenging: while there is probability one that, eventually, the game ends, if, say, it has gone on for 10,000 rounds, there is a 0.8 probability that it will go on for at least one more round. The tree, in other words, never completely ends. Have a look at Figure 3.2. This gives the "start" of what an extensive-form might look like, drawn out, although of course it is very incomplete: It only goes two rounds in, and, at that, it only shows the "top half" of the first two rounds, in which Alice begins with confess. But note a few things: It depicts Alice going "first" in each round, then Bob, with an information set for Bob, so he doesn't know what Alice did that round, but with both Alice and Bob knowing what happened in round 1 when they move in round 2. As for payoffs, look at the payoff vector $(13, 2)$ near the bottom: This is the outcome (the payoffs) if, in the first round, Alice confesses and Bob remains silent (which gives Alice 8 and Bob -3), plus a second round in which the both remain silent (for 5 apiece): Alice totals 13, while Bob nets 2.

And if drawing an extensive-form representation of this game is a challenge, creating a two-by-two strategic-form representation is...much worse. The problem is that Alice and Bob both have an infinite number of strategies they can play. Remember that a strategy must provide a complete description of how a player will play. Since there is a small (but positive) probability that there will be a round 10,000, a strategy for Alice must describe what she will do in round 10,000. Worse than that, it must describe what she will do in round 10,000, dependent on everything that happened in rounds 1 through 9999. Since there are four things that could happen in each round (if we reach round 10,000, we know that nature chose "continue" in each of the first 9999 rounds), that means that we need to specify Alice's choice in round 10,000 for the 4^{9999} possible positions in which she might find herself. And that's only for round 10,000.

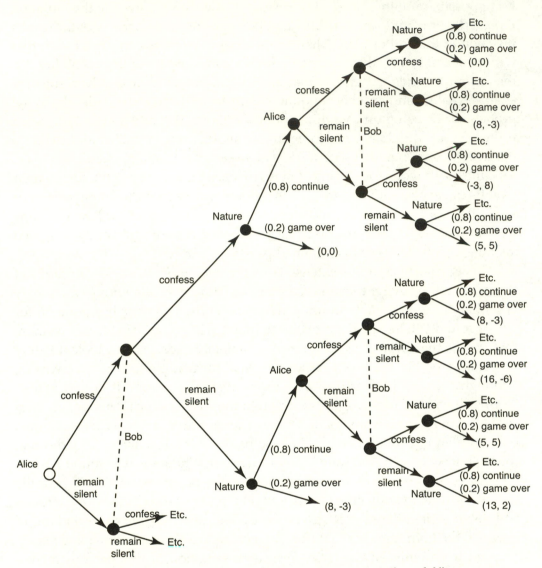

Figure 3.2. The start of an extensive-form game representation of Alice versus Bob in the Repeated Prisoners' Dilemma. Alice's payoffs are listed first.

It may sound hopeless, but by restricting attention to relatively simple strategies, we can still describe some interesting Nash equilibria of this simple yet formidable game. To begin, consider the following four strategies:

1. *Always confess*, which is just what it says: If Alice adopts this strategy, she will always confess, every chance she gets, no matter what happened earlier in the game.

2. *Always remain silent*, which we can (for reasons to be given momentarily) rename *Be a sap*. Just what it says.

3. *The grim strategy*: On the first round, remain silent. On every subsequent round, remain silent if, on all previous rounds, your opponent remained silent. But if your opponent ever confessed on an earlier round, confess. This is a strategy of "I'll cooperate with you as long as you never stab me in the back by confessing. But if you ever confess, that's it: I'm confessing forever, with no forgiveness for what you (once) did to me."

4. *Tit-for-tat*: On the first round, remain silent. On every subsequent round, do whatever your opponent did in the previous round.

For each of these, we can ask, If one player plays this strategy, what is the other player's best response?

1. If your opponent plays *always confess*, your best response, and your only best response, is *always confess*. Nothing you do will affect what your opponent does in the future, so you might as well get as much as you can in each round. That's *always confess*.

2. If your opponent plays *always remain silent*, your best response, and your only best response, is *always confess*. Same reason: Your choice in any round has no impact on what your opponent does in the future, so your best response is to maximize each round what you get that round, which means *always confess*.

In fact, *always confess* is the unique best response to any *nonreactive* strategy by your opponent, meaning any strategy (for your opponent) where what you do in any round has no impact on what your opponent will do in the future.

But suppose your opponent chooses a reactive strategy such as the grim strategy or tit-for-tat. Then matters become more complex.

For one thing, against reactive strategies, you may have many best responses. Suppose, for instance, your opponent plays *grim*, which certainly involves reacting to what you do. Then you never want to *initiate* confessing. As long as you begin and stick with remaining silent, your opponent will reciprocate. That means you will get 5 in round 1, 5 in round 2, if there is a round 2, 5 in round 3, if there is a round 3, and so forth. You could confess at any time, which would net you one 8 in the round that you confess. But, after that, your opponent is going to always confess, and the best you can do subsequently in each round is confess, which gets you 0. And, if you do the math, 5 this round, 5 next round with probability 0.8, 5 the round after that with probability $0.8 \times 0.8 = 0.64$, and so forth[3] is better than 8 this round and 0's forever after (for as long as the game lasts). It would, of course, be different if you knew that this was the last round, or if the probability of the game continuing was small (say, 0.2 instead of 0.8).

---

[3] For those who know the math, the expected value of never initiating confession is $5 + 0.8 \cdot 5 + 0.8^2 \cdot 5 + 0.8^3 \cdot 5 \ldots = 5/(1 - 0.8) = 25$.

But for these numbers, if your opponent is playing the grim strategy, you want to stay away from confession.

But this means that you have many best responses to *grim*. *Always remain silent* is a best response. The *grim* strategy is a best response. *Tit-for-tat* is a best response. Any strategy that never *initiates* confessing is a best response.

What does this mean for Nash equilibria of this game? Recall that a Nash equilibrium is a strategy *profile*—that is, a strategy choice for each player—where each player's choice is a best response to what the other player is doing. Hence, *always confess* against *always confess* is a Nash equilibrium. *Always remain silent* is not part of any Nash equilibrium: The best response to it is *always confess*, to which *always remain silent* is not a best response. Indeed, since *always confess* is the unique best response to any nonreactive strategy, the only Nash equilibrium in nonreactive strategies is *always confess* by both players.

But *grim* is a best response to *grim*, hence it is Nash equilibrium. And, although I haven't justified this, it turns out that, with these numbers, best responses to *tit-for-tat* include *tit-for-tat* and *grim*, so *tit-for-tat* versus *tit-for-tat* is a Nash equilibrium, as is *tit-for-tat* against *grim*. *If your opponent's choice of strategy says, in effect, I'll cooperate (never confess) as long as you reciprocate, but I'll punish you if you try to take advantage of this offer*, and if the punishment is severe enough so you don't want to initiate confession, *and* if your choice of strategy is similarly an invitation to cooperate with a threat to punish, we have a Nash equilibrium.

And that's not all. Consider a strategy I'll call *greedily grim*, which runs as follows: Alternate playing confess (in odd-numbered rounds) and remain silent (in even-numbered rounds), as long your rival always remains silent. But if your rival ever confesses, confess forever after. With a continuation probability of 0.8, your rival will not "put up" with this strategy: If it is an even numbered round, playing a strategy of never confessing gives your rival an expected payoff of $5 + (0.8)(-3) + (0.8^2)5 + (0.8^3)(-3) + \ldots = 7.2222$. (Trust me, or verify using Excel.) By choosing to confess, your rival gets an immediate 8 and then 0 forever, for as long as the game lasts, a total of 8. But if the continuation probability is 0.9, greedily grim is half of a Nash equilibrium: If your rival players *wimpily grim*—always choose remain silent, as long as you follow the rules of greedily grim, but choose confess forever if you ever deviate—then (with continuation probability 0.9) *greedily grim* against *wimpily grim* is a Nash equilibrium. (You can trust me, or you can do the calculations. And if you do the calculations, see if you can show that *greedily grim* versus *wimpily grim* is a Nash equilibrium for continuation probability 0.828 but not 0.827.

The Folk Theorem of Game Theory

The basic idea in the preceding example is formalized in what is known as the *folk theorem* of noncooperative game theory. It is called the *folk theorem* because it seems always to have been known; no one is brash enough to take credit for such a simple idea.[4]

The setting for this formal result is as follows. We have a simple *stage* game played by some number of players. This stage game is played once, then a second time, a third, and so on. Each player receives as total payoff from the sequence of plays the discounted sum of his or her payoffs in each round, discounted with some discount factor $\delta < 1$. You can think of δ as reflecting the time value of money, a probability of continuing, or both.

For each player, we compute the player's *max–min* payoff. This is the worst punishment that all the others can inflict on the player, if the player anticipates what the others will do. For example, in the Prisoners' Dilemma, each player's max-min payoff is 0 because, by confessing, each player can get at least a payoff of 0 no matter what the other player does.

The Folk Theorem (roughly). *Take any outcome of the stage game that gives to each player a payoff that exceeds the player's max–min payoff. Then, if the discount factor δ is close enough to 1, there is a Nash equilibrium of the repeated-interaction game that gives this outcome round after round.*

This is a rough version of a precise mathematical result.[5] You can see the precise result in textbooks on game theory, but the statement here conveys the basic idea. As long as the future matters enough (δ is close enough to 1) any outcome that gives players more than their max–min payoff can be sustained as an equilibrium. In fact, it is easy enough to describe the Nash equilibrium: All the players play the chosen outcome as long as no one deviates. If someone deviates, everyone else punishes the deviator to the fullest extent possible, putting the deviator at his or her max–min payoff level. This is a Nash equilibrium because, if the future matters enough and the chosen outcome gives each player more than he or she gets if punished by the others, it is better for the player to go along with the deal than to deviate and be held afterward to his or her max–min payoff.

A number of questions arise about this result. For instance, can a particular outcome that gives each player more than his or her max–min be sustained as an equilibrium for a particular discount factor, such as 0.8? Also, will the players carry out the mandated punishment of a deviator? This question is particularly germane if, to punish a deviator, a player has to act in a way that hurts herself; in such cases, is the threatened punishment credible? (I won't subject you to the details, but the answer is, We can arrange things so that it is a credible threat.) What happens if more than one player deviates from

---

[4] That said, Robert Aumann received the Nobel Prize in economics for his work on the folk theorem.

[5] The precise result says more. For instance, *grim and greedy* versus *wimpily grim*, which alternates between different stage-game outcomes, is a Nash equilibrium per a precise statement of the result.

the scheme? In formal treatments of the Folk Theorem, all these questions are addressed without affecting the basic result. Rather than presenting the details, we take an applied point of view, stressing the basic idea, which is clear from the example of the (Repeated) Prisoners' Dilemma. But the Folk Theorem's chief weakness is equally clear:

With So Many Equilibria, Why Believe in Any of Them?

Last chapter, we said that being a Nash equilibrium per se was no virtue. You should only believe that some Nash equilibrium will be played *if and when* you believe for some reason that the players involved recognize that this is the way they should behave. Being a Nash equilibrium is a necessary condition for an obvious way to play. But it is far from sufficient, and in some instances, there may be no obvious way to play.

If you keep that notion firmly in mind, what the Folk Theorem tells you is simple common sense: By a mixture of "I'll be nice to you if you are nice to me" and "if you hurt me, watch out!," participants in a situation that resembles a repeated game *might*, in their own self-interest, act in a cooperative manner, as long as at every point, maintaining the cordial relationship is more valuable than taking momentary advantage of the other(s). There are few limits (according to this theory) in what might occur. But the key to sustaining cooperation is the double-edged sword: (1) *I'll cooperate if you do.* (2) *But if you try to take advantage of this, I'll make you pay.*

Conditions that Promote This Sort of Cooperation, and Conditions that Hinder It

The italicized *might* in the last paragraph reflects at least four important conditions that must be met in real-life applications:

1. The participants must want to achieve this sort of cooperative outcome. If one party is psychologically predisposed to reject cooperation, it won't happen. If one party thinks that the other party (or parties) has such a psychological predisposition, it probably won't happen.

2. There must be a common understanding what is "the deal." Ambiguity about what behavior by the parties is permitted and what behavior "crosses the line" is deadly to cooperation of this sort. For this reason, simple deals, based on clear qualitative principles are a good idea.

3. The momentary advantage that one party can take by violating the "agreement" cannot exceed the value to that party of keeping to the deal. This has two practical implications: First, all parties to the deal must get value out of it. If, say, you are dealing with a trading partner, pushing them to a point where they get no value out of the deal means that they have no incentive to

stick to the deal. Second, as conditions change (and in real life, if not in toy games, conditions do change), parties to such an arrangement may need to "reset" the parameters of the arrangement, so that each party continues to see sufficient future value in the arrangement.

4. The key to "good behavior" by all parties to such an arrangement is the threat that, if one party acts outside the arrangement, that party will be punished. But this means that parties to the arrangement must be able to monitor the behavior of their partners. If Party A can't tell whether Party B transgressed, Party A doesn't know whether to punish Party B, and this can encourage Party B to try to transgress.

Noise and the Breakdown of Cooperation

This last point is illustrated by the following elaboration of the Repeated Prisoner's Dilemma. Imagine Alice and Bob playing the Prisoners' Dilemma game repeatedly. In each round, Alice and Bob simultaneously and independently choose their *intended* actions, either to confess or to remain silent. Then, with a given probability, say, 0.75, what they intend is what transpires. But with complementary probability 0.25, what transpires is the reverse of what was intended. And what transpires (not intentions) both determines the players' payoffs and is observed by the other player.

In this new setting, what happens if the two players attempt to always cooperate by remaining silent? Things proceed smoothly for a while, with silence being met with silence. But then, on round 4, say, Bob's action is to confess. Note well, this is what Alice sees and what determines payoffs; Alice doesn't know if Bob intended to remain silent or to confess; she knows that even if he intended to remain silent, there is probability 0.25 that it would appear that he confessed. Should she punish this apparent transgression against the arrangement by, say, confessing in the next round or two?

If she does, she may well be punishing him even though he tried to remain silent. He'll know, if he knows how things appear to her, why she is punishing him. But how will this make him feel? Will he be willing to take this punishment when, in fact, it wasn't deserved? If not, we can anticipate a breakdown of cooperation.

So maybe it would be better for Alice to let it slide. Unhappily, if she does, Bob may get the idea that, at least some of the time, he can intentionally confess, taking advantage of Alice. Certainly, if Alice always lets it slide, Bob will, in his own selfish interests, confess more and more often. Probably, at some point, Alice will decide it is time to punish Bob. (And, this time, Bob will probably deserve it.)

In theory—and I stress, in *theory*—Nash equilibria can be constructed in this situation that provide a measure of cooperation between the two parties. The strategies that give these Nash equilibria are complex animals. When someone confesses, whether intentionally or not, they must be punished, but the punishment can't be too severe, because too-severe punishment causes each party to regard the future value of the arrangement as worth very little, which kills the entire arrangement. A more advanced book on game theory will show you how, in theory, such equilibria work. But, as a practical matter, they seem very unlikely to emerge as "the obvious way to play the game" to the parties involved; the inability to know when one party or another has broken the agreement because of this sort of "noise" is usually deadly for this type of cooperative agreement.

3.2. Collusion in an Oligopoly

So how was the "phases of the moon" arrangement between GE, Westinghouse, and Allis-Chalmers sustained? It began with the realization by all three firms that, because of the other four of Porter's Five Forces, *if* they could restrain themselves in competing against one another, this industry could be a gold mine for them. The next step for them was to arrive at a mutually agreeable deal that each understood: Secret meetings in hotel rooms are gross violations of the antitrust laws, but they make such unambiguous deals a relatively simple task, and that is what happened.

The three needed to divide the market into shares that gave each of the three an incentive to abide by the arrangement. To meet this requirement, each had to be clear on what was the alternative. Presumably, each saw the alternative as all-out, cutthroat competition. Allis-Chalmers probably knew that such competition would be ruinous to it; it would have to leave the industry. So GE and Westinghouse had to give A-C enough of a share of the market so that the value of "one last attractive contract" for A-C would be less than the continued share A-C would get by sticking to the deal. For GE and Westinghouse, the division of what was left was a bit more problematic; why should GE get 17 days out of 30 and Westinghouse only 8? Obviously, Westinghouse would prefer 9, leaving GE with 16. Somehow they agreed; it is probably significant that the shares agreed to were just the historical market shares of the three.

And, then, it was important that each could tell when the others were abiding by the arrangement. The division according to the lunar calendar made this a snap: All three knew unambiguously what "belonged" to GE, to Westinghouse, and to A-C. Monitoring compliance was no problem at all.

The law added a further consideration: Explicit collusive arrangements of this sort are a clear violation of the law. The three knew that, if their scheme became generally known, the Antitrust Division of the Department of Justice would take action. So they had to find a scheme for dividing the market that wouldn't be clear to outsiders. Using the lunar calendar to coordinate their actions was such a scheme.

To be clear, I do not in any sense condone what the three did. One might argue—on both sides—whether corporations have a fiduciary responsibility to their shareholders to push against ambiguities in the law, if the manner of pushing is not unethical in some other sense. But this was a blatant violation of completely unambiguous law. It was wrong, and when discovered, it was right that the companies involved were slapped and slapped hard.

Still, the theory of the previous section makes it clear how this nefarious scheme worked.

And, more generally, it provides a stark example of the theory of the last section applied to the important context of *competitive restraint* in oligopoly.[6] We begin by connecting oligopolistic competition to the prisoners' dilemma. In general, firms in an oligopoly make many different decisions about how to compete, concerning prices they charge, advertising, location of facilities, characteristics of products they offer, and so on. In the prisoners' dilemma, the players have a single, discrete decision: whether to confess or remain silent. Nonetheless, the strategic aspects of oligopolists' decisions often have the general flavor of the prisoners' dilemma: Oligopolists can decide whether to compete in a restrained fashion—charge a high price; advertise in restrained fashion; avoid the territory, whether geographic or in terms of product specification, of rivals—or to compete aggressively. If one firm in an oligopoly competes aggressively, *with no response from its rivals*, then that firm is better off and its rivals are worse off. But if all compete aggressively, all are worse off. I do not mean to denigrate the added difficulties brought on by competition on many dimensions; indeed, we return to those difficulties in just a bit. But the *basic* strategic structure of the prisoners' dilemma captures to a first approximation the strategic structure of rivalry in an oligopoly.

Once you grant this, the relevance of the folk theorem to rivalry in oligopoly is fairly obvious; it indicates the *possibility* of sustainable collusion, either tacit or explicit. I should define this bit of Economese. Oligopolists collude when all restrain their competition with one another. This collusion can be explicit, based on discussions among the oligopolists. In some cases, such as OPEC, it can be both explicit and more or less public, in which case the oligopolists collectively form a *cartel*. But, in the United States, the European Community, and many other places as well, to stay within the antitrust laws, collusion must never be discussed—avoid secret meetings in hotel rooms—but somehow tacitly agreed to, which gives us *tacit collusion*.[7]

---

[6] *Competitive restraint* is one of three phrases that could have been put into this sentence, the other two being *collusion* and, at least in some cases, *cartelization*. I chose the "mildest" of the three here; I'll use these terms somewhat interchangeably in what follows. Don't be misled by my choice here; and see the upcoming subsection on the public interest.

[7] Some formal exceptions to the Sherman Antitrust Act are permitted in the US. A famous example is Major League Baseball; other examples include farm-product cooperatives, where (not-to-exceed) production allocations are given to farmers by a "joint marketing board," to keep prices high.

And what about the list of four conditions back on pages 56 and 57?

1. *The parties involved must want to collude.* This is certainly not guaranteed. For many years, for instance, the three "respectable" daily newpapers in England were the *Times of London*, the (Manchester) *Guardian*, and the *Daily Telegraph*. They enjoyed very restrained competition, with high subscription and lineage (advertising) rates. Then Rupert Murdoch bought the *Times*. Murdoch had no interest in restraining his competition with anyone; both subscription and lineage rates plunged.

    A second example concerns the major commercial airframe manufacturers, Boeing and Airbus. The industry is complex for a variety of reasons but the two, if they wished to, could probably achieve a measure of restraint in how they compete by their selections of product mix. But, while hate is a strong word, it probably isn't too strong in describing how executives at each firm feel about their rival. So the prospect of restrained competition between the two has never been realized.

2. *The parties must have a clear understanding of what is the deal.* When we are speaking of OPEC—an explicit cartel—the mechanism for achieving clarity is obvious: They hold meetings and negotiate. But in most cases, explicit collusion runs afoul of antitrust laws. And achieving clarity of such deals tacitly can prove difficult; see the section further on concerning segmentation strategies.

3. *The future benefits from keeping to the deal must outweigh the advantages that can be gained by short-run "defections" from it.* A story that speaks to this issue concerns the market for civilian air engines. In the early 1980s, the three major manufacturers of these engines were General Electric, Pratt & Whitney, and Rolls-Royce. At the time, Boeing was bringing two new airframes to market—the 757 and 767—and airlines were looking at the three for engines to put on the planes they were ordering. Rolls-Royce, to develop a competitive product, needed development funds from the British government, and the government took the position that they would supply those funds *only if* Rolls-Royce could get some firm orders.

    Pratt & Whitney saw this as an opportunity to deal a death blow to R-R: They "guaranteed" potential customers that their engine would be 8% more fuel efficient than the competing R-R engine, where the force of the guarantee was that P&W would pay any airline that bought P&W engines for fuel costs in excess of 92% of what a R-R engine would have delivered. By this means, P&W hoped to starve R-R of any firm orders, which would mean no development funds, which would mean that the 8% guarantee would be inexpensive to fulfill: *If* R-R developed the new engine, the 8% guarantees would be very costly to P&W, but if R-R didn't develop the new engine, P&W would be safe.

The attempted knock-out blow *almost* worked. It worked, certainly, in that R-R lost orders to P&W; no airline could resist this guarantee. But the British government, seeing what was going on, gave the development funds to R-R anyway, and P&W took a very expensive bath as it fulfilled its guarantees.

The morale: If you want restrained competition, you want circumstances to be arranged so that "brilliant aggressive strategies" never enter the minds of any of the industry participants.

4. *The parties must be able to detect transgressions against the deal.* We return to the example of OPEC. For reasons we'll discuss in a couple of paragraphs, OPEC is no longer very effective as a cartel for maintaining high prices. But, in the 1980s and into the 1990s, OPEC controlled enough of the world's supply of crude oil to be effective: The oil ministers of the member states of OPEC would meet, allocate "production quotas" to each member, and the price of crude would rise. But, then, it would begin to slip, slowly at first, and then more and more rapidly. The problem: The oil ministers could agree on quotas for each member state, but the presumed enforcement was: If someone violates their quota, we'll all pump a lot of oil and drive the price of crude much lower. And the problem was: When the price of crude is high, every member of OPEC has a strong incentive to "cheat" on its quota and put a little more crude into the spot market than it was allowed under its quota. The spot market being pretty opaque, it was never clear who was pumping more than they should. So some cheating—never clear who—would take place. The eventual outcome of this was that the cartel's enforcers, the Saudis, would open the spigots and the price of crude would plummet. And since all members knew this outcome was coming, all had increased incentive to sneak a bit extra into the market before prices fell, hastening the day when prices would fall. After a period of low prices, the oil ministers would meet again, all member states would agree to their quotas with firm pledges of "this time, we mean it," and the dance would begin again.

If it could be determined who had cheated on the deal at the start, a more targeted (and hence, more effective) punishment might have been devised; say, a lower quota for that state "next time." But since the miscreant state(s) could never be identified, the cartel never achieved lasting restraint.

Nowadays, OPEC has little ability to keep the price of crude high, because it no longer controls a large share of recoverable crude. This leads to a fifth condition, one that is important in the real world of oligopolistic competition and collusion:

5. *The parties to the agreement must be able to "control" their industry and retain the extra profits they make through restraint.* There are a number of pieces to this. To begin, if the parties restrain their competition and so make good profits, they

are likely to attract new entrants. Barriers to that entry become important: If new entrants arrive and compete away the profits of the colluders, this lowers the future value of colluding today, potentially fracturing the deal.

And, sometimes, partners to such schemes are not the only suppliers of their product. OPEC, even at the peak of its powers, faced a *competitive fringe* of nonmembers who, of course, increased the amount of crude they extracted whenever OPEC caused prices to rise through internal restraints on production quantitites. And as the competitive fringe became less and less of a fringe and more and more equal to the OPEC countries in terms of percentage of available crude reserves, OPEC's power dwindled to the point where, today, their ability to enforce high prices, even temporarily, is largely gone.[8]

Taking this idea a step further, collusion is more likely when the benefits from colluding are greater. This takes us back to the Porter Five Forces and, in particular, substitutes, suppliers, and customers. That is, few/poor substitutes, relatively weak suppliers, and relatively weak customers, together with high entry barriers, are all conditions that tend to promote collusive schemes.

What's the Ideal Number of Parties to a Collusive Scheme?

It is generally held that a collusive arrangement is more likely to succeed the smaller is the number of parties involved. More participants means, in general, that it is harder to observe what each is doing, to come to agreements, and to avoid misunderstandings. The more prospective participants there are, the more likely it is that some party will simply be unwilling to cooperate. And, typically, the gains from defection for a single participant do not fall as quickly as the gains from collusion; a defector might, temporarily, take a huge share of the market, while in the collusive scheme, the individual participant must be content with its proportional share.

Some of these factors can give rise to a vicious cycle: More participants make it more likely that someone may defect, raising the level of mistrust among the participants, which decreases the perceived future value of the agreement, which increases the odds that some participant will defect.

---

[8] While OPEC can no longer enforce high prices through collective action by its members, individual members and, in particular, Saudi Arabia, can cause spot prices to plummet, by pumping massive quantities of crude. And, starting mid-year in July 2014, the Saudis did just that. Most observers have concluded that this was an attempt by the Saudis to drive the "fringe" of shale-oil producers out of the market; shale-oil production, to be profitable, requires a certain price for crude, and the Saudis' play was to depress prices so much that the shale-oil producers would depart, never to return, even when prices went back up. The nature of this play involves a distinction between sunk and fixed costs in shale-oil production, and we defer until Chapter 14, when we have the necessary tools, the complete story. But, for now: As I write this paragraph late in 2016, it appears that the Saudis have admitted defeat in this play: OPEC has met and set quotas that has caused prices to rise, although there is evidence, once again, of almost immediate cheating on the quotas that were set.

The existence of a competitive fringe complicates matters. The more firms there are that are not "bound" by the agreement but that instead take advantage of the restraint exercised by parties to the agreement, the less future value there will be to keeping the agreement. Or, to put it in more dynamic terms, an industry that has achieved restrained competition amongst its members faces a hard choice when a new firm enters: Band together and try to force the newcomer to rethink its entry decision, or try to welcome the newcomer to the "club?" The former can be very expensive in the short run; the latter is potentially ruinous in the longer run, insofar as it lowers entry barriers.

Market Segmentation

Market segmentation is a very common scheme by which firms in an industry try to moderate their internal competition. Each firm has its own segment of the market—geographically determined, or determined by product characteristics—and firms, content with their own segments, stay out of the segments that have been "colonized" by other firms.

There are two obvious advantages to such schemes: First, they make it relatively easier to tell when one firm "breaks" the deal. If Firm A is the sole provider to some segment of the market and, suddenly, Firm B begins to confront Firm A on Firm A's territory, it is clear to everyone what is going on. This doesn't mean that Firm B will never try such a thing. But insofar as restraint is backed by credible and sufficiently dire threats of what happens if Firm B tries such a thing, at least the firms know when to trigger the threatened actions. And Firm B, knowing that the other firms will recognize what it has done, is then less likely to start the conflict.

Second, qualitative divisions of this sort are more likely to arise tacitly than are divisions that are more quantitative. It can be difficult for firms to signal to one another that "I'll let you have a 35% share of the market, but no more." It is relatively easier to signal "I won't compete with you in Europe, but if you try to compete with me in South America, I'll fight you *and* set up operations in Europe."

There are three negatives to bear in mind when contemplating a segmentation strategy:

1. Market conditions change unevenly in different regions/product lines. Today, Firm A may be content with Territory X, leaving Territory Y to Firm B. But if Territory Y is growing more rapidly or otherwise confers longer-term benefits on Firm B, Firm A may come to regret this deal and, by seeking to change it, destroy the deal.

2. Entry barriers can be adversely affected. An important barrier to entry is the psychological fear that incumbent firms will go to war with a new entrant. But if an entrant invades the segment held by one firm, only that one firm is in a position to impede the entry.

3. Market segmentation can be perceived by legal authorities as a violation of antitrust law and, so, invite the unwanted (by the firm) attention of those authorities. Antitrust law varies from jurisdiction to jurisdiction, so it is impossible to say succinctly how segmentation is viewed in general. But, at least in the U.S., market segmentation stands a greater chance of success on legal grounds the greater the cost-related reasons for the segments. So, for instance, in an industry where transportation costs are significant—think soft-drink or beer distribution—geographic segmentation is more likely to be acceptable under antitrust laws.

The Public Interest

When collusion, whether explicit or tacit, is attained, it comes at the expense of the customers of the industry. In many cases and in many economies, preventing collusion is a matter of law and public policy.

In some cases—most notably in the case of labor unions—laws and public policy work the other way around, allowing "collusion" among sellers. A common story in such cases is that this is needed to redress the too-powerful position of buyers/employers. And, in some cases, governments allow some collusion on grounds of standards setting, technological efficiency, or to prevent "ruinous" competition. At least these are the stories; the public policies we see in such cases mix in various proportions good economic intentions, *stories* of good economic intentions, and interest-group politics.

Still, the balance of such policies and laws runs against collusion. Especially when facing examples of tacit collusion, courts and, ultimately, legislatures can face the following sorts of situations.

1. Suppose competitors, with no overt discussion, fall into a pattern of charging similar prices, with one of the competitors leading the way by announcing price and service policy changes that others in the industry nearly immediately follow.

2. Suppose, in a particular industry, the firms involved fall into a pattern of geographic segmentation, where each company "controls" the market in some region, largely unchallenged by its rivals.

3. Suppose that entry into a particular industry, especially an industry characterized by one of the preceding two patterns, is met by vicious price cutting, driving the entrant out and (thereby) erecting psychological barriers that keep other potential entrants from entering.

Are such practices violations of sensible antitrust policy? How and where does one draw the line between restraint among rivals—to use a term that makes the behavior seem, if not desirable (from the public's point of view), at least defensible—and tacit collusion, to use a term chosen to make the behavior sound nefarious?

Different polities have arrived at different answers to this question. Most notably, the legal tradition within the United States is that to be guilty of antitrust violations, the parties involved must have taken overt acts to collude. It doesn't need to be as blatant as secret meetings in hotel rooms, but intentionality must be shown. In the European Community, in contrast, outcomes matter much more; if the results of behavior are that prices are "unnaturally" high, a violation of antitrust law has occurred. So, as aspiring managers, weighing in the balance your legal responsibilities, your fiduciary responsibilities to shareholders, and your larger ethical responsibilities, you should probably take advice on how the law works where your firm operates.

Regulatory authorities also face ethical dilemmas. Imagine that two strong global firms in an industry wish to merge. Imagine that this merger has the potential of crushing a domestic firm within some country, although the merger will not measurably harm the interests of customers within that country. If the law concerning whether the merger is anticompetitive is murky, should the authorities in the country "misuse" their power to prevent the merger, to protect home-grown firms? Should they use the threat of regulatory action to wring concessions from the merging firms, concessions that do not go directly at the merger itself but protect domestic firms?

Do not expect to find easy answers to any of these questions. The line that divides legal from illegal conduct is often fuzzy, and the line that divides ethical from unethical conduct is fuzzier still. Management has a responsibility to the public, but it also has a fiduciary responsibility to protect and increase the value of its equity. Regulatory bodies, being essentially political, certainly face conflicts of interest. Where the law is unclear, because of legitimate conflicts of interests on both sides, ethics are as well. These are issues that modern economies address daily, with a great deal of controversy.

While I can supply no ultimate answers to any of these questions, I would like to be clear on one point: Students with an interest in public policy, on reading this section, have sometimes asserted that the section itself is unethical, being a primer on "How to Collude." I disagree, on three grounds:

1. In many cases, the law is unclear, and management has a fiduciary responsibility to the holders of its equity. I am certainly uncomfortable with the position that management should push the law whenever and wherever it can. But I am also uncomfortable with the position that management should forebear from perfectly legal actions that would enhance the value of equity.

2. Effective antitrust and anticollusion enforcement begins with an understanding of how collusion and, to look ahead to next chapter, predatory entry deterrence works. Legislators who draft the laws and regulatory authorities that administer them should understand how tacit collusion can be achieved and what structural impediments can be placed in its way. If

you feel that you just read "How to Collude," perhaps a more sympathetic reading would be "How Colluders Collude, and What You Can Do to Make It Difficult for Them."

3. And, should you find yourself the customer of (what you suspect) is a collusive group of suppliers, knowing "how colluders collude, and what you can do to make it difficult for them" can be a very useful bit of knowledge.

3.3. Other Applications of the Folk Theorem

Oligopolistic collusion is an important application of the basic idea of the folk theorem, but it is far from the only managerially relevant application. Whenever two (or more) parties enter in repeated transactions, the folk theorem can come into play as a primer on how to achieve win–win solutions.

For instance, imagine two firms, one that bottles soft drinks and another that makes glass bottles. Because of the costs of transporting empty bottles, it makes sense for the bottle manufacturer and the bottler to locate facilities close to one another. Indeed, it makes sense for them to have adjoining plants, with a conveyor belt that moves empty bottles right onto the bottling line of the soft-drink bottler.

But each firm must worry: Once it has invested in a facility next door to the other party, perhaps the other party will try to take advantage. The bottle manufacturer may worry that the bottler will insist on cutting the price it pays for the bottles. Once the bottle-manufacturing plant is built, what recourse does the bottle manufacturer have? On the other hand, if the best alternative supplier of empty bottles is at some distance, perhaps the bottle manufacturer will exploit this and extract a higher price for its bottles.

Such vertical relations have become extremely important, as manufacturers are increasingly reliant on supply chains. And if you think of the downstream firm as "managing" the supply chain—a situation we will discuss at length in Chapter 5—there are also cases where the upstream firm is the "leader"; think, for instance, of a car manufacturer that sells its cars via a network of franchised dealers (which is the topic of Chapter 8).

What is true for firms is true for countries that are trading partners. At least in the days before GATT and the World Trade Organization (WTO), countries like the United States and Japan maintained relatively open trading relations because each knew that if one tried to take advantage, by slapping on a tariff, say, the other could respond quickly, to the detriment of both sides. (So why have GATT and the WTO? Since there are decided inefficiencies to having a welter of bilateral trading relationships, uniformity in trade rules makes a lot more sense.)

A firm whose workforce is organized and the union that represents its workers provide another example. Without going into all the details, it may surprise you to learn that, in the United States, the presence of a labor union in a firm has a slightly positive impact on firm productivity on average, controlling for obvious factors. The story behind this is, more or less, the Folk Theorem: The ongoing relationship between the labor union and management allows each side to trust the other, with a positive impact on productivity. Each party can trust the other, because each can powerfully harm the other, if the other tries to take advantage. It is worth noting, though, that this is an average effect with a lot of dispersion around the mean. Some labor–management relationships are cooperative and positive, like the grim cooperation versus grim cooperation equilibrium in the Repeated Prisoners' Dilemma; other labor–management relationships are destructive, like an always confess–always confess equilibrium in the repeated game.[9]

A final example concerns peer pressure in small work groups or partnerships. Imagine a situation in which a number of individuals have to exert themselves for the common good. If A works hard, she generates benefits for the entire group, but she bears all the costs of working hard. The same is true of B, C, and D. Suppose that A, while she is working, can observe how hard B, C, and D are working and they can observe her. If this group falls into a behavioral pattern where everyone works hard for the common good, all benefit. And this sort of pattern can be sustained, as long as B, C, and D have a way to punish A for slacking off.

One way to punish A, of course, is for B, C, and D to slack off themselves. But often, in small work groups, there are usually even better ways to sanction slackards. Small workgroups often form social groups. Each member of a well-functioning, well-constructed work group values the social interactions he or she has with other members. So if A slacks off, B, C, and D can punish her by denying her the social interaction she values. Moreover, people usually have a taste for the good regard of their peers. When A slacks off, B, C, and D can show her by word and deed that they think she is a, well, several words come to mind, but I do not want to commit any to paper. Both the threat of social sanctions and the prospective loss of the regard of her peers keeps A's nose to the grindstone and keeps the group, as a group, cooperative and productive.

In this regard, social homogeneity in a small work group may be positive. Worker A is more likely to be careful about incurring social sanctions of her fellow group members, if they all bowl at the same bowling alley or drink at the same pub. Moreover, A is more likely to be concerned with the good opinion of B, C, and D if they are socially similar to her. This is not to say that social homogeneity is the be-all and end-all of small work groups. There are often

---

[9] This is a much more complex story than this simplistic rendition would indicate. For a fuller analysis, including citations to the data of the unionization effect on productivity, see Chapter 7 in J. Baron and D. Kreps, *Strategic Human Resources: Frameworks for General Managers* (New York: John Wiley, 1999).

very good reasons to strive for social diversity in such groups, but there are also some reasons why social homogeneity is valuable. If the reasons to have socially diverse groups are strong, it may make sense for management to build a sense of social identity among members of the work group. Management may want to build social ties where, unaided, they would be weak, say, by putting the team through a shared experience, building diverse teams that share some common hobby or life experience, or by promoting after-hours social interaction.

But do not forget the embarrassment of riches provided by the Folk Theorem. A small, socially homogeneous work group *may* adopt an equilibrium—a specialist in organizational behavior would use the term *work norm*—of hard work to provide all with lots of compensation. But in a different equilibrium, hard work may be frowned on as "rate busting," and a socially homogeneous work group is equally capable of enforcing this sort of norm. The predisposition of the parties involved—everyone should work hard versus no one should rate-bust—must be considered.

These other applications begin with the folk theorem but do not end there:

- We already signaled in several places that credibility and general reputation can be significant factors to consider.

- The governance of relationships in these applications (who makes which decisions when) is very important and requires further analysis.

These two issues are explored in the next two chapters.

Executive Summary

- Cooperation can emerge in repeated interactions if the parties engage in self-interested reciprocity: A does nice things today for B and C, because of the good things they will do for her later if she does *and* because of the bad things they will do to her later if she does not.

- The formal, game-theoretic expression of this simple idea is the Folk Theorem: An outcome of the game that gives to each player a payoff that exceeds the player's max–min payoff can be sustained as a Nash equilibrium if the discount factor α is close enough to 1.

- The chief weakness in the Folk Theorem, and in this basic idea, is that it makes too many outcomes into potential equilibria: The Folk Theorem tells us that cooperation is possible, not that it is inevitable or what form it will take.

- To get this sort of cooperative, ongoing equilibrium, it takes (a) a willingness of the parties to cooperate, (b) clarity as to what is the "deal," (c) at all times, more value to each party to keep the agreement than to take momentary advantage, and (d) the ability of each party to monitor the behavior of others.

- An important application of this basic economic idea concerns collusion, both explicit and tacit, in oligopolies. For collusion to work, the members of the industry must be inclined to collude. But beyond a willingness to collude, important structural conditions must hold: Momentary advantage cannot be too decisive, the future must hold enough promise to keep current actions in check, entrants must be kept out (or domesticated), compliance must be observable, the number of members cannot be too large, and the "agreement" must be clear.

- Many other applications of the basic idea are found in economics, including long-term trading relationships between companies and countries, efficiency in work settings with organized labor, and peer pressure in small work groups.

Problems

This chapter has been conceptual rather than computational. Some very nice models of the concepts can be developed (you got a taste of some of them in Section 3.1), but the mathematics necessary for an analysis of them, dynamic programming, is probably not in the arsenal of most readers. If you know dynamic programming and wish to build your understanding of these concepts by working through some models, try the problems in Chapter 14 of D. Kreps, *A Course in Microeconomic Theory* (Princeton, NJ: Princeton University Press, 1990). Meanwhile, here are two "discussion topics" that rely to some extent on the ideas of this chapter.

3.1 In the United States, real estate brokerage fees for private residences are usually 6% of the gross price of the property.[10] That is, if a property is sold through a broker for $200,000, then $12,000 is paid to the broker(s) involved, either by the buyer or by the seller. (It is a matter of negotiation between the buyer and the seller who pays the fee.) If both buyers and sellers have their own broker, then this fee is split, usually 50–50, between the two brokers.

Brokers provide many valuable services. Because they maintain a network among themselves, they can match prospective buyers and sellers. To help sellers, they can screen out nonserious buyers; and to help buyers, they can select houses that, according to information they are given by the buyer, match the requirements and tastes of the buyer. They help sellers present their properties effectively, and they help buyers recognize important factors to consider when evaluating a particular property. Most agents are members of the Board of Realtors, a professional body that provides arbitration services when a dispute arises between agents or between an agent and client. The Board of Realtors

---

[10] I'm giving a too-simple picture of this industry for pedagogical purposes. In fact, average broker fees are below the "nominal" 6%, for reasons that the problem will mention.

also provides a clearinghouse for information, so individual agents are well informed about what properties are on the market. And it provides a code of ethics for agents.

Another service provided by the Board of Realtors, at least in some states of the United States, is that it registers all sales made through its members. It has a listing of recent sales that describes the property, the purchase price, mode of financing (in some cases), and all commissions and fees. Commission and fee data are made available as a service to the public, so that prospective buyers and sellers can evaluate what will be the net cost of buying or selling property and can understand what are common practices, such as whether buyers or sellers pay particular fees, in the area.

Especially in areas where housing prices have increased dramatically, far above the general rate of inflation, it is something of a mystery why brokerage fees continue to stay at 6%. The marginal cost of providing brokerage services would not seem to rise linearly with the price of property and there are many brokers, so that the brokerage service market seems fairly competitive. One might expect in consequence that commissions on more expensive properties would be less than 6%, and that, as housing prices inflate faster than general inflation, the average commission percentage would decrease, but while this has happened, it hasn't happened to the extent one might expect.

You are advising a state legislator about this. The state legislator wishes to promote competition in real estate brokerage, to benefit consumers. Why, do you think, competition has not forced down commission rates? What can the state legislator do to promote competition in this industry? And, looking over the longer horizon of, say, the past thirty years, what impact (do you expect) the internet has had on real-estate commissions?

3.2 The European Economic Community was formed in part to lower trade barriers and standardize trading relations *within* the community. But another rationale concerned trading relations between member states and countries outside the EEC. Recall, in this regard, that when the U.K. joined, there was much negotiation and dispute about how the U.K.'s relations with its Commonwealth of Nations would (henceforth) be managed.

From the perspective of this chapter, what is/was going on here?

4. Credibility and Reputation

This chapter concerns two linked phenomena: credibility and reputation. First we ask, What makes a promise or a threat credible? Several answers are given, but we emphasize the role that reputation—and the desire to protect it—can play in lending credibility to a promise or threat.

Monopolists are rarely the object of sympathy or pity. After all, according to the standard theory of monopoly,[1] a monopolist examines the demand function for its product, determines which price maximizes profit, declares this to be the price, then watches profit roll in. What other subspecies of economic animal has a board game named after it?

The life of a real monopolist is not so smooth, however:

- When the 086 chip, the central processor of the original IBM PC, was first developed and sold by Intel, personal computer manufacturers were wary of designing computers that would use the chip. They were concerned that once they built a product around the 086 chip, had software developed for it, and established a base of customers who used the chip, they would be at the mercy of Intel, which could raise prices and thereby extract any profits the manufacturer might earn in the PC business. *How could Intel convince computer manufacturers that, once they were hooked on the 086 chip, they would not be subjected to rising prices?*

- In the early days of the copier business, Xerox had a virtual monopoly on the manufacture and sale of plain paper copiers. The technology was vastly superior to available alternatives—do any readers remember the days of carbon paper?—and some potential users, such as high-end law firms, were willing to pay a premium price for a copier. But Xerox encountered some resistance: Potential customers anticipated that Xerox, having sold its copiers to such high-end users at a premium price, might then cut prices for the next tier of users. Anticipating this, many high-end users waited for prices to fall. *How could Xerox convince its high-end customers that it would not lower prices once it saturated the high-end-customer segment of its potential market?*

- For many years, Polaroid enjoyed a virtual monopoly in the instant photography segment of the photography industry. To be sure, instant photography was small potatoes compared to standard photography, but if Polaroid's position was limited, it was enviable. Then, in 1976, Kodak announced that

---

[1] I assume that all readers will have seen a version of the basic theory of monopoly pricing. If this is entirely new to you, it will be discussed in detail in Part II of the book.

it was going to enter this line of business. Kodak tailored its entry strategy in a way that left Polaroid somewhat protected: Profits in instant photography come from selling film rather than cameras, and Kodak entered with a camera–film package incompatible with Polaroid's cameras and film and with a fairly expensive camera. Kodak was as much as saying that it wanted to share in the market and not drive Polaroid out. Polaroid had to choose: It could respond in "businesslike" fashion, accommodating itself to Kodak's entry, which would probably have left it with substantial profit. Or it could choose to go to war against Kodak, an expensive and uncertain proposition, especially given Kodak's immense financial strength. *Both to protect its monopoly against this incursion by Kodak and to forestall other entrants, how should Polaroid react?*

This chapter examines two intertwined topics that bear on these three stories: credibility and reputation. Section 4.1 discusses the basic issue of credibility and some solutions that work in specific instances. Section 4.2 discusses the economic model of reputation, emphasizing how reputation can—in theory—enhance credibility, and what are the real-life complications in building and then maintaining a reputation.

4.1. Credibility

Consider the extensive-form games depicted in Figure 4.1. In this game, called the *Threat Game*, Player B (he) must decide whether to challenge Player A (she). If there is no challenge, B nets 0, and A gets 2. But, if A is challenged, then she must decide whether to fight or acquiesce. Acquiescence nets 1 for A, while fighting costs her 1, so it seems likely that A would acquiesce if challenged. Therefore, Player B can safely challenge A and get a payoff of 1.

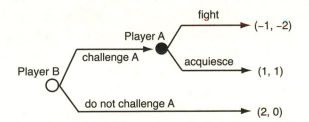

Figure 4.1. The Threat Game. Player B must decide whether to challenge A. If B challenges A, A must decide whether to acquiesce or to fight. Fighting is bad for A once A has been challenged, but if B is convinced that A would fight, B does not challenge A, which is good for A. Therefore, A would like to threaten B that she would fight if challenged. But is this threat credible? (A's payoffs are listed first and B's second.)

Or can he? What if, as he starts to issue the challenge, A bares her teeth, growls, and issues a warning that, *even though* it will cost her 1 to fight, she will fight if challenged. If he believes this threat, he stays out, and she gets 2. Since it does not hurt her to make such a threat—talk is cheap—she can growl away. But precisely because talk is cheap, Player B probably should disregard this threat as mere posturing. Assuming we have the payoffs right, Player A's threat lacks credibility.

Next consider Figure 4.2. This extensive-form game, called the *Trust Game*, has the same basic structure of moves as the threat game, but the payoffs (hence the names of the moves) are entirely different.

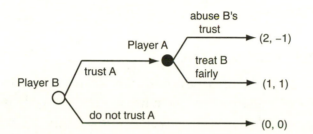

Figure 4.2. The Trust Game. Player B must decide whether to trust A. If B trusts A, A must decide whether to treat B fairly or be abusive. Abuse is best for A once she gets B's trust, but if B anticipates this, he will refrain from trusting A, to the detriment of both. Therefore, A would like to promise B that she will not abuse him. But is this promise credible? (A's payoffs are listed first and B's second.)

Player B must decide at the outset whether to trust A. If B does not trust A, both sides net 0. If B trusts A, A must choose between treating B fairly, netting 1 apiece, or abusing B's trust, which nets 2 for A and −1 for B.

In this game, if B trusts A, A gets a higher payoff by abusing him than by treating him fairly. Seeing this, B would not trust A, to the detriment of both. So, before B decides whether to trust A, perhaps A should smile at B, make soothing noises, and tell him that she promises no abuse. Perhaps she can convince him to trust her. But is this credible? If A plans to abuse B, would she not smile and offer a promise of no abuse? This sort of promise is cheap talk once again, lacking credibility.

These two examples are very different, but they share a basic structure: In each case, B must act, forecasting A's response. In each case, the best action for A once B has acted is clear. And, in each case, to elicit a particular initial action from B, A wishes to convince B that she would not act in her own *ex post* best interests. How can she do this credibly?

The term *credibility* has a number of meanings in English. In this chapter, we use the term as follows: We are always concerned, as in these games, with what some parties (call them Bs) expect, anticipate, fear, or hope would be the future actions of some other party (A). To induce desired behavior by others today, A wants to influence the expectations, anticipations, and, in some cases, fears or hopes of the Bs. Intel wanted to convince potential clients that it (Intel) would not dramatically increase the price of its microprocessors, once it had "hooked" a client base. Xerox wanted to convince potential high-end clients that it would not lower the price of its copiers in the future. Polaroid wanted to convince prospective entrants such as Kodak, and especially Kodak, that entry into Polaroid's domain of instant photography would be an unpleasant and unprofitable experience for the entrant. Is any of this credible? Unless it is, Bs cannot reasonably be expected to adopt the desired expectations, anticipations, fears, or hopes.

So the question becomes, How can A make credible what she wants to be credible?

Tying Your Own Hands, Alone

One way for A to make credible the actions she wants to be credible is to redesign the situation so that those actions are in her interests ex post as well as ex ante. She can take steps that improve the payoff to herself if she takes those actions, or she can worsen her payoff if she does anything else. Since it is typically harder to improve one's payoffs from one action than it is to worsen them from another, we look for steps A can take that effectively tie her own hands, by substantially worsening her payoffs if she takes the "wrong" action.

Contracts promising specific performance are an obvious example of this. If the contract is enforceable by the courts, if it is clear that the Bs will avail themselves of court enforcement, and if the penalty for breach is substantial enough, party A, by entering into a contract, can render the promise of contractually stipulated performance quite credible. Do not go past the first two *ifs* in the previous sentence too quickly, however. Contracts work only to the extent that the courts enforce them, which requires first of all that the aggrieved party sees it in his interests to take the matter to court (see Problem 4.1).

Contracts are promises secured by court-enforced penalties in the event of breach. But they require third-party enforcement, which can be costly. Rather than enter into a contract, party A may simply structure matters so that the Bs, on their own, can punish A for misbehavior or malfeasance.

Consider, for instance, the problem facing Intel, which was to reassure its potential customers that it would not increase microprocessor prices once they were hooked. Intel could write a contract guaranteeing customers access to a certain number of microprocessors at a certain cost, but such a contract would either be extraordinarily rigid (unable to adapt to changes in the cost conditions facing Intel, technological innovations, or changes in the demands of customers) or, if it attempted to be flexible to these things, too complex to be enforceable.

Instead of offering rigid or unenforceable contractual guarantees, Intel simply licensed production of its microprocessors to several competitors. This reassured potential customers that *if* Intel raised prices or rationed supply, the customers would have alternative sources. Intel could not successfully hold up its clients, and so it had no incentive to try.

(The Intel story is more complex than this quick recapitulation indicates, however, because for later generations of the 086 microprocessor, Intel drew back its licenses. Specifically, Intel licensed the 086 chip to 12 other manufacuters and, in fairly short order, was left with only a 30% market share in these chips. For the 286 chip, Intel cut the number of licensees to five and retained a 75% market share. And for the 386 chip, only IBM was given a license, to produce only for IBM's own computers. To the substantial extent that clients of the 086 chip were thereby addicted to subsequent generations of X86 chips, Intel's initial assurances provided by the licenses did not, in the end, provide all that much protection. It is doubtful that potential clients, when deciding whether to adopt the Pentium, would have been very reassured had Intel licensed broadly production of the first generation of Pentiums. So why has Intel not engaged in the holdup originally feared? The stories in the next section, about reputation, may be the answer. And some of Intel's clients might argue that, to some extent, Intel did take advantage of its very strong position as a monopoly supplier of a good to which many downstream manufacturers became somewhat addicted.)

A second example involves the actions of James Casey, the founder of the United Parcel Service, the leading package delivery company in the United States. When Casey first organized UPS, his plans for the business put a premium on getting the cooperation of the truck drivers, who would be largely unmonitorable, since they work out of the eye of any supervisors. To reassure his employees that he would not take advantage of them once they entered employment and set down roots, Casey invited the Teamsters labor union to organize his workforce. This happened at a time when management in the United States was generally extremely hostile to efforts by their workforce to organize. But Casey reasoned that, by inviting the Teamsters in and, from the start, building a constructive relationship with the union, he would give his workforce a hammer with which to pound UPS if UPS management tried to take advantage of the workforce. Therefore, the workforce could trust that UPS management would not try to take advantage, which in turn would benefit the company.

The punishment for misbehavior or malfeasance need not be rendered by a court or the injured party. To make a particular sort of behavior credible, party A might enlist social sanctions. The idea, roughly, is to set things up so that, if A acts badly, she is guilty of the violation of a social norm and will be punished socially accordingly. Promising good behavior in the presence of witnesses— and being demonstrative about this—can sometimes work. Promises made within a family-owned business are generally held to be fairly credible, because breaking a promise to a family member often results in social sanctions from the family. Although there are obvious problems with business done solely in an old-boy network or (only) with "members of the club," promises made within such a closed and close social circle can gain credibility on similar grounds.

Tying Your Hands, So You Must Fight

Notions of contracts and the examples of Intel and of UPS concern situations strategically similar to the trust game: Party A wishes to ensure the Bs that she would not abuse them in the future. On the other side of the coin are situations resembling the threat game, where party A wants to render credible the threat that she will fight any B that challenges her. *Tying your hands*, in this context, means constructing the situation so that, when challenged, it is more costly to acquiesce than to fight. The idea usually is not that A makes fighting more attractive but that she makes acquiescing so unattractive that she must fight.

This phenomenon arises in particular in the context of entry deterrence: A potential rival (B) must decide whether to enter a market; and if it enters, the incumbent firm (A) must decide whether to accept the entry or fight, where fighting is costly to both firms. In this context, the incumbent firm might choose a production technology that has very high fixed costs; it might commit to irrevocable agreements to purchase expensive raw materials, turning variable costs of inputs into fixed costs; it might load up on debt that can be serviced only if it maintains market share; or it might covenant its debt so incumbent management loses control of the firm if its market share slips. Then, the incumbent firm's back is to the wall, and it will fight entry. And the potential entrant, seeing that this is so, will not enter.

A model of this is given by the game in Figure 4.3. Party A moves first, choosing between an optimal technology and a high fixed-cost (FC) technology. The word *optimal* here means that the first choice is better than the second, *fixing the action of Player B*. To see this, simply compare the payoffs to A in the top and bottom halves of the game tree.

The virtue of choosing the high FC technology for A is that it is particularly costly if A acquiesces to B's entry, so costly that, if A chose the high FC technology, it would rather fight than acquiesce to entry. If A chooses the high FC technology, B expects a fight if it enters and so chooses not to enter. Since the cost of maintaining the high fixed-cost technology (if it guarantees no entry) is not high relative to using the so-called optimal technology and suffering from entry, the so-called optimal technology is not optimal after all.

This, in essence, is a Porteresque entry barrier, one that lies on the interface between tangible and psychological barriers. A standard interpretation of an entry barrier is some action that makes entry unattractive to a potential entrant by lowering its payoffs if it enters; for instance, firms in the industry might lock up favored resources or channels of distribution, so that an entrant's costs would be high. What we see here is that it may work equally well for firms in the industry to take actions that commit them to a post-entry course of action that is costly for the entrant. In the game, A's choice of technology has no direct impact on B's payoffs; B's payoffs in each half of the tree are identical. But B's decision whether to challenge A changes decisively in the top and bottom parts

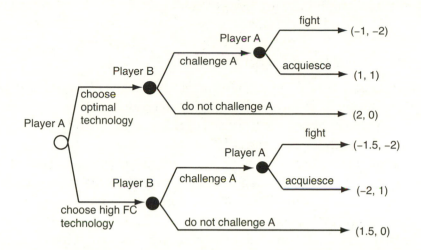

Figure 4.3. Making fighting credible by choosing a suboptimal technology. By choosing the high fixed-cost technology, A lowers its own payoffs at the end of each branch. But, because this choice is extremely harmful to A's payoffs if it acquiesces to entry, B is convinced that A would fight, and so B chooses not to challenge A.

of the game, because of the effect of A's choice of technology on A's payoffs.

This sort of strategem is not danger free. Choosing a high fixed-cost technology can be a good move *if* it keeps at bay rivals, who fear that the technology compels the incumbent to fight. But no such strategem comes with a guarantee. Suppose A chooses the high FC technology then finds that B enters anyway. Party B might do this because its cost structure is such that it prefers to enter, even if it knows a fight will ensue, because it has its own reputation to protect (see the next section) or even out of pique. Then A is in a worse state for having tried to make its threat credible by these means.

For an example along these lines, recall the story from the last chapter about Pratt and Whitney's unsuccessful attempt to knock Rolls-Royce out of a particular segment of the air-engine market. The game involved a third player, the British government, but the idea was the same: Pratt and Whitney issued fuel-efficiency guarantees that would be costly for it *if* Rolls-Royce developed an upgraded engine. Since these guarantees starved Rolls-Royce of orders, they should have ensured that Rolls did not develop the upgraded engine and, therefore, they should not have been costly. This was a brilliant strategic move, *except* that the British government took umbrage and, notwithstanding the economics of the situation, gave Rolls-Royce the money it needed to develop the upgrade, moving Pratt and Whitney to a particularly bad outcome. Or, to cast this in classical military terms, burning your bridges behind you can be a great strategy if it convinces your rival not to attack, because you cannot retreat and your army, realizing this, will fight ferociously. But, if your rival attacks anyway and your ferociously fighting army loses the battle, burning those bridges will look pretty stupid in the history books.

Tying Your Own Hands, and Everyone Else's

The major chemical firms in the United States, such as DuPont and Dow, are among the strongest lobbyists for tough safety and evironmental standards. Since these standards increase the costs of these firms, we might ask why these firms lobby for such tough standards.

One explanation, based on the discussion in the preceding subsections, is that the firms are trying to make a credible promise to various constituencies that they conduct safe, environmentally clean operations.

This is not the only possible explanation. Legislation of this sort binds not only the major chemical firms but also their domestic competitors. Compliance with these sorts of regulations is generally an activity with a substantial fixed-cost component, so it is an activity relatively less expensive for the biggest firms than for smaller competitors. By supporting this sort of legislation, the big firms impose on smaller domestic competitors average costs substantially higher than the costs they impose on themselves.

This strategy (tying your own hands to tie those of your competitors) can go beyond lobbying for government regulations. Go back to the story of Jim Casey, inviting the Teamsters to organize the UPS workforce. One reading of Casey's intentions was given earlier: By empowering his workers, his promises that he would not try to take advantage of them gained credibility. Another reading is that he felt that his management style and business plan was particularly well suited to an empowered workforce; and he had the ability to work in businesslike fashion with the Teamsters, more so than his competitors. His recognition of the Teamsters did not guarantee that the union would subsequently be able to organize his rivals, but it increases the odds that his rivals would find their workforces organized, which, relatively, would be to UPS's benefit.

What if Cheap Talk Is a Little Expensive?

(You may want to skip this section on a first reading, as it gets into some fairly subtle ideas.)

In the preceding discussion of both the trust and the threat games, it was asserted that growling and hissing in B's direction as he decides whether to challenge A in the threat game and smiling at B as he decides whether to trust her in the trust game are unlikely to be effective. These things cost A nothing, and if they were at all efficacious, A would do them regardless of her intentions for subsequent action. So they are meaningless; and B should disregard them. In the language of game theory, they are *cheap talk*, as in "talk is cheap," with the implicit corollary that, when talk is cheap, only actions mean something.

Having said this, it must be admitted that cheap talk does work on some individuals. Individuals in the role of party B sometimes are impressed by hisses and growls or smiles. So, in real-life encounters, don't forswear these apparent indications of your intentions. Maybe your rival will be impressed, even if a game theorist would not be.

This presumes that the hisses, growls, and smiles are costless. In fact, they sometimes cost something, especially when the party who issues them subsequently acts in a manner at variance with her earlier expressions of intent. The cost might be psychological or trace from a loss in general reputation. Abusing a trading partner after smiling at him might, if the smile were observed by others, excite social sanctions. Growling and then backing down might cause a loss of self-esteem or exposure to ridicule.

If the cost of the hisses, growls, and smiles is high enough to guarantee that, once issued, they guarantee the desired subsequent behavior (if, for instance, to back down from a challenge after growling is so costly that, having growled, one is ready and willing to fight), then we are back to the sort of story told earlier. These are actions that, by changing A's payoffs enough, render credible promises of good behavior following smiles or threats of an aggressive response to a challenge in the wake of growls and hisses.

But what if these actions, while costly, are not so costly as to lend full credibility to the desired action? Do they then have any impact? This is a difficult and subtle question. The answers suggested by a game theoretic analysis are not entirely satisfactory. But a game theoretic analysis indicates that they may have an impact. Let me briefly illustrate this point by working with the threat game or, more precisely, the variation depicted in Figure 4.4. Prior to B's decision whether to challenge A, A can take an action, called *costly growling*, that decreases her payoffs everywhere in the game but decreases them in particular if B enters and A acquiesces (does not fight).

Compare Figure 4.4 with Figure 4.3, where costly growling is identified with high FC technology. In both cases, a choice of costly growling–high FC by A lowers A's payoffs relative to no growls–optimal technology. In both cases, B's payoffs are unaffected. But the crucial difference is that, while costly growling is more expensive to A if she does not fight than if she does, the relative expense is insufficient to make fighting better than acquiescing in the event of a challenge. Growling is costly, but not so costly that it makes a fighting response credible.

An application of backward induction to the game tree tells us that Player A would acquiesce if challenged in either half of the tree. Hence, B should enter in either half. Hence, there is no point to costly growling.

Now imagine you are Player B. You have done the analysis just given. You confidently await a lack of throaty noises from A, following which you will enter. And then, to your surprise and consternation, A growls. What do you make of this? How do you respond?

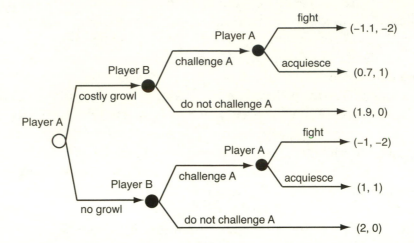

Figure 4.4. Is irrational growling rational? By choosing to growl, A lowers her payoffs at the end of each branch but not by enough that growling makes a fighting response credible. So what impact does growling have? (See the text.)

Your worry—B's worry—is that A will fight you if you challenge her. You were relatively sure she would not do so, because it is not in her interests ex post to do so. But this assurance is predicated on a presumption that A is not a crazy person who might strike out irrationally. And if A is not crazy—if you can be assured that she would acquiesce to entry—why did she engage in this pointless, costly growling? Maybe this is a sign that she is crazy. Maybe you should, on this basis, pick your fights with someone else.

Except, if this growling causes you to forgo the challenge, then growling is an entirely rational thing for A to do. In which case, you should read nothing into it and confidently challenge her. Except, if that is right, then growling is not rational.

To carry out a full analysis of this situation, you need a few techniques from the arsenal of game theorists that I have not introduced. In particular, you need to be able to put within your model the possibility (at least the possibility in the mind of player B) that A might be a crazy person who, notwithstanding the costs of fighting, is willing to fight if challenged. Further, you need to introduce into the model the notion that, if A is crazy in this fashion, she is likely to be growling. Interested readers can consult more advanced textbooks on game theory to see the ideas worked out.

On Kodak's Entry into Instant Photography

The response of Polaroid to Eastman Kodak's entry into instant photography illustrates these ideas. When Eastman Kodak attempted to enter the instant photography business, which had been completely monopolized by Polaroid, it entered in a particularly gentle fashion.[2] Its strategy was tailored to reassure Polaroid that Kodak would not use its immense financial and marketing strengths to knock Polaroid out of the market. In particular, Kodak designed cameras and film that were incompatible with Polaroid's cameras, so that Polaroid would be relatively reassured that it (Polaroid) would be able to continue to make money, selling film to its established customer base. This constituted a tying-our-own-hands strategy by Kodak.

Based on any reasonable financial calculations, it seemed better for Polaroid to acquiesce to Kodak's entry than to fight. This did not seem a fight that Polaroid could win, except by knocking Kodak out of the game with a legal victory in a patent infringement suit. Kodak had enormous financial and marketing strengths, and if the two firms went to war, it was hard to see how a "win" for Polaroid would, on financial grounds, be anything other than a loss.

Notwithstanding these considerations, Polaroid chose war. It launched patent infringement actions. It lowered the prices of its cameras. It brought to market a sequence of improved products, which it had been saving "on the shelf," presumably for just such a situation. And, right at the outset, Polaroid trotted out its founder, Edwin Land, who was quoted in the *New York Times* (April 28, 1976) as saying, "This is our very soul ... our whole life. For them, it's just another field."

It is not hard to imagine Kodak looking at Land's statements and Polaroid's actions and wondering, "What is going on?" Trotting out Land was not entirely costless. If Polaroid plans to accommodate Kodak's entry, putting Land on display means a somewhat painful backing down. So if Polaroid were going to accommodate Kodak, why send Land out in this fashion? Taking into account the patent infringement suits, the new products, and the lowered prices, Kodak had to wonder how far Polaroid was willing to go to defend its turf. Should Kodak be influenced by this? Should it back away from what was beginning to look like a costly fight? If it could be pushed out by such saber rattling, then the saber rattling was rational after all, in which case Kodak should expect Polaroid to back down. But, if Polaroid were going to back down, why rattle those sabers, at some immediate expense, in the first place?

In the event, Polaroid's saber rattling worked. It took quite a while, but every time Kodak tried to signal its firm intentions to stay, Polaroid took what seemed to be another irrational and warlike action. In the end, Kodak folded its hand, leaving instant photography to Polaroid, a monopoly Polaroid maintained until digital photography revolutionized the industry.

---

[2] For details of this case, see the HBS case study *Polaroid vs. Kodak in Instant Photography*, HBS 9-376-266.

4.2. Reputation

We now take up the notion of reputation. The term reputation has a general meaning in common (English) language and a more specific meaning as used in this chapter (and, in most cases, when used by economists). So the first thing to do is to explain the distinctions.

A typical dictionary definition of reputation is *a widespread belief that someone or something has a particular habit or characteristic.* So, for instance, "Dr. Browne [a pediatrician] is always running late because he loves to chat with the parents of his younger patients, especially the younger and prettier moms," is, if widely believed, a part of Dr. Browne's reputation. Digging a bit deeper, we can probably assume that Dr. Browne behaves in this fashion because this behavior directly appeals to him: He likes adult conversation and being in the presence of young and pretty women. The adjectives aren't perfect, but we might call this a *genuine* or *character-revealing* reputation.

Consider as an alternative the following reputation of District Attorney Greene: "He will never make a plea deal with any defendant once the trial begins." This could be genuine if, for instance, Greene believes that, once a jury is empanelled, it is right and proper to let them offer a verdict. But there is another possibility, namely that this behavior is *instrumental.* Greene wants to avoid the cost—to his office and to jurors—of starting a trial, and he feels that, by adhering to this behavior, he pressures defendants into taking plea deals prior to the start of the trial. More than that, he believes that, owing to the uncertainty of a trial and the possible consequences for defendants, pressuring them to take a plea before they see how their trial is going gives him (Greene) more leverage in plea negotiations.

Once a trial begins, Greene sometimes would prefer to take a plea. But he knows that doing so would hurt if not shatter his reputation. Because its impact on future defendants—pressuring them to deal before their trial begins—means more to him than the cost of continuing with today's ongoing trial, he refuses to negotiate any plea. That is, his long-run concern to keep his reputation trumps his short-run desire to settle today's case. This sort of *instrumental* reputation is what this section is about, and it is what economists usually mean when they use the term *reputation.*

A Reputation for Trustworthiness

Imagine that A (she) and B (he) play the trust game repeatedly. To be very specific, suppose that, after each round of play there is a 0.2 chance that the just-completed encounter was the last and a 0.8 chance that they play at least one more time. The payoffs from the sequence of encounters they have is just the expected sum of payoffs. (In exactly the fashion of Chapter 3, you could alternatively imagine that they play the game infinitely many times, with a discount factor 0.8 used to compute net present values.)

As we saw earlier, the only Nash equilibrium in this game played once has B refusing to trust A, because A would abuse B if B were foolish enough to trust to A's good nature. But if we repeat the game in the preceding fashion, the Folk Theorem kicks in and lots of other outcomes are part of equilibria. For instance, suppose that A and B adopt the following pair of strategies:

> B trusts A in the first round and continues to trust A as long as A respects that trust by treating him fairly. But, if A ever abuses B's trust, B grimly refuses to offer trust ever again.

> A treats B fairly in the first round and for as long as she has done so in the past. But if she ever—by mistake, presumably—abuses B, she will abuse him in all subsequent rounds given the chance.

Computation shows that these two strategies constitute a Nash equilibrium for the repeated game. The crucial computation is, Will A treat B fairly when trusted? She can do so and continue to do so, garnering payoffs of 1 in each round, for as long as the game persists. This gives her an expected payoff of

$$1 + (0.8)1 + (0.8)^2 1 + \ldots = 1/0.2 = 5.$$

Or she can act abusively, netting an immediate payoff of 2. But then she would never be trusted again, getting 0 in all subsequent rounds, for an expected payoff of

$$2 + (0.8)0 + (0.8)^2 0 + \ldots = 2.$$

It is pretty clear that she prefers to stick with her part of the equilibrium. And, fixing her strategy, the optimality of A's strategy for him is clear.

Now let me rephrase those two strategies:

> B will trust A in any round if A has the reputation of a trustworthy individual. But B will not trust A if A's reputation is that she is untrustworthy.

> A lives up to her current reputation. She treats B fairly if her (A's) reputation is that of a trustworthy person. But she acts abusively if her reputation is that she is not trustworthy.

> A's reputation begins as a trustworthy person and remains that way as long as she never abuses B's trust. If she does abuse B, she gains a reputation for being untrustworthy, a reputation that can never be shed.

Note that the two players' strategies are described somewhat implicitly here: the actions of A and B both depend on this mysterious new thing, A's reputation. Then the "rule" by which A's reputation evolves is specified. You can turn this into a standard pair of strategies if you wish—in which case you get the strategies given previously—but the point is to phrase things in terms of A's reputation, which is a product of her past behavior.

Of course, since the strategies defined here implicitly are the strategies given before, which form a Nash equilibrium, this is just another way of describing that equilibrium.

The key to this being an equilibrium is the answer to the question, When A has the reputation of being trustworthy, why does she protect this reputation? Why does she forgo the short-run payoff of acting abusively? Preservation of her reputation, while it sacrifices short-run payoff, is better in terms of A's long-run payoff. Protecting her reputation is A's ticket to getting B to trust her, which means good payoffs in the future. In general, a good reputation is worth something, even if it means sacrifice in the short run, if it elicits behavior from others that sufficiently improves the reputation holder's long-run prospects.

Of course, this is not the only equilibrium in the repeated encounter. The Folk Theorem guarantees that there will be a lot more. For instance, consider the reputation-based decision rules just given, but replace the rule for the evolution of A's reputation with *A's reputation is that she is not trustworthy and never will be.* This gives Nash equilibrium strategies where B never trusts A and A would abuse B any time B is silly enough to trust her. There are other equilibria: Where B trusts A and A acts fairly on all even-numbered rounds; where A is trustworthy, hence trusted, on all rounds whose number is not prime; and so forth. When you deal with the folk theorem, you gets lots of equilibria.

A Sequence of Trading Partners

The Folk Theorem, as related in Chapter 3, depends on the folks involved playing the game repeatedly. Specialized to this encounter, the notion is that B, if abused by A, punishes A by refusing to trust her in the future. Suppose instead that A plays the game with one B; call him B1. B1 plays the game once and once only. But A continues (with probability 0.8) to play the game against a different individual, B2. B3 is the other party in the third round, if there is one, and so on. Does this really matter to the equilibria we described?

It does not. Let me restate the first equilibrium for this context, using the language of reputation. Not much changes:

Bn will trust A if A has the reputation of a trustworthy individual and not otherwise, when and if round n comes along.

A behaves in conformance with her reputation, as before.

A's reputation evolves as before: A is perceived at the outset as a trustworthy person, and this remains her reputation as long as she never abuses any B's trust. But, if she does abuse some B, she loses her reputation for trustworthiness, a reputation that can never be reclaimed.

Even though the Bs change, this is still a Nash equilibrium. Now the language of reputation is even more appropriate, since we can imagine Bn asking Bs with earlier experiences with A, "How did she treat you? What's her reputation?" In fact, as long as each Bn asks his immediate predecessor these questions and passes on the information according to the reputation rule, everything works.

To tie this back to credibility, in the trust game played once, according to the payoffs in Figure 4.2, it is not credible that A, if trusted, would treat B fairly. The payoffs facing A motivate her to act abusively once trust is given. Credibility of fair treatment can be restored by a contractual guarantee (backed by the threat of court-ordered sanctions and punishments if A breaches the contract) or by some other structuring of the situation that makes abuse relatively less attractive to A than fair treatment. *Giving A a reputation stake in a repeated game situation is one way that abuse can be made less attractive than fair treatment.* If she is trusted at some date, A does better in the short run by abuse. But traded off against this is the long-run value of her reputation, *assuming* (1) her reputation is valuable, because it induces future Bs to trust her, and (2) abuse would shatter or, at least, damage that reputation. A's desire to protect her reputation, because of its value and fragility, makes fair treatment in any single encounter a credible action.

A Reputation for Toughness: Making Threats Credible

Next imagine that A and B play the Threat Game repeatedly. As before, suppose that, after each round of play, there is a 0.2 chance that the just-completed encounter was the last and a 0.8 chance that they play at least one more time. The payoffs from the sequence of encounters they have is the expected sum of payoffs.

Played once, the sole equilibrium (obtained when you consider how credible is a threat that A would fight) has B enter and A acquiesce. Repeating the encounter opens other possibilities. Consider, for instance, the following strategies for A and B, done up in the language of reputation:

As long as A has a reputation for being tough, B will not challenge her. But he will challenge A if ever A's reputation is that she is a wimp.

A will fight any entry that occurs, as long as she has a reputation for being tough. She will acquiesce if her reputation is that of a wimp.

A's reputation at the outset is that she is tough. It stays that way unless she acquiesces to some entry, after which her reputation is irrevocably that of a wimp.

This holds together as an equilibrium. Moreover, it is an equilibrium where A's threat to fight is now credible. To see this, suppose B challenges A. If A fights, her payoff this round is -1, but she preserves her reputation. Assuming B reverts to the strategy of no entry, this gives A a future stream of payoffs of 2, the expected value of which is

$$-1 + (0.8)2 + (0.8)^2 2 + (0.8)^3 2 + \ldots = 7.$$

(Trust me on the calculation.) If, on the other hand, she acquiesces, she nets 1 immediately, destroys her reputation, and gets a payoff of 1 for the rest of the game, as long as it lasts. This gives her an expected payoff of

$$1 + (0.8)1 + (0.8)^2 1 + \ldots = 5.$$

It is a near thing, but A is better off protecting her reputation than acquiescing and losing it. And if A is going to fight to protect her reputation, B's best response is not to challenge her.

Once again, it is not necessary that one A play one B repeatedly. It suffices that A plays repeatedly, even if A plays a different B in each round, as long as B in round n bases his entry decision on A's reputation, A's reputation evolves as given, and (presumably) B in round n, prior to his entry decision, asks B in round $n - 1$, "What sort of reputation does A have?"

As in the first example, reputation provides credibility. Player A's threat to fight is credible because if she does not fight, she faces a bleaker future than if she does. Acquiescence is relatively more expensive, not in the short run but overall, which is what it takes to make the threat to fight credible.

Sometimes objections to this equilibrium are heard. If the equilibrium describes how the game is played, then A never faces any entry and never has to fight. Put it this way: In the one A against a sequence of Bs version of the game, the answers given by B in round $n - 1$ to B in round n are, "A is tough; she'll fight if you challenge her. But I don't know this from personal experience, because I respected A's reputation and failed to challenge her." Hearing this, B in round n might ask, "Has anyone ever seen A fight?" To which, in the equilibrium described, the answer is, "Nope. She's never been challenged." How did A manage to get this very convenient reputation for toughness? Two answers to this question can be offered:

1. Suppose that a certain fraction of the Bs (say 10%, on average) challenge A no matter what is her reputation, because even if abused, they are better off than if they fail to challenge her. Then, every so often, A faces a challenge, which she must fight to maintain her reputation. A calculation is needed here. If A faces challenges 10% of the time on average no matter what is her reputation and she fights all challenges to forestall others, then instead of averaging 2 per round, she expects to get $(0.9)2 + (0.1)(-1) = 1.7$. If challenged and she fights, her expected payoff is $-1 + (0.8)(1.7) + (0.8)^2 1.7 + \ldots = 5.8$, versus $1 + (0.8)1 + (0.8)^2 1 + \ldots = 5$. The reputation is still worthwhile, but only barely so.

We see this in real life. Procter & Gamble has a reputation for aggressively fighting entrants into its markets. This reputation forestalls most potential rivals, but not all. Those entrants that challenge P&G soon learn that P&G is willing to defend its reputation—which, in the end, is the real source of P&G's very valuable reputation.

2. In both this reputation-based equilibrium and the one in the previous sub-section (for trustworthiness), we started A off with the desirable reputation. In real life, a party A may have to expend some resources to gain the reputation. And, in each of the two cases, this raises some questions.

   In the context of the trust game, A gains the reputation for being trust-worthy by not abusing B. But A has this opportunity *only if* B trusts her. To gain a reputation for being trustworthy, A needs the one B, or some of the Bn, to give her the "benefit of the doubt," at least at the outset. In a setting where most A's abuse anyone foolish enough to trust them, an A who aims to acquire a reputation for trustworthiness may have a hard time getting this off the ground.

   In the context of the threat game, the story is different. If A begins without a reputation for toughness, she will be challenged. This gives her the opportunity to fight her challenger and (perhaps slowly) convince the single B or the later Bn that she is tough. But, if she starts without this reputation, she has to do a calculation at the outset: "How many challenges must I fight, to acquire the desired reputation for toughness?" Depending on this number, on the discount factor, and on the relative costs of fighting versus acquiescing versus not being challenged, she may decide that *acquiring* the reputation isn't worth the cost, even if she would happily *defend* the reputation if she had it. And, if B or the Bn see things the same way, they might well challenge her.

One Enduring Player versus Two

In the two examples we explored, reputation works in the general fashion of the Folk Theorem, but both sides to the encounter need not be enduring. It is important that A is enduring, because her credibility is at stake.

Do not conclude from this that everything the Folk Theorem gives us can be gotten with just one enduring player, facing a sequence of rivals. For instance, imagine one enduring player playing a sequence of Prisoners' Dilemma games against a sequence of rivals, each of whom plays once. The short-lived players have no reputation at stake, hence they follow their short-run interests and confess. Because they do, the enduring player has no reason to do otherwise. In the repeated Prisoners' Dilemma game, it takes two enduring players to get away from confess–confess.

On the other hand, when two enduring players are in a conflict situation, the fact that each has a reputation stake has different consequences. Consider the threat game. Do we really expect an enduring A, playing a sequence of threat games, to be able to acquire and defend a reputation for fighting entry? If an enduring A plays a sequence of Bs, each of whom plays only once, this seems entirely plausible, if the costs and benefits come out the right way. The Bs, since they play only once, have no long-run incentive to press A; each is concerned with what A will do only in their one round of play. Because A has a reputation at stake and the Bs do not, A would seem to have the upper hand. But if A plays a single, enduring B, that B might seek to acquire a reputation for never backing down from a fight by challenging A. If B can convince A that he cannot be cowed by a fighting response by A, A has no incentive to fight. When an enduring A meets an enduring B in the repeated threat game, it seems natural to suppose that a war of attrition would start the encounter, where B challenges A and A fights, until one or the other side "gives in" to the superior staying power of the other. (If you consult the advanced literature of game theory, you'll find substantial theoretical support for these intuitions.)

Reputation and Simultaneous Play with Many Partners

In these reputation stories, either A faces a single rival repeatedly or a sequence of rivals, each of whom conditions his choice of action in his own encounter on A's previous behavior. This establishes a possible long-run vs. short-run trade-off for A, which is the basis for A's reputation.

In some instances, instead of facing the Bs in sequence, A faces them simultaneously, but in encounters that take a while to develop. In such cases, A can be restrained by a desire to maintain a good reputation with all her trading partners simultaneously.

For instance, Toyota deals with many suppliers. For most of these suppliers, Toyota is an extremely important client. Toyota's dealings with its suppliers constitute an ongoing matter, but in many instances, especially since Toyota insists on double sourcing most subassemblies, the balance of power between Toyota and any single supplier is entirely in Toyota's favor. That is, Toyota's good behavior is not really guaranteed by the Folk Theorem applied to the two-player game involving Toyota and the single supplier, because an individual supplier lacks the muscle needed to hurt Toyota, if Toyota misbehaves.

But collectively Toyota's suppliers can punish Toyota. Toyota's network of subcontracting relationships is highly efficient because it is remarkably flexible, flexibility that derives from the fact that the "contracts" between Toyota and its suppliers are very simple, essentially providing that contingencies will be met with goodwill as they arise. If Toyota used this lack of contractual detail and its superior muscle to abuse one of its suppliers and the other suppliers learned of this, their natural response would be to insist on detailed contracts spelling out how the parties would deal with contingencies that might arise. Toyota would lose a lot of the flexibility it has under the current system, at great cost and inconvenience.

That is the point. Toyota maintains a reputation for being a tough-but-fair client of its suppliers. It has the power to be tough and *un*fair in any single case, and looking at its relationship with a single supplier in isolation, it might be in Toyota's best interests to do so. But it does not exercise that power because its actions would be observed by others, so that to do so would compromise its reputation with all its suppliers. Its desire to maintain this reputation, to preserve its relationships, is what protects individual suppliers. (A very detailed account of this story is given in the next chapter.)

Noise in Reputations

In the two examples given at the start of this section, the games are simple and the ability to observe what A does in each round is total. There is neither noise in observables nor ambiguity about what A's reputation is for. In the real world, both noise and ambiguity abound, and both can be deadly to reputation equilibria.

Take the trust game; more specifically, take the repeated trust game with an enduring A facing a sequence of short-lived Bs. Imagine that, every time a B trusts A, A chooses between abuse and fair behavior. But these are only A's intentions: Even if A intends to treat Bn fairly, there is a probability that the Bs see A's actions in round n as abusive.

If A *seemingly* abuses a given B, subsequent Bs must punish A to some extent. If they do not, A has an incentive to abuse all the Bs and blame it on happenstance. But the punishment inflicted on A should not be more severe than necessary to keep A in line. A should be given the opportunity to show contrition if possible. She should be able to get her reputation back, after the punishment. And A and the Bs should jointly look for ways of constructing A's reputation so that it can be monitored relatively noiselessly, to avoid all or at least most of the costs of noise.

Although it is a bit more complex than the model of A and a sequence of Bs, consider in this regard public accounting firms that audit the financial reports of publicly held firms. The "trusting party" in these transactions is the community of investors in the companies being audited, which must trust the auditor to put in the long hours it takes to unravel what is going on at the firm being audited. If the auditing firm works hard and honestly, it is being "fair." If it slacks off or shades its report because of, say, the consulting work it might get from the audited firm, it abuses the trust of the investing community. But, even if the auditing firm works hard and honestly, it might miss something. When that something comes to light, the auditing firm may appear to have abused the public's trust. To be more precise, the investing public would not be able to tell if the undiscovered facts were the result of abusive behavior or honest error. To let the flawed audit go by invites auditors to spend less effort on their audits or worse. But, if too little punishment invites abuse, punishment that is too harsh can also be counterproductive: If the auditors lose their reputation completely after the first honest mistake and such mistakes do happen, then *take the money and run* can become the optimal strategy. In this regard, two observations are worth making:

1. Public accounting firms protect their reputations to garner economic rewards, which arrive in the form of continuing audit engagements, based on a reputation for trustworthiness. In recent years, audit engagement fees have become much lower, as competition in the audit business has become more fierce. This has lowered the value of a good reputation, which means less incentive to behave.

2. An auditor that seems to have missed something defends itself, ex post, by showing that it followed standard auditing procedures. But to verify this means that the standard auditing procedures have to be somewhat formulaic, with less room for subjective judgment by the auditor about what to do at a particular engagement. The same phenomenon appears in the practice of medicine, where the increasing prevalence of malpractice suits (more severe punishment for a seeming abuse of a patient's trust) means greater reliance on the practice of medicine "by the book," instead of using the physician's best subjective judgment.

The general phenomenon of noise enters into the reputation constructions in a second way. In the theoretical analysis of the repeated trust game, it was assumed that each B, when it is his turn to decide whether to trust A, is able to learn how A acted in previous encounters with earlier Bs. More generally and more robustly, it is enough that the behavior of A can be credibly communicated from one generation of Bs to the next. Reputation, in other words, passes by word of mouth, modified perhaps by the current actions of A. But suppose B in round n cannot see how A acted previously and either has difficulty in comprehending what B from round $n-1$ is passing along or finds that testimony less than fully credible. Insofar as A can anticipate these difficulties, A has less incentive to treat fairly B in round $n-1$, as it is less likely that abuse of this B would hurt A's prospects with the next B. If this is so and the Bs anticipate this, then they have less reason to trust A. In other words, in a reputation construction, we must worry about both noise in observing A's actions and, when reputations are communicated by word of mouth, noise in the process of communication of reputation.

In real life, this leads to three further considerations:

1. Reputation constructions, especially of the sort that involve trust, work best when successive generations of A's trading parters can communicate effectively. A common language and a shared culture among the Bs is a plus on

these grounds.

2. It is generally in the interest of A to facilitate this sort of communication among the Bs, because A's reputation is the basis on which the Bs trust A; if A's reputation does not work, there is no trust.

3. While it is often in A's interest to facilitate communication among the Bs, the interests of the Bs to allow for this communication is more complex. If the repeated encounters resemble the trust game, then both A *and the Bs* benefit from clear communication channels. But if the interactions are more adverserial, as in the threat game, then while A benefits from communication among the Bs, the Bs want to cut channels of clear communication; they do not want A to gain the sort of backbone that preservation of her reputation gives her.

Ambiguity

Ambiguity presents problems as well. Imagine a version of the repeated trust game where, instead of a dichotomous choice between fair treatment and abuse, A has a a very large number of choices to make, all of which affect her own payoff and B's. Suppose as well that objective conditions of the game change from round to round. And suppose A wants to cultivate a reputation for being fair but not generous; she is fair enough to merit the trust of B but does not overdo it. Toyota's reputation is precisely this; it is fair with its suppliers, but it certainly is not generous.

The problem is, What does *fair but not generous* mean? What are reasonable demands for Toyota to make of its suppliers? What is a fair level of compensation for them? I do not assert that these things cannot be specified to the satisfaction of the parties concerned; after all, the Toyota-supplier network works quite well. But it is easy to see how, in a real-life example, coming to terms and then keeping to those terms is not easy. When serious ambiguity enters, especially when entirely novel situations arise that call for renegotiating terms, reputations and relationships can founder.

Reputation and Multiple Constituencies

In the real world, actions taken by a particular entity are observed by multiple constituencies. An ideal action in terms of reputation with one party may cause problems in the relationships with other parties. For instance, some firms like to project to their employees an image of being a "family" rather than a business. Such firms eschew organization charts, visible signs of status differentiation, large pay differentials, and so forth. An example of such a "family" is Ben and Jerry's. If such a company decides to expand its operations and needs to raise the capital to do so externally, it has a delicate problem to solve: Bankers and others need to be reassured that the firms they lend money to mean business. Few bankers see the commune atmosphere of a Ben and Jerry's and think,

"Now there's a tight ship, run on sound business principles." Accordingly, one typically sees businesses with this sort of family or commune culture run on internally generated capital, and such businesses typically are closely held.

How Fragile is a Reputation?

In the specific reputation equilibria discussed at the start of this section, A's reputation was extremely fragile. If A ever abused a B in the trust game, no B would trust A again. If A ever acquiesced to B in the threat game, every subsequent B would enter.

Are reputations in real life so fragile? If A damages her reputation by one abusive action or in a moment of weakness, is it really gone forever? Of course not. If, say, A acquiesces to some B in the threat game but then abuses the next 10 or so Bs in a row, A is likely to reacquire a reputation for fighting. A would have a harder time restoring her reputation in the trust game, since no subsequent B would, in the equilibrium, trust her and she would never have the opportunity to show that she is not abusive. In real life, she might obtain the trust of some trading partners, at least some of the time, giving her the opportunity to resuscitate a reputation soiled by a previous action.

When noise, ambiguity, or multiple constituencies enter the story, this consideration becomes crucial, because these factors imply that A will sometimes be perceived as taking actions inconsistent with the reputation she wishes to project. Then it is essential that she be able to repair the damage.

Having said this, let me drop the other shoe. While, in real life, reputations can be repaired, if it is too easy to do so, the reputation becomes worthless. When a soiled reputation is easily repaired, preserving the reputation is less of a concern to the individual who holds it, and therefore it provides less in the way of credibility. Powerful reputations often gain their power *because* they are fragile, which gives the reputation holder the greatest incentive to maintain the reputation.

Inertia and Reputation

The way to gain and maintain a particular reputation is to act in that fashion. It can be useful to talk about what you are doing in the press, through a website, and so forth, especially to explain the underlying principles that govern specific actions you take. But actions usually speak a lot louder than words in this domain.

As a consequence, it can be hard to change a reputation whenever a change suits you. A firm that projected a dog-eat-dog, take-no-prisoners, the-market-is-a-jungle-and-we-mean-to-survive attitude for years will have a hard time if management determines that a change of heart is called for. Going the other way, a company that has not been tough on suppliers in terms of timeliness of deliveries or quality of materials will have a hard time convincing those suppliers that times have changed.

This is not to say that change is impossible. Accompanied by symbolic acts, often including changes in top management or done in a period of crisis, reputations can be turned around. But it is rarely easy.

The Bottom Line on Reputation

A firm's various reputations—with suppliers, workers, rivals, customers, investors, and the local community it inhabits—are often vitally important to its smooth and efficient functioning, both because they set the expectations of others who deal with it and because they can lend credibility to the firm's intention to act in one way or another.

But, as important as reputations are, it is not easy to "dial in" to the desired setting or make your reputation do what you want it to. The bottom line is: In toy games like the trust game or the threat game, the notion of reputation is easy to explain and see. In real life, reputations are very difficult to manage. But they are very important.

Executive Summary

- A credibility problem arises when some party, which must take an action in the future, wishes to be perceived ex ante as planning to take an action that, ex post, runs counter to its own interests. In some instances, typified by the trust game, the problem is that the party wishes to be perceived as planning to be "good," even though "bad" behavior is in its interest ex post. In other instances, typified by the threat game, the party wishes to be perceived as ready to be "bad," even though the ex post costs of being bad outweigh the ex post benefits.

- A variety of methods can be used to solve such credibility problems. The party can tie its own hands, typically by increasing the ex post costs of the action that it does not wish to be perceived as its optimal response. This can be done by signing an enforceable contract, or by noncontractual actions, including actions that empower partners, rivals, suppliers, or customers. Threats or promises may be effective, but these often lack credibility because they cost nothing. (When threats or promises are somewhat costly but not costly enough to ensure they will be carried out, the analysis becomes very subtle.)

- Reputation can lend credibility to threats or promises, if the reputation will be valuable in the future. The theory of reputations is very much like the Folk Theorem of last chapter: A party behaves in a way that is not optimal for it in the short term, because the long-term benefits of behaving in this fashion (maintaining its reputation) outweigh short-term costs. But unlike the last chapter, reputation can work both in cases in which a party deals with one other party repeatedly, in cases where the party deals with a sequence of other parties, and in cases in which the party deals with a number of others simultaneously.

- Noise and ambiguity can kill reputations. This includes noise or ambiguity in the transmission of the reputation from one generation of partners or rivals to the next.

- In real life, the management of reputations is complicated by the diverse audiences that observe what a party does and that interpret those actions in different ways. It can be difficult to shift from one beneficial reputation to another; reputations are often fraught with inertia. And the best (most effective) reputations are those that are fragile; a reputation that can be easily repaired is in consequence less effective in establishing credibility.

Problems

One problem captures most of the ideas of this chapter.

4.1 Two firms, Yaki Industries and Zenith Enterprise, are contemplating a joint venture. Yaki owns a proprietary technology that, unfortunately for Yaki, is unpatentable. This technology, if made available to Zenith Enterprise, could improve Zenith's profit by $20 million, in a market that Zenith serves and that is not connected to any of Yaki's ventures. But, once Zenith has access to this technology, it could use it to invade Yaki's own market as well, which would be very costly to Yaki and quite profitable to Zenith. Zenith proposes to Yaki that it (Yaki) give Zenith access to the technology for a $10 million fee. Zenith issues solemn promises that it will use the technology only in the market it currently serves, netting for it (Zenith) a net $10 million: the $20 million gain mentioned previously, less the $10 million fee. But Yaki is concerned: If Zenith were to renege on its promise and invade Yaki's market with this technology, Yaki would lose a net $10 million (including the $10 million fee), while Zenith's net gain (from both markets, net of the $10 million fee) would be $20 million.

(a) Diagram the "game" played by Yaki and Zenith, where the sequence of actions is this: First Yaki must decide whether to accept Zenith's offer and then, if Yaki accepts the offer, Zenith must decide whether to restrict its behavior as promised or invade Yaki's market. Use backward induction to analyze how this game would be played. Of the games discussed in the chapter, which does this resemble?

(b) In part a, you should have come to the conclusion that Yaki would not accept Zenith's offer, because Zenith could not be trusted to keep its promise. In light of this, Zenith decides to offer Yaki a contract that includes the promise. That way, if Zenith invades Yaki's territory, Yaki can take Zenith to court. The contract would be written so that, if Zenith is taken to court by Yaki and Yaki wins its suit, Zenith must pay Yaki damages of $20 million, which is the amount of damage that Yaki would in fact incur.

This sounds good to Yaki, but it has two concerns. The first is whether it would actually take Zenith to court in the event of a breach of contract. It would receive the $20 million, but there are court costs to consider, costs for which it would not be compensated. The best estimate is that these costs would be $12 million. Zenith's court costs would be $9 million. Assume that, if Zenith breaches the contract and Yaki takes Zenith to court, Yaki is sure to win its case. Does this sort of contractual guarantee make Zenith's promise not to invade Yaki's market credible? Can Yaki sign the contract with Zenith in this case?

(c) Unfortunately, Yaki is not convinced that, if Zenith breaches the contract and Yaki takes it to court, Yaki would win its case. The contract is necessarily a bit murky (what does it mean, precisely, that Zenith invaded Yaki's market?), and the interpretation would be up to a civil-suit jury. In fact, Yaki assesses the probability of only 0.3 that it would prevail in a court case. Assume that the two sides pay their own court costs, win or lose. Also assume that each party is an expected-monetary-value maximizer; that is, both sides are risk neutral. Under these circumstances, would the contract work, in the sense that it provides sufficient guarantees for Yaki to sign?

(d) Suppose we modify part c as follows. If Yaki takes Zenith to court and Yaki wins, the courts might award Yaki punitive damages. The amount of punitive damages will be three times the compensatory damages of $20 million. The odds of getting punitive damages awarded, conditional on Yaki's winning the suit (which has marginal probability 0.3), is $\frac{2}{3}$. Under these circumstances, will the contract work, in the sense that it provides sufficient guarantees for Yaki to sign?

(e) Suppose punitive damages, instead of being awarded to the successful plaintiff, were given to charity. That is, a losing defendant must pay the punitive damages, but the plaintiff receives only the compensatory damages. Under these circumstances, would the contract work, in the the sense that it provides sufficient guarantees for Yaki to sign?

(f) Taking the case of part e, how might reputation in some form or other help get Zenith to a deal, where Yaki would be willing to sign? Think expansively here: The first question to ask yourself is, Whose reputation and for what?

5. Transaction-Cost Economics

Many economic transactions between parties take a long time to play out, so long, that it is impossible for the parties at the outset to specify how the transaction will evolve, as circumstances arise. Transaction-cost economics, a branch of microeconomics, focuses on such transactions and, in particular, on their *governance structure*, the specification of *how and by whom* decisions about "what next?" will be made. We explore this branch of microeconomics in this chapter, seeing that it is intimately connected to the ideas about relationships developed in Chapters 3 and 4. Then we use this theory to look at two questions:

- What is the economic rationale for a firm?

- What is the instrumental case for business ethics?

We conclude, in the executive summary, by drawing together the lessons learned in this first part of the book.

The automobile industry is one of the largest and most important in the world. More than that, at least twice in the 20th century, the automobile industry was the setting for truly significant revolutions in industrial production, first the mass production system pioneered by Henry Ford, and then the Toyota production system. There is a lot to each of these revolutions, but for current purposes, the focus is on Ford's and Toyota's practices with regard to vertical integration.

Imagine a "tree" diagram that describes a car (see Figure 5.1). At the root is the finished car. At one level up the tree trunk are several major branches: The engine, the electrical system, the drive train, the body, the braking system, the wheels, and tires. The body, in turn, is subdivided into the frame (if the car has one), the panels, the seat assemblies, the glass, and so forth. Seat assemblies divide into the seat frame, the cushioning, upholstery, control systems, and so on. Somewhere up the tree from the seat frame are springs, and from the springs (perhaps immediately) is steel wire. You get the point: A car is assembled from an enormous number of pieces, tracing back to sheet steel, steel wire, rubber, glass, and so forth. And, to gild this lily, to make the steel we need iron and coke; to make the coke, coal is needed, and so on.

When Henry Ford entered the industry, the number of parts that went into a car was fewer than today but still impressive. The standard technology for assembling cars at the time was for the assembler to purchase or fabricate most of the pieces and assemble them. When Ford pioneered his machine-paced production line, he integrated into his firm, the Ford Motor Company, the manufacture of many of the parts and pieces that went into his cars. He did not go as far as mining his own coal, but before he was finished, he made his own

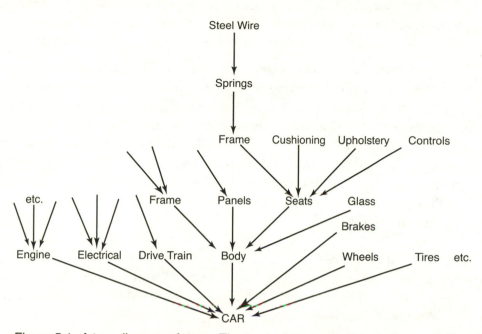

Figure 5.1. A tree diagram of a car. The trunk of the tree is the whole car. Branching off from this are the major subassemblies of the car, each of which splits into smaller and smaller subassemblies.

steel and rubber. The Ford Plant at River Rouge, Michigan, was a wonder of the industrial world, with raw materials delivered at one end of the plant and finished cars rolling out of the plant on the other end.

Why did Ford integrate all these manufacturing operations into his company? One reason was the simple belief that he could, with his superior systems for management and engineering, perform all this manufacturing more efficiently than any would-be suppliers. But there were two other, more specific reasons why he integrated vertically:

1. *Quality control.* Ford felt that purchasing parts and pieces from outside vendors gave him insufficient control of the quality of his inputs. His assembly-line technology, as well as his general reputation for dependable cars, required a level of quality that (he felt) he could get only if he controlled the manufacture of such parts.

   Note that, from Ford's perspective, a crucial aspect of high quality was *conformance to specification.* Of course, he wanted good quality materials, excellent design, and all those things that you naturally think of as contributing to quality. But, for instance, he needed the wheels he used to fit with his axles. As a car moved down his assembly line, the worker tasked with putting wheels on axles couldn't stop and "fix things" if the bolt-holes in the wheel didn't match the bolts on the axle. The bolt-holes and bolts had to line up first time, every time, or chaos on his assembly line would ensue.

This dimension of quality was particularly important to assembly-line operations, and Ford believed that he could get what he needed in this dimension only by taking control of, for instance, the maufacture of the wheels.

2. *Timely deliveries.* Ford's machine-paced assembly line required, to run well, the timely delivery of parts and pieces. In a "job shop" assembly operation, labor can be assigned flexibly to perform tasks that are both needed and for which the inputs are on hand. But, with an assembly line, the pieces have to fit, of course, and *must be there on time.* Ford could, and did, buffer uncertainties in supply with inventories of the parts and pieces. But these inventories represented unproductive capital, and Ford felt that to get a measure of timeliness in his deliveries, he needed to control of the manufacture of all sorts of subassemblies.

Jump ahead 40 years or so, to the 1960s and 1970s. Toyota pioneered a number of practices in how cars are made. Two of the most important pieces of the Toyota production system were zero defects and reduced work-in-process (WIP) inventory on the line.

- Toyota moved from the very high quality control standards of companies such as Ford and General Motors, which still allowed for a small rate of defects, to a policy that accepts no defects at all. Whenever a defect appears on the line, the production line stops and restarts only when the cause is identified and corrective action is taken.

- In what is colloquially called the Kanban system, named for the inventory control tags or *kanban* that drive the levels of WIP inventory, Toyota gradually removed from the production line nearly all the buffering WIP inventory, inventory that keeps the line moving when deliveries to the line are not precisely on time.

In other words, Toyota has increased emphasis on the two concrete motivations Henry Ford had for massive vertical integration. Simultaneously, Toyota exists with a level of vertical integration very much lower than that of the Ford Motor Company of Henry Ford. In terms of the tree diagram, Ford of the 1920s and 1930s is outlined in the solid line in Figure 5.2, while Toyota's boundaries are given by the inside dashed line. (The figure illustrates the notion that Toyota today is much less vertically integrated than Ford was circa 1930. I do not know the precise extent of vertical integration in either case; so please do not take Figure 5.2 literally.)

The Ford Motor Company today has moved dramatically toward the Toyota level of vertical integration, although not as far as Toyota or the other major Japanese car manufacturers, all of whom substantially resemble Toyota in this regard. In other words, it is generally accepted by car manufacturers that Toyota,

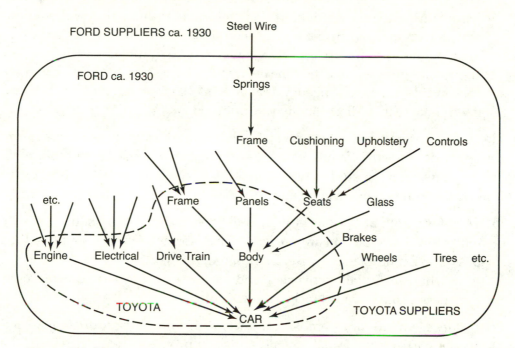

Figure 5.2. Toyota today, and Ford of the 1930s. In terms of the "tree" of a car, Ford in the 1930s took in most of the tree, while Toyota takes in much less.

while increasing its emphasis on quality and timeliness, is correct in the direction it went in terms of vertical integration.

How can we explain this?

5.1. Transaction-Cost Economics

The explanation, which will take several pages, begins with the concepts and frameworks of *transaction-cost economics*.[1]

1. Many important transactions are complex in a variety of ways. They take time to complete, with the parties to the transactions having multiple opportunities to act. They often involve uncertainty, hidden information (information held by one of the trading partners but not by the other), and moral hazard (situations in which one party's actions affect the other party's welfare, but there is no way to guarantee that the first party behaves in an "agreed to" way).[2]

---

[1] This account of transaction-cost economics borrows heavily from the work of Oliver Williamson, who won the Nobel Prize in Economics for this work in 2009. For a fuller and more nuanced treatment, I recommend his book, *The Economic Institutions of Capitalism* (New York: The Free Press, 1985).

[2] Hidden information or, as it is sometimes called, adverse selection, and moral hazard are discussed in depth in Part V of this book.

2. The parties to these transactions are unable or unwilling, either at the outset or during the transaction, to specify how the transaction will adapt to
   all the possible contingencies that may arise. This may be a "failure of
   imagination"—some future contingencies may be simply unanticipated—or
   an unwillingness to take the time needed to discuss and bargain over every
   conceivable future contingency; that is, a "we'll cross that bridge when and
   if we come to it" philosophy may be adopted.

This is not perjorative. No one, no matter how smart, can foresee all the future
contingencies and adaptations to those contingencies in transactions that stretch
out for years. And it would be witless to think through the details of how every
conceivable contingency will be met.

2b. Therefore, both at the outset and as the transaction unfolds, the ultimate
    terms of the transaction are unclear. Those terms are worked out as time
    passes and contingencies arise. In the jargon of Economese, the terms of the
    transaction are initially *incomplete*, and the parties *adapt* to circumstances as
    time passes and circumstances unfold.

For instance, when a car assembler contracts with a firm to produce seat assemblies, both parties hope for a long and mutually profitable relationship. At the
outset of the relationship, neither can predict the volume of cars to be manufactured; whether and when the workforce of either firm, if organized, will go
on strike; or what sort of cars will be in vogue 5 or 10 years down the line. So,
at the outset, the exact terms of trade for this transaction past a few months are
unclear. As time passes and the future unfolds, the two parties must negotiate
over things such as prices, product specification, volumes, delivery times, and
special adjustments if one workforce or the other goes on strike, if one of the
two firm's facility is flooded or damaged by a tornado, and so forth.

   To say all this is not to say that the parties enter the transaction blindly. They
may be quite sophisticated in their attempts to structure the transaction in a way
that is likely to lead to efficient adaptation. "We'll cross that bridge when and
if we come to it" doesn't mean "there are streams and rivers out there, but we
have no idea what they will be like, so we just have to confront them when we
find them." Instead, the notion is that the parties undertake their transaction
thinking:

   There are streams and rivers out there, and our experience and the experience
   of others gives us some idea what sorts of bridging and fording tools to bring
   with us. Based on those experiences, we set out provisioned in a general
   sense for what we think we are likely to find. Of course, we might be
   completely blindsided at some point. In fact, we are more likely than not to
   be blindsided eventually. But we set out ready, to the extent that we can be,
   for the sorts of rivers and streams we expect to have to cross.

The "tools" that are the focus of transaction-cost economics are *decision rights*: When a decision point arrives, who has the authority to make that decision? Are the decision rights (for a particular sort of decision) delegated to one party or another? Or are they shared, in the sense that it takes negotiation and consensus to arrive at a decision? Perhaps there is recourse to a third and supposedly neutral party, who listens to the points of view of the parties directly involved and tells them what happens next. The terminology used includes:

- When one party has most of the authority to make adaptation decisions, we say the transaction is characterized by *hierarchical governance*.

- When decision rights are shared, we have *bilateral governance*. This term includes two very different sorts of arrangements: where decision rights are split—one party (say) can decide on price, and the other on volume; and where negotiated consensus is needed to move from a pre-set status quo.

- When a third, neutral party is involved, we have *trilateral governance*.

These names are not important and, in any case, very, very few transactions[3] fit one of these archetypes perfectly. What are important, instead, in any specific situation, are answers to the following three questions:

- How are adaptation decisions made? Which party(ies) have which decision rights?

- What is the basis on which decision rights are assigned? Answers here include: By formal contractual agreements; as a matter of law; by custom and tradition; and by mutual consent of the parties.

- How should decision rights be assigned to facilitate *efficiency*, where efficiency means, in a manner that maximizes the joint benefits of the transaction/relationship to the parties involved?

Efficiency is enhanced first of all when decision rights are given to the party that is best informed about what sort of adaptation/decision is preferred. So, for instance, in the case of Toyota and its suppliers, because Toyota coordinates the activities of many different suppliers, Toyota is in the best informational position to make decisions about quantities required, timing of deliveries, and so forth.

Efficiency is also enhanced when negotiating and enforcement costs are minimized. Time spent negotiating and coming to agreement is time lost and, if negotiations fail, more than time may be lost. Resources expended enforcing

---

[3] I'm calling the multiyear "thing" between the the two parties a *transaction*, because this is the term used in economics. But if you go by dictionary definitions, the term *relationship* is probably more appropriate than transaction for the multiyear thing, a relationship in which the parties engage in a long, complex sequence of separate transactions. In what follows, I'll use both terms, depending on what sounds best.

agreements are generally not directly productive, except from the perspective of lawyers. This consideration, then, argues for an assignment of decision rights to individual parties, in place of negotiation and consensus.

And, finally, efficiency is enhanced when the parties involved have the incentive to take individual actions that improve the overall transaction/relationship. This is, perhaps, the most complex efficiency factor, because there are lots of incentives about which to worry, and the assignment of decision rights affects them all. Here are three of the most important.

- At the most basic level, it is desirable to arrange decision rights so that parties have the incentive to contribute *consummate effort* to the transaction/relationship. Consummate effort means working hard, but it goes beyond this to mean working smart, being proactive and creative, and so forth. There are a number of reasons why Toyota moved away from the extreme vertical integration of the class Ford and GM models—to be discussed later in this chapter—but suffice it to say for now that a fundamental concern for Toyota was that, by dis-integrating, it provided higher-powered incentives to the manufacturers of its subassemblies to work hard and work smart than would be the case if production were more vertically integrated.

- It is rare that the party who holds a particular decision right has *all* information relevant to making the best specific decision. So when decision rights to a particular decision are assigned, say, to party A, you need to worry: Will party B (or parties B, C, and D) be motivated to share honestly what they know that is relevant.

- And it is often important for parties to a transaction to make *sunk-cost investments* in the relationship. In case you are new to this terminology, a sunk-cost investment is where one party lays out money or resources—anything of value—to create an asset—whether tangible or intangible—that enhances the transaction for both sides, *and where the money or resources invested cannot be fully recouped when and if the transaction goes sour.* It is the last piece of this that justifies the term sunk-cost and that raises the issue: If A is engaged in a transaction/relationship with B, and A makes a sunk-cost investment in this transaction/relationship, A becomes susceptible to a *hold-up* by B.

  When A lays out the money/resources for this asset, she does so in the expectation that, over time, she will get back what she invested and more. In terms that would gain the approval of your finance professor, she invests in assets that have a positive net present value to her. But her returns on the investment—what she will gain from the transaction—are "in the air," and her partner B, seeing that she made an investment which she cannot recoup, may try to take advantage of this by insisting on better terms for himself and worse terms for her.

What Is a Hold-Up?

The concept of a hold-up and its role in this story are so important that I want to provide a caricature example: Suppose a bottle manufacturer and soft-drink bottler are considering a long-term transaction in which the bottle manufacturer will produce bottles at $0.10 apiece, which it expects to transport to the soft-drink bottler for $0.02 apiece and for which it will be paid $0.15 per bottle, a $0.03 margin. Suppose it expects to manufacture and sell to the bottler 50,000 bottles a month, for a net cash flow of $1500 a month. If bottler discounts cash flows at the rate 1% per month, this translates into a net present value (NPV) of $150,000 for the bottle manufacturer. And suppose that the bottler's next best alternative source of bottles would charge it $0.20 per bottle. Assuming (to keep the story simple) the bottler has the same discount rate, its NPV for dealing with this bottle manufacturer is $250,000.

Now imagine that the bottle manufacturer has the opportunity to set up a manufacturing operation adjacent to the bottler's bottling plant. Suppose that, by building this new manufacturing facility, the bottle manufacturer can cut its transport costs to $0.005 per bottle, a net savings of $750 per month, or an NPV savings of $75,000. Of course, setting up this new plant will cost some money—suppose it costs an immediate $50,000 to set this up, so the net gain to the bottle manufacturer of setting up the plant is $25,000. And suppose this co-location will generate other benefits for the bottler (for instance, it allows the bottler to reduce the inventory of empty bottles it holds), worth $500 per month to the bottler, or $50,000 in NPV. This, then, is a win-win for the two trading partners.

Except, this calculation is based on the notion that the price per bottle will stay at $0.15. Suppose that, once the bottle manufacturer invests $50,000 in this new facility, it cannot recoup this money. That is, the investment is a *sunk cost*. What if, once the plant is set up, the soft-drink bottler says: "Before you set up the plant, you were content with a margin of $0.03 per bottle. Seems to me that, since the investment is a sunk cost for you, you should be willing to keep supplying me at this same margin. So, from now on, I'm paying you $0.135 per bottle." This threat is the attempted hold-up. And, since the bottle manufacturer was indeed content with a $0.03 margin per bottle before, *and the investment costs are sunk*, there is no economic (as opposed to psychological) reason for it to resist this hold-up.

We can illustrate the situation with a simple extensive-form game model, shown in Figure 5.3. The bottle manufacturer moves first, deciding whether to invest in the facility or not. If it does not, we get baseline payoffs of $150k (in NPV) for the manufacturer and $250K (measured relative to the next best alternative) for the bottler. If the manufacturer does make the investment, then the bottler chooses: Should it continue to pay $0.15 per bottle (which, I assume, would be accepted by the manufacturer), or make a "moderate demand" of

$0.135 per bottle, or make an outrageous demand of $0.10 per bottle? Finally, the manufacturer must decide, if the bottler demands a lower price per bottle, whether to agree or not.

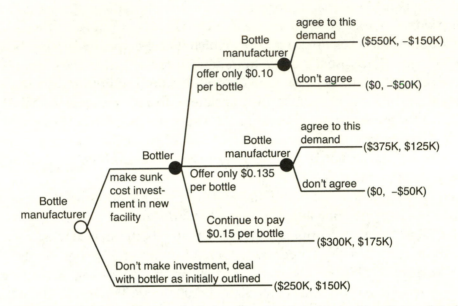

Figure 5.3. An extensive-form depiction of a classic hold-up.. Payoffs are listed for the bottler first (relative to his next best alternative) and then for the bottle manufacturer.

If the bottler makes the outrageous demand of $0.10 per bottle, the manufacturer will say no; it can't cover its variable costs, so even though it made the sunk-cost investment, it is better absorbing that loss and moving on. But if the bottler demands $0.135 per bottle, since the investment cost of $50,000 is sunk, the manufacturer is better off saying "okay" than telling the bottler to get lost. Not that the manufacturer is happy about this. But a $125,000 NPV is better than absorbing the loss of $25,000.

Hence the bottler, given these three options, is best off making the moderate demand of $0.135 per bottle. In real life, it isn't so simple—the bottler will negotiate the price per bottle with the manufacturer. But if the bottler is a strong negotiator, it may be able to get away with this sort of demand. This is the hold-up; the manufacturer, having spent the $50,000 in sunk cost, can't protect that investment.

Now take the backward induction one step further. Anticipating that the bottler will engage in this moderate hold-up, the manufacturer compares an NPV of $125,000 if it makes the sunk-cost investment versus an NPV of $150,000 if it does not. So it doesn't make the investment. And, note, this is inefficient: *If the manufacturer made the investment and the bottler could assure the manufacturer that it would not engage in the hold-up, both sides are better off.* In the situation as depicted, the inability of the bottler to commit credibly not to hold up the manufacturer is leading to an inefficient relationship.

This is, of course, a caricature. But, as a caricature, it illustrates the problem. We are looking at complex transactions/relationships that are incomplete in the sense that the terms will only be determined as circumstances arise and the parties, somehow, decide "what next." Decision rights are established to determine "what next." They can be by mutual consent—but that will tend to raise negotiation costs and, perhaps, subsequent enforcement costs. Into this mix of factors 1 and 2 from pages 99 and 100, we are adding the following third factor:

3. In many (and many of the most important) ongoing transactions/relationship between parties, each party has the opportunity to make efficiency-enhancing sunk-cost investments in the transaction or relationship. But insofar as making these investments makes the parties susceptible to a hold-up by the other side, the parties are demotivated from making these investments. Decision rights should be assigned in a way that changes "demotivated" into "motivated."

How? The caricature example tells the story: To encourage the bottle manufacturer to co-locate, the soft-drink bottler wishes to make a credible promise that it will not try to hold up the bottle manufacuturer, once the new facility is built. Chapter 4 is invoked. If contractual guarantees can be offered, great. But the complexity of the transaction and its incompleteness mean that contractual guarantees in real-life examples will be hard to create. So we fall back on reputation. *Decision rights should be assigned in part with a view to answers to these questions: Which party(ies) can be trusted not to abuse the decision rights they are given? Which parties have the sort of reputation stake that engenders this trust?*

Let's look at three examples:

Toyota and Its Suppliers

Toyota can point to at least two reasons why it prefers to deal with subcontractors of major subassemblies, rather than vertically integrating into the production of those subassemblies. First is economies to scale and scope. The company that supplies Toyota's Jamestown, Kentucky's assembly plant with seat assemblies, Johnson Controls, also makes seat assemblies for Ford, for General Motors, and for a variety of foreign firms that assembly vehicles in the United States. This allows Johnson Controls to take advantage of considerable economies to scale and, especially, scope—Johnson Controls can take knowledge it gains in assembling seats for Ford and improve the seats it supplies to Toyota, and vice versa. At least at the outset, the flow of information in Johnson Controls went from its Toyota operations to its work for other vehicle assemblers. But Toyota is okay with that; this generates value for Johnson Controls, and it increases Johnson Controls' benefits from being a Toyota supplier, benefits that Toyota shares in structuring its relationship with Johnson Controls.

And, second, Toyota believes that this sort of arrangement strengthens the incentives of suppliers such as Johnson Controls to perform in the sense of bringing costs down while keeping deliveries timely and quality at nearly impeccable levels. Johnson Controls enjoys its relationship with Toyota—it doesn't make a fortune in this relationship, but it does make decent margins on relatively steady work, and it values what it learns by being a Toyota supplier—and it knows that, to keep this relationship going, it must perform up to Toyota's high standards. Toyota believes—and its suppliers believe—that a supplier that fails to meet Toyota's standards will be let go, providing higher-powered incentives than Toyota thinks it could achieve with an internal seat-manufacture-and-assembly operation.

The logic in this arrangement goes only so far: Toyota believes that its core competences—what sets it apart and above its rivals—are (1) its ability to manage these relationships, about which we need to say more, (2) its ability to design vehicles, (3) in the manufacture of engines, and (4) its skill in assembling a vehicle from the major subassemblies. So these activities are kept in-house.

What about Henry Ford's original argument that direct control of most aspects of manufacture is paramount? Toyota's relationship with its subcontractors is ongoing and, in the terminology we've developed, *incomplete*, and if they don't get governance—the assignment of decision rights—correct, the overall efficiency of these relationships could be poor. If, for instance, Toyota needed to negotiate with its suppliers on prices and quantities every six months, the negotiation costs could overwhelm the incentive effects and economies to scale and scope.

But the governance of these relationships is, from Toyota's perspective, nearly ideal. Formal contracts are short, both in length and on details. Instead, governance is very heavily hierarchical, with Toyota calling nearly all the shots, including the quantities it demands each week and the prices it will pay. Suppliers like Johnson Controls can of course break off the relationship at any time, if Toyota's decisions become truly outrageous. But, beyond that, it is not too strong a characterization to say that, when dealing with Toyota, it is "Toyota's way or the highway."

Still, Toyota expects its suppliers to invest in their relationship with Toyota, in terms of location of facilities, tooling, information systems, and the like. There is a strong sunk-cost element to these investments, and Toyota's suppliers might worry that they will be subject to hold-ups.

But Toyota doesn't make hold-up-level demands, because it wants to protect its reputation with all its suppliers. If Toyota made such demands on, say, Johnson Controls, Johnson Controls might in its own interest accede. But Toyota's other suppliers would take note and look for the sort of formal contractual guarantees that Toyota wishes to avoid. It isn't that Toyota refrains from taking advantage of Johnson Controls because it might drive JC away. Instead, Toyota refrains from taking advantage of Johnson Controls so that all its suppliers continue to believe that Toyota is a good firm to work for, on the terms that being a Toyota supplier entails. This is reputation, pure and simple.

This system works very well for Toyota, but it takes hard work on Toyota's part to make it work. Toyota sets the prices it will pay for the subassemblies, and to do this "fairly," it has to know a lot about the cost structure of its suppliers. So it invests a lot of resources in understanding that cost structure; most notably, Toyota employees are constantly on the factory floor of suppliers like Johnson Controls, ostensibly to help JC improve its manufacturing techniques, but also to learn what JC does and at what cost.

And Toyota promotes communication among its suppliers. It creates forums where different suppliers meet on a regular basis, to learn from each other, but also to judge in specific cases whether Toyota behaved according to Toyota's reputation. This is a double-edged sword, and both edges are to Toyota's benefit: It keeps Toyota honest in any bilateral relationship it has, because if Toyota abuses one supplier, the others learn about it. The suppliers understand this, and it enhances their trust that they won't be abused. And, at the same time, it creates a "court of public opinion" about how Toyota behaves in any bilateral relationship. If Toyota were to take actions in its relationship with, say, Johnson Controls, that the full cohort of its suppliers deemed "unfair," it would back off.

A final consideration comes directly from last chapter. Toyota relies on its reputation and the value it places on that reputation to engender trust by its suppliers. But reputations, to work effectively, must be clear and consistent. In specific cases, Toyota might see it in its interest and the interests of a particular supplier to do things differently from its normal policies. But this would muddy the reputation it has, putting the system in jeopardy. So it doesn't make those exceptions.[4]

The Employment Transaction

Perhaps the single most important class of economic transactions, in terms of impact on society and individuals, is the employment transaction. In some cases, employment is a simple, spot-market transaction: A is hired to do a day's labor for a set wage, with no implications beyond today's quitting time. But in a much larger fraction of cases, when B goes to work at Company X, there is some anticipation on the part of B and X that this will be an ongoing transaction

---

[4] Readers may recall that, beginning around 2004 or so, Toyota suddenly had major quality issues that led to massive recalls. Did the system fail? I can't say for sure, but I can tell you what Toyota says: Their story was that they had expanded operations too quickly, with suppliers that were improperly trained in the Toyota way. The Toyota system didn't fail, in other words, but Toyota failed its system. I reiterate that this is the story they tell; I can't vouch for it. But it is telling that most other vehicle assembly firms, including Ford and GM, have moved over the years closer and closer to the Toyota way of doing business.

or, at least, there is substantial probability that it will be an ongoing transaction.

And, insofar as it is an ongoing transaction, it is certainly complex and massively incomplete. New hiree B (he) may have a good idea what he will be doing over his first six months on the job, but after that, things depend: they depend on his level of performance, they depend on which jobs need doing at X for which he is better or worse suited, and so on; they depend on lots of stuff, none of which is spelled out in detail when he signs up to work for X.

Both Company X and Employee B make sunk-cost investments in their relationship. Organization X invests in his training, an investment which is almost totally lost if he departs, while he invests in learning specific things about his job at X. Some of the things he learns might be useful elsewhere, but insofar as he learns about things specific to working at X, he'll lose his investment when/if he leaves or is fired. Even more significantly, B "invests" in his long-term relationship with X by moving close to where he works, perhaps putting his children into the local schools, and forming social bonds with both coworkers and neighbors.

So, transaction-cost economics tells us, it becomes important to understand the governance of employment relationships, who has which decision rights in deciding "what next." The stereotypical model is that employment is a hierarchical relationship, with the boss telling the employee what to do. The employee retains the informal right to lobby for something different, but if the boss says do this or that, the employee's choices are to do what he is told or to quit. This stereotypical picture of employment is based on two efficiency considerations. The first is informational: the boss has a better perspective on "the big picture" of what is desirable to do; it might even be said that the job of the boss is to acquire such "big picture" information. And, as the boss (henceforth, she) is coordinating the actions of multiple employees, she has the best information about how to get her employees' work to fit together. And there is reputation: of course, the boss can take advantage of the employee's sunk-cost investments, but if she does so, it will adversely affect her reputation as an employer, making it harder to hold on to the employees she has and to hire new employees.

As with most stereotypes, there is some truth to this one, but the world is much more complex and subtle.

1. Some employees—and an increasing number of them in the modern economy—have access to information that the boss lacks and, holding other considerations equal, would do a better job at deciding "what next." So some decision rights should be and are delegated to employees. My boss, the dean of the Stanford GSB, tells me which courses I will teach. But, absent strong complaints by the students, he leaves it to me to design the courses I teach. Of course, there is the possibility that an individual employee will take advantage of the sunk-cost investments that the "boss" has made in him and attempt a hold-up; and while the individual employee has a personal reputation at stake, this isn't as powerful a reputation stake as has an employer.

So a very large portion of the subject of human resource management concerns motivation: Given that employees will be given decision rights, how do employers motivate them to "do right by their employer"?

2. Employees as a collective body have a greater reputation stake in their ongoing transaction with their employer than does any single employee. So, in cases where employees are organized into a formal collective—as in Works Councils in Germany or, in some instances, into unions—they may be more responsible in the decisions they made, because of that stake. There is no guarantee here. Remember, the folk theorem tells us that "always confess" is one out of many equilibria. Unions *can* have a hostile and destructive relationship with the firm whose workforce they have organized. But when the two sides reach a cooperative equilibrium, efficiency can be enhanced.

3. The stereotype identifies the boss with the organization for which she works. This, of course, is accurate only for sole proprietorships and the like. Bosses make decisions in the organization's name, which in turn impacts the organization's reputation. So the bosses of bosses must motivate the first-line bosses to take decisions that the organization would like them to take.

I repeat, perhaps the single most important class of economic transactions, in terms of impact on society and individuals, is the employment transaction. It is also one of the most complex; not only is employment an economic relationship, but it has strong social connotations as well. As an aspiring (or practicing) manager, you should study this transaction in a lot more depth than we do here.[5]

You and the School You Attend

The third and final example is the transaction between you and the school you attend. (I'm going to assume in this discussion that you are attending a school of management, studying for an MBA or similar degree. Please adapt my language to your particular situation.) This is a complex and incomplete transaction. When, after you were admitted and considered your options and then sent in a deposit to reserve your seat, you had (I hope) a good general idea of what you were getting into. But there were a lot of details—some welcome and some perhaps less welcome—of which you were not aware. Sunk-cost investments are made on both sides of this transaction; looking at it from your perspective, you've paid at least a portion of your tuition; perhaps you turned down some nearly as-good alternatives; you left a good job; you've developed some friendships with classmates. So if a decision must be made—for instance, can you get into a particularly desirable elective, or will you get the star instructor for a specific course?—you may be inclined to stick with the program, even

---

[5] And, if I may offer a suggestion, look at J. Baron and D. Kreps, *Strategic Human Resources: Frameworks for General Managers*, (New York: J. Wiley & Sons, 1999).

if you don't get your desired outcome.

For the most part, the administration holds a near monopoly on the decision rights. They may ask you which courses you want to take, but after learning your preferences by some means, they tell you what happens next. If you think you were mistreated by an instructor, you can appeal. But the rule is, "the dean decides" (unless you appeal on up to the provost and/or president of your institution).

What is your insurance against being held up? Here it is almost entirely a matter of reputation. Two paragraphs previous, it reads "you had (I hope) a good general idea of what you were getting into." And you got that general idea by talking to others who had gone to your school. Someday, a prospective student is going to ask you "How do they treat students at Institution Z?," and if you are mistreated today, you probably won't give the sort of answer your institution would want you to give. The faculty and administration of your school know this—they are very concerned with the institution's reputation—and this is your best guarantee against being abused. I'm not saying that you never feel somewhat hard done by. But when it comes time to add up your experiences, the faculty and administration are very invested in you telling the next group of prospective students, "Overall, its a good/great/fantastic place."

I'd add one important caveat to this story. In a well-managed school, the administration will delegate certain decisions to students collectively. Where a decision has most of its impact on students—when faculty members and administration have a much smaller stake in the decision—it makes good transaction-cost sense to let the students, as a collective, decide. To give an example: At my school, the Stanford GSB, access to elective courses is a very important thing to students. For the most part, the faculty members don't care how students are selected for their courses (with the exception that they don't want students placed in their courses who really don't want to be there). So the administration has given the student-elected Academic Committee more-or-less carte blanche in designing the allocation mechanism, as well as a significant say in cases for which rare exceptions to the allocation rules ought to be made.

5.2. The Economic Role of the Firm

The theory of transaction-cost economics can be employed to help answer the question, What is the economic role of the firm and other, similar organizations?

If you have taken a standard course in microeconomics previously, you will recall that firms, for the most part, are treated as production-technology black boxes. They are entities with the capability of transforming certain bundles of inputs into a corresponding bundle of outputs; they buy the inputs and sell the outputs; and they choose among the production plans of which they are capable to maximize their profit, defined as the income they get from selling their outputs less the cost of their inputs. This is a useful—albeit flawed—model when it comes to trying to understand market outcomes, and in Parts II, III, and IV of this book, we will use this model extensively.

It is, however, not very useful for managers who are operating inside a firm and who want to know, essentially, how to make the firm's production technology as efficient as possible. To answer questions about the internal workings of a firm—to climb inside the black box of the standard microeconomic model of the firm—we must first of all understand the economic role played by firms.

This may seem silly at first. It's obvious that firms exist to organize productive activities. What's the alternative? It is the market. Economists, for a variety of reasons to be discussed in Part IV, have a firm belief in the power of the competitive marketplace to achieve economically efficient outcomes. There are limits to this belief—also discussed in Parts IV and V—but an economist's first instinct is to let markets do what they do, and—within those limits—all will be good.

Firms are an alternative to markets. Imagine Henry Ford, instead of forming the Ford Motor Company, going each day to the marketplace and buying whatever parts he needed for that day's activities from other sole-proprietorship craftspeople and also buying labor services from people with the skill to assemble those parts. That would be a market-based method of automobile assembly. Of course, Henry Ford rejected this method of operation and formed the Ford Motor Company on the grounds that doing so would lead to better, more efficient outcomes (and, ultimately, more goodies for himself). So we are moved to ask, Why? What does the creation of the Ford Motor Company do and do better, in an economic sense, than a market-based organization?

This is not simply a question of academic interest: Remember that Toyota disaggregated the model of a highly integrated Ford Motor Company, believing—and evidence suggests they were right—that a bit more "market" and a bit less "firm" would be more efficient. At some point as a manager, you may be required to decide which activities important to your overall operation should be done internally and which should be done across a market interface. Understanding the different economic roles played by a firm is the first step toward finding a well-informed answer to this question.

Story #1: Unified Governance versus Relational Contracting

Since I've stuck this discussion in a chapter on transaction-cost economics, you can guess that my answer will be based in transaction-cost economics and, in particular, the governance of complex transactions. But the three archetypes for governance that we discussed—hierarchical governance, bilateral governance, and trilateral governance—all concern governance of transactions between two distinct parties. One theory of the economic role of the firm concerns a fourth archetype, called *unified governance*. The image here is: Party A owns access to some factor of production. Party B owns the capital equipment needed to process the material owned by Party A. Some (not specified here) sunk-cost investments in the relationship between A and B are made by B and A. So, the story goes, we have a governance problem, to which any of the three previous archetypes might be applied. *Or*, Party B could buy from Party A the full legal rights to access the factor of production, or A could buy from B the capital equipment. Note well, A isn't leasing the rights to use B's equipment for a while, and/or B isn't buying access to the factors of production for some (short) period of time: One party or the other takes complete and irrevocable control of the other party's assets. That is *unified governance*. Once one party owns both assets, that one party has total command over what happens next, as contingencies arise. In a sense, this is hierarchical governance *plus*, where the plus is: The bought-out party has no further rights; he or she takes the money gained from the sale of the assets and departs the scene.

Story #1 then is that firms are the legal embodiment of unified governance. Firms own arrays of physical capital, and the bosses of the firm can deploy all that capital as they choose, without requiring the "permission" of any other parties.

Of course, the one form of capital that a firm cannot own is human capital (slavery and indenture being illegal). So, even in this story, the firm is involved in *relational contracting*—contracting with legally independent parties—of some fashion with its employees. But at least the firm can have complete control of other assets important to what it does, now and in the future.

Story #2: The Firm as the Nexus of Many Bilateral Transactions

The legal status of a firm is also a contracting convenience in conducting multi-lateral transactions on multiple bilateral basis. This means that, when building and selling a car, a huge number of "entities"—assembly-line workers, engineers, marketing specialists, and suppliers of all sorts—are involved. The firm provides a legal entity with which each of these entities can contract bilaterally (or nearly so); the line worker has a contractual relationship with the firm (and his or her union, which is the reason for the previous parenthetical caveat); the tire supplier does as well; and so forth. It is hard to imagine how the many parties involved would arrange themselves contractually, without this "center" to their activities.

Story #3: Limited Liability and Tax Considerations

Stories 1 and 2 are, at least in part, about the legal existence of a firm, as a legal entity that can own assets and make legal contracts. Firms introduce other legal considerations, among which are the limited liability of the owners of the firm: If the firm as a legal entity borrows money, say, through the issuance of bonds, its owners (equity holders) are not personally liable to pay back that money if the firm fails. And, in terms of tax law, firms have a special status, to which special rules apply. A transaction-cost story for why such arrangement may be useful is available, but it will take us too far afield: When you take a course in corporate finance, challenge your instructor to explain why these "special rules" make economic sense.[6]

Story #4: Firms Provide a Focus for a (Specific) Reputation Stake

When, in describing the relationship between Toyota and Johnson Contols, we say that "Toyota decides what price it will pay to and what quantities it requires from Johnson Controls," we mean "Managers at Toyota decide. . ." Toyota is not a sentient being; it can make no decisions. Managers who work for it make decisions on its behalf.

This is important because, when a manager at Toyota makes a decision, the impact of the decision is primarily on *Toyota's* reputation and not the reputation of the manager. At least, this is true concerning Toyota's reputation with its suppliers. When they get together, they speak of Toyota's reputation, Toyota's actions, and the Toyota way of doing business.

Reputation, to work effectively, to lend credibility, requires wide-ranging and frequent application. If Manager X (he) plays the trust game of Chapter 4 against one party B or against one party B per year, X is not strongly motivated to protect his reputation for being fair. Therefore, the Bs have little reason to trust X or, at least, X's desire to protect his reputation is no reason to trust X. But, if X bands together with a group of somewhat similarly situated individuals, each of whom plays a trust game, if the Xs link their reputations, creating a "brand image," and each X benefits if the "brand" is strong, then each X can be credibly expected to act honorably. In just this fashion, Toyota Manager Y, making decisions on behalf of Toyota concerning its relationship with Johnson Controls, probably does not deal with very many, if any, other suppliers. But if we can tie Y's economic interests to the fortunes of Toyota generally, and Y understands that her individual actions affect the overall reputation of Toyota, then the reputation-borne credibility comes alive.

The firm's role in this story is to be the brand image. It is the focus of the reputation stake, and because "its" reputation is frequently on the line, as long as we appropriately align the interests of those who make decisions in its name with its long-run success, reputation-based credibility can take off.

And, taking this a step further, suppose we tie together the economic interests of various decision makers and say that the firm will be the repository of their joint reputation. From the perspective of creating a joint reputation that works well, we want their activities to be similar and done with a similar phi-

---

[6] An excellent book on how taxes affect how firms are organized—and the implications of this for *your* organization—is M. Scholes, M. Wolfson, M. Erickson, M. Hanlon, E. Maydew, and T. Shevlin, *Taxes and Business Strategy: A Planning Approach*, 5th Edition (Englewood Cliffs, N.J.: Prentice-Hall, 2015).

losophy. Toyota treats its suppliers in one fashion, General Motors in another. If you went to managers in firms such as Johnson Controls, which supplies both Toyota and GM, you would find that they have very well-formed opinions about how the two differ as clients, what sort of behavior can be expected from each, and what sort of behavior can be ruled out. Consistency in the actions of managers making decisions on behalf of a single firm is valuable because it enables trading partners of the firm to understand what the firm's reputation is for. The role of the firm here is to not only to provide a focus for some reputation, but to provide a focus for a consistent and coherent reputation.

Story #5: Firms Create Roles that Affect Expectations and Tastes

Roles affect how individuals relate to one another, in terms of what they expect and how they behave. This lies at the heart of why we see higher powered incentives across a market interface than within a firm; on average, forgiveness for poor performance within a firm is more likely and more forthcoming than forgiveness across a market interface. Moreover, expectations and tastes are organization-specific. Employees A and B of a firm that has a familylike culture of cooperation relate to each other differently than employees C and D of a firm that has a market-like culture of dog-eat-dog. Of course, many social characteristics affect what A expects of B, how A regards B, and what sort of treatment A thinks is appropriate for B. But firms have a role to play here, the more so the more intense is the firm's internal culture.

The Corresponding Challenges for Management

Which of these five different stories is correct? They all are, to different degrees in different cases. The economic role of the firm is a mix of all these things (and others); as you ask, "What do I do to make my firm more efficient?," you should keep them all in mind. Here are a few things to consider.

First, managers must know where to draw the boundaries of the firm, trading off the benefits of unified governance of property and relatively low-powered incentives for employees against a lack of control of physical assets but more high-powered, market-based incentives for those erstwhile employees, now working for a different organization. Henry Ford was a great manager for a number of reasons, among them that he saw how, in his time and context, unified governance (extensive vertical integration) was a key to efficient assembly-line production of automobiles. Toyota's management, in a different time and context, achieved managerial distinction (and riches) by seeing how it could use relational contracting effectively to get back some of the high-powered incentives that Ford's design lacked.

Second, top managers must find ways to link the economic futures of individuals who make decisions on the firm's behalf to the fortunes of the firm. When Manager A takes a decision that affects the reputation of the firm for which she works, she should be motivated to decide in the manner that her firm desires.

At the same time, decision rights within Toyota for decisions that affect Toyota's reputation must be carefully crafted. A firm such as Toyota often finds it helpful, to protect its collective reputation from injury by individuals making decisions in its name, to require a substantial level of consensus before decisions are made. Instead of giving the decision rights on how much Johnson Controls will be paid to a single manager, Toyota can give those rights to a committee of its managers, who are more likely to weigh properly the impact this single decision would have on Toyota's general reputation.

Third, managers must manage the specific reputation of their firm to satisfy a number of goals. The reputation must be strong and easily communicated to trading partners. Special efforts to promote this communication, both with and *among* trading partners, may be warranted. It must be easily communicated to employees of the firm whose decisions affect the firm's reputation. And it must be robust to the sorts of dilemmas and problems the firm will face. Note the conflicts here: a firm with a wide-ranging business, which faces a great diversity of dilemmas and problems, wants a fairly general reputation, one that is adaptable to the great diversity of problems. But the broader and less specific is the reputation, the harder it is to communicate and the weaker the guarantees it provides. For these reasons, managers often limit the scope of what their firm will take on, finding a niche that can be adequately served by a strong, specific reputation.

Fourth, managers must manage the internal culture of the firm, promoting efficient intrafirm transactions. For instance, in organizations where performance is easy to measure, the "technology" of production involves few and controllable interdependencies among workers, and productivity requires substantial effort, a marketlike culture within the organization probably works well. If work is interdependent and individual performance cannot be measured, a culture of cooperation is probably favored.

As you might imagine, these thoughts only scratch the surface of the challenges facing managers, once you think of a firm in these terms.

5.3. Transaction Costs and Ethical Behavior

In summer 2002, the business pages of newspapers and news magazines were filled with stories of allegedly unethical and perhaps illegal behavior by top management of large corporations. The scandals concerned management hiding relevant information from the financial markets through the use of creative accounting, but they went well beyond this in some cases. In general, the scandals involved *pushing the envelope*: Managers are allowed a certain amount of discretion in what they do and what and how they report what they have done.

Some actions and some sorts of reports are proscribed by law, but there is always a gray area, and in many of the cases in the news, management stood accused of pushing as far into the gray area as it could, perhaps going beyond the gray area, but in any event using its skills and creativity to circumvent the spirit of the law. Certainly any willful and knowing violations of the law (at least, of these sorts) are unethical. But most commentators asserted that simply pushing the envelope, without crossing the line, is also unethical.

Is pushing the envelope in this fashion unethical? This may involve an ethical dilemma: Pushing the envelope may serve the interests of shareholders, to whom management has a fiduciary responsibility, although it harms the interests of other stakeholders, such as workers, suppliers, customers, and the general public. Just as in the question of whether implicit collusion is unethical, management sometimes has to balance its responsibility to shareholders with its other responsibilities. But this dilemma did not seem to be present in many of the cases in 2002, where management was, if anything, taking actions that hurt outside shareholders as well as other stakeholders, to line its own personal pockets. Stipulating that this is so, can we say that this sort of pushing the envelope is unethical?

One sometimes hears, in connection with sports, that it is right to push to the edge of rulebreaking; it is the responsibility of the rule makers to provide rules that outlaw undesirable behavior, and it is the responsibility of athletes to do everything they can within the rules to win.[7]

Management, however, is more complex than sports, chiefly because economics is not a zero-sum competition. Doing anything and everything as a manager that is not specifically excluded by law—pushing the envelope to try to see how far you can go—can lead to substantial inefficiencies. The story here involves transaction costs. Parties to complex transactions have myriad opportunities to take advantage of others. These opportunities can be dealt with by formal "contractual" safeguards. But each formal, explicit safeguard comes at some cost, in terms of specifying and enforcing the safeguard and in transactional rigidities and maladaptations caused by formal, specific safeguards. To the extent that certain behaviors are "off the table" because they are regarded as unethical, the parties involved in a specific transaction can economize on transaction costs.

This is the instrumental case for ethics and ethical behavior. If ethical behavior, suitably defined, is guaranteed, then transaction costs can be lowered. For instance, if top management could be trusted to draw up income statements that did not try to paint an overly rosy picture or otherwise mislead investors,

---

[7] There is, though, an evolving cultural aspect to this in sports. In soccer, for instance, diving is (as I write these lines) thought of as an unsavory practice. Holding opponents when defending a corner kick is just as much a violation of the laws of the game, but the sporting press doesn't seem nearly as excited about ending this practice.

less could be spent on auditors, accounting rules and procedures could be less rigid, and capital markets could function more effectively. But, as events in 2002 indicated, ethical behavior, at least defined in this fashion, is not guaranteed.

Indeed, when managers can line their own pockets by issuing misleading reports, why would they behave ethically? In the face of clear and direct incentives to engage in unethical behavior, what prevents an epidemic of it? Several extrinsic motivators may be at work:

- Getting close to the line may take you over it, with criminal and civil penalties imposed by the courts. To stay out of jail, stay away from the line.

- The risk of social opprobrium for those caught pushing the envelope, reinforced by social sanctions, can motivate individuals to stay well within the bounds of acceptable practices.

- Acquiring a reputation as someone who sometimes behaves unethically can mean the loss of economic opportunity in the future, for instance, because potential trading partners are less willing to trade with someone with a poor reputation or because potential trading partners would insist on contractual safeguards.

The strengths of these motivators are endogenous to the social setting: Laws can be changed, and indeed they were in summer 2002. The extent to which unethical behavior excites social opprobrium and sanction depends on society's distaste for the specific behavior. And an unwillingness to trade with someone with a poor reputation for ethical behavior depends at least in part on the availability of alternatives who behave more ethically.

The point I wish to emphasize here is that these are all extrinsic motivators. They work in the fashion of other motivators we studied in this book. In particular, the latter two would seem to fit very well within the frameworks of this chapter and Chapters 3 and 4.

Of course, an individual may behave ethically for intrinsic reasons; that is, because the individual believes that ethical behavior is the right and noble thing to do and would do so even if no one else takes note. I do not deny this important force behind ethical behavior. And I do not deny that behaving ethically is *per se* the right thing to do. But that ethical behavior is instrumental for more efficient transacting, and the existence of extrinsic reasons to behave ethically, add to these more basic reasons.

Executive Summary

This completes Part I of this book, on the economics of relationships. Hence, the executive summary is longer than usual, summarizing not only this chapter but drawing together lessons learned throughout this and the previous four chapters.

We have looked at several different sorts of relationships:

- Chapter 3 is about *reciprocity* and bilateral relationships, with special focus on the relationship between rivals in an industry.

- In Chapter 4, the use of *reputation* to achieve credibility expands focus to multilateral relationships and, in particular, how one's behavior in one relationship—even a short-term or one-off transaction—can impact one's later opportunities.

- And in this chapter, we used the ideas from Chapters 3 and 4 to explore complex bi- and multilateral transactions, with an emphasis on the *governance* of the transaction, the assignment to the parties of decision rights to determine "what next?"

The overarching takeaways are:

- A lot of economic exchange depends on relationships between the parties, where a relationship is, by its nature, an ongoing series of interactions between the parties involved. This involves *both* trading partners and competitors.

- Relationships are built on the expectations that each party has about how the others (will) act and react.

- What others expect of a given party is powerfully and perhaps principally determined by the previous actions of the given party. In the context of relationships, *actions speak very loudly, usually more loudly than do words.*

- Because of this, and because it is impossible to rewrite history, changing the nature of a bad relationship/reputation is usually a lot harder than maintaining a good relationship/reputation. Moral: Be very careful in what you do at the start of a new relationship; the actions you take early on can have remarkable staying power.

- And, as you try to predict how others will behave, look at the situation through their eyes, to the extent that you can. (This is where noncooperative game theory becomes particularly useful, if used carefully.)

- Relationships can be structured so that each party gets a "win." But the first requirement for achieving "win-wins" is that the parties involved must want to accomplish this. If your relationship partners are only interested in beating you and not in achieving a good outcome for all, you probably won't get anywhere with them.

- The Folk Theorem tells us that lots of arrangements *can* be equilibria, in the sense that it is in everyone's best interests to follow along. But being an equilibrium is only relevant for something that is the "obvious way to play." So a further requirement for a relationship to function is that the parties involved must understand their role in the "deal."

- In many if not most "win-win" deals, each party puts itself somewhat at the mercy of the other side. Enforcing the deal involves the double-edged promise/threat: "I'll let you have your win, if you reciprocate and let me have mine. But I'll smash you if you try to take what we've agreed is mine."

- For a threat to punish the other side for cheating to be credible, each party must be able to tell when the other side is cheating. You can only trust what you can verify (unless you are dealing with a saint).

- And the double-edged promise/threat has two corollaries: (1) There must be enough value-at-risk for each party, so they want the deal to continue. (2) The parties must be powerful enough vis-à-vis one another to effectively punish the others for cheating.

- When dealing in a relationship with another partner, it is easy to become fixated on your bilateral relationship. But always remember: What you do is likely to spill over into other relationships you have via reputation effects. Don't ignore those.

- In long-term, open-ended transactions, pay attention to the assignment of subsequent decision rights. You may not be able to anticipate what will happen, but you may be able to anticipate how what will happen will be determined. And in the assignment of decision rights, keep in mind: (1) Which party has the best information for making a good decision? (2) Which party is (often, by virtue of a reputation stake) most trustworthy by the other parties?

What's missing from this picture?

This amounts to a pretty nice picture, but it is far from complete. In particular, and perhaps most important, it doesn't have a lot to say about how the parties get to a desirable relationship, or how one party develops the reputation it wants. "Actions speak loudly" is a good starting point, but which actions, and how can you be sure that the other side is reading your actions the way you want them read? This part is mostly art and ingenuity and not science. At least, it is not economic science, not yet.

And what's wrong with this picture?

And, in at least one important respect, the picture painted by these economic models is flawed. The models, true to the spirit of noncooperative game theory, assume that each party acts in whatever way is best for his/her/its own selfish interests.

But in some (not all) relationships, individuals act in ways that are not purely self-interested. This can cut in either direction: In some cases, one party positively internalizes the welfare of a "trading partner," meaning that the first party is willing to sacrifice some of his or her own personal utility if doing so benefits the second party. The extreme case is perhaps a family relationship; a person will sacrifice rather a lot for his or her spouse, significant other, child, parent, and so forth. But, especially in work environments, we see similar bonds of personal "affection" emerging, manifesting in one party sacrificing to aid another. These relationships are most often between and among people, but such relationships can form between a person and an organization, as in: "That employee will go out of his or her way to benefit the company." In some cases, you can construct an argument of self-interest: Employee A works late and otherwise provides a consummate effort on behalf of her firm in the expectation that this will be noticed and she will get a promotion or a bigger raise. But, the acid test: If employee A will do stuff like this even if there is no chance it is observed by anyone in a position to help A, then A must be internalizing the welfare of her firm.

And, on the other side, there are cases where one party will take actions that are personally costly, as long as they harm a "partner" sufficiently.

These are important considerations that, as I write these lines, are only beginning to be integrated into economics. So we leave the story here, at least for now, and go on to other topics in microeconomics relevant to managers. But while we don't go further into these considerations, *you* should not ignore or forget them.

Part II
Pricing with Market Power

6. Marginal Cost Equals Marginal Revenue

We begin the second part of the book with the basic economic model of a firm that has market power. This involves the use of calculus; we spend a considerable amount of time in this chapter introducing the use of calculus in economic models.

In a mythical land called Freedonia, in a time before trade liberalization became the norm, a domestic steel manufacturing firm named Chicolini Steel—the only manufacturer of steel in the country—produced and sold steel at $680 per ton, well above the (then) world price of $375 per ton. This firm was protected against foreign competition by incredibly high tariffs that effectively barred all imports. There was no possibility that these tariffs would be dropped; Chicolini Steel contributed heavily to both major political parties as well as several smaller parties.

This firm never exported steel: Why export at $375 per ton, when they sell steel at $680 per ton domestically? And, to clinch the argument that there was no reason to export steel, executives at the company noted that the average cost of manufacturing steel, which varied with the rate at which the firm produced steel, was at the time at $405 and would never be below $400 per ton. This company simply could not make positive profits selling steel for $375 per ton. Notwithstanding everything just said, this firm could have increased profits by exporting steel. Why?

6.1. The Simple Model of a Profit-Maximizing Firm

To answer this question, we begin by describing the simple model of a profit-maximizing firm that produces a single output good in a single market.

So, imagine a firm that produces a single good for sale. It has the power to vary its rate or level of production; we'll use the variable x to represent its production (output) level or rate.[1] Corresponding to each x is a total cost to the firm of producing x, given by the function $TC(x)$.

This firm sells its output in some market. Depending on what price it sets for its output, the amount it can sell changes: The higher the price it sets, the less it can sell. We model this by using the variable p to denote the price the firm sets; then the *demand function* it faces, $D(p)$, tells the firm how many units of its product it can sell as a function of its price p.

---

[1] "Rate" or "level?" The simple model we describe is static, so pick whichever term you prefer.

Does the Firm Have Market Power or Is It Competitive?

Can the firm set any price at all that it wishes? Isn't it restrained by the prices set by other firms that sell similar products? Of course, it is restrained by competition. If it faces very little competition, it may be able to sell a lot at a high price; with more competition, customers will go to a competitor. This is what determines the shape and position of the demand function.

In this regard, one extreme case—the case (in our story) facing Chicolini Steel in the global market—is where (1) the good being produced is a *commodity*, meaning that any other producers of this good produce a virtually identical good, and (2) the firm we are modeling is "small" in the entire market, so that its production decisions don't significantly affect the *market* price. In such cases, a going "market price" for the good prevails, and our producer's ability to set its own price is starkly limited:

- If our producer wishes to sell above the market price, its customers will go to other producers who are selling virtually the same product at the market price.

- On the other hand, if our producer undercuts the market price, it draws in the customers of all the other producers and is overwhelmed with demand.

The extreme form of this is where our firm, selling a commodity item and being small, decides how much to produce and sell, *taking the market price as given*, which means that it assumes it can sell nothing at any price above the market price and can sell as much as it wants at (or perhaps slightly below) the market price. A firm in this extreme situation is called a *competitive firm* or a *perfectly competitive firm* by economists.

A firm that is not perfectly competitive has some wiggle room in the price it charges, with the relationship between price set and amount that can be sold given by the demand function $D(p)$. We say that a firm in this situation has *market power*: The amount of market power depends, in general, on how unique is its product, how important the product is to its customers, and how much competition it faces, all of which in this model is encapsulated in the demand function $D(p)$.[2]

The Firm Chooses Its Price and Quantity to Maximize Its Profit

The simple model of a firm with market power, then, describes the firm by its total-cost function $TC(x)$ and the demand function $D(p)$ that it faces. And the model concludes with how the firm chooses the price p it charges and, therefore, the amount $x = D(p)$ it produces and sells:

The firm chooses p and $x = D(p)$ to maximize its profit, where its profit is the

---

[2] Technically, when we discuss the demand *function*, we should write D; $D(p)$ should denote the value of D at the argument (price) p. But we won't be so precise in our notation or terminology.

difference between its total revenue from sales and its total cost of production.

I can hear the objections:

- Real-life firms do not typically choose their price to maximize total revenue less total cost.

- And even if a real-life firm wants to do this, it lacks the required information. It doesn't typically know how much it can sell at every price nor the total cost of every production level.

These are well-founded objections. But remember that this is presented as the simplest model we consider of a firm that has market power. This is a starting point. And, I hope to convince you, despite its obvious flaws, it is a starting point that can be used to gain substantial insights into how real firms set the prices they set. So, please, suspend your disbelief for the next hundred or so pages.

Inverse Demand and Total Revenue

Once we accept this model, if we know demand D and total cost TC, we can, in principle, discover the price the firm will choose. If the firm chooses price p, it sells $D(p)$ units, so its total revenue is $p \cdot D(p)$. The total cost of producing $D(p)$ is $TC(D(p))$. So the firm will choose p to maximize

$$p \cdot D(p) - TC(D(p)).$$

It turns out, though, that rather than looking at the problem as one of picking p, economists typically make the quantity produced x the driving variable.

To do so, we must turn the demand function "inside out." Suppose, to take a simple example, $D(p) = 100 - 2p$. Note what this means: If the firm sets the price of its good to be $p = 0$, $D(0) = 100$; that is, if the firm offers its product for free, according to this demand function, only 100 units are taken by customers. If the firm sets $p = 50$, $D(50) = 0$. No one wants any at a price of 50. (For $p > 50$, this demand function becomes negative, meaning that customers want to sell back to the firm, or something like that. We won't take demand functions seriously when prices are near zero or when demand for the good is close to zero.)

So suppose we ask, What price must be set by the firm, so that it can sell $x = 20$? We're looking for the p that satisfies $D(p) = 20$, or $100 - 2p = 20$, or $p = 40$. The price at which $x = 10$ is $p = 45$. And so forth: You can *invert* the relationship

$$x = 100 - 2p \quad \text{to get} \quad p = \frac{100 - x}{2},$$

which allows you to put in any value of x and get the corresponding p.

We write this *inverse of the demand function* or, for short, *inverse-demand function*, as $P(x)$; for this example, where demand is $D(p) = 100 - 2p$, inverse demand is $P(x) = (100 - x)/2$. As long as the demand function is decreasing—at a higher price, the firm sells less—the demand function can be inverted, and inverse demand is also decreasing, meaning to sell more, the firm must charge less per unit.

Then, if we have the inverse-demand function $P(x)$, we can write *total revenue* as a function of the production level x as $TR(x) = x \cdot P(x)$, and profit as a function of production level x as

$$\pi(x) = TR(x) - TC(x) = x \cdot P(x) - TC(x).$$

And, if we want to know which level of production x the firm will choose (with the choice of price determined implicitly), the answer is, Whatever level of x maximizes $\pi(x)$.

Taking the last mathematical step, we find the value of x that maximizes $\pi(x)$ by taking the derivative of $\pi(x)$ and setting it equal to zero. And since $\pi(x) = TR(x) - TC(x)$, this amounts to:

*Take the derivative of the total-revenue function as a function of x, which economists call the **marginal-revenue function**, written $MR(x)$. Take the derivative of the total-cost function as a function of x, which economists call the **marginal-cost function**, $MC(x)$. The derivative of the profit function is the difference $MR(x) - MC(x)$, so the derivative of the profit function is zero, which is where profit is maximized, where $MR(x) - MC(x) = 0$, which is where $MR(x) = MC(x)$, or where **marginal cost equals marginal revenue**.*

That's quite a mouthful, so let's work out a simple example and then try to explain verbally what the mathematics is telling us.

Example. Imagine a firm with a total-cost function $TC(x) = 10 + 5x + x^2/4$, that faces demand function $D(p) = 100 - 2p$. What price and quantity pair maximizes its profit?

Step 1. Turn demand $D(p)$ into inverse demand $P(x)$. We've already done this. It is $P(x) = (100 - x)/2$.

Step 2. Using inverse demand, compute the total- and marginal-revenue functions. Total revenue is $TR(x) = x \cdot P(x) = x(100 - x)/2 = (100x - x^2)/2 = 50x - x^2/2$, and marginal revenue is the derivative of this, or $MR(x) = 50 - x$.

Step 3. Find marginal cost by taking the derivative of total cost. Total cost is $TC(x) = 10 + 5x + x^2/4$, so marginal cost is $MC(x) = 5 + 2x/4 = 5 + x/2$.

Step 4. Equate marginal cost and marginal revenue, to find the profit-maximizing level of production. MC = MR is

$$5 + \frac{x}{2} = 50 - x \quad \text{or} \quad \frac{3x}{2} = 45 \quad \text{or} \quad x = 30.$$

Step 5. Plug this value of x into inverse demand to find the optimal price to charge: $p = (100 - 30)/2 = 35$. Done.

6.2. Think Like an Economist: Think Margins

What does MC = MR mean, intuitively? Begin with an analogy:

Imagine yourself standing on a hill in a dense fog. You cannot see more than one step in any direction. The question is, Are you on top of the hill?

You cannot tell for sure that you *are* on top, but you sometimes can tell that you are *not*. Ask yourself, Does the hill slope up *on the margin* in any direction? Can you get higher with a small step in any direction? When the answer is yes, then you aren't on top of the hill.

The italicized *on the margin* in the question is superfluous; the question would mean exactly the same thing had I not included it. But I put it there to indicate that the question *Does the hill slope up?* is a question about things in your immediate neighborhood. In general, the term *a marginal change* means a small change.

This test can tell you only that you are not on top of the hill. It cannot assure you that you are on top. Anyone familiar with climbing hills knows that hillsides have what economists, mathematicians, and perhaps hikers call *local peaks*, peaks in their immediate neighborhood that nonetheless are not *global peaks*, or peaks overall. On the surface of the Earth, Mount Everest is a global peak, while Mont Blanc is just a very impressive local peak. If you were standing atop Mont Blanc and you ran the test *Can I get higher in a single step?* you would conclude that you could not. But that does not mean that you had reached the top of the highest mountain on Earth.

This test of *local maximization* is, in part, why *marginal* is one of the most useful words in economics. In economic models, we assume that entities—firms and consumers—purposefully strive to make themselves as well off as possible. We model this purposeful behavior as the act of maximizing some numerical function of "well-offness." In the spirit of the top-of-the-hill test, we constantly ask whether the entities involved can improve their situation by making a small—marginal—change in their activities. They haven't maximized their situation until they have exhausted all possible marginal improvements.

The test seems almost trivial. Yet economists use the adjective *marginal* to an amazing extent. For instance, the index of Parkin's *Economics*, an excellent principles-of-economics textbook, lists as primary entries that begin with the adjective *marginal* the following:[3]

> marginal analysis; marginal benefit; marginal cost; marginal cost pricing rule; marginal grade and grade point average; marginal product; marginal product of labor; marginal propensity to consume; marginal propensity to import; marginal propensity to save; marginal rate of substitution; marginal revenue; marginal revenue product; marginal social benefit and marginal social cost; marginal tax rate; marginal utility; marginal utility in action; marginal utility per dollar spent; and marginal utility theory.

That is a lot of uses for an extremely simple idea. But simple or not, the idea is extremely powerful because it reminds economists, and henceforth you, to think hard about the marginal impacts of small changes in some decision.

And, finally, to bring this back to the simple model of a profit-maximizing firm and MC = MR:

- MC, or marginal cost, is the rate at which your total costs will increase per unit increase in your production level x. If you are at production level x and you move up to, say, $x + 0.1$ units, the change in your total costs will be $TC(x + 0.1) - TC(x)$ which is, approximately, $0.1 \cdot MC(x)$. And, $MC(x)$ is the rate at which total costs decline per unit decrease in production level.

- And, similarly, MR is the rate at which your total revenues will increase per unit increase in x, and it is the rate at which your total revenues will decrease per unit decrease in x.

- For a firm with market power—whose demand and inverse-demand functions are downward sloping—$MR(x)$ = the derivative of $TR(x) = xP(x)$ is, by the product rule, $P(x) + xP'(x)$. Since $P'(x)$ is negative, $MR(x)$ is less than $P(x)$, reflecting the loss in revenue that occurs when price must be lowered to push that last unit of output out the door.

- So suppose that, at your current level of production x, marginal revenue exceeds marginal cost; that is, $MR(x) > MC(x)$. If you increase x by a bit, your revenues will go up faster than will your costs, so your profit will go up. And if $MC(x) > MR(x)$, then by decreasing x a bit, total costs will go down faster than total revenues, increasing your profit. In other words, where $MC(x) \neq MR(x)$, you can vary your production quantity a bit in one or the other direction and increase your profit. You aren't profit maximizing.

This doesn't quite mean that where $MC(x) = MR(x)$ is the profit-maximizing production level. You could be at the bottom of the profit hill, or at a local but not global maximum, for instance. However, in most of the examples that we'll

---

[3] *Economics*, 6th edition (Reading, MA: Addison-Wesley, 2003).

deal with, MC will be an increasing function—as you produce more, it costs more on the margin to make the next unit. And, in most examples, MR(x) will be a decreasing function. And in such cases, MC(x) = MR(x) is where profit is maximized: For lower values of x, marginal revenue will exceed marginal cost, so increasing x (up to the point where MC = MR) increases profit. And for higher values of x, marginal cost will exceed marginal revenue, so increasing x beyond where MC = MR decreases profit. Where MC(x) = MR(x) is, therefore, the very top of the profit hill.

That logic works perfectly in our simple example. The marginal cost function is $5 + x/2$, which is increasing in x. The marginal revenue function is $50 - x$, which is decreasing in x. In case you are more visually minded, they are graphed, with some stick-figure commetary, in Figure 6.1.

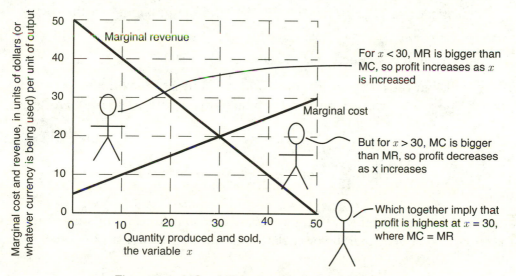

Figure 6.1. MC = MR in the example of this section.

6.3. Some More Complex Examples

I expect that this seems pretty obvious and overly pedantic to most readers. But the basic idea—think in terms of marginal this and marginal that—will serve you well if you learn to apply it to more complex situations. Here are a few examples:

Freedonian Steel

Recall the story at the start of this chapter. Chicolini Steel, the (only) Freedonian steel manufacturer, sells steel domestically at a price of $680 per ton, well above the global steel price of $375 per ton. (Of course, this means that Freedonian companies that buy steel would love to be able to import steel. But we're assuming this is not permitted.) The average cost is presently $405 per ton and is never less than $400 per ton. So, the story ends, it seems logical that this company should not bother selling steel in the global market.

The problem with this "logic" is that it is based on a bunch of *averages*. The domestic price per ton of $680 is the average price that the company gets. And the cost figures of $400 and $405 per ton are explicitly average-cost figures. To decide what is best for this company, we need to know its *marginal* cost of production and its domestic *marginal* revenue.

Here are the numbers: Domestic demand for steel in Freedonia is given by the demand function $D(p) = 250{,}000 - 250p$. And the total cost of producing x tons of steel by this company is $\$10{,}000{,}000 + 200x + x^2/1000$. Hence:

- Inverse domestic demand is $P(x) = 1000 - x/250$. (Do the algebra if this isn't clear to you.) Hence total domestic revenue, if the company sells x tons domestically, is $\text{TR}(x) = 1000x - x^2/250$, and marginal revenue is $\text{MR}(x) = 1000 - x/125$.

- The marginal-cost function is $\text{MC}(x) = 200 + x/500$.

We're told that the company is not exporting. But is it maximizing domestic profit? The production quantity x for which this would be so is where MC = MR, or

$$200 + \frac{x}{500} = 1000 - \frac{x}{125} \quad \text{or} \quad \frac{5x}{500} = 800, \quad \text{which is } x = 80{,}000 \text{ tons.}$$

(Again, DO THE ALGEBRA!) Plug $x = 80{,}000$ into the domestic inverse demand function, and you see that the price that corresponds to domestic sales of 80,000 tons is

$$P(80{,}000) = 1000 - \frac{80{,}000}{250} = 1000 - 320 = \$680,$$

just as in the original story. And we might as well check that cost figure of $405: Total cost at $x = 80{,}000$ is

$$10{,}000{,}000 + 200 \cdot 80{,}000 + \frac{80{,}000^2}{1000} = \$32{,}400{,}000,$$

and so average cost is indeed $405.

I've asserted as well that the average cost of production is never below $400 per ton. To check this assertion, you can write down the average-cost function, which is $\text{AC}(x) = 10{,}000{,}000/x + 200 + x/1000$, take its derivative, and set that derivative equal to zero. Or you can wait until page 140, where the calculation is done for you. For now, trust me.

But the average domestic revenue (or price) of $680, and the average cost of $405, are *not* the relevant numbers to an economist. We need to know the *marginal cost* and *domestic marginal revenue*. So we plug 80,000 into the MC and MR functions and we learn that

$$MC(80,000) = 200 + \frac{80,000}{500} = \$360 = MR(80,000) = 1000 - \frac{80,000}{125}.$$

(Of course, they are the same. If this isn't obvious to you, think it through. What equation gave us the number 80,000?)

And these numbers tell the tale: When I say that the global price of steel is $375, I'm implicitly—now explicitly—saying that the Freedonian steel manufacturer is a price-taker (or is competitive) in the global market. It can sell all the steel it chooses to at this price; it can't sell any at a higher price. Hence its *export total revenue*, if it exports y tons of steel, is $375 \cdot y$, and so its *export marginal revenue* is $375. *On the margin*, it gets $375 for the first ton of steel it sells into the global market, and *on the margin*, one more ton of steel costs it an addition $360. There is profit to be made by exporting!

Or, put another way, the last ton of steel it manufactured and sold domestically (of the 80,000) brought in a marginal $360 in revenues. It could instead sell 79,999 tons domestically and export that last ton. It loses $360 in domestic revenues, but gets $375 for the exported ton, putting it ahead by $15.

So, what is the best production plan for this company? You can set this up as a two-variable maximization problem—the two variables are production x sold domestically and production y sold for export—and use partial derivatives to find the answer. (We discuss the use of partial derivatives in the next subsection.) But the logic of thinking in terms of margins makes finding the answer a lot easier:

- If domestic marginal revenue is below the export price of $375, it can't be that the firm is maximizing profit. Without changing its total costs, it could export one more ton of steel, sell one less ton domestically, and be ahead (in profit) by the amount that $375 exceeds domestic marginal revenue. Conversely, if domestic marginal revenue exceeds $375 *and if the firm is doing any exporting*, it would be better off exporting one ton less and selling that ton domestically. So there are two possibilities: (1) If the firm is exporting steel, to be maximizing its profit, domestic marginal revenue must equal $375, or (2) if domestic marginal revenue is above $375, but the firm is not exporting at all, it is okay.[4]

---

[4] In this second case, the firm would ideally like to *buy* steel on the global market for $375 and sell it domestically, but we'll assume this isn't feasible.

- And the total level of production, which I'll denote by X and which is just $x + y$, should be at the level where the marginal cost of production is \$375 (or, if the firm is not exporting, at whatever is domestic marginal revenue).

We know that, when the firm maximizes domestic profit without exporting, its domestic marginal revenue is less than \$375. So we know that the firm wants to export. Which means it should be producing at the level X where $\text{MC}(X) = 375$, or

$$\text{MC}(X) = 200 + \frac{X}{500} = 375 \quad \text{which is} \quad X = 87{,}500.$$

And its domestic marginal revenue should equal \$375, which is $1000 - x/125 = 375$, or $x = (625) \cdot (125) = 78{,}125$. Exports should be the difference between total production $X = 87{,}500$ and domestic sales of 78,125, so exports should equal $87{,}500 - 78{,}125 = 9375$ tons.

Don't get lost in the math here. The important part is the economic intuition: The firm wants marginal domestic revenue to equal marginal export revenue—which, since the firm is a price-taker globally, is just the global market price—and both of these should equal overall marginal cost. If you understand why this is where the optimal plan is found, and why it is marginal cost and marginal revenues that matter, you've got it.

Multivariable Optimization

I suggested a few paragraphs ago that you could solve the Freedonian steel problem by using two variables and partial derivatives. You are asked to do this in Problem 6.3; I'll illustrate the technique with a different problem here.

Imagine a company that produces two models of tablets, Model X and Model Y. The total cost of producing x Model X's and y Model Y's is given by $\text{TC}(x, y) = 10x + 20y + 1000$: that is, a fixed cost of \$1000, plus \$10 per Model X and \$20 per Model Y. Monthly demand for the two models is complicated because they are *substitute* products: a higher price for Model X means more sales of Model Y, and vice versa. Rather than give you the joint demand functions (what is the level of demand for each product as a function of their two prices), I'll supply you with the joint inverse demand functions: If the firm decides to sell x Model X's and y Model Y's, it must set their prices at

$$P_X(x, y) = 90 - \frac{x}{100} - \frac{y}{300} \quad \text{and} \quad P_Y(x, y) = 120 - \frac{y}{100} - \frac{x}{150},$$

where P_X is the price of a Model X and P_Y is the price of a Model Y. We want to know the levels of the two models to produce and sell that maximize the total profit of the firm.

Step 1. Write profit as a function of x and y:

$$\pi(x,y) = x\left(90 - \frac{x}{100} - \frac{y}{300}\right) + y\left(120 - \frac{y}{100} - \frac{x}{150}\right) - \left(10x + 20y + 1000\right).$$

Step 2. Multiply through and collect similar terms. You get

$$\pi(x,y) = 80x + 100y - \frac{x^2}{100} - \frac{y^2}{100} - \frac{3xy}{300} - 1000.$$

Step 3. Find the partial derivative of profit in each of the two variables. These are, respectively,

$$\frac{\partial \pi}{\partial x} = 80 - \frac{2x}{100} - \frac{3y}{300} \quad \text{and} \quad \frac{\partial \pi}{\partial y} = 100 - \frac{2y}{100} - \frac{3x}{300}.$$

Step 4. The profit function is maximized where these two marginal-profit functions are 0, or where

$$80 - \frac{2x}{100} - \frac{3y}{300} = 0 \quad \text{and} \quad 100 - \frac{2y}{100} - \frac{3x}{300} = 0.$$

Solve these two equations in two unknowns, and the solution is $x = 2000$ and $y = 4000$.

Step 5. (We've answered the question asked, which was to find the profit-maximizing values of x and y. So this final step is an "extra." But since the firm will, presumably, be setting the prices, it is an extra that is worth taking.) Find the prices that correspond to these levels of output, by plugging the levels into the inverse demand functions:

$$P_X(2000, 4000) = 90 - \frac{2000}{100} - \frac{4000}{300} = 56.666\ldots, \quad \text{and}$$

$$P_Y(2000, 4000) = 120 - \frac{4000}{100} - \frac{2000}{150} = 66.666\ldots.$$

Easy enough, as long as you know how to take partial derivatives (and I'm assuming you do), and you remember that *to have maximized a function of several variables, the function's partial derivatives all have to equal 0.*[5]

---

[5] Just as in the case of problems with one variable, setting all the partial derivatives equal to zero is necessary but not sufficient to find the global maximum. (And this is a necessary condition *only* if the objective function—here, profit—is differentiable.) This is the hill-climbing story all over again:

What does all this math have to do with marginal revenue and marginal cost? It's the same story as before, *as long as you are careful about marginal revenue*:

- For both models, in this problem, marginal-cost figures are very simple: If you increase your production of Model X's by a unit, costs go up by 10. If you increase you production of Model Y's by a unit, costs go up by 20. (If this isn't obvious to you, take the two partial derivatives of the total cost function.) So $MC_X = 10$ and $MC_Y = 20$.

- But, *and this is where you must be careful*, marginal revenue is tricky. *Total revenue* is the revenue from the sale of both products:

$$\mathrm{TR}(x, y) = x\left(90 - \frac{x}{100} - \frac{y}{300}\right) + y\left(120 - \frac{y}{100} - \frac{x}{150}\right).$$

That is, total revenue is sum of revenue from the sale of Model X's and revenue from the sale of Model Y's. Rewrite this by distributing the x and y inside the two square brackets, but do not combine like terms:

$$\mathrm{TR}(x, y) = \left(90x - \frac{x^2}{100} - \frac{xy}{300}\right) + \left(120y - \frac{y^2}{100} - \frac{xy}{150}\right).$$

Marginal revenue in Model X's, or MR_X—the rate at which revenues increase per unit increase in x, is the partial derivative of this function with respect to x, which is

$$\mathrm{MR}_X(x, y) = \left(90 - \frac{2x}{100} - \frac{y}{300}\right) + \left(0 - 0 - \frac{y}{150}\right),$$

where I've written each term in the MR_X function in corresponding position to the term that gave rise to it in the TR function.

And this is where students sometimes screw up. The MR_X function consists of two major terms: the marginal impact of an increase in x on the revenues derived from the Model X's—which is the term in the first set of parentheses—and also the marginal impact of an increase in x on the revenue derived from the sale of Model Y's, which is the $-y/150$ inside the

---

You aren't at the peak if the ground under your feet slopes upwards in some direction—which is, if some partial derivative is not zero. But just because the ground under your feet is "flat," doesn't mean you are at the global peak. You could be at a local maximum, or a global minimum, or a saddle-point, or ... There are mathematical techniques that give you sufficient conditions to ensure (at least) that you are at a local maximum—called second-order conditions—and for problems where the objective function is *concave*, any place where all the partial derivatives are zero is assuredly a global maximum. But I won't go into these matters here, except to assure you that, for the multivariate problems in this book, you'll be getting the answer if you find the point where the partial derivatives are all zero.

second set of parentheses. *You need both of these to figure out the marginal impact on total revenue of increases in x,* because an increase in x affects revenue from the Model X's, of course, and also—because increasing x means decreasing P_Y—revenue from the Model Y's. If you only have the first of these, you get the wrong answer.

But if you compute the right MR's and MC's, the answer is to find production levels such that $MR_X = MC_X$ and $MR_Y = MC_Y$, for the same reason as in the case of one-output firms: If one of these is not an equality, there is a direction to move that will enhance profit. And when you solve these two equations in two unknowns (x and y), you get the answer we got before.

Constrained Maximization

Setting derivative or partial derivatives equal to zero works when there are no constraints on the variables; that is, when you can choose any values of the variables that you wish. But many economic problems come with constraints on the variables; the problem is to find the maximizing choice of variables while respecting the constraints.

There are mathematical methods for solving constrained maximization problems using things called Lagrangian multipliers, but their use often obscures what is really going on. Let me give you two examples:

Example 1. A one-variable problem subject to an inequality constraint

Go back to the example that begins on page 126. The firm produces a single product, with total cost function $TC(x) = 10 + 5x + x^2/4$, facing demand function $D(p) = 100 - 2p$. But now I add a constraint. To produce x units of output requires $4x$ hours of labor. And the firm in question, at least in the short run, has only two employees, each working 40 hours a week, who can supply the required labor. So the firm is constrained to choose an x that satisfies $4x \leq 80$ or $x \leq 20$. What should it do to maximize its profit?

Step 1. Whenever you have a constrained problem like this one, the first step is to ask, Does the constraint *bind* at the solution? Practically, you solve the problem without the constraint, to see whether the unconstrained answer satisfies the constraint.

In this case, we know that the optimal, unconstrained solution is $x = 30$. (See the top of page 127.) So, Yes, the constraint binds.

Step 2, for a one-variable problem. Assume, then, that the answer is as close to the unconstrained solution as the constraint will allow. In this case, the answer is $x = 20$.

Easy, right? To be honest, this doesn't always produce the answer in a one-variable problem. It always does for problems you'll encounter in this book, so the recipe just given is good enough for finding answers, for now. But let me carry on the analysis a bit further:

What are the marginal revenue and marginal cost of production at this constrained optimum of $x = 20$? The marginal revenue function is $50 - x$, so $MR(20) = 30$. The marginal cost function is $5 + x/2$, so $MC(20) = 15$. As is intuitive, marginal revenue exceeds marginal cost at $x = 20$, and the firm would love to produce more; the constraint is preventing this.

But now we have a dollar figure for how much this constraint is costing the firm, on the margin. If it could make one more unit, it would make $15 more in profit. So *if the firm could find a way to* **relax** *the constraint, meaning increasing labor supply from 80, it would increase profit to do so as long as a one-hour increase in labor supply cost less than $15/4 = $3.75.* (I apologize for the unrealistic numbers.) Why $15/4$? Because to make a unit more of output, worth $15 in profit on the margin, we need 4 more hours of labor.

Example 2. A multivariable problem subject to a single inequality constraint

The one-variable recipe for dealing with constraints is pretty simple because, if the constraint binds, the answer typically is to get as close to the unconstrained solution as possible. With multivariable problems, the second step is harder, because there will be a number of ways to "get as close to the unconstrained optimum as possible." Here's an example:

The general manager of the Manteca United Soccer Club has a stadium that seats 40,000. 24,000 of the seats are held by season ticket holders, and the remaining 16,000 are allocated to home supporters and visiting-team supporters on a game-by-game basis. These 16,000 are divided between supporters of the two clubs physically, to prevent violence, and seats in each section can only be bought by registered supporters of that section's club, hence different prices can be charged for seats in the two sections.

For the upcoming game against the Wolverton Gladabouts, the question is, How should the 16,000 seats be divided to maximize revenues? To sell W seats to Wolverton supporters, the price per ticket must be set at $£18 - W/2000$. To sell M seats to Manteca supporters, the price per ticket must be set at $£14 - M/8000$. What division of the 16,000 seats maximizes revenue?

Note to start that there is no mention of costs in this problem. There are 16,000 empty seats, and any seat that is not occupied generates no revenue and saves nothing in cost. Put differently, $MC = 0$, and "profit" is simply the level of gate revenues (less any fixed costs, which, being fixed, don't change the how the seats are divided).

We have the same first step as in the previous example: *Find the unconstrained maximum.* You might think that, without constraints and no costs, there is no limit to how much can be made. But, in fact, with downward sloping demand, it will typically be the case that revenues begin to decline as quantity goes off to infinity. This isn't quite a general rule, but it is true for any inverse demand function that has price hit zero at some level of sales, as here.

So, without constraint, total revenue from Wolverton supporters is $18W - W^2/2000$, hence marginal revenue is $18 - 2W/2000$. Marginal cost is zero, so MR = MC where $18 - 2W/2000 = 0$, or $W = 18,000$ seats. And for Manteca, total revenue is $14M - M^2/8000$, so marginal revenue is $14 - 2M/8000$, which is driven to zero when $M = 56,000$. Our general manager may dream about a 98,000-seat stadium that would accommodate 24,000 season-ticket holders, plus 18,000 Wolverton supporters and 56,000 Manteca supporters. But, clearly, the constraint of having 16,000 seats to divide between the two groups of supporters is binding.

In place of *Step 2, for a one-variable problem* we have:

Step 2, for multivariable, single-constraint problems. Assume that the solution is where the constraint holds precisely.

In this case, this is $M + W = 16,000$. One way to proceed is to rewrite the constraint as $M = 16,000 - W$ and then write total revenue as a function of of W alone: Total revenue is

$$W\left(18 - \frac{W}{2000}\right) + M\left(14 - \frac{M}{8000}\right),$$

so this is

$$W\left(18 - \frac{W}{2000}\right) + (16,000 - W)\left(14 - \frac{16,000 - W}{8000}\right).$$

And, from here, you can take the derivative in W, set it equal to zero, and see what you get: If you do the algebra correctly, you'll get $W = 6400$ and so $M = 9600$. (Do the algebra if you are unsure about your ability to do so.)

We can, however, do step 2 a bit more simply using the logic of marginal thinking. (In fact, the algebra is exactly the same, albeit in a different order. But the logic will let you generalize this example to even more complex examples when the trick used in the previous paragraph won't work.) Suppose we allocate W seats to Wolverton supporters. We've already computed that marginal revenue from this group is $MR(W) = 18 - 2W/2000 = 18 - W/1000$. And if we allocate M seats to Manteca supporters, the marginal revenue from this group is $14 - 2M/8000 = 14 - M/4000$. And now for the insight: *At the optimal allocation, the marginal revenues from the two groups must be the same.* Why? Because you can trade one W for one M. If the marginal revenue from Wolverton exceeded the marginal revenue from Manteca at some allocation, taking seats away from Manteca and giving them to Wolverton would mean more revenue. Similarly, at a division for which the marginal revenue from Manteca exceeds the marginal revenue from Wolverton, revenues go up if you take seats away from Wolverton (on the margin) and allocate them to Manteca supporters.

So the answer is where

$$18 - \frac{W}{1000} = 14 - \frac{M}{4000}.$$

Of course, we also have the constraint that $W + M = 16,000$. This is two linear equations in two unknowns, which you can solve and get our answer of $W = 6400$ and $M = 9600$. (Let me check this for you: $W + M$ at these values is 16,000. Marginal revenue from Wolverton is $18 - 6400/1000 = £11.60$. And marginal revenue from Manteca is $14 - 9600/4000 = 14 - 2.4 = £11.60$.)

And, as a final step (necessary for the manager to do, but not for you if you are asked only for the allocation of seats): The ticket price for Wolverton supporters will be $18 - 6400/2000 = £14.80$, while for Manteca supporters, it will be $14 - 9600/8000 = £12.80$. Note carefully: the answer is *not* to set the ticket prices to the two groups to be the same; it is to set the marginal revenues from the two groups to be the same.

6.4. Marginal This and Average That

At the start of the discussion of the Freedonian steel company, I asserted that the logical flaw in the initial argument against exportation was a confusion between marginal revenues and costs and average revenues and costs. The confusion between margins and averages is, in fact, pervasive, and it is to blame for a lot of "logical errors" in the domain of economics. To help you understand the differences between marginal anything and average anything, it is probably a good idea to confront the tensions between the two concepts directly.

I'll keep the discussion to the context of revenue and cost, but pretty much everything I have to say in this discussion generalizes to total anything, average the same thing, and marginal the same thing.

We have a "total" function—total revenue or total cost—as a function of the quantity produced for sale, x. Throughout, we assume that x is one-dimensional; that is, the firm has a single output. (This assumption is *critical*, for reasons to be given at the very end of the chapter.) These functions are written $TR(x)$ and $TC(x)$. From these, we create the average-revenue and average-cost functions

$$AR(x) = \frac{TR(x)}{x} \quad \text{and} \quad AC(x) = \frac{TC(x)}{x},$$

and the marginal-revenue and marginal- cost functions

$$MR(x) = \frac{d\,TR(x)}{dx} \quad \text{and} \quad MC(x) = \frac{d\,TC(x)}{dx}.$$

AR and MR When Demand is Linear

In many, many examples, we'll be dealing with a linear demand function, $D(p) = a - bp$, where a and b are positive constants. The corresponding inverse demand function is $P(x) = (a - x)/b$. The graph of the demand/inverse-demand function is drawn in Figure 6.2; "it" is the solid line. (Disregard the dashed line for the moment.) I've put "it" in scare quotes because economists, for reasons of tradition, *always* put price on the vertical or y-axis and quantity on the horizontal or x-axis. Therefore, one picture shows you both demand and inverse demand. You're probably used to the argument of the function going on the horizontal axis, and that works great for inverse demand. But in the demand function, p is the variable and x is the value of the function, so you have to turn your head to see demand in the usual manner.

In any case, demand/inverse demand is a line segment that runs from $(x = 0, p = a/b)$ to $(x = a, p = 0)$, just as shown.

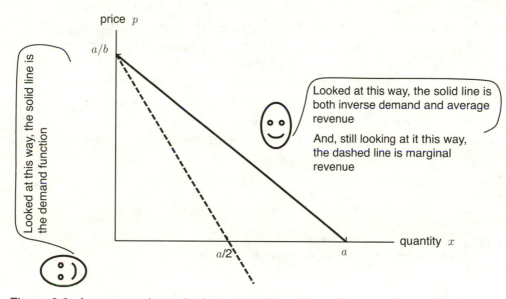

Figure 6.2. *Average and marginal revenue when demand/inverse demand is linear.*

The corresponding total-revenue function is $TR(x) = xP(x) = x(a - x)/b = (ax - x^2)/b$. Therefore, average revenue is $TR(x)/x = (a - x)/b = P(x)$, and marginal revenue is $(a - 2x)/b$. We will be drawing the case of linear demand many times, so please memorize the following:

> *For the case of linear demand, the average revenue is the inverse-demand function, and marginal revenue is a linear function with the same price-axis intercept and twice the slope.*

Average and Marginal Cost: Four Cases

While Figure 6.2 is the picture of demand and marginal revenue that we use repeatedly, when it comes to cost, there are four cases that we'll see repeatedly. The most general of these four cases is when

$$TC(x) = F + Vx + vx^2$$

for positive constants F, V, and v. That is, there is a fixed cost F that is incurred at any level of production, there is a constant variable cost of V per unit, and there is a further variable cost that rises with the production level. Let's deal with this most-general case first and then deal with the special cases that stem from it.

Average cost is $AC(x) = F/x + V + vx$. Marginal cost is $V + 2vx$. As long as $F > 0$, this means that average cost is very, very large for small levels of output. No surprise there: There is a fixed cost to be amortized over the production level, and if the production level is small, each unit of output has to "carry" a lot of the fixed cost. So average cost will be falling, at least for a while.

But, as long as $v > 0$, eventually, average cost must start rising. Put it this way: As x gets very large, the F/x part of average cost gets very small. The V part never changes. But the vx part gets very big.

Therefore, average cost falls for a while and then begins to rise. (We haven't quite demonstrated this "U" shape, but it is true.) Therefore, there is a point where average cost is minimized. You can find this point—which economists call *efficient scale*—by taking the derivative of average cost and setting it equal to zero. I'll do this for you: The derivative of average cost is

$$AC'(x) = -\frac{F}{x^2} + v, \quad \text{which equals zero when} \quad x = \sqrt{\frac{F}{v}}.$$

Note that at this level of output, average cost equals

$$\frac{F}{\sqrt{F/v}} + V + v\sqrt{F/v} = 2\sqrt{Fv} + V.$$

The picture, with marginal cost included, is shown in Figure 6.3.

Note that, in the figure, I have drawn the marginal-cost function cutting through the average-cost function precisely at efficient scale; that is, where average cost is minimized. This is not a coincidence. It reflects the following mathematical fact:

When marginal anything—cost, revenue, anything at all—exceeds average the-same-thing, the average will be rising. When marginal anything—cost, revenue, anything at all—is less than average the-same-thing, the average will be falling.

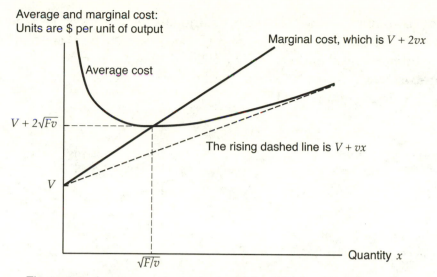

Figure 6.3. Average and marginal cost for $TC(x) = F + Vx + vx^2$.

You can prove this mathematically if you wish to; write $T(x)$ for the total what-ever function, $A(x) = T(x)/x$ for the average function, and $M(x) = T'(x)$ for the marginal function. Then, to see where $A(x)$ is rising and where it is falling, compute (using the quotient rule) the derivative of $A(x) = T(x)/x$.[6]

But if this is too much math, here's the intuition: Suppose we have a line of students and we take the students, one at a time, and average their heights. If the next student in line is taller than the average so far, this student will raise the average. If the next student is shorter than average, this student will lower the average. That's all there is to it.

So why does marginal cost pass through the bottom of average cost? Marginal cost is rising; it is just a linear function. Average cost, we know, is falling at first. So the italicized fact tells us, as long as marginal cost is below average cost, average cost is falling. But, eventually, marginal cost, which is rising with-out bound, is going to catch up to falling average cost. And, precisely at that moment, average cost will turn from falling to rising. That's Figure 6.3.

We can use this fact to find the level of x at which average cost is minimized without taking the derivative of average cost: Average cost is $F/x + V + vx$. Marginal cost is $V + 2vx$. So average cost equals marginal cost where

$$\frac{F}{x} + V + vx = V + 2vx \quad \text{which is} \quad \frac{F}{x} = vx, \quad \text{or} \quad \frac{F}{v} = x^2,$$

which is $x = \sqrt{F/v}$, precisely as before.

That's the hardest case we deal with. The other three cases are specializa-tions. One specialization is where there is a fixed cost F but no v; the marginal

---

[6] In case you try this, let me add: The variable x must be positive.

cost is a constant V, which of course is marginal cost. The second is where there is no fixed cost, or $\mathrm{TC}(x) = Vx + vx^2$ for $v > 0$. And the third specialization is where both F and v are zero, so marginal cost equals average cost equals V. Figure 6.4 shows you the "pictures" for the first two specializations; you should draw the picture for the third.

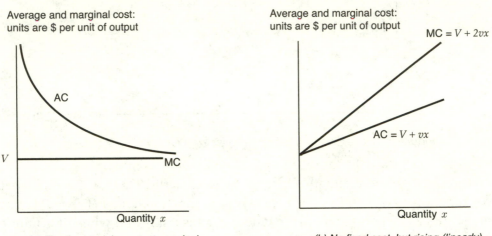

(a) Fixed cost and constant marginal (variable) cost

(b) No fixed cost, but rising (linearly) marginal cost

Figure 6.4. Two special cases of Figure 6.3.

Putting Both Averages and Both Marginals on One Graph

Combining Figures 6.2 and 6.3 into one graph gives us Figure 6.5.

I'll explain why there are three panels in the next paragraph. But, before doing that, it is worth pointing out that having all four functions on one graph tells us where is the profit-maximizing level of x—which is where MC = MR, of course—but also the range of production levels for which profit is positive, namely where inverse demand = AR is greater than average cost, or AC.

The reason for three panels is to clarify the term *efficient scale* and its relationship to the profit-maximizing level of production. *There is no relationship.* Efficient scale is where average costs are lowest. This has *nothing* to do with the revenue side of profit-maximization; it is purely a property of the cost function for the firm. Profit-maximization, on the other hand, combines the cost and revenue sides of the firm. So, depending on the demand conditions faced by the firm, it can maximize profit at less than efficient scale, at more than efficient scale, and—by an amazing coincidence—precisely at efficient scale. (Warning: This conclusion will be subject to some amendment in Part III, when we discuss competitive firms!)

What is the relationship between the quantity that maximizes profit and the quantity that maximizes *profit margin*, defined as the difference between

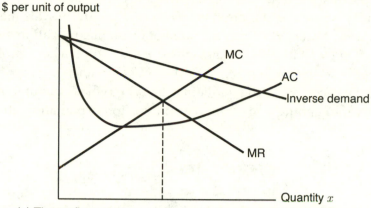
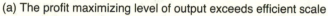

(a) The profit maximizing level of output exceeds efficient scale

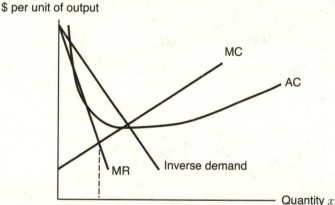
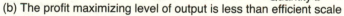

(b) The profit maximizing level of output is less than efficient scale

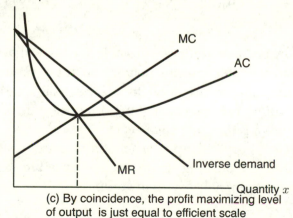

(c) By coincidence, the profit maximizing level
of output is just equal to efficient scale

Figure 6.5. Average and marginal cost and revenue. In these three graphs, we show how Figures 6.2 and 6.3 might fit together. The three panels illustrate that the profit-maximizing level of production, where MC = MR, bears no necessary connection to efficient scale, where AC is minimized.

the price charged and the average cost of production? In general, as long as positive profit is possible, profit maximization occurs at a quantity greater than the quantity where profit margin is largest. We can derive this mathematically by comparing $MC(x) = MR(x)$, the point of profit maximization, with the point where $AC'(x) = AR'(x) = P'(x)$, which is the point where profit margin is greatest: I'll do this by writing $AC(x) = TC(x)/x$ and $AR(x) = TR(x)/x$ and taking derivatives, using the quotient rule. (Skip what's about to happen if the math is overwhelming you—I'll give an intuition explanation after the math.) We have

$$AC'(x) = \frac{TC'(x)}{x} - \frac{TC(x)}{x^2} = \frac{1}{x}\left(MC(x) - AC(x)\right)$$

and, similarly,

$$AR'(x) = \frac{1}{x}\left(MR(x) - AR(x)\right),$$

so where $AC'(x) = AR'(x)$, we have

$$\frac{1}{x}\left(MC(x) - AC(x)\right) = \frac{1}{x}\left(MR(x) - AR(x)\right),$$

which can be rewritten

$$\frac{1}{x}\left(MR(x) - MC(x)\right) = \frac{1}{x}\left(AR(x) - AC(x)\right).$$

Now, supposing positive profits are possible, we know that the maximum profit margin is positive. Which means that at maximum profit margins, the right-hand side of the equation just written must be positive. Which means that, at that level x, $MR(x)$ is bigger than $MC(x)$, and the firm, to maximize profit, wants to produce more.

Intuitively, the story is simple. Where profit margin is highest, the firm can make more profit by pushing its production up a bit: It loses a bit of profit margin, but more than makes it up in volume.[7]

---

[7] Readers who are very well versed in calculus: This of course assumes that all these functions are differentiable, and if you know what that means, here is a bit more: Where profit margin is maximized, a bit more production causes margin to decline, but the decline is second order in the increase because of differentiability and the supposition that we are at the maximum of profit margin. Meanwhile, the increase in profit from increased volume is first-order.

What's Wrong with This Picture, or From AC to MC but Not Back

(You may want to skip this subsection on a first reading.) Have a look at Figure 6.6. What's wrong with this picture? Try to answer this question before reading further.

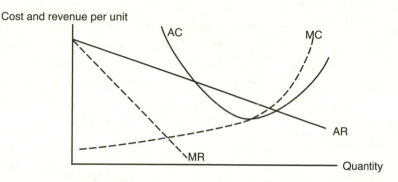

Figure 6.6. What's wrong with this picture?

What is wrong is: At the level of production where MC = MR, AC > AR, so the firm would be losing money if it produced at that level. But at higher levels of production, AR > AC, so there are production levels at which the firm can make a positive profit. Because MC = MR is where profit is maximized, this can't be right.[8]

The point is that you cannot throw any four curves with the "right shapes" on a piece of paper and call them AC, AR, MC, and MR. We already know, for instance, that when AR, which is inverse demand, is linear, MR is linear with the same intercept on the vertical axis and twice the slope. That isn't quite true in the picture—MR is coming down too quickly for the AR function I've drawn—but that is nothing compared to the mismatch between AC and MC.

Suppose I tell you that, at production level $x = 20$, AC(20) = 65 and AC$'$(20) = -2. What can you tell me about MC(20)? For one thing, you know that, since AC is declining, MC(20) must be below AC(20) = 65. But, it turns out, you can do a lot better than that.

Write AC(x) = TC$(x)/x$ and use the quotient rule to evaluate AC$'(x)$:

$$AC'(x) = \frac{TC'(x)}{x} - \frac{TC(x)}{x^2}.$$

But TC$'(x)$ is MC(x), and TC$(x)/x^2$ = AC$(x)/x$, so we can rewrite this as

$$AC'(x) = \frac{1}{x}\Big(MC(x) - AC(x)\Big).$$

---

[8] Another way to see what is wrong is that we just showed that MR > MC where profit margin is largest. That clearly isn't happening here.

Solve for MC(x) and you get MC(x) = AC(x) + xAC′(x). So, in my example, where $x = 20$, AC(20) = 15, and AC′(x) = −2, we have MC(20) = 65+(−2)(20) = 25. *If you have x, AC(x), and AC′(x), you know MC(x).*

So, when anyone draws a smooth curve and calls it AC, the corresponding MC is determined: The drawing tells you for each x the value of AC at x and also the slope of AC at x, which, together with x determine MC at x.

But the reverse is not true. That is, when someone draws a function and labels it MC, you can't supply AC. The reason is: The MC graph can be integrated to tell you how much TC changes over any interval. But if you don't know the value of TC at either endpoint of the interval, you can't pin down the TC function. And knowing TC is equivalent to knowing AC. Essentially, AC depends on MC *and the initial fixed cost, or TC*(0). The initial fixed cost is missing when all you know is the MC function.

6.5. Discrete Optimization, "Margins," and Managerial (Cost) Accounting

Calculus is used in economics along with the modeling assumption that variables are infinitely divisible; that is, they can be split into any fractional parts. This is a modeling conceit: Within a model of the Toyota Motor Company, MC = MR may happen at a production level of, say, 3,298,122.76 cars, but in such a case, producing any level of output in the neighborhood of 3.3 million cars is going to be "good enough." And, since in real life demand and cost functions are never known with the precision of our models, the issue never really comes up.

On some problems in economics, however, it is simply impossible to create adequate models in which choices can be modeled as being infinitely divisible. When the choice is between doing something or not with no intermediate options or when we have only a handful of intermediate options, to find the optimum we must evaluate profit for each of the discrete options and compare them.

That said, the *logic* of this chapter, the logic of thinking about the marginal impact of a decision, is still valid. You simply substitute the term *incremental* for *marginal*.

I can illustrate with a simple example that is a staple of managerial (or cost) accounting courses. Consider a firm that produces for sale three different products, widgets, gidgets, and gadgets. The (highly simplified) income statement for this firm is shown in Figure 6.7; you see there that the production of gadgets is showing a full-cost loss. So, based on this income statement, management of the firm might conclude that the gadget line of products should be dropped.

Perhaps this is the right decision, but the line "allocated o/h" should give you pause. The "o/h" stands for overhead, and what is (presumably) going

Income Statement				
	Widgets	Gidgets	Gadgets	Total
Sales Revenue	$120	$160	$70	$350
Less				
variable costs	$ 70	$ 90	$55	$215
allocated o/h	$ 40	$ 40	$40	$120
Net Contribution to Profit	$ 10	$ 30	($ 25)	$ 15

Figure 6.7. A (simplified) income statement.

on here is that the firm has some expenses that can't be attributed directly to any one of the three product lines, so cost accountants at the firm lump them together, call them overhead and, then, to get an "accurate" picture of how the firm is doing, allocate these costs to the three product lines. As is the practice in some (certainly not all) firms, these cost accountants are allocating the overhead equally among the three product lines.

If the decision facing the firm is *Should we cease production of gadgets?*, based on the Income Statement in Figure 6.7, a further question that must be addressed is, *Will we save any of our overhead costs?* Or, to put it differently, *In terms of our net profit, what will be the incremental effect of dropping Gadgets?* In terms of revenue less variable costs, the gadget line is making a net contribution of $15. Dropping gadgets will, presumably, wipe out the revenues from this line, as well as the variable costs.[9] *If* dropping gadgets will reduce overhead costs by more than $15, then the firm's overall profit will, in fact, go up by dropping the gadget line. But if, instead, dropping gadgets will have little to no effect on overhead, then dropping gadgets will be bad for profit.

Indeed, suppose that the total overhead of $120 is entirely fixed cost. If the firm drops gadgets, it "must" reallocate overhead from $40 for each of three product lines to $60 apiece for each of the two remaining product lines. Then widgets will be showing a full-cost loss. And if they subsequently drop widgets and must allocate all those fixed costs to gidgets, gidgets (and the firm) will show negative income.

Managerial Accounting and Economics

(When appropriate, I try to highlight the connections between microeconomics and the various functions of management, such as Accounting, Finance, Information Systems, Human Resources, Marketing, Operations and Purchasing, and Strategy. Sometimes the connections are made in the main flow of the chapter; occasionally, as in this instance, something of a digression is required.)

---

[9] Will dropping gadgets increase demand for, say, gidgets? I'm going to assume not, but that's another *what's the incremental impact?* issue that needs to be addressed.

I put "must" in scare quotes two paragraphs ago because no such impera-tive exists, at least in the realm of managerial or cost accounting.[10] Managerial accounting is the management function of accounting for the operations of an enterprise for internal, decision-making purposes. And while managerial ac-counting may at times seem like the application of fixed and arbitrary recipes for allocating cost, there is much more to it. To answer the question *How should internal accounts be kept?* first you must answer *Why are accounts being kept?*

Internal accounts are kept first to evaluate the performance of products, managers, services, and so on. If the firm is run in top-down fashion by a central decision maker, then this evaluation is done to inform the decision maker about what things cost, to improve his or her decisions. This is closest to what is going on in the example we just considered, in which the income statement was (mis)used to decide which product lines to keep and which to drop. When accounts are kept to inform a single decision maker, then as the example shows, accounting procedures should reflect the incremental costs and benefits of the decisions that will be taken.

Most large firms and organizations are decentralized, with different decision makers (heads of divisions or business units), who make independent decisions about things in their domain of responsibility. In such firms, accounting mea-sures are used to provide incentives to the autonomous decision makers, either retrospectively, where the firm promotes division heads whose divisions did well, or prospectively, where a manager's annual bonus is explicitly tied to how well his or her division does, according to internal accounts. When the numbers are used in this fashion, answers to the questions *Should fixed costs be allocated?* and *If so, how?* change from when the numbers are used for top-down decision making: If division managers are not charged at all for overhead, what incen-tives do they have for employing the resources whose cost is unallocated? This takes us into issues of transfer pricing and incentives, which we discuss later in this book.

In addition to keeping accounting numbers for internal purposes, firms keep them for a host of reasons having to do with parties external to the firm, such as tax authorities, regulators, legal authorities, large investors, and potential acquirers. Each of these answers to *Why?* suggests different answers to *How?* For instance, when accounts are used by tax authorities, *How?* calls up answers such as *Delay the realization of accounting earnings* and *Use transfer pricing to "transfer" profits to low-tax localities.* Moreover, the question *Why are internal accounts being kept?* often has more than one answer. And the answers to *How?* corresponding to different answers to *Why?* conflict with one another. Since firms usually do not wish to keep different sets of internal accounts, answers

---

[10] For financial accounting, you follow the dictates of FASB/IASB/your national accounting stan-dards board. Those dictates ought to make economic sense, and sometimes they do. But that is mostly the problem of the board members, not your firm's accountants.

to *How?* must be found that balance the different demands the firm puts on its accounting numbers. And since the balance will be different for different organizations, no one-size-fits-all set of accounting practices exists. In particular, blind adherence to GAAP can be quite wrong for some organizations when it comes to their internal accounts.

Economics enters into all these considerations. The simplest story shows that accounting numbers kept for top-down decision making should reflect incremental costs. The stories for decentralization and appropriate incentives are a good deal more complex, because they involve the separate decisions of many different entities, but they still fall in substantial part inside the domain of economics. As for tax or regulatory considerations, accountants often look for ways to beat a given system, while the Cost Accounting Standards Board and the government or regulator look for accounting procedures that are "fair" and reflect to some extent the economic value of activities while being hard for the accountants to manipulate.

6.6. Marginal and Average Costs (and Revenues) For Multi-product Firms

The example of the last section teaches one further lesson. Section 6.4, which concerned the connection between average and marginal costs and average and marginal revenues, is conducted solely in the context of a one-product firm. This is not done for expositional simplification, but because the notion of average cost for a multiproduct firm is, at best, very slippery. Average cost is total cost divided by quantity. For a multiproduct firm, the quantity of each product line is (presumably) easy to identify. But what is the total cost of the individual product line? If all costs can be attributed to one and only one of the product lines, we're in business. But, typically, some costs are shared among the product lines, and to compute the average cost of any single line puts you back in the cost-allocation business.

That's the bad news. The good news is that it is marginal costs (and marginal revenues) of each product line that matters. So you don't need to worry—you shouldn't worry—about average costs. But do remember: Marginal cost is the impact on total cost of the firm of increasing output of a product line, and marginal revenue is the impact on total revenue, not just the revenue earned from the sales in the product line under consideration. (And if this last bit elicits a *Huh?* from you, go back to page 132 and reread the example in the subsection "Multivariable Optimization").

Executive Summary

This is a long and, for many readers, challenging chapter, because it is chock full of both economic ideas and applications of calculus. Remember: Calculus is there to clarify the economic ideas, but this will only happen if you are on firm ground in your understanding of calculus and its connection to "marginal impacts." So if you are shaky on this, start by working on understanding that connection.

As for economic concepts and insights:

- Thinking like an economist in many cases means thinking about the marginal impact of decisions being made. Think margins, not averages!

- The pieces of the basic model of a single-product firm with market power are (a) the demand function the firm faces, typically denoted $D(p)$, (b) the total-cost function TC(x), and (c) the assumption that the firm will select the price it charges/quantity it produces and sells to maximize its profit, or revenue less total cost. (And, despite its flaws as a realistic model of what firms do, it is a model that will generate a lot of insight into the actions of real firms.)

- To find the profit-maximizing price–quantity pair: (a) If necessary, invert the demand function to find the inverse demand function $P(x)$. (b) Construct the total revenue function TR(x) $= xP(x)$ and find its derivative, the marginal cost function MR(x). (c) Find the derivative of the total cost function, the marginal cost function MC(x). (d) Find the level of production at which marginal cost equals marginal revenue. And, as needed, (e) plug this level of production into inverse demand to find the profit-maximizing price to set.

- For a firm with market power, MR(x) $= P(x) + xP'(x)$ which, if P is downward sloping, is less than $P(x)$. The difference between MR(x) and $P(x)$ reflects the loss in revenue that occurs because the price-per-unit must be lowered to sell the extra unit.

- When you deal with multiproduct firms, profit maximization is where the marginal revenue from each good equals the marginal cost of the same good. But *be careful*: Marginal cost and marginal revenue of any good are the marginal impact of increasing production of that good on the the firm's total revenue and total cost, not simply the impact on the total revenue or total cost of that specific good.

- When you face constraints, first solve the problem without the constraints to see if the constraint binds (if the unconstrained solution violates the constraints). If the constraint is satisfied by the unconstrained solution, you're done. If the constraint is violated by the unconstrained solution, you can typically assume that the solution will be found where the constraint just binds.

- The Average Revenue function, denoted AR(x), is just the inverse demand function.

- Average cost (respectively, revenue) falls when marginal cost (resp., revenue) is less than average cost (resp., revenue), and rises when marginal cost (resp., revenue) is above average cost (resp., revenue). Therefore, for total cost functions that have a U-shape (have a fixed cost and rising marginal cost), marginal cost equals average cost at *efficient scale*, the level of production at which average cost is minimized.

- Profit maximization, or MR = MC, bears no particular relation to efficient scale. And MR = MC at a larger quantity than where profit margin (AR − AC) is largest.

- In some cases, it is entirely inappropriate to think of economic "choices" as being infinitely divisible. Some choices—"Do we do this project or not?"—are inherently discrete. In those cases, thinking "on the margin" is problematic. But the logic of thinking on the margin still holds, if you think in terms of the *incremental* effects of your (discrete) decision.

- The concept of average cost is problematic for multiproduct firms insofar as there are fixed costs to allocate. But, since you should be thinking about marginal costs (and revenues) and not about average costs (and revenues), this is not a huge problem.

Problems

6.1 Suppose a firm that produces a single product can sell its output for $p = 100 - x/100$ for each unit that it produces, where x is its level of output. Its total cost function is $\mathrm{TC}(x) = 200 + 20x + x^2/300$. What is the profit-maximizing level of production for this firm, and what is the profit-maximizing price to charge?

6.2 A firm that produces a single product sells its output for $p = 20 - x/1000$, where x is the quantity that it produces and sells. Its total cost function is $\mathrm{TC}(x) = 5000 + 4x$. What are its profit-maximizing levels of production and price?

6.3 Consider the Freedonian steel company example discussed in the chapter.

(a) The story in the chapter asserts that average cost at efficient scale is 400. Using the methods discussed around pages 140 and 141, find efficient scale and verify the figure 400. DO NOT JUST USE THE FORMULAE GIVEN IN THE BOOK. Do the math (either using AC′ = 0 or AC = MC) that gave us those formulae.

(b) Back on page 132, it says you could solve the Freedonian steel problem using two variables, x for domestic steel sales and y for export sales, and the methods of the section on multivariable optimization. Do this. [Hint: The "problem" here is not finding the correct expressions for MR as in the example in the chapter. Instead, it is to find the correct expression for the marginal costs in x and y.]

6.4 On page 132, you are given the system of inverse demand functions for the problem of the two-output firm that sells the two models of tablets. Suppose instead you were given the following system of demand functions:

$$x = \frac{45000 - 900P_X + 300P_Y}{7} \quad \text{and} \quad y = \frac{54000 - 900P_Y + 600P_X}{7}.$$

What would you do? If you are feeling brave, do it and see what answer you get.

6.5. (Here is a slightly harder version of the two-tablet problem.) Let x be the number of Model X's the firm sells and y the number of Model Y's. The two inverse demand functions are

$$P_X = 100 - \frac{x}{100} - \frac{y}{400} \quad \text{and} \quad P_Y = 80 - \frac{y}{50} - \frac{x}{200}.$$

Total costs are given by

$$TC(x, y) = 300 + 20x + 10y + \frac{(3x + y)^2}{1200}.$$

Find the profit-maximizing production rates.

6.6. (a) Suppose that, in the stadium problem, the data are changed as follows. After allocating seats to season ticket holders, the general manager has 30,000 seats to allocate between Wolverton and Manteca supporters. If W seats are allocated to Wolverton supporters, each can be sold for £20 − W/2000. And if M seats are allocated to Manteca supporters, each can be sold for £24−M/3000. What division of seats maximizes gate receipts?

(b) What is the answer if the general manager has 60,000 seats to allocate between the two groups of supporters?

(c) What is the answer if we go back to the case of 30,000 seats to allocate, but we change the formulation as follows: To sell W seats to Wolverton supporters, the price per ticket for the tickets must be set at £20 − W/2000, just as before. But when it comes to Manteca supporters, the general manager can sell as many tickets as desired for £12 apiece, but cannot sell any at any price higher than £12.

6.7 Imagine a single-output firm with the total cost function TC(x) = 10,000,000+ 50x + x^2/16,000, where x is the level of the firm's output.

(a) Draw (roughly) on a single graph the firm's average and marginal cost functions. Your graph should show the general shape of these functions and should identify the firm's efficient scale of production, its marginal cost at that scale of production, and its average cost at that scale of production.

(b) Suppose this firm faces the inverse demand function $P(x) = 250 - x/4000$. For which values of x does this firm have positive profit? (You need to know the quadratic formula to answer with algebra. Do not expect the answer to be in nice round numbers.) For which values of x does this firm have increasing profit? What level of x maximizes this firm's profit?

6.8 Here are four total-cost functions. For each one, if we draw the firms average and marginal cost functions, does the picture look like Figure 6.3, 6.4(a), 6.4(b), or none of these? If the answer is "none of these," what (roughly) are the shapes of AC and MC?

(a) $TC(x) = 40{,}000 + 55x + x^2/9000$

(b) $TC(x) = 60x$

(c) $TC(x) = 250{,}000 + 60x$

(d) $TC(x) = 55x + x^2/9000$

6.9 Suppose the total-cost function of a one-output firm is given by

$$TC(x) = \begin{cases} 20x - x^2/20{,}000 & \text{for } x \le 50{,}000\text{, and} \\ 10x + x^2/20{,}000 + 250{,}000 & \text{for } x \ge 50{,}000. \end{cases}$$

Draw the AC–MC picture for this firm. [Hint: You've never seen one like this, so don't expect this to be easy. If you are adept at graphing using a spreadsheet program such as Excel, that would be a good way to go.]

6.10 Imagine a firm with total-cost function $TC(x) = F + Kx$ facing an inverse-demand function of the form $P(x) = A - Bx$, for constants A, B, and K all strictly positive and $F \ge 0$.

(a) Assuming that $A > K$ and $F = 0$, draw the AC–MC–AR–MR picture for this firm.

(b) Assuming that $A > K$ and $F > 0$, but F is small enough so that, for some levels of production, the firm can make strictly positive profit, draw the AC–MC–AR–MR picture for this firm.

(c) Assume that $A > K$ and $F > 0$ is such that the firm makes negative profit at all levels of output except one, and at that one, the firm makes zero profit. Draw the AC–MC–AR–MR picture for this firm.

(d) Repeat parts a, b, and c, but assuming that the total-cost function is $TC(x) = F + Kx + kx^2$, where k is a strictly positive constant.

6.11 (For people interested in cost accounting) (a) In our simple example of why you shouldn't take seriously full-cost contributions, overhead was allocated equally among the three product lines. You might think that this is the problem, since this clearly makes product lines with small sales volumes look pretty bad; they have to carry a disproportionate share of the overhead. Suppose, therefore, that we allocated overhead in proportion to revenue for each product line. That is, if widgets generate $100 in revenue, gidgets generate $200, and gadgets generate $300, then fixed costs are allocated in the ratio of 1:2:3 over the three product lines. Does this solve the problem? (Try this allocation method on the numbers in Figure 6.7.) [It may occur to you that the "right way" to allocate overhead is in proportion to each line's "variable contribution," defined as revenue less variable costs. But, for reasons that take us outside the scope of this chapter, that method of cost allocation is flawed, as well.]

6.12 Among the many decisions facing designers of American sports stadiums is the number of luxury boxes—plush suites that look out onto the playing field— to build. Suppose that, for a particular stadium under construction, luxury boxes will be sold outright to local businesses and can be constructed at a cost of $2 million apiece. The designer of this stadium plans to build 25 boxes and expects, at this number, to sell each for $10 million, for a net profit of 8×25 = $200 million. An associate asserts that this is crazy. Since boxes can be built at $2 million and sold for $10 million apiece, building only 25 leaves money on the table. What's wrong with this argument?

6.13 Google sells "advertising" on its website in the form of keywords: If some- one searches using a keyword that you "bought," your advertisement appears as a result of the search. (Where your advertisement appears in comparison with other advertisements is a complicated matter that needn't concern us at this point.) Google, in an attempt to help advertisers "optimize" their choice of keywords and levels of investment, offers the following advice at the webpage https://support.google.com/adwords/answer/1722066 :

Suppose you are selling a good for $20 that costs you $10 per unit to produce. Suppose a keyword that you bought generates 1000 sales of this good (Google provides the last figure), and suppose you spent a total of $2000 "buying" this keyword. Then, Google says, you should calculate your "return on investment" of ROI in this keyword as

$$\frac{1000(\$20 - \$10) - \$2000}{\$2000} = 4.$$

That is, every dollar you spend on this keyword provides you with $4 in net profit. Google then offers the following advice:

> "You can also use ROI to help you decide how to spend your budget. For example, if you find that a certain campaign is generating a higher ROI than others, you can apply more of your budget to the successful campaign and less money to campaigns that aren't performing well..."[11]

Is this good advice?

---

[11] From web page https://support.google.com/adwords/answer/1722066. Copyright 2014 Google.

7. Mark-Up Pricing and Elasticity

This chapter looks at the question, *How much should a firm **mark up** goods that it sells?* In the setting of the simple model of firm with market power, the answer is determined by the *elasticity of demand* facing the firm. Elasticity of demand is a central concept in economic analysis, which plays other roles in this book. And it, and the question of mark-ups, leads us to the topic of Chapter 8, *price discrimination*.

People who set prices often think of the problem as one of determining the *mark-up* of a good, this being the difference between the sales price p and the procurement price q, where q reflects the cost of manufacturing the good or, in the case of retail, the price the vendor pays to acquire the good that the vendor resells. Mark-ups can be described in dollar terms, as in "That bottle of wine has been marked up $30," or in percentage terms, as in "That restaurant marks up its wine by 100% over the price it pays for each bottle."

What determines the level of mark-up? It seems reasonable to suppose that it depends on what substitute products are available (better substitutes means smaller mark-ups) and the amount of competition the seller faces (more competition means smaller mark-ups). In this chapter, we take the perspective that things like the availability of substitutes and the amount of competition the seller faces are all subsumed into the demand function the seller faces and, in particular, how responsive is the quantity the seller can sell as she (the seller) changes the price she charges.

That is, we will look at a firm selling a good that has market power—we use the basic model of the last chapter—assuming that the firm sets its price p to maximize its profit—so it sets price and quantity sold where marginal cost equals marginal revenue. And we take the working definition of the **mark-up** to be *the difference between the price the firm charges p and the marginal cost of production/procurement, MC(x).*

But, since MC(x) = MR(x) at the level of sales x that maximizes the firm's profits, we see that...

> ... *the optimal mark-up for a profit-maximizing firm selling x units of a good at a price p per good is the difference between p and the marginal revenue MR(x) that the good generates. To identify the size of this mark-up, we need to understand the difference between price and marginal revenue.*

We already know that price exceeds marginal revenue if demand is downward sloping. This is old business from last chapter, but let me remind you: If

$P(x)$ is the inverse-demand function, $\mathrm{TR}(x) = xP(x)$, so

$$\mathrm{MR}(x) = \frac{d\,\mathrm{TR}(x)}{d\,x} = \frac{d\,[xP(x)]}{d\,x} = P(x) + x\,\frac{d\,P(x)}{d\,x}.$$

Since the derivative of $P(x)$ is negative, the mark-up (measured in dollar terms), which is $P(x) - \mathrm{MR}(x)$, is $-xP'(x)$; the minus sign times the negative derivative $P'(x)$ makes mark-up a positive amount. If we want to talk about the mark-up in percentage terms, it is $100(P(x) - \mathrm{MC}(x))/\mathrm{MC}(x)$, which, using $\mathrm{MC} = \mathrm{MR}$ and the formula for MR just derived, is

$$100 \cdot \frac{P(x) - \mathrm{MC}(x)}{\mathrm{MC}(x)} = 100 \cdot \frac{P(x) - \mathrm{MR}(x)}{\mathrm{MR}(x)} = 100\left[\frac{-1}{1 + P(x)/xP'(x)}\right].$$

So our question becomes,

$$\textit{What determines} - xP'(x) \textit{ and } 100\left[\frac{-1}{1 + P(x)/xP'(x)}\right]?$$

7.1. Elasticity of Demand

To answer this question, we go on what may seem like a tangent:

> The **(own-price) elasticity of demand** along a demand function $D(p)$ at a given price p_0 is the rate of percentage change in quantity demanded per percentage change in the price, starting from the price p_0.

(Until the very end of this chapter, I'll refer simply to the *elasticity of demand* without the modifier *own-price*. The explanation for the modifier comes at the end of the chapter.)

The definition is a mouthful, but we can clarify with an example. Suppose we have the demand function $D(p) = 10{,}000(50 - p)$, and we want to know the elasticity of demand for this demand function at the price $p_0 = 10$.

Step 1. Take a price that is a small change from p_0. Since $p_0 = 10$, a small change is 0.10, so our second price will be $p_1 = 10.10$. (We could equally well use $p_1 = 9.90$, but for the example, we'll use 10.10.)

*Step 2. Calculate the percentage change in price. The change in price is 0.10, which on a base of $p_0 = 10$ is a 1% **increase** in price.*

Step 3. Calculate demand at the orignal price and at the changed price. Then calculate the change in demand. At $p_0 = 10$, demand is $10{,}000(50 - 10) = 400{,}000$.

At $p_1 = 10.10$, demand is $10,000(50 - 10.10) = 10,000 \cdot 39.90 = 399,000$. Hence the change in demand is 1000 units.

Step 4. Calculate the percentage change in demand quantity. The change is 1000 units. Relative to a base level of demand of 400,000 units, this is a 0.25% *decrease* in quantity.

Step 5. The elasticity of demand at p_0 is the ratio of the answer you got in step 4 to the answer you got in step 2. So the elasticity of demand, for the demand function $D(p) = 10,000(50 - p)$ at the price p_0, is $-0.25\%/1\% = -0.25$.

Some immediate comments are in order.

- *Own-price elasticity is a negative number.* Note that, in step 5, I keep track of the sign of the percentage changes. From \$10 to \$10.10 is a 1% *increase* in price, so the denominator in step 5 is +1%. From 400,000 units to 399,000 is a 0.25% *decrease* in quantity, so the numerator in step 5 is −0.25%. This makes elasticity a negative number, and it is a negative number whenever demand is downward sloping.

  Economists agree among themselves on all sorts of stuff, but this is not one of those places. Some books will not carry along that minus sign— they say that elasticity of demand for this demand function at p_0 is 0.25. In this book, we keep the minus sign. Whenever you have a conversation with someone that involves the notion of elasticity, you must clarify which convention you are following.

  If, instead of changing $p_0 = 10$ to $p_1 = 10.10$, we had taken $p_1 = 9.90$, then the percentage change in price would be −1%, while the percentage change in quantity would be +0.25%, and we'd get the same answer for elasticity, −0.25%.

- *The elasticity of demand for a given demand function depends on the price at which it is measured.* If we take the same demand function, $D(p) = 10,000(50 - p)$, and ask, *What is the elasticity of demand at $p_0 = 30$?*, the answer is −1.5. (It's a good idea for you to verify my assertion here.)

- *In general, the size of small change in price that you use in step 1 matters. But for linear demand functions, it doesn't matter.* We deal in this book with very few demand functions that are not linear. But it is good practice to keep the size of the small change small; I used a 1% change, which is usually accurate enough.

Elasticity Using Calculus

The last remark suggests that, when evaluating elasticity of demand for a demand function expressed in an algebraic formula, you can use calculus in your calculations. Let Δp be the small change in price used in step 1, and let Δx be the corresponding change in the quantity demanded. The percentage change in price is then $100\Delta p/p_0$, and the percentage change in quantity is $100\Delta x/D(p_0)$. Hence the formula for elasticity is

$$\frac{100\Delta x/D(p_0)}{100\Delta p/p_0} = \frac{\Delta x}{\Delta p} \cdot \frac{p_0}{D(p_0)}.$$

As the small change in price, Δp, approaches zero, the ratio $\Delta x/\Delta p$ approaches the derivative of $D(p)$, evaluated at p_0. So

> *The calculus-based formula for elasticity of demand is* $\dfrac{D'(p_0)p_0}{D(p_0)}$.

Let me illustrate with the example: When $D(p) = 10{,}000(50 - p)$, $D'(p) = -10{,}000$, and so

$$\frac{D'(p_0)p_0}{D(p_0)} = \frac{-10{,}000p_0}{10{,}000(50 - p_0)} = \frac{-p_0}{(50 - p_0)}.$$

If you plug $p_0 = 10$ into that formula, you get $-10/40 = -0.25$; if you plug 30 in for p_0, you get $-30/20 = -1.5$.

We'll be referring to this elasticity function a lot, so let's make up some notation: For a demand function $D(p)$, we write $\nu(p)$ for the elasticity of demand along this demand function at the price p. So, when you have a nice (differentiable) function for $D(p)$,

$$\nu(p) = \frac{D'(p)p}{D(p)}.$$

The Price Elasticity of Inverse Demand

So far, we've supposed that we have a demand function $D(p)$ and we are looking for the elasticity of demand along this demand function at some price p_0. Sometimes, we are working instead with an inverse-demand function $P(x)$ and we want to know *the elasticity of demand along the inverse-demand function P at some quantity level x_0.*

The name is a little different, and the notation we use is different—we write $\hat{\nu}(x_0)$—but the quantity is the same. It is the ratio of the percentage change in quantity to the percentage change in price.

Example: Suppose inverse demand is given by $P(x) = 50 - x/10{,}000$. (This is the inverse-demand function that goes with demand function $D(p) = 10{,}000(50 - p)$, of course.) Suppose you want to find the elasticity of demand along this inverse-demand function at the quantity $x_0 = 400{,}000$. You can do this any of three ways:

Method 1 Find the price p_0 that goes with the quantity x_0. It is $p_0 = 10$. Find the demand function that goes with the inverse-demand function given. This is the demand function $D(p) = 10{,}000(50 - p)$. Find the elasticity of demand along this demand function at the price p_0. That's your answer. (And, as we already know, in this example the answer is -0.25.)

Method 2 Take a small change in quantity. For instance, change the quantity from 400,000 to 404,000, a 1% increase in quantity. Find the prices corresponding to the original quantity—10—and to the slightly different quantity, $P(404{,}000) = 9.60$. Find the percentage change in price: Price decreased by 0.40 on a base price of 10, which is a 4% *decrease* in price. And take the ratio of the change in quantity (1%) to the change in price (4%), to get the answer: $1\%/(-4\%) = -0.25$. *If you are going to use this method, remember: Elasticity is the percentage change in quantity divided by the percentage change in price. What goes in the numerator and what goes in the denominator do not change whether you are working with the demand function or the inverse-demand function.*

Method 3 When $P(x)$ is given by a formula (as in this case), use calculus and the formula

$$\hat{\nu}(x) = \frac{P(x)}{x P'(x)}.$$

So, in this example, $P'(x) = -1/10{,}000$, so applying the formula gives

$$\hat{\nu}(400{,}000) = \frac{50 - 400{,}000/10{,}000}{400{,}000 \cdot (-1/10{,}000)} = \frac{50 - 40}{-40} = -0.25.$$

(You can trust me that my calculus-based formula for $\hat{\nu}(x)$ is correct. Or, if you remember how the derivative is defined, you can derive it.)

What is the point of the hat in $\hat{\nu}$? Elasticity is a property of the demand function at a particular price–quantity pair along the demand function. When we want to signal that we are specifying the price–quantity pair by fixing the price, we write $\nu(p)$, without the hat. When we want to signal that we are specifying the price–quantity pair by fixing the quantity, we write $\hat{\nu}(x)$. But, for a given demand function and price–quantity pair (p_0, x_0) along the demand function, the elasticity of demand is the same thing. Or, in symbols, if $x_0 = D(p_0)$ (or, equivalently, $p_0 = P(x_0)$), then $\nu(p_0) = \hat{\nu}(x_0)$.

What Does It Mean? And Why Percentage Changes?

Elasticity measures how responsive the quantity demanded is to the price the firm charges. The more negative is elasticity (or, in other words, the farther it is from 0), the more responsive is quantity.

Why not use the derivative of demand, which tells you the rate of change in quantity demanded per unit change in price? Why measure things in percentage changes?

One reason is that size of the derivative depends on the units being used. For instance, suppose the price of gasoline is $4.00 per gallon, at which price demand is 10 million gallons. Suppose that, when the price is $3.96, demand increases to 10.02 million gallons. Then, roughly, the derivative of the demand function is $20,000/(-0.04) = -500$ thousand. But if we measure demand in liters, demand at $4 is 37.854 million litters (roughly), while at $3.96 we get around 37.930 million liters, so the derivative is around -1.9 million. The units we use change the answer. But they don't change the answer if we look at percentage changes: $0.04 is a 1% change in price, and whether we use gallons or liters, the change is 0.2%, so elasticity is -0.2.

If that doesn't convince you, try this: Intuitively, which is more responsive to price changes, the demand for gasoline or the demand for flat-screen televisions? Suppose the price of gasoline is $4.00 per gallon and the price of flat-screen televisions of a particular variety is $1000. Increasing the price of gasoline by, say, $1 per gallon, is likely to have a substantial impact on demand for gasoline. Raising the price of flat-screen televisions by $1 per television is likely to have almost no impact on demand. So the derivative of the demand function for gasoline, where price is measured in dollars, will be a lot larger than the derivative of the demand for flat-screen televisions. Does this make demand for gasoline "more responsive?" The comparison isn't fair: In one case we are raising the price by 25%, in the other by 0.1%.

The fair comparison—one in which the units used to measure both price and quantity are irrelevant—is a comparison using percentage changes in both the numerator and denominator. If a 1% rise in the price of gasoline reduces demand for gasoline by, say, 0.2%, while a 1% rise in the price of flat-screen televisions reduces demand by 1.5%, on that basis it makes sense to say (what, I expect, your inutition told you): Demand for gasoline is less responsive to its price than is demand for flat-screen televisions.

7.2. Elasticity, Price, and Marginal Revenue

Yet another way to see that computing elasticities in percentage-change terms is the right thing to do is to recall the relation between marginal revenue and price:

$$\text{MR}(x) = P(x) + xP'(x).$$

Multiply and divide the term $xP'(x)$ by $P(x)$ and perform a little algebra and you get

$$\text{MR}(x) = P(x) \cdot \left[1 + \frac{xP'(x)}{P(x)}\right] = P(x) \cdot \left[1 + \frac{1}{\hat{\nu}(x)}\right]. \qquad (\star)$$

This formula is so important that I've labelled it $(\star)$. *Please note, $(\star)$ holds for every value of x, not just for the profit-maximizing level of production.*

Remember, elasticity is a negative number, so $1/\hat{\nu}(x)$ is negative. Now consider two cases:

1. Suppose that $0 \geq \hat{\nu}(x) > -1$. (Think in terms of $\hat{\nu}(x) = -0.8$.) This is where a 1% change in price causes a less than 1% change in volume in the other direction. And, in this case, $(\star)$ tells us that marginal revenue is negative. What this means is: If you are at an x where elasticity is between 0 and -1, making and selling another unit—lowering your price so you can sell that additional unit—depresses your revenues. On the presumption that your marginal costs are positive or, at least, not negative, you are definitely making too much x. If you cut back on the volume x, your costs, presumably, will go down. *And, no doubt about it, your revenues will increase.*

    This may surprise you, but it makes sense if you think it through. You cut back on x by raising your price. If you raise your price by, say, 1%, your volume sold goes down by less than 1%. Suppose your volume goes down by 0.8%. Then your total revenue, price times quantity, rises by around 0.2%. Sell less, charge more, and you will make more money; this means total revenue declines with the amount you sell (rises in the price you charge), which is a negative marginal revenue.

2. And if $\hat{\nu}(x) < -1$ (think, $\hat{\nu}(x) = -2$), then marginal revenue is positive. Moreover, we know that marginal revenue is less than price (since $xP'(x) < 0$), and the formula tells us *how much less* in fractional terms: When $\hat{\nu}(x) = -2$, $1 + 1/\hat{\nu}(x) = 1 + 1/(-2) = 1/2$, so marginal revenue is half of price. When $\hat{\nu}(x) = -3$, $1 + \hat{\nu}(x) = 1 + 1/(-3) = 2/3$, so marginal revenue is two-thirds of price. And so forth.

    Again, this is intuitive if you think it through. Lower your price by 1%, and you sell more than 1% more. Your total revenue goes up, so your marginal revenue is positive.

The borderline case is $\hat{\nu}(x) = -1$. In this case, $\text{MR}(x) = 0$. You can move your price up or down, at least locally, and total revenue does not change.

*When $\hat{\nu}(x)$ (which, remember, is $\nu(p)$ for the price p that corresponds to quantity x) is between 0 and -1, we say that demand is **inelastic**. When $\hat{\nu}(x) < -1$, demand is **elastic**. And when $\hat{\nu}(x) = -1$, demand is said to have **unit elasticity**.*

The Case of Linear Demand

Since the case of linear (inverse) demand is very common, it is worthwhile to illustrate these results for that case. Suppose demand is $D(p) = A - Bp$ for positive constants A and B, so that inverse demand is $P(x) = (A - x)/B$. Total revenue is $\text{TR}(x) = (Ax - x^2)/B$ and marginal revenue is $(A - 2x)/B$.

- $\text{MR}(x) > 0$ for $x < A/2$, which is where $p > A/(2B)$,
- $\text{MR}(x) = 0$ for $x = A/2$ and $p = A/(2B)$, and
- $\text{MR}(x) < 0$ for $x > A/2$ and $p < A/(2B)$.

Using the calculus formulae for elasticity,

$$\nu(p) = -\frac{Bp}{A - Bp} \quad \text{and} \quad \hat{\nu}(x) = -\frac{A - x}{x}.$$

All of this is summarized graphically for you in Figure 7.1.

Inelastic Demand and a Profit-Maximizing Firm

When demand is inelastic (when $\hat{\nu}(x)$ and $\nu(p)$ for the corresponding p are between -1 and 0), marginal revenue is negative. What, then, do you say to a firm (with market power, whose demand function is being used in these calculations) that is producing at such a p, x pair and that has positive marginal costs?

You say, "Whoa, you are producing too much. If you reduce x and increase p, your total costs will go down, since you have positive marginal costs, and your revenues will go up, since your marginal revenue is negative." At least, this firm is producing too much if it seeks to maximize profits.

Moral: No profit-maximizing firm with market power and positive marginal costs should produce at a level x where its demand is inelastic.[1]

7.3. Back to Mark-Ups: It's All About Elasticity

We can now answer the question, What determines how much a (profit-maximizing) firm marks up the products it sells? The answer is, *elasticity*. The percentage

---

[1] Just to cover all bases, if the firm's marginal costs are negative—say, because its production is subsidized by the government—it might find that its profit-maximizing point is where demand is inelastic.

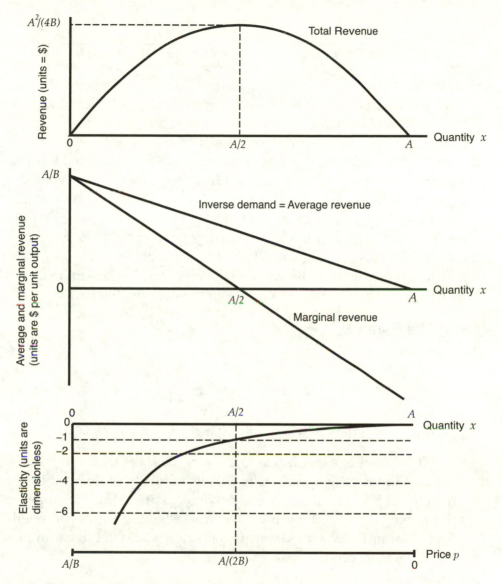

Figure 7.1. *The case of linear (inverse) demand.* The top panel shows total revenue, the middle panel shows demand (or inverse demand) and marginal revenue, and the bottom panel shows the elasticity function. Note that the scale in x and the scale in p are both present in the bottom panel and that elasticity is dimensionless.

mark-up is

$$100 \, \frac{P(x) - \mathrm{MC}(x)}{\mathrm{MC}(x).}$$

If the firm is a profit-maximizing firm, $\mathrm{MC}(x) = \mathrm{MR}(x)$. And at all x (not just the profit-maximizing level of x but, of course, there too) $\mathrm{MR}(x) = P(x)(1 + 1/\hat{\nu}(x))$.

So the percentage mark-up is

$$100 \, \frac{P(x) - \mathrm{MR}(x)}{\mathrm{MR}(x)} = 100 \, \frac{P(x) - P(x)(1 + 1/\hat{\nu}(x))}{P(x)(1 + 1/\hat{\nu}(x))} = -\frac{100}{1 + \hat{\nu}(x)}.$$

If, at the profit-maximizing level of production x, the elasticity of demand is -2, the mark-up is 100%. If the elasticity of demand is -3, the mark-up is 50%. If the elasticity of demand is -4, 33%. And so forth.

Digging one layer deeper, since the size of the mark-up is determined by the elasticity of demand, the size of the mark-up is determined by whatever determines the elasticity of demand. Elasticity is the amount your demand will fall (in percentage terms) if you raise your price by 1%. It then stands to reason that (1) the greater the extent to which there are substitute products out there, and (2) the greater the amount of competition the firm faces, the more the demand for its product will fall, and so the more negative (-3 instead of -2) will be its elasticity of demand and the smaller will be its optimal mark-up. Which is just what we guessed at the beginning of this chapter.

Using the Formula

The formula

$$\mathrm{MR}(x) = P(x) \cdot \left[1 + \frac{1}{\hat{\nu}(x)}\right]$$

can be used in a variety of ways. For instance:

> Based on market experimentation, a firm believes that, for prices for its product in the range from $40 to $45, its elasticity of demand is approximately -2.5.[2] The firm currently charges a price near the upper end of this range, $p = \$44$. At this price, the firm sells 30,000 units per month. The firm's marginal cost at this level of production is $25.00. Is the firm currently maximizing its profit?

To answer this question, we compute the marginal revenue of the firm, charging a price of $44 and selling 30,000 units:

$$\mathrm{MR}(30{,}000) = \$44 \times \left(1 + \frac{1}{\hat{\nu}(30{,}000)}\right) = 44\left(1 + \frac{1}{-2.5}\right)$$

$$= 44 \times (1 - 0.4) = 44 \times 0.6 = \$26.40.$$

---

[2] Note that for a linear demand function, elasticity is never constant. So either this firm's demand function is not linear, or this statement is just an approximation. There are demand functions for which elasticity is constant all along the demand function: If demand is given by $D(p) = Cp^k$ for constants $C > 0$ and $k < 0$, then $\nu(p) = k$ for all p. This sort of demand function is difficult to work with in examples, so we won't use it.

Since its marginal cost is only $25, the firm could increase profit by selling more units.

Problems 7.4 through 7.8 provide more practice in using this formula.

Warning! The Formula is Only Precise
at One Point along the Demand Function

Here's another problem you could be asked to solve:

> A firm is selling a 10,000 units of a product at a price of $20 apiece. It estimates that the elasticity of demand it faces at this price is −4. By how much will its revenues increase if it lowers the price to $19.50?

There are two ways you might try to solve this problem. They both start out in the same fashion: You first have to figure out how many more units will be sold: A $0.50 reduction in price on a base price of $20 is a 2.5% decrease. So, with an elasticity of −4, the firm gets around a 10% increase in quantity, to 11,000 units in total.

And then: 11,000 units sold at $19.50 generates $11,000 \times \$19.50 = \$214,500$. Previously, total revenues were $10,000 \times \$20 - \$200,000$. So the answer is an increase in revenues of $14,500.

Alternatively... And then: The formula says that marginal revenue is MR = $p(1 + 1/\nu) = 20(1 + 1/(-4)) = 20(3/4) = \$15$. So if the firm sells 1000 more units, it will see its revenues increase by $\$15 \times 1000 = \$15,000$.

The two ways of getting "an answer" give *almost* the same answer, but they don't quite agree. The reason is that elasticity typically changes as you move up or down a demand function, and we are using the elasticity at $20 for a range of different prices. Which method is correct? The answer is, It depends. *If* the demand function is linear, the first method gives the absolutely correct answer, and the second method will always give an optimistic picture of what will happen. But if, say, the demand function is a *constant-elasticity* demand function—see footnote 2 on page 164—then the second method gives the correct answer for any particular change in quantity, although the change in quantity that we computed in the first step is inaccurate.

For small changes in the price, the two methods are likely to give answers that are pretty close together, and either one is fine for a "back-of-the-envelope, what-if?" calculation. Since, in real life, you probably won't know the demand function you face exactly, anyway, this is about as good as it will get. (And when it comes to exams and such, your instructor will probably accept either method.)

But now go back to the problem of the firm charging $44 when its marginal cost is $25 and its elasticity of demand is −2.5. The formula is useful in telling us that at that price, marginal revenue is $26.40, more than marginal cost—at least locally, profit will increase if you make more units. But if you try to use the formula to find the price that maximizes profit (by finding which price p gives $MR = p(1 + 1/(-2.5)) = \$25 = MC$, say), and you moreover use this to figure out how much your profit will improve by moving to this price, you are probably pushing the formula further than it can reasonably be pushed. For more on this, try Problem 7.5.

If Firms Don't Know the Demand Function They Face, What Might They Know?

Early on last chapter, when we introduced the simple model of the profit-maximizing firm with market power, we said that assuming firms knew the entire demand function they faced is a heroic (a nice way of saying, unrealistic) assumption. It is much less heroic to think that a firm will have a pretty good idea how its demand will shift for small changes in the price it charges, which means it might know $D'(p)$, where p is its status-quo price, or, equivalently (since of course it knows p and $D(p)$) the elasticity of demand it faces. So, if it also knows its marginal costs, at least locally, it can work out whether it it profit-maximizing, *again locally*, and, if not, what direction to move in terms of price and quantity to increase profit.

7.4. Demand by Groups and in the Aggregate

Firms often consider how demand for their product varies with the type of customer. For instance, an electric utility might wish to think separately of demand from residential, commercial, and industrial customers; a consumer-marketing firm might wish to think separately about demand from different demographic groups.

Imagine, for instance, a firm selling some consumer good. The firm considers demand from three groups, segmented by age: customers 25 years old or less, those 26–55 years old, and those above 55 years old. It charges the same price p to all three groups, and demand functions for the three are, respectively, $D_y(p), D_m(p)$, and $D_s(p)$, where the subscripts y, m, and s represent *youth*, *middle-aged*, and *seniors*, respectively. If the firm fixes its price at p_0, its total demand is the sum of the amount it sells to youths, $D_y(p_0)$; the amount it sells to middle-aged consumers, $D_m(p_0)$; and the amount it sells to seniors, $D_s(p_0)$. Therefore, the total demand *function* it faces is the sum of the three component demand functions, or

$$D_{\text{TOTAL}}(p) = D_y(p) + D_m(p) + D_s(p).$$

This probably seems obvious. But, in models and problems, a lot of confusion arises at this point, on two grounds.

1. If you graph total demand, remember that the price goes on the vertical axis, so this summing of functions is *horizontal* summing. To see what this means, look at Figure 7.2, in which I assume that each of the three component pieces of demand is linear. (See Problem 7.9 for the functions assumed in this figure.)

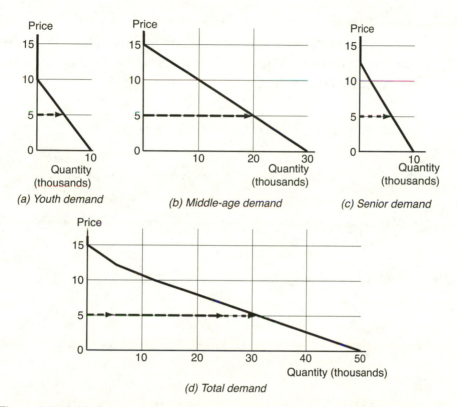

(a) Youth demand   (b) Middle-age demand   (c) Senior demand

(d) Total demand

Figure 7.2. *Add pieces of demand horizontally to get total demand.* Panels a, b, and c of the figure depict demand by youths, the middle-aged, and seniors, respectively. To get total demand, at a given price p, we find the quantity demanded by each group at the price and sum. In a picture, this translates to *horizontal* summing, as shown in panel d.

2. Suppose you were given *inverse* demand functions for each of the three groups, as $P_y(x_y)$, $P_m(x_m)$, and $P_s(x_s)$. To find total inverse demand, do you sum these three functions? *No!* Inverse demand gives the price it takes to elicit a certain level of demand. If we fix a level of demand, say $x = 3000$, and sum $P_y(3000) + P_m(3000) + P_s(3000)$, we are summing the prices it takes to sell 3000 units to each group. This sum is likely to be a price at which no sales are made to any of the three groups. Summing prices makes no sense.

To find total or aggregate inverse demand, if you have inverse demand functions for each group, first invert them to get demand functions for each group. Next sum the demand functions to get total or aggregate demand. And then invert the sum, to get aggregate inverse demand.

As strongly as I can, I urge you to work your way very carefully through Problem 7.9, which gives an example of all this. Until you do, you may not understand fully what you just read.

Elasticity of Total Demand from Elasticities of Pieces

Suppose we have demand broken into pieces, as in the example of the consumer-marketing firm that looks at demand by youths, middle-aged consumers, and seniors. Recall the notation

$$D_{\text{TOTAL}}(p) = D_y(p) + D_m(p) + D_s(p).$$

Suppose that we know the elasticities for each of the three pieces; that is,

$$\nu_y(p) = D'_y(p)\frac{p}{D_y(p)}, \quad \nu_m(p) = D'_m(p)\frac{p}{D_m(p)}, \quad \text{and} \quad \nu_s(p) = D'_s(p)\frac{p}{D_s(p)}.$$

Simple algebra tells us that

$$\nu_y(p)D_y(p) + \nu_m(p)D_m(p) + \nu_s(p)D_s(p)$$
$$= (D'_y(p) + D'_m(p) + D'_s(p))p = D'_{\text{TOTAL}}(p)p,$$

and, therefore,

$$\nu_{\text{TOTAL}}(p) = D'_{\text{TOTAL}}(p)\frac{p}{D_{\text{TOTAL}}(p)} = \frac{\nu_y(p)D_y(p) + \nu_m(p)D_m(p) + \nu_s(p)D_s(p)}{D_y(p) + D_m(p) + D_s(p)}.$$

*In words, when total demand is the sum of a number of segments or pieces, summed over demographic groups, different classes of customers, or even individual customers, the elasticity of total demand is the weighted average of the elasticities of the pieces, **where the weights are proportional to the amounts demanded by each piece.***

Marginal Revenue for Aggregate Demand Functions

We deal with several examples in the book where demand is the sum of demand by different demographic groups and where the demand functions for the different groups are linear. When this happens, be warned that marginal-revenue function is "interesting"; see Problem 8.4 and the discussion of this problem in the *Online Supplement*.

Disaggregating Demand and Price Discrimination

Suppose you are managing an amusement park such as Disneyland. You note that demand for entry into your park comes from two distinct groups: (1) tourists, who come from far away for a short stay at your park, and (2) locals, who can come often should they choose to do so. As I expect is simple commonsense, you'd like to charge the tourists a high admission price and the locals a much lower price.[3] Why? Because the elasticity of demand by tourists is likely a lot closer to -1 than is the demand by locals. Indeed, suppose that demand at your current admission price (assuming you are charging a single price of admission) is 75% from tourists and 25% from locals, your current elasticity of demand is -2.5, and the elasticity of demand by the locals is -8. To get these numbers, the elasticity of demand for tourists must satisfy the equation

$$0.75\,\nu_{\text{Tourists}} + 0.25(-8) = -2.5,$$

the solution to which is $\nu_{\text{Tourists}} = -2/3$. This means that if you *raise* the price for tourists, your revenue from tourists will go up.

Clearly, you would like to find some way to charge these two different groups different prices. And, of course, Disneyland and other amusement parks know very well how to do this: They offer admission for different lengths of "stay," including season passes. Tourists don't buy season passes and so, if season passes cost, say, the same as five-days' worth of separate admission, locals may well see this as a great deal.

This is an example of price discrimination (or, more accurately, bundling), which is the topic of Chapter 8.

7.5. Other Elasticities

The elasticity we've discussed in this chapter, *own-price elasticity*, is just the start of the story. Economists discuss how large is the percentage change in demand for one good—say, wheat—if the price of a second good, such as rice, rises by one percent; this is called a *cross-price elasticity*. The percentage change in demand for a good per-percentage change in the income of a (group of) consumer(s) is an *income elasticity of demand*. There are also elasticities of supply (although these make most sense when firms are price takers). Whenever economists talk about the X-elasticity of Y, they mean the percentage change in Y, per one-percent change in X. Hence, in this chapter, the modifier *own-price* comes from

---

[3] There is a lot more to pricing at an amusement park than simply charging for admission. Do you charge for individual rides? Do you charge more during peak seasons? I'm focused here on only one aspect of the complex pricing decisions that face the manager of Disneyland-type operation; we will look at some other aspects later in this book.

the fact that we are discussing the percentage change in demand for a good, per one-percent change in the good's *own price*.

The only two types of elasticity found in this book are the own-price elasticity of demand and, in Part III, the elasticity of supply. But if you go deeper into microeconomics, and especially if you wind up in the marketing or strategic management functions, the language of other elasticities may enter into conversations in which you take part.

Executive Summary

- The (own-price) elasticity of demand for a good (whose demand function is given by, say, $D(p)$, and at a specific price p_0), is the rate of percentage change in the quantity demand per percentage change in the price.

- You can compute own-price elasticity at p_0 by taking a second price, p_1, close to p_0, and computing

$$\frac{100[D(p_1) - D(p_0)]/D(p_0)}{100[p_1 - p_0]/p_0} = \frac{[D(p_1) - D(p_0)] \cdot p_0}{[p_1 - p_0] \cdot D(p_0),}$$

or, if D is a nice (differentiable) function, by computing

$$\frac{d\,D(p_0)}{d\,p} \cdot \frac{p_0}{D(p_0)} \text{ (or, in slightly different notation) } \frac{D'(p_0) \cdot p_0}{D(p_0)}.$$

In either case, this is a negative number (as long as demand is downward sloping). We use $\nu(p_0)$ to represent the elasticity of demand function as a function of the price p_0 at which it is evaluated, for a fixed demand function.

- If you are working with quantity x as the driving variable instead of price p, so you are working with an inverse demand function $P(x)$, the elasticity of demand at x_0 is the elasticity of demand at $P(x_0)$, which you can compute as

$$\frac{[x_1 - x_0] \cdot P(x_0)}{[P(x_1) - P(x_0)] \cdot x_0} \text{ where } x_1 \text{ is a quantity close to } x_0,$$

or, using calculus, as

$$\frac{P(x_0)}{x_0 P'(x_0).}$$

In either case, this is denoted by $\hat{\nu}(x_0)$.

- The case of linear demand is summarized on page 163. Since we work a lot with linear demand functions, it is worth "bookmarking" this page.

- Elasticity determines how much marginal revenue falls short of price. The key formula is

$$\text{MR}(x) = P(x)\left(1 + \frac{1}{\hat{\nu}(x)}\right).$$

Note: this formula holds at every quantity. It does not only hold at the profit-maximizing quantity although, of course, it holds there as well. (You should also bookmark this formula!)

- If $\hat{\nu}(x)$ falls between -1 and 0, we say that demand is *inelastic* at x. This implies (using the formula just above) that marginal revenue is negative when demand is inelastic: A profit-maximizing firm with nonnegative marginal costs never produces at a level of production where demand is inelastic.

- If $\hat{\nu}(x)$ is less than -1, we say that demand is *elastic* at x. Where demand is elastic, marginal revenue is positive.

- At the profit-maximizing level of production x, a firm with market power marks up its product (over its marginal cost of production) by $-100/(1+\hat{\nu}(x))$ percent. That is, the closer to -1 is $\hat{\nu}(x)$ (where x is the profit-maximizing quantity, hence $\hat{\nu}(x) < -1$), the bigger is the percentage mark-up.

- Firms may not know the full demand function they face, but they are likely to know how that function behaves locally: that is, they will know to some degree of precision the elasticity of demand they face at their status-quo price. Hence, even if they don't know their overall profit-maximizing price, if they also have a good idea about their (local) marginal cost, they can see (locally) if a change in quantity and price will improve profit.

- We sometimes deal with demand for a particular product by different demographic groups or classes of customers. When it comes to summing up these different pieces of overall demand, a price should be fixed and the quantities demanded summed; in terms of the graphs, you should sum horizontally.

- The overall elasticity of demand, when demand comes from different segments of customers, is the weighted average of the elasticities of demand from each segment, weighted by the relative size (in terms of quantities demanded) of each segment.

Problems

7.1 Consider a firm with the demand function $D(p) = 2000(50-p)$ and the total cost function $\text{TC}(x) = 10{,}000 + 10x$.

(a) Just for the practice, find the profit-maximizing price and quantity for this firm.

(b) What is the elasticity of demand $\nu(p)$ for this firm's demand function at $p = 40$? You only need to compute this once, but you should know (at least) three different ways to find this number.

(c) What is the elasticity of demand $\hat{\nu}(x)$ at the quantity you computed in part (a)? Once again, there are many ways to do this—do it once, but make a list of as many different ways to find this number as you can.

(d) What is the optimal mark-up for this firm, expressed as a percentage mark-up over marginal cost?

7.2 A firm sells its product for $8 apiece and sells 10,000 units per month at that price. It estimates that for small changes in price, a 1% change in price means a 3% change in the quantity sold (in the opposite direction).

(a) What would be the change in total revenues or receipts for this firm if it lowered its price by $0.10?

(b) What would be the change in total revenues or receipts for this firm if it lowered the quantity it sells by 150 units?

7.3 A profit-maximizing firm sells its goods at a price of $40 apiece. Its marginal cost of production at its profit-maximizing level of production is $10. For this firm, what is $\nu(\$40)$?

7.4 Brigadier Motors (BM), a profit-maximizing firm, produces a single variety of light truck. It sells this truck for $20,000, at which price it sells approximately 1.6 million light trucks per year. BM estimates that, at this price–quantity pair, the elasticity of demand for its light truck is -4. Given that all this is true, what is the marginal cost of a BM light truck?

7.5 Go back to pages 165-6 and the problem discussed there. We said that $44 was not profit maximizing but, per the information given, $41.67 would be. By how much (approximately) would the firm's profit increase if it lowered its price to $41.67? (Warning: This is not easy. Why is there a problem?)

7.6 Go back to page 168 and the firm selling to the three consumer groups mentioned there. Suppose that the inverse demand functions facing this firm for the three groups are, respectively, $P_y(x_y) = 10 - x_y/1000$, $P_m(x_m) = 15 - x_m/2000$, and $P_s(x_s) = 12.5 - x_s/800$. Find the aggregate or total demand and inverse demand functions facing this firm.

7.7 (a) A consumer marketing firm has been test marketing a new product in a number of markets. This firm believes that demand for its product comes entirely from women between the ages of 15 and 35, and that demand by the 15- to 25-year-old group is quite different from consumers in the 26- to 35-year-old segment. Specifically, per 1000 women between 15 and 25 in a market, the firm would sell $X_1 = 500(10 - P)$ units at the price P (to those women), while it would sell $X_2 = 250(15 - P)$ per 1000 women between 26 and 35. What demand function would this firm face in a market that has 40,000 women in the age group 15–25 and 25,000 women in the age group 26–35?

(b) It is unlikely that a real firm would have the sort of knowledge assumed in part a. It is much more realistic that the firm would know "local" data about the demand by various segments, local in the sense that the data are for small changes in price only. For example, the firm might know, on the basis of consumer surveys or test marketing, that at a price of $8:

- Per 1000 women aged 15–20, it can expect to sell 600 units of the good, with a price elasticity of -1.0.

- Per 1000 women aged 21–25, it can expect to sell 500 units of the good, with a price elasticity of -1.2.

- Per 1000 women aged 26–30, it can expect to sell 600 units of the good, with a price elasticity of -1.5.

- Per 1000 women aged 31–35, it can expect to sell 300 units of the good, with a price elasticity of -2.0.

(Note that these data are not consistent with the data given in part a.) In a market with 25,000 women aged 15–20, 15,000 aged 21–25, 10,000 aged 26–30, and 5,000 aged 31–35, how many units can the firm expect to sell at a price of $8 per unit? Approximately how many can it expect to sell at a price of $8.16?

(c) Suppose this firm has a constant marginal cost of production of $c = \$2$ per unit. Assuming the firm faces falling marginal revenues, is the price of $8 per unit too high, too low, or just right for profit maximization, based on the demand data given in part b?

7.8 A bakery in the seaside town of Malvino sells freshly baked bread at a store it operates along the highway to two categories of customers: residents of the town and tourists. During the summer season, the bakery prices a loaf of bread at $2.50, at which price it sells 90 loaves a day to locals and 300 loaves a day to tourists passing through on their way to the local state beach. During the winter season, they have been lowering their price to $2.25, and they find that they sell 135 loaves per day to locals. The bakery's marginal cost for a loaf of bread is $1.20.

The owner of the bakery wonders: Suppose we could find a way in the summer to charge locals a different price than we charge tourists. Perhaps we could give locals "discount coupons" or have them join a "frequent customer club" or just set up a second storefront at the bakery itself, which is in a part of the town to which tourists never go, and offer the bread at a lower price there. Suppose we lowered the price to locals to $2.25, while raising the price to tourists to, say, $2.75. Would this be a profitable move?

To answer this question, of course, the bakery must decide how these changes will impact demand. In real life, the bakery might experiment with different prices, but suppose that the owner of the bakery knows that, at the price of $2.50, the elasticity of demand by tourists is -1, while for locals it is -5. Shifts of $0.25 on a base price of $2.50—that is, 10%—are pretty large, but supposing we can use the elasticity figures for this range of price changes, what will be the impact on the bakery's bottom line of this two-price policy?

And, assuming the bakery decides it wants to do this and that a second storefront location is the best way to implement this strategy, if you are on the town's zoning commission, how do you feel about letting the bakery open a store in this "industrial zone?"

8. Price Discrimination

Firms selling goods sometimes charge different customers different prices for the "same" good. There are various techniques for doing this, including volume discounts (or the reverse — higher marginal prices for large purchases); employing periodic sales, coupons, and outlet stores; differentiating the good, which is why *same* is in scare quotes; or simply using demographic characteristics of the customer, as in discounts for senior citizens. In all these practices, the motivation is the same: charge higher prices to customers whose demand is more inelastic and lower prices to customers whose demand is more elastic, to increase revenue. (We will see some other motivations in our discussion.) Economists call such practices *price discrimination*.

This chapter concerns the following phenomena:

- The same textbook can often be bought for very different prices. In December 2014, a particular textbook bought from Amazon.com (US) cost $151.50. At Amazon.fr (France), the exact same book cost $177.57. (The price is quoted in Euro, and I'm converting using the then current exchange rate.) Across the Pyrenees, at Amazon.es (Spain), it cost $118.87. Amazon.co.jp (Japan) sold it for $92.33. Or you could by a soft-cover edition of the same book from Amazon.es for $62.77 and from Amazon.co.jp for $55.31. (To be clear, these are all in English. They are not translations.) Of course, some of the difference in price between hard- and softcover versions is due to the difference in the costs of producing a softcover vs. a hardcover book. But not too much; it costs about $1.00 more to make a book with a hard cover than one with a soft cover. Why, then, is the retail price of a hardcover book so much more? And why is the price in Spain of a hardcover edition 67% of the price in France?

- In October 2000, the cheapest round-trip ticket from San Francisco to Chicago, departing Sunday morning and returning Tuesday morning, cost over $2300. But the same itinerary, with a departure time shifted 15 hours earlier, cost less than $450.

- Manufacturers of packaged foods such as ready-to-eat cereals distribute coupons for their products in so-called advertising mailers, which are freely available. These coupons effectively reduce the profit margin of the company by up to 40%, *and* they are costly to prepare, distribute, and administer. Why not save the administrative expense and simply sell the goods at the cheaper price?

- Order phone service for a new business and you will be amazed at the array of billing plans available. The choice can be so bewildering that phone companies have sometimes offered to compute a customer's bill, on a month by month basis, according to whichever scheme the company offers that would be cheapest for the customer. What are phone companies trying to accomplish with all this?

- If two individuals, one a man and the other a woman, bargain separately with a new car dealer for the purchase of a new car and the two follow precisely the same bargaining script, on average, the man will be offered the better deal. Why?

All these phenomena are examples of or are closely related to price discrimination. The term *price discrimination* is used because, at their heart, all these phenomena involve discriminating among customers, charging different customers different prices, to exploit differences in the demand characteristics of the customers.

Why would a firm want to charge different customers different prices? Consider the two individuals depicted in Figure 8.1. The first says that he is not very sensitive to the price being charged. He wants some amount of the good, and if the price he is charged doubles, he will decrease his demand, but only by a bit. The second says that he is sensitive to price; lower the price a bit, for him, and he will respond with a substantial increase in his level of purchases. I have two questions regarding these individuals:

- If you could charge them different prices, to which one would you charge a lower price and to which one a higher price?

- The names of these two individuals are Mr. Pretty-elastic-demand and Mr. Not-very-elastic-demand. Who is who?

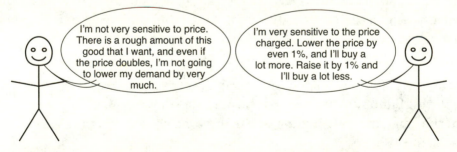

Figure 8.1. Two consumers. If you can charge one of these two a higher price and one a lower, who will get the higher price? And, given what they have to say, which one has more-elastic and which less-elastic demand?

Of course, you want to charge a high price to the individual who is not sensitive to price—he is willing to pay through the nose for what he wants—and you want to charge a relatively low price to the other individual, to get him to buy a substantial quantity. The first is Mr. Not-very-elastic-demand; the second is Mr. Pretty-elastic-demand.

Firms can rarely charge each individual a tailored-to-the-individual price. But sometimes they can segment their customers into *groups,* where the different groups have different elasticities of demand, charging the more-inelastic-demand group a higher price, thereby increasing revenues.

8.1. Why Price-Discriminate?

To illustrate how this might work, let's solve Problem 8 from last chapter. The story is:

> A bakery in the seaside town of Malvino sells freshly baked bread at a store it operates along the highway to two categories of customers: Residents of the town and tourists. During the summer season, the bakery prices a loaf of bread at $2.50, at which price it sells 90 loaves a day to locals and 300 loaves a day to tourists passing through on their way to the local state beach. During the winter season, they have been lowering their price to $2.25, and they find that they sell 135 loaves per day to locals. The bakery's marginal cost for a loaf of bread is $1.20.
>
> The owner of the bakery wonders: Suppose we could find a way in the summer to charge locals a different price than we charge tourists. Perhaps we could give locals "discount coupons" or have them join a "frequent customer club" or just set up a second storefront at the bakery itself, which is in a part of the town to which tourists never go, and offer the bread at a lower price there. Suppose we lowered the price to locals to $2.25, while raising the price to tourists to, say, $2.75. Would this be a profitable move?
>
> To answer this question, of course, the bakery must decide how these changes will impact demand. In real life, the bakery might experiment with different prices, but suppose that the owner of the bakery knows that, at the price of $2.50, the elasticity of demand by tourists is −1, while for locals it is −5. Shifts of $0.25 on a base price of $2.50—that is, 10%—are pretty large. But supposing we can use the elasticity figures for this range of price changes, what will be the impact on the bakery's bottom line of this two-price policy?
>
> And, assuming the bakery decides it wants to do this and that a second storefront location is the best way to implement this strategy, if you are on the town's zoning commission, how do you feel about letting the bakery open a store in this "industrial zone?"

The calculations are easy: $0.25 is a 10% change in price. If we lower price to the locals by 10% and their elasticity of demand is −5, they will buy 50% more bread. On a base of 90 loaves a day, this means the bakery will sell 135 loaves to the locals, consistent with the figures for winter sales. Meanwhile, a $0.25 or 10% rise in price for the tourists, combined with an elasticity of demand of -1 for them, means a 10% fall in their demand, from 300 loaves a day to 270 loaves (in the summer). The bakery has been selling 390 loaves a day at $2.50 per day; at a marginal cost of $1.20 per load, this means daily profit[1] of $390 \times (\$2.50 - \$1.20) = \$507$. The new scheme, in comparison, means a daily profit of $135 \times (\$2.25 - \$1.20) = \$141.75$ from the locals, and $270 \times (\$2.75 - \$1.20) = \$418.50$ from the tourists, or a grand (daily) total of $560.25, which is quite an improvement.

As for the zoning commission: There may be things to consider about commercial traffic in the industrial zone and such, but the first-order effects are that your constituent (and potential campaign contributor), the bakery, improves its profit by a lot, and the local population—the voters—get more bread at a significantly lower price. Sounds like a winner to me!

This is but one possible strategy for the bakery, raising the price for the tourists while lowering it for the locals by the same 10%. There is no claim that this is the optimal scheme and, in fact, it would be quite a coincidence if it were optimal. To figure out the optimal scheme, we'd need to know what are the full demand functions for the locals and the tourists, and while such things are easy to "know" within the context of an economics textbook, they generally are hard to find in the real world. Still, since this is a textbook, Problem 8.4 provides you with the information you need to optimize fully for the Malvino Bakery.

What is this example telling us? Suppose a firm is charging a single price p. Suppose it is maximizing its profit by equating marginal cost and marginal revenue. Since marginal revenue is (always)

$$p\left[1 + \frac{1}{\nu(p)}\right],$$

this is also marginal cost. Suppose demand comes from two groups, the A's and the B's. Overall elasticity of demand at price p, or $\nu(p)$, is (as we saw last chapter) a weighted average of the elasticities of demand of the A's and the B's, where the weights are proportional to the amount the two segments demand. Writing $\nu_A(p)$ for the elasticity of demand of A's at p, and $\nu_B(p)$ for the elasticity of demand of the B's, suppose $\nu_A(p) < \nu_B(p)$; that is, the A's have more elastic demand. *And now suppose that the firm could, somehow, charge different prices for the A's and B's.* Since $\nu(p)$ is an average of $\nu_A(p)$ and $\nu_B(p)$, we know that $\nu_A(p) < \nu(p) < \nu_B(p)$. But then writing MR_A for the marginal revenue of selling one more unit to the A's and MR_B for the marginal revenue of selling

---

[1] Presumably, the bakery has some fixed costs, such as rental or perhaps labor costs. So this is *variable* profit.

one more unit to the B's, we know that, at the quantities demanded by the A's and B's for a single price p,

$$\mathrm{MR}_A = p\left[1 + \frac{1}{\nu_A(p)}\right] > \mathrm{MR}_{\text{Both Groups}} = p\left[1 + \frac{1}{\nu(p)}\right] > \mathrm{MR}_B = p\left[1 + \frac{1}{\nu_B(p)}\right].$$

And, since $\mathrm{MC} = \mathrm{MR}_{\text{Both Groups}}$ at the quantity being produced,

$$\mathrm{MR}_A > \mathrm{MC} > \mathrm{MR}_B.$$

By lowering the price to the A's and selling them more units, its revenues will increase more than will its costs, and by raising the price to the B's and selling them fewer units, its costs will fall more than will its revenues. That's the motivation behind price discrimination.

8.2. But How? Different Methods for Achieving Price Discrimination

But how is our bakery going to charge locals less and tourists more? In the problem, they planned on using geography and convenient access. The tourists who pass through Malvino typically drive through on the Coast Highway—they are on their way to a state beach and don't venture into the town. The bakery sells its bread in a store right on the Coast Highway. So if the bakery opens a second outlet, inside the town, hidden from the tourists but known to the locals, it can probably charge a high price at the store on the highway and a lower price in town. And note that, if opening this second location takes a zoning variation (because, say, they want to put the second outlet in a residential neighborhood), from the perspective of the City Council, it is all good: More profits for the bakery, which means more taxes and, perhaps, more political contributions, *and* lower bread prices for the relevant local public.

A different scheme, but one you may have encountered, is practiced in particular by local supermarkets in vacation locales such as Hawaii. The supermarkets have two prices for many goods, the "regular" price and the "club" price. Anyone can join the "club," but (we're sorry to tell you) it takes a couple of weeks for an application to be processed, and your club card is mailed to your personal residence: "Only staying a week? Too bad, but maybe, if you apply, you'll come back some day."[2]

Another variation on the same basic theme is the practice of couponing. The idea is that customers with very elastic demand are much more likely to take the

---

[2] I'm told that if you are in Hawaii and a major chain supermarket is nearby, like Safeway, your "membership" privileges from back home will work there as well.

time and effort to look for coupons in mailers and newspapers, while customers whose demand is closer to inelastic haven't got the time or inclination to do so. So, to lower the price to the first group, coupons are printed and distributed.

Periodic sales present another example. In the United States, at least, so-called "white goods"—sheets and other bedding, towels, and so forth—go on sale on predictable dates, typically in January. The idea: Customers with more inelastic demand often need their white goods when they need them. If you *need* a new set of sheets in September, you probably aren't willing to wait until January. But some people don't need new sheets as much as they'd like to refresh their collection periodically, which makes their demand much more elastic. This group, of course, is much more willing to wait.[3]

To give one last example: Advertisements for vendors heard on the radio, read by a radio personality, sometimes end with the tag line, "Tell them [the vendor] that Joe Radio-guy [the radio personality] sent you and they'll pay the sales tax," or " . . . they'll take 5% off," or " . . . they'll give you a free waffle iron." Why does the mention of Joe Radio-guy's name get you favored treatment? In part—when the add-on is relatively cheap, such as a waffle iron—this is a way for the seller to gauge the success of its advertisements. But when the price break offered is large—sales taxes can be on the order of 8% in the United States—another explanation is that Joe Radio-guy's audience has more elastic demand for the goods being sold than the population as a whole. This offer allows the vendor to charge this more elastic demand segment of the population a lower price.

Discrimination by Demographic Grouping

In the examples just given, the groups form somewhat endogenously. The tourists passing through Malvino could buy cheap bread if they took the time to find the in-town outlet; coupons are available to anyone willing to take the time to find them; and so forth.

But in some instances, one customer is offered a better price than another, and the second *cannot* access the better price. Typically, this is done by demography, as in: A cheese shop that offers a 10% discount to seniors; a public transportation company that gives discounted weekly passes to students; or a baseball club that offers discounted ticket prices to youth sports teams. Note that the language here is all about *discounts*; the inference that you are meant to draw if you are not eligible for the discount is that you aren't being charged a higher price than you would be, otherwise. Which might be true, if the company is engaging in price discrimination out of the goodness of its heart and not to enhance revenues. But, if the cheese shop is lowering the prices it charges seniors because seniors

---

[3] The publication *US News* has a website that lists, month by month, the traditional sales seasons for a variety of different sorts of goods. See http://money.usnews.com/money/personal-finance/articles/2013/01/17/your-month-to-month-guide-to-great-sales.

have more elastic demand than the shop's overall clientele, the clientele that remains after the seniors are removed has a less elastic demand than before: If the shop is setting all its prices to maximize its profit, nonseniors face higher mark-ups than they otherwise would.

Terms and Conditions and Other "Quality" Distinctions

To "separate" the segments of the population, sellers who want to discriminate will sometimes differentiate what they are selling, adding "terms and conditions" to low-price goods that the more-elastic group is willing to accept but that are unacceptable to the more-inelastic group.

Perhaps the most prevalent example of this is airline pricing. Recall the example at the start of the chapter: To fly round-trip from San Francisco to Chicago in October 2000, departing Sunday morning and returning Tuesday, cost a minimum of $2300. But if you were willing to leave from SF 15 hours earlier (and give up on cancellation fees), the ticket would cost $450.

This could have several explanations. There may have been a lot of empty seats on the Saturday-departure plane, so the airline was holding a "fire sale" to get rid of some of its unused inventory. But, at the same time, airlines recognize that business travelers, who rarely pay for their own tickets—making them the very definition of inelastic demanders—are loath to spend the extra night away from home. Vacation travelers, on the other hand, whose demand is much, much more elastic, might even see the extra night in Chicago as a plus. Variations on this include: discounts for round-trip tickets versus the same trip composed out of one-way segments; discounts for travel booked weeks in advance; and discounts for tickets with no-change conditions.

Or consider the difference in the price between hard- and softcover textbooks. There is a production-cost difference, but it is trivial compared to the difference in prices. That said, libraries buy hardcover books and, at least when it comes to textbooks, libraries have much more inelastic demand than do other purchasers, who often are willing to purchase a softcover book.[4]

Indeed, manufacturers of various types of consumer electronics that are sold with and without various features find it economical to manufacture all the devices with a full set of features. Then, to satisfy demand for the lower-price, less-featured models, they disable features. That is, the marginal cost of manufacture of the less-featured models, which are sold at a lower price, is higher than the marginal cost of the full-featured, higher-price model.

Perhaps the most stunning (alleged) example of this sort concerns a plastic cement that is used both in dentistry, where demand is highly inelastic for very small quantities, and in construction, where demand is much more elastic and

---

[4] A library can buy softcover books and, if they wish, put "hard covers" on them; in fact, some university libraries do just that. Compare with the case of subscription prices for scholarly journals: Libraries that wish to subscribe must pay a much higher subscription fee than individuals, a classic example of discrimination by demography (libraries versus people).

for bucketfuls of the stuff. So, the manufacturer (it is alleged) formulated and sold two "versions" of the material. The first was the cement, sold at a very high price per ounce, for dental purposes. The second version included in the cement was a mild poison that would have no effect if the material was used in construction, but would kill anyone who walked around with this in their teeth, sold for a much lower price per bucketful.

Nonlinear pricing

Nonlinear pricing describes situations where the total the buyer pays for x units is a nonlinear function of x. This includes both cases where the price charged for the marginal unit goes up (you can by the first ten units for $12 apiece, but anything past ten will cost you $15 each) and where the price charged for the marginal unit goes down (the first ten you buy will cost you $12 apiece, but any further units will cost you only $8 each).

As a price-discrimination scheme the idea is: There are customers who buy in bulk, and those who buy only a few. If the elasticities of demand of these two groups are quite different, then there may be room for non-linear pricing of one form or the other. Which form is appropriate depends, of course, on which group—the bulk buyers or the small-lot buyers—has the more elastic demand; in the end, one always wants to charge the more elastic-demand group the lower marginal price.

Bundling

Bundling refers to the practice of selling goods separately and in bundles, as in: You can buy tickets to the symphony concert-by-concert, or you can buy a season ticket, or you can buy a bundle of five concerts, where the bundle is either fixed or, in some cases, where you can assemble the bundle.

When the bundle price is just the sum of the individual item prices, the bundling is not being done for discriminatory purposes. (But, in some cases, you get certain extra privileges if you buy a bundle: e.g., buy a season ticket to a major league baseball team, and you have priority for buying postseason tickets. In such cases, since the privilege has value, the bundle is in effect sold at less than the sum of all its parts.)

Bundling becomes interesting as a discriminatory scheme, though, if the bundle costs less than the sum of its parts. For instance, in December 2014, Disneyland offers admission to its park for one day at $96, for two consecutive days at $89 per day, for three consecutive days at $75.34 per day, for four consecutive days at $62.50 per day, and for five consecutive days at $53.20 per day, or $266 total. You could also buy an annual passport (admission on 315 days of the year—major holidays and all Saturdays in the summer excluded) for $519. And, to throw in a bit of discrimination by geography, the Disneyland website mentioned special deals for Southern California residents that I, using a computer located in Northern California, was unable to view.

What's going on here? A caricature of the situation will illustrate. Suppose Disneyland had a two-day season. Suppose there are 10,000 potential visitors. Each visitor attaches a dollar value to attending the park on day 1 and on day 2. For instance, one potential visitor sees the park as being worth $23 on day 1 and $45 on day 2. (It would make sense to say that the values are connected—if this consumer visits the park on day 1, it is worth less to her to attend on day 2. But I won't put that consideration into my model.) The reason for having 10,000 potential visitors is that I will assume that the population of visitors have values $1 to $100 for day 1 and $1 to $100 for day 2, with every one of the 10,000 combinations represented by one and only one person in the population.

Suppose there is $20 marginal cost of admitting a visitor, and Disneyland decides to charge an admission price on day 1 and an admission price on day 2, with the same price on each day applying to each visitor. The optimal prices to charge, to maximize total revenue and total cost, are $60 for day 1 and $60 for day 2. (Since the variable x is discrete, you must use a spreadsheet to verify my calculation. And I depend on the person whose value is exactly $60 being willing to attend when the price is $60. Alternatively, you can approximate my situation with two linear demand curves $D(p) = 100(100 - p)$ for each day and do the usual MC = MR.)

Can Disneyland make any more revenue by bundling? A bundle here would be for admission on both days, for a price less than $120. (At a price of $120 or more, the bundle costs no less than two single-day admissions.) How about trying a bundle at $110? Follow along on Figure 8.2.

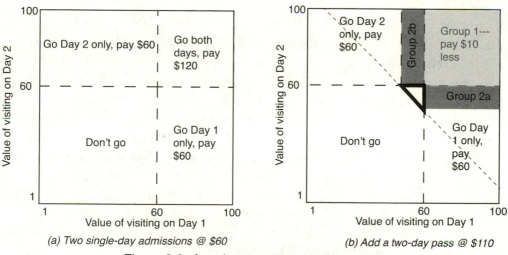

(a) Two single-day admissions @ $60   (b) Add a two-day pass @ $110

Figure 8.2. A caricature example of bundling.

In panel a, we see the situation with only single-day admission at a price of $60. Everyone whose value of visiting on Day 1 exceeds $60 goes on Day 1, and everyone whose value of visiting on Day 2 exceeds $60 goes on Day 2. This gives us a block of folks (in the upper-right corner) who go both days.

Now introduce a two-day pass priced at $110.

- Anyone who would, without the bundle, choose to enter the park both days will buy this bundle, costing Disneyland $10 in revenue. These are the folks in panel b labelled as Group 1. There are $41 \times 41 = 1681$ such people: The cost to Disneyland of offering the bundle in terms of these 1681 consumers is $16,810 in lost revenue.

But some new attendees arrive:

- Consider first the group who previously only attended on Day 1. These people have value $v_1 \geq 60$ and $v_2 < 60$, using the obvious notation. Might they now be induced to buy a two-day pass? They will, if $v_2 \geq 50$: It costs an incremental $50 to buy the two-day pass instead of one one-day pass, so as long as they get $50 or more additional value, this is a good deal for them. They are represented in panel b by Group 2a. And there is a symmetric Group 2b. Each group has 410 members, and from each, Disneyland is ahead $50 - $20 = $30 in profit; this is an incremental $50 in revenue less a $20 cost, for a total net gain of $30 \times 2 \times 410 = $24,600 more in profit.

- And of the folks who didn't go at all, previously, there are small handful whose value of going both days, $v_1 + v_2$, exceeds the cost of a two-day pass. For instance, there is the person with $v_1 = $58 and $v_2 = $55. In panel b, they are the folks in the heavily outlined triangle. There are 45 such people, and Disneyland nets $110 in revenue less $40 in cost, or $70, from each, for a net gain of $45 \times $70 = $3150.

So, overall, Disneyland makes an incremental profit of $3150+$24,600−$16,810 = $10,940 by offering the two-day pass at $110, in addition to one-day passes at $60 for each day.

Can Disneyland do better? Think, for instance, of lowering the two-day pass price by, say, $5, to $105. Disneyland loses $5 more for each member of Group 1, and it makes $5 less from members of Groups 2a and 2b and the folks in the triangle. But more folks join Groups 2a and 2b, and the triangle gets bigger.

Even in this ultrasimple model, it is not trivial to find the best scheme for single-day prices and a bundled two-day price. It is not impossible to do in Excel, but I found it more convenient to use the language R, and I found the profit-maximizing deal to be where the one-day (only) price is $68 and the two-day pass cost $109. This generates a net profit of $349,038, versus $338,940 for the scheme with one day for $60 and two days for $110.

This example doesn't immediately fit the theme of this chapter, which is that price discrimination schemes work by separating more- and less-elastic de-manders. But we can make it fit, as follows: You want to separate more- and less-elastic customers because, by lowering the price to the more-elastic customers, you can sell more to them for a marginal revenue above your marginal cost. And once you've separated them, you can raise your profit by raising the price to the other, less-elastic customers. Of course, if you must set a single price for each group, you lose some revenue for the more-elastic group by lowering the price on units they would have purchased at the single price; the point is, for them, you make up your losses and more with increased volume.

So, roughly, it is with bundling. When you bundle, say, two goods at a price less than the sum of the two individual prices, you lose money on those who would have bought both goods anyway. But some folks who would only have bought one of the goods now buy the second as well (as part of the bundle), producing revenues in excess of your costs. And—the icing on the cake—there are some potential customers who would have bought no goods from you if the goods are singly priced. But if their value for the bundle exceeds the bundle price, you can sell to them. And, of course, as long as the bundle price exceeds the marginal cost of producing the bundle, that's good for you.

Let me reiterate, there is a lot more to how Disneyland prices all the goodies it has on offer, including bundles with and without parking, bundles that include early admission to the park, bundles that involve stays at a Disneyland hotel, and so forth. And then there is one of the most basic aspects of Disneyland pricing: A customer buys admission to the park for the day and then can ride as many rides as desired and (given the lines) feasible. But food is not "free" after admission. If the airlines are the major leagues when it comes to discriminatory pricing to maximize revenue, Disneyland may well be the MVP.

Experience Goods and "Introductory Price Offers"

Traditional performing arts organizations—symphony orchestras, ballets, opera companies—offer discounts both for seniors and for students. To some extent, this is driven by the elasticities of demand of these two groups. But when it comes to students, a further, revenue-based reason comes into play: The organization believes (and has good reason to believe) that the experience of consuming their product entices the audience member into further attendance. For students, the idea, at least in part, is to "build the audience of the future" by getting them in the door today.

When new products are introduced or when, say, a new restaurant opens, similar "introductory price offers" will be observed, and for the same reason. These are, typically, available to all, so this doesn't really fit the notion of price discrimination. But, in some cases, special deals are offered by established businesses to new customers that are not available to ongoing customers; this mixes a (presumably) greater elasticity for not-yet-customers with an investment in future revenues by sacrificing some revenue today.

Educational discounts for computer hardware and software are other examples that mix both aspects: Students (and academics more generally) probably have more elastic demand for these goods than do businesses. And, at the same time, hardware and software firms believe that a student who adopts their products when in school is more likely to keep using those products after school, and even may induce others to use them, too.

Nth-degree Price Discrimination

If you consult economic textbooks, you may run into a classification scheme for different "degrees" of price discrimination: There are first-, second-, and third-degrees of price discrimination. But different sources use the classification system in different ways, so I avoid this bit of terminology. That said, the "ideal" in terms of price discrimination is to tailor the prices charged individual customers to the individual customer. This is the "first degree," and I discuss how this works when, in Chapter 10, we have models of the demand behavior of individuals.

8.3. Price Discrimination Based on Other Grounds

In the previous discussion, price discrimination was *revenue*-based. The idea is to extract more revenue from the diverse set of customers facing the firm. There are also *cost-based* reasons to price-discriminate.

This arises primarily in the service sector, where the "good" being sold is some service, and the marginal cost of providing the service to some customers is higher than it is to others. Of course, if the marginal revenue of providing the service to a member of Group A is the same as the marginal revenue of providing the service to a member of Group B, but the marginal cost for Group A is higher, the firm wants to raise prices for Group A and lower them for Group B.

Consider, for instance, the provision of automobile insurance. On average, drivers under the age of 25 have more accidents, and male drivers of this age are particularly prone to accidents. This doesn't mean that every teenage boy is a peril to others on the road. But, as a class, it costs insurance companies a lot more to insure young drivers and, in particular, young male drivers, than it does other groups. Hence, insurance premia for these groups reflects the costs of providing the insurance.

Regulation provides a fourth reason you sometimes see price discrimination and, in particular, nonlinear pricing for "essential services" such as water and electricity. In most cases, the per-unit price a household pays for water and electricity rises with the amounts purchased per (say) month. Is this revenue-based price discrimination? For it to be so, we would need to believe that the demand of high-volume households is more inelastic than that of low-volume households. And that doesn't seem quite right: Low-volume households (as well as high-volume households) *need* those first few kilowatts/thousands of gallons to survive and, in many cases, would pay more if necessary to get what they *need*, which is the very definition of inelastic demand. Once basic needs are met, demand is probably more elastic.

But water and electricity providers are regulated, and regulators are particularly keen that "lifeline" quantities of water and electricity are affordable by virtually all households. The water and electricity providers, if they could, would increase revenue by jacking up the per-unit prices they charge for the essential quantities of what they provide. But they are not allowed to do so.

8.4. If Price Discrimination Sounds Great, Watch Out for the Following

To people who will be on the selling side of markets, price discrimination has a lot of initial appeal. However:

- When you try to charge different people different prices, you must be able to control (to some extent, at least) what happens to the goods after they leave your hands. Consider, for instance, a cheese shop that offers a 10% discount to seniors (enforced, in close cases, by examination of the individual's ID). What prevents a senior from buying cheese for himself, and also for his (adult) children and/or some younger friends and associates, all at the discounted price? What prevents an enterprising senior from buying massive quantities and then going door to door, reselling the cheese or setting up a cheese-for-sale stand just outside the front door of the cheese shop?

  Or consider nonlinear pricing schemes. If the per-unit price decreases with volume, what prevents a customer from buying in bulk and reselling? What prevents a group of small-lot purchasers from banding together to make and then split up a single large-lot purchase? And if the per-unit price increases with volume, what prevents a large-lot customer from making a number of small-lot purchases or, perhaps, getting some friends to make small-lot purchases (at the lower per-unit price) on his behalf?

  Of course, it was exactly this resale consideration that caused the plastic cement manufacturer (allegedly) to put the slow-acting poison in the goods sold for construction purposes. The cheese shop could (and shops in this situation sometimes do) limit the dollar amount that qualifies for the senior purchase or, relying on moral suasion, say that "discounts apply to purchases for own use, only." But, in many cases, vendors cannot perfectly control the resale of their goods and, to the extent that there are enterprising customers out there, some "slippage" is likely to occur.

  Services—especially personal services—are better candidates for price discrimination in this regard. A beautician who offers a 10% discount on manicures and pedicures for senior citizens doesn't need to worry about grandma reselling her mani-pedi to her adult daughter. An insurance company, insuring a 45-year-old driver, doesn't need to worry that the driver will resell this insurance to her 18-year-old son. And, in the case of "services" such as electricity and water, since the service is delivered to a specific address, resale, while not entirely impossible, is certainly cumbersome.

- The principle behind price discrimination is reasonably clear. But implementation of this principle in practice is typically difficult. In a simple model, where we assume that we know the demand characteristics of certain groups of customers, finding the best price-discrimination scheme is still difficult. (This is why, when illustrating the principle, we employ caricatures like the Malvino Bakery and a theme park that is open for only two days a season.) In the real world, where demand elasticities must be estimated, finding good price-discrimination schemes is an art. Elasticities of different groups can point you in the right direction, but how far do you go? When it comes to a simple scheme like couponing, how do you trade off the size of the intended audience for the coupons against their aggregate price elasticity? For an airline, is it best to set advance-purchase requirements at 22 days, or 14, or 7? When I say that airlines are the major league of third-degree price discrimination or that Disneyland is an all-star at bundling and other, similar schemes, it is because they combine an excellent understanding of the basic principles with a vast amount of experience putting those principles to work.

- And, then, there is the ethical question:

8.5. Is Price Discrimination Ethical?

When asked, "Is it ethical for the local deli to offer a 10% discount to senior citizens?," most (but not all!) Stanford MBA students say that it is ethical. I imagine that this opinion would be widely shared.

But, what about the following case? Legal scholar Ian Ayers[5] sent trained investigators to new car dealerships in the Chicago area armed with very precise scripts about how to negotiate the purchase of a new car. The investigators were dressed alike; appearance and behavior, except for gender and race, were kept as uniform as possible. Ayers's investigators kept track of the progress of their negotiations, noting the levels of price concessions they got from the dealer at different time points (that is, what would be conceded in the first 30 minutes, and so forth). The question Ayers addressed with the data collected was, Would dealership salespersons respond differently to customers who were following

---

[5] In Ayers, "Fair Driving: Gender and Race Discrimination in Retail Car Negotiations," *Harvard Law Review*, Vol. 104, 1991, 817–71. I have elected to use the terms that Ayers uses, namely *white* and *black* for race and *male* and *female* for gender.

the same script and were dressed similarly, depending on the customer's race and sex? He found that white males received significantly greater concessions from dealers (over a given time period) than white females, black males, and black females: In terms of the offers they received, white females, on average, were offered 40% higher mark-ups than white males. Black males were offered around twice the mark-up of white males. Black females were offered around three times the mark-up offered to white males. Of course, none of the deals were consummated—Ayers's research budget did not stretch that far—so perhaps the females and black males would have gotten the same deals being offered to white males had they been a bit more patient. But if females and black males have to negotiate longer to get the same deal, this is still a form of discrimination. Why might this be?

One possible explanation is pure prejudice, meaning actions in the face of countervailing economic considerations, to serve some noneconomic goal such as harming people of color and women. Ayers considered this possibility, and he asserts that the data he collected do not support it. Instead, he asserts that this is a case of economic discrimination based on group membership. White females, black males, and especially black females have more inelastic demand for new cars than white males. For economic or social or other reasons,[6] females and black males are less likely to haggle *on average* than white males. Please note the "on average" in this sentence. A black female who is also ready and willing to drive a hard bargain might, in the end, get the concessions offered a white male. But she has to wait longer and work harder to get those concessions, which in itself is discriminatory.

Suppose Ayers is right about this. Suppose that, on average, it makes economic sense, *meaning it increases profits*, for new car dealers to discriminate in this fashion against females and black males. Should such discrimination be legal? And since it might be hard to enforce a law against it if it is illegal, is it ethical? Most individuals with whom I discussed these questions believe both that it should not be permitted under law and, even absent an effective and enforceable law against it, that such behavior is ethically reprehensible. I share these judgments. But, assuming you agree, let me challenge you: Should discounts for seniors be legal? Are they ethical? And if you answer Yes to both questions, what is the philosophical or ethical basis for the distinction between discounts

---

[6] The reason could be entirely endogenous, in the following sense. Suppose you are bargaining over the price of some good you wish to purchase. The seller has already named a price you would be willing to pay, if you are convinced this is the best deal you can get. Of course, this doesn't mean you should agree; how much more you press for a lower price depends on what you think you can get. So, if the selling side of automobile sales believes that some demographic groups are more likely on average to settle for higher prices than are members of a second group, and if the sellers therefore are less likely to concede, it can be optimal for the first group to settle for higher prices, which validates the hypothesis that group members are willing to settle for higher prices. Note well, I didn't say that this is *fair*. It isn't fair. But it is an optimal individual response to an unfair *bargaining equilibrium*.

for seniors at the deli and gender- and race-based discrimination at the car dealership? (Please do not argue, "In the first case, seniors are getting discounts, so no one is hurt." When seniors get discounts, the price to nonseniors—at least, the profit-maximizing price to nonseniors—goes up.)

Let me throw a third example into the mix: When banks make mortgage loans, they try to estimate the likelihood of default by the client. Among the data they might use are the personal employment history of the buyer and the neighborhood of the property. With regard to the neighborhood, properties in some neighborhoods show a higher propensity to default and, in a now-illegal practice called redlining, banks would "red line" certain neighborhoods and refuse to make any mortgage loans for properties in those neighborhoods. Since the practice is illegal, the ethics of the practice are moot. But would redlining be ethical if it were legal?

And with regard to personal employment history, is it ethical to use those data? Suppose that we found that, statistically, personal employment history differentially disadvantaged members of one race over another—what is known in the United States as the test of *disparate impact*. If we saw disparate impact in the data, does that make the use of personal employment history unethical? Does that mean that using these data should be illegal?

This is a textbook in economics, not law and not ethics. So I will not try to answer those questions. My point is that economic discrimination is, by definition, discriminatory. This raises substantial issues that transcend simple economics, issues that, if you plan to price-disciminate, you must consider.

Executive Summary

- Price-discrimination schemes of various sorts are very often based in the desire to improve profit by raising prices for customers with more inelastic demand (and/or higher marginal costs of service) and lowering prices for customers with more elastic demand (and/or lower marginal costs of service).

- Among the many schemes used are: discrimination by demographic group (e.g., discounts for seniors); by self-selected group (couponing); by differentiating the goods sold (length-of-stay requirements for airline tickets); nonlinear prices, both quantity discounts and unit prices that rise with the quantity purchased; and bundling (selling a package of items for less than it would cost to buy them separately).

- Finding the "best" price-discrimination scheme is, in most cases, a very complex problem. And, in any case, firms rarely have the data they would require to optimize. So price discrimination in practice is more an art than the application of set procedures. But it is a highly analytical art when practiced by the best practitioners: namely, the airlines, Disneyland, and similar firms.

- Price discrimination "works" only insofar as the seller can control the resale of the good in question.

- Price discrimination raises issues both legal and ethical that must be considered.

Problems

8.1 On October 10, 2000, a particular book about human resource management was being sold by Amazon.com for $102.75. At precisely the same time, this book could be purchased at the Amazon.uk website for the sterling equivalent of $36.29. (This is not an international student edition or anything like that. It is the same book, published by the same publisher, in the same format.) What do you think is going on here? (A one-sentence answer is appropriate.)

8.2 Suppose a firm sells to senior citizens and others at a single price of $10 per unit. At this price, it sells 10,000 units in total; 2,000 to seniors and 8,000 to the others. At the price of $10, demand by seniors has elasticity −3, while demand by the others has elasticity −1.5.

(a) Suppose the firm decides to raise the price it charges nonseniors by $0.10. At the same time, it lowers the price facing seniors. How much should it decrease its price to seniors, to keep the total quantity sold at 10,000?

(b) (The answer to part a is that it should lower the price to seniors by $0.20. Use this number even if you cannot solve part a.) What will be the (approximate) impact on the firm's profits if it simultaneously raises its price to nonseniors to $10.10 and lowers the price to seniors to $9.80?

(c) Note that I say nothing about the marginal costs of production of this firm. Why don't you need to know this to answer part b?

8.3 A manufacturer with a constant-marginal-cost production technology sells 10,000 units at a price of $10 per unit. The elasticity of demand facing this manufacturer at this price is −3. The price of $10 is profit maximizing.

The manufacturer decides to engage in a coupon campaign. In this campaign, coupons offering an instant discount of $0.50 per unit purchased to anyone holding a coupon are distributed to a segment of the entire buying public. (In real life, you need a separate coupon for each unit purchased. If you think of coupons as operating in this fashion, imagine that that members of this segment of the population will have access to as many coupons as they wish to use.) Marketing specialists estimate that the segment of the buying public that would obtain a coupon purchases 3000 units at a net per-unit price of $10 per unit and has an elasticity of demand of −6 at that price per unit. The remaining 70% of the population have no access to coupons and so must pay the full price, which—until part c—is $10 per unit.

(a) How would this coupon campaign affect the firm's profit? (There are several steps to solving this, so you might need to consult the solutions, to see how to proceed. Also, check your solution to part a before going on with the rest of the problem.)

(b) Suppose the manufacturer keeps the noncoupon price at $10 and optimizes over the coupon value. What coupon value should be selected, and what is the impact on profit?

(c) Suppose the manufacturer optimizes over both the noncoupon price and the coupon value. That is, the $10 price may change as well as the amount off provided by the coupon. What noncoupon price and what coupon value should be chosen, and what is the impact on profit?

(d) Suppose that an alternative coupon program would get the coupons into the hands of 40% of the consuming population, but this 40% has an (average) elasticity of demand of -5.2. Only one of the two coupon programs can be used. Which is better for the manufacturer?

If you are checking your answers in the *Online Supplement*, so that your computations are the same as mine, compute changes in quantity demanded given price changes in the following "simpleminded" fashion: If a group has a price elasticity of -6 and its price falls by $x\%$, then its quantity demanded rises by $6x\%$. I suggest, very strongly, that you solve this problem with Excel. Part a isn't too bad done by hand, but the rest gets to be quite an algebraic mess.

8.4 Regarding the Malvino Bakery problem:

(a) If the tourists have an elasticity of demand of -1 at the price $2.50 and buy 300 loaves, and the locals have an elasticity of -5 at that price and buy 90 loaves, what is the overall elasticity of demand at $2.50?

(b) And what is marginal revenue at $2.50? (How does this compare with the marginal cost of $1.20?)

(c) Suppose demand by tourists is given by the linear demand function $D_T(p) = 120(5 - p)$, while demand by locals is $D_L(p) = 180(3 - p)$. Verify that these demand functions are consistent with the elasticities of -1 and -5 at the price $2.50 as asserted in the problem. Then calculate the optimal (separate) prices to charge the two groups, given these demand functions.

(d) *(This part has the possibility of confusing you, so apprach with caution.)* You already know (how) that marginal cost equals marginal revenue from both segments together at $2.50. Why do you know this? But, it turns out, this is a problem in which finding a quantity at which MC = MR isn't quite enough to be certain that this is the profit-maximizing level of production, because the marginal-revenue function exhibits some pretty strange behavior. Using the two demand functions for the two segments, (1) find overall demand, (2) then find overall inverse demand, (3) use this to find overall total revenue, and then

(4) find and graph marginal revenue for both populations together. Finally, (5) superimpose the constant marginal cost of $1.20 on your marginal-revenue function. What is going on, here? How do you find the true profit-maximizing point?

8.5 Nonlinear prices can give rise to a number of counterintuitive phenomena. Here is a (hard!) example to illustrate some of the things that can happen.

To give a model in which we can explore nonlinear prices, we must first have a way to model the choice behavior of individual consumers whose choice involves the amount of some good to buy. Chapter 10 discusses this in some generality, but here is a version good enough for the time being.

Imagine that the good in question must be consumed in integer units. That is, a given consumer can choose not to consume any of the good, or one unit, or two, or three, and so forth. We'll assume in this problem that no consumer wishes to consume more than five units of the good, as long as the price is greater than zero.

There will be three consumers in this model. Each one is characterized by "dollar values for each level of consumption." For instance, the first consumer is characterized by the following string of values:

$$v_1(1) = \$10, \quad v_1(2) = \$18, \quad v_1(3) = \$23, \quad v_1(4) = \$25, \quad v_1(5) = \$26.$$

What this means is that, for this consumer, consuming one unit of the good is worth $10 to her, consuming two units is worth $18, and so forth. Now suppose that the cost to purchase this good is given by: To buy one unit costs $5. To buy two units costs $10 in total. To buy three units costs $13. To buy four or more costs $10 + \$3(n - 2)$, where n is the number of units she buys. That is, the first two units she buys cost $5 each, but any units beyond the first two cost $3 each. Then she computes:

- If I buy one unit, my net benefit is $v_1(1) - \$5 = \$10 - \$5 = \$5$.

- If I buy two units, my net benefit is $v_1(2) - \$10 = \$18 - \$10 = \$8$.

- Three units gives me a net $v_1(3) - \$13 = \$23 - \$13 = \$10$.

- Four units gives me a net $v_1(4) - \$16 = \$25 - \$16 = \$9$.

- And five units gives me a net $\$26 - \$19 = \$7$.

My best purchase amount is three units, so that's what I'll purchase. (And, if there is a tie for best net benefit at several different levels, we'll assume that consumers always purchase the largest level that ties for best.)

That's consumer #1. Consumers #2 and #3 behave in similar fashion, although they have different dollar-value functions:

$$v_2(1) = \$20, \ v_2(2) = \$39, \ v_2(3) = \$44, \ v_2(4) = \$48, \ v_2(5) = \$50, \text{ and}$$
$$v_3(1) = \$30, \ v_3(2) = \$50, \ v_3(3) = \$60, \ v_3(4) = \$62, \ v_3(5) = \$62.5.$$

Suppose the firm's marginal cost of producing this good is a constant $4 per unit.

(a) If this firm must choose a single per-unit price (use linear pricing), the optimal per-unit price for it to charge is $19 per unit. Why?

(b) One prevalent form of nonlinear pricing involves an "entry fee" F and a per-unit price p. If the customer wishes to buy any quantity, she must pay the entry fee F, after which she may buy as many units as she wishes at a per-unit price of p. Suppose the seller chooses $p = 15$ and $F = 5$. How will each of the three consumers respond?

(c) In terms of maximizing its revenue, what is the best entry fee and per-unit-price combination? You may restrict attention to values of F and p that are integers greater or equal to 1. (You should not attempt to use calculus on this problem. You must look at each discrete possibility. The solution in the *Online Supplement* uses an Excel spreadsheet.)

(d) Redo parts a and c if the firm's marginal cost of production is $2 instead of $4.

8.6 In the example of bundling that is presented in the chapter, the values a given consumer attach to Day 1 and Day 2 are independent. That is, if I pick one of the 10,000 consumers at random and tell you the value from 1 to 100 she attaches to Day 1 attendance, this gives you no information at all about the value she attaches to Day 2 attendance. Also, attending on, say, Day 1 does not affect the value of attending on Day 2: If, for instance, the consumer values Day 1 attendance at $69 and Day 2 attendance at $44, she values attendance both days at 69 + 44 = $113.

The case of independent values is special—in general, the valuations consumers put on two objects that can be bundled are correlated—and, insofar as we are talking about closely related items that are, to some extent, substitutes, buying one may lower the value attached to the other. The question is, How do these things affect the value of bundling as a marketing strategy?

To investigate these things, consider the following model. There are two objects involved—think of them, as attendance on Day 1 and on Day 2. The distribution in the population of prospective customers of dollar values for each has a Normal distribution, with a mean of $50 and a standard deviation of $20. But these values can be correlated, either positively or negatively; CORR denotes their correlation, so that $-1 \leq$ CORR ≤ 1, with CORR $= 0$ being the case of independence.[7]

(a) First suppose that the value of attending both days is just the sum of the values on the two different days, as in the example in the chapter. How do the optimal bundling strategies change with changes in CORR? How does the value of bundling change as CORR changes? In particular, is bundling a more valuable strategy (vis-à-vis just pricing each day separately) when CORR is closer to 1 or closer to -1? (Even if you have no idea how to attack this, what does your intuition tell you is the answer to the question, Is bundling more valuable for positively or negatively correlated items?)

(b) Now suppose that v_1 and v_2 are the values for a given consumer of good 1 and good 2. If (as we will assume, although it is true of the optimal pricing strategy) the one-item price p is the same for the two goods (because they have the same distribution), and if the customer decides to buy only one good, she will certainly buy whichever item/day has the larger one-day value. Suppose, then, that if $v_2 > v_1$ and the consumer buys both goods, her dollar value for the package is only $0.8v_1 + v_2$ (and vice versa if $v_1 > v_2$). That is, consuming one of the two reduces the dollar value of also consuming the second by 20%. What are the optimal pricing schemes (as a function of CORR) in this case?

This is a difficult problem, and even if you don't carry through the analysis, try to describe how you would do this. (Hint: If you don't know about Monte Carlo simulation, it is probably impossible to do. You can still set it up analytically, but pushing through to a solution will take a huge amount of math.)

---

[7] To be mathematically precise, the two have a joint Normal distribution.

9. Channels of Distribution and Double Marginalization

Manufactured goods are typically sold via multilayered channels of distribution, from manufacturer to wholesalers to retailers to consumers. This chapter uses some of the concepts and techniques we have developed to study this situation. In particular, it studies the problem of *double marginalization*, the loss in overall profit that takes place because each party in the distribution chain, to get its share of the pie, marks up the price of the goods. The chapter goes on to show how dealership or franchise fees can ameliorate the problem.

In October 2014, Governor Rick Snyder of Michigan signed into law a bill that, according to the language in the bill, prevents electric-car manufacturer Tesla from selling its vehicles directly to the public. Snyder asserted, as he signed the bill, that in fact the law did no such thing; Michigan laws already forbid car manufacturers from selling directly to the public, he asserted, and the new bill merely "clarified" and "strengthened" the existing law. Public sources do not agree entirely on what the law does and does not allow. Clearly, it prohibits Tesla from setting up a company-owned "store" in Michigan where customers could purchase a Tesla. It also prohibits Tesla from setting up a "gallery" where customers could view Teslas and talk to company employees about the vehicle. It seems to prohibit Tesla from advertising the sale of their cars in Michigan, but it is unclear how Michigan can regulate websites posted outside of Michigan. And various reports on the law differ on whether Michigan residents can purchase Tesla vehicles on-line.[1] But the intent is clear: Michigan wants Tesla to sell its vehicles through an independent dealership network. And Tesla's response has been clear: They do not wish to do that.

Michigan is far from unique; while Tesla has begun direct marketing in at least 23 states, Tesla has met opposition in other states, including Massachusetts (where the courts recently ruled against a legislative attempt similar to that in Michigan), Texas, New Jersey, and Missouri. In Michigan and elsewhere, the opposition comes primarily from the politically powerful and well-organized state Automobile Dealers Associations as well as the National Automobile Dealers Association in Washington, D.C. But, at least in the case of the Michigan law,

---

[1] Of course, nothing stops a customer from driving to the nearest out-of-state Tesla store, which is in Ohio, purchasing the vehicle there, and then driving it home. Except, perhaps, the hassle of paying sales tax in Ohio and then dealing with Michigan's attempt to collect the sales tax, if indeed Michigan makes that attempt (as does, for instance, California).

auto manufacturer General Motors issued a statement in support of the new law.[2]

The public argument put forward by the automobile dealers against direct sales is that competition among dealers provides the public with lower prices. They argue that, if a manufacturer such as Telsa could be the sole seller of its vehicles, it could use its market power to mark up prices dramatically. Telsa argues back that this legislation is pure rent-seeking by the automobile dealers, who fear the loss of their lucrative businesses. By allowing direct sales, Tesla concludes, costs to the public would be lower and, especially for an innovative product such as an all-electric vehicle, the quality of information provided in the sales process would be enhanced.

This is not the first time this issue has arisen. Until 1984, Porsches were sold in the United States through the Volkswagen–Audi dealership network. In 1984, the marketing agreement between Porsche and Volkswagen USA was expiring, and Porsche announced that it would not renew the agreement, but instead would create a new model for retailing its cars. In particular, Porsche said that *it* would set a nonnegotiable price for its cars, and authorized dealers would be order-takers and vehicle-deliverers only. Porsche would pay these dealers a commission for acting as the sales agent, although the proposed commission would be significantly less than the margin dealers typically made on the sale of car of Porsche's quality; Porsche would pay an 8% commission, compared with an estimated margin of 18% in the then current arrangement. Predictably, the VW-Audi dealers thoughout the United States objected, threatening to take Porsche to court.[3]

Background: Automobile Retailing in the U.S. in 1984 and Today

Both in 1984 and, for the most part, today, automobile retailing was and is done through by independent dealerships, which buy cars from auto manufacturers and resell the cars to the public. Stock trading among the dealers is common. Dealerships are "authorized franchises" of the major manufacturers. It has become increasingly common, at least in urban areas, for a dealer to sell more than one brand of car under the same (or adjoining) roof. And many dealerships are owned or controlled by large holding corporations; in northern California, for example, many dealerships in 1984 were part of either the Mike Harvey Group or the Lucas Group; today the Del Grande Dealership Group (DGDG) is ubiquitous. Dealers and manufacturers have arm's-length relationships; a manufacturer sells its cars wholesale to its dealers, who then get the best prices they can selling cars to consumers.

---

[2] See, for instance, "Michigan to Tesla: Dealers only," by Doron Levin, *Fortune*, October 22, 2014. Available online at fortune.com/2014/10/22/tesla-michigan-dealerships/; "Michigan Joins List of Tesla-Hating States; Bans Direct Sales of Cars," by Chis Morran, *Consumerist*, October 21, 2014.

[3] See *Automotive News* of February 20 and 27 and March 12 and 19, 1984. This example was suggested to me by Peter Reiss.

Dealers, back in 1984, could usually get a very good price from consumers. The invoice that a dealer would show the customer, however reluctantly, was (and is) often an overstatement of what the dealer would wind up paying for the car. This is so in particular because dealers are sometimes given an off-invoice "rebate" for cars that move quickly through the dealership. Moreover, many cars were sold for an amount greatly in excess of the invoice price. Dealers guard this sort of information closely, but it is asserted that, at the time, over 90% of the sales were at amounts within $1000 of the manufacturer's suggested retail price (MSRP), a figure that represents the highest and most glorious aspirations of dealers.[4]

Dealers had two major advantages vis-à-vis customers. They had better information on what were the "best deals" for new cars; a well-informed and patient buyer could wait out a dealer, but many buyers lacked the ability and or information to do so; in effect, dealers could engage in substantial price discrimination. And, especially as dealerships came under one corporate roof, "collusion" among them became increasingly easy.

Dealers, while independent of manufacturers, have certain responsibilities as part of their dealership contracts. They are required to contribute to cooperative national and regional advertising, and to maintain repair and servicing facilities and an inventory of spare parts.

This manner of marketing presents substantial problems of incentives. Most notably, while the manufacturer wants the independent dealer to sell a large number of cars by taking a smaller-percentage profit, dealers are more interested in holding back cars, waiting for the customer who would pay the sticker (MSRP) price. Since dealers carry the cost of inventory, they have some incentive to sell cars quickly. And some special arrangements between the manufacturer and dealers increase each dealer's incentive to sell cars quickly. But, in general, dealers' incentives do not align with those of the manufacturer.

Given these problems of incentives, you might wonder why automobiles are retailed in this fashion. The institution of independent dealerships goes back to when Alfred P. Sloan was building General Motors, and the most widely accepted explanations are that Sloan felt that (1) independent dealers would have a better chance of building a loyal customer base and a better sense of the local conditions in the market, especially as it related to trade-ins, and (2) independent dealers, by holding stock in their inventory, would decrease inventory-holding costs to GM.

For whatever reason, independent dealerships became the norm. And, since dealers are an easily organized group, with strong ties to local government, many laws were passed at the level of state government to protect the interests

---

[4] Very occasionally, a new model car in very high demand and short supply can sell for more than the MSRP. The "sticker" on the car would be amended to include the rather blatantly titled "Dealership Markup."

of dealers from exploitation by manufacturers. These laws, which are usually posed more generally to apply to all franchiser–franchisee relationships, essentially prohibit the franchiser from ever changing the nature of its economic relationship with the franchisee, except with the agreement of the franchisee. The economic relationship, in other words, is fixed by its initial form, except for changes that benefit both parties.

The internet has made the very comfortable existence of dealers somewhat less comfortable. Internet-mediated sales have increased competition, to some extent: Dealers are increasingly willing to quote prices on the phone or over the internet, which lowers the costs to the buyer of comparison shopping. And "independent purchasing agents," who will (for a commission) shop for a customer, are typically much better informed than the customer on what deals can be had. Finally, new-car buyers today can quickly gather from internet websites such as Edmunds.com data about recent "reasonable" sales prices for specific models in specific locales. Shake-ups in the autombile industry, notably the bankruptcies of General Motors and Chrysler in 2009, have added to the perception that sunk-cost investments by dealerships (in facilities, in particular) carry significant risk. But dealers continue to wield signficant political power, and they continue to protect what they have.

The Porsche and Tesla Stories, Continued

Porsche's proposals in 1984 did not meet with the approval of the Volkswagen–Audi dealers who had been selling Porsche cars. Invoking state laws concerning franchises, many lawsuits were filed. Porsche maintained that it was not in violation of those laws, because the Porsche–Audi dealers had franchise arrangements with VW USA and not with Porsche; as Porsche was no longer being sold through VW USA, new arrangements were unconstrained by the prior arrangements. VW USA, fearing that it would be named as a party to the lawsuits against Porsche by its dealers, itself initiated a suit against Porsche, claiming that *its* relationship was covered by franchise laws.

When the dust settled, Porsche retreated from its proposed new way of marketing cars. It continued to assert that its legal case was strong, but there was insufficient time for it to establish the sort of agency network it wanted, and so it would undertake traditional dealership relationships. Of course, whatever the standing of its legal position, once it did this, it was stuck. And, while the internet has caused the industry to evolve since then, not much changed structurally until recently, when Tesla—unconstrained by any previous dealership agreements—proposed to sell directly to the public. Automobile dealers in general have mobilized against this, seeking and in some states getting laws that would stop *any* manufacturer, even a new one, from selling directly to the public. How this will end up is an open question; Governor Snyder, in his signing statement (a month before the 2014 elections), claimed that "next year" the

State Legislature should look into whether the voting public would be better off under some other arrangement. As of September 2016, though, Michigan was still denying Tesla the dealership license it would need to sell directly to the public.

The questions are, Why did Porsche try to change the nature of its arrangement with the dealers of its vehicles? Why does Tesla want to sell directly to the public?

9.1. A Simple Model of Two-Step Distribution

To answer these questions, we analyze a very simple and stylized model of a manufacturer, her, and an arms-length retailer, him. Imagine a manufacturer who produces a product at constant marginal cost, say, $11 per unit. This manufacturer sells the good to the retailer, at a price set by the manufacturer, denoted by p; the retailer is allowed to buy as many units as he desires at p per unit. The retailer then turns around and sells the units he has bought to the public, at a price denoted by P. The retailer, we will assume, is the sole seller of this good to the public. To keep the math and pictures simple, we assume a zero marginal cost of retailing, other than the cost of goods sold, so the marginal cost to the retailer is p, the wholesale price set by the manufacturer. Although the numbers are hardly suggestive of the marginal cost or demand function for Tesla or Porsche automobiles, I refer to this item as a *car*.

Suppose the retailer faces the inverse-demand function

$$P(x) = 131 - \frac{x}{100},$$

where x is the number of units the retailer sells, and $P(x)$ is the price he gets per unit. We tackle the following questions:

- What wholesale price p should the manufacturer set, to maximize her profit? What retail price will be set by the retailer, how much will be sold, and what will be the profits of the two firms?

- Suppose that the manufacturer could retail cars on her own, without the middleman, and at no additional cost of retailing. What happens then?

- Suppose the manufacturer could retail cars on her own, but at a marginal cost of k per vehicle sold, as compared to 0 marginal cost for the retailer. That is, the retailer has a cost advantage in retailing. (One of the alleged reasons that Sloan went through dealers is that they had a cost advantage in retailing. So this question is meant to get at the issue: How much of an advantage is needed to make two-step distribution better for the manufacturer?) At what levels of k does the manufacturer prefer to deal through the retailer and at what levels would she prefer to sell direct? At what levels of k would the buying public *prefer* that sales come through the retailer?

• Suppose the manufacturer decides that she must market her cars through the retailer, say, because she is much less capable at consumer marketing than the retailer. Is there any sort of scheme she might employ in her dealings with the retailer, which would enable her to do better than by simply charging a wholesale price p? (If this question seems mysterious to you, remember that this chapter follows a chapter on price discrimination. But also remember: Dealerships often swap stock.)

We answer these questions, then take our analysis back to the Porsche and Tesla stories, to see what this model teaches us. If you wish to try your analytical skills, try to answer these questions for the model on your own, and see what you think the answers are saying about the real-world problems of Porsche and Tesla. Then proceed to read the analysis that follows.

The Best Wholesale Price to Charge

What is the best wholesale price p for the manufacturer to set? Our approach to this question employs the backward-induction technique of Chapter 2: We assume that the manufacturer moves first, setting a wholesale price p. The retailer takes p as a given and chooses the number of cars x to buy from the manufacturer, mark up, and sell to the public. So in the first step of our analysis, we ask: Given p, what x is best for the retailer?

Suppose the manufacturer sets a wholesale price of p. This, then, is the *marginal cost* facing the retailer. His inverse-demand fuction is $P(x) = 131 - x/100$, so his marginal-revenue function is $MR(x) = 131 - 2x/100$, and hence the amount he will purchase from the manufacturer, at a wholesale price of p, is the solution to $MR = MC$, or

$$131 - \frac{2x}{100} = p \quad \text{which is} \quad x = 50(131 - p).$$

Although we won't need it for another paragraph, we can also derive here the retail price that the retailer will set as a function of the wholesale price p. It is

$$P = 131 - \frac{50(131 - p)}{100} = \frac{131 + p}{2}.$$

Hence, the manufacturer knows that if she sets a wholesale price of p, her level of sales will be $x = 50(131 - p)$. This is *her* demand function, and her inverse-demand function is obtained by solving for p: If she wants to sell x vehicles to the wholesaler, she must set her wholesale price p so that

$$x = 50(131 - p) \quad \text{or} \quad p = 131 - \frac{x}{50}.$$

Therefore, her marginal-revenue function is $MR(x) = 131 - 2x/50$, and she maximizes her profit (at a constant marginal cost of 11) where her MR equals her MC, or

$$131 - \frac{2x}{50} = 11 \quad \text{which has solution} \quad x = 120 \cdot 25 = 3000.$$

To sell 3000 vehicles to the retailer, she sets p, the wholesale price, to be $131 - 3000/50 = 71$, giving her a profit of $(71 - 11) \cdot 3000 = \$180{,}000$. The retailer, in turn, marks up the 3000 cars he buys to a price of $131 - 3000/100 = \$101$ (or use the formula $(131 + p)/2$), for a profit to him of $(101 - 71) \cdot 3000 = \$90{,}000$.
    Done.

What if the Manufacturer Could Sell Directly to the Public?

In this case, the manufacturer faces the retail inverse-demand function $131 - x/100$, so she faces the marginal-revenue function $MR(x) = 131 - 2x/100$, and her profit-maximizing level of sales is the solution to $MR = MC$ or

$$131 - \frac{2x}{100} = 11 \quad \text{which is} \quad x = 6000.$$

This goes with a retail price of $P = 131 - 6000/100 = \$71$, and a profit to the manufacturer of $(71 - 11) \cdot 6000 = \$360{,}000$.
    The manufacturer is better off (greater profits). The public is better off (more cars at lower prices). But, of course, the retailer is unhappy and will begin lobbying his state legislator.

And if the Manufacturer Can Sell Directly,
But at a Cost Disadvantage?

Suppose that the manufacturer can sell directly to the retail market but, if she does, she incurs an additional marginal cost per car sold of k. We've done MR = MC often enough, so I'll just supply the answers:

- She sells $x = 50(120 - k)$ cars.

- The (retail) price per car is $P = (142 + k)/2$.

- Her profit is $25(120 - k)^2$.

So, assuming she has this retailing cost disadvantage vis-à-vis the retailer,

- the consuming public prefers that she sell directly to them as long as $(142 + k)/2 < 101$, which is $k < 60$ (because, if $k < 60$, there are more cars that cost less when she sells directly), and

- she prefers to sell direct as long as $25(120 - k)^2 > 180{,}000$, which is when $k < \$35.148$, more or less.

What Does It All Mean? The Costs of Double Marginalization

To understand what is going on here, focus on the case of $k = 0$, where the manufacturer is just as able as the retailer to sell the product to consumers. The model says that, in this case, selling directly to the public results in a $71 retail price, 6000 units sold, and a profit of $360,000. But, with two-step distribution, the retail price is $101, only 3000 units are sold, and total profit—the sum of the retailer's and the manufacturer's profits—is only $270,000, divided $90,000 to the retailer and $180,000 to the manufacturer.

As long as the retailer has no cost advantage in retailing, it is not hard to see why total profit with two-step distribution is no larger than profit from selling directly to the public. Whatever distribution system is used, some quantity x is produced and sold to the public. Revenue earned from consumers is $xP(x)$, and the cost to manufacture x units is $TC(x)$. If the costs of retailing are 0, then total profit—the sum of the two firms' profits in two-step distribution—is $xP(x) - TC(x)$. In direct-to-the-public distribution, the manufacturer chooses x to maximize $xP(x) - TC(x)$. So, whatever x is chosen in two-step distribution, total profit can be no larger in two-step distribution than in selling directly to the public. And, to the extent that two-step distribution results in a quantity different from the profit-maximizing quantity for the direct-to-the-public system, total profit with the two-step distribution system must be less.

Moreover, two-step distribution definitely results in a lower quantity x than selling directly to the public. *For the manufacturer to make a profit, she must set her wholesale price p at a level that exceeds her marginal cost.* But her wholesale price is the marginal cost of the retailer. So, *the retailer's marginal cost exceeds the manufacturer's marginal cost.* With direct-to-the-public distribution, the manufacturer equates her marginal cost to retail marginal revenue. With two-step distribution, the quantity is set by the retailer, who equates his higher marginal cost to retail marginal revenue. Since his marginal cost is higher, his profit-maximizing quantity is less than hers.[5]

To summarize, two-step distribution means a lower quantity than direct-to-the-public distribution, and therefore it means higher prices for consumers. And it yields a smaller total profit.

But, let me reiterate, this is true *only* as long as the manufacturer is not at a cost disadvantage to the retailer in retailing. We find two-step distribution precisely because retailers have lower costs of retailing than manufacturers or because retailers, being closer to the market, are better able to engage in the sort of price-discrimination strategies we studied last chapter. In particular, when it comes to new car sales, local dealers are more likely to be able to discern which customers have more inelastic demand and which more elastic demand, or who will pay MSRP, if the salesperson will just wait them out, and who will

---

[5] While I've illustrated this only for this simple example, it is true very generally, as long as the marginal revenue function at the retail level is continuous.

go elsewhere if the salesperson is intransigent. (So, as the internet levels the car-bargaining playing field, the cost advantage held by independent dealerships is reduced, and the costs of two-step sales relative to direct sales is increased.)

Economists call this phenomenon *double marginalization*. To explain this terminology, see Figure 9.1. In panel a, the black line is retail market (inverse) demand, $P(x) = 131 - x/100$. Retail total revenue is $TR(x) = 131x - x^2/100$ and retail marginal revenue is $MR_R(x) = 131 - 2x/100$, depicted by the gray line.

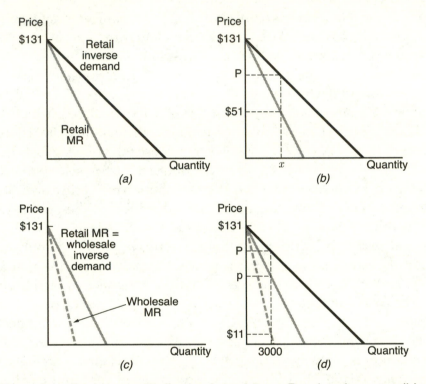

Figure 9.1. Double marginalization in a picture. Panel a shows retail inverse demand and retail marginal revenue. Panel b shows how, given a wholesale price p, such as $p = \$51$, the retailer equates this, his marginal cost, to retail marginal revenue to find the quantity x to buy, marking up the retail price to P. Hence, *the retail marginal-revenue function is the wholesale inverse-demand function.* (This is emphasized because it is the key. Don't read on until you understand this point.) In panel c, we see the "second marginalization": Retail inverse demand is marginalized once to get retail marginal revenue = wholesale inverse demand, which is marginalized a second time to get wholesale marginal revenue. Finally, in panel d, we see that manufacturer marginal cost (\$11) is equated to the wholesale marginal revenue to get the quantity (3000 units) sold; this determines the wholesale price p and the retail price P. Of course, this is a much smaller quantity—in this linear example, half—than we would get with direct distribution, if the manufacturer's marginal cost of distribution were 0.

Suppose the manufacturer sets a wholesale price of \$51. This is the retailer's marginal cost, and to maximize profit, he equates this wholesale price to his retail marginal revenue. So, as shown in panel b, a wholesale price of $51 gives the quantity where $\mathrm{MR}_R(x) = \$51$. And, in general, a wholesale price of p gives the quantity where $\mathrm{MR}_R(x) = p$. But this means that wholesale demand—the amount the manufacturer could expect to sell as a function of wholesale price—is traced out by retail marginal revenue. In other words, retail marginal revenue *is* wholesale inverse demand.

Wholesale marginal revenue is the marginal-revenue function obtained from the wholesale inverse demand function = retail marginal revenue function = $131 - 2x/100$. Do the math, and you'll find that this means that wholesale marginal revenue is $131 - 4x/100$, the dashed gray line in panel c of Figure 6.5.

Panel d finishes the story. Given manufacturer marginal cost, the manufacturer sets her wholesale price to sell the quantity where her marginal cost equals her wholesale marginal revenue. The retail price is then read off the retail inverse demand function at this quantity.

Hence, the terminology *double marginalization*: We begin with retail inverse demand and "marginalize" it for each step in the distribution chain—that is, twice in two-step distribution—to get the marginal-revenue function that is equated to manufacturer marginal cost.

Having Your Cake and Eating It, Too:
Charging the Retailer an Up-Front Fee

Of course, the analysis just completed does not imply that we never see retailers. Retailers exist. And, in fact, we have already seen one reason why: Retailers may have a cost advantage over manufacturers in retailing.

So, based on the issues we've discussed, it would seem that the choice between two-step and direct-to-the-public distribution turns on the cost of double marginalization versus the retailing cost advantages possessed by dedicated retailers. Manufacturers can have their cake or they can eat it, but they cannot do both—or so it might seem.

To be very concrete about things, suppose the retailer has a marginal cost of $0 for retailing, and if the manufacturer retails directly to the public, her marginal cost of retailing is $30. With these numbers, our earlier calculations tell us that the manufacturer would rather sell directly to the public, setting a retail price of $86 and making a profit of $202,500.

Suppose someone in the marketing department of the manufacturer comes up with the idea of charging the retailer an up-front fee in addition to a per-unit cost. In other words, the manufacturer will tell the retailer:

> "You can buy as many units as you wish at a cost to you of p per unit, and you can retail them at any price you wish. But before you buy any, you must pay me an up-front fee of F."

What is the manufacturer's profit-maximizing combination of F and p? Does it do better than marketing directly to the public? To answer these questions, we have to answer the question, Which combinations of F and p will the retailer accept?

In real life, this takes us into some psychological considerations. Suppose the retailer accepts this offer and pays F. That payment is now a *sunk cost* for the retailer, meaning nothing he does is going to get this money back, so he may as well forget that he paid it and optimize in what remains. And then, with a per-unit cost of p as his marginal cost, he would choose to buy and resell $50(131 - p)$ units, setting a retail price of $131 - 50(131 - p)/100 = (131 + p)/2$, for a profit gross of F equal to

$$50(131 - p)\left(\frac{131 + p}{2} - p\right) = 25(131 - p)^2.$$

Will he pay F to make a gross profit of $25(131 - p)^2$? This is where, in real life, the psychology of the situation enters. Clearly he will not do so if F exceeds $25(131 - p)^2$. But suppose F is \$1 less than $25(131 - p)^2$. Would he accept the offer then, to make a net profit of \$1? Will he accept only if F is at least \$1000 less than $25(131 - p)^2$, so that he makes a net \$1000? How much net profit must the manufacturer leave on the table for the retailer, to induce him to accept the offer?

This is a hard question. It has to do with the retailer's next best profit opportunity as well as his psychology; would he spurn a profitable offer net of his opportunity cost, if he thought he was being exploited by the manufacturer? There is no way that we can resolve these issues and, in any event, we're exploring a model and not making a real-life recommendation (at least, not yet). So in what follows, I'll make the modeling assumption that the retailer will accept the offer as long as F leaves him with a net profit of at least \$1000. That is, F must be less than $25(131 - p)^2 - 1000$, to induce the retailer to say yes.

But if, as we assume, the manufacturer knows this \$1000 figure and, as we also assume, the manufacturer is able to calculate that, facing a wholesale price of p, the retailer's gross profit would be $25(131 - p)^2$, *then* the manufacturer has no reason to make F any less than $25(131 - p)^2 - 1000$. Why leave the retailer more net profit than is necessary to induce him to say Yes?

So, assume that, if the manufacturer sets a wholesale price of p, she will set $F = 25(131 - p)^2 - 1000$. And then her net profit will be

The fixed-fee F +

[the per-unit price p less her marginal cost] $\times$ [the quantity she sells]

which, replacing the words by symbols, is

$$25(131 - p)^2 - 1000 \quad + \quad [p - 11] \times [50(131 - p)].$$

What value of p maximizes this net profit?[6] First, we simplify the expression:

$25(131 - p)^2 - 1000 + (p - 11)50(131 - p) =$

$\quad (25)(131)^2 - 50(131)p + 25p^2 - 1000 + 50(131)p - 50p^2 - 11(50)(131) + 11(50)p =$

$\quad [(25)(131)^2 - 1000 - 11(50)(131)] + [11(50) + 50(131) - 50(131)]p + [25 - 50]p^2 =$

$\quad [\text{some contant}] + 5500p - 25p^2.$

Take the derivative of this expression with respect to p and set it equal to 0: You get $5500 - 50p = 0$, or $p = 11$. So grinding through the math says: The manufacturer should set the per-unit price at $p = 11$, *which is her marginal cost of production*, and set the fixed fee at $25(131 - 11)^2 - 1000 = \$360,000 - \$1000$, or *$1000 less than the profit she would make if (1) she sold directly to the public and (2) her cost of retailing was the same as the retailers (namely $0)*. Moreover, the number of cars the retailer buys from her to resell is $50(131 - 11) = 6000$, or *as many cars as she would choose to sell to the public, if 1 and 2 in the previous sentence held.*

And, if you think about it, this makes perfect sense. The total profit to be shared between the retailer and the manufacturer is the total revenue from the sale of whatever cars are made, less the manufacturing cost of making those cars. Any money that changes hands between the retailer and the manufacturer has zero net effect on this sum. Of course, this is true if the retailer is doing the retailing, since he has $0 cost of retailing (in this model).

Moreover, the manufacturer is going to structure the deal so that the retailer gets a fixed $1000. So the manufacturer wants to set things up so that the retailer, once he accepts the offer, chooses to buy the number of cars x that maximizes total retail revenue less total manufacturing costs. We know that this is $x = 6000$. And we know how the manufacturer can induce the retailer to make this choice: By choosing $p = 11$, $11 becomes the retailer's marginal costs of operation, and the retailer will set his MC of $11 to the retail marginal revenue, getting $x = 6000$, creating the biggest pie possible for the two to split, and (we are assuming) settling for his slice of $1000.

The manufacturer, in other words, can have his cake (oops, shift in metaphor from pie to cake) and eat it too, or eat all but $1000, which is not bad for taking advantage of the retailer's cost advantage in the act of retailing the cars.

---

[6] In all previous exercises where we employed calculus to find the profit-maximizing price and quantity, we worked with quantity as the driving variable, which allowed us to use the MR = MC mantra. We are about to use price as the driving variable, expressing profit as a function of p, taking the derivative with respect to p, and setting it equal to zero. You might want to think though how we would formulate and solve this problem, if we followed our former pattern of working in x instead of p.

Multiple (Monopoly) Retailers

To take this simple model a step closer to Porsche (but not Tesla), imagine that the manufacturer deals with not one retailer but several, where the retailers *do not compete*. Each one has his own territory and his own downward-sloping (inverse) demand function. In terms of the Porsche story, think of a situation in which there is one retailer in Los Angeles, one in San Francisco, and one in San Diego, and even the trek from LA to San Diego (or vice versa) is too far for a customer. (But the three dealers can and do trade stock among themselves).

We'll model this as follows. In the first market, retail inverse demand is $P_1(x_1) = 131 - x_1/100$. In the second, it is $P_2(x_2) = 151 - x_2/50$. And in the third, it is $P_3(x_3) = 171 - x_3/200$. [7] In each of the markets, we'll assume that the marginal costs of retailing by the retailer are zero, while the marginal cost of retailing for the manufacturer is $30 in the first market, $20 in the second, and $50 in the third. The marginal cost of manufacturing the cars remains a constant $11.

We want to repeat our earlier analysis in this situation, which means finding the best price p for the manufacturer to charge the retailers, compared to what happens if the manufacturer sells directly to the public, compared to what happens if the manufacturer can charge the retailers a franchise fee plus a per-unit cost.

But as we do this, we must be careful regarding three issues:

1. If the manufacturer works with retailers, can she charge retailer #1 a different per-unit price than she charges #2 and/or #3? Since we are trying to mimic as much as possible in this simple model the car-retailing context, we should be guided by that and, I think, there is no clear answer to this question. On the one hand, dealers in real life do trade stock. But they must barter stock: A dealer is not allowed to sell a car it gets from the manufacturer to another dealer. [8] That would argue for allowing different per-unit prices. But there are only a few dealers and the economics of relationships might well kick in: If the per-unit price for the LA dealer is lower than the price for the San Francisco dealer, the dealer in LA might do the selling and paperwork for a sale booked from San Francisco, expecting a quid pro quo in the form of, say, a favorable trade of stock. So I'll be agnostic on this point and solve the model under both assumptions: Case 1A will be where per-unit prices can

---

[7] The third market is LA, with the largest demand and also some consumers who are willing to pay huge prices for their Porsches. Note that the size of the market is, more or less, determined by the denominator of the x term, while the price-line intercept tells you how much the first consumer will pay for a Porsche. The second market is San Francisco—smallest volume-wise, but still some customers willing to pay huge prices, although not as huge as in LA. And the first market—medium size and the smallest price intercept, is San Diego.

[8] More precisely, it *can* sell a car to another dealer: It can sell its cars to anyone it wants. But a sale entails the imposition of sales taxes and registration fees. Stock trading is permitted without such expensive transaction costs.

be different; case 1B will be where the per-unit or wholesale prices must be the same.

2. Can the manufacturer sustain different retail prices in the three markets? (For that matter, can the three retailers?) The sense of the model—that these are three distinct markets each served by a single seller—suggests that we should allow this in the model.[9]

3. When we examine what happens if the manufacturer uses a fixed fee plus a per-unit price, should she be allowed to charge different fixed fees to the different retailers? I think the answer here is a definite Yes. I expect that the franchise fee for a dealership in west LA would, because of the opportunity this represents, be higher than the franchise fee charged in some smaller and less affluent market. Of course, my "expectations" in this regard are not dispositive; I'd probably need to talk to people in the industry, to see which assumption is reasonable. But, for current purposes, this is what I'll assume.

And with this, the results are presented in Table 9.1.

The derivations of Cases 1A and 2 follow precisely the schemes employed in our analysis of a single market. Case 1B is a bit different, in that you must find one price for all three markets at once. This can be done analytically, using the techniques used in Chapter 8 for Malvino Bakery, but employing Excel and Solver may be quicker in this instance. Case 3 is as before, and the intuition is the same: The manufacturer sets the per unit price at $11, her marginal cost, to induce the retailers to choose the sales volume that maximizes the size of the total pie. Her franchise fee for each is just their gross profits (the whole pie), less the $1000 slice that she is constrained to leave to them. Note that the issue of whether she can charge a different per-unit price doesn't arise in this case: If she can "personalize" the franchise fee to each, even if she could charge different per-unit prices, she wouldn't want to: She wants to charge each of them her marginal cost as their per-unit price, for the reasons just given.

9.2. Back to the Real World of Tesla and Porsche

Does this very simple model tell us anything of value concerning Tesla and Porsche?

While the model is extremely simple, I believe that the phenomenon that it illustrates, double marginalization, is what is driving Tesla's desire to sell its vehicles directly and what motivated Porsche, years ago. Two factors, one general and one specific to the cases of Tesla and Porsche, point to the cost of double-marginalization being relatively high for those two manufacturers:

---

[9]   A richer model in which the markets were somewhat linked would be a next step in modeling this context, but it is step that is a bit too complex for this book.

	Market 1	Market 2	Market 3	Totals
Data				
Retail demand intercept	131	151	171	
Retail demand slope	−1/100	−1/50	−1/200	
Manufacturer's cost of retailing	30	20	50	

Case 1A: Manufacturer sells to retailers who resell, wholesale prices can differ

	Market 1	Market 2	Market 3	Totals
Wholesale prices	$71	$81	$91	
Retail prices	$101	$116	$131	
Volume of sales	3000	3500	8000	14,000
Manufacturer's profit	$180,000	$245,000	$640,000	$1,065,000
Retailer's profit	$90,000	$122,500	$320,000	$532,500

Case 1B: Manufacturer sells to retailers who resell, wholesale prices must be same

	Market 1	Market 2	Market 3	Totals
Wholesale prices	$83.857	$83.857	$83.857	
Retail prices	$107.429	$117.429	$127.429	
Volume of sales	2357.15	1678.575	8714.300	12,750.03
Manufacturer's profit	$151,735	$122,296	$634,898	$928,929
Retailer's profit	$55,562	$56,352	$379,695	$491,609

Case 2: Manufacturer sells directly to the public (different retail prices allowed)

	Market 1	Market 2	Market 3	Totals
Retail prices	$86	$91	$116	
Volume of sales	4500	3000	11,000	18,500
Manufacturer's profit	$405,000	$3600	$1,210,000	$1,975,000
Retailer's profit	$0	$0	$0	$0

Case 3: Manufacturer uses retailers, sets a franchise fee plus a per-unit wholesale price

	Market 1	Market 2	Market 3	Totals
Franchise fee	$719,000	$489,000	$2,559,000	
Wholesale per-unit	$11	$11	$11	
Retail prices	$71	$81	$91	
Volume of sales	12,000	7000	32,000	51,000
Manufacturer's profit	$719,000	$489,000	$2,559,000	$3,767,000
Retailer's profit	$1000	$1000	$1000	$3,000

Table 9.1. Alternatives with three different markets.

• Information gleaned from the internet has greatly leveled the bargaining playing field when it comes to a new car purchase. Hence, the general advantage of having a dealer try to extract as much as possible from a particular buyer—something that would be harder to do with direct sales—is reduced, relative to times past. And the internet has also diminished advantages that local dealers once had in the used-vehicle markets. (Think of these two factors as decreasing the sales-cost advantage that an independent retailer would have vis-à-vis the manufacturer.)

- Both Teslas and Porsches are the sorts of cars that "sell themselves." These vehicles inhabit niches in which there are few (if any) competitors. This means that demand for these vehicles tends to the more inelastic side of the spectrum and, while it is a further modeling exercise that I will not provide here, this exacerbates the costs to the manufacturer of going through a retailer. It certainly means that the salesperson has less of a selling job to do: someone who walks into a Porsche or Tesla showroom is likely to be more "decided" that this is the car he or she wants than the corresponding customer walking into a Toyota showroom. Again, the relative retailing disadvantage to direct sales is less, making the costs of double marginalization relatively higher.

What about the argument put forward by the auto dealership group in Michigan, that having independent dealers fosters competition, which is good for the consumer, compared to the "monopolist" model of direct retailing? On its face, this argument is silly: The dealers have to deal in the first instance with a monopolist manufacturer, which sets the price they face. That said, it is interesting to think about the impact of multiple competing dealers on our model. To model this requires tools that we do not have yet, so I'll simply assert: If the dealers have no market power—if they are competitive—the costs to the manufacturer of double-marginalization go away. (You'll have the tools to reach this conclusion after finishing Part IV.) But there are at least three reasons to believe that dealerships have and exercise market power (which means, there are positive costs of double-marginalization):

1. Even if dealers competed fiercely, because they are geographically dispersed, each probably retains some market power. This is, presumably, more so the smaller the volume of sales of the vehicles and (hence) the fewer the number of dealerships in any broad geographical region, a condition that pertains to Tesla and Porsche.

2. And I doubt that the dealerships in a particular geographical region compete fiercely with one another. For one thing, many dealerships are "joined" through corporate ownership. And even if they were not joined in this fashion, dealers have an obvious desire to engage in *collective* competitive restraint. Moreover, they have good reasons to cooperate on things like stock trading, to get a customer just the right car with the right optional equipment and color. This sort of cooperation gives dealerships a hammer with which to discipline a dealership that competes fiercely. As long as dealerships can identify rivals who are chasing sales with very low prices—and asking customers, "What price is X offering?" provides that information— the conditions for restrained competition in the fashion of Chapter 3 are met.

3. Finally, the dealerships fought Porsche fiercely, and they are fighting Tesla

just as hard, if not harder. Presumably they wouldn't be so concerned if competition among them meant that there wasn't much treasure to be guarded. They fight because the current arrangement suits them—they are getting a good-sized slice of the pie. And the only way they can do this, under current institutional arrangements, is by marking up the price they are charged, when they sell to a retail customer. The auto manufacturers cannot be happy with that.

Why Not Charge a "Dealership" or "Franchise" Fee?

Why don't automobile manufacturers, insofar as they recognize the problem of double marginalization, resort to charging their dealers a fixed franchise fee and then sell their vehicles wholesale at marginal cost?

1. To a small extent, they do charge a "franchise fee," insofar as dealerships are required to contribute to regional advertising budgets. But this is pretty small potatoes.

2. For existing dealership arrangements, manufacturers presumably are barred from doing this by the laws that say that franchise relationships cannot be changed except by mutual consent. Note that this isn't completely dispositive: Go back to our original formulation of the model. The manufacturer probably won't get the retailer to agree to a franchise fee that leaves him with $1000 in profit, since under existing conditions the retailer makes $90,000. But what if the franchise fee is set to leave the retailer with, say, $100,000. That is, the franchise fee F is set to be $260,000, and the per-car cost to the retailer is set at $11. The retailer will happily sign that contract, marking up the price of cars to $71, making a gross $360,000 and so a net $100,000, better than before. And the manufacturer gets no profit out of the sale of her cars (the wholesale price is the marginal cost of manufacture), but she does pocket the franchise fee of $260,000, which is $80,000 better than the $180,000 she is making out of current arrangements.

   The point is that double marginalization not only reduces the slice of profit that the manufacturer receives, but it reduces the size of the entire pie that is split between manufacturer and retailer. By setting the per-unit price to the retailer at $11, the size of the pie increases by $90,000, and so there ought to be some mutually agreeable arrangement for the two parties that gets them there. (But keep reading.)

   It is pure speculation, but Porsche may have decided not to propose such an arrangement because (they felt) this was more blatantly a change in the relationship they had with dealers, hence would present a weaker legal case. As for Tesla, at least for now, they seem to be going for direct marketing or nothing, presumably feeling that the dealerships add little to the marketing of Tesla cars.

3. Our simple model presumes that the retail demand function is certain and known to retailer and manufacturer alike. But, in real life, the demand for cars over a period of, say, a year is quite uncertain. Many exogenous factors impinge, such as the state of the national economy. And local factors affect local dealers. For instance, I expect that the period 1998–2000 was remarkably profitable for the Porsche dealership in Silicon Valley, as the dot-com revolution led to exploding wealth in the region, but that, in 2001, the Porsche dealership in the area did a good deal less business.

The point is that, if Porsche were to charge a fixed yearly up-front fee, dealers would carry almost all the risks in year-end profits. This takes us into material that is not covered until Chapters 18 and 19 but, in short, it is likely that the dealerships would require compensation to carry all this risk; a better (more efficient) risk-sharing arrangement would be for the manufacturer to bear at least some of the risks. We might imagine fancier schemes, where the size of the fixed fee a dealer owes the manufacturer at the end of the year is tied to the state of the national and local economies, but such schemes are hard to administer. The one thing the manufacturer cannot do is to tie the fixed fee to the dealer's actual annual profit; the fixed fee and per-unit charge scheme works precisely because the dealer's marginal cost is set equal to the manufacturer's marginal cost. Tying the fixed fee to the actual dealer's profit destroys this.

Why Do Laws to Protect Franchisees Exist?
And Why Was GM in Favor of the Law, in Michigan?

Before leaving the cases of Tesla and Porsche, two final comments about this story are worth making. Both companies are being impeded by laws put on the books that protect dealerships and other franchisees. Why are these laws on the books?

In part, this is a matter of pure interest-group politics. Franchisees are an easily organized group; they are easy to find and very concerned with laws affecting their economic status. And, as small- to medium-size business owners, the owners of franchises are the sort of interest group that can have substantial influence, through contributions they make, on local legislators.

But there is more to the story than this, and it goes back to some concepts and frameworks from Part I of the book. Most franchisees, when they establish their franchise, incur substantial sunk costs. Car dealers invest in lavish showrooms and repair facilities. Fast food franchisees often invest in their facility. These costs are not entirely sunk—the franchisee can recoup some of his or her investment—but the amount recovered is far from $1 recouped for each $1 invested, let alone $1 plus some reasonable return.

If a franchiser could freely change the terms of the franchise agreement, this would put the franchisee in danger of being held up, just as in the fashion described in Part I: The franchisee presumably makes the initial sunk-cost investment in the expectation of a stream of profits from the franchise. If the franchiser can, say, suddenly impose a substantial fixed annual franchise fee, the initially forecast stream of profits might disappear. The franchiser may have a reputation for not doing this to protect, which may give franchisees some assurance that they won't be held up. But offering franchisees legal protection does have some economic merit, if we (as society) want those sunk-cost investments to be tenable.

Finally, why did GM offer support for the new law in Michigan? I can only speculate, but (1) GM knows that existing laws prevent it from doing direct-to-the-public retailing, and so it didn't want Tesla to have a competitive advantage, and (2) it may simply have seen this as a way to forestall a rival that, in time, might become a formidable competitor.

9.3. First-Degree Price Discrimination in the B2B setting

We can now continue the discussion of price discrimination begun last chapter by explaining *first-degree price discrimination.*

In first-degree price discrimination, each individual customer is provided with whatever take-it-or-leave-it offer makes the maximum profit for the seller, subject to being acceptable to the customer. In the case of our manufacturer selling to the retailer, this was the offer $F = \$359{,}000$ and $p = \$11$, although we could equally well phrase the offer as "You may have precisely 6000 vehicles to sell, if you pay me \$425,000 for them. Take it or leave it." The 6000 vehicles is selected as the number that makes the profit pie to be shared as large as possible; the \$425,000 is selected as the highest take-it-or-leave-it "price" for the package that the retailer will take, at least within our model. [10]

More generally, but still in a B2B (business-to-business) context, the seller of the good considers the buyer and computes, "For each quantity x of the good I might provide to the buyer, how much will the buyer's profit increase over his profit if I refuse to sell to him?" Let $IP(x)$ denote this incremental profit. "And if I offer him a take-it-or-leave-it offer of x units for some amount of money, what is the largest amount $R(x)$ I can demand to which he will acquiesce?" Presumably, this amount $R(x)$ is no larger than $IP(x)$, but if we imagine that the buyer is guided solely by profit maximization and not by the emotions he will feel concerning such an exploitative offer, and if we further imagine that the seller can convince the buyer that there is no room to negotiate (both of which are highly suspect assumptions), then presumably $R(x)$ is just a bit less than

---

[10] If the retailer has precisely 6000 cars to sell, he puts the price at \$71, that being $P(6000) = 131 - 6000/100$. This means his revenue is $\$71 \cdot 6000 = \$426{,}000$. He'll take the offer, we are assuming, if it leaves him with \$1000 net, so he'll take it if the fee to him for the 6000 cars is \$425,000.

$IP(x)$. The offer made to this buyer, then, is the amount x that maximizes the seller's total profit: If the seller has, say, ten customers of this sort, the seller will maximize

$$R_1(x_1) + R_2(x_2) + \ldots R_{10}(x_{10}) - \text{TC}(x_1 + \ldots + x_{10}),$$

where R_i is the R function for customer #i, and x_i is the amount in the take-it-or-leave-it offer to customer #i. Of course, in terms of marginal revenues and marginal costs, these variables will be chosen so that, simultaneously, $R_i'(x_i) = \text{MC}(x_1 + \ldots + x_{10})$.

The keys to this are that (1) the seller can prevent resale between the buyers, which is generally necessary in any price-discrimination scheme, (2) sellers see themselves in a weak bargaining position, so that take-it-or-leave-it offers are credible, and (3) the seller can discern the function R_i for each of its clients.

Requirement #1 is what it is; it is more likely to hold when the good in question is a service, but even when it is a physical good, this requirement is sometimes satisfied. Requirement #2 is a matter of the psychology of bargaining. And requirement #3? This may seem unlikely, but in a B2B setting, it is not impossible, if the seller has a great deal of insight into the "books" of all its customers.[11]

That's for a B2B setting; what about B2C (Business-to-Consumer)? That is, what if the customers are consumers rather than other firms? The basic logic is unchanged, as long as, for each customer-consumer, the seller knows the biggest take-it-or-leave-it price the consumer will pay for a package of x units, for each x. That is, the seller must continue to know $R_i(x)$ for each customer i, where i is now a consumer. When customer i is a profit-maximizing firm, a good case can be made for $R_i(x)$ being close to $IP_i(x)$, the incremental profit firm i can make with x units of the good versus with none. But what is $R_i(x)$ for customers who are consumers? To answer this question, we need a detailed model of individual consumer behavior, to which we turn in Chapter 10.

Executive Summary

Multistep distribution is a fact of life in all sorts of businesses, and so the costs of double (and triple and quadruple) marginalization are also facts of life. With the rise of the internet, direct-to-the-consumer (and, in B2B settings, the business customer) distribution becomes increasingly viable and attractive. (Although we don't have the tools to deal with this, you can imagine that the competition provided to retailers by direct-to-the-public, internet marketing, will lessen the mark-ups that retailers will want to employ [by making their demand more elastic], and so will help ameliorate the costs of double-marginalization.)

---

[11] It is reversing the role of buyer and seller, but you might reconsider in this light the relationship between Toyota and its suppliers, as described in Chapter 5.

(But, on the other side, the rise of retailing giants such as Walmart and Amazon worsens the costs of distribution for manufacturing. In the model of this chapter, the manufacturer was assumed to dictate the wholesale price to the retailer. Imagine if the retailer could say: "I'm paying no franchise fee, and since your marginal cost of production is $11, I'm willing to be generous and pay you $12 per car.")

The franchise fee plus per-unit wholesale price has its problems—and it won't be until Chapters 18 and 19 that we are in a position to understand those problems—but it is well worth contemplating, the more so when a manufacturer in one country employs local retails to sell its product globally.

Problems

9.1 Redo the analysis of this chapter with the following assumptions: Retail inverse demand is $131 - x/100$. The total cost of manufacturing x units is $TC(x) = 10{,}000 + 11x + x^2/100$. If the retailer is used, his cost of retailing x units is $1000 + 10x$. If the manufacturer sells directly to consumers, her cost of retailing x units is $5000 + 30x$. To get the retailer to sign an agreement to pay a fixed fee F and a per-unit price of p, the retailer must be left with a net profit of $1000.

Part III
Bang for the Buck:
Optimization Under Constraint

10. The Utility-Maximizing Consumer

The *utility-maximizing consumer*, who chooses subject to a *budget constraint*, is the basic economic model of individual behavior. This chapter presents this model and discusses its rationale and some empirical flaws. The chapter also serves as an introduction to methods for solving optimization problems under constraints and, in particular, to the concept of *bang for the buck*.

In the models we've explored so far, the only entities making conscious choices have been firms, which choose production levels to maximize profit. But, in economics, other sorts of "actors" make choices. Preeminent among these are individuals, who choose how much to buy and consume, how much to save, how to invest those savings, where to work, how hard to work, and so forth. For a variety of purposes, including a better understanding firm behavior, we must model choices made by individuals.

This chapter introduces the model of the *utility-maximizing consumer*, which economists use for this purpose. We eventually use this model as the foundation for modeling savings and investment choices, effort choices on the job, and so forth. It would better suit the variety of applications we have in mind to call this the model of the utility-maximizing *person*, but economists use the term *consumer* instead of *person*, and we follow suit. Indeed, in this chapter, all our illustrative examples concern a consumer choosing what to eat for lunch and, in places, how much money to leave in her pocket for future purchases. So, as far as our examples are concerned, the term *consumer* is entirely appropriate. But do not be misled by this; we apply this model much more broadly in later chapters.

10.1. The Model: Utility Maximization

The model of the utility-maximizing consumer is conceptually quite simple. A set of consumption bundles are offered to the consumer, from which she must choose one. Let X denote the set of all consumption bundles that might ever be available to her. Then her problem is to choose one x from a subset A of X, where A represents the set of *available* bundles. The consumer's behavior in the face of any choice problem is modeled as follows.

> For each consumer, every bundle x in X has a numerical value $U(x)$, called her *utility* of x. When faced with the problem of choosing from the set A, the consumer chooses whichever element x of A has the highest utility (for her) among all elements x of A.

Each consumer has her own subjective utility function, reflecting her own preferences and tastes. If Consumer H likes apples more than pears, bundles with more apples and fewer pears have higher utility, *according to H's utility function*, than otherwise identical bundles with more pears and fewer apples.

For instance, imagine a world in which there are only three goods: bread, cheese, and salami. We fix units for each good, say, loaves of bread, kilos of cheese, and kilos of salami. A *bundle* of goods is an amount of bread, cheese, and salami, such as three loaves of bread, three-quarters of a kilo of cheese, and a kilo of salami. Listing bread first, cheese second, and salami third, we write this bundle compactly as the vector $(3, 0.75, 1)$. Another bundle would be $(1.5, 1, 0)$, meaning a bundle consisting of one and a half loaves of bread, a kilo of cheese, and no salami.

This can be confusing, so be careful. Do not think of x as a number, standing for a number of loaves of bread or kilos of cheese, so that the consumer chooses to fill her shopping basket with several points from X. Instead, x is a consumption *bundle*, a three-dimensional vector that describes everything in the consumer's shopping basket; and the consumer chooses a single x from X as a result of her trip to the market.

Imagine a consumer who is choosing among the following four bundles:

$$(3, 3, 2), \quad (2, 1, 6), \quad (5, 0.1, 0.1), \quad (1, 4, 0.5).$$

Imagine as well that this consumer is modeled as having the *utility function*

$$U(b, c, s) = 3\ln(b) + \ln(c) + 0.8\ln(s),$$

where b, c, and s are the levels of bread, cheese, and salami, respectively, in the bundle (b, c, s), and $\ln(\cdot)$ is the natural logarithm function. To the nearest 0.01, the utilities of the four bundles are

$$U(3, 3, 2) = 3\ln(3) + \ln(3) + 0.8\ln(2) = 4.95,$$
$$U(2, 1, 6) = 3\ln(2) + \ln(1) + 0.8\ln(6) = 3.51,$$
$$U(5, 0.1, 0.1) = 3\ln(5) + \ln(0.1) + 0.8\ln(0.1) = 0.68, \text{ and}$$
$$U(1, 4, 0.5) = 3\ln(1) + \ln(4) + 0.8\ln(0.5) = 2.67.$$

Hence, a consumer with the utility function posited will choose $(3, 3, 2)$ from among these four bundles. (If you are thinking, "Doesn't the cost of the various bundles matter?," you are thinking good thoughts. We'll get prices and the cost of different bundles shortly. But, for the time being, we'll assume that the choice is among the four bundles, without any payment required.) If the choice were among $(2, 1, 6)$, $(5, 0.1, 0.1)$, and $(1, 4, 0.5)$, then the chosen bundle would be

$(2, 1, 6)$, and so on. The point is that, once we know the utility function of the consumer, her behavior in every choice situation is clear: Her choice behavior is completely described by (1) her utility function and (2) the assertion that she always picks whichever bundle ranks most highly (among those bundles that are available to her) according to that utility function.

Comments on the Basic Model

1. The essence of the model is that each consumer has a single utility function that works for all subsets A from which the consumer might choose. We do not allow the consumer's utility function to change depending on the range of choices available to her; if we did, the model would have no content. We'll get back to this shortly.

2. In some cases, more than one bundle in the set of bundles on offer may have the highest utility. In this case, we imagine that the consumer is happy to take any one of the bundles that have highest utility, without a further care about which of those bundles she gets. When two bundles give the same utility so that, according to the model, the consumer does not care which bundle she gets, we say she is *indifferent* between the two bundles.

3. The numerical utility function is not what matters, but rather the order this function establishes among bundles. Suppose we took three other consumers, whose utility functions are

$$V_1(b, c, s) = 6 \ln(b) + 2 \ln(c) + 1.6 \ln(s) + 2701,$$
$$V_2(b, c, s) = [3 \ln(b) + \ln(s) + 0.8 \ln(s)]^3, \text{ and}$$
$$V_3(b, c, s) = b^3 c s^{0.8}.$$

These functions establish exactly the same order among bundles as U, in the sense that, for any two bundles (b, c, s) and $(b', c's')$,

$$U(b, c, s) \geq U(b', c', s') \text{ if and only if } V_i(b, c, s) \geq V_i(b', c', s'),$$

for $i = 1$, 2, or 3. (Depending on the amount of math you know, you may need to take my word for this.) Therefore, these three consumers' choices in any situation would be exactly the same as that of our original consumer. Put somewhat differently, in terms of our model of consumer choice behavior, it does not matter whether we think of our original consumer having the utility function U or one of the three V_i functions.

4. This is not to say that every utility function gives the same choice behavior, of course. Two utility functions that establish different orders over consumption bundles lead to different choice behaviors. For example, a consumer

whose utility function is $V(b, c, s) = b + c + s$ would choose the bundle (2,1,6) from among the four we are considering, rather than (3,3,2), and someone with utility function $W(b, c, s) = 3b + c + s$ would choose (5,0.1,0.1). (Be sure you understand these two assertions.) Different consumers may order bundles differently and therefore make different choices, at least in some situations.

5. With respect to the particular utility function $U(b, c, s) = 3\ln(b) + \ln(c) + 0.8\ln(s)$, note that $\ln(x) < 0$, for $x < 1$. Hence, $U(0.5, 0.5, 0.5) = 3\ln(0.5) + \ln(0.5) + 0.8\ln(0.5) = -3.327 < 0$. Does this mean that half a loaf of bread, half a kilo of cheese, and half a kilo of salami is worse than nothing at all?

   It absolutely *does not* mean that. The numerical quantities of utility have no particular meaning, and this is as true for the number 0 as it is for any other number. Thinking of 0 utility as being the utility of "nothing at all" makes as much sense as it does to think of 0° C or 0° F as meaning "no temperature at all." Presumably, you think that more bread or cheese or more salami is better than less. That is, if (b, c, s) is one bundle and (b', c', s') is another and if $b > b'$, $c > c'$, and $s > s'$, then you expect (b, c, s) to be higher in utility than (b', c', s'). Sure enough, since the natural logarithm function is increasing, that is the case; at least for the function $U(b, c, s) = 3\ln(b) + \ln(c) + 0.8\ln(s)$.

6. A problem with the utility function $U(b, c, s) = 3\ln(b) + \ln(c) + 0.8\ln(s)$ concerns bundles where one or more of the quantities b, c, or s is 0. Look, for instance, at a bundle $(10, 10, 0)$, or 10 loaves of bread, 10 kilos of cheese, and no salami. Because $\ln(0) = -\infty$, $U(10, 10, 0) = -\infty$. What do we make of this, in terms of our consumer?

   A consumer whose utility function $U(b, c, s)$ is $3\ln(b) + \ln(c) + 0.8\ln(s)$ needs positive quantities of each of the three goods; she cannot make do with none of any one. Any positive amount, however small, of all three is better than any bundle of goods that has none of one or more of the three commodities. You may decide that this is a silly utility function; that consumers can usually stand to be without salami and would willingly choose, say, (100, 100, 0) over (0.001, 0.001, 0.001). But this is just saying that you do not find the particular utility function $U(b, c, s) = 3\ln(b) + \ln(c) + 0.8\ln(s)$ to be very believable; you want instead a function where $U(100, 100, 0) > U(0.001, 0.001, 0.001)$. For instance, the function $W(b, c, s) = 3\ln(b) + \ln(c + 3) + 0.8\ln(s + 5)$ describes a consumer who must have some positive amount of bread—any consumption bundle (b, c, s) where $b = 0$ gives utility $-\infty$— but who will survive quite nicely without any cheese or salami: For this utility function $W(100, 100, 0) = 3\ln(100) + \ln(103) + 0.8\ln(5) = 19.738$, while $W(0.001, 0.001, 0.001) = 3\ln(0.001) + \ln(3.001) + 0.8\ln(5.001) = -18.337$.

10.2. What's the Content of This Model?

That's the model. Most of the remainder of this chapter is devoted to working with the model algebraically and graphically and to connecting it to demand functions. But before getting to this, I want to address two questions:

1. Why would anyone put any credence in this model?

2. What, if anything, does this model preclude in terms of consumer behavior?

These two questions are closely connected: On the one hand, if no behavior is precluded by this model, then giving the model credence *as a model* is no problem at all, since it is *tautological*. You can anticipate that this can't be true; no one, not even an economist, would devote a chapter to a model that is tautological. But, then, exactly what behavior is precluded, and is it sensible to think that such behavior ought to be precluded by what is in fact the central model of individual behavior in all of microeconomics?

If your objective is only to be able to "do the problems and pass the test," you can skip ahead to Section 10.3. But, at some point, you should confront these dual questions and the answers that economists give to them as, in many ways, the essence of economic thinking is captured by the answers.

What Behavior is Precluded?

Essentially, what this model precludes is the protagonist's behavior in the short cartoon in Figure 10.1.

Figure 10.1. What the utility-maximizing consumer model precludes.

A gentleman seeking a slice of pie and a cup of coffee, when given a choice between apple and peach pie, chooses apple pie. But when told that the choice is, in fact, between apple, peach, and banana cream, he chooses peach. This is inconsistent with the utility-maximization model because, if he chooses apple when apple and peach are available, his utility for apple pie must be at least as great as his utility for peach pie. If banana cream is added to what is feasible for him, he could choose this new option, if its utility (for him) exceeds that of apple. But his first choice reveals that he places as much utility on apple pie as on peach, so introducing the third option cannot result in him strictly preferring peach.[1]

The answer to the question, What is precluded?, goes back to comment 1 on page 221: *The essence of the model is that each consumer has a single utility function that works for all subsets from which the consumer (she) might choose.* Imagine an individual who is asked to choose from various sets of objects she is offered, sets that are subsets of some larger set X of all conceivable choices she might make. Imagine we ask the consumer, From every subset A of X, what do you choose? Consider the following two properties of her choices:

- From any finite subset A of X, the consumer is ready to make a choice. She might say that several elements of A are tied for best and she is willing to have any one of those, but she is never so flummoxed by the situation that she freezes with indecision.

- Suppose x and y are two bundles in some set of bundles A, and the consumer says she is willing to have x out of A. Then, for any other set of bundles B that contains both x and y, if the consumer is willing to take y out of B, she must be happy to take x as well.

The first of these should present no problem. But the second takes a bit of thought. It is the second, of course, that our cartoon character is violating.

The point is that, up to some technical conditions that would interest only a Ph.D. student, these two properties are what it takes: Any consumer whose choice behavior obeys these two rules chooses *as if* she were maximizing some utility function. That is a mathematical result that I do not expect you to see through—the proof isn't easy and, in fact, some technical problems must be dealt with that do not change the economic intuition at all—so you have to take my word for it.[2]

But looks can be deceiving. In particular, the second property says, in as many words, that the consumer cannot be tricked by how a set of options is

---

[1] Well, *cannot* here is not entirely correct. Perhaps there is information that he lacks about the relative merits of apple and peach pie as provided by this cafe, information that is revealed to him when he learns that they have banana cream. For instance, suppose there is much more skill required to make a good peach pie than apple, and he doubts that the baker at this cafe has the requisite skill. But, if the baker can produce banana cream, his doubts are eased. Such clever rationalizations of just about any behavior can be produced. But we assume away such elaborated stories concerning things like information provided by the feasible set.

[2] If you do not want to take my word for it, see Chapter 1 in David M. Kreps, *Microeconomic Foundations I: Choice and Competitive Markets*, Princeton University Press, 2013.

framed. She knows what she likes—how she ranks the options she might have— and her relative likes and dislikes are not affected by the set of objects from which she is allowed to choose.

Designers of websites believe that context matters to real consumers. When designing a particular webpage that they hope will inspire a viewer to purchase, say, a particular item, they put two versions of the item on the same page. Version 1 is a standard model, with a price of, say, $40. Version 2 is a very slightly enhanced model, with a price of $60. The web designer wants to sell the first version; the purpose of the very steeply priced version 2 is to try to convince the prospective buyer that version 1 is a bargain. Or the designer may put on the page with the $40 model a very much inferior model at a price of, say, $35. Again, the idea is to convince the buyer that the $40 model is a good deal. This sort of stuff works, and to the extent that it does, it constitutes a violation of the second property.

More generally, a lot of advertising attempts to frame items in ways that cause consumers to change their purchase behavior, something that the standard economic model of the utility-maximizing consumer rules out. We observe violations of the standard model in the real world that are systematic enough that people make sizeable incomes creating violations that benefit sellers of goods. And, in other contexts, especially where time is involved and choices are dynamic, we observe other sorts of violations.

Notwithstanding this, economic models are almost invariably populated by utility-maximizing consumers. As with the profit-maximizing firm, this is done with one of two rationales in mind: The violations that occur are not sufficiently important empirically to worry about; or, in terms of the conclusions drawn, those violations we do see have insignificant impact. The best attitude to have is one of informed skepticism. Studying consumer marketing, especially those pieces that rely on social and cognitive psychology, will alert you to egregious and systematic violations. But, as long as you are alert to those violations, the economic model is still useful.

10.3. The Consumer's Problem, and Equating Bangs for the Buck

The most often-used context in which utility-maximizing consumers appear in economics is the so-called *consumer's problem*:

- The object being chosen is a consumption bundle, which is a vector listing amounts of various commodities. That is, a commodity bundle is a vector $(x_1, x_2, \ldots, x_k)$, where k is the number of commodities, representing x_1 units of the first commodity, x_2 units of the second commodity, and so on, to x_k units of the kth commodity. You can continue to think in terms of $k = 3$, with the three commodities being bread (in loaves), cheese (in kilos), and salami (in kilos), although keep in the back of your mind that the story is meant for much more general situations.

- Each commodity has a market price; p_j denotes the market price of the jth good on the list, measured in dollars per unit of the jth good. Imagine, for example, that bread costs $1.60 per loaf, cheese is $5.00 per kilo, and salami is $8.00 per kilo. Then, $p_1 = \$1.60$, $p_2 = \$5.00$, and $p_3 = \$8.00$.

- The consumer has an amount of wealth she can spend on her consumption bundle. In the abstract, we denote this amount of money by the variable y. But you can think, concretely, about our consumer having $120 to spend.

The consumer's problem is to purchase the best bundle she can afford. She can afford any bundle $(x_1, x_2, \ldots, x_k)$ whose total cost is less than her wealth y. We assume that her purchase activities have no impact on the prices of commodities—these stay fixed at the levels p_1, p_2, and so on—so that the total cost to her of the bundle $(x_1, x_2, \ldots, x_k)$ is $p_1 x_1 + p_2 x_2 + \ldots + p_k x_k$. Therefore, she can afford any bundle $(x_1, x_2, \ldots, x_k)$ that satisfies her *budget constraint*

$$p_1 x_1 + p_2 x_2 + \ldots + p_k x_k \leq y.$$

In our example, she can spend all her $120 on bread, which will give her 75 loaves of bread, no cheese, and no salami, or the bundle $(75, 0, 0)$. Or she can spend all her money on cheese, getting 24 kilos of cheese, no bread, and no salami, or the bundle $(0, 24, 0)$. Or she can spend all her money on salami, getting 15 kilos of salami, no bread, and no cheese, the bundle $(0, 0, 15)$. These are the extreme purchases she might make. But she can also, for example, purchase 35 loaves of bread, 6 kilos of cheese, and 4.25 kilos of salami. This will cost her $\$1.60 \times 35 + \$5 \times 6 + \$8 \times 4.25 = \$56 + \$30 + \$34 = \$120$, or precisely what she has to spend.

She can, if she wishes, spend less than all her money. That is, one of the bundles she can afford is the bundle $(30, 5, 4)$, or 30 loaves of bread (total cost $48), 5 kilos of cheese (total cost $25), and 4 kilos of salami (total cost $32), for a total expenditure of $48 + $25 + $32 = $105. If this turns out to be best for her, then this is what she will buy.

How is "best" to be judged? By the consumer's utility function U, whose arguments are consumption bundles $(x_1, x_2, \ldots, x_k)$ and whose values are numbers. So, to summarize, the *consumer's problem* is to

$$\text{maximize } U(x_1, x_2, \ldots, x_k), \quad \text{subject to } p_1 x_1 + p_2 x_2 + \ldots + p_k x_k \leq y.$$

One thing must be added: We assume that the amounts of the commodities consumed must be nonnegative. That is, the constraints $x_i \geq 0$ are assumed to hold as well.

Using Calculus to Solve This Problem: Bangs for the Buck

The consumer's problem is a relatively simple constrained-maximization problem. Starting on page 135, we discussed the solution of constrained-maximization problems, and the techniques discussed there will work here, *if* there are only two commodities. But with three or more commodities, those techniques are inadequate. To solve the consumer's problem, we need something a bit more robust.

To enlist calculus, we assume that the utility function U is differentiable in all k arguments, and we write $\mathrm{MU}_i(x)$ for the marginal utility of good i, evaluated at the bundle x. That is,

$$\mathrm{MU}_i(x) = \left.\frac{\partial U}{\partial x_i}\right|_x.$$

And we define, for each commodity i, a new function, the *bang for the buck of commodity i*, evaluated at the bundle x and the price vector p, by

$$\mathrm{BfB}_i(x) = \frac{\mathrm{MU}_i(x)}{p_i}.$$

Mathematical facts. *Suppose prices are given by strictly positive vector p and the consumer has y to spend. Suppose the consumer is seeking to maximize her utility of consumption $u(x_1, \ldots, x_k)$ subject to her budget constraint $p_1 x_1 + \ldots + p_k x_k \leq y$ and to nonnegativity constraints $x_i \geq 0$ for $i = 1, \ldots, k$.*

a.   *A consumption bundle $x^0 = (x_1^0, \ldots, x_k^0)$ (where each $x_i^0 \geq 0$) such that $p_1 x_1^0 + \ldots + p_k x_k^0 < y$ is **not** a solution to this problem if, for any i, $\mathrm{MU}_i(x^0) > 0$ or $\mathrm{MU}_i(x^0)x_i^0 < 0$.*

b.   *A consumption bundle $x^0 = (x_1^0, \ldots, x_k^0)$ (where each $x_i^0 \geq 0$) such that $p_1 x_1^0 + \ldots + p_k x_k^0 = y$ is **not** a solution to this problem if, for any i such that $x_i^0 > 0$ and for any other j, $\mathrm{BfB}_j(x^0) > \mathrm{BfB}_i(x^0)$.*

c.   *If the function U is **concave**, then a consumption bundle x^0 that passes the tests posed in a and b just above **is** a solution to the consumer's problem.*

That is quite a mouthful, but it is much less complex than it may seem at first. To begin, let me translate and then dispose of part a. This says that, if a consumer is not spending all her money, then the marginal utility of each good must be zero or negative, and it can only be negative if the amount of the good being consumed is zero. Reason: Because the consumer has money left over to spend, if any good had positive marginal utility, she'd improve her utility by buying a bit more of it. And if some good had (strictly) negative marginal utility, she'd be better off consuming less of it, which she'd be able to do if she were consuming a strictly positive amount of it. That's the translation. And to dispose of part a: in almost all problems we'll look at, the function u will be strictly increasing in each argument, so that consuming more is better for the consumer than consuming less. That may not be a fact of life in all cases—think of consuming, say, kilos and kilos of cotton candy—but with a few exceptions that we'll note when the time comes, we'll avoid such cases. And, then, $MU_i(x) > 0$ for all i, hence the consumer will *always* be spending all her income. So only part b (and part c) are relevant.

(The obvious objection to this is that consumers rarely spend all their money on a trip to the grocery store. We'll deal with this in just a bit.)

To translate part b: *For x^0 to be a solution to the consumer's problem, it must be that, at x^0, the bang for the buck of every commodity on which she spends money is at least as large as the bang for the buck of any other commodity.* Since this must hold for every commodity on which she spends money, it implies that *the bang for the buck of every commodity on which she spends money must (i) **equal** the bang for the buck of any other commodity on which she spends money and (ii) be at least as large as the bang for the buck of any commodity on which she spends zero.* And, part c: *Moreover, if u is a concave function, the condition just italicized is not only necessary for x^0 to solve the consumer's problem, but sufficient as well.*

A Simple Example, and One a Degree More Complex

To see this in action, go back to our consumer with utility function for bread (in loaves), cheese (in kilos), and salami (in kilos) given by

$$U(b, c, s) = 3\ln(b) + \ln(c) + 0.8\ln(s).$$

Suppose this consumer has \$120 to spend, and the prices of the three goods are \$1.60 per loaf of bread, \$5 per kilo of cheese, and \$8 per kilo of salami.

The three marginal utility functions for this consumer are

$$MU_b = \frac{3}{b}, \quad MU_c = \frac{1}{c}, \quad \text{and} \quad MU_s = \frac{0.8}{s}.$$

Hence the three bang-for-the-buck functions are

$$BfB_b = \frac{3}{1.6b}, \quad BfB_c = \frac{1}{5c}, \quad \text{and} \quad BfB_s = \frac{0.8}{8s} = \frac{1}{10s}.$$

If we suppose that, at the solution to her problem of maximizing utility, the consumer will buy strictly positive amounts on each of the three goods—and because of properties of the log function at and near zero, we know this will happen—rule b says that, at the solution, these three BfBs must be equal, or

$$\frac{3}{1.6b} = \frac{1}{5c} = \frac{1}{10s}.$$

Flipping these three fractions, this means that, at the solution, $1.6b/3 = 5c = 10s$. We also have the budget constraint:

$$1.6b + 5c + 8s = 120.$$

But if $1.6b/3 = 5c$, then $1.6b = 15c$. So in the budget constraint, you can replace $1.6b$ with $15c$. And if $5c = 10s$, then $4c = 8s$, so you can replace $8s$ with $4c$. Hence, the budget constraint is

$$1.6b + 5c + 8s = 15c + 5c + 4c = 24c = 120,$$

which means $c = 5$. And from there, we can solve for $b = 15c/1.6 = (15 \times 5)/1.6 = 46.875$ and $s = 5c/10 = 25/10 = 2.5$. That's the answer.

(It is a good idea to check such answers: Her expenditure is $46.875 \times \$1.60 + 5 \times \$5 + 2.5 \times \$8 = \$75 + \$25 + \$20 = \$120$. And $\text{BfB}_b = 3/1.6b = 3/(1.6 \times 46.875) = 3/75 = 1/25$, $\text{BfB}_c = 1/5c = 1/25$, and $\text{BfB}_s = 1/10s = 1/25$. It all checks out.)

To make it a level more complex, suppose that, instead of the utility function with which we just worked, we had a consumer with utility function $U(b, c, s) = 3.2\ln(b+2) + \ln(c+1) + .4\ln(s+8)$. [3] The prices will be as before, and we assume as before that the consumer has \$120 to spend. What is the solution to this consumer's problem?

The bang-for-the-buck functions are

$$\text{BfB}_b = \frac{3.2}{1.6(b+2)} = \frac{2}{b+2}, \quad \text{BfB}_c = \frac{1}{5(c+1)}, \text{ and BfB}_s = \frac{.4}{8(s+8)} = \frac{1}{20(s+8)}.$$

We begin by guessing that b, c, and s will all be strictly positive at the solution. Hence, their BfBs must be equal, or

$$\frac{b+2}{2}(= 0.5b + 1) = 5c + 5 = 20s + 160.$$

Using $0.5b + 1 = 5c + 5$, we get $1.6b = 16c + 12.8$, and $5c + 5 = 20s + 160$ gives us $8s = 2c - 62$. So the budget constraint, when we substitute in for $1.6b$ and $8s$, is

$$16c + 12.8 + 5c + 2c - 62 = 120, \quad \text{or} \quad 23c = 169.2, \quad \text{or} \quad c = 7.357.$$

---

[3] If you are a bit shaky with the first example, this may be more confusing than helpful.

And then, when we use this value of c to find the corresponding value of s, we get a strictly negative value of s ($= -5.91$). That can't be the answer. Our initial guess that all three goods will be consumed in strictly positive amounts doesn't work.

So, since salami was the problem under that first guess, I'll guess that, at the solution, $s = 0$. Then the bangs for the buck for bread and cheese must be equal (if both of those are strictly positive), which is

$$0.5b + 1 = 5c + 5, \quad \text{or} \quad b = 10c + 8.$$

The budget constraint is

$$1.6b + 5c = 120, \quad \text{or} \quad 16c + 12.8 + 5c = 120, \quad \text{or} \quad 21c = 107.2,$$

which gives $c = 5.1048$ and, therefore, $b = 59.048$. (Remember, $s = 0$, so it doesn't enter the budget constraint.) To check my math, I first compute the amount expended:

$$59.048 \times \$1.6 + 5.1048 \times \$5 = \$120.0008,$$

which is round-off error. And I check the three BfBs at the bundle $b = 59.048, c = 5.1048$, and $s = 0$:

$$\text{BfB}_b = \frac{3.2}{1.6(59.048 + 2)} = 0.03276, \quad \text{BfB}_b = \frac{1}{5(5.1048 + 1)} = 0.03276, \quad \text{and}$$

$$\text{BfB}_s = \frac{1}{20(0 + 8)} = 0.00625.$$

This satisfies the required condition: All the money is spent, the BfBs of goods being consumed are equal and exceed the BfBs of goods not being consumed. And since this utility function is concave (take my word for it), we know we have the solution!

Why Are the "Mathematical Facts" on Page 227 Really Facts?

The mathematical facts back on page 227 and their translations give you a machine for solving the consumer's problem. If you are willing to trust me that these facts are indeed facts, you can skip ahead to the next section. But it isn't that hard to see why they are facts; here is the explanation.

We are asking the question, Is a consumption bundle $x^0 = (x_1^0, \ldots, x_k^0)$ the solution? Part a of the mathematical facts should be no mystery to you: If, at x^0, some money is left over, and if some good has positive marginal utility, clearly the consumer will do better to spend some of the leftover money on that good.

But suppose there is no money left over. The consumer can still contemplate *shifting* expenditure from one good to another. That's what equal bangs for the buck is about. Suppose, for instance, the consumer contemplates spending a small amount, ϵ, less on good i, using the freed-up cash to buy a little more j. Now it had better be that $x_i^0 > 0$, or else spending a little less on good i isn't feasible. But if $x_i^0 > 0$—more precisely, if $p_i x_i^0 > \epsilon$, so she can spend ϵ less on good i—what happens? As p_i is the price of good i, this means she gets ϵ/p_i less of good i to consume. And, to a first-degree approximation, the impact this small change (assuming ϵ is small) has on her utility is $MU_i(x^0) \times (-\epsilon/p_i) = -[MU_i(x^0)/p_i]\epsilon = -BfB_i(x^0)\epsilon$. This allows her to spend ϵ more on good j, which means ϵ/p_j more of good j to consume, which means a change in her utility of $MU_j(x^0) \times [\epsilon/p_j] = BfB_j(x^0)\epsilon$. So the net impact on her utility (to a first-order approximation) of spending ϵ less on good i and ϵ more on good j is

$$[BfB_j(x^0) - BfB_i(x^0)]\epsilon.$$

This is an increase in utility if $BfB_j(x^0) > BfB_i(x^0)$. So, if x^0 is the solution to her problem, it must be that whenever $x_i^0 > 0$, $BfB_i(x^0) \geq BfB_j(x^0)$ for all other j. That is precisely mathematical fact b.[4]

The argument just provided explains why $MU_i(x^0)/p_i$ is called the bang for the buck of good i, although it would be clearer to call it the *marginal* bang for the *marginal* buck. If you spend a bit more on good i, for the marginal buck more spent you get $\$1/p_i$ more of good i. And, on the margin, your utility (if you are the consumer) rises by this amount times the marginal utility of good i. Interpreting "bang" as utility, that's the explanation.

10.4. Will the Consumer Spend All Her Wealth?

In the general formulation of the consumer's problem, the budget constraint reads $p_1 x_1 + p_2 x_2 + \ldots + p_k x_k \leq y$. The consumer is allowed to spend less than all her money, if doing so gives her higher utility. What does it take to conclude that the consumer will indeed spend all her money?

Suppose some commodity, say, good i, is always desirable. That is, no matter what else the consumer is consuming, as long as we hold the levels of consumption of goods other than i fixed, more of good i gives higher utility. In this case, the consumer will never stop short of spending all her money; any money left over can be used to purchase a bit more of good i, improving her situation.

---

[4] For mathematical fact c, you need to know about concave functions, so I'll leave that for you to ponder. But for those who do know these things, here is how to proceed: Suppose x^0 is not the solution. Then there is some x' that is better. And then, because u is concave, if you move along the line segment from x^0 to x', at every step, you are better off than at x^0. This is true, in particular, for small changes from x^0. You can take it from there.

However, I imagine that on most trips to the deli to buy lunch, you leave with lunch *and* some money in your pocket. You do not spend every penny on food, and this is so even though you are not completely satiated: At least one good, if increased in your lunch menu, would increase your utility. The reason you leave with money in your pocket is that you plan to spend that money sometime in the future. Money is worth something to you outside of its use in buying lunch.

The utility functions we looked at so far fail to capture this, because money left over does not enter as an argument. And anything that is not an argument of the utility function cannot be something that is, in the model, desirable. The key, then, is to think in terms of utility functions that have as arguments things like bread, cheese, salami, *and* money left over. As long as money left over has high enough marginal utility, the consumer being modeled will choose a bundle with money left in her pocket.

An example illustrates the point. To model the idea that a consumer buying a lunch of bread, cheese, and salami also values money left over, we can employ the utility function

$$U(b, c, s, m) = 3\ln(b) + \ln(c) + 0.8\ln(s) + m^{1/2},$$

where the new variable m is money left over. Her budget constraint, which previously was $1.60b + 5c + 8s \leq 120$, becomes $1.60b + 5c + 8s + m = 120$ or, what may be easier to understand,

$$120 - (1.60b + 5c + 8s) = m.$$

Written this second way, the budget constraint says that the money she has left over is what she begins with, $120, less the cost of her purchases, $1.60b + 5c + 8s$. Because of the mix of logs and square roots in the utility function, this is not that easy to solve algebraically with calculus. But a numerical solution gives the answer: $b = 26.85, c = 2.864, s = 1.432$, and $m = \$51.265$ (all approximately). That's still a lot of bread, but at least our consumer leaves with some money in her pocket.

In general, whenever the consumer's utility is increasing in money left over, which is in virtually every case, the consumer's budget constraint is satisfied with an equality; anything the consumer does not spend, she puts back in her pocket.

Is it appropriate to constrain money left over to be nonnegative? We typically assume that the consumer cannot borrow, so $m \geq 0$ is indeed appropriate. But, in applications such as the purchase of graduate education, it is entirely appropriate to allow for the possibility of borrowing. We do this by putting money-left-over into the utility function and into the budget constraint without requiring $m \geq 0$; the interpretation of $m \leq 0$ is that this represents *debt*, where debt's impact on the consumer's utility is, typically, that she doesn't like it; the more negative is m (the larger is her debt), the smaller is her level of utility.

A Particularly Convenient Form of Utility Function

Consider a consumer whose utility function for bread, cheese, salami, and money left over takes the form

$$U(b, c, s, m) = 20\ln(b) + 8\ln(c + 1) + 5\ln(s + 2) + m.$$

Imagine that this consumer faces prices $p_b = \$2$, $p_c = \$4$, and $p_s = \$10$ and has $100 in her pocket. What consumption choice maximizes her utility, subject to her budget constraint?

Hypothesize that, when she solves her problem, the consumer will have money left over in her pocket; she will not spend the whole $100 on lunch. (We check this hypothesis later.) Then the rule says that the bang for the buck of money must equal the bangs for the buck of other commodities that are consumed in positive amounts and it must equal or exceed the bangs for the buck of commodities whose consumption level is 0.

The bang for the buck of money left over, for this utility function, is remarkably simple: It is the marginal utility of money left over, divided by the price of money left over. The marginal utility of money left over for this utility function is 1. And the price of money left over—the amount of money it takes to "buy" another dollar in the consumer's pocket as she leaves the deli—is 1. So her bang for the buck in money is $1/1 = 1$.

Now go on to the three food commodities:

- The bang for the buck of bread is its marginal utility, $20/b$, divided by its price, $2, or $10/b$. This, the rule says, must equal the bang for the buck of money left over, which is 1, so at the solution to the consumer's problem, $10/b = 1$, or $b = 10$.

- For cheese, we get $[8/(c + 1)]/4 = 2/(c + 1)$ as its bang for the buck. Setting this equal to the bang for the buck of money gives $2/(c + 1) = 1$, or $c = 1$.

- The bang for the buck of salami is $[5/(s + 2)]/10 = 1/(2s + 4)$. When $s = 0$, this is $1/4$, and it decreases as s gets larger, because the marginal utility of salami decreases. Therefore, the bang for the buck in salami is never going to equal 1, for nonnegative amounts of salami.

We conclude that the consumer maximizes her utility, subject to her budget constraint, if she consumes 10 loaves of bread, 1 kilo of cheese, and no salami. At these consumption levels, the bang for the buck in bread equals the bang for the buck in cheese equals the bang for the buck in money left over (all equal 1) and all exceed the bang for the buck of salami. The rule is satisfied, and so this is the solution.

Now confirm the hypothesis that this bundle leaves the consumer with money left over: 10 loaves of bread cost $20, and 1 kilo of cheese costs $4, so the consumer spends $24 out of her initial $100, leaving $76 in her pocket.

As consumer problems go, this one is remarkably easy to solve, because the consumer's utility function, defined for a string of "real" commodities x_1, x_2, and so on, and for money left over m, takes the form

$$U(x_1, x_2, \ldots, m) = v_1(x_1) + v_2(x_2) + \ldots + m.$$

In words, the contribution of each of the "real" commodities to utility is a function of the amount of that commodity alone added to the total, and the contribution of money left over is simply the amount of money left over.

In Economese, we say that this utility function is additively separable by commodities and quasi-linear in money left over. But regardless of terminology, this form of utility is so convenient analytically that we use it incessantly in examples and to illustrate basic ideas in what follows.

For this special utility function, once the consumer is rich enough, her consumption of the "real" commodities does not depend on her level of wealth, y. In the example, we saw that, with the prices given and with $y = \$100$ in her pocket, the consumer purchased 10 loaves of bread, 1 kilo of cheese, and no salami, at a cost of $24, leaving $m = \$76$. Suppose that, instead, the consumer had $1000 in her pocket. Then, as long as the prices are the same, she would choose 10 loaves of bread, 1 kilo of cheese, and no salami, leaving $m = \$976$ in her pocket. If she has any amount of money exceeding $24, she consumes 10 loaves of bread, 1 kilo of cheese, and no salami, with any money left after these purchases going to money left over.

Why is this? You can get some intuition by looking at the marginal utilities of the various goods. Since money left over enters the utility function as $\ldots +$ m, it has a constant marginal utility of 1 unit of utility per dollar. The other commodities have decreasing marginal utility, in this case because the logarithm function is concave. So the consumer, in matching bangs for the buck, consumes each commodity to the point where its marginal utility divided by its price equals the constant marginal utility of money, 1, divided by its price, $1. To consume any more of the commodity would reduce its bang for the buck below that of money left over. Consuming any less would be consuming too little. And since the bang for the buck of money never diminishes, this remains true no matter how rich the consumer becomes.

Is this a reasonable model of human preferences? Does the marginal value of money, measured on a scale where the marginal values of other commodities decreases, stay constant? Would your purchases of commodities remain constant, once your wealth rose to some level, no matter how much richer you became? The answer to all these questions is probably No, in general, but Yes in specific cases. When you walk into a cafeteria or deli to purchase lunch, you probably do not consider your bank account balance, to see what food to buy. If I increased your bank balance by, say, 10%, it would not affect what you buy for lunch. Now if I doubled or tripled your bank balance, you might buy a different lunch—lobster salad and caviar, instead of turkey and swiss on rye—but when you purchase lunch, you do not contemplate purchases that would take half your bank account balance, so what you choose with half or double your current wealth really is not at issue. Therefore, this ultraconvenient utility function is probably adequate for modeling consumers—relatively well-to-do consumers, perhaps—who are in the market for lunch, a week's groceries, or other such minor, day-to-day purchases. But this sort of utility function is not a good model when we discuss the purchase of a house, investments, or education, things that do take an appreciable fraction of one's income.

In summary, we use this ultrasimple form for utility in examples and to illustrate some concepts because it is so convenient. But it involves implicit assumptions that are not always valid.

Two final comments:

- The preceding discussion concerned the $\ldots + m$ part of the utility function. The "additive separability" assumptions (that the rest of the utility function looks like $v_1(x_1) + v_2(x_2) + \ldots$) also involve implicit assumptions. But these are beyond the scope of this book; consult a more advanced economics textbook to learn about them. For most economic purposes, the $\ldots + m$ part is a more restrictive assumption, which is why I concentrate on it.

- Earlier in this chapter I said that the numerical quantities of utility don't have any particular meaning. With this special form of utility, that is no longer true: Utility is measured on a scale where $1 more left over provides precisely one unit of utility more. For this utility function, utility is measured on a dollar scale.

10.5. Pictures: Indifference Curves and Budget Sets

Economists love to draw pictures of their concepts, and the theory of the consumer is no exception. These pictures are limited by the talents of the artist, and economists typically are not artists, especially when it comes to diagrams with more than two dimensions. So the pictures are limited to examples where there are two commodities, which for this discussion will be bread and cheese.

Indifference Curves

The first step is to draw a "map" of the consumer's utility function. Figure 10.2 is typical. This depicts the *indifference curves* or level sets of the consumer's utility function u. Two bundles are on the same indifference curve if they have the same utility. The arrow in the picture, which typically is not drawn, indicates that moving up and to the right—more c or more b—puts you on indifference curves with greater utility, which just means that this particular utility function increases if either b or c increases.

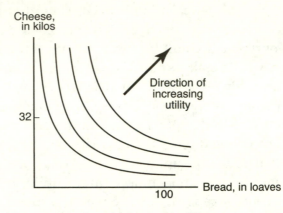

Figure 10.2. A typical set of indifference curves.

Think in terms of a topographical relief map. The coordinates, measured north–south and east–west, give the amounts of b and c. Imagine coming up out of the page is a mountain, whose height at coordinates (b, c) is $U(b, c)$. This mountain rises (perpetually) as you move north or east. Figure 10.2 shows the topographical contours, or families of bundles that are at the same height or utility.

The four functions graphed in Figure 10.2 are *not* the utility function U. They represent sets of points (b, c) such that, along each curve, $U(b, c)$ equals a constant, with the constant changing for each curve; the constants get larger as we move northeast. For example, if $U(b, c) = 3\ln(b) + \ln(c)$, then one indifference curve would be the set of points (b, c) that satisfy $3\ln(b) + \ln(c) = 5$. A second curve, further to the north and east, would be all the points (b, c) that satisfy $3\ln(b) + \ln(c) = 5.6$, and so on.

The shapes you see in Figure 10.2—indifference curves that proceed from the northwest to the southeast and are convex to the origin—are standard. The northwest-to-southeast character is a consequence of the assumption that utility strictly increases in the two goods. As for the convexity, this reflects what economists call *convexity* of preferences: If we have two bundles, (b, c) and (b', c'), where the first is preferred by the consumer to the second (or if the consumer is indifferent between them), then the bundle $(0.5b + 0.5b', 0.5c + 0.5c')$, the simple average of the two, is at least as good as (b', c'). In most applications, this property of preferences is reasonable.[5]

---

[5]   If u is concave, the preferences represented by u have this property. In fact, u can be *quasi-*

While this is the typical picture, no natural law says that preferences should conform to these properties. In particular, for some goods, such as a very sweet dessert, the utility eventually declines as the amount of the good increases. In Problems 10.6 and 10.10, we examine indifference curves for this sort of good.

Consumer Choice from Indifference Curves

Imagine a consumer choosing from among the five points shown as heavy dots in Figure 10.3(a). If we superimpose the consumer's indifference curve map, as in Figure 10.3(b), it is easy to figure out what our model predicts the consumer will choose. She will select whichever of the five points is on the indifference curve of highest elevation.

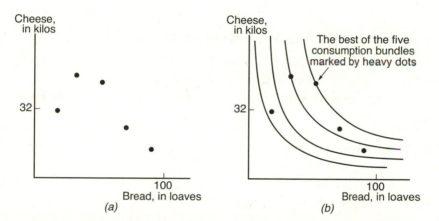

Figure 10.3. Choosing among five consumption bundles. To choose among the five bundles shown as heavy dots in panel a, you first lay on the graph the consumer's indifference curves. The point on the highest (most northeastern) indifference curve is the winner, as shown in panel b.

Suppose next that our consumer has $160 to spend, the price of bread is $1.60 per loaf, and the price of cheese is $5.00 per kilo. In this case, the picture is given by Figure 10.4.

Panel a shows the line segment joining the bundles (0 bread, 32 kilos of cheese) and (100 loaves of bread, no cheese). That is, these are all the bundles the consumer can buy and exhaust her budget of $160. The shaded region in panel b is then her "feasible consumption set" or budget set; all bundles of bread and cheese with nonnegative components that cost $160 or less. And, in panel c, her indifference curves are superimposed, and her optimal choice is shown: This is the point in her budget set that is on the highest indifference curve among all points in her budget set.

---

concave, and it will represent convex preferences. But you'll need to consult a more advanced textbook to understand what this means.

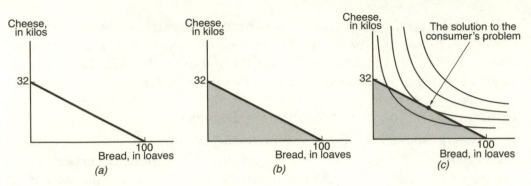

Figure 10.4. *Solving the consumer's problem graphically.* If bread costs $1.60 a loaf, cheese costs $5 a kilo, and the consumer has $160 to spend, we get the budget line (panel a) and budget set (panel b) shown here. Superimposing the indifference curves then allows us to find the solution to the consumer's problem (panel c).

Equal Bangs for the Buck in the Picture

Note that, in panel c of Figure 10.4, at the solution to the consumer's problem, the consumer's indifference curve through that point is tangent to the budget line. This is the graphical manifestation of the equal-bangs-for-the-buck rule. Here is why:

- An indifference curve for a two-commodity world is a curve given by the equation $u(x_1, x_2) = k$, for some constant k. Suppose x_1 increases by a small amount, ϵ. This increases utility by approximately $\epsilon \, \mathrm{MU}_1$, where MU_1 is shorthand for the marginal utility of good 1. If x_2 simultaneously decreases by some amount δ, utility falls by $\delta \, \mathrm{MU}_2$. If δ and ϵ are chosen so that the net effect of the two changes is to stay on a single indifference curve, then

$$\epsilon \, \mathrm{MU}_1 - \delta \, \mathrm{MU}_2 = 0, \quad \text{or} \quad \frac{\delta}{\epsilon} = \frac{\mathrm{MU}_1}{\mathrm{MU}_2}.$$

Recalling that δ is the amount of decrease of commodity 2, the slope of the indifference curve at the point is $-\delta/\epsilon$, so that

$$\text{the slope of an indifference curve at a point is} \quad -\frac{\mathrm{MU}_1}{\mathrm{MU}_2},$$

where the marginal utilities are measured at that point.

- The budget line is the line $p_1 x_1 + p_2 x_2 = \text{constant}$. So the slope of this line, viewed as defining x_2 as a function of x_1, is $-p_1/p_2$.

- Hence, the tangency of the budget line and the indifference curve implies

$$-\frac{\mathrm{MU}_1}{\mathrm{MU}_2} = -\frac{p_1}{p_2} \quad \text{which can be rewritten as} \quad \frac{\mathrm{MU}_1}{p_1} = \frac{\mathrm{MU}_2}{p_2},$$

which is the equal-bangs-for-the-buck condition.

10.6. Individual Demand Functions

The previous two sections concern the consumer's problem at a given set of prices. Suppose we solve that problem for all possible prices. More specifically, suppose we fix the prices of all the goods except good i and answer the question, What amount of good i is chosen by this consumer as a function of p_i, holding fixed the consumer's wealth and the prices of all other goods? This function is the consumer's demand function for good i.

In general, this is a very hard problem to solve algebraically. But for some special utility functions, it can be done. In particular, it can be done rather easily for a consumer whose utility function is

$$U(x_1, \ldots, x_k, m) = v_1(x_1) + \ldots + v_k(x_k) + m :$$

that is, is additively separable and quasi-linear in money-left-over, if we add an assumption that v_i is a concave function, which means that v_i', the marginal-utility-of-good-i function, is a decreasing function.

Recall that, as long as the consumer has enough money at the start to have money left over at the end, the optimal level of good i to consume at price p_i is given by

$$\frac{v_i'(x_i)}{p_i} = 1, \quad \text{or} \quad v_i'(x_i) = p_i.$$

Graph the function v_i' with its argument x_i on the horizontal axis. Find p_i on the vertical axis and move across until you hit v_i'. The quantity at which you hit v_i' solves the equation $v_i'(x_i) = p_i$, which is this consumer's demand at price p_i.

In fact, draw this picture and you discover that, subject to a caveat coming up, the graph of v_i' is the "same" as the graph of the demand function. Look at Figure 10.5. Think of this first as the marginal utility function $v_i'(x_i)$; that is, the argument runs on the horizontal or quantity axis and the value of the function is measured on the vertical axis. Now turn the page 90°. If the argument of the function is price p_i, the value of this function—keep the page turned 90°—is the demand at that price.

Why are there quotes around "same" in the preceding paragraph? Looking at this as the graph of the function v_i', the argument of the function x_i runs from 0 to infinity. In Figure 10.5, $v_i'(0)$ is finite and $v_i'(x_i)$ is always strictly positive, no matter how large is x_i. Turn the page 90°, so that price is the argument and the function is demand, and we see something slightly different: Price runs from 0 to infinity, and demand at high enough prices is 0. (How high? Demand

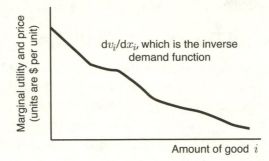

Figure 10.5. The consumer's demand curve for good i. For a consumer with utility function $U(x_1, \ldots, x_k, m) = v_1(x_1) + \ldots v_k(x_k) + m$ and enough initial wealth that, after choosing her optimal consumption bundle, she has money left over, her demand for good i is given by the equation $v_i'(x_i) = p_i$. If we graph the function $v_i'(x_i)$, we see her (inverse) demand function.

is 0 whenever the price $p_i \geq v_i'(0)$.) On the other end of the price spectrum, demand is not really defined for the price $p_i = 0$. In this case, if the good is being given away, the consumer would ask for infinite quantities of it.

This is a utility function where $v_i'(0)$ is finite and v_i' does not hit 0 for any finite level of consumption. Problem 10.13 explores a number of other possibilities.

Please note: everything just derived is based on the assumption that demand is given by $v_i'(x_i) = p_i$, which in turn depends on the consumer being rich enough that, after all her purchases are made, she has some money left over. You have to verify that this is so in applications, at least for the range of prices you are interested in; see Problems 10.4 and 10.5.

10.7. First-Degree Price Discrimination and Consumers

First-degree price discrimination, you will recall, consists of tailored take-it-or-leave-it offers to each individual customer, designed to extract the maximum amount of payment each customer would be willing to pay for the number of goods offered. In a B2B setting, we compare the gross-of-payment profit the customer (which is a firm) would make with the goods with the profit the firm would make without any goods; the difference is, roughly, the most the firm would be willing to pay. Now we have the tools needed to adapt this idea to a B2C context, asking: Suppose a given customer (now a consumer) has y in total to spend and we offer the consumer x^* units of the good. For what amount of money y^* is the consumer's utility with x^* units of the good and $y - y^*$ to spend on other goods equal to her utility if she has none of the good and y to spend? That amount, y^*, is (roughly) the maximum she would pay on a take-it-or-leave-it basis; it remains to find the optimal level x^* (and its corresponding y^*) for the firm.

What information is needed to pull this off? If the customer is a firm, the seller must understand the economics of the firm and, in particular, how much having the goods on offer improves its profit. This is a lot of information to possess, but in some contexts it is not completely unreasonable. But when the customer is a consumer, the seller must "know" the consumer's utility function. That is *not* knowledge that it is reasonable to have.[6] So, on these grounds, first-degree price discrimination in a B2C context is more of an ideal than a practical scheme for pricing goods for sale.

That said, for money-left-over utility functions, first-degree price discrimination can be further developed on at least a theoretical basis. To see more, consult Problem 10.14.

Executive Summary

- In the economic model of the utility-maximizing consumer, the consumer's utility function associates a numerical value to each conceivable choice. Given any feasible set of choices, the consumer chooses the option from the feasible set that maximizes her utility.

  - The utility function establishes an order among the consumer's possible options. Two utility functions that establish the same order are equivalent in the sense that they give the same choice behavior by consumers.

  - In models of some choices by individuals, money left over is included as an argument of the utility function, where the "utility" from money left over is derived from the value of things that might be purchased (outside the model) with the money left over.

- The *consumer's problem* is to choose the best (utility-maximizing) bundle from among all those she can afford, given prices and her monetary resources.

  - At the solution of the consumer's problem, the bangs for the buck of commodities at strictly positive levels must be equal and must be at least as large as the bangs for the buck of commodities that are not consumed.

  - This rule is typically very easy to apply in models where money left over enters the utility function linearly.

- The model of the utility-maximizing consumer is rationalized by economists as an as-if model. No one believes that consumers consciously maximize a utility function.

---

[6] It has been alleged that internet vendors, by keeping careful track of each individual consumer's history of purchases, can begin to develop a good sense of "willingness to pay" numbers on an individual-consumer basis. Internet vendors generally deny that they do this—although there is no doubt that they tailor pop-up advertisements to the user's history of past views—but the data are, to some extent, there for them to process. Also, when there is a limited number of the goods available to sell, clever auction schemes can be used to get close to the "maximum willingness to pay" of the consumer who wins the goods in the auction.

But, if the consumer's choice behavior conforms to two relatively simple principles—
the two bullet points on page 224—the consumer acts *as if* she maximizes utility.

- Systematic violations of one of these simple rules can be observed in real life.
  Consumer marketers and advertising executives are well compensated for their
  skills in manipulating how consumers frame their choices.

- Nothwithstanding which, economists continue to use the model of the utility-
  maximizing consumer, in the belief that the violations are usually insignificant
  or in the hope that the conclusions drawn from models so constructed are not
  grossly affected by violations.

Problems

10.1 Three consumers rank bundles consisting of b loaves of bread, c kilos of
cheese, and s kilos of salami according to the following three utility functions:
Consumer 1 ranks them according to the utility function $U_1(b, c, s) = \ln(b) +
0.5 \ln(c) + 0.5 \ln(s)$. Consumer 2 ranks them according to the utility function
$U_2(b, c, s) = b^4 c^2 s$. And Consumer 3 ranks them according to the utility function
$U_3(b, c, s) = b + 2c + 2\ln(s)$. Suppose these three consumers are given their choice
from the following three bundles:

   Bundle 1 $= (b, c, s) = (4, 0.5, 0.25)$; Bundle 2 $= (2, 1.25, 0.5)$; and
   Bundle 3 $= (1, 0.5, 2.5)$.

Which bundle will each consumer choose?

10.2 Suppose that a particular consumer has utility function (for bundles of
bread, cheese, and salami) given by

$$U(b, c, s) = 6 \ln(b) + 3 \ln(c) + \ln(s),$$

and the consumer has $20 to spend. The prices of bread, cheese, and salami
are, respectively, $1.20 per loaf, $3 per kilo, and $4 per kilo. What amounts of
bread, cheese, and salami will this consumer choose, if she chooses in a way
that maximizes her utility, subject to the constraint that she spend no more than
$20?

10.3 Suppose a consumer with $160 to spend has the utility function (for bundles
of bread, cheese, salami, and money left over) given by

$$U(b, c, s, m) = 6 \ln(b) + 2 \ln(c) + \ln(s) + m.$$

What choices maximize this consumer's utility? Assume $p_b = \$1.20, p_c = \$3$,
and $p_s = \$4$.

10.4 (a) Solve the consumer's problem for a consumer with the utility function $U(b, c, s) = 8 \ln(b + 2) + 6 \ln(c + 1) + 2 \ln(2s + 1)$, if the prices are $p_b = \$1$, $p_c = \$2$, and $p_s = \$4$, and the consumer has $18 to spend.

(b) Solve the consumer's problem for a consumer with the utility function $U(b, c, s) = 8 \ln(b + 2) + 6 \ln(c + 1) + 2 \ln(2s + 1)$, if the prices are $p_b = \$1$, $p_c = \$2$, and $p_s = \$4$, and the consumer has $6.50 to spend.

(c) Solve the consumer's problem for a consumer with the utility function $u(b, c, s, m) = 8 \ln(b + 2) + 6 \ln(c + 1) + 2 \ln(2s + 1) + m$, where m is money left over, if the prices are $p_b = \$1$, $p_c = \$2$, and $p_s = \$4$, and the consumer has $50 to spend. What if the consumer has $500 to spend? What if the consumer has $18 to spend? What if the consumer has $6.50 to spend?

10.5 (a) Solve the consumer's problem for a consumer with utility function $U(b, c, s) = 10 \ln(b) + \ln(c + 1) + 0.5 \ln(s + 4)$, if the prices are $p_b = \$2$, $p_c = \$5$, and $p_s = \$10$, and if the consumer has $83 to spend.

(b) Solve the consumer's problem for a consumer with the utility function $U(b, c, s) = 10 \ln(b) + \ln(c) + 0.5 \ln(s + 4) + m$, where m is money left over, if the prices are $p_b = \$2$, $p_c = \$5$, and $p_s = \$10$, and the consumer has $83 to spend. What if the consumer has only $6.60 to spend?

10.6 Imagine a consumer who wants to purchase some cotton candy. This consumer's choice behavior (in terms of her purchase of cotton candy) is described by utility maximization for the utility function $U(c, m) = 4c - c^2 + m$, where c is the amount of cotton candy consumed (measured in sticks) and m is the amount of money the consumer has left over (measured in dollars). Note that, past the level $c = 2$, this function decreases in c; this consumer is decreasingly well off if she consumes more than two sticks of cotton candy.

(a) Suppose we graph the indifference curve of this individual through the point ($5.00, 1 stick). At what dollar value m^* does this indifference curve pass through the 1.5 stick level? That is, for what value of m^* is (m^*, 1.5 sticks) on the same indifference curve as ($5.00, 1 stick)?

(b) Graph this consumer's entire indifference curves through the points ($5.00, 1 stick) and ($6.00, 1 stick).

10.7 Go back to Figure 10.3 and number the five dots consecutively, moving from left to right. Then, for the consumer whose indifference curves are shown in panel b of Figure 10.3, what is the rank order of these five in terms of consumer well-being? (To get you started: The leftmost dot is worst, and the rightmost dot is second worst.)

10.8 Suppose that a consumer has $24 to spend for bread and cheese, where bread costs $1.20 per loaf and cheese costs $3 per kilo. On a piece of graph paper, draw the budget set of this consumer.

10.9 In Figure 10.6, I depict four indifference curves for an individual trying to decide how much wine to buy (where we consider money left over as the second good).

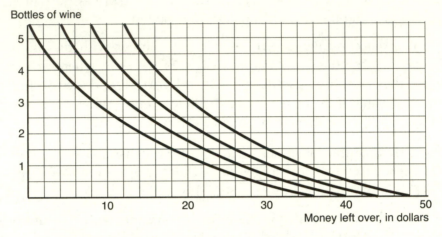

Figure 10.6. Problem 10.9: Some indifference curves.

(a) Suppose the price of wine is $10 per bottle, and the consumer has $40 to spend. How many bottles of wine will he buy? (Do not try to be too precise about this.)

(b) If the consumer has $40 to spend and the price of wine is $30 per bottle, how many bottles will the consumer purchase?

10.10 Imagine a consumer choosing bundles consisting of an amount of cotton candy and an amount of double chocolate fudge. The consumer has a certain amount she can spend on these two confections and she forfeits any money she does not spend on them. Her preferences can be described (very roughly and descriptively) as follows. She likes both confections but only in limited amounts. If we write (c, f) for the bundle consisting of c sticks of cotton candy and f pounds of double chocolate fudge, then her most preferred bundle out of any conceivable bundle is $(2, 3)$, or two sticks of cotton candy and 3 pounds of fudge.

Try to draw indifference curves for this consumer that are consistent with the statements just made. One example will do. Try to make these as "realistic" as you can; that is, as much in accord as possible with the general tenor of the brief description given.

10.11 A consumer with $10 to spend on bread, cheese, and salami has the utility function $U(b, c, s) = 4\ln(b) + \ln(c+1) + 0.5\ln(s)$. Describe as completely as you can the demand function of this consumer for cheese, if the price of bread is $2 per loaf and the price of salami is $2.50 per kilo.

10.12 (a) Suppose a consumer has utility function

$$U(b, c, f, m) = \ln(b) + \ln(c + 3) + (2f - f^2) + m,$$

where b is loaves of bread, c is kilos of cheese, f is kilos of fudge, and m is money left over. The consumer has $100 to spend, which (you may assume) leaves him with money left over after purchasing the optimal amounts of bread, cheese, and fudge, at any prices for those three goods. What are his demand functions (or, if it is easier, his inverse demand functions) for the three goods?

(b) What is the most he will spend on the three goods? To answer this question, you have to find prices for the three goods that maximize his expenditures on each. (This is a little tricky when it comes to cheese.)

10.13 (This problem is primarily for readers who love math.) Figure 10.5 depicts a demand function that hits quantity 0 at a finite price and that (seemingly) goes to infinity as the price approaches 0. This is not the only possibility. Imagine a consumer choosing the amount x to consume, where the alternative to purchasing x is to leave money in her pocket. More specifically, imagine a consumer with the utility function $U(x, m) = v(x) + m$ for a concave function v. For each of the four possibilities for v that follow, find the consumer's demand function for the good x as a function of its price p.

(a) $v(x) = x^{1/2}$

(b) $v(x) = 10 \ln(x + 1)$

(c) $v(x) = 6x - x^2$

(d) $v(x) = \begin{cases} \ln(x), & \text{for } x \leq 1, \text{ and} \\ 3x - x^2, & \text{for } x \geq 1. \end{cases}$

Using these examples as guides, complete the following sentences. For this sort of problem, in which the utility for x and money left over has the form $v(x) + m$ (where, to be fastidious, v is a strictly concave function),

Demand is strictly positive no matter how high price gets if _____, but if _____, demand hits zero when price rises to _____.

Demand approaches ∞ as price declines to 0 if _____. But if _____, then demand stops at the level _____ when price goes to 0.

10.14 Imagine a single consumer whose utility function takes the money-left-over form $U(x_1, x_2, \ldots, x_k, m) = v_1(x_1) + V(x_2, \ldots, x_k) + m$, where m is money left over after purchases of goods 1 through k and the function v_1 is strictly concave. Suppose that the consumer starts with enough money so that, after her purchases of these goods, she has a strictly positive amount of money left over. Therefore, if good 1 were sold in the standard method of a set price p_1 and the consumer allowed to choose how much of the good to buy at that price, she would choose x_1^* that solves $v_1'(x_1^*) = 1$. It is also the case that, no matter how good 1 is sold, as long as the terms of sale in no way affect the consumer's ability to purchase other goods, we can ignore the other goods in deciding how much good 1 the consumer buys.

The firm selling good 1 has constant marginal cost c. Suppose the firm can make the following offer to the particular consumer: "If you pay a fixed fee F, you can buy as much or as little as you want at the price-per-unit p." What are the optimal (profit-maximizing) levels of F and p for the firm to set? What is the connection with first-degree price discrimination?

11. Technology and Cost Minimization

This chapter concerns economic models of production technology and the connection between these models and the total-cost function:

- Technology is modeled with production functions and, graphically, with isoquant diagrams. Concepts such as flexibility and returns to scale are discussed.
- Given a model of technology and prices for the inputs to production, we find the cheapest way the firm can attain a given level of output, which provides us with the total-cost function.

11.1. Modeling Technology

In this chapter, we envision firms as enterprises with the ability to turn various combinations of input into various levels of output. The *technology* of the firm is, essentially, a complete description of the firm's abilities in this regard.

Production Functions

The technology of a firm that produces a single output from several inputs is represented by a *production function*. Supposing there are ℓ different inputs or *factors of production*, an *input vector* is a vector of the form $(y_1, \ldots, y_\ell)$, meaning y_1 units of the first input, y_2 units of the second, and so forth. The *production function f* takes as argument a vector of inputs $y = (y_1, \ldots, y_\ell)$ and maps this input vector into the greatest amount of the single output $f(y)$ that the firm can wring out of the input vector y.

So, for instance, suppose a firm makes widgets out of labor input (measured in hours) and sheet metal (measured in square meters), and suppose that with 9 hours of labor and 8 square meters of sheet metal, it can produce 24 widgets. Then this firm's production function would have $f(9, 8) = 24$. Typically, in economic models, production functions are defined for every input vector y, so (for instance) we might have $f(11, 9) = 27.5954$, not worrying too much what might be meant by 0.5954 of a widget. And, within models, production functions are often specified "algebraically," for instance $f(y_1, y_2) = 4y_1^{1/2} y_2^{1/3}$. This functional form for a production function may seem unnecessarily complex but, as you'll see, it is very convenient for later purposes. It is an example of a *Cobb-Douglas production function*.

In real-life organizations, the number of different inputs to the production process is huge, much too large for writing out in a function. Put another way, the manufacture of a complex product such as a widget presumably involves not only labor and sheet metal, but several different varieties of labor, raw materials other than sheet metal, the use of capital equipment, electricity to power the capital equipment, and so forth. And yet, in economic models, you will find many production functions that go (only) one input further than the example just given: factors of production are labor, raw materials, and (the additional factor) capital equipment. These are employed in highly simplified and stylized models to answer questions such as, If the government subsidizes the use of capital equipment (say, through the tax code), how will that affect the employment of and wages paid to labor? And when these models are employed, a variable like *labor input* is to be thought of as an *aggregate* measure of all the different types of labor employed. My point is: the sort of models of production technology and its connection to cost functions that are discussed in this chapter and next are, from the perspective of a (prospective) manager, generally useful for qualitative insights and *not* for the detailed management of a production process. That's why you are (I hope) studying production and operations management in addition to economics.

More than One Output?

Production functions allow many inputs, but they are limited to a single output. How do we represent technologies for multiproduct firms?

In cases where the production processes of different outputs are technologically independent—the amount of output #1 derived from some combinations of inputs does not depend on the amounts of other outputs produced—there are no problems: Simply treat each output independently, with its own production function. But very often outputs generate *production externalities* for one another, meaning the menus of input needed to get x units of output #1 will depend on the production levels of other output. These externalities can be positive, where more of one output makes it easier to get more of another; for instance, if the technology for output #1 generates excess heat, that heat might help in producing output #2 or if different outputs share productive resources or know-how. The externalities also can be negative; for instance, if two outputs rely on river water for cooling, supplemented as needed by refrigeration, then more of output #2, by raising the water temperature, can increase the amount of supplemental refrigeration needed in the production of output #1.

When they exist, externalities complicate the representation of the production technology of the firm. Formal models are not impossible in such cases, but they are not simple, so we do not deal with them here.[1]

Returns to Scale

Suppose we increase all the inputs in some production technology by 10%.

---

[1] If you are curious, see Chapter 9 of Kreps, *Microeconomic Foundations I* (Princeton: Princeton University Press, 2013).

What happens to the amount of output? In particular, does the amount of output increase by more than, less than, or precisely 10%? The technology's *returns to scale* are the issue here.

- The production function f has *increasing returns to scale* when, assuming there are ℓ inputs, for input vectors $y = (y_1, \ldots, y_\ell)$ and all scale factors $a > 1$, $f(ay_1, ay_2, \ldots, ay_\ell) \geq af(y_1, y_2, \ldots, y_\ell)$.

- The production function f has *decreasing returns to scale* when, for all input vectors $y = (y_1, \ldots, y_\ell)$ and all scale factors $a > 1$, $f(ay_1, ay_2, \ldots, ay_\ell) \leq af(y_1, y_2, \ldots, y_\ell)$.

- The production function f has *constant returns to scale* when, for all input vectors $y = (y_1, \ldots, y_\ell)$ and for all scale factors $a > 0$, $f(ay_1, ay_2, \ldots, ay_\ell) = af(y_1, y_2, \ldots, y_\ell)$.

Two clarifying remarks are in order:

1. In the first two of these definitions, $a > 1$ means that we are looking at how output reacts to increasing the scale of the inputs. In the third, since we have an equals sign, we can get away with scaling inputs up *or down* proportionately.

2. In the first two definitions, we have weak inequalities in terms of output. So the first would be more accurately termed *nondecreasing* returns to scale and the second, *nonincreasing* returns. Moreover, constant returns to scale, for this reason, is a special case of *both* increasing and decreasing returns. (The terms *strictly inceasing* and *strictly decreasing* returns to scale are used when the inequalities on the outputs hold with strict inequalities.)

The most important remark is that each of these definitions requires the inequality (or equation) to hold for *every* set of inputs and *every* proportional scaling of those inputs. To understand this remark, begin by answering the questions: *Why might a technology have increasing returns to scale?* and *Why might it have decreasing returns?*

- One set of reasons for increasing returns—what most people think of first— is purely technological. Making steel in blast furnaces, generating electricity by burning coal, and shipping cargo by both road and sea are all examples where, at least up to some fairly large scale, processes are more efficient at larger and larger scale.

- Another set of reasons for increasing returns appeals to specialization of labor and mass production. An artisan who makes every part of a car and then assembles the pieces is likely to be less efficient than a team that pro- duces cars at a scale sufficient to have specialists in motor assembly, casting, bumper attachment, and so forth.

- Some expenses relative to production need not increase proportionally with the scale of production, especially expenses that are knowledge-related. The knowledge derived from a fixed amount of R&D expenditure can be used in production plant A just as well as in plant B, even if A is twice the size of B. So if we double all the inputs, including the amount of R&D, we get more knowledge, which might then more than double the output.

- The standard stories for decreasing returns concern the costs of coordination and management. With increases in scale, management is less able to monitor and coordinate what is going on. Incentives for individual workers are less effective in larger and larger facilities. So an increase in all input means a smaller than proportional increase in output.

All these can be true and, for some technologies, *all* are true; but they do not apply uniformly. The first three forces are typically more powerful at low levels of output, giving "increasing returns," and the last predominates at high levels of output, giving "decreasing returns."

The quotes in the previous sentence explain the remark begun just prior to the four bullet points. The formal definitions of increasing, decreasing, and constant returns to scale require satisfaction of the appropriate inequality for all scale changes and all baseline vectors of inputs. A technology that has increasing returns for low levels and decreasing returns for higher levels of output satisfies none of these definitions, and so the terms *increasing* and *decreasing returns* don't apply, formally. But they certainly apply informally, and we sometimes use them informally, as in: Firm X has increasing returns to scale up to around 10 million units produced annually, but it suffers from decreasing returns at larger scales. (What do these things imply for the shape of the total-cost function? Read on.)

Since I introduced Cobb-Douglas production functions earlier, it may be worthwhile to connect them to returns to scale. First, for a production function f defined for an ℓ-input technology, so an input vector is a vector $y = (y_1, \ldots, y_\ell)$, the general Cobb-Douglas production function takes the form

$$f(y_1, \ldots, y_\ell) = K y_1^{\alpha_1} \cdot y_2^{\alpha_2} \cdot \ldots \cdot y_\ell^{\alpha_\ell},$$

for positive constants K and $\alpha_1, \alpha_2, \ldots, \alpha_\ell$. Such a production function has increasing returns to scale if $\sum_i \alpha_i \geq 1$, it has decreasing returns of $\sum_i \alpha_i \leq 1$, and it has constant returns to scale if $\sum_i \alpha_i = 1$. (Proving this takes a very little bit of algebra.)

Isoquant Diagrams

Isoquant diagrams provide a depiction of a firm's production capabilities, if the firm produces one output using two other goods as inputs. (*Iso* is the Greek prefix for "equal," so *isoquant* is meant to be read as "equal quantity.") For each level of output x, the x-*unit isoquant* depicts all combinations of the two inputs that (efficiently) product x units of output.

For instance, consider a firm whose production function is $f(y_1, y_2) = 4y_1^{1/2}y_2^{1/3}$. For this firm, $f(9, 8) = f(4, 27) = 24$. So the *24-unit isoquant* for this firm passes through both these points. See Figure 11.1. These two points are marked with heavy dots, and the 24-unit isoquant—all combinations of the two inputs that give 24 units of output—is the curve that runs through them. The 12- and 18-unit isoquants for this production function are also shown.

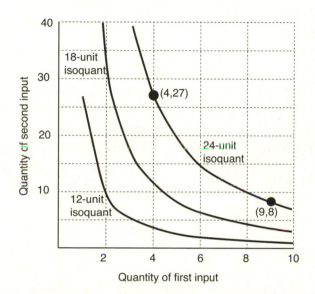

Figure 11.1. *Isoquant diagrams.* For a good produced out of two inputs, we graph, for various levels of output, all the combinations of the two inputs that give that level of output.

Substitution of Inputs, Fixed Coefficients, Marginal Rates of Substitution, and Flexibility

Suppose someone says, The production process at that firm (or plant) is *flexible*. What might this mean?

One possible meaning is that the firm is able to shift output mixes or levels quickly and relatively costlessly. This sort of flexibility—concerning changes in output—is a topic of the next chapter. In terms of production functions, a different notion of flexibility is relevant: How easily can the firm substitute one factor of production for another, while maintaining its level of output? The firm might want this sort of flexibility if, say, the prices of their inputs fluctuate: If the price of input #1 suddenly skyrockets, it would be nice to be able to dial down the use of that input, substituting with others whose price has not gone up.

The notion that one input can be substituted for another in a production process may strike you as somewhat odd. If the product is a widget, how can labor hours replace sheet metal? Doesn't each widget require some fixed amount of sheet metal? Perhaps it does, although you might imagine that, with more time spend cutting up the sheet metal, the amount of wastage might be reduced. Still, to a first approximation, one imagines that each widget requires a certain amount of raw material, worked on by fabricators for a set amount of time, using (if we introduce capital equipment into the production function) equipment such as metal shears and stamping machines for a set amount of time.

We can write down the general production function of this type. Suppose that each unit of output requires b_1 units of input 1, b_2 units of input 2, ..., and b_ℓ units of input ℓ, and no substitutions are possible. Then if we have a vector of inputs $y = (y_1, \ldots, y_\ell)$, the amount of output that can be produced is the smallest of $y_1/b_1, y_2/b_2, \ldots, y_\ell/b_\ell$. If, for instance, $\ell = 3$, $b_1 = 2$, $b_2 = 4$, and $b_3 = 1.5$, and if we have available inputs $y = (80, 160, 45)$, then the most output we can produce is 15 units; we have more of inputs 1 and 2 than we can use, because the supply of input 3 is the limiting factor. Hence, for this type of technology, called a *fixed-coefficients technology*, the production function is

$$f(y_1, \ldots, y_\ell) = \min\left\{ \frac{y_1}{b_1}, \ldots, \frac{y_\ell}{b_\ell} \right\}.$$

(Actually, this is a fixed-coefficients, *constant-returns-to-scale* production function. If, say, the production function were $f(y) = \left[\min\{y_1/b_1, \ldots, y_\ell/b_\ell\} \right]^{1/2}$, we'd still have fixed coefficients for inputs, but by taking the square-root of the minimum, it becomes a fixed-coefficient, decreasing-returns-to-scale production function. If the exponent is 1.3, say, instead of $1/2$, we have increasing returns to scale. All that said, the story as to why we would have fixed coefficients in inputs goes best with constant returns to scale.)

But when we take a longer-horizon look at a firm's technology, it makes sense that the firm has some flexibility in the mix of inputs used. Think of General Motors, assembling vehicles. Once their plant has been set up, with a production line put in place, and their vehicle designs are fixed, each vehicle probably has a fixed list of inputs required. But, as they are designing a new production facility, they can think in terms of more or fewer robots being installed, with more robots meaning less labor required and fewer robots meaning more labor; when designing a vehicle, substitution of materials is possible.

Flexibility in the substitution of inputs, then, goes with production technologies whose isoquants resemble those in Figure 11.1. Take the point $(4, 27)$, which lies along the 24-unit isoquant. The *marginal rate of substitution of input 1 for input 2* at that point is the answer to the question, If the amount input 2 is reduced by a small amount—call it ϵ—at what corresponding rate must input 1 be increased to keep production at level 24? For production functions given algebraically, this can be computed as follows: First, write down the equation that defines the 24-unit isoquant,

$$f(y_1, y_2) = 4y_1^{1/2}y_2^{1/3} = 24.$$

Next, solve for y_1 as a function of y_2. This involves isolating y_1 on one side of the equation, with y_2 (and any other input levels, which are treated as constants) on the other side:

$$y_1^{1/2} = \frac{24}{4y_2^{1/3}} = 6y_2^{-1/3} \quad \text{or} \quad y_1 = 36y_2^{-2/3}.$$

The (marginal) rate at which y_1 must be increased per unit decrease in y_2 is then the derivative of this function (or the partial derivative in y_2 if there are more than two inputs):

$$\frac{dy_1}{dy_2} = -24y_2^{-5/3}, \text{which, evaluated at } y_2 = 27, \text{is} -0.0987.$$

The minus sign reminds us that to decrease y_2, we must decrease y_1 to maintain the output level 24, and vice versa. If you very carefully draw the tangent line to the 24-unit isoquant at $(4, 27)$, you'll find that its slope, in terms of changes in y_1 per unit change in y_2, is indeed -0.1, more or less.

And, finally, to tie all this back to flexibility. Suppose the firm is producing 24 units of output and, to do so in cost-minimizing fashion, using 4 units of the first input good and 27 units of the second. It gets a bit ahead of the story, but this would be the right thing to do if the price of input good 1 were about ten times that of good 2. Now suppose the price of good 2 rises; to be dramatic, suppose it doubles. The firm will probably want to respond in two ways: it will want to cut back on its output (its marginal costs have risen) and it will want to employ more input good 1 relative to the amount of input good 2 is uses. How "flexible" it is in this regard then has to do with how much substitution is can accomplish. The less "bendy" are the isoquants, which means the less the marginal rate of substitution changes as the firm changes its input mix, the more flexible it is. The more bendy are the isoquants—where the ultimate in bendiness is a right-angle turn at the current level of production, which is the case of fixed coefficients—the less substitution it can do, and the less flexible it is. See Figure 11.2 for pictures of this.

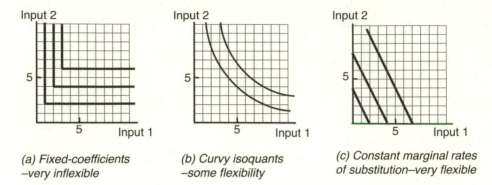

(a) Fixed-coefficients
–very inflexible

(b) Curvy isoquants
–some flexibility

(c) Constant marginal rates
of substitution–very flexible

Figure 11.2. Three isoquant diagrams. With fixed coefficients, the isoquant diagram is a series of right angles, whose verticies lie along a ray corresponding to the fixed ratios of inputs that are required. This sort of technology has no flexibility in shifting between inputs. When isoquants are straight lines, as in panel c, the marginal rates of substitution do not change, and the firm has a lot of flexibility. For curvy isoquants, as in panel b, the firm has some flexibility, although the more it substitutes one input for another, the "worse" the required marginal rate of substitution becomes.

11.2. From Technology to Cost Functions: The Cost-Minimization Problem

Imagine a firm whose technology is given by the production function f. Suppose also that the price of input i is r_i dollars per unit, for $i = 1, \ldots, \ell$, regardless of how much or little this firm purchases. (That is to say, the firm is a price-taker in the market for its inputs.) Then the cheapest, most cost-efficient way for the firm to produce x units of output is the solution to the following problem, called the *cost-minimization problem:*

Minimize $r_1 y_1 + r_2 y_2 + \ldots + r_\ell y_\ell$

subject to $f(y_1, \ldots, y_\ell) \geq x$,   and $y_1 \geq 0, y_2 \geq 0, \ldots, y_\ell \geq 0$.

The output constraint is written with an inequality, but as long as the production function is continuous and $f(0) = 0$ (no inputs means no output), and the prices of all input goods are strictly positive, $f(y)$ will equal x at every solution to this problem.[2]

This cost-minimization problem is a part of the firm's overall profit-maximization problem. The firm, seeking to maximize profit, can be thought of as tackling that problem in two steps. First, for each possible level of output x, it solves the cost-minimization problem, finding the cheapest way it can make x.

---

[2] Why? If you like logical proofs, see the solution to Problem 11.8 in the *Online Supplement.*

This gives it the total-cost function TC(x). Then, once TC(x) is computed, the firm chooses the optimal level of output x by looking at total revenues less total costs. This is where MC = MR comes in.

Solving the Cost Minimization Problem with Calculus

When the production function f is differentiable, as is the case for Cobb-Douglas production functions, you can enlist calculus to solve the firm's cost minimization problem in a manner that, mathematically, is similar to the way the consumer's problem was solved in Chapter 10.

We need one piece of notation: Given f and an input vector y, define the *marginal physical product of input i at y* by

$$\text{MPP}_i(y) = \left.\frac{\partial f}{\partial y_i}\right|_y.$$

In words, this is the rate at which the level of output increases as we increase the level of input i, holding all other inputs fixed at their levels according to y. To keep matters simple, I will assume that f is nondecreasing in y; that is, greater levels of input cannot result is less output.

*Mathematical facts. The input vector y is **not** a solution to the firm's cost-minimization problem (for producing x units of output) unless $f(y) = x$ and, for each input good i such that $y_i > 0$ and for any other input good j,*

$$\frac{r_i}{MPP_i(y)} \leq \frac{r_j}{MPP_j(y)}.$$

Conversely, if $f(y) = x$, if the stated condition holds (so that $r_i/MPP_i(y) = r_j/MPP_j(y)$ for all i and j such that y_i and y_j are both strictly positive), and if f is concave, then y is a solution to the firm's cost-mimization problem at x.

To illustrate, consider a firm that uses three inputs—capital, labor, and material, denoted by k, l, and m, respectively—with production function

$$f(k, l, m) = k^{1/4}l^{1/8}m^{1/8}.$$

Suppose that the prices of the three inputs are $r_k = 16$, $r_l = 1$, and $r_m = 0.25$. What is the firm's total-cost function TC(x)?

The first thing to note is that, for this (Cobb-Douglas) production function, output is zero if any one of the three input goods is at level zero. Therefore, to make any level of output $x > 0$, the firm must use strictly positive amounts of all three inputs. The mathematical fact therefore implies that, at the solution to the firm's cost-minimization problem (for any level of $x > 0$, including $x = 100$), it must be that

$$\frac{r_k}{\text{MPP}_k} = \frac{r_l}{\text{MPP}_l} = \frac{r_m}{\text{MPP}_m}.$$

And what are these ratios?

$$\text{MPP}_k = \frac{\partial f}{\partial k} = (1/4)k^{1/4-1}l^{1/8}m^{1/8} = \frac{1}{4k}k^{1/4}l^{1/8}m^{1/8} = \frac{1}{4k}x,$$

where the last step is because the input vector (k, l, m) must produce x units of output. Hence

$$\frac{r_k}{\text{MPP}_k} = \frac{16 \times 4k}{x} = \frac{64k}{x},$$

and, similarly,

$$\frac{r_l}{\text{MPP}_l} = \frac{1 \times 8l}{x} = \frac{8l}{x} \quad \text{and} \quad \frac{r_m}{\text{MPP}_m} = \frac{0.25 \times 8m}{x} = \frac{2m}{x}.$$

So, for (k, l, m) to be a solution, it must be that

$$\frac{64k}{x} = \frac{8l}{x} = \frac{2m}{x}.$$

Solve for k and for m in terms of l, and you get $k = l/8$ and $m = 4l$.

To produce x units, we need $k^{1/4}l^{1/8}m^{1/8} = x$. Substitute $l/8$ for k and $4l$ for m, and this becomes

$$(l/8)^{1/4}l^{1/8}(4l)^{1/8} = \left(\frac{l}{2}\right)^{1/2} = x, \quad \text{or} \quad l = 2x^2.$$

Since $k = l/8$, $k = x^2/4$. Since $m = 4l$, $m = 8x^2$. Hence the minimized total cost for producing x units, or TC(x), is

$$\text{TC}(x) = \$16 \times \frac{x^2}{4} + \$1 \times 2x^2 + \$0.25 \times 8x^2 = 8x^2.$$

That's a very nice formula. Can you expect such a nice answer every time? The answer is, Yes and No. With Cobb-Douglas production functions, functions of the form $f(y_1, \ldots, y_\ell) = Ky_1^{\alpha_1} \ldots y_\ell^{\alpha_\ell}$, the total-cost function is always of the form TC$(x) = K'x^\beta$, where $\beta = 1/(\alpha_1 + \ldots + \alpha_\ell)$, for some constant K' that depends on the prices of the inputs. So, in this example, there the sum of the three power coefficients is $1/4 + 1/8 + 1/8 = 1/2$, we get a constant times x^2 for total cost. However, the constant, which I emphasize will be different for different prices for the inputs, will rarely work out so nicely: The prices of the inputs in this example were selected to give such a nice constant. (You are asked to work out the general formula for TC in Problem 11.7.)

As for why the mathematical facts are, indeed, facts: The logic here is pretty close to the logic for the bangs-for-the-buck facts in Chapter 10. Suppose that, at input levels y such that $f(y) = x$, for some input i that is used in strictly positive amounts and for some other input j, we had $r_i/\mathrm{MPP}_i(y) > r_j/\mathrm{MPP}_j(y)$. Then imagine reducing the amount of input i by the small amount $\epsilon/\mathrm{MPP}_i(y)$, while increasing the amount of input j by the small amount $\epsilon/\mathrm{MPP}_j(y)$. The first change reduces output by ϵ and the second brings it back up by ϵ, so the net of these changes in production quantity is 0. These changes leave the production fixed at level x.[3] And, if $r_i/\mathrm{MPP}_i(y) > r_j/\mathrm{MPP}_j(y)$, they lower cost by $\epsilon(r_i/\mathrm{MPP}_i(y) - r_j/\mathrm{MPP}_j(y))$. So y cannot be cost minimizing.

If you compare what is going on here with Chapter 10, you may wonder why prices are in the denomimator of the bang-for-the-buck but in the numerator in this chapter. This is explained as follows: In Chapter 10, the variables are the levels of consumption of various commodities, the objective is to maximize utility, and the constraint is the budget constraint. We look at the ratio of the marginal impact of a small change in each variable on the objective to its impact on the constraint. Here, the variables are the amounts of various inputs used, the objective is to minimize the cost of the input vector, and the amount of output is the constraint. So, *just as in Chapter 10*, we look at the ratio of the marginal impact of a small change in each variable on the objective to its impact on the constraint.

Cost Minimization for Fixed-Coefficient Production Functions

The techniques just employed work when the production function f is differentiable. But for one important class of production functions—fixed-coefficient production functions—f is not differentiable. What then?

Happily, it is relatively easy to figure out the total-cost function that goes with a fixed-coefficient production function from first principles. In general, a fixed-coefficients production function has the form

$$f(y) = G\left(\min\left\{ \frac{y_1}{b_1}, \ldots, \frac{y_\ell}{b_\ell} \right\} \right),$$

---

[3] Since f is, in general, nonlinear, these two changes are unlikely to get production back to x exactly. In particular, if f is concave, they probably leave you a bit short of x. The increase in input j must be slightly larger than $\epsilon/\mathrm{MPP}_j(y)$, but the extra increase will be $o(\epsilon)$ and, if you know what that means, you'll see why it doesn't affect the conclusion I'm about to give.

where G is some increasing real-valued function with $G(0) = 0$, and b_1 through b_ℓ are constants that determine the fixed-coefficient ratios of the different inputs. As we said earlier, the story that goes with fixed coefficients is most natural when G is the function $G(x) = x$; then the constants b_1 through b_ℓ are the amounts of each input needed to produce a single unit of output. So we'll solve for total cost here for this most-natural case; Problem 11.9 will give you a chance to extend this to more general G.

And in this special case, things are trivial: To produce x units of output, it takes $b_1 x$ units of input 1, $b_2 x$ units of input 2, ..., and $b_\ell x$ units of input ℓ. Any more of any one of the inputs is more than is needed; any less is too little. So, if r_i is the cost to the firm of a unit of input i, we have

$$\text{TC}(x) = (r_1 b_1 + r_2 b_2 + \ldots + r_\ell b_\ell)x.$$

Returns to Scale and Total Cost

Suppose a firm's production function has increasing returns to scale, or decreasing, or constant. What are the implications for the total-cost function?

Take the case of increasing returns. Consider any level of output x and any scale factor $a > 1$. If the cost-mimimizing input vector to make x units of output is y, we have $\text{TC}(x) = r_1 y_1 + \ldots + r_\ell y_\ell$. And because there are increasing returns, $f(ay) \geq x$, so the cost-minimizing way to produce ax cannot be larger than $r_1 a y_1 + \ldots + r_\ell a y_\ell = a\text{TC}(x)$. That is:

- *If f has increasing returns to scale, then for all output levels x and scale factors $a > 1$, $TC(ax) \leq aTC(x)$. Hence, $AC(x)$ is a nonincreasing function, which, of course, implies that $MC(x) \leq AC(x)$.*

Similarly:

- *If f has decreasing returns to scale, then for all output levels x and scale factors $a > 1$, $TC(ax) \geq aTC(x)$. Average cost is nondecreasing and marginal cost is everywhere above (or equal to) average cost.*

- *If f has constant returns to scale, then $TC(x)$ is a linear function $TC(x) = kx$ for some constant k, which implies that $AC(x) \equiv MC(x) \equiv k$.*

And the U-shaped average-cost functions that we draw repeatedly go—this time only roughly—with technologies with increasing returns to scale for smaller levels of output but, past a certain scale of operations, with decreasing returns to scale in production.

Rising Marginal Cost and Technology

To complement the results just given, it would be nice to know what it takes to conclude that marginal cost is nondecreasing. Since marginal cost is the derivative of total cost, this is the same as: What does it take in terms of f to guarantee that TC is convex?

- *If f is concave, TC is convex, and so MC is nondecreasing.*

You can take my word for it, or here is the proof: Take any two levels of output x and x' and some intermediate level $x'' = ax + (1 - a)x'$ for a between zero and one. Let y be the cost-minimizing level of inputs for producing x and y' be the same for x'. Then, if f is concave,

$$f(ay + (1 - a)y') \geq af(y) + (1 - a)f(y') = ax + (1 - a)x' = x''.$$

So the input vector $ay + (1 - a)y'$ suffices to produce x'', and TC(x'') is no larger than the cost of the input vector $ay + (1 - a)y'$, which of course is just aTC$(x) + (1 - a)$TC(x').

What does "f is concave" mean? This means that the amount of input that can be realized from the average of two vectors of inputs is at least as large as the average amount of output produced by those two vectors of inputs. This implies decreasing returns to scale, in particular, but is more restrictive than that.

Solving the Cost-Minimization Problem Graphically

For the case of two-input production technology, we can use an isoquant diagram to solve the firm's cost-minimization problem graphically.

Consider, for instance, the production function $f(y_1, y_2) = 4y_1^{1/2}y_2^{1/3}$, whose isoquant diagram is shown in Figure 11.1 and is reproduced in the three panels of Figure 11.3.

Suppose the price of the first input is 6, while the price of the second input is 1. Then proceed as follows:

Step 1. *Using convenient values of y_1 and y_2, draw on the isoquant diagram a single* **iso-cost** *line, a line along which the costs of the two inputs remain constant.* In this case, the $30 iso-cost line is quite convenient, as it passes between the points $(5, 0)$ and $(0, 30)$. This is shown as the dashed line in panel a of Figure 11.3.

Step 2. *To find the cost-input vector for a given level of output, slide the iso-cost line parallel to itself until you hit the isoquant of the desired level of output.* In panel b, this is done for the output level 24. Intersection occurs at the point just a bit below $(5, 20)$. (To check my graph, I used calculus and found that the actual values are, roughly, $y_1 = 4.93$ and $y_2 = 19.75$.) This gives a total cost for 24 units of a bit less than $50 or, using the more precise values for the two input levels, $49.3126.

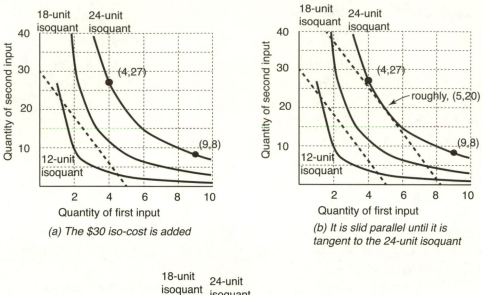

(a) The $30 iso-cost is added

(b) It is slid parallel until it is tangent to the 24-unit isoquant

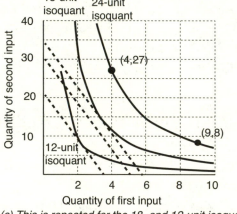

(c) This is repeated for the 18- and 12-unit isoquants

Figure 11.3. Solving the cost-miminization problem graphically.

In panel c, I follow the same procedure for the 12- and 18-unit isoquants, getting $TC(12) = \$21.46$ and $TC(18) = \$34.92$. (Actually, I cheated and used calculus. But those are roughly the values you get graphically.)

I do this to point out a "remarkable" fact. If you join the three cost-minimizing input vectors, they lie along the ray $y_2 = 4y_1$. Of course, this is not in the least bit remarkable: This happens whenever the production function is of the Cobb-Douglas type. (And, of course, the ratio of one input to another changes with changes in the prices of the inputs, unlike with a fixed-coefficients technology, where the ratios never change.) For more on this, see Problem 11.7.

Inputs without Clearly Defined Prices

We have been assuming that the total cost of a list of quantities of inputs is clear. Each input has a price r_i, and the bill for the list of inputs $(y_1, \ldots, y_\ell)$ is $r_1 y_1 + r_2 y_2 + \ldots + r_\ell y_\ell$.

Things are not so easy in real life. Sometimes it is hard to ascribe a price to each input. One important class of difficulties, which we'll deal with next chapter, concerns inputs that are durable. For example, suppose one input is time on a metal lathe. If the firm rents its metal lathes, then there is no problem; $r_{\text{metal lathes}}$ is just the rental rate of a lathe. But most firms purchase equipment like metal lathes and use them for more than a single production period. How should the cost of such durable inputs be computed? See Chapter 12.

A second class of difficulties concerns inputs for which there is no clearly established market price, because the item in question is one of a kind. The typical example here is managerial time, especially the labor input of owner–managers. Most owner–managers are paid a wage by the firm, and it might seem appropriate to say that the cost of the owner–manager to the firm is just the wage paid. But, for a variety of reasons including both tax and financing considerations, it is rare that the wages an owner–manager pays herself equals the "economic cost" her time represents. In principle, the correct economic cost of her time is the opportunity cost of her time; that is, what she could earn in her best alternative opportunity. This represents the economic cost of her time, because if the firm did not employ her in supervising and managing its operations, she could instead earn this amount of money and contribute it to the firm's income. But, while the principle is fairly clear, in practice it is often difficult and sometimes impossible to compute opportunity costs. And, whether easy, difficult, or impossible, firms rarely keep their books in this fashion.

The message is a double-edged caution. First, we simplify unrealistically when we assume we can easily associate a cost to every input. Second, the accounting that firms do will not always correspond precisely to the appropriate economic costs of different inputs, so that economic profits and accounting profits are different, for this reason and for more to come in the next two chapters.

Executive Summary

- Production functions are used to describe the technological capabilities of one-output firms: What is the most output they can create from different vectors of inputs?

- If there are only two inputs, isoquant diagrams offer visual representation of the firm's technological capabilities.

- Increasing, descreasing, and constant returns-to-scale technologies are defined and related to the behavior of the average cost function.

- The firm's cost-minimization problem, in which its total-cost function is derived from a production function and the prices of the firms inputs, is defined and solved, using "bang-for-the-buck" style logic.

Problems

11.1 A firm that manufactures widgets (and only widgets) has a fixed-coefficients and constant-returns-to-scale technology, in which each widget made requires 10 units of labor, 12 units of material 1, 16 units of material 2, 3 units of electricity, and 5 units of machine-tool time. The costs of the various inputs are $15 per unit of labor, $1 per unit of material 1, $2 per unit of material 2, $0.20 per unit of electricity, and $20 per unit of machine-tool time. What is the total-cost function of this firm?

11.2 In Figure 11.3 and the discussion of it on pages 259 and 260, we found, using the graph, that if $f(y_1, y_2) = 4y_1^{1/2} y_2^{1/3}$ and if the price of the two inputs were $6 for input 1 and $1 for input 2, then the cost-minimizing production plan for making 24 units of output employed a bit less than 5 units of y_1 and a bit less than 20 units of y_2. I asserted that, by using calculus, I could get these numbers pinned down to (approximately) $y_1 = 4.93$ and $y_2 = 19.75$.

Suppose instead that the price of input #1 were $4 and the price of input #2 were $1. Using a graphical approach, find the cost-minimizing combination of inputs for making 24 units of output. Then check your graphical abilities by deriving these numbers using calculus.

11.3 Use calculus to solve the following cost-minimization problem. The firm has production function

$$f(y_1, y_2, y_3) = 10y_1^{1/2} y_2^{1/3} y_3^{1/6}.$$

The three inputs have prices $r_1 = 6$, $r_2 = 1$, and $r_3 = 0.5$.

(a) What is the least-cost input vector for making 120 units?

(b) What is the total-cost function of this firm?

11.4 Figure 11.4 shows the 100-unit isoquant of a firm that makes a single product, utemkos, out of labor and materials. This isoquant comes from the production function

$$f(l, m) = l^{1/2} m^{1/2}.$$

(The isoquant is as exact as I could make it, exact enough for this problem, but it probably is not perfectly matched with this production function.) The production technology that goes with this production function has constant

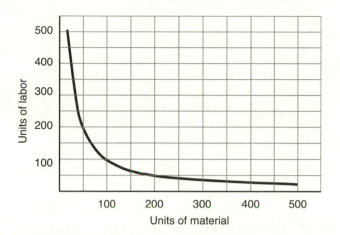

Figure 11.4. Problem 11.4: The 100-unit isoquant.

returns to scale. The price of materials is $1 per unit. The price of labor is $4 per unit.

(a) First using the graph of the 100-unit isoquant, then using calculus, find the value of TC(100).

(b) Suppose the firm faces an inverse demand curve of the form $P(x) = 12 - (x/2000)$, where x is the number of utemkos produced and sold and $P(x)$ is their price. What price will the firm charge to maximize its profits and how many units will it make? (Hint: If you chose to work graphically in part a, you can still answer this question, if you use the fact that this production technology has constant returns to scale.)

11.5   A firm makes a patented product, called xillip, out of two inputs, raw material and labor. Letting x stand for the amount of xillip produced, m be the amount of raw material, and l the amount of labor input, the firm's production function is given by $x = m^{1/3}l^{1/6}$. In addition, the firm must have a license to produce xillip, which costs it $300 per production period, regardless of how much xillip it produces. The price of a unit of raw material is $1, and the price of a unit of labor is $4. The (inverse) demand function for xillip is $P(x) = 160 - 2x$. Find the profit-maximizing production plan for this firm in two steps. First, find the total-cost function for this firm. Then, find the profit-maximizing production level by equating marginal cost to marginal revenue.

11.6   Look at the isoquant diagram in Figure 11.5. In this figure, I give you the ten-unit isoquant only.

(a) Suppose I told you this firm has constant returns to scale. Where would the 20-unit isoquant pass through the dashed line shown? Mark the appropriate

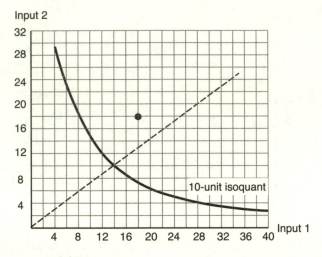

Figure 11.5. Problem 11.6: An isoquant diagram.

point on the graph with an X.

(b) Suppose I told you that the firm has decreasing returns to scale. On which of the following isoquants might the heavy dot lie: The 12-unit isoquant, the 14-unit isoquant, the 16-unit isoquant, or the 18-unit isoquant? More than one of these might be correct—note that I ask you for isoquant(s) on which the dot *might* lie.

11.7 Recall that the general Cobb-Douglas production function, for a firm with a single output and ℓ inputs, takes the form

$$f(y_1, \ldots, y_\ell) = K y_1^{\alpha_1} y_2^{\alpha_2} \ldots y_\ell^{\alpha_\ell},$$

for strictly positive constants K and α_1 through α_ℓ.

(a) Show that this production function has increasing returns to scale if $\sum_i \alpha_i \geq 1$, it has decreasing returns to scale if $\sum_i \alpha_i \leq 1$, and it has constant returns to scale if $\sum_i \alpha_i = 1$.

(b) Suppose this firm faces prices for its inputs r_1 through r_ℓ. Suppose that it wishes to produce level x of output and, to that end, solves its cost-minimization problem. Show that, at the solution $y = (y_1, \ldots, y_\ell)$ to this problem, the amount the firm spends on input i, or $r_i y_i$, divided by α_i, is the same all $i = 1, \ldots, \ell$. This is easier than it may seem.

(c) Express $\mathrm{TC}(x)$ as a function of x, K, the α_i, and the input prices r_1 through r_ℓ. This isn't that hard, as long as you remember high-school algebra and, in particular, all the rules for dealing with exponents. But it is tedious.

11.8 On page 254, I asserted that if we define the firm's cost-minimization problem with a weak inequality in the constraint $f(y) \geq x$, if f is continuous, and if $f(0) = 0$, then at the solution to the problem $f(y)$ must equal x. Prove this, please. (This takes a bit more mathematical sophistication than do most of the problems in this book.)

11.9 Suppose f has fixed coefficients but not constant returns to scale. Specifically, suppose

$$f(y) = G\left(\min \left\{ \frac{y_1}{b_1}, \ldots, \frac{y_\ell}{b_\ell} \right\} \right),$$

where G is an increasing real-valued function of one variable with $G(0) = 0$, and b_1 through b_ℓ are strictly positive constants that determine the fixed-coefficient ratios of the different inputs. Let H be the inverse of G: that is, $H(G(z)) = z$ for all nonnegative numbers z. What is $TC(x)$? (If you find this too difficult, work with the special case $G(z) = z^{1/2}$.)

Problem 11.10 introduces you to a different sort of cost-minimization problem, one where a firm has access to different "facilities" that can produce its output. Given a total amount of output that it wants to produce, the firm wishes to allocate production among its facilities in a cost-minimizing manner. In the *Student's Guide*, the solution to this problem goes into substantial detail about the problem and extensions of it.

11.10 Consider a one-product firm that has access to three sources for its output. If x_1 units are produced by the first source, the total cost is $TC_1(x_1) = x_1^2/1000 + 3x_1$. If x_2 units are produced by the second source, the total cost is $TC(x_2) = x_2^2/2000 + x_2$. The third source is direct purchase from another firm at a price of $6 apiece. The firm can produce its output using any mix of the three sources it chooses.

(a) Suppose the firm wishes to produce/procure 5000 units. What is the cost-minimizing way to do this, in terms of allocating the 5000 units among the three possible sources? What about if it wishes to produce/procure 10,000 units?

(b) (This is hard if you don't know how to proceed. But if you are facile with Excel and have access to an optimization add-on such as Solver, you can do it that way.) Suppose the firm faces demand curve $D(p) = 400(16 - p)$. What level of production maximizes its profits, and how should that level of production be divided among the three technologies?

While, for the most part, the concepts discussed in this chapter are not used to figure out detailed production plans for real-life firms, there are cases where the ideas here become applicable, namely when the production facility can be modeled with a linear activities model and linear programming can be employed. The final two problems give you an introduction to these applications.

11.11 A firm that makes a particular bulk chemical can use either of two processes. The first involves hydration and then distillation. The second involves a completely separate catalytic process. The inputs to the process are the raw materials (a different bulk chemical purchased at $1 per kilogram), labor time to run the processes, and time using the capital equipment. Specifically, to process a kilogram of raw materials in the hydration–distillation process requires 0.03 labor hours at $20 per hour, and to process a kilogram in the catalytic process requires 0.09 labor hours at the same wage rate. Suppose this firm can vary the amount of raw materials it purchases and the amount of labor hours it hires, but it cannot change the capacity it has for the two processes. It can run the hydration–distillation process at up to a level of 1000 kilograms of input per hour and the catalytic process at up to 500 kilograms of input per hour. For every kilogram of input to the hydration–distillation process, the firm gets out 0.4 kilograms of final output. For every kilogram of input to the catalysis process, the firm gets out 0.5 kilograms of final output.

What is the total cost function of this firm? Ignore the fixed costs of the machinery.

11.12 (If you know linear programming, you might find it helpful to try to solve this problem by formulating the cost-minimization problem as a linear programming problem.) Suppose that we complicate Problem 11.11 as follows. We imagine that the firm cannot reduce its labor bill below 18 billed labor hours per hour of operation. It can, however, add to its labor bill (at $20 per labor hour) up to a level of 60 labor hours used per hour of operation. Beyond 60 labor hours per hour of operation, the firm must pay $30 per labor hour. What is the total cost function of this firm? Again ignore the fixed costs of machinery.

12. Multiperiod Production and Cost

Quality is free. Philip Crosby
There are no free lunches. Milton Friedman

This chapter concerns three aspects of multiperiod production:

1. Changing production plans can raise costs in the short run.
2. Some factors of production are long-lived capital assets. In theory, these are easy to deal with, but practice is harder. Accounting practices for dealing with durable assets—depreciation and the like—require explanation.
3. Actions taken today affect capabilities tomorrow.

In the early 1980s, one of the biggest fads in management was the experience curve, the notion that unit costs fall with experience. Management gurus and consultants preached that the winning strategy in industries with several firms was to accumulate production volume faster than one's rivals, to gain an ultimate cost advantage. In the early 1990s, Total Quality Management (TQM) was the fad of the day. The idea in TQM is captured succinctly if a bit too simply by Philip Crosby's dictum that quality is free: a firm can improve its quality at no cost or even lower its unit costs by raising its quality.

Experience-curve strategies and TQM are a lot more than fads. They contain powerful and important ideas. But often they were used faddishly: adopted by managers who did not understand them, with predictably disastrous results. To be used wisely, they first must be understood.

Both the experience curve and TQM concern the cost structure of a firm, and so, in an economics textbook, understanding them ought to begin with economic models of cost, the subject of Chapter 11. But, it is difficult to find a connection between the experience curve or TQM and concepts like total-cost or production functions or isoquants, *as defined in Chapter 11*. This is because, in Chapter 11, the firm's technological capabilities are fixed and static. The firm has certain technological capabilities and exists in a market environment with given factor costs and facing a given demand curve; it makes input and output decisions to maximize its immediate profit. The experience curve and TQM concern dynamic production effects, where production decisions taken today affect the firm's technological capabilities tomorrow.

The experience curve and TQM, while important, are only a part of the story of dynamic production. In this chapter, we discuss three general categories of dynamic production phenomena:

1. Today's production routines constrain, at least for a while, what the firm can do tomorrow. It can repeat what it is doing today fairly easily, but *changing* a production technique or level may temporarily raise the costs of production; in a word, changing production routines may engender *friction*.

2. Some inputs are durable. This includes physical capital, such as metal lathes and oil refineries, but also includes harder to measure assets such as the firm's human capital, and even extends to such intangibles as its reputation and relationship with suppliers.

3. Perhaps the least tangible productive asset is *know-how* or technology itself. Production decisions taken today can affect the firm's technological capabilities tomorrow. The firm can engage in direct R&D concerning its products and processes and it can *learn by doing*, which is what the experience curve and TQM are ultimately all about.

The dividing lines between *friction, durable productive assets*, and *know-how* are fuzzy: Friction can result from the inability, at least in the short run, to procure or redeploy durable factors of production. Know-how is often embodied in the human capital assets of the firm. Still, when modeling dynamic production, these three categories are treated somewhat distinctively and so provide the structure of this chapter.

As we start in, it is worth observing that only the first of these three topics will be actively used in the rest of the book, in particular in Part IV. But you should not on that account avoid the other topics. Dynamic production is an important subject, in which basic microeconomics meets courses in Corporate Finance, Managerial Accounting, Production/Operations Management, and Human Resources. We cannot do justice in one chapter to all the nuances of those subjects. But we can and do begin to make connections, so when you study those subjects, you'll see the connections among them and with the economic notions of production and cost.

12.1. Profits Today, Tomorrow, and Next Year

Before getting to the different categories of dynamic effects, we first must confront the firm's basic objective: profit maximization.

In a single-period story, profit is revenue minus (economic) cost. This is clearly defined and one-dimensional; we know what constitutes greater profit. But, with multiperiod production, decisions can be taken that raise net cash flow—gross receipts less gross expenditures—tomorrow, or next year, or 5 years from now, but mean lower net cash flow today. Is $5 more in 5 years "worth" $1 less in this year's cash flow? Is it worth $4 less this year? How do we model the resulting trade-offs?

The standard model in economics assumes that, in place of profit maximization, the firm chooses among alternative streams of cash flows to maximize the market value of its net cash flows; that is, the amount of money that would be paid in the market to own the net cash flows. Moreover, and based on the theory of financial markets, the market value of a firm's stream of net cash flows is the sum of present values of those net cash flows, discounted at rates derived from the market price of debt.[1] So, in the spirit of the earlier assumption that the firm maximizes its profit in a single-period setting, in multiperiod settings we assume that the firm makes choices with the objective of maximizing the present value of its stream of net cash flows.[2]

12.2. Frictions

Suppose that the Boeing Corporation currently produces 787s at a rate of four per month, at a monthly cost of $60 million per month. It has been doing so for quite some time and, for the forseeable future, if it continues to produce at that rate, it will make no changes in its production routines. Let TC(4) denote its current rate of total cost (on, say, a monthly basis).

We want to know, What will it cost Boeing per month to increase the rate of its production to, say, five 787s per month?

If you asked this question of Boeing engineers and production specialists, they probably would respond, "It depends." One thing that it depends on is how quickly must change be made. It is (probably) a lot more expensive per month for Boeing to move to a production rate of five next month than it will be if they have a year to make the necessary adjustments. Indeed, it may be impossible for Boeing to increase its rate of production by 25% in a single month.[3]

If "it depends," what do we make of the total cost function? What is TC(5)? Is it the rate of cost expenditure if Boeing moves to a production level of five in a month? Or in three months? Or in twelve? And, to complicate matters, consider the labor-cost piece of TC(5). Presumably, Boeing must increase labor supply, if it is going to increase its rate of output. It will take time to find new employees and so, in the shorter run, Boeing might increase labor supply by asking existing employees to work overtime, at overtime rates. Overtime rates

---

[1] I assume you know about discounted present values. If this is new to you, please consult a textbook on corporate finance or your corporate-finance instructor, both on the methods of dealing with discounted cash flows and the market-based rationale for using discounted cash flows.

[2] And please note: this is a descriptive modeling assumption. (1) It is not a normative prescription; I do not assert that maximizing the value of shareholder equity is morally the right thing to do. On this point, please read Section 15.5 carefully when you get to it. (2) It is a modeling assumption. Real-life firms chase more complex and multi-dimensional objectives, and insofar as "what real firms do" varies importantly and systematically from this simplifying assumption, we need to be cautious in how we use these models.

[3] Engineers at Boeing would also tell you that Boeing's production technology has what is called a strong *experience-curve* effect, which is discussed near the end of this chapter.

are higher than regular-time rates, so the total labor cost in the short term is likely to be higher than in the longer term. And, also, new employees must be trained. This is an additional short-run cost, but it is a different sort of short-run cost: If, say, Boeing wishes to increase production rates to five per month for two months only and then go back to a production rate of four, it may choose to use overtime only. If, on the other hand, it wishes to increase production rates to five per month for the foreseeable future, it may use overtime to get a quick increase in production rate, but it will probably also begin hiring more employees, incurring the further cost of training them. And what if it wishes to increase to five per month for nine months or twelve? Does it just rely on overtime, or does it hire and train new employees, knowing that after nine (or twelve) months, it may want to lay off some of the new hires? This calls for the sort of net-present-value calculation to which we alluded last section.

Economists often employ the following model of this situation. The *long-run total-cost function* or $\mathrm{LRTC}(x)$ tells us how much it costs to produce at the level x in the long run, once the firm has made all cost-minimizing adjustments to its production routines for producing at the rate x. The firm, the model supposes, is producing at some *status-quo* production rate x_0, incurring total cost $\mathrm{LRTC}(x_0)$. If the firm wishes to change its production rate to x_1—and assuming it plans to stay at the level x_1 for the foreseeable future, in the long-run its cost per period will become $\mathrm{LRTC}(x_1)$. But in the *short* run, as it moves toward producing this new level, it will cost more than $\mathrm{LRTC}(x)$ to produce at level x, because of the frictions incurred in changing production routines. Please note: the firm may have a target level of production x_1 in mind, but because of the frictional expenses incurred in the shorter run, it may get there in stages, producing various levels x between x_0 and x_1.

In reality, the firm is likely to get to x_1 from x_0 more or less continuously. But the standard economic model has the firm move in discrete steps: The model supposes that there is a *short run* and, starting from the status-quo level of x_0, the total cost of producing at level x in this short run is $\mathrm{SRTC}(x)$. There might be an intermediate run, with corresponding intermediate-run total-cost function $\mathrm{IRTC}(x)$. Depending on how elaborate is the model, there might be a *very short run*, a *short run*, an *intermediate run*, a *longer intermediate run*, and finally a *long run*, each with its own total-cost function. To keep the discussion simple, however, we'll deal for the time being with only two runs, a short and a long run.

The usual model makes the following further assumptions connecting the short- and long-run cost functions:

1. If the firm continues to produce at the status-quo level x_0, and if there are no changes in the production technology or costs of inputs, it can continue

in the short run to do just as well as it has been doing:

$$\text{SRTC}(x_0) = \text{LRTC}(x_0).$$

2. But for any level of production $x \neq x_0$, the firm can do better at minimizing its costs if it has more time to make adjustments,[4] so

$$\text{For all } x \neq x_0, \text{LRTC}(x) < \text{SRTC}(x).$$

These two assumptions together imply that the "picture" of the SRTC and LRTC functions is as in Figure 12.1. Note that this drawing makes a further assumption that both functions are smooth (differentiable). This, together with my two assumptions, implies that LRTC and SRTC are tangent to one another at the status quo x_0.

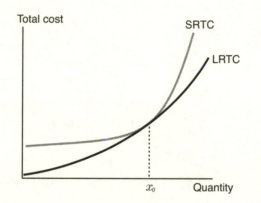

Figure 12.1. SRTC and LRTC given our assumptions.

Please note: Assumptions 1 and 2 and smoothness of the two total-cost functions are modeling *assumptions*. In specific applications, they may not hold. It is possible, for instance, that a firm is able to do things in the short run, for short periods of time, that it cannot sustain in the long run, which can mean $\text{SRTC}(x_0) < \text{LRTC}(x_0)$. It is possible that 1 and 2 hold, but that SRTC has a kink at the status-quo level of production; see Story 3 on page 276. And in cases where the cost of inputs suddenly change, both 1 and 2 may fail; see Problem 12.4.

---

[4] The proviso that there are no changes in production technology or cost of inputs is a maintained part of this assumption. You can ignore this proviso for now, but it will deepen your understanding of this assumption if at some point you tackle Problem 12.4.

Many SRTC Functions, Depending on the Status-Quo Level

We assume that the long run is long enough so that the firm can do all the fine-tuning and adjusting of its production schemes and routines to suit the level of production x. That is, the status-quo level x_0 has no effect on the LRTC function.

But that is manifestly not the case for the SRTC function. That is what the firm can achieve in minimizing its costs in the short run, *starting from the status-quo level* x_0. If the firm started at some other status-quo level, say, x_0', it would have some other SRTC function. In particular, Assumption 1 says that $\text{SRTC}(x_0) = \text{LRTC}(x_0)$. That's for the SRTC function that is based on x_0 as the starting point for changes: A better way to write this would be to stick a subscript on the SRTC function, denoting the starting point, as in SRTC_{x_0}. Then we'd have $\text{SRTC}_{x_0}(x_0) = \text{LRTC}(x_0)$ and, for $x \neq x_0$, $\text{SRTC}_{x_0}(x) > \text{LRTC}(x)$. An elaboration of Figure 12.1 is shown in Figure 12.2, where I've included a second SRTC function for a different starting point.

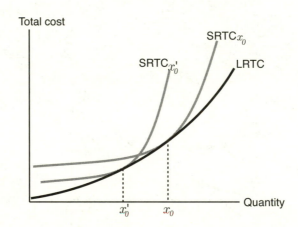

Figure 12.2. *Different status-quo production levels give different SRTC functions.*

In the discussion to follow, I'll assume that the status-quo production level is fixed, and I won't attach the subscript indicating it to the SRTC function. But keep in mind that SRTC depends on the production level from which the firm begins.

Implications for AC and MC

What are the implications of Figure 12.1 for the average-cost and marginal-cost functions?

We'll have two of each, a long-run average-cost function and a short-run average-cost function, and a short-run and a long-run marginal-cost function. The notation SRAC, LRAC, SRMC, and LRMC is used.

Since $SRAC(x) = SRTC(x)/x$ and $LRAC(x) = LRTC(x)/x$, the two average-cost functions inherit the properties assumed in 1 and 2 from the total-cost functions: $SRAC(x_0) = LRAC(x_0)$ and, for all $x \neq x_0$, $SRAC(x) > LRAC(x)$.

But the story for the two marginal-cost functions is more complex and, for some students, confusing. Remember, the marginal-cost function for either -run is the derivative of the total-cost function for the same -run. Since, in Figure 12.1, I've drawn the total-cost functions as smooth at x_0, and since this means that SRTC and LRTC are tangent there, we have

$$SRMC(x_0) = LRMC(x_0).$$

But what about for $x \neq x_0$? Looking at Figure 12.1, you see: For $x > x_0$, $SRTC(x)$ is steeper than $LRTC(x)$. For $x < x_0$, $SRTC(x)$ is less steep than is $LRTC(x)$. Hence

For $x > x_0$, $SRMC(x) > LRMC$. And for $x < x_0$, $SRMC(x) < LRMC(x)$.

Putting these together, we have the picture shown in Figure 12.3.

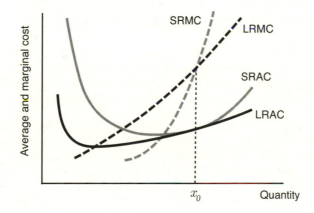

Figure 12.3. SRAC, LRAC, SRMC, and LRMC.

Note that the relationships between the average- and marginal-cost functions that we discussed in Chapter 6 hold for each -run. When $SRMC(x) < SRAC(x)$, SRAC is falling. When $SRMC(x) > SRAC(x)$, SRAC is rising. Therefore, SRMC cuts through SRAC (for this U-shaped SRAC function) at minimum SRAC, or what we can call short-run efficient scale. And similarly for LRAC and LRMC.

Typically, everything depicted in Figure 12.3 makes sense to students seeing this for the first time, *except for* the fact that $SRMC(x) < LRMC(x)$ for $x < x_0$. "How," students have asked, "can the short-run marginal cost be less than its long-run counterpart?" To explain this inutitively, remember that *marginal* costs reflect changes in total-cost levels. If, from the status-quo level x_0, the firm wants to raise its production level, this will cost more in the short run than in the long run. Hence, for $x > x_0$, SRMC$(x) >$ LRMC(x). *And if the firm wants to lower its production rate from x_0 to some smaller x, it will **save less** in the short-run than in the long-run. Hence the change in costs—what marginal cost picks up—will be less. That is, for $x < x_0$, SRMC$(x) <$ LRMC(x).*[5]

Why Is the Short Run Different from the Long Run?
From Technological "Frictions" to Figure 12.1.

Cost functions, per Chapter 11, are derived from two things: the firm's technological capabilities, given (in Chapter 11) by its production function; and the prices being charged for its various inputs into the production process. We can use Chapter 11-style analysis to "derive" pictures like Figure 12.1. Here are three stories of this sort:

Story 1. An input whose level is fixed in the short run. Consider a firm that uses two inputs, m (materials) and l (labor), with production function given by $f(m,l) = m^{1/3}l^{1/6}$. In addition, this firm faces a fixed cost of \$300 per period. The price of m is \$1 per unit, and the price of l is \$4 per unit. Using the methods of Chapter 11, you can show that the firm's total-cost function, if it can freely vary its two inputs, is TC$(x) = 300 + 3x^2$, and so its marginal-cost

---

[5] The following footnote is probably best avoided if your math is a somewhat shaky: the mathematically astute reader will recognize that these relations between short- and long-run marginal costs are not guaranteed by Assumptions 1 and 2 for all $x > x_0$ and all $x < x_0$. They are only guaranteed to hold in a neighborhood of the status-quo level x_0. Nonetheless, we'll assume throughout that they hold for all $x \neq x_0$.

Students who remember the Fundamental Theorem of Calculus—the derivative of the integral of a function f is the function f—are sometimes still troubled by Figures 12.1 and 12.3. The X-run marginal-cost function is the derivative of the the X-run total-cost function, so the integral of the X-run marginal-cost function should give you the X-run total cost function, where X can be either short- or long-. Per Figure 12.3, if SRMC is less than LRMC for quantities below the status quo, doesn't this imply that the SRTC of quantities below the status quo is *less* than LRTC? Which, seemingly, contradicts Figure 12.1 and, indeed, our general rule that short-run total costs are always at least as large as long-run total costs.

If this troubles you, remember: the Fundamental Theorem of Calculus says that $\int_0^y$ XRMC$(x)dx =$ XRTC$(y) -$ XRTC(0) or, rewriting this, XRTC$(y) =$ XRTC$(0) + \int_0^y$ XRMC$(x)dx$. So while it may be true that $\int_0^y$ SRMC$(x)dx < \int_0^y$ LRMC$(x)dx$ for $y < x_0$, since the integrands have this property, you still have to consider the SR and LR fixed costs, SRTC(0) and LRTC(0). As you see in Figure 12.2, LRTC$(0) <$ SRTC(0)—fixed costs are higher in the short run than in the long run—and, indeed, if you work your way through all this math, you'll discover that, since SRTC$(x_0) =$ LRTC(x_0) (where, remember, x_0 is the status-quo level of production), we must have

$$\text{SRTC}(0) - \text{LRTC}(0) = \int_0^{x_0} \text{LRMC}(x)dx - \int_0^{x_0} \text{SRMC}(x)dx.$$

function is $MC(x) = 6x$. This firm has been facing the inverse demand function $P(x) = 160 - 2x$, so marginal cost equals marginal revenue at $x_0 = 16$, at which point it employs 64 units of l and 512 units of m. (If this seems familiar, it may be because you did Problem 11.5, which asked you to derive all these things.)

Suppose, from this status-quo production plan and level of output, the firm decides to change its level of output. (Why might it do this? Read on). Suppose that, in the short run, the firm can freely vary m, but it is stuck with $l = 64$; it takes time to hire new employees or to discharge them. So the firm is, in the short run, stuck with $l = 64$. It can still vary its output level but, now, in the short run, to change its output level to x, it must choose m so that $f(m, 64) = m^{1/3}64^{1/6} = 2m^{1/3} = x$, which means $m = x^3/8$. Hence, in the short run, its total cost function is

$$SRTC(x) = \$300 + (\$4 \times 64) + (\$1 \times x^3/8) = 556 + x^3/8.$$

This is the long-run fixed cost of \$300, plus the short-run fixed cost of 64 units of l, which is \$4 × 64, plus the cost of material input required to get production up or down to x units.

Either analytically or using Excel, you can verify that if $300 + 3x^2$ is the long-run total-cost function and $556 + x^3/8$ is the short-run total-cost function, than both Assumptions 1 and 2 from pages 270 and 271 hold (and both functions are differentiable). Use Excel to graph them, and the picture will look just like Figure 12.1. And if you graph the corresponding average and marginal cost functions, you will get Figure 12.3.

Story 2. Both inputs can change, but one of them costs more to increase and saves less to decrease. The story is the same as in Story 1, except that, in the short run, the firm can increase or decrease l. But it does so at disadvantageous prices: Any short-run increase in l costs \$6 per unit increase, and any short-run decrease only saves \$2 of the \$4 the firm was paying. (Think of this as: l represents labor inputs, and the firm can get more labor by paying existing employees time-and-a-half for overtime and can reduce l by furloughing workers, but must pay them half the wages they were earning while they are furloughed.) The resulting short-run total-cost function is difficult to compute, so I'll do it for you:

$$SRTC(x) = \begin{cases} 428 + 2.3811x^2, & \text{if } x \le 12.6992, \\ 556 + x^3/8, & \text{if } 12.6992 \le x \le 18.3154, \text{ and} \\ 172 + 3.434143x^2, & \text{for } x \ge 18.3154. \end{cases}$$

(See the solution to Problem 12.2 in the *Online Supplement* for an explanation.) You can check, using Excel, that this gives us a picture just like Figure 12.1.

Story 3. Just like Stories 1 and 2, but with fixed coefficients and constant returns to scale. Suppose a firm with two inputs, m and l, has a fixed-coefficient, constant-returns-to-scale technology, where the fixed ratio of the inputs is $m = 8l$. Specifically, suppose that to make one unit takes 4 units of l and 32 units of m. If the prices of m and l are \$1 and \$4, respectively, the long-run total-cost function is LRTC$(x) = (\$4 \times 4 + \$1 \times 32)x = 48x$. Suppose the status-quo level of production is 16, so the firm (at the status quo) is using 64 units of l and 512 units of m.

If, in the short run, the firm cannot change the amount of l it uses, then the short-run total cost of any quantity greater than 16 is infinity or, put in plainer English, the firm can't produce more than 16 in the short run. It can produce less, and for $x \leq 16$, SRTC$(x) = 300 + \$4 \times 16 + \$1 \times 32 \times x = 556 + 32x$. This doesn't quite give the picture of Figure 12.1; properties 1 and 2 from pages 270 and 271 hold (after a fashion for $x > 16$), but the tangency of the two SRTC functions is no longer valid.

Alternatively, if, in the short run, the firm can change m freely and can change x under the cost conditions of Story 2, we get

$$\text{SRTC}(x) = \begin{cases} 128 + 40x, & \text{for } x \leq 16, \text{ and} \\ 56x - 128, & \text{for } x \geq 16. \end{cases}$$

The picture is similar to Figure 12.1, except that LRTC is the linear function $48x$ and, while SRTC(16) = LRTC(16) (and both equal \$768), SRTC has a decided kink at $x = 16$. (It is a good exercise for you to derive this SRTC function. Or see the solution to Problem 12.3 in the *Online Supplement*.)

These are only three of many, many possible stories. Some of them, like Stories 1 and 2, give pictures that look like Figure 12.1; others, like Story 3, can provide a kink in SRTC at the status-quo point. And there are other possibilities: Suppose, for instance, that the firm can, for short periods of time, push its workforce to extraordinary levels of effort. In such case, SRTC might be less than LRTC for levels of production above the status quo.

And a different picture emerges if we suppose that (a) the firm is unable to shift its employment of one or more inputs in the short run, and (b) because of a shift in market conditions, the price of a short-run fixed factor of production (or input) changes. Consider, for instance, the firm in Story 1, producing 16 units through a combination of $l = 64$ and $m = 512$. Suppose that, suddenly, the price of l rises to, say, \$6. (The price of m stays \$1.) At the old prices, the production function called for an 8:1 ration of m to l at every scale of production. At the new prices, cost minimization calls for a 12:1 ratio. *If* the firm chose to maintain output levels at $x = 16$, it would want to decrease l and increase m and, in the long run, it can do this. But in the short run, if it is stuck at $l = 64$, it can't do this.

So this would be a case where, owing to a shift in the prices of inputs, SRTC at the status quo is strictly greater than LRTC. For more on this, see Problem 12.4.

Story 1, Continued: Reacting to a Shift in Demand

Consider the firm in Story 1, whose long-run total-cost function is $TC(x) = 300 + 3x^2$ and which has been facing inverse demand $P(x) = 160 - 2x$. Hence MC = MR is $6x = 160 - 4x$, leading to a profit-maximizing level of output of 16 units and a profit-maximizing price of $138. This is the status quo.

Suddenly, inverse demand shifts upward to $P(x) = 200 - 2x$. *This shift was not anticipated by the firm and, moreover, the firm anticipates that this shift is permanent.* How will it react?

In the long run, the firm will equate LRMC of $6x$ to the new MR, which is $6x = 200 - 4x$ or $x = 20$ and a profit-maximizing price of $160.

But, before that can happen, the firm will make short-run adjustments in what it is doing. Following Story 1, we suppose that the firm's SRTC function from the status-quo level of production $x_0 = 16$ is $SRTC(x) = 556 + x^3/8$. Hence, its SRMC is $3x^2/8$ and, in the short run, SRMC = MR is

$$\frac{3x^2}{8} = 200 - 4x, \quad \text{which has solution} \quad x = 18.3685,$$

for a price of $200 - 2 \times 18.3685 = \$163.2630$.

Note the implications of this for the price charged by the firm: At the status-quo level of $x = 16$ and the old inverse-demand function $160 - 2x$, price is $128. In the short run, price jumps to $163.26; in the long run, it moves back down a bit, to $160—higher than at the start, but lower than in the short run. This, of course, happens because the firm moves in steps from the old quantity of 16 to the new long run quantity 20.

There is a final chapter to this short story: When, in the long run, the firm settles at $x = 20$, it will be employing 80 units of l and 640 units of m. This establishes a new status quo and, in particular, a new short-run total-cost function, predicated on $l = 80$ being fixed in the short run. From this new status quo, if the firm wishes to change from 80 units of output to some new level x, it must choose m to satisfy $m^{1/3}80^{1/6} = x$, or $m = x^3/\sqrt{80} = x^3/8.9443$, for a (new) short-run total-cost function $SRTC(x) = 300 + (\$4 \times 80) + (\$1 \times x^3/8.9443) = \$620 + x^3/8.9443$.

See Figure 12.4 for a pictorial depiction of this story. The picture concerns the original and new marginal revenue functions, long-run marginal cost, and (from the status-quo $x_0 = 16$) short-run marginal cost, since it is easiest to follow the action on the "picture" of the various marginal functions.

Let me reiterate: This is a very simple and assumption-bound model of what in real life is a complex phenomenon. Real-life firms probably adjust their quantity continuously, not in two steps. In real life, there are different

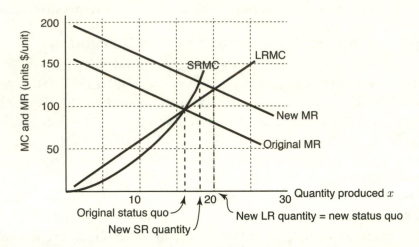

Figure 12.4. *Reacting to a upward shift in (inverse) demand.* At the original demand, MR = MC at $x_0 = 16$. When demand shifts up, so does MR. The firm, in the short run, increases quantity produced to the point where SRMC = new MR, which is $x = 18.3685$; in the long run, it settles where LRMC = new MR, at $x = 20$.

ways to adjust labor supply, involving different combinations of ongoing costs (e.g., using overtime for incumbent employees) and sunk costs (search, hiring, and training costs of new hires). And the best combination will depend on how persistent the shift in demand is likely to be, based on net-present-value calculations.[6]

That said, this very simple model is useful as a illustrative caricature of reality. In particular, it alerts us to the facts that (1) firms face frictions in adjusting to shifting environmental variables (such as shifts in the demand that they face) and (2), because of those frictions, their adjustments to changes in environmental shifts take time. And, as you'll see in Chapter 14, this model is employed to discuss the dynamics of price and supply decisions in *competitive industries*, although you'll need to wait until Chapter 14 to see what that means.

12.3. Durable Assets

We turn now to the second sort of multiperiod effect in production: durable assets. This change in topic is accompanied by a change in style; we eschew functions, algebra, calculus, and pictures, and settle for chat.

---

[6] The case *Oil Tanker Shipping*, HBS Case 9-384-034, illustrates some of these real-life complexities, although it adds a further complication that firms in the oil-tanker-shipping business are competitive. You shouldn't try to tackle that case until you have absorbed Chapter 14 but, once you have finished Chapter 14, it is a great case for connecting economic theory to considerably more messy reality.

The Range of Durable Assets

The range of a firm's durable assets is huge. Obviously included here are real assets, such as buildings and land; large fixed assets such as blast furnaces, stamping machines, and assembly lines; and more temporary equipment, such as jigs, fixtures, and tools. But the list of durable assets contains a lot more than these obvious items. It includes:

- Human capital, or the stock of skills, training, and so on held by the firm's workforce.

- Goodwill, including the goodwill of suppliers, employees, union officials if the workforce is unionized, government officials, and so on.

- Demand-side assets, such as a strong reputation with a customer base built up from years of high-quality production and service or from a strong advertising campaign.

The firm doesn't hold legal title to its workers' human capital but often effectively controls it.[7] And while goodwill and reputation are largely intangible, they can be very valuable and powerful, as discussed in Part I.

Including Durable Assets in Economic Models

The whole point of durable assets is that they are useful for more than one production period. Money is spent today, to purchase the asset, and "value" from it accrues in later periods. Moreover, assets—whether physical or less tangible—can depreciate as time passes, at a rate that is usually somewhat, and sometimes mainly, under the control of the firm. So expenditures on maintaining or enhancing assets today—paying to keep the tools in good repair, to enhance a machine's performance, or to maintain a firm's reputation for producing high-quality goods—subtract from today's cash flows but add to tomorrow's. Depreciation here does not mean accounting depreciation but rather real depreciation, a temporal change in the asset's ability to contribute to the production process. Physical assets tend to *de*preciate in this sense, while intangible assets, such as human capital and customer goodwill can and often do *ap*preciate.

In theory, durable assets are easily handled. In a multiperiod setting, rather than speak of the profit of a firm, we work with the stream of net cash flows. We assume that the firm chooses its production plans, including which assets to invest in and how to maintain them, to maximize the sum of appropriately discounted net cash flows.

Therefore, the decision whether to purchase a particular blast furnace—or invest in worker training or customer goodwill—amounts to a present-value calculation: The blast furnace involves an immediate expenditure but provides increased revenues or decreased production cost, hence increased net cash flows,

---

[7] See Baron and Kreps, *Strategic Human Resources* (New York: Wiley and Sons, 1999), Chapter 4.

in future years. The blast furnace is purchased if the purchase decision increases the overall net present value (NPV) of the firm's stream of cash flows.

As many readers know from experience, firms sometimes employ other techniques, such as internal rates of return or payback periods, to evaluate whether to employ a particular durable asset. I leave it to finance textbooks to explain why NPV calculations are superior.

And, as many readers will know, NPV calculations require a discount rate, so it is necessary to specify which discount rate to use. Finance textbooks should be consulted concerning the *risk-adjusted cost of capital*, with the rationale that this reflects the market valuation of $1 today compared to a (risky) $1 next week or month or year or decade.

Finally, as many readers also know and the rest can guess, the less tangible is a durable asset, the harder it is in practice to do these calculations. What would be the impact on the future cash flows of an investment in the goodwill of suppliers? What would be the impact of an investment in training workers or putting up a gym where they can play basketball at lunchtime? To reiterate, durable assets are easy to deal with *in theory*. In practice, the NPV prescription can be hard to fill, and managers have to rely on their instincts about what would or would not add value to the enterprise.

Accounting Depreciation and the Construction of Income Statements

Suppose durable assets could be evaluated in this fashion in practice. Compare the notion of computing the NPV of the stream of cash flows with accounting procedures and, in particular, the strange accounting practice of depreciating durable assets, where firms "recognize" depreciation in their income statements by taking a charge against current income for depreciation of assets, using rules such as straight-line depreciation.

- What, if anything, does accounting income have to do with economic profit?

- Why do accountants depreciate assets?

- From an economic perspective, what sins of omission or commission do accountants commit?

Let me say at the outset, these are difficult questions, and the various concerned communities—accountants, economists, lawyers, managers, regulators, and tax authorities—argue vociferously about answers. Completely satisfactory answers are impossible, and even reasonably satisfactory answers require concepts that we ignore until late in the book. But this is a good place to begin a discussion of these questions.

To answer these questions, we first discuss the uses to which income statements are put. There are several uses and I focus on only the most important: Income statements provide information to outsiders—especially outside investors—about the "ongoing health" of the enterprise. This provides outsiders with the information they need to do business with and in the enterprise. A potential investor in XYZ Corporation wants some indication of how well XYZ is doing, and this investor turns first to XYZ's annual report and income statement.

Suppose that XYZ is offered a license to produce a given product for the next 5 years. Suppose the firm can make excellent use of this license, because it has established channels of distribution that are ideal for the product. Purchasing the license is a good deal; the present worth of the incremental net cash flows from buying the license is substantially positive. But the license costs the firm a lot of money up front, with the incremental revenues coming only in the future. Purchasing this license ultimately generates value for shareholders but, insofar as the license must be paid for immediately, it *depresses* the firm's current-period cash flow.

In an ideal world of very smart investors, XYZ Corporation would issue the following information: "We have bought a license costing us N this period that, we believe, will add an extra M per year to our bottom line for each of the next 5 years." Investors check on the bona fides of this claim, compute the sum of the discounted incremental cash flows, and are happily impressed by the wise decision of the managers of the firm.

Unhappily, investors, instead of doing these calculations, look at "reports" in which all the firm's current activities are summarized into a single consolidated income figure. So, how should XYZ report the financial consequences of its license purchase?

Suppose XYZ takes the purchase price of the asset and charges it against the firm's cash flow a bit at a time; say, one-fifth of the purchase price for each of the 5 years the license runs. In this way, in each of the 5 years, if those rosy claims are correct, the firm will realize positive cash flow from using the license more than sufficient to cover that year's portion of the purchase price of the license.

Accountants call this *straight-line depreciation*. Instead of charging the full purchase price of the license against current income, the license is depreciated in the accounting sense over its lifetime, with a fraction of its purchase price charged against income in each period it runs.

This is not ideal on at least two grounds: First, if credit is to be given for a good management decision, why not "recognize" the full NPV in year 1, when the license is purchased? Second, suppose that the incremental cash flow from the license will be very large in years 4 and 5, but not much at all in years 1, 2, and 3. Then, charging years 1 through 3 with one-fifth of the license fee makes those years look worse than they really are.

Why settle for the less-than-ideal procedure of straight-line depreciation? The reason is that accounting numbers, to be useful to the investing public, have to be somewhat objectively produced. Firms often have an incentive to paint a rosier picture of their situation than is true. If income figures were produced entirely subjectively, they would be unreliable. There must be rules and standards for how accounting numbers are produced, and there usually must be an independent authority—the external auditor—willing to vouch that those rules and standards were applied correctly, if investors and other parties are to trust the income statement.

Of course, the more formulaic and objective are the rules, the less well the accounting numbers reflect how the firm is doing in this period. Straight-line depreciation of an asset, for instance, is a good all-purpose rule that fits fairly well in a wide variety of circumstances and reduces the degrees of freedom of those generating the income report, *but therefore* it fits very few circumstances perfectly.

When accountants debate the rules of their profession—the Generally Accepted Accounting Procedures (GAAP), what the International Accounting Standards Board (IASB) or its national counterparts permit—the debates should be and often are framed along these lines. First, for the item under discussion, what is an ideal measure of its impact on the long-term profits of the firm? Then, to the extent that the ideal would allow for manipulation by management, what objective and formulaic rules can be devised that do rough justice to the wide range of specific situations that arise?

That is the basic story. I close with three remarks:

1. Some accountants and accounting theorists would dispute the notion that income should measure how current decisions affect the flow of profits to the firm, now and in the future. The other major category of information provided by accountants is the *balance sheet*, a statement of the firm's productive assets and liabilities. Income, by this alternative perspective, should be a measure of the current flow of realized "profit"; if management makes a wise purchase of an asset whose value to the firm is more than its purchase price, the value of the asset should be recognized on the balance sheet. I have a lot of sympathy for this philosophical position. But it does make it harder to understand some accounting procedures that go into the determination of income; why not just report cash flow and recognize the value of the asset on the balance sheet?

2. In the late 1990s, so-called dot-com companies posed a challenge to accounting conventional wisdom. These companies had substantial market value, even when they were showing quarter after quarter of accounting losses. If accounting income is meant to be a measure of how well its management is doing, this measure did a poor job for the dot-coms.

   The problem was that the dot-com companies invested heavily in "assets" that traditional accounting procedures have a hard time with, such as market share, channels of distribution, customer base, know-how, and human resources. These assets might pay back some day, and pay back handsomely, or so the market believed. But expenditures for them appear as immediate, direct charges in the current income statements. Accountants "ought" to have counted such expenditures as investment, with depreciation charges (only) appearing as appropriate on income statements. But they did not do this, and companies that consistently showed accounting losses simultaneously had substantial market capitalization.

3. I cannot resist closing with a slap at the terrible job done by many countries— certainly by the United States—in accounting for assets when it comes to the national budget. No serious attempt is made, at least in the United States, to take into account whether yearly expenditures are for infrastructure, such as highways, or for expendibles, nor is depreciation seriously measured. This is not a book in macroeconomics—and I'm far from an expert on that mysterious branch of economics—but I think I know enough to say that, when people start talking about the federal budget surplus or deficit, without regard to the formation or degradation of long-lived national assets within the budget, they are not engaged in either meaningful or intelligent debate.

12.4. Know-How

The third sort of multiperiod effect we discuss concerns know-how. In a sense, know-how is a durable productive asset, and it could be dealt with in the same way as human capital or customer goodwill: An investment in know-how improves future cash flows, and whether a particular investment in know-how is undertaken or not should depend on whether it improves or degrades the net present value of the firm's cash flows. Know-how should, but rarely does, turn up on the firm's balance sheet, and charges for the depreciation of know-how, or credits for its appreciation, should appear on the income statement.

But know-how is placed in its own category, because, while we certainly think of production functions with arguments such as metal lathes, blast furnaces, and skilled labor, know-how *is* the production function itself.

Some forms of investing in know-how are fairly tangible and direct. A manufacturing firm might purchase a license that gives it access to a patented production process; the license should, and often does, go on the firm's balance sheet, and its cost is amortized over the lifetime of the license. Other forms are direct if not so tangible, such as expenditures on R&D. But among the most interesting forms of investment in know-how are indirect investments, such as the experience-curve effect and TQM.

The Experience Curve

In the manufacture of aircraft, computer chips, and a host of other products, a remarkable empirical regularity is that direct costs of production fall a fixed percentage when cumulative output doubles, at least on average. If you are told that a certain manufacturing process follows an 80% learning or experience curve, this means that the firm can expect the 2000th unit it makes to cost 80% of its 1000th unit, and the 3000th to cost 80% of unit number 1500. There are all sorts of fancifications of this idea, concerning how unit costs decline for firms with multiple plants, how they change when a firm moves from a less-advanced to a more-advanced model of the same general product, and so on, but the basic idea is fairly clear. Firms, if they pay attention, learn by experience less costly ways of producing whatever they produce, and the sequence of unit costs falls in a very predictable pattern.

The consequences can be substantial. In the late 1970s and early 1980s, management consulting firms did quite well pushing the idea of the experience curve, which was loosely translated to say that the long-term profitable firms are those with the largest market shares. In infant industries or early in a product life cycle, firms should be willing to sell their products for less than their current direct costs, because by so doing they are riding down the experience curve, to a point, sometime later, when large positive cash flows would be realized. In bidding to sell a brand new model of aircraft, aircraft manufacturers often bid very low relative to their current direct costs in order to ride down the learning curve: The suppliers of military aircraft plan to take a loss on their initial sales in the hope of making profits on reorders or orders to foreign governments; and the suppliers of civilian aircraft chase initial sales very aggressively to build up the volume of production.

Whenever the experience curve is operating, production in and of itself is an investment in lower production costs, hence higher profits in the future. From the perspective of a proper economic calculation, losses incurred in early periods, measured in terms of revenue less the direct cost of production, may not be losses at all, since some of the cost of production is really an investment in knowledge. A controversy on this point arose concerning the sale of dynamic random-access memory chips (DRAMs) by Japanese firms in the United States. American manufacturers insisted that the Japanese were dumping DRAMs on the American market, where *dumping* means selling at a loss to forestall domestic (American) producers from entering. Certainly the Japanese were selling their DRAMs at prices well below direct manufacturing costs, and as the Americans were quick to argue, this non-profit-maximizing approach to price setting could only be for some nefarious purpose. The Japanese manufacturers retorted that using direct costs of manufacture is not economically correct; they claimed that they were simply pricing their chips in the way that would maximize their overall long-term profits, whether the American manufacturers were in the market or not.

Modeling the Experience-Curve Effect

Modeling the experience-curve effect requires rethinking the concept of a total-cost function. Up to this point, whenever we write $TC(x)$, we think of the variable x as the *rate* of production, the number of units made during a specific time period, such as a month or a year. Hence, we focus entirely on the extent to which costs are driven by the rate of production. But, with an experience-curve effect, the total cost of producing x units in a given production period is a function of x *and* the cumulative amount produced before the current production period, which we denote temporarily by X. Writing $TC(x, X)$ for this total cost function, we assume that TC is increasing in x and decreasing in X.

In the simplest form of the experience curve, things are even simpler. It is claimed that unit costs fall a set percentage with each doubling of cumulative output, *no matter what is the rate of production*. This is rather incredible, because for one thing, it means that the cost of the 10,000th unit is the same whether the firm takes 5 weeks or 5 years to produce 10,000 units. Notwithstanding the (in)credibility of this claim, it means that $TC(x, X)$ can be simplified as follows:

- The cost of producing unit n is given by c_n, whenever unit n is made.

- If the firm produces X units prior to the current production period and x units during this period, total costs this period are $c_{X+1} + c_{X+2} + \ldots + c_{X+x}$.

- Moreover, for some $\gamma < 1$, $c_2 = \gamma c_1$, $c_4 = \gamma c_2$, $c_6 = \gamma c_3$, $c_8 = \gamma c_4 = \gamma^2 c_2 = \gamma^3 c_1$, and so on.

- *Therefore,* if the firm has produced X units prior to the current production period and x units during this period, total costs this period are (approximately)

$$\frac{c_1[(X + x)^\beta - X^\beta]}{\beta}, \quad \text{for } \beta = \frac{\ln(\gamma)}{\ln(2)} + 1.$$

That last step takes more math than I expect readers to know, so just take it on faith, or see the derivation in the *Online Supplement*.

The Formula Meets the Real World

This is a pretty remarkable model, on two grounds. It says that the rate of production is unimportant to costs: whether Boeing produces 10 787s a year for 10 years or 20 a month for 5 months, the cost of the 101st plane is the same and independent of Boeing's production rate when the 101st is produced. Further, costs fall in such a regular pattern that we can determine the unit and total costs of any unit from just two parameters: the cost of the first unit and the steepness of the experience curve.

In fact, this is a bit too remarkable; the world is not quite this simple. Costs depend on rates of production as well as on cumulative experience. Experience lowers costs but at rates that vary with time and are somewhat random. Previous experience can count and there are spillover effects: Boeing did not start a new experience curve when it began producing 787-10s but profited from its experiences producing 787-8s and 787-9s. Different parts of a large product have different experience-curve rates; for instance, the rate of decline in costs for wings is larger than for cabins. Moreover, this price reduction is not free: Specific actions taken by the firm can affect the rate of cost reduction, which in just a few paragraphs takes us to TQM.

Still, the idea that costs are lowered by cumulative output means that a firm chasing maximal profits should "overproduce" and "underperform" in terms of revenue less cost early in a product's life cycle. Put in terms that hearken back to earlier chapters, MC = MR remains true, but the computation of marginal cost can be tricky. To see this fleshed out, try the exercise Pricing Down the Experience Curve? in the *Chapter 12 Material* in the *Online Supplement*.

Natural Resource Extraction

In contrast to the experience-curve story, where costs fall with the level of cumulative output, in some cases production costs *rise* with cumulative output. The most prevalent case is that of natural resource extraction—for instance, extracting oil reserves, coal mining, or ore mining—where it becomes harder and more expensive to extract resources as the pool or vein is depleted. In this case, the "cost" of extracting the easy-to-get resource (oil, coal, or ore) should be thought of as greater than just the cost of physical extraction, insofar as this extraction imposes higher costs on later production periods. The economics of the situation, and models of cost structures, are the same as that of the experience curve, except that $c(x, X)$ —the cost of extracting x units in the current period if X units were extracted previously—increases in both x and X.

Total Quality Management

If the experience curve was to be found in every nook and cranny of the management press and management education in the early 1980s, the big buzz words ten years later were *Total Quality Management*. There is no single form of TQM but rather a number of varieties and variations. Moreover, a number of other buzz words or terms are used somewhat interchangeably with TQM: *world class manufacturing*, *lean production systems*, *kanban systems*, and the *Toyota Production System*. These share the following characteristics:

- Management and workers together must strive incessantly and continually to improve the production process, pursuing products of higher and higher quality, measured by conformance to specification.

- The production process and product specifications should be carefully and systematically documented, and conformance to spec should be watched especially carefully.

- Problems related to quality or production process should be dealt with as they occur; they should not be papered over or left for some later day.

- Workers must take responsibility for their own product quality; they must know how to recognize quality problems and be able—both in terms of a wide knowledge of the entire production process and the authority to implement changes—to solve problems as problems arise.

- The production process should be continuously subjected to increasing stress, in the form of lower work-in-process inventory, shorter production runs and more frequent changeovers, and so on, because stress gives the workers and managers the opportunity to see and correct problems in the production process.

- Suppliers must be tightly integrated into the production process and part of the TQM effort.

In traditional (economic) discussions of quality choice by a firm, it is assumed that the firm pays increased costs to obtain higher-quality output. Firms may be willing to pay those costs, if higher-quality output means a better reputation with consumers of the output and thus even higher revenues. But increased quality means increased total cost, to be traded off against increased revenues.

In contrast, the purported advantage of TQM is succinctly captured in a slogan coined by one of its developers, Philip Crosby: Quality is free. Crosby's slogan denies the existence of a trade-off between higher revenue and higher costs from higher quality. He claims that if the firm pursues better quality, using the general scheme of management he details, then higher quality costs the firm nothing. In fact, the firm might find that it costs less to produce at higher quality.

Economists respond reflexively to statements that *X is free* with the aphorism *There are no free lunches*.[8] So, in the early days of TQM, economists tended to dismiss TQM as a sham; nothing is free, certainly not quality. But TQM should not be dismissed; viewed correctly, it makes good sense, even economic sense, which is not inevitably the same thing.

From the perspective of economics, the magic at work in TQM—if and when TQM does work—comes from the idea that the firm's production technology can be improved if the firm invests in product and process improvements. This

---

[8] This phrase was coined with reference to the "free lunches" offered by saloons in the 1800s; customers who thought that they could eat for free were quickly disabused of the notion. Robert Heinlein, in *Stranger in a Strange Land*, popularized the phrase "There ain't no such thing as a free lunch," or TANSTAAFL. Independently, the economist Milton Friedman brought the phrase into the lexicon of economics, as a guiding principle of the Chicago School of economics.

involves learning how to make existing products more efficiently and reformulating product design so that the products are more manufacturable. The way to obtain the knowledge needed to improve product and process is to understand deeply the existing process and learn from mistakes or flaws that come up when employing the existing process. By chasing higher quality or greater conformance to specification, one focuses on the cases where conformance to specification is poor, which is precisely where the product or process needs to be and can be improved. Hence chasing higher quality in the form of greater conformance to specification is precisely chasing the sort of product and process improvements that, in the longer term, mean both higher quality and lower cost.

TQM is a lot more than this. The ways to invest most effectively in improved process and product design involve the management of work-in-process inventory, where the terms *kanban* and *lean production systems* come in, workforce practices that give workers knowledge and authority, tightly integrated relations with suppliers, and so on. Those details are what make TQM effective or not, because they are the means by which one will or will not succeed in obtaining knowledge about process and product design. The essence of TQM lies in these details, details I do not get into here. (The "tightly integrated supplier" part of the story was discussed back in Chapter 5; remember Toyota's relationships with its suppliers.) But, from the point of view of basic microeconomics, TQM is about an investment in know-how, involving a trade-off between today's cash flow and tomorrow's. Crosby's *quality is free*, in this respect, should be reformulated as *quality is a great investment in know-how that will quickly pay for itself*, even if it involves a rise in today's costs.

Executive Summary

- This chapter looks at some issues concerning multiperiod production.

- In place of profit maximization, we assume firms maximize their market value, which is operationalized as maximizing the sum of the discounted net cash flows. The justification for this operationalization, as well as the identification of the appropriate discount factors, is part of financial market theory and corporate finance.

- The first dynamic effect considered is friction in production, a higher cost in the short run than in the long run for changes from the status-quo production plan.

- If SRTC is at least as large as LRTC for every level of production, and if they are equal at the status-quo level of production, then SRMC = LRMC at the status quo, SRMC $\geq$ LRMC for increases from the status quo, and SRMC $\leq$ LRMC for decreases from the status quo.

- The second dynamic effect considered is the role of durable productive assets. Most of the discussion here concerns the accounting measure of income and, more specifically, depreciation. Accounting income is meant to be a single-dimensional measure of how the enterprise is doing, used to inform investors and other outsiders. But, so that outsiders can trust these numbers, they must be computed in reasonably objective fashion, which compromises accuracy. Depreciation takes the cost of durable assets, at least some durable assets, and distributes that cost over the useful life of the asset.

- The third dynamic effect concerns the special durable asset know-how. Two specific "models" of the indirect accumulation of know-how—the experience curve model of production costs and total quality management—are described.

Problems

12.1 Suppose a firm that uses three inputs, k, l, and m, has production function

$$f(k, l, m) = k^{1/2}l^{1/3}m^{1/6}.$$

The prices of the three inputs are, respectively, $p_k = 48$, $p_l = 16$, and $p_m = 1$. The firm faces inverse demand $P(x) = 192 - x$.

(a) What is the (long-run) total-cost function for this firm?

(b) What quantity x_0 maximizes its profit?

(c) In the short run, from the status-quo position you compute in doing parts a and b, the firm can vary l and m freely but cannot change k at all. What is its short-run total-cost function from this status-quo point?

(d) Suppose (inverse) demand changes (permanently) to $P(x) = 200 - x$. What are the short-run and long-run (= new status-quo) production levels of the firm, assuming it maximizes profit in each -run?

12.2 (a) Using Excel or some similar program, plot LRTC and SRTC for Story 2 (page 275), for x in the range 10 to 20.

(b) Derive the short-run total-cost function given on page 275 for Story 2. This will probably be difficult, so let me give you a hint. If the prices were $p_l = 6$ and $p_m = 1$, the cost-minimizing ratio of m to l would be 12 to 1, and, at $x = 18.3154$, the optimal level of l would be 64. If the prices were $p_l = 2$ and $p_m = 1$, the cost-minimizing ratio of m to l would be 4 to 1, and, at $x = 12.6992$, the optimal level of l would be 64. Even with this hint, this is probably going to be very difficult; see the solution in the *Online Supplement* if you are stymied.

12.3 Derive the SRTC function displayed in the middle of page 276. (This should not be that hard.)

12.4 Go back to the basic story of a firm with production function $f(m, l) = l^{1/3}m^{1/6}$, where $p_l = 4$ and $p_m = 1$, where the firm has additional fixed costs of

300, and where inverse demand is given by $P(x) = 160 - 2x$. As recorded in the text of the chapter, this firm has LRTC function $300 + 3x^2$ and so maximizes profit by employing $l = 64$ and $m = 512$, giving $x = 16$ and output price \$128. In the long run, this firm can freely vary l and m at market prices; in the short run, its level of l is fixed but it can freely vary m.

Now suppose that, suddenly and unexpectedly, the price of l rises to \$6. The managers of this firm are convinced that this price rise is permanent. How do they respond in the short run and in the long run?

(You might want to begin by finding the LR and SRTC functions in the new circumstances and, using Excel, plot them. What has happened to Assumptions 1 and 2 from pages 270 and 271? Why has this happened?)

For a fairly long and complex problem about the experience curve, please see the *Online Supplement*, following the solution to Problem 12.4.

Part IV
Competitive Markets

13. The Most Famous Picture in Economics

Supply equals demand is the most famous phrase in economics, and the picture that goes with it is economics' most famous picture. This fame is well deserved. The expression and picture encapsulate powerful and empirically relevant concepts. In this chapter, we explore the expression and picture.

Most people who have taken a course in microeconomics, if they remember anything at all, remember the maxim that *supply equals demand* and the corresponding picture, Figure 13.1.

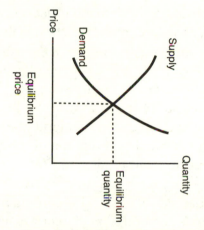

Figure 13.1. Supply, demand, and equilibrium.

One part of this picture—the demand function—is old business for us by now. Added to the demand function are (1) the *supply function* and (2), where the supply function intersects the demand function, the *equilibrium price and quantity*.

Before going into detail about items 1 and 2, let me explain why the labels are all turned on their side: Economists always draw this picture with price on the vertical axis and quantity on the horizontal axis. But, in terms of the two functions, demand and supply, *price* is the independent or driving variable. So, to remind you of this (to get you to tilt your head or to rotate the page by ninety degrees), I've labelled the figure in this unusual fashion. Henceforth, I don't do this. But remember, price is the independent variable in this figure.

13.1. The Supply Function

Throughout Parts II and III, we were thinking of firms that supplied some good (or goods) to the market, facing a demand function, and so setting price. In this chapter and the next one, and for large chunks of the three chapters that follow that, the story changes dramatically. Whoever is supplying this good to the market—be they individuals who are endowed with quantities of the good that they would sell for the right price, or firms that are producing the item for sale—is "small" relative to the entire market in the good and so sees and accepts that there is a price of the good upon which their individual supply decision has no impact. Instead of deciding which price–quantity pair to select off of the demand function that the individual seller faces, the individual seller must decide on how much to supply, *given the price prevailing in the market*. This is the "perfectly competitive firm" described back on page 124, accompanied by assumptions that makes this model plausible: Suppliers are small relative to the market, the goods supplied by different suppliers are so nearly perfect substitutes that they can be treated as being precisely the same, and information about the equilibrium price is known to everyone on either side of the market.

Because of this interpretation, the demand function isn't quite what it was in Part II. In Part II, we thought of the demand function as that facing the individual firm. In Figure 13.1, the demand function gives the quantity demanded of all the many suppliers of the good. In the language of economics, it is the *whole-market* or *industry-demand function*. To unify what we did in Part II with this story, you can think of each supplier as facing his or her or its own individual demand function: This would be (a) zero demand at any price more than the equilibrium price, (b) an essentially infinite queue of customers at any price less than the equilibrium price, and (c) demand for as much or as little as the individual supplier wishes to supply, at the equilibrium price.

Just as we spoke in Chapter 7 of demand as coming from different segments or customers, with aggregate demand being the *horizontal sum* of the the different pieces, so it is with supply: Each individual supplier, given a price p prevailing in the market, has his or her or its desired level of supply $s(p)$, where the lower case s is meant to indicate that this is an individual supply function. And aggregate supply is the sum of these individual supply functions, which I'll write $S(p)$. Or course, since price is on the vertical axis, if you want to take the sum graphically, you sum horizontally.

It is typical to assume that supply functions—both individual and aggregate or market-wide—are upward sloping: At higher prices, suppliers want to supply at least as much and perhaps more.

There will be cases, in particular in the stories of next chapter, where the supply function is horizontal[1] at a given price p_0—that is, no supplier is willing to supply anything at any price below p_0, and the full set of suppliers are willing

---

[1]   The use of "horizontal" and "vertical" in describing supply and demand functions has tremendous potential for creating confusion, since it isn't clear whether this means (say) "horizontal" as you look at the page with your head upright or turned on its side. With apologies for what is undoubtedly poor language but is standard in economics, "horizontal" will mean as you look at the graph with your head upright.

to supply any desired quantity at price p_0 or above. (This last bit probably seems incredible, but (1) remember that we are dealing in models, which in some details may not fit reality, and (2) what is important in such cases is that, at this magic price p_0, suppliers are willing to supply enough of the good to satisfy the level of demand, $D(p_0)$, at that point.) In such cases, we say that supply is *perfectly elastic at price* p_0.

And there will be cases in which, at virtually any price, the supply of the good in question is the same constant amount x_0. This would be the case, for instance, where supply comes from individuals who are endowed with the good and have no use for it: Whatever is the price being offered, they are ready to sell what they have. Or, if supply is coming from producers that, in the very short run, cannot change their rate/level of production, we would have this case. In agriculture, once crops in a season are planted, it is up to nature to determine the size of the harvest. And, whatever is the size of the harvest, that is what is supplied to the market.[2] In all such cases, we say that supply is *perfectly inelastic at the quantity* x_0.

More generally, we can talk about the *supply elasticity* of a good, that being the rate of percentage change in quantity per one-percent change in price.[3] Since quantity moves in the same direction as prices when it comes to supply, supply elasticities are positive numbers between 0—the perfectly inelastic case—and infinity, the perfectly elastic case.

13.2. Equilibrium

Suppose that, somehow, a price for the good was set. Where could it be set that would leave everyone happy? If this price p is at a point where supply exceeds demand, or $S(p) > D(p)$, more would be offered for sale than would be bought. Some of the good would sit on shelves or in warehouses or silos, unwanted and unpurchased. Sellers with excess supply on their shelves would try to unload this merchandise by holding a sale, and prices would fall. On the other hand, if the price p is at a point where demand exceeds supply, or $D(p) > S(p)$, then the shelves would empty and customers would still come in looking for the good. Some buyers might go to the sellers and offer to pay more than p, to guarantee that they get some of this good. Some sellers might get the bright idea that they could charge a slightly higher price and still sell the amount they want. So the price p would rise. Only if the price p is at a level where supply equals demand, or $S(p) = D(p)$, would markets clear. At that price, just as much would be desired for purchase as would be supplied. We call this price p the

---

[2] Unless farmers agree in advance to withhold some of their harvest if the total harvest is very large. This sort of thing does happen, when farmers sell their crop through a marketing board. There is also the possibility that some supply comes from storage from previous crops.

[3] If $S(p)$, industry supply, is differentiable, this supply elasticity at price p is $S'(p)p/S(p)$. You'll need this formula in Chapter 16, and I'll remind you then.

equilibrium price and the corresponding quantity $x = S(p) = D(p)$ the *equilibrium quantity*. Note well, if supply is an increasing function of price and demand is a decreasing function, then there will be at most one equilibrium price and quantity.

13.3. Does It Really Work? When? How? Market Makers and Figure 13.1

As models go, supply equals demand is pretty incomplete. Put it this way. The demand function records how much buyers want to buy at each price, once they know the price. The supply function records how much sellers want to sell at each price, once they know the price. But which comes first, the equilibrium price or supply and demand decisions by sellers and buyers? The first two sentences of this paragraph seem to say that the price comes first; folks see the price and decide how much to supply and demand. But equilibrium price is the result of supply and demand decisions of individuals. Presumably, there is some dynamic process of equilibration in the market. But what is that process? Whatever it is, Figure 13.1 tells us nothing about it. (An economist would say that Figure 13.1 and the model it depicts is a *reduced-form* model.)

Economists have enormous faith in markets. They believe that in most cases,

1. *if* a large number of people and/or firms want to purchase the item and a large number of people and/or firms want to sell,

2. *if* the item is a commodity item in the sense that it doesn't matter to buyer/seller from whom/to whom the item is bought/sold, and

3. *if* buyers and sellers have access to relatively good information about what is happening with other buyers and sellers,

then most transactions will take place at or near the price where supply equals demand. The source of their faith is sometimes the result of their upbringing as economists; that's what the books say, so it must be true. But substantial empirical evidence supports this belief. The evidence doesn't suggest that *price will reach a point where supply equals demand* is a law of nature, but it does suggest that, *when the preceding conditions are met*, it comes close to being a law of nature.

But for this model to work—for it to give accurate predictions about what will happen in terms of exchange between those who want to sell the good and those who want to buy—takes some sort of market institution, set up and run by market makers. The activities of those market makers within the institutions they set up and run is what is missing. The economist's faith in this model and in markets stems from a further belief that, when people/firms have an item they want to sell, and when other people/firms would like to purchase that item—that is, when there are potential *gains from trade*—someone/thing will step forward and make the market.

This isn't quite sufficient to make supply equals demand a useful (that is to say, accurate) model of what will happen, on two grounds.

A. The market maker rarely if ever makes the market out of the goodness of his/her/its heart but instead to make a profit. A single market maker (or market intermediary) will probably have market power, which can be exploited to drive a wedge between what sellers get for the goods they sell and what buyers must pay. There is no wedge in Figure 10.1—only a single price—which is fine as an approximate model if, in real life, the wedge imposed by the market maker is small. But, for the wedge to be small, one typically needs either that (a) there is competition among market makers, and/or (b) the activities of the market maker are regulated.

The specialist system of the New York Stock Exchange provides an example of b: The market in each stock is made by a single market maker, the *specialist* in that stock, who acts both as auctioneer, matching buy and sell orders, and as a "trader of last resort." Specialists are, essentially, employed by the NYSE to perform this function, and they are charged with "making an orderly market." This means, among other things, that the *spread* between their buying and selling prices at any point in time—the wedge they employ—must be kept at a reasonable (small) level, with the threat that the Exchange will take away their franchise if they are too greedy.

B. Market makers are not magicians. They typically are expert in assessing from the data they receive where supply will equal demand, but in a market where supply and/or demand fluctuates wildly, they can make mistakes. The model works best when supply and demand are reasonably stable over time; it becomes problematic when there are wild gyrations on one side or the other.

The bottom line here, concerning the use of the model of supply equals demand, is that it does work, and work well, both to explain what *has* happened and to predict what *will* happen in all sorts of economic contexts. Indeed, the internet and the access to information that it provides to wide audiences of prospective buyers and sellers has, if anything, enhanced the applicability of this model.

But when it comes to you applying this model, be sure to ask, Do conditions 1, 2, and 3 from page 296 hold? Conditions 1 and 2 are "structural"; condition 3 is more a matter of whether the market institutions support the free and accurate flow of information. And be sure to think about the market institutions and the market maker(s); does condition A from last page hold, and are supply and demand stable enough so that who/whatever is making the market can figure out where supply will equal demand?

13.4. Example: The Kerala Fish Market

To illustrate the power of supply equals demand and the importance of information and market-making, consider the following example taken from "The Digital Provide: Information (Technology), Market Performance, and Welfare in the South Indian Fisheries Sector," by Robert Jensen.[4]

Jensen studies the local beach markets for fish along the southwest (Kerala) coast of India. Fish are an important part of the diet in the region, and so the fish markets are a vital piece of the economy. Each day, fisherman go to sea in their boats and return to one of the beach markets to sell their catch. The Kannur District has several such beach markets, and a fisherman returning with his catch must choose one and only one to visit. Because of variation in the size of each day's catch by each fisherman, the total amount brought to these markets can vary enormously. Worse still, because of variations in each fisherman's catch, supply at one beach may be small while another beach may have a glut of fish. Demand at the beach markets is much more stable, so prices at the beach markets vary enormously, depending on whether, on a given day, a glut of fish is being supplied or not enough to satisfy demand. On a given day, prices at one beach—where there is a glut of supply—may be very low, while at a nearby beach market, prices may go through the roof. And the next day, prices at the two beaches may reverse. This is supply equals demand with a vengeance—erratic supply and stable demand leads to fluctuating prices (for goods which cannot be stored or brought out of storage).

Then, beginning in 1999, cell-phone service was implemented in Kerala, with coverage extending far enough out to sea so that fishermen could exchange information with buyers at the different beach markets and with each other about who had caught how much fish and who was going to which of the beach markets. Fishermen used this information to choose which beach market to head for, generally heading for beaches where supply looked like it would be low relative to that beach's demand. The results were dramatic:

Figure 13.2(a) shows the percentage adoption of cell phone service among fishermen in the Kannur district.[5] Phone service was added in this district in week 98 of the four year period studied by the author, and phones were quickly adopted by a large percentage of the fishermen. And Figure 13.2(b) shows the results, in terms of prices at five beach markets in the district for which Jensen gathered data. Before phone service, prices fluctuated wildly and, while this is hard to see in the graph, prices at one beach market were often very different from at another. Then phones were introduced, and supplies to the five markets studied (and, presumably, to other markets in the district) were better coordinated: Prices vary much less and, while there is some variation,

---

[4] *The Quarterly Journal of Economics*, Volume 122, 2007, 879–924.

[5] Figure 13.2 is adapted from Jensen, *ibid.*, and is reprinted by permission of Oxford University Press.

prices in the different markets move more or less in sync. The article gives more details and statistics; it is well worth reading.

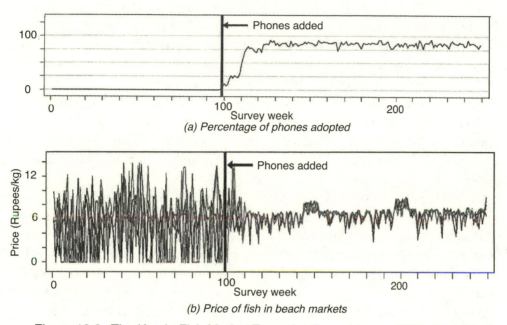

Figure 13.2. *The Kerala Fish Market Example.* From Jensen, 2007. Reprinted by permission.

The point is: supply equals demand worked at each beach market prior to the introduction of cell-phone service. But the outcome was not very efficient, since supply at each beach varied enormously. The introduction of better information (through technology) allowed the beach markets to become, approximately, a single market where, once again, supply-equals-demand worked on a daily basis, but now (because the unification of the markets reduced day-to-day variability in supply) with a much better overall outcome.

This is a dramatic example of how supply equals demand works and also of the importance of information in allowing it to work. But it is not cherry-picked. The article presents data on two other districts of Kerala, and the pictures are just the same. (Moreover, because cell-phone service was introduced at different dates in the three districts, we see that this effect is clearly tied to the introduction of phone service in each.) And, beyond markets for fish in Kerala, the power of supply equals demand—and the importance of market-making and information technology—are stories that repeat over and over; consider, for instance, the impact of technology allied with entrepreneurial market-making in the cases of Airbnb and Uber.

13.5. A Case-Let: General Motors and the Truck Coupons

Between 1973 and 1987, General Motors sold pickup trucks in the United States with gasoline tanks that sit outside the main structural frame of the truck.[6] In the summer of 1992, two groups founded by Ralph Nader filed a petition with the National Highway Traffic Safety Administration (NHTSA), alleging that these tanks were vulnerable to rupture if the truck was hit from the side, possibly leading to a fire or an explosion. The petition asked that GM be compelled to recall the trucks and correct this problem. Passion on the subject reached fever pitch when *Dateline NBC*, a television newsmagazine program, ran a story on these trucks in which toy-rocket engines were secretly placed on the trucks to ignite any gas that did leak after a staged accident. Confronted with legal action by GM, NBC retracted the story, fired its producers, and apologized for the incident.

The NHTSA investigated the matter and, in 1993, requested a voluntary recall. GM declined, aggressively disputing the contention that the trucks in question were any more dangerous than trucks without this feature. In the end, GM avoided a mandatory recall. Simultaneously, however, GM faced a number of class-action lawsuits by owners of the vehicles, seeking compensation for the loss in value of their trucks or the cost of repairs. In contrast to its aggressive stand against the NHTSA, GM sought to settle the class-action suits, and in July 1993, GM and the lawyers for the class asked to presiding courts to approve a negotiated settlement.

In the proposed settlement, GM—without admitting any fault or liability—agreed to give each currently registered owner of these trucks a coupon worth $1000 toward the purchase of any new GM light truck, including minivans, full-sized vans, pickup trucks, and sport-utility vehicles, such as the Blazer and Suburban. (Only one coupon could be used per vehicle purchased.) The coupons could be used, at full value, by the registered owner of the old vehicle or by any member of the registered owner's immediate family. A coupon could also be transferred once to any third party, for whom it would be worth $500 off the purchase price of a new light truck. The coupons would be good for 15 months after being issued, with issuance initially set for the fall of 1993.[7]

GM was quick to point out its generosity, given that many of the older trucks involved in the suit were up to 21 years old, had cost only $2000 or so new, and, according to the *Kelly Bluebook*, the semiofficial guide to market prices of used vehicles in the United States, had a retail value of around $1800. The newest of

---

[6] I am grateful to Jeremy Bulow, who first called this story to my attention and who has contributed enormously to the analysis that follows. Also, the real-life story gets complex in places, so I will simplify somewhat for expositional purposes.

[7] The "transferred only once" rule did not preclude a market maker from buying coupons and then reselling them to someone who wished to buy a GM light truck.

the affected vehicles had current retail values around $8000. GM emphasized that the old trucks were just as safe as other pickup trucks of similar vintages and that this wasn't an admission of liability or error but merely a matter of trying to appease loyal owners of GM products. "It does not affect the NHTSA case in any way, shape, or form," said a GM spokesperson, quoted in the *Wall Street Journal*.[8] "This is not a recall. There is absolutely no modification of the vehicle. This separates the customer satisfaction concerns from the technical concerns."

The *Wall Street Journal* was impressed by the settlement offer. Approximately 4.7 million of these trucks were still on the road, so GM would be issuing 4.7 million coupons. The *Journal* calculated that the potential liability of 4.7 million coupons at $1000 apiece is $4.7 billion (which was about GM's net profit in 1995). This is a lot of money, but GM didn't seem too worried; the same spokesperson pointed out that for each coupon cashed, GM would be selling a vehicle, "so there is a revenue component."

The judge to whom this settlement was proposed was less impressed and did not approve the settlement, on the grounds that it provided very little value to members of the affected class. Following this setback, GM and the lawyers for the class continued their negotiations. In the summer of 1999, they reached agreement on terms of a revised settlement, which was tentatively approved by the presiding judge. The terms of the new settlement, simplified here, were as follows:

- 5.8 million coupons were to be mailed out to registered old-truck owners. The change from 4.7 to 5.8 million was because trucks manufactured from 1987 and 1991 were now included in the settlement.

- These coupons would provide a $1000 rebate to the original bearer or family members, or a $500 rebate to any third party to whom it was transferred, for a period of 15 months after the coupons were mailed out. Then, unless the original bearer was a fleet owner—defined as a registered owner of three or more of the vehicles—or a government agency, the coupons provided a $500 rebate for the original bearer and a $250 rebate if transferred, for an additional 18 months. For fleet owners and government agencies, the coupons would be worth a flat $250 for an additional 35 months, if used by the original bearer, but these coupons could not be transferred after the first 15 months.

- The coupons provided rebates on any GM vehicle—not only GM light trucks—except for products produced by the Saturn Division.

- For original bearers, the $1000 rebate was in addition to any other rebate that GM might offer. But for third-party users, at least for the first 15 months,

---

[8] *Wall Street Journal*, July 20, 1993, A3.

the use of other rebates offered by GM would reduce the rebate provided by this coupon; if the other rebates used totaled less than $250, the coupon would provide an additional rebate of $500 less the total of the others, so the total amount rebated would be $500. If the other rebates used amounted to more than $250, the coupon would provide an additional rebate of $250.

- In addition, GM would provide $4.1 million for a research project on fuel system safety in gasoline-powered vehicles.

Wrangling about this settlement didn't end at this point. In the summer of 1999, for instance, GM was upset that the lawyers for the affected class were proposing that when notifying members of the class about the settlement, they would include the information that the Certificate Redemption Group (CRG) of Houston, Texas, was willing to buy coupons from anyone at $100 apiece. Spokespersons at CRG, when interviewed, suggested that they expected to be able to sell the coupons at $150 to $200 apiece, so that, if 3 million coupons were tendered to them, they would make a tidy profit of $150 to $300 million. The *Wall Street Journal* of July 16, 1999, reported that GM was unhappy about this and had appealed to the courts to stop the inclusion of this statement in the notification to the class. Following this, the presiding court put the settlement on hold. The coupons were finally mailed to truck owners in the spring of 2001.

Consider the following three assertions:

1. Back in 1994, the judge who refused to approve the original settlement was entirely correct to refuse. I estimate that the original proposed settlement would have cost GM (only) tens of millions of dollars. That may seem like a lot of money, but $10m is approximately 0.2% of GM's net profit at the time. More to the point (in terms of what motivated the judge), the 1993 proposed settlement would have generated virtually no value to most of the injured class—that is, to members of the injured class who were not willing to purchase a new GM light truck for themselves (or their family)—and less than $400 in value to those of the injured class willing to purchase a new GM light truck.

2. The 1999 proposed settlement was far more costly to GM and far more generous to the bulk of the injured-class members. I estimate that each member of the injured class would get around $200 in value (and maybe more) and the cost to GM would be on the order of $1.5 billion.

3. Suppose that, under the terms of the 1999 proposed settlement, GM picked 11.6 million names out of the phone book and mailed each person a coupon, providing the same entitlement as given to the 5.8 million members of the affected class. In other words, suppose GM tripled the number of coupons in circulation. Would the cost of this program to GM then triple? Absolutely not! My guess is that the cost would go *down* to the neighborhood of

$100 million, and most members of the injured class would be left with no discernible value.

Concerning the first assertion, about the initial proposed settlement, in a fifteen-month period beginning in/around fall of 1993, GM (at its current price points) expected to sell around two million "light trucks," with about 30% of those sales going to the 4.7 million members of the affected class. Moreover, it estimated a price elasticity of around −4, at an average price-point for these trucks of $20,000. GM did not believe that the demand elasticity of the affected class would be much different from the overall elasticity; previous owners, they thought, might be inclined to be more loyal, hence somewhat less elastic. But members of the affected class might be less loyal because of their experience with this issue.

Concerning the second and revised offer, GM expected to sell around 4.8 million vehicles of various sorts per year for the forseeable future, with perhaps 20% going to members of the affected class (now numbering 5.8 million). The elasticities of demand for various GM cars and trucks were different, but an overall elasticity of around −4.5 was a good working figure.

The question is, What is the logic behind my three assertions? You may want to construct a model of the situation. I provide such a model in the *Online Supplement* for the first proposed settlement, with the following simplifying assumptions: GM sells a single type of "light truck" whose marginal cost is $15,000. Demand for this light truck is, in the neighborhood of $20,000 at least, linear. GM can move the price it charges for its light truck as it sees fit.[9]

While the analysis of this case-let involves some ideas from Part II of this book, the most important and significant facts regarding my three assertions involve the topic of this chapter. So you'll need to find somewhere to invoke supply equals demand.

Executive Summary

- The most famous picture in economics is the picture of supply equals demand, Figure 13.1.

- The picture is made up of two functions, supply and demand. We've discussed demand in detail in Part II; you'll learn more about supply in Chapter 14. But, importantly, when you start talking about the supply function, you are no longer in the realm of Part II: The supply function records how much sellers of a good want to supply as a function of the market price, *which sellers take as given.*

- The picture, and the model it represents, concludes with: Exchange between buyers and sellers will take place at the price—and in the quantity—where demand equals

---

[9] The details of the second proposed settlement are complex, and building a model for that situation is difficult. But if you model the first offer and use it to see why my first assertion is correct, you should be able to see the basic logic behind the second and third assertions.

supply.

- Supply equals demand as a model doesn't have a thing to say about the process by which an equilibrium price emerges.

  - It works well, empirically, in situations with many buyers, many sellers, a commodity item, and lots of freely available information.

  - It can be observed to work in many real-life markets.

  - But, while the prediction that the price will find the level where supply equals demand depends on the institutional details of how the market is made—more precisely, it depends on the market functioning somehow—it doesn't describe those institutions. To know when it is safe to use this model, you must have a feel for whether the unmodeled market institutions are adequate to the task, whether—based on competition or regulation—market makers are not exploiting their privileged position to drive a large wedge between the buying and selling prices, and whether conditions of supply and demand are stable enough so that market makers can figure out where the two intersect.

Problems

Besides analyzing the case-let provided in Section 13.5, here is a toy problem that illustrates the mechanics of supply equals demand and that introduces taxes imposed on the sale of a good in a competitive market.

13.1 This problem concerns a market for a commodity item in which there are many sellers, all firms that produce the item, and many buyers, who are consumers. Supply of the product depends on the price received by the firms and increases as that price increases. If firms receive p per unit, they will supply (in total) $S(p) = 1000(p-4)$ units of the good for $p \geq 4$. (If the price is less than 4, they will supply none.) Consumer demand depends on the price that consumers must pay per unit for the good. Calling the price per unit to consumers q, consumer demand is given by the demand function $D(q) = 2000(10 - q)$ for $q \leq 10$. If the price exceeds 10, consumers demand no units of the good.

(a) Suppose this good is sold in a market where consumers pay an amount that exactly equals the amount (per unit) taken in by producers. That is, suppose that $p = q$. Where does supply equal demand? (You might want to draw a picture of supply and demand in this market, just to get the practice.)

(b) Suppose that this good is sold in a region where there is a 10% sales tax. That is, if the posted price per unit of the good is p (which is what the sellers of the good receive, free and clear), then for each unit of the good purchased, a consumer must remit $q = 1.1p$. What is the equilibrium in this market? How much tax revenue does the government take in?

(c) Suppose that this good is sold in a region where sellers must pay the government 10% of their gross revenues (but no sales tax is imposed on buyers). That is, if purchasers of the good pay q per unit purchased, the seller receives q gross, but only $p = 0.9q$ net of the mandatory payment to the government. What is the equilibrium in this market? How much tax revenue does the government take in?

14. Competitive Firms in Competitive Markets

Firms with market power, to maximize profit, set MR = MC. But what happens if the firm is competitive? And what happens if firms can enter and leave a particular industry?

14.1. The Supply Decision of a Competitive Firm

Imagine a firm that produces a single good. Let $TC(x)$ denote the total cost to the firm of producing and selling x units of the good.

Suppose that this firm is (perfectly) competitive, in the terminology introduced back on page 124. The good it produces is (essentially) produced by many other firms, and customers don't care from whom they buy. Prices charged by producers are widely known. And the feasible scale of production of this firm is small relative to the whole market, so small that its supply decisions will have very little impact on the market price of the good. In other words, the firm is a price-taker: it takes the market price p as given in the sense that it assumes that it can sell as much as it wants at price p or below, and it can't sell anything at any price above p.

In this case, if the firm produces x units, its total revenue is px, and so its marginal revenue is p. Marginal cost equals marginal revenue, the condition for profit maximization, becomes *price equals marginal cost.*

The Supply Function of a Price-Taking Firm, Part 1:
The Supply Function "Is" (Almost) the Marginal-Cost Function

If the firm takes p as given, how much does it produce and supply to the market as a function of p? This amount, regarded as a function $s(p)$ of the price p, is called the firm's *supply function.*

Begin with a firm that has no fixed cost—$TC(0) = 0$—and rising marginal cost. Facing price p, such a firm chooses $s(p)$ so that the marginal cost of unit $s(p)$ is p or, in symbols,

$$s(p) \text{ is defined by } MC[s(p)] = p.$$

This is pretty simple graphically. Panel a of Figure 14.1 depicts a firm's total-cost function; panel b, its marginal-cost function. For any price p on the vertical axis in Figure 14.1(b), the quantity the firm supplies is the quantity x with this marginal cost, so the supply function $s(p)$ is as depicted in Figure 14.1(c).

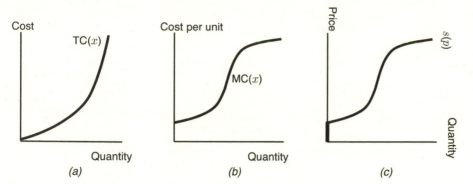

Figure 14.1. Case 1: The supply function for a firm with rising marginal cost. Panel a depicts the total-cost function for a firm with rising marginal cost and no fixed cost; panel b depicts the corresponding marginal-cost function. The firm's supply function is shown in panel c.

Because the argument of the firms supply function is p and not x, I've turned the labels in Figure 14.1(c) on their side.

The firm's supply function "is" (almost) the firm's marginal-cost function. We have scare quotes around *is* because $MC(x)$ and $s(p)$ are not at all the same function. Marginal cost gives a dollar per unit (cost) figure as a function of quantity. The firm's supply function gives quantity as a function of dollars per unit (price). More precisely, one function is the inverse of the other. But they look the same in terms of the picture, so it is typical, if a bit sloppy, to say that supply "is" (almost) marginal cost.

Why (almost)? Because, in Figure 14.1(c), we have the heavy line segment along the vertical axis for low prices as part of the supply function, which is not part of the marginal-cost function. At prices below the lowest marginal cost the firm faces, $p = MC(x)$ cannot be solved and the firm supplies nothing.

The Supply Function of a Price-Taking Firm, Part 2:
Rising Marginal Cost with a Positive Fixed Cost

Now suppose the firm has rising marginal cost and a positive fixed cost. This gives us the standard bowl-shaped average-cost function, as in Figure 14.2(b).

Nothing changes in this case for prices below the minimum marginal cost—the firm supplies 0 at such low prices—or at prices above the minimum average cost, where the firm's supply runs along with the marginal-cost function. But writing p^{**} for the minimum marginal cost and p^* for the minimum average cost, the story is more complex for prices between p^* and p^{**}. Moreover, this more complex story depends on the answer to the question, Can the firm, by producing nothing (or otherwise going out of business), avoid its fixed cost?

If the fixed cost is unavoidable, then it is irrelevant to the firm's supply decisions. The firm's supply is just as in Figure 14.1(c), which is repeated in

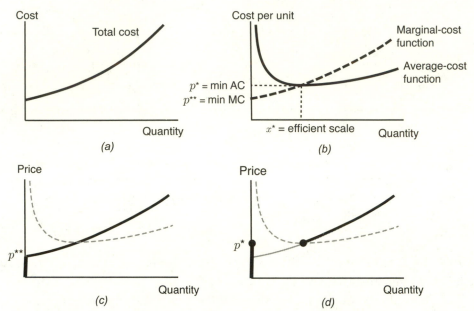

Figure 14.2. Case 2: Rising marginal costs and a positive fixed cost. Panels a and b depict the total-, marginal-, and average-cost functions. Supply below p^{**} is 0 and above p^{*} it lies along the marginal-cost curve, but what is it between p^{**} and p^{*}? If the firm must pay the fixed cost even if its production level is 0, then supply runs along the marginal-cost curve for these prices, as in panel c. If the firm can avoid the fixed cost by producing no output, then supply at these prices is 0, as in panel d. And at the crucial price p^{*}, which equals minimum average cost, supply is either 0 or at efficient scale.

Figure 14.2(c). (I won't rotate the labels anymore, but remember, for the firm's supply function, the argument is the price, p.)

Suppose, on the other hand, that the firm completely avoids its fixed cost by producing 0. Then at prices below p^{*}, the firm produces 0: To produce any positive amount means negative profit—the price is less than the minimum average cost, so it is less than average cost at whatever scale of production the firm chooses—while producing 0 means a profit of 0. And, at p^{*} specifically, the firm either produces 0 and earns a profit of 0 or it produces at its efficient scale,[1] which also gives a profit of 0. Production at any other level means negative profit, so the only two possibilities are producing 0 or producing at its efficient scale. This is depicted in Figure 14.2(d).

The possibility remains that, by producing 0, the firm can avoid some but not all its fixed cost. I leave it to you to puzzle through this case; see Problem 14.1.

---

[1] Reminder: Efficient scale is the level of production at which average cost is minimized.

The Supply Function of a Price-Taking Firm, Part 3: Constant Marginal Costs

In a third case, the firm has no fixed cost and and linear total cost, so that marginal cost is constant. In this case, we get extreme behavior by the firm. At any price below its constant marginal cost, it supplies nothing. At any price above its constant marginal cost, it supplies infinite amounts because, believing as it does that it has no effect on price, it believes that it can make ever-increasing profits with ever-increasing output. At a price equal to its constant marginal cost, it is happy with *any* level of supply. See Figure 14.3.

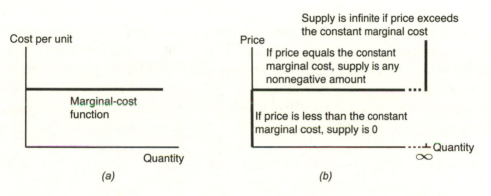

Figure 14.3. Case 3: The case of constant marginal cost and no fixed cost.

Do not be too impressed by Figure 14.3. The extreme behavior it depicts comes from taking the model much too seriously. Marginal cost cannot be constant forever, and even if it is, the firm will realize that eventually, at some scale of production, it will drive prices down. A model that says the firm will go from supplying nothing at the price $p - \$0.01$ to supplying any amount at p to supplying infinite amounts at $p + \$0.01$ should be thought of as an idealization of a firm whose supply responses vary enormously over a small range of prices.

Other Cases: Natural Monopoly and Oligopoly

In all the algebraic examples we deal with in this book, marginal cost is either rising or flat and, if flat, the fixed cost is 0. So this covers all the cases we will see later *in this book*. But what about, in real life, the other possibilities? The key to an industry's being perfectly competitive is that, at any price that is a reasonable candidate for the equilibrium price, individual firms maximize their profits at a scale that is small relative to the size of demand at that price. This is consistent with marginal costs that fall and then rise, for instance, as long as marginal costs for each firm rise fast enough. The mathematics in such cases is a little harder than the three cases we have explored, but most of the important insights we'll develop over the rest of this chapter still hold.

Sometimes, however, the technology of production simply does not support a perfectly competitive market. Imagine, for instance, that marginal cost is constant or falling for levels that are large relative to market demand, and firms also have a substantial fixed cost. Examples include electric power and natural gas distribution, and local phone service (prior to the development of cell-phone technology). These are cases of *natural monopoly*: One firm can serve the market efficiently; a second firm would have to pay the fixed cost without gaining a marginal cost advantage. Hence, a monopoly is natural both in terms of efficient production and as the result of market competition: The largest firm can always undercut the prices charged by its rivals. Industries in which the technology favors relatively large firms simply aren't consistent with perfect competition. We do not discuss them further, but they exist and are of concern to governments; if you are curious, the terms to look for are *regulation* and *natural monopoly*.[2]

And, in other cases, while the efficient scale of production permits several large firms to coexist, it doesn't allow enough so that firms become price takers. Think of cell-phone service (where the network of towers keeps efficient scale large), so-called trunk-carrier airlines (where landing slots and counter space at major airports keep the numbers low), and petroleum-product refining. Government policy regarding these industries aims at preventing collusion; a back-reference to Part I of this book comes here.

14.2. Equilibrium with Competitive Firms

Now we can look at the equilibrium of a *perfectly competitive market*, in which all the buyers and sellers are price-takers. The setting is a market for some commodity item. Demand for this good is given by a demand function. We assume that demand slopes downward, but we say no more about where it comes from.

All supply comes from competitive firms. If there are N firms in the industry and, for $n = 1$, 2, and on up to N, $s_n(p)$ is the amount supplied by firm n at the price p, then the industrywide supply curve is given by

$$S(p) = s_1(p) + s_2(p) + \ldots + s_N(p).$$

That is, the total supply at any price is just the sum of individual firm-level supplies at that price. (Remember: Graphically, this is a horizontal sum.)

---

[2] While I will not go into detail, let me at least say: It used to be, at least in the U.S., that the government regulated the prices charged by such natural monopolies as electricity and phone-service providers. But then, to promote efficiency, policy changed: These industries were deregulated. There was still the issue of transmission lines, a very substantial fixed cost that was the reason these firms were, initially, regarded as natural monopolies. But the government got around that problem by requiring the owners of the transmission lines to "carry" the electricity / phone calls of their competitors at a reasonable (regulated) price. Why this arrangement was regarded as more efficient takes us beyond—but not too far beyond—the scope of this book.

Three Toy Examples

Three toy examples illustrate this. First, imagine that the good in question is supplied by 50 firms. Suppose that each firm has a total-cost function given by $TC(x) = 2x + 0.01x^2$. Fixed costs are 0, and each firm's marginal-cost function, $MC(x) = 2 + 0.02x$, is an increasing function that equals 2 at $x = 0$.

Because these firms have rising marginal cost and no fixed cost, each firm supplies nothing below its minimum marginal cost of 2 and a positive amount for prices above 2. At a price $p > 2$, the supply of the firm is the solution to price equals marginal cost, or

$$p = 2 + 0.02s(p) \quad \text{or} \quad p - 2 = 0.02s(p) \quad \text{or} \quad s(p) = 50p - 100.$$

Industry supply is the sum of the supplies of the individual firms. Since all 50 firms are identical, supply at any price p is just 50 times the supply of any single firm. So, at prices $p \leq 2$, industrywide supply is 0. At prices $p \geq 2$, supply is

$$S(p) = 50s(p) = 50(50p - 100) = 2500p - 5000.$$

In the second example, we complicate matters by supposing 100 firms supply the good. Fifty have the total cost function just given, and so the supply function of those 50 is as computed. The other 50 have total cost function $TC(x) = 3x + 0.005x^2$. So for these other 50, $MC(x) = 3 + 0.01x$. Hence, each of these firms supplies 0 at prices below 3, and at prices above 3, each supplies the amount $s(p)$ that solves

$$p = 3 + 0.01s(p) \quad \text{or} \quad p - 3 = 0.01s(p) \quad \text{or} \quad s(p) = 100p - 300.$$

Thus industrywide supply comes in three pieces: At prices p below 2, no firm supplies anything, so $S(p) = 0$. At prices p between 2 and 3, each of the first 50 firms supplies $50p - 100$ and each of the second 50 supplies nothing, for a total of

$$S(p) = 2500p - 5000.$$

At prices p that are 3 or more, each of the first 50 supplies $50p - 100$, or $2500p - 5000$ in total, and each of the second 50 supplies $100p - 300$, or $50(100p - 300) = 5000p - 15,000$ in total. Hence, at prices 3 or more, total supply is

$$S(p) = 2500p - 5000 + 5000p - 15,000 = 7500p - 20,000.$$

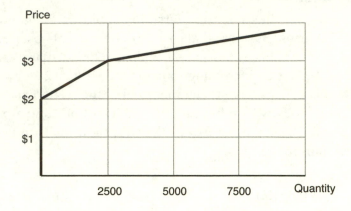

Figure 14.4. The supply function in the second example. This example has 50 firms with the marginal-cost function $2 + 0.02x$ and 50 with the marginal-cost function $3 + 0.01x$. No firm has any fixed cost. The first 50 firms begin to supply at the price $p = 2$, and the second 50 begin when the price reaches $p = 3$, giving the kinks shown.

A graph of this total supply function is shown in Figure 14.4. Note the kinks at $p = 2$, when the first 50 firms suddenly kick in and start producing, and at $p = 3$, when the second 50 begin producing.

A real-life lesson lurks in this toy example. If the equilibrium price in this industry is $2.50, we would see 50 firms producing. If, in trying to construct the supply curve of this industry, we consider only these 50 firms, we would not come up with the supply curve in Figure 14.4, because we would miss the second 50 firms that will *enter* this industry when and if price exceeds 3. In constructing industrywide supply curves, you must consider whether firms will enter (or leave) the industry in response to changes in price and, if so, what would be the impact on supply.

The third example introduces firms with avoidable fixed costs. Specifically, imagine that the industry consists of 50 identical firms, each of which has the total-cost function

$$\mathrm{TC}(x) = 100 + 2x + 0.01x^2 \ \text{ for } \ x > 0, \ \text{ and } \ \mathrm{TC}(0) = 0.$$

The fixed cost of 100 is paid only if the firm produces a strictly positive amount. Then, from our earlier analysis, we know that the firm's supply curve traces along its marginal-cost curve $\mathrm{MC}(x) = 2 + 0.02x$ *as long as the price exceeds the firm's minimum average cost*. If price is below the minimum average cost, then the firm supplies nothing.

We can find the firm's minimum average cost by differentiating average cost and setting the derivative equal to 0 or by equating average and marginal cost.

Doing the latter, average cost is

$$AC(x) = \frac{100}{x} + 2 + 0.01x,$$

so average cost equals marginal cost where

$$\frac{100}{x} + 2 + 0.01x = 2 + 0.02x \quad \text{or} \quad \frac{100}{x} = 0.01x \quad \text{or} \quad \frac{100}{0.01} = 10,000 = x^2,$$

which is $x = 100$. Plug this value of x back into the average or marginal cost function, to find that the minimum average cost is

$$AC(100) = \frac{100}{100} + 2 + 0.01(100) = 1 + 2 + 1 = 4.$$

The supply of a single firm, therefore, is: 0 if $p < 4$; either 0 or 100 if $p = 4$; the solution to $p = 2 + 0.02x$, which is $s(p) = 50p - 100$, if $p > 4$.

The industry supply curve is the horizontal sum of 50 of these supply curves. At prices $p < 4$, $S(p) = 0$. At prices $p > 4$, $S(p) = 2500p - 5000$. And, the hard part, at $p = 4$, $S(p) = 0, 100, 200, \ldots, 4900$, or 5000. The idea here is that, at $p = 4$, we can have any subset of the firms supplying 100 apiece and the rest supplying nothing. If k of the 50 firms supply 100 apiece, total supply is $100k$. And k can be 0, 1, 2, on up to fifty. The picture is Figure 14.5.

Figure 14.5. Supply in the third example. The third example has 50 firms with rising marginal and avoidable fixed costs. These firms have efficient scales of production of 100 units, at which point their average cost is $4. Therefore, each individual firm supplies nothing if price is below $4; it supplies along its marginal-cost function if price is above $4; and, if $p = 4, it supplies either 0 or 100. Hence, at $p = 4, supply is a succession of "dots"; supply is 0 if all 50 choose 0, or 100 if 1 chooses 100 and the other 49 choose 0, or 200, 300, up to 5000 if all 50 supply 100.

Equilibrium

Now for the punchline. A demand function is specified. The industry supply function is computed. Equilibrium is where the two intersect.

For instance, in the first example, with 50 firms, each of which has the total cost function $\text{TC}(x) = 2x + 0.01x^2$, industrywide supply is

$$S(p) = \begin{cases} 0, & \text{if } p < 2, \text{ and} \\ 2500p - 5000, & \text{if } p \geq 2. \end{cases}$$

If demand is given by $D(p) = 10{,}000 - 500p$, the equilibrium price is where supply equals demand, or

$$10{,}000 - 500p = 2500p - 5000, \quad \text{which is} \quad 15{,}000 = 3000p, \quad \text{or} \quad p = 5.$$

At this price, supply equals demand equals 7500, which means that each of the 50 firms supplies $7500/50 = 150$ units. We can also work out each firm's total revenue, total cost, and profit: total revenue is $150 \times 5 = 750$, total cost is $2 \times 150 + 0.01 \times 150^2 = 525$, and profit per firm is $750 - 525 = 225$.

And If There Is No Intersection?

In some models we build, a problem arises at this point: Supply does not intersect demand anywhere. This happens in particular in cases where supply has the form of Figure 14.5: a sequence of "dots." I'll discuss this situation in a bit.

14.3. Short- and Intermediate-Run Analysis

Suppose that demand suddenly shifts in a competitive market that had reached equilibrium. How does the market respond?

We use the ideas of Chapter 12 and assume that firms in this industry have available some feasible short-run responses and a richer variety of intermediate-run responses. (We reserve the *long run* for later purposes.) Following the discussion in Chapter 12, each firm will have short- and intermediate-run total- and marginal-cost functions, where the two marginal-cost functions cross at the firm's *status-quo* level of production, and the short-run marginal cost function is steeper than the intermediate-run marginal-cost function. Assume that any fixed costs are unavoidable, hence irrelevant, in both the short run and the intermediate run.

The picture of a market in an intermediate-run equilibrium is Figure 14.6. Firms' supply functions trace their marginal-cost functions, and industry supply

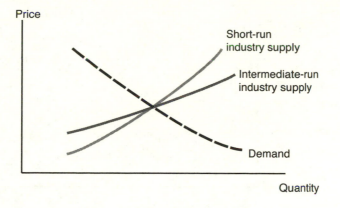

Figure 14.6 Short-run (SR) and intermediate-run (IR) supply, in a market in an intermediate-run equilibrium. Mimicking the shape of the firm-level short- and intermediate-run marginal cost functions, short- and intermediate-run industry supply functions cross at the status-quo equilibrium, with short-run supply appearing more vertical than intermediate-run supply.

is the horizontal sum of firm-level supply, so we get short-run and intermediate-run industry supply curves that cross at the status-quo level of industry production, with the short-run supply curve steeper than intermediate-run supply.

(The use of the term *steeper* here might cause some confusion, in the same sense as terms like "vertical" and "horizontal" supply functions are confusing: Does this refer to your head looking at the page upright or turned ninety degrees? As before—cf. footnote 1 from Chapter 13 on page 294—"steeper" here means, looked at with your head upright. That is, for any given change in price from the status quo, the supply response of the industry is less in the short run than in the intermediate run.)

Suppose demand suddenly shifts out. (Follow on Figure 14.7.) Prices jump up, causing the firms supplying the good to increase their output, moving along the short-run supply curve. A short-run equilibrium is attained where the new demand function and short-run supply curve intersect, at a price–quantity pair that is higher than before.

As time passes, firms make adjustments unavailable to them in the short run. At the new short-run equilibrium price, this would lead to an overabundance of supply. So prices begin to slip back toward their initial level. The intermediate-run equilibrium is achieved when demand intersects intermediate-run supply, at a price between the old equilibrium price and the short-run equilibrium price and at a quantity larger than both.

That is how things work out *in the model*. In real life, the price dynamics we observe are not so pat. For one thing, no single definition of "short run" or "intermediate run" applies consistently to all firms. Some firms in the industry can adjust their production levels more quickly, given an economic incentive

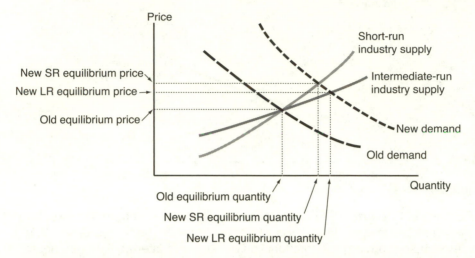

Figure 14.7. Dynamic price and quantity adjustment to an upward shift in demand. After demand shifts out, in the short run, the price rises and supply increases. In the intermediate run, supply continues to rise so the price drops back toward its original level.

to do so; others respond more slowly. Moreover, demand in real life rarely jumps up or down unexpectedly and then stays at its new level. For one thing, firms can sometimes anticipate a demand shift and proactively prepare for it. In markets for physical goods, the ability to take goods in or out of inventory mutes the price jumps we see. And when demand begins to move in one direction or another, it can take its time getting to wherever it is going; firms in the industry find themselves aiming at a moving target.

But cases do exist in which the model predictions can be seen quite vividly. In, for instance, the spot market for crude oil *transport* from sources in the Persian Gulf, to refineries in Asia and in Europe, demand to move crude oil (and refined products) sometimes shifts up dramatically. This happens, for instance, when the Persian Gulf region becomes politically embroiled: Refiners and retailers have a sudden urge to get product out and away, before the bombs (may) start to fall. Because transportation is a service, it can't be inventoried; so prices shoot up dramatically. (It helps that demand is highly inelastic.) Then, as the operators of oil tankers begin to react by getting their ships to the Gulf, prices begin to retreat, just as our simple model predicts.

14.4. The Long Run, Entry, and Exit

If there is a short run and an intermediate run, there must be a long run. In the model, new firms can enter the industry in the long run, and firms in the industry can liquidate all their obligations and exit. We assume firms enter when they see the opportunity to make an *economic profit*, and they exit, eventually, if they take *economic losses*.

Economic Profit versus Accounting Income

The term *economic profit* needs definition. Profit to an economist is total revenue less total cost.[3] Included among the costs that make up total cost is a charge for the capital bound up in capital equipment, land, and so forth. If the firm borrows funds to finance its capital, interest on the borrowed funds is the appropriate charge. But suppose, moving toward greater realism, the firm raises funds for capital purchases by issuing equity. The firm's accounting income statement contains no charge for equity capital, because accounting income is supposed to measure what is left over for equity holders, after all other claimants on the firm's revenues have been paid. In this very important respect, accounting income is *not* the same thing as economic profit.

Bear this distinction clearly in mind when evaluating the assumption that *firms enter the industry if economic profit is positive and leave if it is negative*. An economic profit of 0 does not mean zero accounting income. An economic profit of 0 requires enough accounting income that equity holders are "satisfied" with their investment, so that their return on their investment matches the overall market rate of return. The assumption that firms enter when economic profit is positive means, essentially, that an industry whose equity holders are getting more than the market average rate of return is likely to attract investment. And the assumption that firms leave when economic profit is negative translates into this: Industries that provide equity holders with subpar returns see capital being withdrawn. Keep the distinction between economic profit and accounting income clear, and our assumptions about entry and exit are quite reasonable *for a first-cut, toy model*.

Back to the Story

This entry and exit process adds a third supply curve to the picture of Figure 14.6, which is even less steep than the intermediate-run supply curve.

If we imagine, in the spirit of Figure 14.7, a sudden increase in demand, we would expect to see (1) a sharp rise in price and a smaller increase in quantity in the short run, (2) then a fall in price to above the original equilibrium level and a continued increase in quantity in the intermediate run, and finally, in the long run, (3) a further increase in quantity and a further fall in price to a level still no smaller than the original equilibrium price, driven by the entry of new firms.

Free and Unlimited Entry with the Best Available Technology

Suppose for now that, in a particular industry, *no firm has an advantage over any*

---

[3] This is true in static or single-period models. For now, restrict your attention to such simple situations.

other in terms of its technological capability. Whatever technology is available to any firm is available to all, including to potential entrants. Further suppose that *there is an unlimited supply of potential entrants.*

Pay attention to the italics. These are assumptions that may or may not be true, even approximately, in specific cases. For instance, in agriculture, there is better farmland and there is worse, and there is a limited supply of the better. Since the quality of the land determines to some extent the yield, farmers lucky enough to own better land have a "more productive" technology. On the other hand, in the manufacture of relatively cheap clothing, done in Southeast Asia, say, for markets in the richer economies of Western Europe, North America, and Japan, there is a vast supply of potential manufacturers, all of whom have access to the lowest cost technology, fueled by cheap labor. (This assertion is descriptive, not normative.)

Under these assumptions, firms cannot earn positive economic profits in a long-run equilibrium. If one firm earns a positive economic profit, potential entrants just as capable as this firm observe the market price, compute that they can make a positive economic profit at that price, and therefore enter the market, causing the price to decline. This process continues as long as positive economic profits are being earned. The process of entry stops only when the price falls to a level at which no firm makes a positive economic profit. Similarly, if firms incur economic losses, they depart, and they continue to depart until all make an economic profit of 0.

This story is perhaps clearest and cleanest if the technology gives a U-shaped average-cost curve because of a fixed cost that can be avoided (only) by leaving the industry. Then, firms make positive profits when price is above minimum average cost and take losses when price is below minimum average cost. So, as long as price is above minimum average cost, firms enter. When price is below minimum average cost, firms depart. The long-run equilibrium must be as follows:

> *If the best technology in an industry is freely available to all producers, if unlimited numbers of potential entrants are ready to enter the industry using this technology, and if this best technology has U-shaped average costs, then the only long-run equilibrium price in a perfectly competitive market is at the level of minimum average cost. At the long-run equilibrium, each active firm produces at efficient scale and earns an economic profit of 0.*

Pictures of This

How does this look in pictures? What are the dynamics when there is a shift in demand? Consider Figure 14.8. Suppose the technology of the single firm is, as in panel a, a U-shaped average cost with minimum average cost p^*. The long-run equilibrium price must equal p^*. So, if we have the (inverse) demand function shown in panel b, the equilibrium must be as indicated. Note that the efficient scale is marked at q^*; imagine that at the long-run equilibrium, N active firms each produce q^*. (What if demand at the price p^* is not an integer multiple of q^*? We get to this in the next subsection.)

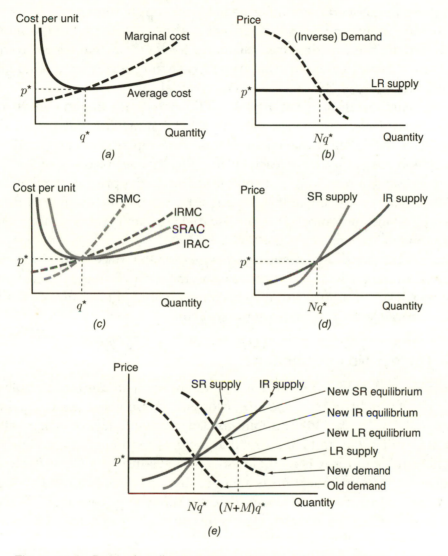

Figure 14.8. *Dynamic adjustment to an increase in demand in the short, intermediate, and long run for an industry with a long queue of potential entrants all of which have access to the best technology.* See the text for an explanation of each panel.

Suppose that, in a period of time shorter than the time it takes for entry and exit to occur, firms that are active can react to changes in market price along the marginal-cost function in panel a. We call this time period the *intermediate run*; this gives (in panel c) the labels IRMC and IRAC. And, in a still shorter time period, the *short run*, firms that are active can react to prices but in more limited fashion; exactly as in Chapter 12, this gives a short-run average-cost function (SRAC) that is "above" IRAC and just touching at the status-quo level of production q^*, and a short-run marginal-cost function that is (a) steeper than IRMC and (b) passes through IRMC at q^*, just as depicted in panel c.

This gives the short-run and intermediate-run supply functions for the industry that are shown in panel d. These are the horizontal sums of the short- and intermediate-run marginal-cost functions, for the N active firms. Transferring these to panel e and superimposing a demand function that suddenly shifts outward, we have the dynamics: (1) an initial sharp rise in price following which incumbent firms make short-run adjustments, leading to a short-run equilibrium price–quantity pair; a fall in price back toward, but not all the way to, p^*, as incumbent firms make intermediate-run adjustments, until an intermediate-run equilibrium is reached; and, finally, since prices above p^* attract new entrants, a new long-run equilibrium with the price back at p^*, all active firms again producing at the efficient scale q^*, and the number of firms increased by whatever number M it takes so that the quantity demanded along the new demand function at price p^* is $(N + M)q^*$.

Although it it not shown in panel e, please note that once a new long-run equilibrium is reached, with $N+M$ active firms, the short-run and intermediate-run supply curves shift outward; they become the horizontal sums of $N + M$ times the respective single-firm marginal cost curves.

What If There Is No Intersection?

What happens if demand at p^* does not precisely equal an integer multiple of q^*? This is relevant because, while I drew long-run supply as a horizontal line in Figure 14.8, I really should draw long-run supply as a sequence of separated dots, in the spirit of Figure 14.5, except that the dots continue forever, since an unlimited number of firms is ready to enter and produce at efficient scale q^* if the price is p^*. (Remember, this is a model. In reality, we just need enough firms around so that, each producing q^*, they satisfy any reasonable level of demand at p^*.) If $D(p^*)$ is not an integer multiple of q^*, then demand does not intersect long-run supply.

What happens here, *in terms of the model*, is that the industry is slightly unsettled. Suppose $D(p^*) = 34.3q^*$, so 34 firms are too few and 35 are too many. Then, if 34 firms are in the market, each makes a small profit. This attracts entry, and a 35th firm enters. This causes each of the 35 to take small losses, so one of the 35 leaves. This pushes profits slightly into the black, attracting a new entrant, and so on.

In real life, where firms are not completely, precisely identical, we are apt to see something slightly different: The 34 most efficient firms (ranked by their minimum average cost) are in the market, making slightly positive economic profits. Suppose the next most efficient firm can make a profit at the price that clears markets with these 34 firms. If it understands that its impact on prices, while slight, will be enough to cause it to sustain a loss, it will not enter. If it doesn't realize this, it may enter, and the experience of entry will teach it this lesson. Hence, we will probably settle out with 34 firms, each making an economic profit so small that no other firm is sufficiently motivated to enter. Which, from the point of view of predictions about price and equilibrium quantity, is virtually what the model, taken literally, predicts.

Rents

True or false? *In the long run, in a competitive industry, (economic) profits of all firms are zero.* Of course, the answer is, False, in general. This assertion is true *IF* there is unimpeded entry into the industry and *IF* all firms, whether active or potential entrants, have access to the same technology. Those are two big ifs, and when they don't hold, firms in a competitive industry can make positive economic profits.

(If, you have ever heard an economist say—or read a textbook that claimed— that firms in a competitive industry *always* make zero profit, and you want to understand why I'm saying something different, read the rest of this subsection. If you never heard such a claim or don't care to understand what was behind it, skip ahead to the next subsection.)

Economists are so fond of the italicized slogan in the first paragraph that they sometimes reduce it to a tautology. This bit of semantic legerdemain works as follows: imagine a farmer whose land is superior to the average farm land. For the same expenditure on seed, fertilizer, and so forth, it yields more crop. This farmer may well be a price-taker in the market for his crop, but his superior yield means that he earns positive economic profits. *However,* because his land is more productive, it is valuable and should command a higher *rent* than less fertile land. If the farmer owns the land, so there is no question of rent actually changing hands, we should still think in terms of the rent the land could command if the owner rented it out instead of farming it himself. How much rent? The economic definition of *rent* is "just enough so that the italicized slogan is correct."

When it comes to farmland, the term *rent* is particularly appropriate. But the term *rent*, or sometimes *quasi-rent*, is also applied in cases where an industrial firm owns a patent on a particularly cost-effective technology or even when the technology is not patentable but still superior to the technology held by competitors. This fortunate firm does not make positive economic profits; instead, its patents, or just its production technology, earn rent, just enough rent that the firm's profit is zero. The term is applied whenever some input to production— land, a patented process, superior technology—is in relatively fixed supply, so that the process of entry does not "compete away" the value generated by the input for its owners. The term *rent* is used because this terminology, like most economic terminology, was set (in English) in 18th and 19th century England, when the chief example was in fact agricultural land. (Filers of income tax in the United States: If you ever wondered why rents and royalties are covered by the same laws and reported on the same form, this is the economic rationale. I leave it to you to discover the etymology of the term *royalties*.)

This is simply semantics. When you hear people (who speak the language of economics) talking about economic rents or quasi-rents, this is what they have in mind. And when you hear an overenthusiastic economist say that, in competitive markets, economic profits *must* be zero, understand that this bit of tautological semantics is involved.

Do Firms Produce at Their Efficient Scale?

In Chapter 6, when the notion of efficient scale was first introduced, I pooh-poohed the idea that a profit-maximizing firm must produce at its efficient scale. A profit-maximizing firm produces where marginal cost equals marginal revenue, which can be above or below its efficient scale.

When we look at competitive markets, however, the notion that a firm produces at its efficient scale gets a new lease on life. Any profit-maximizing *competitive* firm making an economic profit of zero must be producing at its efficient scale, and what is more, the equilibrium price must be equal to its minimum average cost. This does not depend on free entry: If the price is below the minimum average cost, the firm cannot be active and sustain a nonnegative profit. If the price is above the minimum average cost, at some scale of production it will make a strictly positive profit. Zero profit thus means the price equals the firm's minimum average cost, and the only place the firm can make that zero profit, aside from being out of the industry, is at its efficient scale.

So, to the extent that a competitive firm makes an economic profit of 0, it must be producing "efficiently." Moreover, a profit-maximizing competitive firm that turns a strictly positive profit must produce *above* its efficient scale. (See Problem 14.10.)

Is Long-Run Supply Flat?

(Skip or skim this subsection on a first reading, as it goes into some fairly subtle matters.)

Suppose the very best technology for making some product is freely available to all firms. Is the long-run equilibrium supply curve really horizontal? It was drawn that way in Figure 14.8 and will continue to be so in models in which the least-cost technology is available to a vast horde of potential entrants. Why? If all firms have access to the same technology, including hordes of potential entrants, then equilibrium price in the industry must be the minimum value of average cost. At any higher price, firms make positive profits, attracting entry. At any lower price, firms sustain losses and depart.

This bit of logic is not perfect, however. Long-run costs depend on technology *and* the prices of inputs. If the long-run supply of inputs is not flat—if the price of an input rises with its usage by the industry in question—then, as the scale of industry production rises, each firm's long-run average-cost function rises, minimum average cost rises, and the long-run supply curve of the industry is not flat. Long-run profit will stay at 0 in such a case. But the price needed to achieve a long-run profit of 0 for each firm must rise, to cover the increased cost of the inputs.

To be clear here, to say the supply of inputs is not flat is not to say that individual firms act as if they have market power in the input market. As long as all firms are relatively small, they regard their purchases of the input as on a scale that does not appreciably affect the input's price. But when all those competitive firms expand their demand for the input, the scale is sufficient for the input's price to rise. This is exactly parallel to the idea that, while each firm inside the industry might regard itself as a price-taker in the output market, the industry as a whole can and does affect the price of that output.

This means that industrywide supply is not (really) the horizontal sum of individual supply functions. Indeed, this could be true even assuming that entry into or exit from the industry is not possible. Individual firm supply functions are drawn assuming that input prices are fixed, which they are, at least approximately, for small individual firms. But this may not be true for the industry as a whole.

Think, for instance, of grain farming, which is as close to a competitive industry as you can find. No individual farmer—not even an agribusiness giant—can have much of an impact on the price of fertilizer. Therefore, individual firm supply functions take the price of fertilizer as constant. But the industry as a whole makes tremendous demands on the fertilizer industry, demands that can push up the price of fertilizer as more land is brought under cultivation or land already cultivated is cultivated more intensively, using more fertilizer to increase yield. Thus industry supply is "steeper" than the horizontal sum of individual firm supply functions.

For an example that illustrates this, see the discussion in the *Online Supplement* following the problems for Chapter 14. Let me warn you, this is tough stuff, and if you can work your way through that discussion, you have command of this chapter.

14.5. Sunk Costs: One Step Closer to Reality

Toy models of dynamic industry (and equilibrium price) responses to shifts in demand (or to a sudden change in factor prices), typified by the "story" of Figure 14.8, are fodder for microeconomics problem sets and exams; the odds are good, I imagine, that you will see more than one such exercise.

But they are not reality, and certainly they shouldn't be confused with reality, which is generally much messier. They help us to understand reality, by providing a baseline toy model but, as is true of all toy models, they miss features of the real world that *you* must factor in, formally if you can and informally otherwise, as you try to understand or predict what will happen in a particular real-world industry.

What's missing? For one thing, firms do not have access to the same technology, and the simple picture of a long-run supply function that is "flat" at minimum average cost of the best available technology may not apply. In fact, you have the tools you need to deal with such complications; try Problems 14.8 and 14.9.

A second missing feature is that different suppliers have different levels of flexibility in responding to price changes. There is no one "short-run" time frame that applies to all firms. One firm may be making its "intermediate-run" changes when other firms in the industry are still back in the "short run." Worse still, gap-filling firms may enter a given industry while less flexible incumbent firms are adjusting their own activities and then exit once the incumbent firms have made those adjustments.

But perhaps the most important missing feature are the complications brought on by *sunk* costs as opposed to *fixed* costs. In this section, I'll provide a toy model and then tell two real-life stories that show how this more elaborate toy model advances our understanding of the much messier reality.

A Toy Model with Sunk Costs

(Warning: This model requires that you understand net-present-value calculations. If you don't know about these things, you can still probably get the gist of what is going on. But it will be tough going in places.)

Demand for a product is given by $D(p) = 1000(100 - p)$ per month. Supply comes from competitive firms, all of whom (if they are active) have total-cost functions $TC(x) = 100 + 5x + x^2/100$, where x is the rate of output per month. The term 100 is a *fixed* cost; it is paid each month by the firm regardless of the scale of production x, as long as the firm is active, but (assume) this fixed cost can be avoided by producing 0. Note that efficient scale for this firm is 100, with minimum average costs of 7. So, if the story ended here, the long-run equilibrium would be $p = 7$, market demand would be 93,000, and so 930 firms would be active.

So far, this is just like the models we've studied previously, but now for the new feature. To enter the industry, a firm must pay a *sunk* cost of 150,000. This means that it pays 150,000 up front (say, in the first period it produces), and it can never recover any of this if and when it exits the industry.

Consider a firm that is thinking of entering the market. It will enter if and only if it forecasts a stream of monthly profits whose net present value (NPV) more than covers the fixed cost of entry. Suppose (remember, this is just a toy model!) a firm forecasts a constant stream of (economic) profit of π per month, extending forever. Suppose the firm discounts profits at 1% per month, compounded. Then the NPV of the stream of profits the firm forecasts is

$$\pi + \frac{\pi}{1.01} + \frac{\pi}{1.01^2} + \frac{\pi}{1.01^3} + \ldots = 101\pi.$$

So if the firm forecasts that $\pi > 150,000/101 = \$1485.15$, it will enter. If $\pi < \$1485.15$, it stays out. When $\pi = \$1485.15$, we have our long-run equilibrium.

How do we find the long-run equilibrium? Note first that, because all the firms have the same per-month total-cost function and face the same price, every active firm will produce where its marginal cost equals the market price (as long as that price is above 7). So if we let x denote the production per firm and p the equilibrium price, one equation that must hold is $5 + 2x/100 = p$.

And, in equilibrium, supply must equal demand. If there are N active firms, each producing x, supply is Nx and demand is $1000(100 - p)$, so we have a second equation, $1000(100 - p) = Nx$.

So, *if we fix the number of active firms at* N, we have two equations in two unknowns (p and x); solve for them (treating N as a parameter) and get

$$x = \frac{95,000}{20 + N} \quad \text{and} \quad p = 5 + \frac{190}{20 + N}.$$

The number of active firms is set by the condition that each firm, at this price and producing this quantity, has a monthly profit (or cash flow) of (roughly) $1485.15. Solving for N algebraically is a mess, so I resorted to Excel: I found that if $N = 219$, the profit flow per month for each firm is $1479.98, while for $N = 218$, the profit flow per month is $1493.28. So, somewhere between 218 and 219 active firms, we have the long-run equilibrium in this toy model. The corresponding equilibrium price is around $12.95, total (market) supply and demand is roughly 87,050, and individual-firm production levels are roughly 397 per month.

Note: because of the sunk cost of entry, firms are realizing positive (economic) profits per month,[4] they are supplying significantly more than their efficient scale, the equilibrium price is significantly higher than the firms' minimum average cost of $7 and, at the scale of production of each firm, their average cost is $9.23 (roughly).

---

[4] The presence of the sunk cost complicates the comparison of economic profit—which is now probably better termed *monthly cash flow*—and accounting income; depending on the nature of the sunk-cost investment and how it was financed, it may be that that it is being depreciated in the computation of accounting income. But it may not. The comparison is a mess.

Now imagine a shift in demand. If demand increases, the price rises immediately. Active firms adjust their quantities, which causes the price to fall back toward $12.95. But the fall is insufficient to bring monthly profit back down to around $1485, so inactive firms consider entering. Of course, these inactive firms have to do some forecasting: How long will the increased demand last? (If it is only temporary, the NPV calculations become complex; the more-than-$1485 trigger for new entry is no longer applicable.) How many other firms will enter? This last question is both hard to answer and critical: If there are only fixed and variable costs, and if too many inactive firms enter, some of them can leave quickly without too much damage to their bottom line. But if too many firms pay the sunk-cost $150,000, as long as the resulting price is above $7, they will stick around (unless they go bankrupt for failing to service debt that was used to finance the sunk-cost entry expense). Keep this possibility in mind when you read Story #1 to follow.

On the other hand, suppose demand falls. The price declines. Active firms cut back on their production, which causes price to rise back toward $12.95. But even after the active firms adjust their production levels, price falls short of $12.95, the price required to get per-firm monthly cash flow up to $1475 or so. Because the sunk costs were sunk, active firms only leave if the price falls below $7. And even that isn't necessarily so: suppose the fall in demand is temporary, and a firm that exits must repay the sunk cost to reenter. Then an active firm has to forecast the length of time until demand gets back to where it was and do an NPV calculation: Is it better to exit and avoid losses for a while or to ride out the storm? And still more complicated would be a case where an active firm, to become active again, doesn't need to pay the full $150,000 "entry fee"; there is a "reentry sunk cost" to be paid that is smaller than the full $150,000. (And keep this possibility in mind when reading Story #2.) Or suppose that exiting, even temporarily, means paying a sunk-cost exit fee. And, finally, remember that all this is relevant *only if* the fall in demand leads to a fall in price below $7. Until prices go that low, active firms are unhappy—they aren't generating the cash flow that they anticipated would cover their original sunk cost of entry, and if they have heavy debt financing, they could fail to be able to service their debt—but sunk costs are sunk and, as long as monthly profit (economic profit) is positive, they are going to stick around, barring bankruptcy.

The last two paragraphs may make your head hurt. But it is precisely these sorts of considerations that drive real-world applications.

Story #1: High-Fructose Corn Syrup

The Harvard Corn Wet Milling Industry cases (HBS 1-378-186 and 4-378-206) tell a very common, if a bit dated, story about how, in the presence of sunk costs, entry decisions by industry participants can go horribly wong. The basic story runs as follows.

In 1972, the corn wet-milling industry was a mature and stable oligopoly, with a few old and well-established firms that milled corn to make cornstarch and corn syrup. Then, a chemical process was invented that could turn corn syrup into high-fructose corn syrup (HFCS), a much sweeter corn syrup that could, potentially, be used as a sugar substitute (at much lower manufacturing costs) in food products, including the massive market in soft drinks (Coca-Cola, Pepsi, and so forth). The potential for market expansion and profit was enormous, and all sorts of firms—firms already in the industry, agro-industrial giants, and others—more or less simultaneously decided to enter. The problem was that, to enter, firms had to build a processing facility, the efficient scale of which was quite large and quite expensive and which was, to a very large extent, a sunk cost. It is probably inaccurate to say that market participants were price-takers. But the NPV calculations they had to do were similar to those in our toy model and, since this is the real world, they had to forecast (1) how big the market would be (would Coca-Cola adopt HFCS?), (2) how long would the market last and, most significantly, (3) how many other firms would enter. The market was large and it lasted for a long time (it is only recently that diet consciousness has begun to push back against the use of HFCS). But all evidence suggests that entrants gravely underestimated the number of other firms that would enter. Sunk costs being sunk, productive capacity reached levels at which prices, while covering monthly operating costs, fell to levels such that industry participants never realized the flow of cash flows/profits that would have made their initial investments worthwhile.

Story #2: Saudi Arabia and Shale-Oil Producers

A more recent story concerns the alledged attempt by Saudi Arabia to drive shale-oil producers out of business.

Crude oil extraction is certainly not a competitive industry. There are several producers that have the ability to move the price of crude oil; the most important of these is Saudi Arabia. But there is a sea of price-taking producers, including shale-oil producers; this simply means that their capacity for production is too small to have any meaningful impact on the market price. Those producers are "competitive": The product they sell isn't quite a commodity, in that there are different grades of crude oil. But the differences are well understood, and the price differences between different grades are very well established. And there is copious information about market prices and market conditions. So, for this sea of small producers, the assumptions of perfect competition hold, with the complicating feature that the market prices they face are, to a very large extent, set based on Saudi Arabia's decisions how much to pump and sell.[5]

---

[5] The cost functions of oil extractors and, in particular, shale oil extractors over this period exhibit two significant complicating features. First, in any sort of mineral extraction, the more you extract, the harder it is to extract the next bit. This is like the experience curve in manufacturing—cf.

Now, for the story. Starting in the fall of 2014, the price of a barrel of crude oil fell sharply. In July 2014, the price was around $100 per barrel; by January 2015, it was below $50, and in January 2016, it bottomed out below $30. The fall in price was largely due to the Saudis, who increased their own output rate significantly. Demand for oil is fairly inelastic, and it is clear that the Saudis would have increased their immediate revenues by selling less (because of the higher prices that would result); so the obvious question is, Why were they pumping and selling so much?

Several explanations were offered, but the explanation that has been most widely accepted is that the Saudis were targeting the shale-oil producers, trying to drive them from the market. An article in Bloomberg (September 2015) entitled "Saudis are Winning the War on Shale"[6] put it this way:

> The Saudis are teaching the market that they are the go-to suppliers at any price level and that they're always going to be there, unlike those fly-by-night American operators. They're also teaching investors in U.S. shale that as soon as they plow more money into the sector, they, the Saudis, will boost output and drive prices lower, ruining the economic models on which the investment decision was based. That's a lesson they want to sink in, because there's still a lot of talk about shale's nimbleness in responding to changing price conditions.

This is not a story about fixed costs. If shale-oil producers only had fixed and variable costs, they could depart from the market when prices are driven below their minimum average costs and return as soon as the Saudis cut back on production and prices rise to a level where they (the shale-oil producers) can make a profit. The story—that is to say, the Saudi's strategy in this explanation—only makes sense if it is about sunk costs of entry: The Saudis were saying, in effect, that they wouldn't and, in the future, won't permit shale-oil producers to recoup their sunk costs of entry. If prospective investors in shale oil absorb this "lesson," they will not invest in shale oil, and the Saudis can then return prices to levels that they desire.

If that was the strategy, it didn't seem to have worked. Late in 2016, the Saudis pulled back on production; early in January 2017 (when I wrote this paragraph), price was back above $50 per barrel, at which price the shale-oil producers can profitably produce. Why did the strategy fail? At least two explanations have been offered. First, the cost of shale-oil extraction fell as shale-oil producers got better at what they do, enough so that, even at $30 per

---

Chapter 12—but in reverse. On the other hand, and specific to shale-oil extraction, the technology is new, and there have been significant cost-reducing advances in the technology. This point will be important in the story to follow.

[6] See http://www.bloombergview.com/articles/2015-09-11/saudis-are-winning-the-war-on-shale

barrel, they were not going to go away.[7] And the Saudis couldn't afford to drive prices even further down. And, second, while a lot of the sunk costs in shale-oil production was initially debt financed—so that initial shale-oil producers went bankrupt—the sunk-cost assets that they had created were bought up at fire-sale prices by savvy investors, ready to reenter. In other words, the sunk-cost assets initially created were held in readiness, and the cost of reentry was much lower than the intial (sunk) costs of entry.[8] The Saudis, seeing this, understood that they could never drive shale-oil production out of the industry (or so analysts speculate); they have cut back on production, and prices are rising again.

14.6. Why Do We Care about Perfect Competition?

You now probably know more than you ever wanted to know about perfect competition. Indeed, many students of management, studying economics for the first time, react to all this by claiming that the first bit of knowledge was probably more than desired, since there are no perfectly competitive industries in the world.

This claim is incorrect. Some very important industries come close enough that the model is a good predictor, at least over some time frames. Broad classes of examples include many sectors of agriculture, some sectors of labor markets, and reasonably heavily traded financial securities. The case of financial securities is especially interesting, because prices are set in highly organized exchanges, exchanges that engage in activities, such as the disclosure of financial information, to make their markets come closer to the competitive ideal. And, as the case of the Saudis and the shale-oil producers show, even in markets with some "big" producers, if the market also has an active competitive fringe whose output is significant, understanding perfect competition and the basic dynamics it creates can help you to understand significant real-life events.

This is not to say that the models we've looked at are flawless. Especially when it comes to entry and exit decisions, when there are sunk-cost aspects to entry and exit, models of perfect competition might work well for a fixed set of participating firms but can fail badly—at least, they are hard to apply—in longer time frames where entry and exit are issues. The story of HFCS provides a good example; if you would like to see a case study for which the models work well in the short run but have sunk-cost-created problems in the longer run, I strongly recomment the case "The Oil Tanker Shipping Industry in 1983" (HBS 9-384-034).

Finally, perfect competition provides the benchmark case for understanding how well or poorly markets function as an economic system. This is where we

---

[7] See "Texas shale oil has fought Saudi Arabia to a standstill," by Ambrose Evans-Pritchard, *The Telegraph*, July 31, 2016, page B1.

[8] See "Saudis 'will not destroy the US shale industry'," by Ambrose Evans-Pritchard, *The Telegraph*, Jaunuary 24, 2016.

are headed in the next chapter.

14.7. Monopolistic Competition

A variation on perfect competition that is important to some branches of economic modeling, particularly theories of growth in macroeconomics, is so-called *monopolistic competition*. Roughly speaking, an industry is monopolistically competitive if firms face downward sloping demand and needn't worry about how "competitors" will respond to their own pricing decisions (the monopoly part), but there is enough "competition" so that economic profits of industry participants are forced down to zero. I put "competitors" and "competition" in scare quotes, because that's the genius of this type of model.

I won't develop this theory here; while the rise of e-commerce is, perhaps, making it more realistic, I have real problems with monopolistic competition as a microeconomic model of important real-life industries. But since your macroeconomics instructor in particular may want you to have had some exposure to this model, in the *Online Supplement Material for Chapter 12*, I provide a brief treatment (along with my objections to the model as being a model of real-life industries).

Executive Summary

- A competitive (price-taking) firm believes it can sell as much or as little as it wishes at a going market price.

- For a competitive firm, MC = MR is replaced by *price equals marginal cost*, or $p =$ MC, since a competitive firm's marginal revenue is the price it faces. This implies that, for a competitive firm with no fixed costs and rising marginal cost, its marginal cost function "is" its supply function. If it has rising marginal costs and a positive and *avoidable* fixed cost, its supply is the marginal cost function but only at or above its minimum average cost.

- In a competitive market, aggregate supply is the horizontal sum of the supply functions of individual firms.

- In an industry with free entry and exit, firms enter if they can earn a positive economic profit, and they exit if they are in the (economic) red.

- If the best technology is available broadly to firms in the market and to a host of potential entrants, and if entry and exit are free, the long-run equilibrium price must equal the minimum average cost of the best available technology, active firms will produce at their efficient scale, and all firms will earn 0 economic profit.

- If a perfectly competitive market in long-run equilibrium confronts a sudden shift upward in demand, prices will shoot up at first, and then gradually decline as incumbent firms adjust to the new environment and, as available and necessary, new firms enter. Or, at least, that's what our models predict: In reality, where firms can expand operations or enter willy-nilly, the industry can reach a position of overcapacity (as happened in the corn wet-milling industry with the introduction of HFCS).

- Even with free entry and exit at the best available technology, long-run supply can slope upward if changes in industry output affect the prices of inputs to the industry. If we imagine no change in the prices of inputs, long-run supply is horizontal.

- Adding sunk costs (of entry or exit) to models of entry and exit brings these models closer to reality, but at the same time complicates the models enormously, because these features require the model builder to confront net-present-value calculations and forecasts by both incumbent and prospective industry participants of what prices will be in the future. As illustrated by both the story of HFCS and the Saudis attempt to drive shale-oil producers out of crude-oil extraction, those forecasts can go quite wrong.

- Perfect competition is interesting because some important industries are close to perfectly competitive; it is also interesting as a benchmark, especially as we turn, in the next chapter, to issues of economic efficiency.

Problems

14.1 A competitive firm has total cost function $TC(x) = 5$ million$+5x+x^2/10{,}000$. Regarding its fixed cost of \$5 million, \$4 million can be avoided if the firm produces 0, but \$1 million is completely unavoidable: Even if the firm ceases production, it must pay this \$1 million. What is the supply function for this competitive firm?

14.2 A competitive firm has marginal cost function $MC(x) = 3 + x/20{,}000$. The total cost function for this firm is $TC(x) = F_1 + F_2 + 3x + x^2/40{,}000$, where F_1 and F_2 are fixed costs: The firm can avoid paying F_2 if it produces 0, but it cannot avoid F_1. (That is, $TC(0) = F_1$.) Efficient scale for this firm—the level of x that minimizes average cost—is $x = 60{,}000$. This firm supplies positive levels of output for all prices above \$5. What are the values of F_1 and F_2? (Answer [so you can check your work]: $F_1 = \$50{,}000$ and $F_2 = \$40{,}000$.)

14.3 A competitive firm has the marginal-cost function $MC(x) = 8 - x/10 + x^2/2000$ and the total-cost function $TC(x) = 8x - x^2/20 + x^3/6000$. What is this firm's supply function? Suppose the firm has a fixed cost of \$10,000, and the entire fixed cost can be avoided if the firm produces 0. What is the firm's supply function in this case? (A little tricky, as this has a marginal-cost function that falls and then rises.)

14.4 A consumer with the money-left-over utility function $u(x) + m = 10\ln(x + 1) + m$ is endowed with 100 units of x and \$1000. This consumer can buy or sell the commodity in question, depending on its price. If, for instance, the price of x is \$4 per unit and the consumer sells 25 units, she ends up with 75 units of the good and $1100 in money left over, for an ending utility level of $10\ln(76)+1100$. If she buys 25 units, she ends with 125 units of the good and $900 in money left over, for an ending utility of $10\ln(126) + 900$. Given the price p of the good, the consumer buys or sells, doing whatever makes her ending utility as high as possible. As a function of the price p, what will this consumer do?

14.5 Suppose a particular perfectly competitive industry has 10 identical firms, each with the total-cost function $TC(x) = 4x + x^2/2$. There is no possibility of entry into or exit from this industry. If demand for the item in question is given by $D(p) = 10(20 - p)$, what is the equilibrium in this market?

14.6 Suppose that, in a perfectly competitive industry, every firm has total-cost function $TC(x) = 10$ million $+ 2x + x^2/100{,}000$. Demand is given by $D(p) = 500{,}000(42 - p)$.

(a) If the industry consists of five firms, with no possibility of entry or exit, what is the equilibrium?

(b) If there is an unlimited number of potential entrants for this industry and firms can enter or exit freely (and pay the fixed cost only if they are actively producing), what is the equilibrium?

14.7 Suppose that, in a particular perfectly competitive industry, the technology for making the product (by any single firm) has the total-cost function $TC(x) = 100 + 3x + 0.04x^2$. An unlimited supply of firms could enter this industry, all with that total-cost function. Firms incur the fixed cost only if they are in the industry.

(a) If demand for the product is given by $D(p) = 200(10-p)$, what is the long-run equilibrium in this industry? What is the price of the good in equilibrium, how much is traded, how many firms are active, how much does each firm produce, and what profit is made by each firm?

(b) Suppose demand for the product suddenly shifts to $D(p) = 200(12 - p)$. In the short run, firms cannot change their production quantities at all. What is the new short-run equilibrium? In the intermediate run, firms in the industry can change their production quantities according to the total-cost function just given. What is the intermediate-run equilibrium in this industry? In the long run, firms can enter and leave the industry. What is the new long-run equilibrium in this industry?

14.8 Suppose, in the industry of Problem 14.7, four firms have a superior production technology, which gives each the total-cost function $TC(x) = 50 + x + 0.04x^2$. An additional eight firms have the cost function from Problem 14.7. There are no other possible entrants into this industry.

If demand for the product is given by $D(p) = 200(10-p)$, what is the equilibrium in this industry?

I have not told you whether the fixed costs of the 12 firms can be avoided. Does this matter to the answer to this problem? How?

14.9 Suppose that, in Problem 14.8, instead of eight firms with the cost function from Problem 14.7, an unlimited number of firms possess this cost function. Assume that all fixed costs can be avoided if a firm produces no output. If demand for the product is given by $D(p) = 200(10 - p)$, what is the equilibrium in this industry?

14.10 I assert that a profit-maximizing competitive firm that turns a strictly positive profit must produce above its efficient scale. Back on page 144, I asserted that a profit-maximizing firm with market power always produces at a level greater than the level that maximizes profit margin (the difference between average revenue and average cost). What's the connection between these two assertions?

14.11 Suppose that, in the toy model with sunk costs given beginning on page 324, the sunk cost of entry is $100,000. Redo the analysis to find the "long-run equilibrium" in terms of number of active firms, equilibrium price, production per active firm, and cash flow per month of active firms. (Do not expect the answer to have a whole-number number of firms.) What if the sunk cost of entry is $50,000?

15. The Invisible Hand

This chapter has two objectives:

- It discusses the concepts of *consumer* and *producer surplus*, dollar-valued measures of the value that consumers and producers receive from participating in market exchange.
- Using these concepts, it shows why economists rhapsodize about markets and prices: Competitive markets are *efficient*, meaning they lead to the largest possible level of total surplus. But this statement must be qualified, and some of the qualifications are discussed here as well.

If you surveyed the general populace, asking people to name phrases that economists use, *supply equals demand* would be the hands-down winner. But a contender for second place would probably be *the invisible hand*.

The invisible hand, a phrase coined by the father of economics, Adam Smith, refers to the role prices play in achieving a good allocation of resources in the economy. Economists, or at least economists who respect markets, are fond of rhapsodizing about the price mechanism. "Imagine," one of them might say, "many consumers and producers, with many conflicting preferences and capabilities, whose activities need to be coordinated. And the price mechanism does this so well, telling consumers the 'cost' of a particular item while telling producers the 'value' of the item in the marketplace." Warming up to her subject, our market-respecting economist explains, "Prices and the market mechanism are like an invisible hand that correctly and efficiently coordinates consumer desires and producer activities, achieving an unimprovable result."

Indeed, and with some justice, the invisible hand is sometimes cited as one reason that Soviet-style communism failed. The former Soviet Union was run as a centrally planned and administered economy. That is a pretty big operation to run from headquarters; and without in the least disparaging the talents of the commissariat and others who did the planning, the planning did not always work well.

In comparison, in price-driven economies, prices decentralize the planning process. To be very clear about this, decentralization is what gets the good results. Individual consumers have a lot of information and the time and incentive to process it, as they seek to maximize their utility. Firms have a lot of information and the time and incentive to process it, as they chase higher profits. Prices play an informational role: They sum up very concisely everything profit-maximizing firms and utility-maximizing consumers need to know about each other's desires and capabilities. Firms and consumers, guided by equilibrium prices and their own self-interest, reach an overall outcome that centrally planned and administered economies seemingly cannot match.

Needless to say, there is a lot more to why Soviet-style communism failed. The corrupt political system played a role, as did a lack of incentives for individuals to take risks and innovate. But there is little doubt that running by fiat an economy the size of the former Soviet Union, or even one the size of, say, Portugal, is a daunting task. The central planners sitting in Moscow may have been able to decide how many shoes to make for sale in Novosibirsk. But they probably had no clue about styles. And, if they got the styles wrong, the shoes might sit on the shelves of shoe stores in Novosibirsk, as the consumers of Novosibirsk made do with their somewhat worn old shoes. In comparison, the owner of a private shoe store in Zurich has a very strong incentive, and the time required, to learn what would be deemed a stylish pair of footwear in Zurich. Even if the bureaucratic planner sitting in Moscow had the incentive to follow the latest fashion trends in Novosibirsk, which is doubtful, he still would have lacked the time and opportunity to glean the required information. Prices—or, more properly, the decentralization of decision making and information gathering, allied with the incentives provided by the market system—get the job done.

And what "job" does the market system "get done?" We discover in this chapter that the invisible hand, *if certain conditions are met*, produces an *efficient* outcome, but not necessarily one that is *equitable*.

15.1. Consumer and Producer Surplus

For most of this chapter, we look at a perfectly competitive market, where all supply comes from firms and all demand comes from consumers.

Figure 15.1 depicts the usual supply equals demand picture, with the equilibrium price and equilibrium quantity at the point where supply intersects demand. Note the two shaded regions. The darker region is bounded by the equilibrium price and the demand function to the left of the equilibrium quantity. The area of this region is called the *consumer surplus*. The lighter region is bounded by the equilibrium price and the supply function, to the left of the equilibrium quantity. The area of this region is called the *producer surplus*. I assert the following:

- Producer surplus measures, in dollars, the profits producers obtain from trading in this market.

- Consumer surplus measures (approximately), in dollars, the benefits consumers obtain from trading in this market.

- Hence, these two quantities, when summed, measure in dollars the (approximate) value generated by the existence of this market.

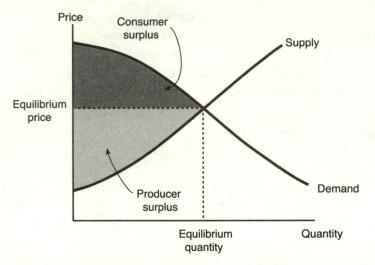

Figure 15.1. Consumer and producer surplus. Consumer surplus (the area of the darkly shaded region) measures in dollars the benefits that consumers obtain from the equilibrium outcome. Producer surplus (the area of the lightly shaded region) measures in dollars the benefits to producers of this market outcome.

In what sense is this true? And why is consumer surplus only an approximation? This will take a few pages.

Producer Surplus

Producer surplus equals *the profits of the firms in the industry* as long as three conditions are met: (1) Firms are price takers. (2) The supply function is drawn assuming all prices that involve the firms except for this one price do not change. (3) The firms have no unavoidable fixed costs.

Condition 1 is probably superfluous, as we wouldn't be drawing a supply function otherwise. As to Condition 2, this concerns the material that begins on the bottom of page 322 in Chapter 14: The empirical supply function—what we would see in data we collected—may involve changing prices for factor inputs, in which case producer surplus will (typically) overstate profits earned by firms in the industry.

Condition 3, however, is important. If the firms have unavoidable fixed costs, then the area marked out by producer surplus is the sum of industry profits plus those unavoidable fixed costs. This has two immediate consequences:

- Most of the time when we employ the concept of producer surplus, we will be measuring the *change in producer surplus* as the price of the output good changes from one value to another. See, for instance, Figure 15.2, where we shade the change in producer surplus when the price producers are paid for the goods they produce and sell rises from p_0 to p_1. Whether or not the firms have unavoidable fixed costs is irrelevant to this difference since, if they do, when we take the difference between producer surplus at p_0 and producer surplus at p_1, they cancel out. Subject to Conditions 1 and 2 holding, *when it comes to computing the* **change** *in producer surplus for a change in the output price, the change in producer surplus is* **precisely** *the change in industry profits.*

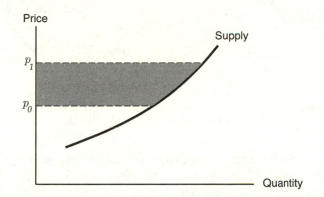

Figure 15.2. The change in producer surplus for a price increase.

- We will sometimes want to know: What is the change in producer surplus in the short run versus in the (say) intermediate run? The pictures of short-run and intermediate-run supply will have the usual appearance, as in Figure 15.3, where p_0 is the status-quo price. Suppose the price of the good falls to p_1. Then the change in short-run profits—how much less the firms make in the short run—is larger than the change in intermediate-run profits, which makes sense. And if the price of the good rises, the change in short-run profits—which for a rise in the output price is how much more firms make—is smaller than the change in intermediate-run profits, which also makes sense.

  What confuses some students is that, if we look not at changes in short-run and intermediate-run producer surplus, but at the levels of short-run and intermediate-run producer surplus at the status-quo price, it appears that the short-run producer surplus is larger. But, at the status-quo price, the two ought to be equal. The difference is that costs that are unavoidable in the short run can be avoided in the intermediate run. The difference between the total short-run producer surplus and the total intermediate-run producer surplus, both measured at the status-quo price, is precisely those short-run fixed costs.

Why is it that these areas measure (changes in) industry profits? In the simple case where firms have no fixed costs and therefore supply along their marginal-cost functions, this isn't hard to prove: First you prove it for each individual firm—Figure 15.4 gives the proof in pictures—and then you use the fact that industry supply is the horizontal sum of individual firm supply functions and the calculus fact that the sum of integrals is the integral of the sum. For the more

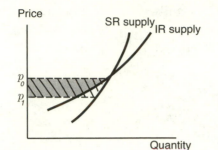

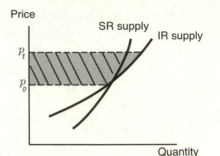

(a) For a fall in price, the change in IR producer surplus is less than the change in SR producer surplus–profits fall more in the SR than in the IR

(b) For a rise in price, the change in IR producer surplus is greater than the change in SR producer surplus–profits rise more in the IR than in the SR

Figure 15.3. Short- and intermediate-run changes in producer surplus for a fall in price from the status quo (panel a) and a rise (panel b). In both panels, the change in IR producer surplus is solid gray and the change in SR producer surplus is the hatched area.

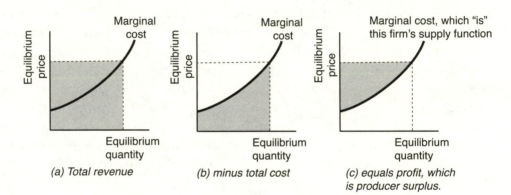

(a) Total revenue

(b) minus total cost

(c) equals profit, which is producer surplus.

Figure 15.4. Producer surplus = profits for a single producer with no fixed costs.

general case, you can take my word for it.[1]

There is one thing to add about producer surplus: the nice pictures we have drawn are all for the case of firms in a perfectly competitive industry where, moreover, producers are selling along the industry supply function. In some applications to come, the government may stop firms from selling as much as they want, or it may compel them to sell more than they would like (at the prices they are paid). In other applications, we'll want to think about "producer surplus" for a firm with market power. In all cases, the rule *producer surplus = producer's profits* applies. The dollar-valued measure of how firms do is their profits; the dollar-valued measure of how they are affected by some government policy or another is, How much and in what direction do their profits change?

---

[1]   If you are disinclined to take my word for it, a very general proof is provided as Corollary 12.4 in Kreps, *Microeconomic Foundations, I*.

Consumer Surplus

The story for consumer surplus is not so simple. You can take my word for it: The heavily shaded area in Figure 15.1 is an *approximate* dollar-valued measure of the benefit consumers get from being able to consume at the equilibrium price the quantity they demand. Changes in consumer surplus, driven by changes in the price charged, measure in dollar terms the welfare gains (if prices go down) or losses (if prices go up) from the price change. And if you are content to take my word for it, skip ahead to the next section.

But if you want to know a bit more: We first ask, How would one construct a dollar-valued measure of the change in consumer welfare? Suppose, for instance, the price of the good is currently p_0, and we want to know, How much better off will consumers be, if we lower the price to p_1? We can go to each consumer and ask the following questions:

1. How much money would you be willing to give up, to cause the price of the good to decrease from p_0 to p_1?

2. How much money would we have to give you if, instead of lowering the price to p_1, we kept it at p_0, so you wouldn't mind that we didn't lower the price?

The answers to these questions for consumers are, generally, not quite the same. Which one is bigger depends on the good in question and, specifically, the answer to the question, If I give you more money to spend but don't change the price of the good, will you buy more of the good, less of the good, or the same amount? But, whichever is bigger, in a fairly general sense, the heavily shaded area in Figure 15.1 will lie between the two. And if the price change is small, and/or if the consumers' demand levels don't change much (holding the price fixed) as we change the amount of money they have to spend, the two numbers are close to one another and, therefore, close to what we are calling consumer surplus.

If you want to see this developed in gory detail, see Chapter 12 of Kreps, *ibid.* But I don't recommend that, unless your math skills are really good. Instead, I'll conclude with a couple of pictures that may help your understanding. These pictures are for a special case of consumer demand: Each consumer wants one and only unit of the good in question, as long as the price of the good is below that consumer's *reservation price*. Consumer A, for instance, has a reservation price of $34; if the good costs $34 or less, she'll buy one unit. And her level of welfare gained from this transaction is her reservation price less what she has to pay for the goood; if the price of the good is $20, she is $34 − $20 = $14 to the good.

In this case, the demand function for the good is: At any price p the number of units demanded is the number of consumers whose reservation price is p or greater. Now look at Figure 15.5. The "staircase" on which the three consumers are sitting is the (inverse) demand function, with one step per consumer, each step one unit wide, with the top of each step at that consumer's reservation price. For the supply function depicted, the equilibrium price is $4. And you see that the shaded area on which each consumer sits—one unit wide by reservation-price-less-equilibrium-price high—is the dollar surplus that consumer gets from consuming the good at the equilibrium price.

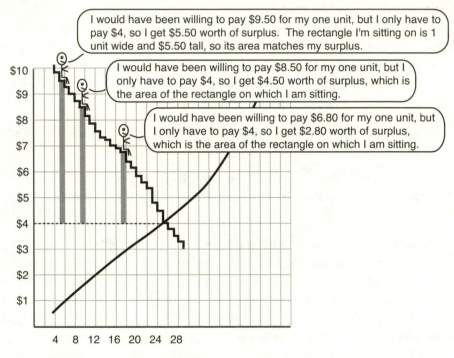

Figure 15.5. A few consumers and their surpluses.

Now take all of these consumers together, as in Figure 15.6, and you have the full measure of consumer surplus. The reservation-demand model is, of course, a special case. But it gives you an idea what is going on.

Consumer Surplus in Nonequilibrium Situations

As with producer surplus, we sometimes want to apply the concept of consumer surplus in contexts other than the supply-equals-demand equilibrium of a competitive marketplace. The concept does not change in the least when applied to consumers in a market where the supplier has market power, or any setting in which there is a market price for the good set by some means, which consumers take as given and at which they buy whatever amount they desire. Slightly more complex are contexts in which the good is sold using a price-discriminating scheme, but usually these can be figured out if you are careful.

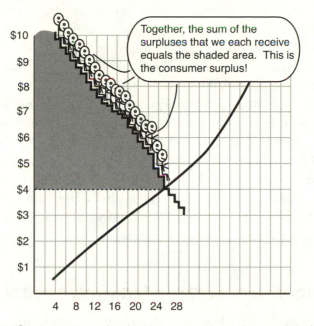

Figure 15.6. Consumer surplus in the reservation-price model of demand.

Other contexts can be harder to deal with. Suppose, for instance, the government nationalizes the shoe industry and produces 10 million pairs of shoes. Suppose further that the price per pair that would give demand of 10 million pairs is $50 per pair, but the Commissar for Footwear decides that a price of $10 per pair is more equitable. Demand at $10 per pair is presumably significantly more than 10 million pairs, and so the 10 million pairs must be rationed among consumers. Queues form at the shoe department. Bribes are paid to shoe salespersons. A black market in shoes springs up, where people sell or barter shoes they do not want for things they do. And, as an economic analyst, you must work out the consumer surplus engendered by the 10 million pairs that are sold—at least officially—for $10 per pair.

You cannot carry out this task without making a lot more assumptions. You need to know on whose feet those shoes will eventually be found, because you need to know how much benefit the shoe wearers get. As we are about to discover, a nice thing about competitive markets is that the folks who "value" the items for sale the most—who are willing to pay the most—get the items. (The scare quotes around *value* will be explained later.) This allows for the computation of consumer surplus. But, when nonmarket allocation schemes are used, unless we know the identity of the folks who get the goods and the dollar-valued surpluses they enjoy from consuming those goods, we are stumped. For more on this, see Problem 15.6.

Firms as Customers and Consumers as Suppliers

In the case of producer surplus, we are imagining that supply comes from competitive firms. In the case of consumer surplus, we are imagining that demand comes from end-use consumers. But what about B2B transactions, where the costumer is a firm? What about markets in which some of the supply comes from consumers (e.g., the market in GM Truck Coupons)?

If we rename producer surplus as *provider surplus* and consumer surplus as *customer surplus*, nothing changes. We use the same measures taken from the picture of supply and demand, and they mean the same things: For (profit-maximizing) firms who are customers, their contribution to overall customer surplus measures the profits they enjoy for getting to buy the goods at the price they pay. For consumers who are suppliers, their contribution to overall provider surplus is an approximate dollar-denominated measure of how much they enjoy selling the good at the price they get.

15.2. Competitive Markets Maximize Total Surplus

Now that we have standards by which to judge the benefits received by consumers and producers from particular market outcomes, we can see in what sense the equilibrium achieved by a perfectly competitive market is ideal.[2] The result is simple to state:

> *A competitive-market equilibrium maximizes total surplus, which is the sum of consumer and producer surplus.*

This result is true in substantial generality, but it does require that some conditions are met. In particular,

- each consumer's utility from consumption depends only on his or her own level of consumption and not on how the goods are produced or what other consumers get to consume, and

- each firm's total cost of production depends only on what the firm itself produces.

In Chapter 17, we learn that this pair of assumptions is crucial if the invisible hand is to perform ideally; to use the language of Chapter 17, this assumes that there are no consumption or production *externalities*.

While the result is easy to state and is true in substantial generality (as long as the assumptions are met), proving it rigorously is not so easy and involves

---

[2] I'll continue to use consumer and producer, instead of customer and provider, because that's the standard language used by economists. But understand that all these ideas apply just as well to B2B transactions as well as consumers who sell out of their endowment of goods they choose to sell rather than consume.

some abstract math. So I won't try to prove this but, instead, I'll try to indicate semi-intuitively why it is true.[3]

In any arrangement we could make between the firms supplying the good and the consumers buying and consuming the goods, three things happen:

1. Some amount x of the good is produced, with production quantities allocated among the firms.

2. This amount is allocated to the consumers in various amounts, to be consumed.

3. The consumers pay some amounts of money, which is distributed among the firms that do the producing.

The first step in the argument is to recognize that, as far as the sum of surpluses goes, we can ignore the money that changes hands in part 3. Every dollar that a consumer pays is a dollar that some firm receives. (This assumes that no money gets "lost," which is a third assumption, I suppose.) This dollar is one dollar less for the consumer who pays it and one dollar more for the firm that receives it. When we add the consumer and producer surpluses, this exchange of money nets out to zero.

So the key to maximizing the total surplus is whether

a. the right amount of the good is being produced,

b. the low marginal-cost firms are doing the producing, and

c. the high marginal-value consumers are doing the consuming.

As far as b goes, producers are producing up to the point where the price equals their marginal cost. That is, they are each producing units whose marginal cost is less than the market price, and the marginal unit each produces has a marginal cost equal to the price. Hence, b is satisfied.

And as for c, each consumer is buying goods (in the equilibrium) to the point where her dollar-measured gain in surplus equals the price. That is, she buys units of the good whose surplus value exceeds the price, and the (last) marginal unit she buys gives her marginal surplus equal to the price. Any other allocation of the goods would have to take units away from consumers whose marginal value (measured in dollars) is more than the price and give it to consumers whose marginal value (again measured in dollars) is less than the price. So the right folks are getting the good.

And the right amount is being produced, which is a: the marginal cost (measured, of course, in dollars) of the last units produced equal the price, which equals the dollar-valued marginal surplus those goods provide to consumers.

---

[3] If you like rigorous logical proofs, what you are about to read will not satisfy you. If that is so, in the *Online Supplement Material for Chapter 15*, you will find three increasingly general proofs of this result.

Produce less than this amount, and the marginal cost would be below the dollar-valued marginal surplus—total surplus goes up if more is produced. Produce more, and the marginal cost exceeds the marginal surplus; too much is being produced.

Prices Are the Invisible Hand

I want to emphasize that prices—equilibrium prices—are the brains behind the invisible hand. The shoe retailer in Zurich, knowing the equilibrium price and her marginal cost of each type of shoe, stocks those pairs whose marginal cost to her is less than their price. Prices signal the marginal value to consumers of one more pair of each type, so while her concern is to maximize her profit, doing so vis-à-vis the equilibrium price gets the socially "right" shoes on her shelves.[4] And the shoe buyer in Zurich chooses between pairs of shoes to maximize his personal utility. One pair may be worth a lot more to him (on the margin) than another, but if the second pair is cheap enough relative to the first, he goes with the first pair. He doesn't think, "The second pair costs less (on the margin) for society to produce, so it is better for total surplus that I buy those." But responding to the prices of different pairs of shoes as he maximizes his utility, in effect, has him do just that.

Competitive Firms That Don't Maximize Profits

When, back in Chapter 6, I introduced the model of the profit-maximizing firm, I said that profit maximization per se wouldn't affect many of the conclusions that we reach. For instance, we used the model of a profit-maximizing firm to discover the basic idea behind price discrimination: raise prices to low-elasticity customers, cut price for high-elasticity customers. That conclusion remains valid for a firm (with market power) that sets its price(s) in the pursuit of something other than maximized profit.

But for the invisible hand to do its magic, profit maximization of the objective of firms is pretty close to crucial. If, say, the Zurich retailer stocks shoes from a local and inefficient shoe manufacturer because the two went to college together, the "wrong" shoes are being produced from the perspective of total surplus.[5]

This Does Not Work When Firms Have Market Power

What if the market is not perfectly competitive? Suppose it is served by a single profit-maximizing firm that has market power; that is, that faces a downward sloping demand function. Figure 15.7 presents demand, marginal revenue, and marginal cost. There is no supply function in this case, because a firm facing a

---

[4] The scare quotes around "right" are because right here means, "that maximize total surplus."
[5] Although, presumably, the Zurich retailer gets some utility out of helping her old college friend, and "total surplus" should reflect a dollar value of that.

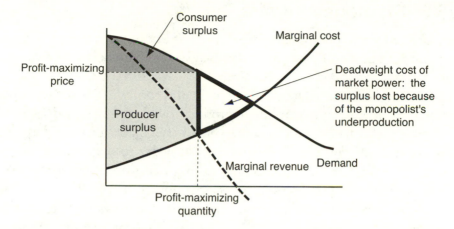

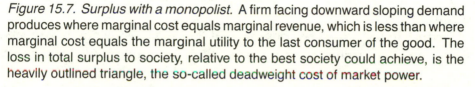

Figure 15.7. Surplus with a monopolist. A firm facing downward sloping demand produces where marginal cost equals marginal revenue, which is less than where marginal cost equals the marginal utility to the last consumer of the good. The loss in total surplus to society, relative to the best society could achieve, is the heavily outlined triangle, the so-called deadweight cost of market power.

downward sloping demand function sets the market price of its output rather than responding to an exogenously given market price.

The market price in this case is determined by the intersection of marginal cost and marginal revenue, giving the quantity and price marked on Figure 15.7. The area of the darkly shaded region is the amount of consumer surplus, and the area of the lightly shaded region is the firm's profit, gross of any fixed cost the firm faces. (See Problem 15.4.) Therefore, the combined shaded area is the total surplus generated in this market. It falls short of the maximal amount of surplus that could be generated by the area of the heavily outlined triangle. *The firm, in pursuit of maximal profits, produces at the level where its marginal cost equals its marginal revenue. This is less than the level that maximizes total surplus, where the firm's marginal cost equals the dollar-denominated marginal surplus.*

What About the Government's Share?

So far in this book, money that changes hands goes from consumers to firms, with each dollar going out of one pocket winding up in another. But, in the next chapter, a third category of "player" is added to the story: There are firms, consumers, and the government, which may impose taxes or provide subsidies and the like. In the next chapter and in Problem 15.7, when we evaluate outcomes that involve net inflows or outflows of cash from or to the government, we treat net government revenue on a dollar-for-dollar on-par basis with consumer and producer surplus. That is, the total surplus equals the net consumer surplus, plus the net producer surplus, plus the government's net revenue. In Chapter 17, we question whether and why a dollar in the government's hands might be worth more or less than a dollar held by the private sector of the economy.

15.3. Efficiency versus Equity

So subject to some qualifications—that stuff about no externalities, which we explain in Chapter 17—competitive markets maximize total surplus. But is total surplus a good standard of comparison for social outcomes? What does it capture and what does it miss? Or, to put it differently, in the last section we were talking about the "right" amount to produce, by the "right" producers, allocated to the "right" consumers. It is somewhere between explicit and implicit in that discussion that "right" is measured by "in order to maximize total surplus," hence "right" means low marginal-cost producers and high marginal-surplus consumers. But is it really right to seek maximum surplus?

In any arrangement that causes the good to be produced and assigned to consumers, with money changing hands, two qualities to look for are efficiency and equity.

Efficiency in the sense used here is what the previous section was all about: maximizing total surplus, no matter how it is distributed among firms and consumers.[6] *Equity*, on the other hand, concerns whether the combined transfers of goods and money result in a fair distribution of the surplus that could be created by production and exchange.

Efficiency is measured by the sum of individual surpluses (which, to sum, must be in the same units; which is why we looked for dollar-denominated measures). To complement this, we'd like to know how to measure the level of equity in a particular social arrangement.

Political philsophers, of whom there is some intersection with economists, have wrestled with this question without coming to any widely accepted answer. But it is probably true that almost all the political philosophers who have thought about this reject total surplus as a useful measure of equity on at least two grounds: (1) It treats firms on par with consumers. Now, this isn't as bad as it may first seem. Someone owns the firm and gets the benefit of the firm's profit. But we'd probably want to know how those profits are distributed among shareholders before equating $1 in profit with $1 in consumer surplus. (2) And $1 in surplus for, say, Daddy Warbucks (a very rich plutocrat) is probably not equivalent in an equity sense to $1 in surplus for a poor laborer whose children go to bed hungry each night. If efficiency—total surplus, in other words—is your guide, you would take $1 in surplus away from the laborer if it gets you $1.10 more in surplus for Daddy Warbucks and consider yourself $0.10 to the good. Whatever equity means, it doesn't mean that.

---

[6] If you consult a more advanced book on microeconomics, efficiency has a different meaning: given the fancier name *Pareto efficiency*, it means an arrangement or outcome where it is impossible to make (at least) one of the participants better off without making at least one other participant worse off. Pareto efficiency is the sort of efficiency we use here, if money can be used by more well-off parties to compensate less well-off parties. But the story is complex. And since this involves the possibility of monetary compensation and not the actuality of it, it still misses on equity. Once again, I send you to Kreps, ibid., Chapter 8, for the gory details.

When asked to evaluate the equity of a given institutional arrangement on the basis of economic principles, economists are prone to answer, "As an economist, I have no comment." They may have their own notions of equity, but they tend to leave to philosophers the question of what constitutes equity. Philosophers are ready to take up this challenge; John Rawls and Robert Nozick, two modern philosophers, staked out strong and fairly opposing positions on what constitutes equity. But this is economics, not philosophy, so in this book, we use total surplus as a formal measure of the efficiency of institutional arrangements, leaving trade-offs between efficiency and equity to informal judgment.

Do not misunderstand. Just because something is formalized does not make it important, nor are those things that lack formality unimportant. We separate equity and efficiency, and, using total surplus, we speak formally about efficiency. But do not feel in the least bit restrained from sacrificing a bit or even a lot of efficiency to serve equity. What we do in this chapter is provide the tools that let us measure how much efficiency is being sacrificed.

15.4. Other Aspects of Welfare and Efficiency

Since we began this chapter speaking vaguely of the triumph of capitalism over state socialism, I should say a few more things regarding this topic.

This chapter concerns the *allocative* ability of the price system to achieve an efficient level of production and distribution of goods and services in a settled or static economy. The main result is that if firms and consumers respond to prices by maximizing profit and utility—and if firms and consumers are price takers and there are no externalities—then prices direct the economy to efficient production and distribution. This is not to say that a commissariat could not do just as well. But it is easy to believe that by decentralizing decisions on matters such as the number and styles of shoes to have available in shops in Novosibirsk, markets (and profit- and utility-maximization motives) outperform central planning.

But the story we've told in this chapter is inadequate for some other aspects of "efficient" economies. For instance, a large portion of what makes for material wealth is innovation and the creation of new products. A quite different story about incentives for innovation would have to be spun concerning the *creative* abilities of an economy. In particular, the story about allocative efficiency told in this chapter seems to imply that governments, to improve efficiency, should increase the level of competition. Antitrust activity seems to be clearly indicated. And things that stifle competition by protecting intellectual property, such as patents, would seem to be a bad idea. But innovation is spurred when innovators have the prospect of enjoying the fruits of their innovative activities. Some political economists would argue that the triumph of capitalism was not because the market-driven economies of the West resulted in a better assortment of shoes on the shelves of shoe stores in Los Angeles and Zurich than in Novosibirsk. Instead, the triumph followed because capitalism and private enterprise (with protections built in for private property, including intellectual property) provide innovators the incentive to innovate and investors the incentive to seek out and finance worthwhile innovations.

We lack the tools needed to flesh out this sort of story at this point. We will be in reasonable shape to do so nearer the end of the book. But it is worth noting that seeming implications of the story told here—about antitrust activity, patents, and the like—*may* be muted and even reversed when the process of innovation is added to the mix.

Another important aspect of economic efficiency concerns the ability of individuals within the society to transact with one another in a relatively low-cost manner. This takes us back to Chapter 5 and transaction-cost economics and, in particular, the discussion there about the instrumental case for ethics in business. People who sing praises to the wonderfulness of competitive markets sometimes gild this lily with statements such as "greed is good." "Self-interest" is certainly a part of the story of the allocative efficiency of competitive markets. But when it leads to practices intended to monopolize a particular market or even just to take maximal advantage of trading partners, it can lead to allocative inefficiencies of one sort or another.

Finally, efficiency depends on what individuals value. We have used models of firm and consumer behavior in which self-interest is paramount. But, in real life, individuals have a positive taste for things like equity and providing for those less fortunate. In formal economic terms, when consumers have these sorts of tastes, we say that there are externalities in consumption. We deal with externalities in Chapter 17 and see there that they can cause real problems for the rosy picture this chapter paints. For now, record that the clear division between equity and efficiency relied on in this chapter is not entirely realistic.

15.5. Should Firms Maximize Profit?

Throughout this book, we have assumed that firms seek to maximize their profit. At various points, we've observed that this is not an empirical law of nature but instead a modeling assumption, made in the hope that the insights that we learn are at least somewhat robust to this assumption.

But rather than asking if the maximization of profit is descriptively, empirically accurate, we can ask the normative question: Is profit maximization the "right" thing for managers of a firm to do?

Two arguments are made, and sometimes entangled, that profit maximization is morally correct. The first takes off from the ideas of this chapter—profit maximization leads to surplus maximization or efficiency—so it is good for "society." I hope that you now know enough to understand that this is a flawed argument: *Firms with market power, by maximizing their profits, don't maximize social surplus.* And please note that we've assumed in our analysis that a given firm either has market power or is competitive. But a firm that seeks to maximize its profit typically finds that enhancing its market power enhances its profit. So the observation that profit-maximization by competitive firms maximizes social surplus needs the following amendment: Profit-maximization by competitive firms maximizes social surplus, as long as the profit-maximizing firms remain competitive.

And even if firms in a market are and remain competitive, other issues arise. We'll see in Chapter 17 that firms can generate externalities and, if they do, maximizing profit doesn't maximize social surplus. We discussed back in Chapter 5 that "unbridled and naked greed" in the moment can raise transaction costs, leading to worse social outcomes. And, even if none of these objections holds in a specific context, maximizing social surplus, while perhaps efficient, is not necessarily equitable.

The second argument that is offered is that the owners (equity holders) in a firm are the residual claimants to the firm's profit, and management has a fiduciary responsibility to operate the firm in the interests of its owners. If you grant the premise—that management has fiduciary responsibility to operate the firm in the interests of its owners—and if the firm is fully competitive, then the conclusion that management should seek to maximize profit (or the value of its equity) is indeed valid.

However: In the real world, firms are not generally competitive. General Motors has market power when it comes to setting the price of Cadillacs. And a small shareholder who buys a new Cadillac each year doesn't want GM to price Cadillacs in a way that maximizes its overall profit; this shareholder may prefer that GM price Cadillacs at $10 apiece. A shareholder who lives downstream from a plant operated by the firm in which she holds shares might well be willing to have the firm give up some of its profit to clean up effluent that it is dumping into the river that runs past her home. The point is that, except in the case of perfectly competitive firms that generate no externalities for its shareholders, those shareholders can and often do disagree concerning which actions by the firm are in their individual best interests. So, granting the premise that management has a fiduciary responsibility to operate the firm in the interests of its owners, there is reason to believe that maximizing profit—or anything else—does not satisfy that lofty goal for all shareholders, unanimously.

This is not to say that management doesn't have a fiduciary responsibility to the owners of the firm that it manages. This doesn't give management license to pad their own pockets or those of their cronies at the expense of shareholders. But when you hear that "profit maximization is the morally right thing to do," please understand that there is very much less to this assertion than meets the eye.

Executive Summary

- In a perfectly competitive market, producer surplus (the area between the price per unit and the industry supply curve out to the level of production) gives the sum of profits of suppliers of the good, gross of any unavoidable fixed costs.

- Consumer surplus (the area between the demand curve and the price per unit out to the level of consumption) gives an approximate dollar-valued measure of the benefits consumers take from purchasing and consuming the good. Used to measure the change in benefits for a change in price, consumer surplus gives a very accurate approximation when (a) the change in price is small and/or (b) when the consumers' demands for the good in question aren't very sensitive to the amounts of money they have to spend.

- In a perfectly competitive market, the market equilibrium maximizes the total surplus generated in the production, exchange, and consumption of the good.

- The good is produced in an overall cost-minimizing manner by the industry, with the marginal cost of the last unit produced equal to the equilibrium price.

- The good is consumed in an overall sum-of-benefits-maximizing manner by consumers, with the marginal surplus value of the last unit consumed equal to the equilibrium price.

- The cost of the marginal unit produced matches the surplus its consumption engenders, because each is equal to the price: The right amount is being produced.

- The transfer of money from consumers to producers is a net wash in terms of total surplus.

- Economists phrase this as, A competitive market equilibrium is efficient. This is how *the invisible hand* works. However, keep in mind the following three points.

- Efficiency is not equity. Economists generally avoid formal measures or definition of equity, but this does not mean that equity should be ignored: It is perfectly reasonable to sacrifice some efficiency to achieve a more equitable outcome.

- A firm that faces downward sloping demand and sets its price rather than taking price as given, sets its marginal cost equal to its marginal revenue: Since marginal revenue is less than price (for downward sloping demand), which equals marginal surplus, this means that too little is produced to achieve full efficiency.

- The invisible-hand story of this chapter concerns *allocative efficiency*. Policies intended to promote innovation can be in conflict with some of the prescriptions that might otherwise flow from this discussion.

Problems

15.1 Suppose the supply of a particular good is given by $S(p) = 1000(p - 4)$, while demand is given by $D(p) = 3000(20 - p)$. What is consumer surplus at the equilibrium of this market? What is producer surplus?

15.2 Problem 14.9 described a perfectly competitive industry with four firms having the total cost function $TC(x) = 50 + x + 0.04x^2$ and an unlimited supply of firms having the total cost function $TC(x) = 100 + 3x + 0.04x^2$. In all cases, fixed costs are avoided by not producing. Suppose demand is given by $D(p) = 200(10 - p)$. What are the consumer and producer surpluses at the competitive market equilibrium of this industry? How does producer surplus relate to the profit levels of the firms?

15.3 Refer to Problem 14.7. An industry has free entry and exit for an unlimited number of firms, each having total-cost function $TC(x) = 100 + 3x + 0.04x^2$. The industry demand is initially given by $D(p) = 200(10 - p)$, and the long-run equilibrium has price \$7, total quantity 600, 12 active firms each producing 50, with \$0 profit per firm. In the short run, firms cannot change their production quantities. In the intermediate run, the 12 active firms can change their production quantities. In the long run, firms can enter or leave. In Problem 14.7, we found the short-, intermediate-, and long-run equilibria if demand shifts to $200(12 - p)$. Compute the consumer and producer surpluses for the original equilibrium and then for the short-, intermediate-, and long-run equilibria following the shift in demand. Warning: To make meaningful comparisons with the status-quo situation, when you compute the status-quo level of producer surplus, do it *three times*. (Making sense of that last sentence is, more or less, the whole point of this problem.)

15.4 Figure 15.8 depicts the average- and marginal-cost functions for a firm with a fixed cost and rising marginal cost. It also gives a demand function and marginal-revenue function for the firm, assuming this firm serves the market by itself and (therefore) has market power. Find the regions whose areas are the firm's profit gross of its fixed cost and net of its fixed cost, when it chooses price and quantity to maximize its profit. (Refer to Figure 15.7 if you need a hint for part of this.)

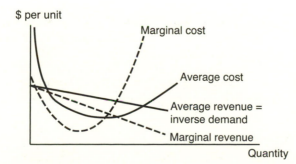

Figure 15.8. Problem 15.4: The situation facing a firm with market power.

15.5 Imagine a monopoly whose marginal-cost function is $MC(x) = 4 + x/1000$, facing a demand function given by $D(p) = 3000(20 - p)$. What producer and consumer surpluses result if the monopoly maximizes its profit? Compare your answers with the answers to Problem 15.1.

15.6 Suppose the demand for pairs of shoes in the People's Republic of Slynavia is given by $D(p) = 250{,}000(90 - p)$. (To keep the discussion simple, assume that each consumer wishes to buy at most a single pair of shoes.) The Commissar for Shoes can produce 10 million pairs of shoes to sell. A price of \$50 per pair would lead to demand for 10 million pairs. But the commissar decides that a price of \$10 per pair would be more in keeping with the government's ideology. At this price, 20 million pairs are demanded; hence, the shoes must be rationed.

(a) Suppose, in the rationing scheme employed, each of the 20 million consumers who wish to purchase a pair of shoes at \$10 per pair has an equal chance of getting 1 of the 10 million pairs available. That is, each has a 0.5 of getting a pair, *which he or she then wears*. What measure of consumer surplus is appropriate for this outcome?

(b) To explain the italicized *which he or she then wears*, the rationing outcome described has some consumers who value a pair of shoes at \$80 without shoes, while others who value a pair at \$20 wearing a pair. It seems likely in such cases that a black market in shoes will spring up. Suppose this is a well-functioning black market, where an equilibrium black-market price emerges and trades are made at that price. What is an appropriate measure of consumer surplus generated by the sale of shoes (by the state, for \$10 per pair) for the eventual outcome?

15.7 Imagine a market for a good in which demand is given by $D(p) = 10{,}000(10 - p)$. Twenty-five identical firms supply this good, each of which has the total-cost function $TC(x) = 4x + x^2/200$. All these firms are competitive; they act as if they have no impact on the prices they face.

(a) What is the equilibrium price and quantity? At this equilibrium, what are the levels of consumer and producer surplus?

(b) The government imposes a tax of \$1 per unit on this good, collected from the manufacturer. That is, if the firm produces x units of the good for sale, it must give the government \$$x$. What is the impact of this tax in terms of price, quantity, producer surplus, and consumer surplus?

(c) Add together producer and consumer surpluses from part a. Add together producer surplus, consumer surplus, and government net revenue from the tax in part b. Why is the second sum less?

16. Taxes, Subsidies, Administered Prices, and Quotas

In Chapter 15, we developed tools that allow us to discuss efficiency and inefficiency connected with market outcomes. In this chapter, we use those tools to study the impact on markets of a variety of government "interventions," such as taxes, subsidies, price floors, price ceilings, and quotas on imports.

Governments often intervene in markets: They impose taxes on some goods and subsidize others; they set price ceilings (for instance, in the case of rent control); they set price floors (to support the agricultural sector, in particular, but also in setting minimum-wage levels); they ban or set quotas or impose high tariffs on certain imports, typically to protect domestic industries or politically powerful interest groups. The results of these interventions are: Some parties are better off; some are worse off; and, if the market is competitive, a measure of inefficiency or loss of total surplus is entailed. In this chapter, we show how to use the tools developed in earlier chapters to see who are the winners, who are the losers, and—using surplus as our measure—by how much the winners win and the losers lose.

Presenting detailed analyses of all of these different types of government intervention would require a chapter of enormous length. So we will look in depth at an analysis of taxes and then price ceilings, concluding at the end with a few anecdotes about other interventions.

16.1. Taxes (and Subsidies)

We begin with taxes. To keep matters simple, we will examine taxes that are fixed (dollar) amount per unit of the good, regardless of the price of the good. And we will assume that the tax is paid by the producer/seller out of his or her revenue. That is, if the tax amount is t per unit (in dollars or whatever is the local currency), p will denote what buyers pay per unit for the good, and $p - t$ is the amount that sellers keep per unit that they sell.

This situation describes precisely how so-called *excise* taxes work; cases include taxes imposed on gasoline (petrol) and alcohol. The "opposite" rules— taxes are a percentage of price and are paid by the buyer in addition to the price of the good—are more prevalent, at least in the United States, as they characterize so-called sales taxes. Value-added-taxes are more complex. We work with the simple "excise-tax" formulation because it makes for the simplest pictures of what is going on; the impact of other forms of taxes follows the general principles of this sort of tax, although the formulas are a bit different.

The impact of a tax of t per unit sold, paid by the seller, can be thought of as affecting the producer on either the cost side—it raises the seller's marginal cost by the amount of the tax—or on the revenue side, where it lowers the seller's marginal revenue by the amount of the tax. We employ both ways of "coding" the tax's impact on the producer in what follows, choosing whichever way of thinking is most convenient to the calculation being done.

A Tax on a Competitive Industry

What is the impact of a tax on a competitive industry? As you read, follow along on Figure 16.1.

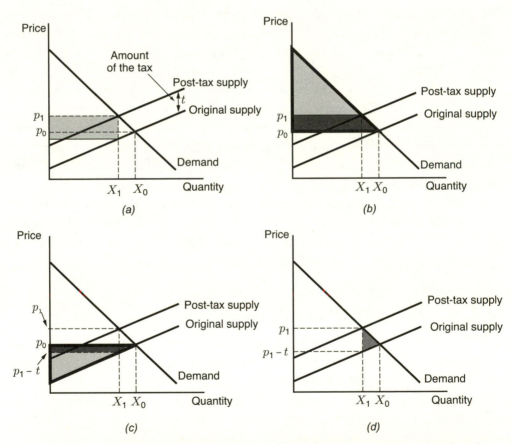

Figure 16.1. Effects of a tax. A tax of t per unit is imposed on a product in a competitive industry. This raises the inverse-supply function by the amount of the tax. Price rises and quantity falls, the consumer and producer surpluses both fall (panels b and c), and total surplus declines by the area of the shaded triangle in panel d.

1. Prior to the tax, the equilibrium price and quantity are, say, p_0 and X_0.

2. The impact of the tax is to "raise" the supply function. Suppose that $S(p)$ is the amount supplied by sellers at each price p, that is, $S(p)$ is the pre-tax supply function. Once the tax (of t per unit) is imposed, sellers only realize $p - t$ per unit when the price is p, so their supply falls at each price p from $S(p)$ to $S(p - t)$. This has the effect in the figure of "raising" the supply function vertically by t: If, to get supply X in total prior to the tax requires the price p, to get this same quantity X after the tax requires a price of $p+t$.[1]

   Warning: When you work on toy problems, proceed as follows. Suppose that pre-tax supply is $S(p) = 200(p - 4)$. Suppose a \$0.10 tax is imposed. To find the post-tax supply function, *do not* add \$0.10 to $S(p)$. Instead, replace p with $p - 0.1$ in the function S: The post-tax supply function is

$$S_{\text{Post-tax}}(p) = 200((p - .1) - 4) = 200(p - 4.1).$$

   If you remember to put price on the vertical axis and graph the functions $S(p) = 200(p-4)$ and $S_{\text{Post-tax}}(p) = 200(p-4.1)$, you will see that, graphically, post-tax supply is 0.1 units (in prices) "higher" than pre-tax prices, reflecting the fact that, for a given price, we get *less* supply. Please try to understand this; it isn't hard once you get it, but it can be quite confusing until you do.

3. Since the tax shifts the supply function "upwards" (meaning, less supply at every given price), the point where supply equals demand after the tax is at a higher price. Let $\Delta P = p_1 - p_0$; ΔP is the amount by which the price-to-the-consumer rises. Note that, as shown, prices (typically) rise by *less* than the full amount of the tax, t. And let $\Delta X = X_0 - X_1$; ΔX is the amount by which the total quantity bought and sold declines.

Here is an example. Suppose in the toy problem with pre-tax supply of $S(p) = 200(p-4)$ and a tax of \$0.01 per unit, demand is $100(10-p)$. Then before the tax is imposed, supply equals demand where $200(p-4) = 100(10-p)$, which is $p = \$6.00$. The tax shifts supply to $200(p-4.1)$ (see two paragraphs above), so supply equals demand with the tax at the price p where $200(p-4.1) = 100(10-p)$, which is $p = \$6.067$. The price has risen by \$0.067, or two-thirds of the amount of the tax. (These numbers are selected to "match" Figure 16.1, panel a, more or less.)

- The higher price p_1 and the lower quantity X_1 mean that consumer surplus is decreased. In panel b, the area of the heavily outlined triangle is pre-tax

---

[1] The correct way to say this mathematically is: Let $P_{\text{Supply}}(X)$ be the *inverse-supply function* before the tax; that is, for each X, $P_{\text{Supply}}(X)$ is the solution of $S(p) = X$. And let $\hat{P}(S)$ be the inverse-supply function after the tax is imposed. Since to get a given quantity X from suppliers after the tax takes a price t higher than before the tax, $\hat{P}_{\text{Supply}}(X) = P_{\text{Supply}}(X) + t$ for every value of X. (I put this in a footnote because I've found that it is more confusing than helpful for many students.)

consumer surplus, while the area of the smaller shaded triange is post-tax consumer surplus. The difference, the area of the heavily shaded trapezoid, is the reduction in consumer surplus, which I henceforth denote by ΔCS.

- Producers, net of the tax, are receiving less per unit (net of the tax) and are selling less. So their profits (or producer surplus) declines. In panel c, the area of the heavily outlined triangle is the old producer surplus, while lightly shaded triangle is the new, lower producer surplus. (Producers net $p_1 - t$ per unit sold, so their producer surplus is computed just as in Chapter 15, but assuming that the "market price" is $p_1 - t$, which it is, for them.) So the reduction of producer surplus, denoted ΔPS, is the area of the heavily shaded trapezoid.

- If you sum the old consumer and producer surpluses and compare that sum with the sum of the new consumer surplus, the new producer surplus, *and the tax revenues, which are* tX_1, you get a difference equal to the shaded triangle in panel d. This is called the *deadweight loss* from the tax, which we abbreviate DL. Think of it as follows: the (marginal) costs to society of producing units $\#X_1$ to $\#X_0$ are given by the (pre-tax) supply function for those levels. The (marginal) values to society from consumption of these units are given by the demand function. Since the demand function is above the (pre-tax) supply function for these units, not having them produced is a loss to society: they are worth more on the margin than they cost. And the dollar-denominated size of that loss is the area of the little triangle (the integral of the difference between their marginal values and their marginal costs).

What determines the amount of the tax passed on to consumers, the size of the deadweight loss, and other such things? It is (approximately) the elasticities of supply and demand at the original equilibrium values p_0 and X_0. Let ν_D denote the elasticity of demand at p_0 (recall that this is a negative number), and let ν_S denote the elasticity of supply at p_0 (along the pre-tax supply function).[2] Also, let $r = t/p_0$; that is, r is the ratio of the tax to the pre-tax price. Assuming the elasticities of supply and demand don't change much over the range of prices from p_0 to p_1—which is true if the tax t is small relative to p_0 and the supply and demand functions are smooth—we have the following (approximate) formulas:

---

[2]   We only briefly formally defined the elasticity of supply so to reiterate: It is the rate of percentage change in supply per percent change in price; the calculus formula using the supply function $S(p)$ is $\nu_S(p) = S'(p)p/S(p)$. For upward-sloping supply, ν_S lies between zero (if supply is vertical) and $+\infty$ (if supply is horizontal). Supply is inelastic if $\nu_S < 1$ and elastic if $\nu_S > 1$; higher ν_S is *more elastic* supply.

$$\Delta P = t\frac{\nu_S}{\nu_S - \nu_D}, \quad \text{or} \quad \frac{\Delta P}{p_0} = r\frac{\nu_S}{\nu_S - \nu_D} \quad \text{and} \quad \frac{\Delta X}{X_0} = \frac{r}{\frac{1}{\nu_S} - \frac{1}{\nu_D}};$$

$$\Delta CS = \Delta P\left[\frac{X_0 + X_1}{2}\right] = t\left[\frac{\nu_S}{\nu_S - \nu_D}\right]\left[\frac{X_0 + X_1}{2}\right] \approx tX_0\left[\frac{\nu_S}{\nu_S - \nu_D}\right];$$

$$\Delta PS = (t - \Delta P)\left[\frac{X_0 + X_1}{2}\right] = t\left[\frac{-\nu_D}{\nu_S - \nu_D}\right]\left[\frac{X_0 + X_1}{2}\right] \approx tX_0\left[\frac{-\nu_D}{\nu_S - \nu_D}\right]; \text{ and}$$

$$\text{the deadweight loss from the tax } = \frac{1}{2}\Delta X \cdot t = \frac{1}{2}r^2\left[\frac{p_0 X_0}{\frac{1}{\nu_S} - \frac{1}{\nu_D}}\right].$$

Please note that these are all approximations, in general. For ΔCS and ΔPS, I provide two levels of "approximation." The first and second listed expressions take into account the little triangles at the end of the two respective trapezoids (Figure 16.1(b) and (c)); the third expression approximates the average of pre- and post-tax quantity with pre-tax quantity alone, which is a good enough for quick estimates when t/P_0 is small.[3]

If you are wondering how these formulas are derived, see the solution to Problem 16.2 in the *Online Supplement*.

We can use these formulas to derive two further relevant numbers:

- The first is the *relative burden of the tax on consumers versus producers.* There are two ways this might be defined: First, what proportion of the full tax t is passed on in higher prices for consumers (with the complementary proportion being imposed on the sellers)? And, second, what is the ratio of the loss in consumer surplus to the sum of what they lose and what producers lose? The answer is the same for either definition: The *relative burden of the tax on consumers (versus producers) is $\nu_S/(\nu_S - \nu_D)$.*

  This means that the tax hurts consumers relatively more the more elastic is supply and the less elastic is demand.

---

[3] And I have to add a technical qualification: If demand and supply are both extremely elastic, it is possible that the imposition of the tax shuts down the market: Even at $X_1 = 0$, the distance (in prices) between the supply and demand functions is less than t. Practically speaking, these approximations work when t is a small fraction of P_0 *and* when r is small relative to $1/\nu_S - 1/\nu_D$, so that ΔX is also small relative to X_0.

- Taxes are often imposed to raise revenues for the government. To the extent that this is so, we are interested in the *efficiency* of the tax, which is defined as the ratio of the deadweight loss caused by the tax to the amount of tax revenues raised. (Please note carefully that a smaller ratio is a *more* efficient tax; a case can be made for calling this ratio the *inefficiency* of the tax.) Assuming $1/\nu_S - 1/\nu_D$ is large relative to r (cf. fn. 2), the efficiency of the tax is

$$\frac{r}{2}\left[\frac{1}{\dfrac{1}{\nu_S} - \dfrac{1}{\nu_D} - r}\right].$$

What Is a "Good" Tax?

If we measure the "goodness" of a tax by its efficiency alone, good taxes are those that have low rates r and for which that ugly term in the square brackets is small. Do not be misled by the "low r" part of this, thinking that this means low tax revenues. Our efficiency measure is dollar-denominated deadweight loss per dollar of revenue raised. Roughly speaking, two small-r taxes typically produce less deadweight loss than a third bigger-r tax, if the two together produce the same tax revenue as the third.[4] And the ugly term is small if either supply or demand is inelastic. If we add the further consideration that we want the brunt of the tax to be borne primarily by the producers (and I'm not endorsing this as necessarily desirable), we want to find products where the supply is relatively more inelastic than demand.

Two other considerations, not captured by these formulas, are often brought into the discussion. First, insofar as we want to *discourage* some activities and encourage others, we tax those we want to discourage. Hence, for instance, it is common for taxes on items like liquor and cigarettes to be relatively high; these are often called *sin* taxes.

And these formulas treat all consumers equally. But, on equity grounds, it is often held to be desirable *not* to tax goods whose consumption is relatively concentrated among the less well-off; taxes ought to be *progressive*, not *regressive*. So, for instance, consider the hefty taxes imposed on gasoline: The elasticity of demand for gasoline is pretty low—a good thing—and for a variety of reasons, public policy is to discourage the use of gasoline (and encourage fuel efficiency). But the gasoline tax is very decidedly regressive.[5]

---

[4] This is because the deadweight loss is the area of a triangle whose height and base are both proportional to r; note the r^2 term in the formula for deadweight loss.

[5] The average percentage of household income spent on gasoline, hence on gasoline taxes, falls as household income increases.

It is also worth observing that while shorter-run supply may be relatively inelastic (good for low deadweight loss and also for having producers bear more of the burden of the tax), in the longer run, supply typically becomes more elastic. Demand can also become more elastic as time passes, although the effect is typically more pronounced for supply. Hence a tax that looks good at the outset may, over time, lose its allure; deadweight losses rise, and the burden of the tax is (typically) increasingly shifted onto consumers.

Taxing a Firm with Market Power

What about a tax imposed on a firm with market power? Assuming a fixed tax per unit, paid by the producer, this shifts the firm's marginal-cost function up by the amount of the tax, leading to a new intersection of marginal cost and marginal revenue. See Figure 16.2, where I've drawn a pretty large tax (relative to the pre-tax equilibrium price) so you can see the various "regions." Panel a shows the pre-tax quantity x_0 and the pre-tax price p_0. Panel b shows the pre-tax consumer surplus (shaded) and producer surplus (the heavily outlined "trapezoid.") Panels c and d show the impact of the tax in two different ways. In panel c, we think of the tax as raising the producer's marginal costs by the amount of the tax, giving the new quantity x_1 and price p_1. In panel d, we think of the tax as lowering the producer's marginal revenue by the amount of the tax. Since the new equilibrium quantity x_1 is where the (new) MC and MR meet, whether you think of the tax as raising marginal costs (panel c) or lowering marginal revenue (panel d), we intersection at the same quantity x_1 and so the same price p_1. Both panels also show the loss in consumer surplus as the shaded "trapezoid."

Panel e uses the "reduced marginal revenue" formulation of panel d to show the new producer surplus (outlined "trapezoid") as well as loss in producer profit/surplus (shaded). Note that the loss in producer surplus is quite large, relative to the loss in consumer surplus. Finally, panel f shows the tax revenues $t \cdot x_1$ as a shaded rectangle, as well as the deadweight loss, which is now a sizeable (heavily outlined) trapezoid instead of a triangle .

The general formulas for things like the increase in price, the relative burden on consumers, and the efficiency of the tax are complex in general. The problem, roughly speaking, is that the key to all our formulas, the reduction in quantity from x_0 to x_1, depends on the slope of marginal revenue, and the slope of marginal revenue depends in turn on the *second* derivative of demand. Rather than dive into those complexities, I'll give you formulas based on the substantial simplifications that result if demand is linear. In this case, we know that marginal revenue is also linear (and with twice the slope of inverse demand); we also know the size of the gap between marginal revenue and inverse demand, which is important in calculating both the loss in producer surplus

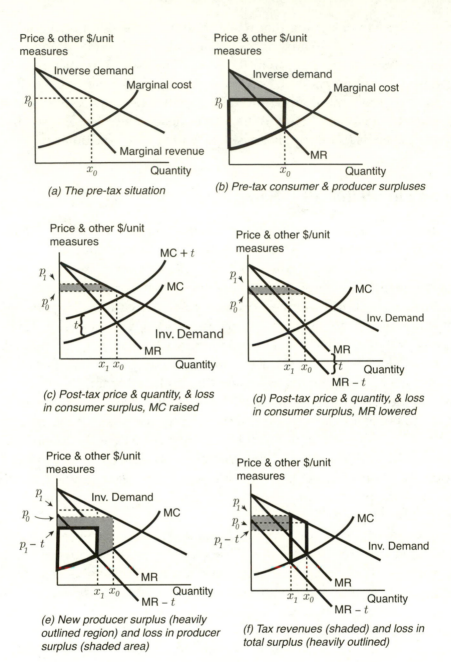

Figure 16.2. The effect of a tax on a firm with market power. See text for explanation.

(see Panel e of Figure 16.2) and the deadweight loss of the tax (see panel f).[6]
Because there is no supply function, it makes less sense to talk about the

---

[6] These formulas remain relatively good approximations for general demand, *if* (inverse) demand is "close to" linear over the range of relevant quantities and prices; that is, if the derivative of (inverse) demand doesn't change much.

elasticity of supply. So in the formulas I provide here, I'll work with two parameters: The derivative of marginal cost at the pre-tax quantity x_0, which I'll denote by d, and the negative of the slope of inverse demand, which will be b. (That is, inverse demand is assumed to have the form $P(x) = A - bx$ for some $b > 0$.) Also, I will give "second-level" approximations, meaning approximations that ignore the little triangles at the end of various trapezoids. As with the formulas on pages 357 and 358, I do not present the derivations: These are supplied in the *Online Supplement* as the solution to Problem 16.3 (for those who are interested).

$$\Delta P = p_1 - p_0 = \frac{t}{2 + d/b} \quad \text{and} \quad \Delta X = x_0 - x_1 = \frac{t}{d + 2b}.$$

$$\Delta CS \approx \frac{tx_0}{2 + d/b} \approx \text{DL}.$$

This is an overestimate of ΔCS and an underestimate of DL.

$$\Delta PS \approx tx_0.$$

Therefore, the proportion of the burden of the tax on consumers (as a fraction of the full burden on consumers and producers) and the efficiency of the tax are both roughly $1/(2 + d/b)$.

Note that the burden on consumers is always less than 50%; it is 50% exactly if the firm has constant marginal cost ($d = 0$). And, in general, taxes on firms with market power are relatively inefficient: If $d = b$, efficiency is $1/3$ regardless of the rate of tax r, for example. (Compare with the case of a tax on a competitive industry: For given elasticities of supply and demand, as r approaches zero, our efficiency measure, which is better when lower, also approaches zero.)

Finally, what we said about shorter- and longer-run effects of a tax on a competitive industry applies here: if marginal cost "flattens out" in the longer run, meaning d gets smaller, an increasing share of the tax is borne by consumers. But the consumers' share of the burden is never more than $1/2$.

Subsidies

Per-unit subsidies are like negative taxes. Most of the analysis we did for taxes can be repeated for subsidies, and similar pictures emerge. Problems 16.5 and 16.6 give you the opportunity to replicate for subsidies the analysis done for taxes. If you look at these problems, you'll discover that:

- When the production of a good is subsidized for a competitive industry, the good is overproduced relative to the level of output that maximizes total surplus; the true cost of the last few units exceeds the marginal surplus generated by those units in consumption, which generates a deadweight loss.

- But subsidizing a producer who has market power can result in an *increase* in total surplus: The producer with market power is, without the subsidy, underproducing relative to the surplus-maximizing quantity; the subsidy motivates the producer to produce more. Of course, there are distributional consequences; the general populace is (through other tax revenues, presumably) subsidizing both the producer and the consumers of this good. But see Problem 16.6 for a twist to this story.

16.2. Administered Prices: Price Ceilings

Governments can, and sometimes do, support the price of a good at a prespecified level, or they can put a ceiling above which the price may not go. And, sometimes, they simply announce what prices will be.

The Best Case for Price Ceilings: Firms with Market Power

The best case that can be made for price ceilings is when a well-picked ceiling is imposed on a firm with market power. Follow along with Figure 16.3.

Panel a shows the pre-ceiling situation, with a surplus loss relative to maximal feasible total surplus because the firm produces the quantity x_0 (and charges p_0) where MR = MC, not where inverse demand hits MC. In panel b, a ceiling price p^* is shown, so the firm's average-revenue function is now p^* up to the quantity x^* where p^* hits inverse demand, then down along inverse demand. This then gives a discontinuous marginal-revenue function for the firm: Up to the level x^*, marginal revenue is p^* per unit; beyond this level, we jump down to the original MR function.

In panel b, the p^* selected is below the old price set by the firm with no price ceilings, but above the price where MC = inverse demand. Hence (panel d), the firm's (post-ceiling) marginal revenue exceeds marginal cost for all levels of production below x^* and jumps to below marginal cost just past x^*; x^* maximizes its profits. Panel d also shows the gain in consumer surplus (shaded) and the *gain* in total surplus (the heavily outlined trapezoid): Total surplus is *larger* because x^* is closer than x_0 to the surplus-maximizing quantity where MC = Inverse demand.

Hence, to maximize total surplus, p^* should ideally be chosen to be the price where MC = inverse demand. (Finding this price is a lot easier in a textbook drawing than in real life!)

Panels e and f show what can happen if p^* is set too low. In panel e, p^* is set below the level where MC = Inverse demand but above the level where MC = original MR. The quantity produced is x^{**}, where MC = p^*. There is still a net surplus gain, and consumers gain considerably.

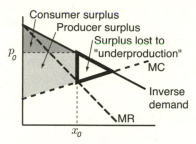

(a) The pre-ceiling situation

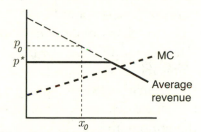

(b) A price ceiling p^* is applied. Note that p^* is above where MC hits inverse demand.

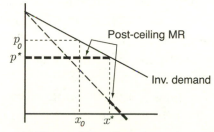

(c) The resulting marginal revenue function is discontinuous

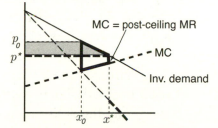

(d) MC passes through the jump in MR, the monopolist chooses x^*, consumers are better off, and total surplus increases

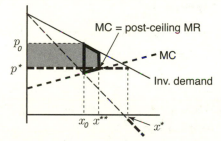

(e) If the ceiling price is chosen below the price where MC = inverse demand, but above where MR = MC, we get this picture. Consumers gain a lot, and there is still a surplus gain.

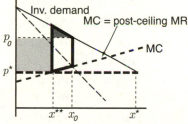

(f) But if p^* is chosen below the intersection of MR and MC, total surplus is reduced. (Consumers gain the rectangle and lose the triangle.)

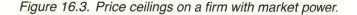

Figure 16.3. Price ceilings on a firm with market power.

But what if p^* is selected below the level p where MC = MR? See panel f. Then there is a deadweight loss (the heavily outlined trapezoid), because the quantity x^{**} the firm selects is below what is would do with no ceiling price. Some consumers are better off and some are worse off: The lightly shaded rectangle shows how much the gainers gain, while the heavily shaded triangle shows how much the losers lose, relative to the pre-ceiling situation.

In fact, what happens in the cases depicted in panels e and f is more problematic than these pictures show. At the price p^*, demand by consumers is for x^* of the good. But the firm is supplying a quantity x^{**} that is less than x^*. So some form of rationing of supply to the overabundance of demanders is needed. The pictures in panels e and f are "optimistic" in that they assume the limited supply goes to those demanders who get the greatest surplus value from the goods; if this is not the case, the panel e overstates the surplus gains and panel f understates the total surplus loss. Also, in situations where demand outstrips supply, black markets often spring up; we have no tools for quantifying the social costs of a black market, but those costs shouldn't be ignored.

So, the bottom line is: As long as whoever is setting the ceiling price sets it above where MC = inverse demand—and ideally, from the perspective of both consumers and total surplus, the best ceiling price in this range is where MC = inverse demand exactly—price ceilings are great: They raise total surplus and cause a transfer of surplus from the producer to consumers, which, one presumes, is what motivated the desire to impose a price ceiling in the first place. This is the strongest case typically made for price ceilings.

(I won't go into details, but in cases like panels e and f, the authority who sets the price ceiling sometimes *also* compels the firm to serve x^*—the firm doesn't get to pick the level that would maximize its profit given the ceiling. This—sort of—is the case of regulated utilities.[7])

Price Ceilings in a Competitive Market

The story for price ceilings imposed on competitive markets is more mixed. The pre-ceiling equilibrium quantity in a competitive market maximizes total surplus, so when a price ceiling is imposed, suppliers supply less (assuming supply is not completely inelastic), and there is bound to be a reduction in total surplus. But consumers are better off with lower prices; presumably the ceiling is imposed to transfer surplus from producers to consumers.

Proponents of price ceilings for a competitive market typically draw Figure 16.4.

The pre-ceiling equilibrium is at price p and quantity x. If the price ceiling p^* is imposed, the quantity supplied falls a bit, to x^*. Most consumers gain from the lower price; the gains are the shaded rectangle in panel b. But a few lose, their loss is the tiny shaded triangle in panel b. Producers lose the shaded trapezoid in panel c, so the net loss in surplus is the sum of the two shaded triangles in panel d.

The story isn't quite that simple, however. At the ceiling price p^*, demand is for x^{**}. So we have unhappy demanders, wanting to buy a total of $x^{**} - x^*$ units at the bargain price of p^* but finding only bare shelves. The surplus calculations in Figure 16.4 make the optimistic assumption that the x^* available units go to those demanders with the highest surplus value for them; one can make the case that, if a black market in the good is tolerated, something close to

---

[7] "Sort of," because regulated utilities are more likely to have cost structures more complex than the simple rising marginal cost of our picture.

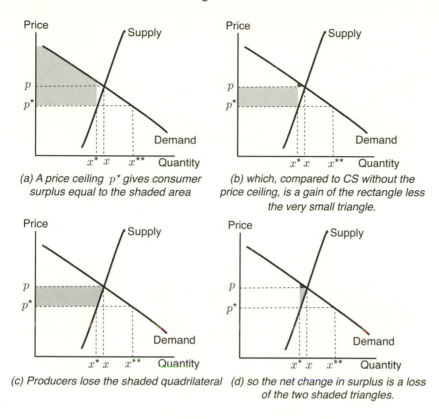

(a) A price ceiling p^* gives consumer surplus equal to the shaded area

(b) which, compared to CS without the price ceiling, is a gain of the rectangle less the very small triangle.

(c) Producers lose the shaded quadrilateral

(d) so the net change in surplus is a loss of the two shaded triangles.

Figure 16.4. A price ceiling in a competitive market.

this will happen, because high-value consumers will buy units from low-value consumers at a mutually agreeable price. Indeed, if the black market is well run, the black-market price will be $P(x^*)$ (where P is the inverse-demand function), which means a transfer of "welfare" from producers to whichever consumers are lucky enough to get goods at the "official" ceiling price of p^*. But is it good for society to tolerate an active black market?

And, the story depicted in Figure 16.4 looks good partly because supply is inelastic. If supply is elastic, the picture is less rosy. See Figure 16.5.

Consumers in aggregate are still better off—the shaded rectangle in panel b is larger than the shaded triangle—but it is a lot closer. And the net loss in total surplus (panel d) is a lot larger. Plus $x^{**} - x^*$ has grown (and, in this respect, the worst case is where both demand and supply are elastic), meaning either more units consumed by the "wrong" people or a bigger black market or both.

Bottom line: A good case can be made for administered price ceilings for a firm with market power, if the ceiling is well chosen. The case for price ceilings in a competitive market is not as good—total surplus decreases—but if supply is inelastic, the deadweight loss is relatively small and the redistribution from firms to consumers might be desirable. However, this case weakens the more

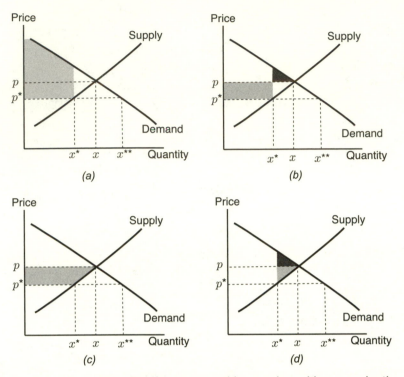

Figure 16.5. A price ceiling for a competitive market with more elastic supply.

elastic is supply and, since supply tends to become more elastic in the longer run, price ceilings for competitive markets that look good in the short run can look increasingly problematic as time passes.

16.3. Administered Prices: Price Floors

Price floors are sometimes set, with a notion that the sellers of the good in question need "support." The two most common instances are agricultural price supports and minimum-wage laws.

We don't need to worry about price floors administered for a firm with market power, since a firm with market power chooses its price and could pick the higher price if it so desired.[8] However, especially with the case of wage earners, we might want to consider how price floors work when the *demand* side has market power. We haven't developed tools for analyzing such situations—what in many economic textbooks is called *monopsony*—so I'll simply assert:

---

[8] Well, not quite: for one thing, the government might impose a price floor not to benefit the seller but instead to discourage consumption of the good in question. Normally, though, taxes are the preferred method for doing this. And a price floor might be imposed on a small group of competitive firms to stop them from engaging in ruinous competition or, in cases where there is one giant firm driving smaller competitors to the brink, to stop the giant firm's predatory practices.

Just as well-administered price ceilings can increase total surplus when the supplier has market power, well-administered price floors can increase total surplus when the demand side of the market has market power. And, with this, we'll discuss price floors for markets that are competitive on both sides.

If the immediate problem with price ceilings in competitive markets is more demand than there is supply (at the ceiling price), with price floors there typically is more supply than there is demand. Governments that want to support agricultural activities typically deal with this in one of three ways:

1. At the supported price, the government buys up and stores (more or less permanently) or destroys any supply that is not bought by consumers. The European Economic Community followed this sort of strategy for many years as part of the Common Agricultural Program, accumulating, for instance, mountains of butter and other dairy products.[9]

2. The government purchases everything that is supplied at the support price and then resells to consumers at the (significantly) lower price that clears the market. This, in essence, is a per-unit subsidy to farmers, with the subsidy the difference between the support price and the market-clearing price. When supply is elastic and demand is inelastic, the bill to the government of this subsidy can be astronomical.

3. The government can ration the right to supply. The government determines what demand will be at the price it desires to support and limits the amount that individual producers can supply so that total supply matches that demand. (Agricultural "marketing boards" do this, essentially, privately. This makes sense when demand for the good in question is inelastic; total revenue increases as the amount supplied to the market decreases, so farmers make higher profit if they band together and act in the more-or-less collusive fashion.) Or, in some cases, producers are paid by the government *not* to produce.

From the perspective of total surplus maximization, Program 1 is a clear loser. Assuming the support price is the same in 1 and 2, since in each program farmers get to supply as much as they want at the support price, they are just as well off. But consumers get much less to consume in Program 1 than in Program 2. Still, governments sometimes resort to programs in the style of 1, for reasons that transcend the analysis here. For instance, if the EC subsidized foodstuffs (Program 2), the subsidized consumer price would likely be such that producers from other parts of the world could not compete; unless the EC wishes to start a trade war, this can give the advantage to Program 1. And both Programs 1

---

[9] In 1986 alone, the EC purchased and stored 1.23 million tons of butter. Reforms in the CAP eliminated this butter mountain by 2007, although shortly thereafter, the EC was back to buying butter. See, for instance, http://www.nytimes.com/2009/01/22/world/europe/22iht-union.4.19606951.html?_r=0 .

and 2 can involve tremendous government expense, but they aren't the same expense. Depending on the elasticities of supply and demand, either program can be more "economical" in terms of government expenditure than the other.

Since I'm not going to undertake an analysis of these programs, I'll leave this here, with a final thought: Minimum-wage legislation introduces issues different from those you see in agricultural supports, concerning in particular the possibility that supply (people willing to work at minimum wage) exceeds the demand (jobs for those people). The government could hire, at the minimum wage, anyone who wants but cannot find a job—akin to Program 1—and some argue that, to a small extent, governments do some of this, especially in times of recession. The government could subsidize the employment of minimum wage workers—akin to Program 2—but for the most part, it does not. Perhaps there is a way to ration the small number of available jobs to those wanting work, but I don't see a workable scheme.

What is left is the other side of the black-market coin: discrimination in who gets hired (which, the government will then try to stamp out administratively), under-the-table kickbacks in the form of hours worked off the clock (which, again, the government tries to stamp out), under-the-table kickbacks in the form of straight cash kickbacks to the employer (or in the form of "charges" for meals and clothing supplied, and so forth). And there is the worry that, in the longer term, a higher-minimum wage will mean fewer minimum-wage jobs, as firms find it economical to subsitute away from minimum-wage labor in their production technology.

Increasing minimum wages is, without question, a desirable policy for those who have minimum-wage jobs and, after their mandated pay is increased, who keep those jobs. But that isn't the complete picture.

16.4. Quotas and Tariffs

A quota is a program in which the importation of a particular good is limited. Quotas are imposed for a variety of reasons, including retaliation in trade disputes, but the usual reason for a quota is to protect a domestic industry that is politically powerful. The protection can aim at helping the industry develop, especially if it is a relatively new industry and production costs have an experience-curve effect, or to protect an old, inefficient industry. For instance, Japan has for many years limited the importation of rice to protect its "traditional" and politically very powerful rice farmers.

Issues connected to current policy and trade disputes over Japanese rice imports are quite complex, and I will not attempt a complete model of the situation. But it is worth indicating that the economics of such quotas can sometimes lead to surprises. In particular, Thai rice exporters (to Japan) might be much better off under a system of Japanese quotas on rice importation, where

Japan permits only, say, 40% of its domestic rice consumption to be imported, instead of free importation.

The key is to ask, What determines the price of rice in Japan under the two scenarios? If free importation of rice is allowed to Japan, the price of rice must fall to meet the intersection of world-wide supply of and world-wide demand for rice. The domestic market in rice in Japan is fairly large, but the world rice market is quite a bit larger; and while the world supply of rice is not flat—it slopes somewhat upward—allowing free importation of rice into Japan would not raise the world price of rice by all that much.

But if an importation quota is set at 40% of the Japanese domestic market, then it is the marginal cost of the last active (domestic) rice producer that equals the market price. Some domestic producers are reasonably efficient, but in comparison with international producers, Japanese rice growers have high marginal costs. Under this scenario, the price of rice in Japan, driven by domestic marginal costs of production, is two or even three times the international price.

Quotas, then, make the importation of rice into Japan very lucrative for the Thai producer, whose marginal costs are around the world price of rice. Profit margins in the world market, because of the very high level of competition—that is, the very elastic supply—are quite thin. With a 40% total quota, those international producers lucky enough to get the right to import into Japan would be looking at profit margins over 100%.

Of course, this makes the right to import rice into Japan very valuable and, as you might imagine, it evokes all manner of—what's a polite way to say it?—activities devoted to getting a slice of the quota.

Who are the winners and who are the losers? Those global rice producers lucky enough to get a share of the Japanese import quota are the big winners. Japanese rice farmers, who continue to have a market for their rice in Japan, are little winners: They don't make a lot of money, but at least they aren't driven out of business by the much more efficient Thai producers. And Japanese consumers are the big losers, paying a much higher price for their rice than they would if free importation were allowed.

Two remarks are worth making here:

1. Instead of a quota on rice imports, the Japanese government might consider imposing a tariff on rice imports, or it might use a combination of tariffs and quotas. In that way, it could extract some of the profit that would otherwise accrue to international producers.

   But they don't do this, and two reasons are often cited. First, the Thai government might register a complaint with the WTO about a tariff while being "okay" with a quota: Quotas can mean big profits for Thai producers, while tariffs transfer those profits from the Thai producers to the Japanese treasury. And while Japanese consumers don't fully appreciate how much more they are paying for their rice because of the quota, they (the story goes) would be much more sensitive to a tariff.

2. In the 1980s, the Japanese automobile manufacturers voluntarily restricted the number of cars they exported to the United States, in what was called the voluntary-export-restraint (VER) program. The new car market is not perfectly competitive, and economists continue to try to estimate the impact of the VERs on American consumers, the U.S. domestic producers, and the Japanese producers. These estimates are controversial. But, by all accounts, this restriction did not hurt the Japanese manufacturers, and some analysts insist that the Japanese manufacturers made money out of the VERs: By administratively restricting their imports to the United States, the Japanese car manufacturers restrained their internecine competition and pushed up the price of Japanese cars in America. The increase in profit margins on a smaller number of cars was enough to keep profits where they would otherwise have been or even to improve those profits. And American car buyers paid for this, in higher prices for their cars.

But if this is the right story, it didn't last for long. Each Japanese car manufacturer wanted a larger share of the U.S. market than it was given by the Japanese Ministry of International Trade and Industry (MITI), which assigned export quotas to the different Japanese firms. The way around the VERs in the short run was to form joint manufacturing partnerships with American firms; a lot of that happened very quickly. And, in the longer run, Japanese manufacturers had substantial incentive to manufacture in the United States, which has provided a number of excellent blue-collar jobs to American workers.

16.5. Is Government Intervention in Competitive Markets Always Bad?

You may have gotten the impression from this chapter that any government intervention in a competitive market leads to a net loss in total surplus. At least, that happened in every competitive-market story we tell and every competitive-market model we examine. (Of course, this wasn't so for markets in which the supplier had market power.) And it is clear why: As discussed in Chapter 12, in an unfettered competitive market, the invisible hand of prices leads to maximal total surplus. If the government intervention only involves a transfer of value from one group of market participants to another, without changing the amount produced, who produces, and who consumes, it wouldn't change total surplus. But if it affects any one of those, total surplus will decline.

This doesn't mean that a case can't be made for government intervention on redistributive (equity) grounds. We might be willing to sacrifice some efficiency for enough increase in equity.

Another argument in favor of some government interventions (but one with which I'm a bit less comfortable) is that the government knows better than do consumers what is good for them (the consumers). So, for instance, we have taxes on liquor and cigarettes. There are surely cases where citizens make bad personal choices. But my editorial position is that consumers by and large are smarter than policy makers think, and policy makers should be more reluctant than they are to think they (the policy makers) know best.

A third and very powerful argument involves externalities. Since that's the topic of next chapter, no more will be said here.

And there is a fourth argument in favor of some interventions: They can undo or mitigate other government interventions. While it is true that, in the absence of externalities, any government intervention in an otherwise unfettered competitive market can only muck things up in terms of total surplus, this is not true of a government intervention into a competitive market that has already been...mucked. Since there are few pristine and unfettered competitive markets around, the proper response to an incremental government intervention is (you knew it was coming) to understand the incremental impact this has on the market outcome.

Executive Summary

- Concerning taxes imposed on a competitive industry: (1) The tax causes prices to rise and quantity produced/consumed to fall. (2) The fall in quantity (from the nontax equilibrium level) causes a deadweight loss in total surplus, which is greater (for a given size tax) the more elastic is supply or demand. (3) The burden of a tax on consumers—whether measured by the proportion of the tax that is passed on to them in the form of higher prices or by the proportion of their surplus loss to the sum of their loss and that of suppliers—is borne relatively in proportion to how inelastic/elastic are supply and demand: the more elastic is supply, the greater the burden on consumers; the more elastic is demand, the smaller the burden. (4) The efficiency of the tax—the ratio of the deadweight loss in surplus to the amount of revenues raised–is lower (which is better) when the tax rate is small and when demand and/or supply is less elastic. (Formulae in support of all of these conclusions are found on pages 357 and 358.)

- Concerning taxes imposed on a firm with market power, formulae for similar measures are found on page 361, in the special case where demand is linear. Deadweight loss is generally "bigger" in this case than if a similar tax is placed on a competitive industry, especially as measured by the efficiency of the tax.

- Price ceilings placed on a firm with market power, if well chosen, can enhance total surplus as well as accomplish redistributive aims of improving the lot of consumers at the expense of the producer/seller. In the case of competitive markets, redistribution can still be accomplished by a price ceiling, but total surplus will decline, and the decline in surplus grows as supply becomes more elastic.

- Any price ceiling on a competitive firm, and a "too low" price ceiling imposed on a firm with market power, will cause more demand than supply, which in turn can lead to black markets springing up. And, in such cases, there are no guarantees that high-surplus consumers get to consume the goods, which may increase surplus loss/decrease (in the case of a firm with market power) surplus gain.

- Price floors to enhance the welfare of suppliers usually lead to more supply than demand, a condition that must be somehow managed.

- Quotas on imports are often enacted to protect domestic producers but can benefit foreign producers as well by pushing up the domestic price of the good. They are paid for, by and large, by domestic consumers. Instead of a quota, a tariff can be employed, transfering profits from foreign producers to the domestic treasury (which is why an exporting nation might object to a tariff when it is okay with a quota).

- Government intervention in competitive markets can be justified on (1) equity grounds, (2) because the government wishes to discourage consumption of some goods, (3) because of externalities, and (4) to undo or mitigate the effects of other government interventions.

Problems

16.1 (a) Consider a good for which the supply function is $S(p) = 2000(p-4)$ (for prices 4 and above) and the demand function is $D(p) = 1000(10 - p)$. What are the equilibrium price and quantity for this market? If a tax of \$0.30 is imposed on the good, what are the new equilibrium price and quantity? What is the loss in consumer surplus, and what is the loss in producer surplus? What is the relative burden of the tax on consumers, relative to its total burden on producers and consumers? How much is the deadweight loss from the tax? You can answer these questions directly by solving for the equilibrium price and quantity with and without the tax and computing various surpluses; or you can try the formulae given in the text. (I suggest you do the former, although it would be ideal if you did both, just to check that the formulas really work.) (b) Redo part a but for a firm with market power whose marginal cost function is $MC(x) = 4 + x/2000$. (Demand doesn't change.) To help you out with this: The firm's total-cost function is $TC(x) = 2000 + 4x + x^2/4000$.

16.2 If you did Problem 16.1, you know that the formulas really do work. So now the question is why. Derive the formulas given on pages 357-8 for a tax placed on a competitive industry. The key is to begin with the right picture.

16.3 And derive the formulas on page 361 for a tax imposed on a firm with market power.

16.4 Suppose, in a competitive market, the supply function is $S(p) = 5000(p-2)$ and the demand function is $D(p) = 2000(16 - p)$. If a tax of $0.70 is placed on the good, by how much does the equilibrium price rise? By how much does the equilibrium quantity fall? What is the deadweight loss from the tax? Do you need to solve for the equilibrium price and quantity to answer these questions?

16.5 Derive formulas similar to those given in the text for taxes on a competitive industry, but for a subsidy of size s per unit, paid directly to the manufacturer by the government.

16.6 (a) Consider a firm with market power that faces the inverse-demand function $P(x) = (100 - 0.001x)$ and has a constant marginal cost of production equal to $20. The government decides to subsidize the production of this good, offering the firm $4 for every unit of the good the firm manufactures and sells. What is the impact of this subsidy program on consumer, producer, and total surpluses?

(b) National and state governments often "privatize" the provision of concession services at national or state parks and recreation areas. The concessionaire is chosen by a competitive bidding process; firms that wish to hold the concession bid for the right to do so. An issue that often arises is the level of "services" the government provides the eventual concessionaire; in effect, the government can subsidize the costs of running the concession. Assume that the government does not wish to regulate the prices set by the eventual concessionaire. It is then sometimes asserted that the government should charge the concessionaire for all marginal-cost items the government provides. Why might this argument be wrongheaded?

If you are interested in the brief story about Japanese rice related in the text, try the next two problems.

16.7 Rufus T. Firefly, prime minister of the country of Freedonia, faces an economic crisis. The citizens of his country are demanding the free importation of sorghum, and sorghum producers are threatening to vote en masse for his rivals if he allows this.

For the citizens of Freedonia, sorghum is a crop with a long tradition. The ancient folk fables of the Freedonian people stress the importance of sorghum to the tribes that established Freedonia. National rituals are built around the ceremonial use of sorghum. In addition to its ceremonial uses, sorghum is an important ingredient in the national staple, sorghum pancakes.

Demand for sorghum in Freedonia is given by the demand function $D(p) =$

$5000(10 - p)$, where p is the price of a kilogram of sorghum in the local currency and quantities are in kilograms. There is not much good sorghum-growing land in Freedonia, and the supply function of sorghum from domestic sources is $S(p) = 25,000(p - 4)$ for prices $p \geq 4$. (Sorghum suppliers are perfectly competitive.) If the price of sorghum is less than 4 per kilo, domestic supply is 0. Sorghum imports are currently banned. (If this sounds like Japanese rice, the resemblance is entirely intentional.)

(a) What is the current equilibrium (price and quantity) in the sorghum market? Assuming sorghum producers have fixed costs of 0, what are the profits of sorghum producers?

The world price of sorghum (in local currency) is 3. If Freedonia allowed the free importation of sorghum, the world price of sorghum would be unaffected: Freedonians could purchase as much sorghum as they wish at 3 per kilo.

(b) What would happen if Freedonia allowed the free importation of sorghum? What would be the new equilibrium price and quantity? What would happen to the domestic suppliers of sorghum? By what amount would consumer surplus rise?

(c) Owing to the unhappy consequences for domestic suppliers of sorghum that you found in part b, Prime Minister Firefly considers subsidizing domestic sorghum producers. For each kilogram of sorghum sold by a domestic producer, the producer would receive a fixed amount. At the same time, the free importation of sorghum would be allowed. Firefly wishes to set the level of this subsidy so that domestic sorghum producers sell just as much sorghum as they did in the initial equilibrium of part a. What level of subsidy accomplishes this? At this level of subsidy, what is the market equilibrium in sorghum?

(d) In the market equilibrium of part c, if you take into account the welfare of consumers (measured by consumer surplus) and domestic producers (measured by producer surplus) and account for the cost of the subsidy program, are Freedonians in sum better or worse off than in the equilibrium in part a?

16.8 Suppose that, in the situation of Problem 16.7, Prime Minister Firefly considers a different course of action: He would allow the importation of some sorghum, by granting to each of 10 good friends and political supporters the right to import up to 1000 kgs of sorghum. These friends would be able to purchase their sorghum at the world price of 3 per kg, then resell it at whatever price the domestic market would bear. Any supply of sorghum above the 10,000 kgs imported by this method would be provided for by domestic sorghum producers, who would receive no subsidy from the government. What would be the result of this in terms of the equilibrium in the sorghum market? Relative to the market equilibrium computed in part a of Problem 16.7, are domestic consumers better or worse off and by how much? Are domestic sorghum growers better or worse off and by how much? What profits are enjoyed by the 10 friends of Prime Minister Firefly? Combining the welfare of domestic consumers, domestic producers, Firefly's friends, and the government (in terms of any subsidy costs or tax revenues), under which of the three programs (no imports, free importation combined with subsidized domestic production, or a quota on imports with licenses given to domestic importers) are Freedonians best off?

16.9 On page 367, I described three "programs" by which the government could support the price of a good above the equilibrium price that would be set in a competitive market. In the first program, the government allows producers to produce as much as they want at the supported price and it allows consumers to buy as much as they want (less than is supplied) at the supported price, with the government buying up (and storing or destroying) the excess supply. In program 2, the government essentially subsidizes production of the good: Suppliers are paid the supported price, consumers buy at the price that clears this supply (less than the supply price and, in fact, less than what would be the equilibrium price), and the government pays the "difference."

Draw "pictures" that describe these two programs. Identify the gain in producer surplus, the change in consumer surplus, government expenditures, and the deadweight lost in total surplus from the program. Then: To stay "under the radar of the public," the government might choose the first program (which has substantially larger deadweight loss) because it involves less government expenditure. What sorts of supply and demand functions (in terms of elasticities) are consistent with this story?

16.10 In the chapter, I asserted that, if the world supply curve of rice is nearly flat, it is clear that foregone Japanese consumer surplus from any combination of quotas and tariffs is greater than the surplus gains of Japanese domestic producers and the government. Hence, these quotas and tariffs must be the result of interest-group politics. I doubt that the second conclusion surprises you, but what is the logic that underlies the first assertion?

16.11 Suppose that a particular perfectly competitive industry has 10 identical firms, each with the marginal-cost function $MC(y) = 4 + y$. Suppose that the demand function for the item in question is $D(p) = 10(20 - p)$.

(a) What is the equilibrium in this market?

(b) Suppose that, of the 10 firms in the industry, 5 are polluters and 5 are not. The government, to cut down on the amount of pollution, imposes a tax of $1 per unit produced on the five polluters and gives a subsidy of $1 per unit produced to the five others. What is the equilibrium after these taxes and subsidies are imposed? Do revenues from the tax on the five polluters equal the subsidies paid to the five nonpolluters?

(c) Continuing with part b, suppose that the total social surplus in this situation is computed as the sum of producer surplus (profits), consumer surplus (in the usual fashion), and net government revenues (tax revenue less subsidies paid), less $2 for each unit produced by a polluter, which you can think of as the loss to society from the pollution. Compute each of the four components separately, then compute total social surplus for the equilibria of parts a and b. How do they compare?

17. Externalities

This chapter concerns externalities, instances where the activity of one party affects the welfare of another. When externalities are present, market outcomes need not be efficient, because parties do not take into account, or internalize, the externalities their choices cause. Hence, a case can be made for government intervention into markets to promote efficiency. We

- define and give examples of externalities,
- discuss why they can result in market inefficiency,
- list various means for dealing with them,
- discuss the regulation of a specific externality, pollution, focusing on so-called cap-and-trade legislation, and
- see how the concept of externalities applies broadly to the internal operations of most large and complex organizations.

17.1. What Are Externalities?

When the economic activity of any entity, whether a firm or a consumer, affects the welfare of another entity, the first activity generates an *externality*. When the second party benefits, the externality is *positive*; when the second party is hurt, the externality is *negative*:

- Someone smoking a cigarette in an elevator probably generates a negative externality for anyone unlucky enough to be riding at the same time.

- When my neighbor spends hours and hours cultivating her front garden, she generates a positive externality for me, because I enjoy looking at her garden. And if I fail to tend my own front yard, I generate a negative externality for her.

- When a firm with a factory on a river discharges effluent into the river, it generates negative externalities both for downriver consumers and firms that use the river water and must now expend resources cleaning it before using it.

Beyond these straightforward examples of externalities are other less obvious but important categories:

- *Network and Standards Externalities.* These are generally positive. Stanford University's decision to join in a communications network generates a positive externality for other members of the network, since being able to communicate with Stanford is presumably good for institutions already on the network. Similarly, the decision by an electronics firm to build its products in conformance to some industry *standard* benefits other firms whose products conform, since this increases the base over which the standard is valid.

- *Congestion Externalities.* Suppose, leaving work or school today at rush hour, you take a highway on your way home. By so doing, you increase by a small amount the amount the commute time of others who have chosen to drive on the same highway. By adding to the *congestion* on the highway, you generate negative externalities for others. Of course, the time of day can be important: If you drove home at 3 A.M., you probably would not measurably affect anyone else.

- *Commons Problems.* A category of negative externalities very close to congestion externalities consists of *commons problems*. The name comes from the practice of allowing privately owned sheep to graze on the village commons. If my sheep are eating grass on the commons, your sheep have less grass available; my sheep are generating a negative externality for you and, contemporaneously, your sheep are as well for me. A very significant example of this concerns fisheries, where each party's private interests are to overfish the fishery.

  Somewhere between congestion externalities and commons problems are externalities in multidivisional firms in which the divisions share some common service providers, such as IT. When Division A puts demands on the service provider, it can negatively impact the service that is provided to Division B.

- *Public Goods.* A *pure public good* is a commodity whose consumption by one party in no way hinders its consumption by another party. The good can be consumed by anyone who cares to do so, without affecting the enjoyment that others take in its consumption.

  It is hard to think of anything that is a pure public good. Clean air, national defense, the services of a lighthouse, turnpikes, and national parks and recreation areas are all sometimes used as examples, although there are clear congestion effects to contend with in at least the cases of turnpikes or national parks. Still, these examples capture the flavor of a public good.

  The public good has the possibility of *exclusion* if we can control the entities who take advantage of the good. For example, we can restrict access to turnpikes and national parks, so insofar as these approximate public goods, they are public goods with the possibility of exclusion. But it is hard to stop residents of some area from enjoying clean air, if clean air is provided at all; this is public good without exclusion.

  The provision of a public good is an activity that usually has very strong and substantial positive externalities: As long as it generates positive value for folks, it does so for everyone. If I provide clean air, by cleaning air that is dirty or by failing to pollute, I generate positive externalities for others. Because so many others enjoy the clean air—because clean air approximates a public good—the amount of positive externality I generate can be huge.

- *Market Power.* When a firm with market power uses that market power to, say, raise the price of its own good, it affects the welfare of its customers. When Intel lowers the price it charges for its processors, it adversely affects the welfare of AMD (a competitor) and positively affects the welfare of HP (a customer). Because it works through the price system, the exercise of market power is sometimes called a *pecuniary* externality.[1]

    A closely related externality in the context of multidivisional firms is when the price Division A sets for its products affects demand for the products of Division B. If the leadership of Division A is rewarded based on the performance of Division A, this motivates the leadership to set prices for its products in a way that can hurt and, sometimes, can help how well Division B does.

17.2. Why Do Externalities Lead to Inefficiency?

When firms or consumers generate externalities, the outcome of a market equilibrium may not maximize total surplus, even assuming that markets are perfectly competitive. To see why, review the argument from Chapter 15. In a competitive-market equilibrium, when there are no externalities, the marginal consumer benefit equals the equilibrium price, which equals the marginal cost of production. This gives the efficient outcome.

But this involves equating the marginal *private* consumer benefit and the marginal *private* cost of production. When consumption by an individual generates externalities, the marginal *social* benefit of the consumption activity (the marginal impact on overall surplus) is not the same as the marginal private benefit to the consumer in question. And, when the production activities of a firm generate production externalities, the marginal *social* cost of production is not the same as the marginal private cost of production. To be efficient, we want to have marginal social benefits equal to marginal social costs. A market equilibrium typically does not achieve this.

Suppose, for instance, a firm generates negative externalities for consumers

---

[1] Students sometimes ask, "Since the entry of many firms in a perfectly competitive industry lowers the profits of firms already producing, isn't this a pecuniary externality?" The answer is a hedged No. Externalities are actions by single agents—consumers or firms—that directly affect the welfare of other agents. In a perfectly competitive market, the entry of a single firm has a very small impact on the equilibrium price; the fact that the impact is very small and not zero is why the No is hedged. Note in this regard that, in a competitive market, if A buys goods from B, we don't say that A has generated an externality for B or vice versa, because if A didn't buy those goods from B, B would find another buyer. And if B didn't sell those goods to A, A would find another vendor.

and other firms by polluting. When it pushes its private marginal cost to equal price, it does not take into account the amount by which its pollution lowers the utility (or surplus) of consumers generally or the profit (surplus) of other firms. It probably produces more output than is socially optimal, unless it is made to take into account—to *internalize*—the externalities it produces.

17.3. Dealing with Externalities

Externalities are dealt with in a number of ways.

Social Norms

Social norms can sometimes control externalities. My front garden, if well tended, generates positive externalities for my neighbors, as do their front gardens for me. If each of us maximizes his or her own private utility, each of us would spend less on our front gardens than is socially optimal. But we can fall into an arrangement where each of us spends more time because of the social pressure to do so; if I suddenly let my front garden go to seed, so to speak, my neighbors might quit speaking to me, stop pruning bushes that lie along our common property lines, and so on, to signal to me that my behavior is unacceptable. Or one of my neighbors might point out to me that my yard is an eyesore and ask me, "What are you going to do about that?" In fact, since I value the good opinion of my neighbors (and I fear being taken to task), I keep up my front garden even if they would in fact do nothing tangible to punish me if I didn't keep it well tended.

There is an important point here, which really belongs to the social psychology of norms, but is worth making even in an economic textbook: I just told two stories about norms of behavior. The first is that I conform to the norm of a well-tended front yard because, if I do not, my neighbors will take actions that adversely affect me. The second is that I conform to the norm because I *internalize* my neighbors' good opinion: Being in their good graces is directly valuable to me, increasing my utility. A variation on the second story is that I internalize conformance to the norm simply because it is a norm, and conformance to norms per se increases my utility. Whichever story appeals to you is fine; each works in different contexts and, as you can imagine, the most powerful institutional arrangements are often those that enlist them simultaneously.

Property Rights and the Coase Theorem

A second method for dealing with externalities involves the establishment of clear and unambiguous "property rights." If an upstream firm pollutes a river, society might decide (1) that the downstream parties have a property right to clean water or (2) that the upstream party has the right to dispose of its effluent as it sees fit. Property rights can be established either way. But, once the property rights are clearly established, individuals bargain over how they exercise those rights. If downstream parties have the right to clean water, then the upstream firm can offer to pay to be allowed to dispose of its effluent in the river. If the upstream firm has the right to dispose of its effluent as it sees fit, then downstream parties can offer to pay the upstream firm to restrict its pollution. Of course, the establishment of property rights has substantial distributive consequences; the upstream firm wants the right to dispose of its effluent, so if it restricts its pollution, it is paid for that, rather than having to pay to pollute. In either case, as long as property rights are clearly and unambiguously delineated, the story goes, we can trust that parties bargain to a socially efficient outcome.

This approach to externalities is known as the *Coase Theorem*, after its origina-tor, Ronald Coase,[2] who asserted that if property rights are clearly established, the problem of externalities vanishes. The approach of the Coase Theorem to dealing with externalities (clearly establish property rights, then let "markets" [bargaining] determine the outcome) has been fashionable among economists and legal theorists recently, but it is not without problems. One problem con-cerns the costs of bargaining. Suppose we give the firm the property right to pollute and leave it to the parties downstream to bargain over abatement. If many parties are downstream, each will want the others to offer the upstream polluter money to reduce pollution, in order to free ride on the efforts of the others. You can think of this problem as resulting from the inability of one party to exclude others from the enjoyment of some good. If I pay the upstream party to refrain from polluting the stream, I cannot exclude your enjoyment of the clean water that results, so you benefit from my efforts. To deal with this, we might try to give all the downstream parties the right to clean water, so that the firm must compensate each for any pollution it causes. Then a different sort of bargaining problem occurs: downstream parties have private information about the value they place on an unpolluted stream, and each wants to claim that the cost to it is higher than it really is, to increase its compensation. Also, if we establish that downstream parties have a right to unpolluted water and the stream is polluted, we may have a problem ascertaining who is responsible for the pollution, hence who must pay compensation.

The Coase Theorem is a useful starting point for analysis. It tells us to think of all problems of externalities as problems in which there are "missing markets" because of unassigned or hard-to-assign property rights; if property rights were assigned, then markets would be created to facilitate the bargaining. But it is often impractical to assign property rights and have the parties bargain. Hence, we move to a third category of answers to the problem of externalities, namely collective action.

---

[2] Nobel Laureate 1991, basically for this result.

Collective Action

Some forms of collective action are informal, such as boycotts against or social sanctions imposed on entities that generate negative externalities. Groups such as the Audubon Society or the Kiwanis often engage in the provision of positive externalities. But the majority of collective action is taken more formally, by political collectives (governments):

1. Public goods are provided, using revenues raised from broad-based taxes.

2. The provision of positive externalities is encouraged, often through tax incentives or subsidies.

3. Activities that generate negative externalities are either directly regulated—proscribed entirely or subject to limits—or discouraged through the imposition of fines and fees.

17.4. On the Regulation of Pollution: Cap and Trade Legislation

To illustrate the formal (government) regulation of externalities, as well as a practical application of the Coase Theorem, consider how a government might regulate the pollution of a natural resource such as a river or the air.

Imagine a firm, sitting upriver from other firms and consumers, that disposes of effluent in the river. This pollutes the river and affects the welfare of the firms and consumers downstream.

Controlling pollution generates benefits *and* costs. If pollution lowers the welfare of consumers downstream, lowering or abating pollution raises external welfare, a benefit. But abating pollution has a cost, usually borne privately by the polluter. The social optimum is where the *marginal external cost of pollution* equals the *marginal cost of abating pollution*. We can use pictures to illustrate this.

The firm's profit depends on its level of pollution, see Figure 17.1.

Panel a graphs the profit of the firm as a function of its level of pollution. This function rises for a while, because the firm spends less on abatement the more it pollutes, hits a maximum, and then turns over; profit falls as pollution rises when the effects of pollution are so severe that they damage the firm's profit, say, by affecting the health and well-being of its workers. Panel b shows the firm's marginal profit as a function of the level of pollution, or the derivative of the profit function.[3] Marginal profit is 0 where profit is maximized. In the

---

[3] *This footnote is for readers interested in the precise mathematics behind Figure 17.1. If it confuses you, ignore it.* Since earlier in the book we used the term "the marginal-profit function," and meant something other than what you see in panel b, let me clarify. Profit is a *multivariate* function; it depends on the level of output of the firm, the amount it pollutes, and probably other things as well. To keep things simple, suppose that pollution level ℓ and output level x are the only two variables, so profit is a function $\pi(x, \ell)$. In Figure 17.1, we are thinking of ℓ as the "free" variable; so

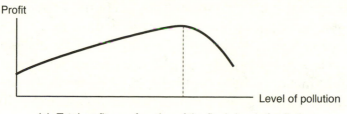

(a) Total profit as a function of the firm's level of pollution

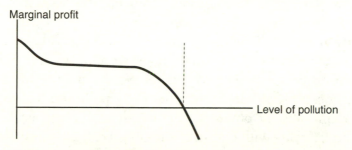

(b) Marginal profit as a function of the firm's level of pollution, which
equals the firm's marginal cost of abatement

Figure 17.1. *Profit and the marginal cost of abatement.* Panel a shows the profit
level of the firm as a function of its level of pollution; panel b shows the derivative
of this, the marginal-profit function. Since the cost to the firm of abating a unit of
production is the same as the marginal profit it gives up by this action, another
name for marginal profit is the *marginal cost of abatement.*

figure, the marginal-profit function is decreasing; this will be explained two
paragraphs hence.

The marginal-profit function in Figure 17.1(b) has a second name, *the marginal
cost of abatement.* This function describes the marginal *cost* to the firm of *decreasing* or abating its level of pollution by a unit, which is just its marginal profit
from increasing pollution by the same unit. The term *the marginal cost of abatement* is used because, in many contexts, it makes sense to think of the cost of
reducing pollution, in terms of water filtration plants, smokestack scrubbers,
or whatever, instead of thinking in terms of the marginal impact on profit from
polluting more. Do not be put off by the semantics: This is just the derivative
of the function in Figure 17.1(a).

Viewed in this fashion, the reason that the function is decreasing can now
be given. This means that for any two levels of pollution, it costs more on the
margin to reduce by one unit the smaller level. That is, going (down) from 100

---

insofar as the optimal level of x changes with changes in ℓ, we write $x^*(\ell)$ for the optimal value of
x given ℓ; then panel a depicts the function $\ell \to \pi(x^*(\ell), \ell)$, while panel b depicts the total derivative of $\pi(x^*(\ell), \ell)$ with respect to p. Earlier in the book, when we spoke about marginal profit (in
x, which equals marginal revenue less marginal cost), we would (in this context) be looking at the
total derivative of $\pi(x, \ell^*(x))$ in x, where $\ell^*(x)$ is the optimal level of ℓ for a given level of output x.

units to 99 is less expensive than going from 50 to 49, which is less expensive than going from 49 to 48, and so forth. This, of course, is an assumption about the costs of abating pollution and not a law of nature. But, as assumptions go (and ignoring complications caused by fixed costs in the abatement process), it is a reasonable assumption. Figure 17.2(a) shows the surplus of the external population as a function of the level of pollution. This is a dollar-valued measure of the welfare of everyone downstream of this firm as a function of the pollution put by this firm into the river. For consumers, this includes a measure of the loss in their welfare from the pollution. For firms, this takes into account their lost profits, because they now must clean up the water they use, for example. It is a heroic assumption to think we can assign a dollar value to the welfare of consumers and firms, as a function of the level of pollution. As a practical matter, finding this function—or even trying to get a sense of its approximate value— is enormously complex. Imagine, for instance, pollution that might result in permanent damage to the environment or extinction of a species: How do we associate a dollar value with that? But suppose it could be computed. Then we have a function, as in Figure 17.2(a), that decreases as the level of pollution of the upstream firm increases.

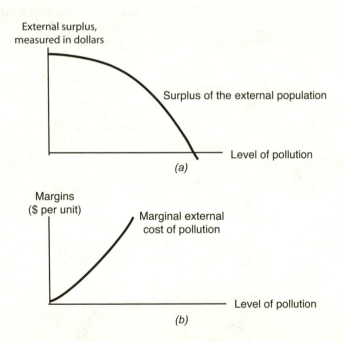

Figure 17.2. *The surplus of the external population and the marginal external cost of pollution.* The dollar-valued surplus of the external population, depicted in panel a, falls as pollution rises, and in the figure, it falls more rapidly, the greater is the level of pollution. Therefore, the marginal external cost of pollution (panel b), which is the same as the marginal external benefit from abating pollution, is an increasing function of the level of pollution.

The negative of the derivative of this function is graphed in Figure 17.2(b). This is the marginal external cost of the pollution or, alternatively, the marginal external benefit from abating pollution. This function is increasing, the idea being that the first few units of pollution are, on the margin, not too bad, but as pollution builds up, each additional (marginal) unit makes the situation increasingly worse.

In Figure 17.3, panel a superimposes the profit of the firm and the surplus of the external population. Panel b graphs the sum of profit and the surplus of the external population. And, in panel c, the marginal external cost of pollution and the marginal cost of abatement are superimposed.

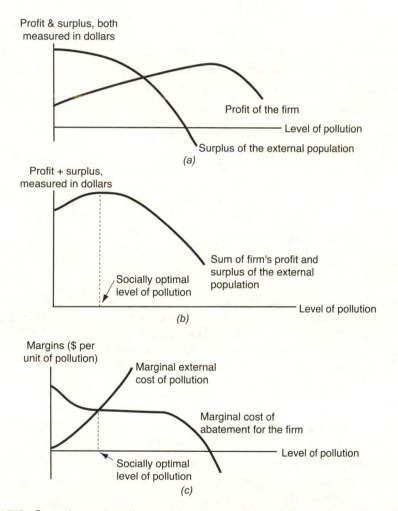

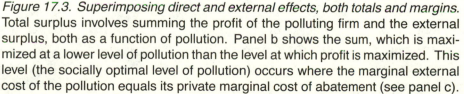

Figure 17.3. *Superimposing direct and external effects, both totals and margins.* Total surplus involves summing the profit of the polluting firm and the external surplus, both as a function of pollution. Panel b shows the sum, which is maximized at a lower level of pollution than the level at which profit is maximized. This level (the socially optimal level of pollution) occurs where the marginal external cost of the pollution equals its private marginal cost of abatement (see panel c).

Note that, in the middle panel, the sum of the two rises at first. Going up to the top panel, you see that this is so because the rate at which the surplus of the external population is falling, the marginal external cost of pollution, is less than the rate at which profit is rising, the marginal cost of abatement. The sum of the two continues to rise until the rate of decrease in the surplus of the external population equals the rate of increase in profit. At this point, the sum is as great as it is going to be; thereafter, falling external surplus outweighs any increase in profit. Eventually, profit falls as pollution increases, accentuating the decrease in the surplus of the external population.

Of course, this maximizing point in terms of the sum occurs where the two margins are equal; see Figure 17.3(c).

Analysis

We can now proceed to some analysis. First, suppose the picture is as in Figure 17.4. If we engage in a laissez-faire economic policy (meaning that we do not interfere in the firm's activities), a profit-maximizing firm would choose the level of pollution at which the marginal cost of abatement is 0.

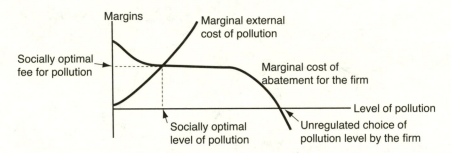

Figure 17.4. *Setting an optimal level of pollution or an optimal fee for pollution.* If the marginal cost of abatement and marginal external cost of pollution functions are known, then the socially optimal level of pollution is where they cross. This can be implemented by directly regulating the level of pollution or by setting a fee for pollution equal to the *optimal pollution fee* shown.

But if we choose the socially optimal level of pollution, we would go to the point where profit plus external surplus is maximized, the point where the marginal external cost of pollution equals the marginal cost of abatement.

This is the sense in which, when there are externalities, the unfettered marketplace fails to produce a social optimum. The firm does not take into account its external effects on the welfare of others. In this case, it pollutes more than is socially optimal.

How can the government enforce this social optimum? Two policy instruments are available. It can regulate directly the level of pollution that the firm is allowed to put into the river, or it can charge the firm a fee or fine per unit of pollution (see Figure 17.4). If the firm is allowed to pollute only to the point marked the *socially optimal level of pollution*, that is what the firm will choose to do. Or, if firm is charged a fee per unit of pollution equal to the *socially optimal fee for pollution*, then it will pollute to the point where the marginal cost of abatement equals this fee, which is again the socially optimal level of pollution. Either instrument works.

In reality, however, no one—and certainly not the government—knows precisely the position of these curves. Each is estimated by analysis and data collection, and especially concerning the social cost of pollution, debates over how this should be measured are intense. The government uses these estimates to set its policy, knowing that it might be missetting things. So it makes sense to ask, Is it worse to misset the level of allowable pollution or to misset the "fee" the firm is charged per unit of pollution?

If an allowable level of pollution is set too high, we have a social cost equal to the area of the shaded triangle in Figure 17.5. A similar picture, but with the triangle on the other side of the intersection of the two curves, results if the standard is set too stringently.

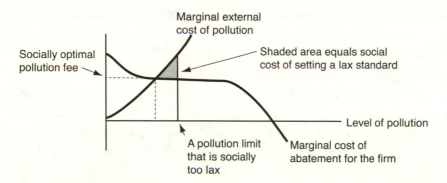

Figure 17.5. *Missetting a pollution standard.* If the firm is directly regulated and the level of allowable pollution is set too high relative to the social optimum, a net social cost equal to the area of the shaded triangle results.

On the other hand, if we misset a fee for pollution, we get the sort of picture shown in Figure 17.6. Here we set the fee too high, and the firm responds with a suboptimally low level of pollution. Again we get a shaded triangle as the social cost of setting the pollution fee incorrectly. (A fee lower than optimal would produce a welfare triangle as in Figure 17.5.)

So which is better, fees or standards? This depends on how well the government knows the shapes and positions of these two curves, as well as their slopes. Suppose, for example, the government has a very good idea of the marginal social cost of pollution and, moreover, this cost is relatively flat. Then we can impose a fee equal to the marginal social cost (firms pay society for the pollution they cause) and let the firms find the optimal level of abatement. On the other hand, if the marginal social cost of pollution is relatively low up to some

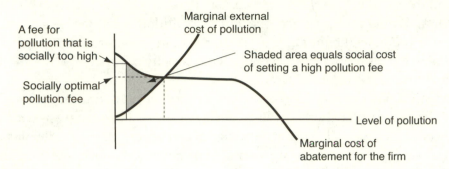

Figure 17.6. Missetting a pollution fee. If a fee for pollution is used, and if it is set too high relative to the optimal pollution fee, the firm responds by abating pollution more than is socially optimal, with a net social cost equal to the area of the shaded triangle.

level and then very steep (that is, some sort of tipping point in pollution exists), and if the government is unclear on the firm's marginal costs of abatement, so that it cannot tell how much firms will abate pollution given a pollution fee, then fixing the allowable level of pollution is likely to be a safer course of action.

Cap and Trade: Resaleable Licenses to Pollute

Do not be misled by the simplicity of these pictures. A lot of the ongoing debate centers on how to measure the external costs of pollution. What value do we put on the destruction of species in the water? What weight should be put on the welfare of unborn generations? How do we value unforeseen or hard-to-predict changes in the environment, in the case, for instance, of climate change? Until such issues as these are settled, it may seem a bit silly to worry about the issue of fees vs. licenses. However, once these primary issues are settled— usually on political grounds—questions about the mechanism for controlling externalities can be tackled with this sort of analysis. Then, to control pollution most efficiently, market mechanisms that employ Coasian logic can be fruitfully employed.

For example, the U.S. government regulates the amount of sulfur emissions by electricity-generation facilities with resaleable licenses to pollute. The government has decided on an amount of pollution of this sort that it will permit. The "level of permitted pollution" is set by cost analyses similar to those sketched in the previous subsections but also is based on a substantial amount of political and interest-group lobbying. Essentially, the government started from existing levels of pollution and is gradually tightening what is permitted.

The government has decided how much pollution of this sort it wants to allow in total. Therefore, it makes sense to hand out pollution quotas rather than setting a pollution fee. Then the problem arises: Given a total amount of pollution it wishes to permit, how should it divvy up this quota among the various polluters? Ideally, the government wants to set pollution levels for each polluter in a manner that equates the polluters' marginal costs of abatement. At least, this is ideal from the point of view of maximizing the social surplus, given the fixed amount of total pollution allowed. But the government is not particularly well informed about the marginal costs of abatement of the various firms that pollute. Suppose, for instance, Public Service Electric and Gas (PSE&G) of New Jersey, because of its installed technology for generating electricity, can abate pollution more cheaply on the margin than Consolidated Edison (Con Ed) of New York. From a social surplus point of view, the government should give Con Ed a break and let it pollute, while turning the screws on PSE&G. But the government does not know these things. The government can ask the firms involved what are their marginal costs of abatement, but the firms, knowing how these data will be used, have a strong incentive to overstate their costs. Moreover, is it fair to penalize PSE&G and reward Con Ed because PSE&G has technology that can abate pollution cheaply relative to that of Con Ed?

Hence, instead of setting quotas for each company, the government gives each polluter a number of licenses, each of which gives the holder the right to put so many tons of pollutant (oxides of sulfur) into the atmosphere. And, the novel part, the companies can trade these licenses among themselves. The idea is this: If PSE&G holds, say, 1000 tons' worth of licenses and can, at relatively little cost, abate its pollution to only 400 tons per year, it would probably increase profit by selling 600 tons' worth of licenses to firms, such as Con Ed, that find abatement expensive. Assuming the market in these licenses is well run and competitive—in fact, it is both—an equilibrium market price in licenses to pollute will become established, so that each firm abates to the point where its marginal cost of abatement equals the equilibrium market price. Of course, this has a very strong Coasian flavor: The government gives each company a property right to pollute to a given level, a property right that can be traded in the market.

The program has a further interesting feature. The pollution licenses establish a maximum amount of permitted pollution. But imagine that some broad-based conservation group, the Sierra Club, say, decides the government has allowed too much pollution. To the extent that the Sierra Club can raise the necessary funds, it can enter the market for licenses, buy up a number of them, then "retire" them by sitting on them. In fact, this has happened. And, if the government believes that groups like the Sierra Club face substantial free-rider problems when they try to raise money for this sort of thing, it could offer some "assistance," by using the tax laws, for instance.

Additionally, the program provides information that regulatory authorities might find helpful: The equilibrium price of a license to pollute one unit of pollution is, as we just noted, the marginal cost of abatement for all the firms involved. If the government set the number of licenses issued based on some notion of what would be the marginal cost of abatement for the industry at that number of licenses and finds, to its surprise, that the marginal cost is quite a bit different, it could rethink how many licenses to issue or, more dynamically, how fast to withdraw licenses from the system.

The decision how to allocate licenses among firms can be contentious. Suppose licenses are issued initially at firms' historical levels of pollutant emission. Then firms that have done a better job abating pollution historically, will object that this scheme punishes them for prior good behavior, arguing instead that (perhaps) licenses should be allocated based on levels of output of the final good. Firms with technologies that pollute more heavily—utilities in coal-producing regions that employ coal instead of natural gas—object that this alternative scheme punishes them for economizing on transportation costs of fuel. In a Coasian sense, this is the inevitable squabbling that results when unassigned property rights are assigned; everyone (of course) wants the assignment of rights to favor themselves.

This description of resaleable pollution licenses, while somewhat simplified, conveys the program's basic purpose: The government solves the allocation problem (how to allocate a fixed amount of pollution) by letting the market solve the problem for it. This is an excellent example of how government regulation of externalities can use the "invisible hand" to advantage, in situations where full regulation might screw things up.

17.5. Externalities within Organizations

Unless you aspire to manage in the public sector or an industry subject to some form of government regulation, you might have concluded that this chapter is of no more than general interest. But the basic ideas of this chapter, repackaged just a bit, are often of great interest to aspiring managers, when the repackaging concerns externalities within organizations. Think in terms of a large, multidivisional firm. Often, to allow for efficient decentralization of decision making, divisional management is given the authority to make operating decisions for its own division. Divisional earnings are measured, and division top management is rewarded based on the performance of the division in terms of these measures.

The problem is that each division, seeking to maximize its own earnings, may lower the earnings of other divisions. To the extent that this is true, the first division exerts a negative externality on the second, and earnings maximization by each division leads to lower profit for the firm as a whole.

How can one division's activities affect the profit of another? One obvious mechanism involves competition among divisions for customers. When the Chevrolet division of General Motors advertises heavily to sell its cars, it presumably depresses the sales and earnings of the Buick division. Or different units within a corporation may compete for scarce factors of production. It is not unheard of, for instance, for one division to compete with other divisions for specific human resources. Division A may hire away from Division B an employee crucial to Division B but merely useful to Division A, offering the employee a promotion or higher salary or both.

To take a concrete example, imagine a corporation with three identical divisions that have a shared service facility. We let y_i for $i = 1, 2$, and 3 be the level of services received from this shared facility by Division i. We imagine that the gross benefit to Division i in terms of improved divisional earnings is given by the function

$$y_i - 0.25y_i^2 - 0.1(y_1 + y_2 + y_3)$$

measured in millions of dollars. The key is the last part of this expression, $-0.1(y_1 + y_2 + y_3)$, which models the idea that the greater is the level of total demand placed on this facility, the smaller the value received by each division fixing its own service demands. In addition, the shared service facility must be paid for; if the demands placed on the facility are y_1, y_2, and y_3, the facility costs 0.5 in fixed costs plus $0.2(y_1 + y_2 + y_3)$ in variable costs.

(This is not a very realistic functional specification of a congestion effect. A more realistic model would say that the degradation in service quality is fairly low until the total demands on the facility approach the facility's capacity, at which point degradation rises very quickly. But dealing with a realistic model of congestion is difficult mathematically, so I illustrate the basic ideas with the simple model proposed here.)

What are the best utilization levels from the perspective of the entire corporation? Taking into account the divisional benefits and the cost of the facility, as a function of y_1, y_2, and y_3, total benefits to the corporation are

$$y_1 - 0.25y_1^2 + y_2 - 0.25y_2^2 + y_3 - 0.25y_3^2 - 0.3(y_1 + y_2 + y_3) - [0.5 + 0.2(y_1 + y_2 + y_3)],$$

which, collecting terms, is

$$0.5y_1 - 0.25y_1^2 + 0.5y_2 - 0.25y_2^2 + 0.5y_3 - 0.25y_3^2 - 0.5.$$

Maximizing this in the three variables gives $y_1 = y_2 = y_3 = 1$, for a net gain to the corporation of $0.25 million.

Now imagine that the firm allows each division to choose its own level of service. Imagine, first, that the firm does not charge the divisions anything for the service and each division chooses its utilization level to maximize its gross divisional earnings, taking as fixed the demands put on the facility by the other divisions. The divisions are identical, so we can figure out what happens by focusing on Division 1: It chooses y_1 to maximize $y_1 - 0.25y_1^2 - -.1(y_1 + y_2 + y_3)$.

Since y_2 and y_3 are outside of this division's control, the problem is to maximize $0.9y_1 - 0.25y_1^2$, which gives $y_1 = 1.8$. By symmetry, we also get $y_2 = y_3 = 1.8$. And, if you do the math, this gives each division a gross benefit of 0.45, against a cost to the firm in providing these services of 1.58. Therefore, the net benefit to the firm is $3 \times .45 - 1.58 = -0.23$ (millions of dollars). The firm actually loses money from providing this service.

Of course, it is clear why this is happening: The divisions do not internalize the variable cost $0.2(y_1 + y_2 + y_3)$ of providing this service. The firm should charge divisions a "transfer price" of 0.2 times the demands they place on the facility, in the accounts maintained on divisional profit. And if the firm does this, Division 1 chooses y_1 to maximize $y_1 - 0.25y_1^2 - 0.1(y_1 + y_2 + y_3) - 0.2y_1$, which comes down to maximizing $0.7y_1 - 0.25y_1^2$ in y_1, which is $y_1 = 1.4$. Divisions 2 and 3 are symmetric and also come up with this utilization level. And net earnings gain for the firm is $0.13 million. (Do the math if you are unsure where this number comes from.) This is better than in the previous paragraph but still not as high as we got two paragraphs ago; the divisions still overutilize the shared facility.

Why? Because while each division now internalizes the direct variable costs incurred by the firm in providing the service, the division fails to take into account the impact of its demand on the quality of service received by the other two divisions.

What are the remedies? Just as in the regulation of pollution, two basic remedies are available. The firm can dictate the utilization levels for each division, rationing each division to 1 unit of service. Or it can raise the transfer price for the service to a level sufficiently high that each division internalizes the external effects it has on its fellow divisions. This means raising the transfer price from 0.2 per unit to 0.4 per unit. If it uses this transfer price, each division, on its own, chooses $y_i = 1$, and the firm's total profit is maximized.

In this ultrasimple example, corporate headquarters can work out both the amount of the service to "dictate" to each division and the size of the transfer payment that causes each division, on its own, to "do the right thing." But in real life, where there is uncertainty in the mind of headquarters about the costs and benefits attending to this sort of problem, one instrument or the other may be preferred. More specifically, to the extent that headquarters cannot accurately estimate how valuable the shared service is directly to each individual division but it has a rough handle on the size of the externality each imposes marginally on the others, using transfer prices and decentralizing the decision is better. However, there are a lot of suppositions in the previous sentence; the most that can be said in general is that headquarters has to be aware of these sorts of externalities and, in some fashion or another, be ready to deal with them. For more on this story, see Problem 17.3.

17.6. Innovation as a Prospective Positive Externality

In Section 15.4, the tension between innovation and allocative efficiency was mentioned. A few more words on this topic are now appropriate.

Innovation of a new product, process, or service represents a *prospective* positive externality. Consider, for instance, a new drug for treating some disease. Widespread distribution of this drug to all who are suffering from the disease will provide sufferers with obvious benefits. So, to promote allocative efficiency, widespread distribution is warranted. But to motivate innovation, which is a costly (and risky) process, the successful innovator must be rewarded for her efforts. If we rely on markets to provide this reward, the innovator is likely to charge users a high price, which restricts distribution to the few who can afford it. In the case of innovation then, because it represents a prospective positive externality, allocative efficiency is more or less directly opposed to providing the rewards that spur innovation, at least insofar as we rely on market-based rewards to the innovator. So, for instance, we have limitations on patent rights: the innovator enjoys the fruits of her innovation for a period of time, after which widespread distribution of the innovation is allowed. A drug manufacturer can be the sole distributor of a new drug for a while, but after a period of time, the manufacture and sale of "generic copies" are permitted.

This compromise between allocative efficiency and incentives to innovate is, of course, imperfect. You should ponder whether it might not be more efficient to have the government provide rewards to innovators in exchange for immediate widespread distribution of the innovation, as well as the issues such a system would raise. (Because innovation is generally risky, you might wait until after Part V of the book to consider the merits and demerits of such a system.)

Executive Summary

- When the actions of one economic entity (consumer or firm) affect the welfare measured in the utility or profit of another, the first imposes an *externality* on the second. The externality is positive if the second party's welfare is improved and negative if the second party's welfare is diminished. Examples of externalities include some obvious cases, such as pollution, but also network, standards, congestion, and shared-commons externalities.

- Public goods provide extreme cases of externalities: A public good is a good that can be consumed simultaneously by as many people as wish to do so without diminishing the welfare other consumers receive from the good. True public goods are hard to find, but things like clean air come close. The provision of a public good generates substantial positive externalities because of the large number of beneficiaries.

- The argument that says that a competitive market equilibrium maximizes surplus does not hold when there are externalities, because in a competitive market equilibrium, consumers and firms pay attention to the private utilities and profits they garner and do not take into account the full impact of their activities on social costs and benefits. Thus, when externalities are present, there is scope for beneficial government intervention in markets. But saying there is scope for beneficial government intervention is not the same thing as saying the government intervention will be beneficial.

- Externalities can be dealt with informally, through social norms. In theory, they can be dealt with through the assignment of property rights and reliance on markets and bargaining. Often, they are dealt with through government or legal action; governments provide public goods using tax revenues, they promote the provision of positive externalities, and they regulate the creation of negative externalities.

- In the regulation of specific negative externalities, the government can either directly set limits to the externality-generating activity (Firm X can put only N tons of sulfur dioxide into the atmosphere) or impose fees on the activity (Firm X must pay $\$M$ for every ton of sulfur dioxide it puts into the atmosphere).

- The resaleable-pollution-licenses program is an example of the regulation of a negative externality that takes advantage of market processes to allocate efficiently a fixed amount of allowable pollution.

- This sort of problem is not only a matter for governments regulating the economic decisions of individual consumers or firms; it can also be found in large organizations, where decentralized decision making combined with intraorganizational external effects can lead to suboptimal (less-than-profit-maximizing) decision making.

Problems

17.1 The business district of the capital of Freedonia, Freedonia City, sits on an island. Most of the people who work in this district commute from the mainland. Specifically, 400,000 people make this commute. Freedonians are in love with their cars, so each of the 400,000 people drives to and from work in a private car; there is no carpooling.

There are two routes from the mainland into (and out of) the business district, the Rufus T. Firefly Bridge and the Chicollini Tunnel. The times it takes to commute across the bridge and through the tunnel depend on the number of individuals n_B and n_T who take the bridge and the tunnel, respectively. Specifically, if n_B people come via the bridge, the commute time via the bridge is $30 + n_B/20,000$ minutes, and if n_T people come via the tunnel, the commute time via the tunnel is $40 + n_T/5000$ minutes.

(a) Suppose each of the 400,000 people who make this commute takes either the bridge or the tunnel; that is, $n_B + n_T = 400,000$. People choose whether to take the bridge or the tunnel depending on which takes less time, so in equilibrium, the numbers n_B and n_T are chosen so that the two commute times are equal.

What are n_B and n_T?

(b) We define the total commute time as n_B times the commute time via the bridge plus n_T times the commute time via the tunnel. In your answer to part a, what is the total commute time?

(c) Suppose the mayor of Freedonia City could control the number of people who come via the bridge and via the tunnel. How would she allocate the 400,000 commuters between the bridge and the tunnel to minimize total commute time?

(d) Except for the congestion on the bridge and the tunnel, there is zero marginal cost of getting consumers across the bridge and through the tunnel. For this reason, transit across the bridge and through the tunnel have been kept free. But the mayor and city council of Freedonia City are considering whether to impose a toll on one or the other. If a toll of t_B is imposed on the bridge and t_T on the tunnel, consumers will rearrange their commute so that $10t_B+$ commute time across the bridge (in minutes) equals $10t_T+$ commute time through the tunnel (in minutes). In other words, 10 minutes of commute time is worth $1 to commuters. Find values for t_B and t_T, where one is 0, so that, facing these tolls, commuters arrange their commute in the manner that minimizes total commute time.

17.2   The Freedonian people love fish caught in Lake Bella, a large lake in the middle of Freedonia. This fish is a great delicacy, and Freedonians are willing to pay quite a lot for it. In addition, the life of a Lake Bella fisherman has deep roots in Freedonian folklore. (In Freedonia, all fishermen are in fact men; this society is decades behind the times.) Each fisherman requires a boat, which has a fixed cost of $10,000 and otherwise spends $(10 + X/1000)x + x^2/100$ to catch x pounds of fish, where X is the total amount (in pounds) of fish caught in Lake Bella by all the fishermen. (That is, the more fish caught in total, the more expensive it is for a single fisherman to catch x lbs. of fish.) Fishermen choose how much fish to catch based on the price p for fish (per ton), which they regard as fixed (they are price takers); they understand their costs and take the total catch X from the lake as fixed and outside their control. Demand for fish from Lake Bella is given by the demand function $D(p) = 5000(60 - p)$.

(a) Suppose that precisely 10 fishermen fish Lake Bella. (They can neither enter nor exit and they cannot avoid the fixed cost of the boat by refusing to fish.) What is the market equilibrium in the Lake Bella fish market?

(b) Suppose there is free entry to and exit from this market. What is the long-run equilibrium in the Lake Bella fish market? What are consumer and producer surplus?

(c) Suppose the Freedonia Fish and Game Department imposes a $6-per-pound tax on fish caught in Lake Bella. This tax is paid for by fishermen. What is the (free entry and exit) equilibrium in the Lake Bella fish market? Compare total surplus in this equilibrium (including government net revenues) with total surplus in the answer you got to part b. Can you explain the answer you are getting?

17.3 Consider a firm with the sort of shared resource–congestion problem sketched in the final section of this chapter. Imagine that the shared facility has a capacity for, say, 500 units of work per month. Congestion (and concommitant service degradation) is minimal if demands placed on the facility total 450 units or less but becomes substantial as total demand on the facility approaches 500 and skyrockets if demands on the facility total more than 500. The firm is determined, therefore, to limit demands on the facility to 450 units per month.

Five divisions place demands on this shared facility, so the firm thinks first of dictating to each that it (the division) can use the facility up to 90 units of service per month. But headquarters worries that this is a suboptimal allocation of the 450 units available. Perhaps one division gets more (marginal) benefit out of its 150th unit of service, than another gets from its 70th.

How, in the spirit of resaleable pollution licenses, can the firm mitigate against this problem? If headquarters can increase the capacity of this facility at a cost per unit per month that it knows, but it is unsure of the value of the facility to its divisions, how can it decide whether to increase the capacity?

17.4 Among the ways to protect your car or truck from theft are "crowbar" devices that lock the steering wheel in place and the LoJack™ theft-recovery system. The LoJack system works by hiding a small RF transmitter in your car; when you report that your car has been stolen, the system is activated, and law enforcement agencies can then quickly locate and recover your car. Car insurance companies will "subsidize" your use of either method by reducing the premium charged for the theft-portion of your insurance; they have discussed whether, collectively, they should increase the subsidy for LoJack relative to the subsidy for using the "crowbar." The difference in premia reduction could be due to differences in theft/recovery rates in the two systems, although were this the case, it would make sense for each insurance company to act unilaterally in this fashion. The fact that the discussions were about collective action in decreasing the premium for LoJack indicates that something more is going on here. What do you think that something is (and please remember that this is a chapter on externalities)?[4]

---

[4] Thanks to Jeremy Bulow, who suggested this problem.

Part V
Uncertainty and Information

18. The Expected-Utility Model

The choices consumers make in many important economic contexts have uncertain consequences. Consumers undertake transactions with other parties in which one of the parties has information that the other party lacks, and in which the specific performance of one party in fulfilling the transaction cannot be guaranteed. This chapter provides the basic (descriptive) model of choice under uncertainty, the expected-utility model, that we use in the final three chapters to study the economics of such situations.

Uncertainty is a fact of economic life. For individuals, major decisions concerning education, career, housing, saving, and investment have substantially uncertain consequences. For firms, this is true concerning which products to develop and market, technologies to employ, and employees to hire. And these are only partial lists. Vitally important markets—in securities, insurance, options, and futures—exist largely to help individuals and firms deal with the uncertainties they face.

And parties often engage in transactions in which one party has access to valuable information the second party lacks, or where the first party's "fulfillment" of the transaction cannot be contractually guaranteed. For instance, the seller of a used car will typically have a lot more information about the quality of the car than does the buyer. A landlord, renting a house to her tenant, must worry that the tenant will not take sufficient care of the her property.

Yet here we are, quite far into a book about microeconomics, and the few discussions about uncertainty and information that we've had have been loose and imprecise. In this final part of the book, we rectify this. We create models that provide insight into three important economic issues:

- In Chapter 19, we investigate the role of financial and insurance markets in spreading and sharing in risks.

- In Chapter 20, we look at markets like the used car market in which *adverse selection* can cause a breakdown in market functioning and in which *screening* and *signaling* can, to some extent, repair these breakdowns.

- And in Chapter 21, we investigate issues of *moral hazard*, where (for instance) a tenant lacks the incentive to take good care of the apartment he rents, and where the landlord can employ *incentives* that, to some extent, can rectify this situation.

The models we use to study these issues are built from a model of how individuals make choices with uncertain consequences. Specifically, we employ the *expected-utility model.*[1] In this chapter, we provide the basics of this model of individual choice behavior, including a discussion of which empirical phenomena it captures and what it misses.

18.1. The Model

The first step in building the *expected-utility* model is to say how *uncertain prospects* are described. This is done in two ways.

Lotteries with (Objective) Probabilities

In the first way, an uncertain prospect is described as a probability distribution over a set of prizes. We think of the consumer choosing among gambles or prospects that will (in time) provide her with some prize—it could be a bundle of goods, an amount of money, or both goods and money—and when she chooses, although she doesn't know which prize she will get, she can associate with each prize its probability of being realized.

We'll use pictures like those in Figure 18.1 to depict the sort of objects among which the consumer must pick, referring to them as *prospects*, *gambles*, and *lotteries*, all interchangeably. Possible prizes are listed at the end of separate branches; their respective probabilities are placed on the branches. In the first of these gambles, all the prizes are monetary, but the other two gambles show that any sort of prize can be considered.[2]

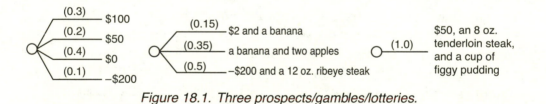

Figure 18.1. Three prospects/gambles/lotteries.

Lotteries Based on "States of the World"

The assumption that we can write down the probabilities of the different prizes is quite heroic. Suppose you are considering among other gambles a wager on the winner of the next World Cup Tournament. You will win $100 if a South American team wins, lose $100 if a European team wins, and neither win nor

---

[1] You may have heard this model called the von Neumann–Morgenstern expected-utility model or the Savage model (Savage being the name of an economist and not a comment on the consumer making the choices); there are distinctions, which we later explain.

[2] In this book, all gambles will have finitely many possible prizes, as in the three gambles in Figure 18.1. The model is sometimes applied by economists to gambles with a continuum of prizes; then the sums that we use to evaluate expected utility are replaced by integrals.

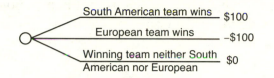

Figure 18.2. A gamble with no obvious objective odds.

lose if a country not from South America or Europe wins. In other words, you are looking at, among other possible choices, the gamble depicted in Figure 18.2. Figure 18.2 clearly depicts this gamble. But where do we find the probabilities to place on the branches? Indeed, gambles like this are often taken because the bettors disagree about the odds: You may think that it is more likely that a South American team will win than that a European team will, while the person with whom you are betting thinks the opposite. Therefore, each of you is content to make this bet. The point is, you and your betting partner probably couldn't agree on the probabilities of each branch; your disagreement is what makes the bet possible.

This sort of thing gives rise to the second way that economists represent prospects/gambles/lotteries. First, they identify a set of *states of the (later) world*, a list of all relevant future conditions that might hold, where the test of relevance is whether the outcome of some gamble being considered depends on those conditions. So, for instance, if we are looking at *all* possible bets based on the the winner of the next World Cup Tournament, our list—called the *state space*, would be something like {Brazil wins, Argentina wins, Germany wins, Italy wins, Spain wins, . . . , New Zealand wins}. (If we are looking only at bets based on the three outcomes in Figure 18.2, a state space with only those three states would suffice.) The list of states must be exhaustive—if necessary, add a "none of the previous" state of the world—and mutually exclusive. And, then, a gamble is a function from the set of states of the world to the set of possible prizes.

Expected Utility

For most of this chapter, we'll work with the first sort of model, where gambles are probability distributions over prizes as in Figure 18.1. (We'll return briefly to the second sort of model in a few places.) And now it is easy to describe how the expected-utility model of consumer choice works:

> *The expected-utility model of consumer choice says that a consumer associates to each possible prize a number, her personal (subjectve) utility of that prize. And, faced with a choice of one gamble out of some set of gambles, the consumer will choose whichever gamble has the highest **expected utility**, where the expected utility of a gamble is the sum over all prizes of the probability of the prize times its utility to her.*

So, for instance, suppose a particular consumer had a choice among the three gambles shown in Figure 18.1. Suppose she must choose one and only one of the three. Suppose her utility values for the eight different prizes are given by Table 18.1.

Prize	Utility
$100	7
$50	4
$0	−1
−$200	−6.5
$2 and a banana	−0.8
a banana & two apples	−0.75
−$200 and a 12 oz. ribeye steak	−6.25
$50, an 8 oz. tenderloin steak, and a cup of figgy pudding	4.6

Table 18.1. Utilities of the prizes from the gambles in Figure 18.1.

Then we compute: For the first gamble in Figure 18.1, its expected utility is

$$(0.3)[7] + (0.2)[4] + (0.4)[-1] + (0.1)[-6.5] = [1.85].$$

Let me spell this out. There are four prizes: $100, $50, $0, and −$200. The utility of $100 is [7], and its probability is (0.3), so the first term in our sum is (0.3)[7] = [2.1]. The utility of $50 is [4] and its probability is (0.2), so the second term in the sum is (0.2)[4] = [0.8]. The third prize contributes (0.4)[−1] = [−0.4] (probability .4 times utility −1) to the sum, and the fourth and final prize contributes (0.1)[−6.5] = [−0.65]. (I put probabilities inside parentheses and utility levels inside square brackets to avoid confusion.) The sum of the four terms is [2.1] + [0.8] + [−0.4] + [−0.65] = [1.85], which is the *expected utility* of the first gamble. The second gamble has expected utility

$$(0.15)[-0.8] + (0.35)[-0.75] + (0.5)[-6.25] = [-3.5075].$$

And the third gamble has expected utility

$$(1.0)[4.6] = [4.6].$$

The gamble with the highest expected utility is the third; the model says that she chooses the third gamble.

That's all there is to the model itself. But a variety of questions immediately arise: (1) Why do economists use this particular model? (2) Where does this utility function come from? (3) How does this model connect to the model of utility maximization from Chapter 10? And (4) how do we handle gambles of the sort shown in Figure 18.2, where the probabilities are not supplied?

Expected Utility with States of the World: Subjective Expected Utility

The fourth question has a simple answer: When the choices are formulated with states of the world, as in Figure 18.2, the model of choice is amended as follows:

> *The first step is for the consumer to give her personal best assessment of the likelihoods of the various states of world, in the form of a probability distribution. She then uses the probabilities she has supplied to compute subjective expected utilities as in the first model.*

So, when a consumer is evaluating the gamble in Figure 18.2, she begins by giving her best assessment that Argentina will win, that Brazil will win, etc. Or, for purposes of evaluating the gamble in Figure 18.2, what is her best assessment that a South American team will win, that a European team will win, and that the winning team is from outside Europe and South America. If, for instance, her best assessment is that a South American team will win with probability 0.6, that a European team will win with probability 0.38, and that a team from outside those areas will win with probability 0.02 (and it is an important part of this model that her numbers add up to 1—she must supply a probability distribution), then her expected utility for the gamble in Figure 18.2 is

$$(0.6)[\text{her utility of the prize } \$100] \; + \; (0.38)[\text{her utility of } -\$100]$$
$$+ \; (0.02)[\text{her utility of } \$0].$$

These subjective probabilities should be *her* best assessments of the odds. Ask another person to evaluate this gamble and, according to this model, he should supply his personal best assessment (which may be different), as well as his utility function (about which, more to come.)

To distinguish the expected utility model where the objects of choice have probabilities assigned, as in Figure 18.1, from the model where the consumer has to supply her assessments, as in Figure 18.2, economists say the first is the expected utility model with *objective probabilities*, while the second is the *subjective expected utility model*.[3]

---

[3] And, returning to footnote 1, the first sort of model, with objective probabilities, is more or less due to von Neumann and Morgenstern, while the subjective expected utility model is generally attributed to Savage.

How Does This Connect to the Utility-Maximization Model of Chapter 10?

In the model of consumer choice in Chapter 10, each possible object of choice is assigned a utility (according to the consumer's personal preferences), and the consumer, faced with some set of feasible choices, picks whichever object maximizes her utility.

In the story here, the objects of choice are gambles, such as the three gambles in Figure 18.1 or the gamble in Figure 18.2. So if we were to apply the model of Chapter 10 to these objects, we'd say that, per the consumer's preferences, she attaches a utility to each of these gambles.

We are, in essence, doing just that. But, because the objects are gambles, we are assuming that the consumer's utility for a gamble takes a very special form: The utility of a gamble is its expected utility. Which is a very confusing way to say things, because we are using the same word, utility, to mean two different things: In Chapter 10, utilities measure how much the consumer likes an object she might choose. But here, the objects of choice are gambles or lotteries, and *utilities* are associated with the prizes in the lotteries. To make the distinction, we could use an upper-case U and the word Utility to describe the function in Chapter 10 and use a lower-case u and the word utility to describe the function on prizes here: If we did this, we could succinctly explain how the two concepts connect with the following formulation:

> *The (upper-case U) Utility of a gamble is the **expected** utility (lower-case u) of the prizes in the gamble, where expectations are computed with the supplied probabilities in the objective-probability formulation and with the consumer's subjective probabilities in the states-of-the-world formulation.*

In sympathy with this formulation, we henceforth will use a lower-case u to denote the function on prizes that gives their utilities in the expected-utility model. (We already used upper-case U's in Chapter 10.)

Where Does the (Lower Case "u") Utility Function Come From?

Each consumer has her personal utility function, which reflects her personal attitude toward risk, just as (back in Chapter 10) each consumer has her own Utility function, reflecting her (relative) tastes for things like a bundle of one loaf of bread and a kilo of cheese versus half a loaf of bread, half a kilo of cheese, and half a kilo of salami.

Which is unlikely to satisfy you as an answer, on two grounds. First, and as you are bound to know, we do not see individuals, faced with a choice among lotteries, actually computing expected utilities as a step in making their choice. I'll get to this objection next section.

Second, the phrase *which reflects her personal attitude toward risk* is almost certainly mysterious at this point; what does it mean? It will be easier to answer this question closer to the end of the chapter, so I'll leave it hanging for now, with the understanding that I owe you an answer to the question, *How does one of these utility functions reflect an individual's attitude toward risk?*

18.2. Why (and How) Do Economists Use This Model?

So much for questions 3 and 4 (and, to some extent, 2). The question *Why do economists use this model?* remains. To answer *why*, we first must be clear on *how* economists use this model. It gets used in two ways: *descriptively*, to describe (within a larger model) the choices made by consumers who face uncertain outcomes; and *normatively*, as advice on how individuals and, in particular, you ought to make such choices.

Using the Model Descriptively: An As-If Model

Our interests in this book are descriptive: We want to have a model of people making choices when there is uncertainty, so we can investigate the issues listed at the start of the chapter. But, to be very clear, no economist asserts that a real-life consumer, making such choices, actually computes expected utilities and chooses the available option that has the highest expected utility. Just as with the basic model of the Utility-maximizing consumer in Chapter 10, this is an *as-if* model. The assertion is that the choices consumers make are by and large *as if* they were maximizing expected utility for some utility function. This as-if model of choice captures some common patterns of behavior that are seen when consumers make these sorts of choices.

But this is a model, not reality, and even as an as-if model, it misses other patterns of behavior that we often observe. Viewed as an as-if, descriptive model, we must sort out: *What are the behavioral patterns that this model captures, and what patterns does it miss?*

Using the Model Normatively: Good (?) Advice for You

At the same time, economists believe that the expected-utility model provides people such as yourself with a good tool for making complex decisions under uncertainty. While the choices people (including yourself) are *more or less* as if they were maximizing expected utility, they (and you) would do better to use this decision-making model in a systematic fashion. There is a story that goes with this assertion—which includes a list of reasons why, in some instances, this decision technique misses the normative mark—but the story takes us away from the main points of this chapter. So I leave this to Appendix 4 in the *Online Supplement.*

18.3. Working with the Model: Mechanics

Since economists (and, for the remainder of this book, we) use this model descriptively, the question *What behavioral patterns or tendencies does it capture and what does it miss?* would seem to be next on the agenda. But, on expositional grounds, it is easier to answer that question if we first discuss the mechanics of working with the model.[4]

For the remainder of this chapter, and for all subsequent applications in this book, we deal with lotteries with objectively specified probabilities and monetary prizes; that is, with lotteries that look like the first lottery in Figure 18.1. Since prizes are monetary amounts, utility functions are functions that associate to (real-valued) numbers—the dollar prize—other (real-valued) numbers—the utility of the prize. So we can present a particular utility function either graphically or algebraically. A typical utility function presented graphically is shown in Figure 18.3; as for utility functions specified algebraically, we will work in examples with three specific functional forms:

$u(x) = -e^{-\lambda x}$ for a nonnegative constant λ;

$u(x) = x^a/a,$ for a constant $a < 1$ and $\neq 0$, defined (only) for $x > 0$; and

$u(x) = \ln(x),$ where $\ln(\cdot)$ is the natural log function, also only for $x > 0$.

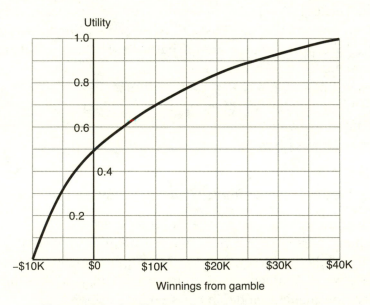

Figure 18.3. A utility function for monetary prizes.

---

[4]   And, as a practical matter, you may be more concerned about the mechanics, at least insofar as your concerns are less philosophical and more practically oriented towards doing problem sets and passing exams.

What Does the Argument of the Utility Function Represent?

Suppose I offer some consumer a lottery in which she can win $10,000 with probability 1/2 and lose $5000 with probability 1/2, where she has the right to refuse the offer. Alternatively, suppose she currently has a bank account balance of $24,000, and I offer her a gamble where, with probability 1/2, her bank account balance will be $34,000 and with probability 1/2 it will be $19,000 and where, as before, she may refuse my offer. Clearly, these are two different ways of describing the same thing.

But if we say "this person's utility function is u" and we use the expected-utility maximization model to describe how she chooses, in the first case we'll be comparing

$$(0.5)[u[\$10{,}000) + (0.5)[u(-\$5000)] \quad \text{with} \quad u(0),$$

while in the second case we'll be comparing

$$(0.5)[u(\$34{,}000) + (0.5)[u(\$19{,}000)] \quad \text{with} \quad u(\$24{,}000).$$

There is no guarantee that, for a given function u, the comparison will come out the same.

The point is that the argument of a given utility function is *not* a units-free number. Back in Chapter 10, I had to specify the units of bread, cheese, and salami, so that $U(1, 2, 0.5)$ meant the consumer's utility of one *loaf* of bread, two *kilos* of cheese, and half a *kilo* of salami. And, similarly, in the context of expected utility, I have to give *units* of the dollar amounts. This is not only a matter of specifying whether the currency is dollars or yen. I must also specify whether the dollar (say) amount represents net winnings or loss from this gamble, or the size of the individual's bank account following the gamble.

In any application—and this includes problems you are given to solve—be careful on this point. So, for instance, in drawing the utility function in Figure 18.3, I am careful to label the x-axis with "winnings from gamble."[5]

Why Doesn't the Utility of $0 Equal 0?:
Utility Is Measured on an "Interval Scale"

Students are sometimes put off by the fact that, for the utility function in Figure 18.3, $u(0) = 0.5$. And if we use the utility function $u(x) = -e^{-\lambda x}$, $u(0) = -e^0 = -1$. "Shouldn't," these students ask, "the utility of 0 always be 0?"

---

[5] And, to foreshadow later developments: If we are describing the choice behavior of real human consumers, whether you *frame* a choice in one units or another can matter. You may have recognized that the two ways of describing the consumer's choice in the first paragraph of this subsection are the same. But lots of real-life consumers can get "fooled" by this sort of changes in how the lotteries are framed. We'll get back to this point.

The answer is, No. The model has the individual comparing the expected utility levels of different gambles with one another. Suppose an individual has the utility function in Figure 18.3 and we offer her a choice of either not gambling or taking a gamble in which she wins $40K with probability 0.6 or loses $10K with probability 0.4. The utility of $-$$10 K$ is 0, and the utility of $40K is 1, so the expected utility of the risky gamble is $(0.6)[1]+(0.4)[0] = 0.6$, while not gambling means a "prize" of $0 with certainty, for an expected utility of $(1.0)[0.5] = 0.5$. The model says she will choose the gamble.

Put another way, saying that the utility of $0 should be 0 makes as much sense as saying that a temperature of zero degrees (and you can choose either Fahrenheit or centigrade here) means no temperature at all. Which makes no sense at all.

That said, suppose we model an individual's choice as being according to expected utility with utility function u. Suppose we take a positive constant A and any constant (positive or negative) B, and we replace $u(x)$ with $v(x) = Au(x) + B$. Then the choices made by the individual with utility function v will be the same as those made by an individual with utility function u. A "measurement theorist" (and, believe it or not, there are such) would say, "In the expected-utility model, utility is measured on an interval scale"; what is important is that if (as in the utility function in Figure 18.3) the utility of $0 is halfway between that of $-$$10K$ and $40K, that this is preserved if you rescale the units of utility.

So if you really, really want the utility of $0 to be 0, and you are dealing with the utility function of Figure 18.3, just subtract 0.5 from every utility measurement you get from the graph. This will make the utility of $-$$10K$ become -0.5 and the utility of $40K become 0.5, so the expected utility of a 0.6 chance at $40K and a 0.4 chance at $10K$ becomes $(0.6)[0.5] + (0.4)[-0.5] = 0.1$, which is more than the (new) utility of $0, which is (by design) 0. The individual chooses just as before.

More Money Is Better than Less Money

It is generally true that if you offer an individual a choice of more money for sure versus less, she'll take the greater amount. In terms of utility functions, this means u should be strictly increasing. In every example we do (and, in particular, in the case of the functional forms on page 415), this will be true.[6]

---

[6]   Take, for instance, $u(x) = -e^{-\lambda x}$. Even after we discuss why the utilty of $0 need not be 0, students object to the leading minus sign, which makes u(any amount of money) a negative number. "Doesn't this mean that an individual with this utility function never gambles?" It does not: Since $u(0) = -e^0 = -1$, any gamble with an expected utility above -1 is preferred to not gambling at all. The point of the leading minus sign is that $e^{-\lambda x}$, where λ is a positive number, is decreasing in x. Putting that leading minus sign there turns it into a function that is increasing in x. And, if you are following this, think about $u(x) = x^a/a$ for cases where $a < 0$.

The Certainty Equivalent of a Gamble

Suppose we model an individual as having the utility function shown in Figure 18.3. Suppose we offer her a choice among a gamble with prizes $0 and $40K, where $40K has probability 0.4, a gamble with prizes $0 or $20K, where the probability of $20K is 0.7, or $15K for sure. Which does she take?

First, we read off the graph the utility values of the possible prizes: $u(0) = 0.5, u(15K) = 0.77, u(20K) = 0.84$, and $u(40K) = 1$, where the reading of the graph at the levels 15K and 20K is, unquestionably, inexact. Inexact or not, if we go with these utility values, the three expected utilities are, respectively,

$$(0.6)[0.5] + (0.4)[1] = 0.7, \quad (0.3)[0.5] + (0.7)[0.84] = 0.738, \quad \text{and} \quad 0.77.$$

The model says she takes the sure thing. But we might want to know, How much better is $15K for sure than the other two gambles?

We could say, $15K for sure is 0.039 utils better than the second bet and 0.07 utils better than the first, but since "utils" have no real meaning, this tells us nothing.

But we can do better: Take the first gamble, with expected utility level 0.7. *What dollar amount has this utility?* To answer this, you go to the graph, find the utility level 0.7 on the y-axis, go across until you hit the utility function, and drop down: The answer is, to the limits of my ability to read this graph, $10K. This number—the dollar value whose utility (for this individual) equals the expected utility (for this individual) of the first gamble is her *certainty equivalent* (or CE) for the first gamble. It is the amount of money *for certain* that gives her the same level of (expected) utility or satisfaction as the gamble.

And, for the second gamble, with expected utility 0.738, my reading of the graph suggests a CE of somewhere in the neighborhood of $12K.

Since the for-certain $15K has a certainty equivalent of $15K (and, if this statement is mysterious to you, reread the last few paragraphs until the mystery is gone), we'd say that: This individual, with this utility function, is roughly $3K better off with a sure $15K than with the second gamble (whose CE = $12K, roughly) and $5K better off than with the first gamble (whose CE is $10K, roughly).

As long as an individual's utility function u is continuous and increasing—and this will be true in all examples we'll have occasion to use—every gamble or lottery she faces has a unique certainty equivalent. Continuity of u guarantees existence (remember the Intermediate Value Theorem from your calculus course, long ago); if u is increasing, there can't be more than one.

The ability to find the CE of a gamble is important in applications, because in many cases it is important to have some notion of how much better one gamble is than another, measured in units (dollars) that are economically meaningful. The example just worked through gives you the technique for finding CEs when you are given a utility function in graphical form; but you will also need to do this when utility is given in one of the functional forms provided on page 415. Here is how:

- Suppose $u(x) = -e^{-\lambda x}$. Suppose a particular gamble has expected utility EU. The certainty equivalent of this gamble is the solution z to the equation

$$u(z) = EU \quad \text{or} \quad -e^{-\lambda z} = EU \quad \text{or} \quad e^{-\lambda z} = -EU \quad \text{or} \quad -\lambda z = \ln(-EU),$$

and hence $CE = z = -\ln(-EU)/\lambda$.

- Suppose $u(x) = \ln(x)$. A gamble with expected utility EU has certainty equivalent z that solves $\ln(z) = EU$, which is $CE = z = e^{EU}$.

- Suppose $u(x) = x^a/a$. A gamble with expected utility E has certainty equivalent z that solves $z^a/a = EU$, which is $CE = z = (aEU)^{1/a}$.

I strongly urge you to practice using these formulas in Excel by doing Problems 18.1 and 18.2.

CEs Can Be Negative

Going back to the individual with the utility function depicted in Figure 18.3, what is her CE for a gamble where she wins \$40K with probability 0.4 and loses \$10K with probability 0.6? The utility of \$40K is 1.0 and the utility of $-\$10K$ is 0, so the expected utility of this gamble is $(0.4)[1] + (0.6)[0] = 0.4$, *which is less than the utility of not gambling at all*. If you go back to the graph, you'll find that the dollar value with utility level 0.4—which is her CE for this gamble—is roughly $-\$6K$. This means that, if you told this individual that she MUST either accept this gamble or pay you \$5K, she will undoubtedly grumble, but in the end, she'd rather pay \$5K than take the gamble. But if you insist that she pay \$7K, she'll grumble even more loudly and, in the end, if she can't find some escape clause, tell you to conduct the gamble. (You might object that this scenario is unrealistic. But it is not unrealistic at all. Think about insurance markets: The consumer is willing to pay a premium to get insurance, which "releases" her from an disadvantageous gamble that she faces.)

The CE Is the Selling Price, But Not (Necessarily) the Buying Price

Suppose an individual—call her Alice—owns the following lottery: With probability 0.4, she wins \$40K. With probability 0.6, she wins nothing (that is, \$0.) Suppose Alice is an expected-utility maximizer, and Figure 18.3 depicts her utility function.

We know from the previous subsection that her expected utility for this lottery is, roughly, 0.7, and her CE is around \$10K. Imagine we approached her and asked, "We want to buy that lottery from you. We are willing to pay you

$11K for it. Will you sell?" Of course, she is likely to bargain a bit. But if she becomes convinced that $11K is our best offer, since this is more than her CE for the lottery, she will sell. In this sense, her CE is her (lowest) *selling price* for this lottery; more generally, the CE of any lottery is the lowest price that an individual will accept in exchange for a lottery that she owns.

But now imagine that you own this lottery and you'd like to sell it to Alice. Would she be willing to *pay* you up to $10K for it? If she pays $10K, then her net from the transaction is a 0.4 chance to gain $30K and a 0.6 chance that she loses $10K (what she paid). The utility of $30K is around 0.93, while the utility of $-\$10K$ is 0, so this venture, if consummated, gives her expected utility equal to $(0.4)[0.93] + (0.6)[0] = 0.372$. Not buying at this price gives her utility 0.5 for sure. So there is no way she'd pay $10K.

Would she pay $5K? The only way to find out is to work through the deal: This would result in a 0.4 chance at $35K (utility roughly 0.97) and a 0.6 chance of a net loss of $5K (utility 0.31 or so), for an expected utility of $(0.4)[0.97] + (0.6)[0.31] = 0.574$, better than the utility 0.5 of not taking the deal. So she would pay $5K.

How do you find the most she would be willing to pay, which we call her (highest) *buying price*? For a utility function given graphically, you must engage in trial and error. We know the number is somewhere between $5K and $10K, so maybe try $7K next. I read the graph as saying that $u(\$33K) = 0.96$ and $u(-\$7) = 0.17$, so if she bought at $7K, her expected utility would be $(0.4)[0.96] + (0.6)[0.17] = 0.486$; this is below the utility of $0, so she won't pay $7K, and now you can try (say) $6500. With the graph, I'm skeptical that you can be accurate enough to pin things down; I'd be content with saying that her buying price is (probably) a bit less $7K.

Which raises the questions: *Why would she sell the gamble (if she owned it) for $10K, but she wouldn't buy it for $10K, or even $8K? Why is there this difference between her buying and selling prices? And, in this case, she'll sell it for more than she would pay to buy it. Is that some sort of (empirically) general truth?* We have a bit more mechanics to attend to, and then we'll get to the answers to these questions.

Buying Prices for Functionally Specified Utility Functions, and the Magic of the Negative Exponential Utility Function

If I gave you a model in which the individual's utility function was specified functionally, you could find his buying price using Excel and GoalSeek or Solver or similar. Let me work through an example. (This example includes some valuable "tricks" for solving problems that you should know, so you should work your way through it slowly and carefully. Have Excel or similar by your side: You will need it.)

Bob is an expected utility maximizer with utility function $u(x) = x^{0.2}$, where

x is his bank balance. Bob currently has a bank-account balance of $120K. In addition, he owns a lottery which will cause him to win $110K with probability 0.3 or lose $10K with 0.7. What is his selling price for this lottery?

In terms of his bank account balance, he will either wind up with a balance of $230K with probability 0.3 or $110K with probability 0.7. This gives him an expected utility of

$$(0.3)[\$230,000^{0.2}] + (0.7)[\$110,000^{0.2}] = 10.6784947,$$

where I'm using Excel to do the calculations for me. Hence, Bob's certainty equivalent *bank balance* is $10.6784947^{1/0.2} = 10.6784947^5 = \$138,851.37$ And, therefore, he would be willing to sell his gamble for any amount in excess of $138,851.37 less $120,000; his selling price is $18,851.37.

Now change the story a bit. Bob has the same utility function and bank balance, but he doesn't own the gamble. Someone is trying to sell him this gamble. What is the most he would pay to get this gamble?

Suppose Bob pays P. Then with probability 0.3, his bank account balance will be $\$230,000 - P$, while with probability 0.7, it will be $\$110,000 - P$. His expected utility will be

$$(0.3)[(\$230,000 - P)^{0.2}] + (0.7)[(\$110,000 - P)^{0.2}].$$

To find his buying price, or the most he would pay, we have to find out what value of P makes this equal to his current position, which has utility $120,000^{0.2}$. At this point, you almost certainly have to proceed numerically; when I did so (using Excel), I got (to the nearest penny) $P = \$17,964.43$.

Now suppose we ask the same two questions about Cathy, whose bank account balance is $200K and whose utility function is $-e^{-0.00001x}$. (For this sort of utility function, values of λ on the order of 0.00001 turn out to be quite reasonable.) And, while we're at it, we ask the same two questions about Daniel, who has the same utility function as Cathy but only has $50K in the bank.

For Cathy, her expected utility (if she already owns the gamble) is

$$(0.3)[-e^{-0.00001 \times 310,000}] + (0.7)[-e^{-0.00001 \times 190,000}] = -0.1182128.$$

Converting this to her certainty equivalent bank balance, we get

$$-\frac{\ln(0.1182128)}{0.00001} = \$213,526.894.$$

So Cathy's selling price for the gamble is $13,526.894.

What about her buying price, if she doesn't already own the gamble? And what about Daniel? It turns out that her buying price is $13,526.894. And Daniel's buying and selling price are both $13,526.894. If you wish, you can get out Excel and verify these assertions. Or you can trust me. Or (to give you a third possibility), if you remember that $e^{A+B} = e^A \times e^B$, you can prove these remarkable facts. (So it isn't magic—it is mathematics.)

But there is something going on here and, in particular, with this negative exponential utility function, that has economic meaning. And to understand that something, we abandon mechanics and (finally) get to the question, *Why do economists use the expected utility model? What behaviorial traits does it capture?*

18.4. Real-Life Behaviors That the Model Captures

The expected-utility model, viewed as an as-if or descriptive model of choice of risky gambles or lotteries, takes each lottery individually and gives a summary measure—the lottery's expected utility—of how "good" or "valuable" is the lottery. This summary measure does some obvious stuff: It puts more weight on prizes with greater probability. For gambles with monetary prizes and utility functions that are strictly increasing (both of which hold in all examples we'll look at), it attaches greater value to lotteries whose prizes are bigger, holding the odds fixed.

If you have taken a course in statistics, and even if you haven't, you will know of a summary statistic that does both these things, namely the *expected value*—or, since the prizes are monetary, what we'll call the *expected monetary value* (or EMV)—of the lottery. In computing the EMV of a lottery, you multiply the probability of each prize times the prize itself (not its utility) and sum up. So, for instance, a lottery in which you can win $100,000 with probability 0.4 and lose $20,000 with probability 0.6 has EMV

$$(0.4)(\$100,000) + (0.6)(-\$20,000) = 40000 - 12000 = \$28,000.$$

Were we to model individuals as choosing whichever lottery has the largest EMV (among those that they can have), we'd have a model that captures some aspects of real-life choice. But this model misses an important first-order factor in real-life choice, *risk aversion*.

Risk Aversion

Risk aversion refers to the general tendency to "discount" the value of a lottery below its EMV because of the riskiness of the gamble. Put it this way. Suppose you offered your classmates (or any group of individuals that you know) a choice between (1) the gamble of last paragraph, a gamble where they win $100,000 with probability 0.4 and lose $20,000 with probability 0.6, or (2) $28,000 for sure.

My guess, and I suspect your guess, is that most—perhaps not all, but most—folks would prefer the sure thing. And they'd prefer the sure thing by quite a lot. Even if the sure thing was only $27,000, many and perhaps most would prefer the sure thing. Were the sure thing a check for (only) $20,000, maybe more would say take the gamble; who and how many would prefer the gamble to $20,000 depends on things like the gambling instincts of the individual, how much the individual has in the bank, and such like. And even at the initial terms of the gamble or $28,000 for sure, some folks would take the gamble. But, most people, in most situations, faced with a lottery in which there is risk, value the lottery at something less than its EMV for sure.

There are some specific contexts in which this tendency is reversed. Many people buy lottery tickets that promise a tiny chance at a huge prize, where the huge prize times the tiny chance is less than the cost of the lottery ticket. (But if we are trying to model typical behavior, you should consider all the folks who could buy lottery tickets but choose not to do so.) Empirical evidence has been collected that shows that bettors at a racetrack who have had a bad day are more likely to take "bad bets" to try to get back to even.

But, economists believe, by and large, in most contexts, most folks exhibit some aversion to risk.

You may have encountered how financial models incorporate risk aversion into their models of investor choice: A gamble—which is now graced with the nicer-sounding name, an investment—is valued at its EMV less some positive constant times its variance—so called mean–variance preferences. The positive constant can be different for different individual investors; bigger constants go with greater risk aversion. For purposes of financial market theory—such as the Capital Asset Pricing Model, or CAPM—this is an adequate *model*. But for some of the issues we investigate in the next three chapters, it doesn't work as well as the expected-utility model.

The expected-utility model per se doesn't imply risk aversion. But if an individual maximizes expected utility and her utility function u is concave—that means it bends over, or has decreasing derivative, as in the case of the utility function in Figure 18.3 and in all the functional forms for utility listed on page 415—then the individual will exhibit risk averse behavior.[7] (If u is convex, the individual will be risk seeking, meaning that for any gamble, her CE will be at least as large as the gamble's EMV. And she is risk neutral—her CE for any gamble is equal to the gamble's EMV—if and only if her utility function is linear.)

Although there are some cases where individuals are risk seeking, and with a caveat to be explained one subsection further on, for the remainder of this book, expected-utility maximizers will occasionally be risk neutral and more often risk averse.

---

[7] This assertion is proved with a mathematical result called Jensen's inequality.

Bob Is More Risk Averse than Is Alice...

Back on page 405, I asserted that an individual's utility function reflects the individual's attitude towards risk, without explaining how it does this. Now we can fill in that hole. By *the individual's attitude towards risk*, I mean her level of risk aversion. Some people are more risk averse; others are less.

To be precise, we say that *Bob is more risk averse than is Alice if Bob's CE for any given gamble is less than or equal to Alice's CE.* This is true whenever Bob's utility function u_B is more concave than Alice's utility function u_A.[8] I won't give you proofs but simply assert:

- For $u(x) = -e^{-\lambda x}$, bigger λ means more risk averse. That is, if $u_A(x) = -e^{-0.00001x}$ and $u_B = -e^{-00002x}$, then Bob is more risk averse than is Alice.

- For $u(x) = x^a/a$, for $a < 1$, smaller a is more risk averse. And, comparing $u(x) = x^a/a$ with $v(x) = \ln(x)$, u is less risk averse than v if $a > 0$ and more risk averse than v if $a < 0$.

Risk Aversion "Vanishes" as the Scale of the Gamble Decreases

Have a look at the three gambles depicted in Figure 18.4.

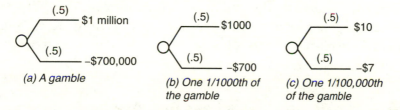

Figure 18.4. *The scale of a gamble affects its desirability.*

Assuming you cannot avoid a bad outcome by declaring bankruptcy, my guess is that, offered the gamble in panel a, you would turn it down; you would certainly accept the gamble in panel c, and while you probably would accept the gamble in panel b, you might turn it down. Moreover, you would be willing to pay close to $1.50—gamble c's EMV—for gamble c; you would pay something less than $150, maybe $100 or so, for gamble b; and you would be quite willing to pay me to avoid having to take gamble a.

What this illustrates is a common behavioral pattern, that risk aversion is about "big-scale" gambles. As the scale of a gamble decreases, risk aversion plays less and less of a role in determining how desirable is the gamble. One way to "unpack" this property is the following:

---

[8] Technically, this means that $u_B(x) = f(u_A(x))$ for every x, for some concave function f. Again, Jensen's inequality gives the proof. Assuming that both u_A and u_B are very smooth—they are twice continuously differentiable—this is equivalent to $-u_B''(x)/u_B'(x) \geq -u_A''(x)/u_A'(x)$.

Take any gamble, such as the gamble in Figure 18.4(a). Regard the prizes as additions to Alice's current bank account, whatever that is. Call this gamble G. Now, for $0 \leq a \leq 1$, let $G(a)$ be the gamble but with every prize scaled to be a times its original size. So, for instance, if G is the gamble in panel a, the gamble in panel b is $G(1/1000)$ and the gamble in panel c is $G(1/100,000)$. Of course, as the gamble is scaled in this fashion, its EMV scales proportionally; that is, $EMV(G(a)) = a \times EMV(G)$. For instance, the EMV of the gamble in panel a is \$150 million, so the EMV of the gamble in panel b is $(1/1000)(\$150 \text{ million}) = \$150$. Finally, let $CE(a)$ be Alice's certainty equivalent of gamble $G(a)$.

Then, $(EMV(a) - CE(a))/a$ decreases as a decreases: The proportional amount Alice discounts a gamble from its EMV declines as its scale declines. And as a approaches zero, $(EMV(a) - CE(a))/a$ approaches zero: As the scale of gamble approaches zero, Alice becomes "almost risk neutral" about the gamble.

I wish there were an easier way to say all this, and if it doesn't quite make sense to you, don't worry: In Chapter 19, this behavioral tendency will become clear, together with its profound implications for things like securities and insurance markets.

But for now, I assert (a) this is a common behavioral tendency of real-life individuals, and (b) it is a tendency that holds for any expected utility maximizer whose utility function (for additions to or subtractions from her current wealth) is smooth (differentiable) at the value zero. Keep this in mind when you get to Chapter 19.

As Alice Grows Richer, She Is Less Risk Averse: Why Buying and Selling Prices Aren't the Same

In the previous subsection, we looked at how risk aversion changes if we fix an individual's wealth and scale gambles that will be added to that level of wealth. Now consider fixing the gamble and changing the individual's level of wealth. The general behavioral tendency here is for people to be less risk averse the wealthier they become.

Not every (risk-averse) expected-utility maximizer exhibits this tendency. It depends on the specific utility function u. The utility functions $u(x) = x^a/a$ for $a < 1$ and $\neq 0$ do have this property, as does $u(x) = \ln(x)$, if the argument x is interpreted as the individual's (after-the-lottery) wealth level. And, in general, a very smooth utility function $u(x)$ (where x is the individual's after-the-lottery wealth level) will have this property if $-u''(x)/u(x)$ is decreasing in x.

This general tendency explains why buying and selling prices for a lottery are not the same and, moreover, why it is typically case that the selling price is greater than the buying price. Suppose Alice owns a lottery and, besides, has wealth level W. Her selling price for the lottery—the least amount she will accept in exchange for the lottery—is her certainty equivalent for the lottery at wealth level W. Now imagine that she has wealth level W but does not own the lottery and is looking to buy it. If she pays P for the lottery, she reduces her wealth level to $W - P$. If she exhibits the general tendency to be more risk averse the poorer she is, her certainty equivalent for this lottery at wealth $W - P$ will be less than it is when her wealth level is W. That is, the lottery, if it is all risky, will be worth less to her if she has to pay for it than if she owns it and is selling it.

Negative Exponential Utility and Constant (In Wealth) Risk Aversion

In this regard, consider the utility function $u(x) = -e^{-\lambda x}$ for some positive constant λ. Back on pages 412-3, we noted that if an expected utility maximizer had this utility function, her buying and selling prices for a lottery would be identical. And, in fact, if we interpret the argument x as after-the-lottery wealth or bank-account balance of the individual, the buying price and selling price of a lottery will not change with changes in the individual's initial wealth.

This is because, for this utility function, the individual's level of risk aversion is independent of her level of wealth. [9] If her CE for some gamble when she has $10,000 in the bank is, say, $1500, then $1500 is her CE for the gamble when she has $10,000,000 in the bank. Obviously, this is *not* a very prevalent behavioral tendency.

But for gambles which are a small proportion of the individual's net worth, it can be a reasonable modeling assumption that, for such gambles, the individual's attitude towards risk doesn't shift much. That is, for someone with, say, $1 million in the bank, gambles whose prizes range from $5000 to −$3000, while posing significant risk, won't shift the individual's wealth enough to shift her level of risk aversion. Hence, in such cases, using these negative exponential utility functions can be acceptable in models of the individual's behavior. And, assuming it is acceptable, it is extremely convenient, as you will see in Chapter 19.

Is It Irrational to Be Risk Averse?

To summarize this section: Economists use the expected-utility model because, by using it with a concave utility function, it captures the behavioral tendency of individuals to be risk averse. It captures the idea that as the scale of a gamble declines, risk aversion declines, ultimately vanishing as the scale of the gamble

---

[9] There are two ways to see this. If you evaluate $-u''(x)/u(x)$ for this utility function, you will find that it is λ, no matter what is x. Accordingly, for this utility function, λ is called the individual's *level of risk aversion*. Or if you think of x as the individual's after-the-lottery wealth level and write $x = W + z$, where W is the individual's before-the-gamble level of wealth and z is the result of the gamble, then $-e^{-\lambda x} = -e^{-\lambda(W+z)} = -(e^{-\lambda W})(e^{-\lambda z})$. All that W does is to multiply $-e^{-\lambda z}$ by the positive constant $e^{-\lambda W}$, which we said on page 408 doesn't change the individual's attitude toward risk.

approaches zero. And, with the "right" sort of utility functions, it can capture how risk attitudes vary with the individual's level of wealth. To summarize this summary, the expected utility model does a pretty good job of capturing risk aversion and phenomena associated with risk aversion.

Students occasionally argue that the "law of large numbers" implies that it is irrational to be risk averse: If you always choose the gamble with the largest EMV, in the long run, as the law of large numbers kicks in, you will come out ahead. Hence (the argument goes), people shouldn't be risk averse, and it is bad modeling to "make" them so.

This is wrong in (at least) two ways. It might be correct if the individual faces a large number of small gambles. But, for small gambles, we've seen that maximizing expected utility is pretty much the same as maximizing EMV. And if the gambles you face are "large," with significantly different prizes, then (a) you probably don't face enough of them for the law of large numbers to be effective, and (b) in the rare cases where you do face a large number of large gambles, the consequences of a large number of losses can be devastating.

That's the first reason. The second is that we are engaged here in *descriptive* modeling; we want to have models of how people behave. The notion that some behavior or other is "irrational" and should be avoided belongs to normative theory; the preceding paragraph really belongs in Appendix 4 of the *Online Supplement* (and, in fact, will be repeated there, word for word). People do behave in risk-averse fashion—you see this clearly in all manner of insurance markets—so modeling them as being risk averse is the right thing to do *descriptively*.

18.5. Behavior Missed by the Expected-Utility Model

While the expected-utility model does capture the important behavioral properties just discussed, it misses other behavioral properties that we see in the choices people make, depending (in part) on how it is applied. We will use the expected-utility model for the remainder of this book, but it may be worthwhile to quickly review three objections to this model as a descriptive model that are often raised.

The Substitution Principle and the Allais Paradox

Consider the two pairs of gambles shown in Figure 18.5. If you were offered a choice between A and B, which would you take? How about between C and D? Psychologists D. Kahneman and A. Tversky asked a large number of subjects these questions and recorded how they answered.[10] But before telling you how their subjects answered, which would you choose?

---

[10] In D. Kahnemann and A. Tversky, "Prospect Theory: An Analysis of Decisions Under Risk," *Econometrica*, Vol. 47, 1979, 263-91.

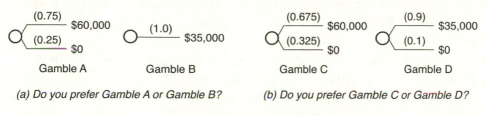

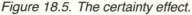

(a) Do you prefer Gamble A or Gamble B?   *(b) Do you prefer Gamble C or Gamble D?*

Figure 18.5. The certainty effect.

Kahneman and Tversky found that many of their subjects preferred B to A and, at the same time, C to D. This pattern is inconsistent with the expected-utility model. If an expected-utility maximizer chooses Gamble B in the first case, she is saying that

$$(0.75)[u(\$60,000)] + (0.25)[u(\$0)] < u(\$35,000),$$

at least, for her utility function. Multiply each side of this inequality by 0.9 and add to each side $(0.1)[u(\$0)]$, and you get

$$(0.675)[u(\$60,000)] + (0.325)[u(\$0)] < (0.9)[u(\$35,000)] + (0.1)[u(\$0)].$$

An expected-utility maximizer who prefers Gamble B in Figure 18.5 to Gamble A must prefer Gamble D to Gamble C.

And what do you say about the two choices in Figure 18.6?

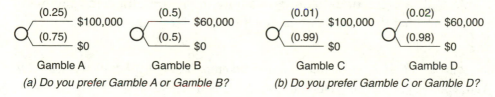

Gamble A   Gamble B   Gamble C   Gamble D
(a) Do you prefer Gamble A or Gamble B?   *(b) Do you prefer Gamble C or Gamble D?*

Figure 18.6. The small-probability effect.

In this case, many of Kahneman and Tversky's subjects chose Gamble B in the first case and Gamble C in the second case, which is, by much the same logic, inconsistent with the expected-utility model.

Kahneman and Tversky give names to what they see empirically. They call the choices of B and C in Figure 18.5 the *certainty effect*; the idea is that individuals attach too much "value" to certainty, and so "overvalue" option B in 18.5(a). And they call the pair of choices B and C in Figure 18.6 the *small probability effect*; it is as if the individual, faced with the choice between C and D in 18.6(d) reasons, "I'm only going to win if I'm lucky, so if I'm lucky, I might as well go for the better prize (namely C)."

Both of these violations of the expected-utility model are special cases of what is called the *Allais Paradox*.[11] The essence of these "counterexamples" and of Allais's original critique comes down to what is known as the *substitution principle*: Suppose we have a lottery in which one of the prizes is $100, say with probability 0.3. Suppose the individual says that $100 is her certainty equivalent for a gamble with prizes $200 and $0, where $200 has probability 0.6. Then, according to the substitution principle, if we took the first gamble and replaced the branch with prize $100 with two branches, one with prize $200 and one with $0, where the first has probability $(0.3)(0.6) = (0.18)$ and the second with probability $(0.3)(0.4) = (0.12)$, we'd have a new lottery that the individual would view as being just as good as the original lottery. In words, we can substitute for any prize a lottery that is just exactly as good as that prize, without changing the value.

Indeed, subject to some technicalities,[12] the expected-utility model of choice is fully characterized by adherence to the substitution principle together with no examples of the sort of behavior illustrated by Figure 10.1 back on page 223. Allais, and the specific examples of Kahneman and Tversky, show that the substitution principle is not, in general, empirically valid. Hence, they conclude, the expected-utility model is in this sense, and for the sort of effects illustrated by the two examples, empirically invalid.

The Ellsberg Paradox

Daniel Ellsberg (of Pentagon Papers fame) proposes the following choice problem.[13] Imagine an urn with 300 colored balls of equal size and weight. One hundred are colored red. Some of the other 200 are colored blue, while the remaining balls are green. It is unknown how many are blue and how many are green, only that the blues and greens total 200. Now answer the following question.

> *You will be paid $100 if a ball drawn at random from the urn has a specified color. Would you prefer that the color that pays $100 is red, blue, or green?*

Asked of colleagues at the Rand Institute, where he worked, Ellsberg found that a substantial number of his associates said that they strictly preferred red. When asked why, they said that they knew the odds of a red ball were 1/3, and while they knew that the odds of green plus the odds of blue were 2/3, they didn't know the odds of green or blue. They preferred a gamble where they knew the odds to one where they didn't, hence red was their strict preference.

---

[11] M. Allais, "Le comportement de l'homme rationnel devant le risque: critique des postulats et axiomes de l'école Américaine," *Econometrica*, Vol. 21, 1953, 503-46.

[12] That you can read about, if you wish, in Kreps, *Microeconomic Foundations*, Chapter 5.

[13] This example is loosely adapted from D. Ellsberg, "Risk, Ambiguity, and the Savage Axioms," *Quarterly Journal of Economics*, Vol. 75, 1961, 643–69. For expositional purposes, I simplify Ellsberg's original example.

We haven't spent much time on choice among lotteries where the probabilities are not given but must be assessed, and now is not the time to begin. But suffice it to say that the model economists use, in which individuals must provide their best assessment of the odds they face and choose according to (subjective) expected utility, is inconsistent with the behavior Ellsberg found empirically. Someone conforming the you-must-give-your-best-assessment-of-the-odds model of choice will probably assess that the odds of red are $1/3$. But then she must assess blue has odds p and green has odds q, where $p + q = 2/3$. Either p or q will exceed $1/3$, or both must equal $1/3$. If one or the other exceeds $1/3$, that should be the individual's choice. If they both equal $1/3$, the individual shouldn't strictly prefer red; she should be indifferent.

It is pretty much beyond (empirical) doubt that people are averse to taking gambles where they don't know the odds; this is sometimes called *uncertainty* or *ambiguity* (about the odds) *aversion*. The standard models of choice under uncertainty employed by economists doesn't allow for this.

Framing

Imagine you are advising the staff of the public health agency of your country (such as the Centers for Disease Control in the United States) concerning an immunization program that deals with a prospective flu epidemic. You are given a choice between two options that are described to you as follows:[14]

> If nothing is done, the prospective flu epidemic will result in the death of 600 people. (Either death or complete recovery is the outcome in each case.) You can undertake either of two possible vaccination programs, and doing one precludes doing the other. The first will save 400 people with certainty. The second will save no one with probability $1/3$ and 600 with probability $2/3$. Which do you recommend?

You might wonder why you, a specialist in management, are being asked for advice concerning this sort of life-and-death medical question. But decide how you would choose, if the choice were yours to make. Then try the following:

> As an advisor to the staff of your country's public health agency, you are informed that a new flu epidemic will hit your country next winter. To fight this epidemic, one of two possible vaccination programs is to be chosen, and undertaking one program precludes attempting the other. In the first program, 200 people will die with certainty. In the second, there is a $2/3$ chance that no one will die, and a $1/3$ chance that 600 will die. Which do you prefer?

These two questions were asked of a large number of medical professionals, and the modal pair of responses was to choose the first program in the first

---

[14] This example is also from D. Kahneman and A. Tversky, op.cit.

formulation of the question and the second program in the second formulation. My experience has been that the modal student of management makes the same pair of choices. In the first formulation of the question, it seems better to be sure of saving someone, while in the second formulation, it seems better to avoid consigning anyone to certain death. But, if you think about it, you'll see the questions are, in terms of actual consequences, the same. The first options in each formulation are the same (400 live with certainty and 200 die), and the second options in each are identically a 2/3 chance of no deaths and a 1/3 chance of 600 deaths. If you prefer the first option in the first question and you think in these logical terms, you should prefer the first option in the second question. But, as the data indicate, the different ways the questions are framed confuse many people; choices do depend on how the possible options are framed.

The Zero Illusion

Framing effects are observed in all sorts of contexts, not only when matters of life and death cloud judgment. A very significant example involves the so-called *zero illusion*. Ask yourself, Would you rather pay $300 or take a gamble based on the flip of a coin, where you will lose $600 if the coin comes up heads, but you neither win nor lose anything if it comes up tails? Then reask this question, framing the outcomes in terms of your bank account balance. I do not know the level of your bank account balance, but if it is, say, $25,220, the question framed this second way is, Would you rather have a bank account balance of $24,920 for sure, or flip a coin where your bank account balance will be $24,620 if the coin comes up heads or $25,220 if it comes up tails? In pictures, these are the choices depicted in Figure 18.7.

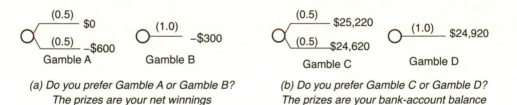

(a) Do you prefer Gamble A or Gamble B?   (b) Do you prefer Gamble C or Gamble D?
   The prizes are your net winnings   The prizes are your bank-account balance

Figure 18.7. The zero illusion.

You can fill in your own answers, after adjusting the numbers to reflect your current bank account balance. In a significant number of cases, people strictly prefer the gamble if the choices are framed in the first way, but they strictly prefer the sure thing in the second framing. The explanation of this is usually that, in the first framing, the individual focuses too heavily on the zero point, hence the name zero illusion: Rather than accept a loss for sure of $300, the individual is willing to gamble—she is risk *seeking*—since this presents an even chance of losing nothing. But when framed in terms of bank account balances, the psychologically loaded term *loss* is missing and the choice reverses.

At this point, please flip back to page 407 and the discussion there. In particular, please reread footnote 5. As we put the expected-utility model to use in the final three chapters, we'll assume that our individual consumers do not suffer from the zero illusion or other framing illusions. Their choices will be consistent, however the lotteries they face are framed. Used *in this fashion*, the expected-utility model misses a behavioral tendency that in some contexts is important. One can use the expected-utility model in ways that are sensitive to this behavioral tendency—if you are curious, look up *reference-dependent preferences*—but we will not do so, as they complicate our story and add little to the applications of we study in the final three chapters.[15]

Executive Summary

- Beginning with this chapter, we add uncertainty to the story. As a first step, this chapter presents the expected-utility model, the leading model of individual choice under uncertainty in economics.

- As applied to gambles that are probability distributions over prizes, the model is quite simple: Each prize has a utility level, and the consumer will choose whichever gamble (or lottery, or prospect) gives the highest expected utility.

- If uncertain prospects are described with states of the world (and the prizes obtained in each state), the consumer first assesses probabilities for the states of the world and then computes (and maximizes) expected utility.

- This is a *model* of the choices people make and, moreover, it is an "as-if" model. No one asserts that consumers compute expected utilities and choose whichever gamble has the highest expected utility. But we model them as choosing "as if" they were doing so.

- A consumer's Certainty Equivalent (CE) for a given gamble is the amount of money obtained with certainty that, in the opinion of the consumer, is just as good as the gamble. The expected monetary value (EMV) is just the probability-weighted average of the prizes (when the prizes are all monetary). Consumers are typically *risk averse*, meaning that for each gamble, the CE of the gamble is less than its EMV.

- The justification for this model as an as-if, descriptive model of choice is that it allows us to capture consumer behavior that is risk averse, but where risk aversion decreases as the scale of the gamble diminishes.

---

[15] This is also true of the behaviors described in the other subsections of this section, the Allais and Ellsberg Paradoxes. Models of behavior more complex than expected utility have been invented that permit the sort of behavior described in these paradoxes—the most notable is Prospect Theory, developed in the article by Kahneman and Tversky that I've been referencing—but these models complicate the issues we discuss without adding insights that are of first-order importance.

- And, applied for some utility functions, it allows us to capture the idea that an individual's aversion to risk diminishes as the individual becomes richer.

- For a very special class of utility functions, the negative exponentials, or $u(x) = -e^{-\lambda x}$ for a positive constant λ, the individual's level of risk aversion is independent of her wealth level.

- While the expected-utility model captures some commonly observed behavioral tendencies of individuals choosing among risky options—which is why economists use this model descriptively—it fails to capture other behavioral tendencies.

- Expected utility is also advanced as a normative decision-making tool: a technique or tool that you should employ. The normative theory of expected utility is not discussed in this chapter but is presented in Appendix 4 of the *Online Supplement*.

Problems

All the decision-makers in these problems are expected-utility maximizers.

18.1 Consider the three gambles depicted in Figure 18.8 and three decision-makers, each of whom chooses among gambles based on expected utility. For each of these three, the utility function argument is the amount of winnings/losses from the gambles being contemplated.

(a) Jo MBA, whose utility function for the range of prizes in these gambles is depicted in Figure 18.9.

(b) Professor David Kreps, whose utility function for the range of prizes in these gambles is given by $u(x) = -e^{-0.00001x}$, where x is the dollar value of the prize.

(c) Professor Sanjay Patel, who like Professor Kreps has constant risk aversion for this range of prizes but who is more risk averse than Professor Kreps. Professor Patel's utility function is given by $u(x) = -e^{-0.00002x}$.

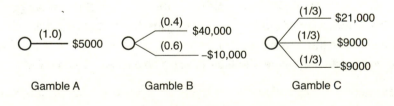

Figure 18.8. Three gambles.

For each of these three individuals, find the individual's expected utility and certainty equivalent for each of the gambles. How would each of these individuals rank the three gambles?

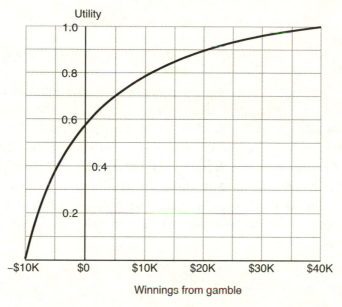

Figure 18.9. Jo MBA's utility function.

18.2 To the three individuals in Problem 18.1, we add three more:

(a) Alice, whose utility function for her final bank account is $u(x) = x^{1/2}$ and who starts with \$50,000 in the bank.

(b) Bob, whose utility function for his final bank account balance is $u(x) = x^{1/2}$ (just the same as Alice) but who is poorer than Alice; Bob starts with (only) \$15,000 in the bank.

(c) Bill, whose utility function for his final bank account balance is $u(x) = \ln(x)$ and who starts with \$50,000 in the bank, just like Alice.

For Alice, Bob, and Bill, find their expected utilities for each of the three gambles in Figure 18.8 and find their certainty equivalents. Caution: When you find their certainty equivalents, be very clear on what units you are using.

18.3 Jack and Jim are twins who have the same utility function, given by $u(x) = \sqrt{x}$, where x is the amount of money they have in the bank after the results of any gambling they undertake in the course of this problem. Jack begins with \$5000 in the bank, while Jim has \$50,000. Each is contemplating a gamble in which, with probability $1/4$, he wins \$40,000, but with probability $3/4$, he wins nothing.

(a) Would Jack rather take this gamble or receive \$7500 for sure? How about Jim?

(b) What is Jim's certainty equivalent if he must pay \$7500 but then gets to take the gamble? What is the most Jim would pay to be allowed to take this bet?

(c) (There's a trick to this part!!!) Can you answer part b for Jack?

18.4 A decision-maker faces the following decision under conditions of uncertainty. This decision-maker has $1 million in assets. Most of those assets, $750,000, are the individual's equity in his house. The remaining $250,000 are absolutely secure. Unhappily, there is a risk that the individual's house will burn down in a fire, which would be a total loss of the $750,000. The individual can insure his house against the loss from this fire. The premium for the insurance is $40,000, and it will insure the individual completely; that is, if the individual chooses to purchase this insurance policy, his assets will be $960,000, whether or not there is a fire. (There is no mortgage on the house, so $750,000 is the full amount paid by the insurance company.) The probability of a fire is 0.05.

(a) What is the expected net earnings, the premium less the expected amount paid out to the client, to the insurance company from this policy?

(b) If the individual in question were risk neutral, would he buy this insurance policy?

(c) If the individual in question is an expected utility maximizer, with the utility function $u(x) = \sqrt{x}$ where x is the individual's total assets, would this individual buy the insurance?

(d) (Use Excel and Solver on this.) Suppose the individual of part c can buy partial insurance. Partial insurance works as follows: If the individual buys, say, α insurance, where α is a constant between 0 and 1, he must pay the premium $\alpha \times \$40,000$ up front. Then, in the event of a fire, the individual gets a payout from the insurance company of α times his loss or, in this problem, $\alpha \times \$750,000$. If the individual can insure partially and, in particular, can pick the level of insurance he purchases, what level of insurance would he select?

18.5 Suppose we offered Professor Patel from Problem 18.1(c) his choice of the following three gambles:

- Gamble A pays $50,000 with certainty.
- Gamble B pays $100,000 with probability 0.8 and $0 with probability 0.2.
- Gamble C pays $200,000 with probability 0.7 and $0 with probability 0.3.

(a) These winnings are added to Professor Patel's existing assets, which at the moment are $500,000. And Professor Patel's utility function $u(x) = -e^{-0.00002x}$ is in units of his total assets so, for instance, if Professor Patel chooses gamble A, his (expected) utility will be $-e^{-0.00002 \times 550,000}$. What is Professor Patel's choice? What is his certainty equivalent (in terms of net assets) from taking each of the three gambles?

(b) Suppose that, instead of $500,000, Professor Patel's initial assets were $1 million. What would be his choice in this case? What is his certainty equivalent (in terms of net assets) from taking each of the three gambles?

(c) Suppose that, instead of $500,000 or $1 million, Professor Patel's initial assets were $0. What would be his choice in this case? What is his certainty equivalent (in terms of net assets) from taking each of the three gambles?

(d) Professor Patel's twin brother, Professor Krishna Patel, claims he is twice as excitable and 100 units more optimistic than his brother. Therefore, he says, his (Professor K. Patel's) utility function is $-2\,e^{-0.00002x} + 100$. What choices does he make concerning these three gambles?

18.6 (This problem foreshadows the topic of Chapter 19; it is well worth trying. If you have problems with the exponential utility function, please see the discussion in the *Online Supplement*.)

Jan MBA has the opportunity to take a gamble that will net her either a gain of $50,000 or a loss of $25,000, each with probability 1/2. Jan chooses among gambles to maximize her expected utility, with utility function

$$u(y) = -e^{-0.0000211y},$$

where y is Jan's net proceeds from the various deals she is currently contemplating.

(a) Will Jan choose to take this gamble, if the alternative is a sure thing of $0?

(b) Suppose Jan could securitize this gamble, which means she prints up 100 "shares" in the gamble, each of which gives a 1/2 chance at a gain of $500 and a 1/2 chance of a loss of $250. Suppose Jan has 99 friends, each of whom has precisely the same utility function as Jan. Would one of those 99 friends be willing to pay Jan $100 for a 1% share of the gamble?

19. Risk Sharing and Spreading: Securities and Insurance Markets

This chapter discusses the economic rationale for equity, insurance, and futures markets: by taking a risk and breaking it into pieces, with the pieces shared among many individuals—in other words, by *securitizing* the risk—risk aversion on the part of individual risk bearers is largely defeated. That's the main message of this chapter but, after delivering this message, the chapter goes on with two caveats and an extension:

- Countervailing forces prevent risks from being shared completely, chief among which are adverse selection and moral hazard (which are discussed in depth in the following two chapters).
- Even if the risks are spread widely, the value of any share of a risk depends on how much riskiness it adds to the general portfolio of risk that individuals bear.
- For a given risk and a fixed population of investors, the problem of sharing the risk efficiently is confronted.

During the late 1990s, the words *initial public offering* (IPO) were viewed as the key to fame and fortune for students of management. Students flocked to create entrepreneurial ventures, looking forward to the day when (1) the venture would be taken public, (2) money would roll in the door in wheelbarrows, and (3) the Porsche could be traded in for a Ferrari. At least, that was the dream.

More generally, securities, futures, and insurance markets are vitally important to managers of virtually every stripe. So it is imperative, at least for aspiring managers, to understand these markets as economic phenomena:

- What economic role do these markets play?

- How do they create value?

- What limits their ability to create value?

The academic discipline of finance is primarily concerned with these questions, and most students of management take at least one, and often a lot more than one, course in finance. I will not upstage the finance courses you might take or finance books you might read, but having introduced risk aversion, it makes sense to give the basic answers to these three questions.

At the outset, it must be said that these markets play several economic roles. In particular, security and other financial markets are the means by which firms obtain liquidity; that is, these markets allow firms to have cash on hand for current transactions, in anticipation of profits to be made later. I am not concerned here with the liquidity role of financial markets; instead I focus on the way in which these markets create value by sharing and spreading risk.

19.1. The Basic Idea

The story begins with risk aversion. Consider a gamble with equally likely prizes $50,000 and −$25,000. This gamble has a positive expected value of $12,500, but the chance of a loss is significant and the size of potential loss is large. Therefore, many risk-averse individuals would turn down this gamble if it were offered.

For instance, suppose this gamble is offered to Jan MBA, an expected-utility-maximizing decision maker whose utility function is $u(x) = -e^{-0.0000211x}$.[1] Jan computes the expected utility of this gamble:

- The prize $50,000 has utility level [-0.3481924].

- The prize −$25,000 has utility level [-1.6946903].

- Therefore, the gamble has expected utility $(0.5)[−0.3481924]$ + $(0.5)[−1.6946903] = [−1.0214414]$, corresponding to a certainty equivalent around −$1005.

- In contrast, if Jan does not take this gamble, she has prize $0 for sure, which has (expected) utility [-1].

So, Jan is better off declining this gamble.

Suppose instead that this gamble had equally likely prizes of $500 and −$250. Then Jan's expected utility from this gamble is (you do the computations!) [−0.9973972], which corresponds to a certainty equivalent of $123.516. Jan would happily accept this scaled-down version of the original gamble. This is nothing more than the observation made in the last chapter, that risk aversion diminishes to the point of vanishing as a gamble is scaled down.

Suppose Jan is smart enough to recognize that, while she would not be happy taking on the full gamble herself, she would be happy to take on a 1% share of it. How can she lay off 99% of the risk? One possibility is to find a bunch of friends and associates who, if they are about as risk averse as she, would each happily accept a small share of the gamble. More specifically, if she could find 99 friends whose utility function matched her own, she could give each a 1% share: All would be happy—this gift is worth $123.516 to each of them—and she is left with a 1% share worth $123.516 to her.

Should Jan give away 99% of the venture? Would it not be better for her to retain a larger share? In fact, you can use Excel and Solver to discover that, if

---

[1] Because Jan has a constant-risk-aversion utility function, it doesn't matter whether the argument x is her net winnings from an immediate gamble or her final bank account balance. We'll treat x as her net winnings in what follows.

Jan is giving away shares in this gamble, she does best for herself by retaining around 43.8% of the gamble, which gives her a certainty equivalent of $2684 (see Problem 19.1).

But Jan is more clever than this. Giving away shares in this gamble is giving away a valuable item. Perhaps she ought to *sell* shares in her venture. For instance, if she could find 99 friends and associates who have the same utility function as she, she could sell 1% shares in this gamble to each for up to $123.516. That is, if she sets a price for a 1% share at, say, $123, anyone with the same utility function that she has would be willing to pay this price; after paying this price, someone with the same utility function as hers would be left with a net certainty equivalent of $0.516.[2] This means big bucks for Jan: If she sells 99 shares, each a 1% share in the gamble, for $123 apiece, she nets $99 \times \$123 = \$12,177$, to which we add her certainty equivalent of $123.516 for the 1% share she retains; overall, she is ahead by $12,300.516. And she was going to turn down the gamble!

Securitization for Fun and Profit

The story has Jan selling or giving shares to friends and associates who happen to have the same utility function as she. It is unlikely, to say the least, that she would find friends and associates with precisely her utility function. But the basic economic phenomenon illustrated by this story does not depend on finding folks with precisely the same utility function. It simply depends on the property of expected-utility maximizing consumers that we discussed last chapter: As we scale down the risk, the ratio of the certainty equivalent to the EMV goes to one (as long as the EMV of the gamble is positive and the consumer's utility function is smooth at 0.)[3]

So, for any large collection of expected-utility maximizing consumers, a big gamble or prospect or, to use terminology more appropriate to this story, risky venture G can be *securitized*—broken into small shares—and sold in bits and pieces to the consumers for (roughly, in general a bit less than) the EMV of the gamble. The more consumers there are around, on whom small shares can be flogged, the closer the original holder of the prospect can get to recovering the full EMV. This is so even if the owner is risk averse. The owner's original risk aversion is unimportant, since in the end neither the owner nor anyone else bears much of the risk.

The basic idea of risk sharing is one with which you probably are already at

---

[2] Remember from the last chapter: for a consumer whose utility function has constant risk aversion—that is, that has the form $-e^{-\lambda x}$—the maximum the consumer would pay to assume a gamble is the consumer's CE for that gamble alone.

[3] *(This footnote is for folks who like precise arguments and don't mind a bit of math.)* This isn't quite what was said last chapter. There, the condition that the EMV is positive wasn't present, and the statement was that $(EMV(a) - CE(a))/a$ approaches zero as a, the scale factor, approaches zero. But, $EMV(a) = a\,EMV$, so this is the same as $EMV - CE(a)/a \to 0$, or $CE(a)/a \to EMV$, or $CE(a)/(a\,EMV) = CE(a)/EMV(a) \to 1$, which is what I'm claiming here. Of course, to divide by EMV in the last step, it must be that $EMV \neq 0$.

least vaguely familiar, because it is a chief feature of modern capitalist society. Securities markets, where equity, somewhat risky debt, and instruments even more complex than debt or equity are traded, are precisely a manifestation of defeating risk aversion by risk sharing. Rather than have Henry Ford or his heirs bear all the risk of Ford Motor Company, Ford at one point took Ford Motor public, selling shares in this venture to the public, because the public was better able to bear the risk of the venture than he and his heirs could by themselves. New examples appear every day, as privately held companies go public. Entrepreneurs share risk with venture capitalists, who provide capital to a venture in return for a share in the risky proceeds. You might argue that this is more a question of the availability of funds to the entrepreneur (that is, of generating liquidity); but if it were only a question of the availability of funds, then debt contracts, in which the payment to the venture capitalist does not depend on how well the venture does, would be the rule instead of equity arrangements, where the venture capitalist shares in good times and in bad. (Because of the law of limited liability—you cannot collect from a bankrupt— even nominal debt carries some risk, hence provides some risk sharing. But equity arrangements increase the amount of risk sharing, and their relative prevalence indicates that risk sharing is at least part of the motive for the venture capital arrangements we see.) Still another form of risk sharing via securitization are real estate investment trusts, which spread the risk (of both default and early repayment) of holding a single mortgage.

On the other side, when risks that individuals hold have negative expected payouts, we have insurance markets. Think of an individual who owns a house subject to risk of fire damage. Suppose, to keep it very simple, the house is either going to burn to the ground, a loss of $200,000, or not burn at all; and suppose that the probability it will burn to the ground is 0.001 in any given year. The EMV of the gamble facing the house owner is $(0.001)(-\$200,000) + (0.999)(\$0) = -\$200$. But, if the owner is at all risk averse, his or her certainty equivalent is likely to be a good deal more negative. When buying insurance, the owner pays a premium, say, of $300 per year to have the insurance company bear the risk of the $200,000 loss in case of fire. The insurance company is willing to bear this risk for a premium payment of $300 because it is close to risk neutral, and so the premium more than compensates it for the risk it assumes. *And it is close to risk neutral because it shares the risk out over many different shareholders in the company.*

A less obvious form of risk sharing involves futures markets. In the futures market for, say, wheat, one can buy or sell wheat for delivery some months hence. Consider a wheat farmer (he) whose crop is in the ground. This farmer faces two sorts of risks. First are the risks concerning his own yield: Will it rain? Will his fields be attacked by locusts? Second are the risks concerning the value of his harvest when it comes time to sell. If wheat sells $3.00 per bushel today, will its price be $3.00 or $3.30 or $2.70 in 4 months? Note that a $0.30 change in the price of a bushel of wheat means a 10% swing in the farmer's gross revenue, fixing his yield, which would mean an enormous swing in net income. The futures market gives this farmer a chance to "insure" against the second sort of risk, by selling a portion of his crop forward, while it is still in the ground, at a fixed price. On the other side, it allows large purchasers of wheat, such as mills, to buy forward and insure against rising prices.

This is the main message of this chapter. If you spread risk thinly, you defeat risk aversion, and in a world of risks, defeating risk aversion creates value. This is one rationale for securities markets, and it is the overwhelming rationale for futures and insurance markets.

Once you absorb this main message, you are likely to have come to the following conclusions:

1. *Risks should be spread out to such an extent that no risk-averse individual is left holding a substantial fraction of the risk.* (Why? Because if anyone is left holding a substantial fraction of some risk, that person will value the risk at something less than its EMV. Spread it out, and this person will be able to capture the full EMV.)

2. *Therefore, in consequence of conclusion 1, the value of any gamble to its initial holder is just its EMV, since this is its value in the market once it has been securitized and shared out.*

What a wonderful thing it would be if conclusion 2 were true. Having learned all that stuff about utility functions, we could forget about them and use expected monetary values, with the proviso that one should be sure to securitize and spread risk widely.

But, if you look at the real world, conclusion 1 is not true. The Ford family did not sell off all but a small fraction of their shares in Ford Motor Company. In general, many firms have significant fractions held by founders or their families. Other firms have significant fractions held by single investors. We see publicly held companies being taken private, through leveraged buyouts and the like. Why does conclusion 1 fail?

And even supposing conclusion 1 holds, conclusion 2 is not quite right.

The remainder of this chapter explores why conclusion 1 fails and, in cases where it holds, why conclusion 2 is not really right. Then we close with a subject that will be important in later chapters, efficient risk sharing.

19.2. Why Risk Is Not Always Spread Thinly

There are many reasons why conclusion 1 fails:

- There can be differences of opinion about the gamble a particular venture represents. Suppose Jan MBA believes that her gamble will yield $50,000 with probability 0.7 and −$25,000 with probability 0.3, while everyone else in the world thinks the odds are 50–50. Then she cannot sell the shares for more than $125 per percent. But, given her optimistic forecast, even at $125 per percent, she would want to retain 53.54%. (Can you replicate this 53.54%?)

- As something of a twist on the first reason, while the entrepreneur may be able to convince others that she is not unduly optimistic, to do so would compromise her venture. Suppose Jan could convince others that the probability of making $50,000 is 0.7, but doing so would expose her ideas to many potential competitors whose competition would destroy her profitable opportunity. She might then be willing to bear some of the risk of a profitable venture, even if, for the risk sharing she does, she gets less than what she knows to be the full value of the shares she sells.

- By retaining a significant share of a venture, an individual often retains or acquires controlling rights, such as a seat on the board of directors or, for a big enough share, the right to appoint the board. This has a value that may outweigh the gains from risk spreading.

- Transaction costs are associated with securitizing and selling pieces of a gamble. Some are fairly trivial in nature if not in expense, such as the costs of printing the securities, finding customers, and exchanging the shares for money. Beyond these more mundane transaction costs are two categories of transaction costs that are often both significant and subtle: the costs of *adverse selection* and *moral hazard*.

Chapters 20 and 21 concern adverse selection and moral hazard, so I do not give a complete treatment of these issues now. But, in the context of securitization of gambles, let me briefly indicate what are the issues.

Imagine that someone approaches you on the street, wanting to sell you shares in a gold mine. He represents to you that this is a risky venture; the prospectus he offers you gives you information from which you can construct a probability distribution for your returns. But you know that the prospectus is incomplete. Material facts are not given; for instance, the results of some preliminary borings that the seller might have done are not present. So you wonder, Does this individual have information that is pessimistic in terms of the mine's prospects? You should worry about this, because if some gold miners have optimistic private information and others have pessimistic private information, those with pessimistic private information are more apt to want to sell their shares in the venture (see Problem 19.5). In other words, the gold mines being "sold on the street" are apt to be an *adverse selection* of all gold mines, in terms of their prospects.

Or imagine that someone approaches you on the street, wanting to sell you shares in her entrepreneurial venture. The prospectus she offers makes it clear that the returns from this venture depend very significantly on how much effort she puts into the development of the product this venture will produce. And you worry, Once she sells out a significant fraction of the venture, will she be motivated to put in the long, arduous hours needed to make the venture a success? She may promise to do so, but is a promise good enough? Even if you could be sure she would work hard, would she spend the venture's money on fancy rugs for her office, corporate planes, and the like? Would she spend her time and the venture's money creating a spin-off that she would leave to manage, leaving the venture in which you hold shares in the lurch? In this case, you face a *moral hazard*.

To summarize, we can see clear reasons why conclusion 1 fails in some cases. And as long as 1 fails, conclusion 2 is incorrect. If a risk-averse individual bears significant risk, the individual's risk aversion plays a role in determining the overall value of the venture.

19.3. Correlation between Gambles: Why Conclusion 2 Can Fail Even When 1 Holds

As if that were not bad enough, even if conclusion 1 holds, conclusion 2 can fail. The reason is that when a new risk is shared among lots of people, the new risk goes into a portfolio of risks the people already hold.

Imagine a centralized risk-sharing institution. Call it the NYSE or NASDAQ, if you wish. Anyone who has a risky venture can take it to this institution, where it is parceled out in small bits to people around the world. At any point in time, lots of people are holding on to little pieces of a whole lot of risky ventures. These risky ventures are not necessarily independent. Many are entrepreneurial and corporate ventures, most of which have a general tendency to do relatively well when the economy is doing well and relatively poorly when the economy is in recession. Therefore, when we look at the portfolio of risk, composed of many pieces of little ventures, held by any individual, there is some overall or systematic risk to that portfolio.

Along comes a new entrepreneur with some risk to share. If this new risk is independent of the systematic risk in everyone's portfolio, then the marginal impact of a little piece of the new risk on everyone's certainty equivalent is roughly the EMV of the little piece. Then conclusion 2 holds.

However, if this new risk is positively correlated with the value of everyone's portfolio (if it pays off well when, on average, the balance of other risks pay off well, such as when the economy is doing well), then even a little piece of the new risk compounds some of the risk in people's portfolios, and they do not see its incremental value as equal to its expected monetary value; its incremental value is something less.

On the other hand, if this new risk is negatively correlated with the value of everyone's portfolio (if it pays off well when, on average, the balance of other risks are paying off poorly, as might be true of a gold hoarding scheme, because the price of gold tends to rise when the economy is going sour), then the value of a piece of it for everyone can *exceed* its expected monetary value, because it provides insurance.

The point is that the valuation of a particular shared risk, in this world where all risks are shared, has to do with how the particular risk covaries with the risky portfolio all the risk sharers hold. Expected utility, which ignores the benefits of risk sharing altogether, is not right in isolation, and expected monetary value is not right either.

So, what is right? At this point, the modern theory of finance must be consulted. A pillar of the modern theory of finance is the capital asset pricing model (CAPM). Most treatments of the CAPM are done using mean–variance preferences instead of the expected utility framework we use here, but the conclusions of the CAPM (that the value of a share depends on its expected return and the correlation of that return with the market portfolio) is entirely in line with what we see here.

With this as an introduction, we could concentrate on large, perfectly competitive markets where the items for sale are shares in some risk. This becomes the theory of competitive financial markets, the domain of the CAPM, which I leave to your finance courses, books, and instructors. Instead, beginning with next two chapters, we go back to the list of reasons why conclusion 1 fails (why risk is *not* thinly spread): in particular, the problems of adverse selection and moral hazard. To do justice to these topics, one final technical matter concerning risk sharing must be addressed. But first, this is a good opportunity to discuss a specific instance of securitization that helped to *destroy* a whole lot of value.

19.4. Did Securitization Cause the Great Recession?

In 2008, a meltdown in the financial sector of the global economy triggered what has come to be known as the Great Recession, a period of negative to no to slow growth from which, as I write this section in 2015, the economy still has not fully recovered. *What caused the Great Recession?* is a controversial question, with all sorts of different explanations provided by different commentators. And, in my opinion, no single answer is correct; it was a chain of events and weaknesses in the financial system, one piled on top of others, that led to the collapse. But one of the triggering factors was the result of securitization gone bad, and, since I've been painting a picture about how much value is created through risk sharing and securitization, it is probably worthwhile to see how the process can contribute to a disaster.

The risks that were securitized were mortgages and, in a small but ultimately significant amount, subprime mortgages, "subprime" meaning mortgages given to individuals who, under usual standards, posed too high a risk of default.[4]

To create "investment grade" securities out of these mortgages, the following clever bit of securitization was employed. First, a portfolio of, say, 1000 mortgages was created; suppose for simplicity they are all for the same $200K, with an interest rate of 10%, and a monthly payment set to amortize the mortgage in thirty years. Five different securities were created out of the returns from that portfolio. The first security was secured by, say, the 300 "best" mortgages in the portfolio, where "best" was measured in an ex post manner; the second security was secured by the next 200; the third security by the 200 after that; the fourth by the following 200; and the fifth by the 100 worst. It worked this way:[5] Suppose there are 100 shares created out of each of the five levels or, to use the technical term, tranches. When interest + principal payments came in in the first month, suppose all 1000 mortgages "perform." Then each share of the first tranche gets 1/100th of 3/10ths of all the incoming funds; each share of the second tranche gets 1/100th of 2/10ths, and so on. Suppose that, in month 2, two of the borrowers default.[6] This only affects members of the fifth tranche—each share of the fifth tranche gets 1/100th of the monthly payments of 98 mortgages, and the shareholders of this tranche eventually recover a share of whatever is realized from the two unperforming mortgages. The point is that nothing happens to the monthly payments of holders of the first through fourth tranches until the 101st mortgage defaults (or pays off prematurely), and then it is only tranche four that is affected until 300 mortgages are "unperforming."

So, assuming there is virtually no chance that over 700 mortgages will default (or pay off prematurely), the holder of a share of the first tranche has a virtually guaranteed regular flow of monthly payments. If there is only a slight chance that over 500 mortgages will default, except for that slight chance, shareholders of the second tranche can expect regular payments.

This securitization and repackaging of the proceeds from the pool of 1000 mortgages was very attractive to all sorts of institutions. In particular, banks are regulated in a way that increases their demand for assets that are perceived to be safe, and shares of the first and second tranches were widely regarded as extremely safe. (More to the point, the rating agencies declared them to be "investment grade" securities, which is what the banks really required.) The

---

[4] "Subprime" technically was defined as: at a rate 300 basis points over that charged for a conforming mortgage. But this description will do for this story.

[5] I'm simplifying for expositional purposes.

[6] "Not performing" means either (a) in default or (b) paid off prematurely.

market prices for shares in the better tranches were high. A booming business in packaging mortgages in this fashion was created. But to be in this business, one needs a supply of mortgages, and at the level of mortgage origination, incentives were to get folks to take on mortgages, including folks who had no business doing so given their prospects for steady future income. (Indeed, a significant number of mortgage loans that were made *never* performed: The borrower failed to make the *first* payment.) And all those folks with easy mortgage money pushed up the price of houses.

What went wrong? The models built to price these securities and to assess how safe they were, and the data used to assess parameters for these models, did not adequately take into account a variety of factors that made default on mortgages highly correlated. When housing prices fell and the economy began to weaken, loans that were not merely subprime but sub-subprime defaulted in numbers unimagined by the models. Which caused a further weakening in the economy, which exacerbated the problem. When things began to go a bit sour in the economy, these securities acted as amplifiers, and the economy went a lot sour.

That's the trigger. To finish the story, one needs to talk about how this impacted the balance sheets of banks and other financial institutions who were holding all these originally over-valued and more-risky-than-anyone-thought assets, and how that set off further shocks to the global economy (because of how major banks were tied together financially). I won't finish the story, but I do want to draw a moral about securitization. *The nice theoretical constructs of this chapter, concerning how securitization can create value through the sharing of risk, work when and if the individuals buying and selling these securities understand them. In a market where a new kind of security is "selling like hotcakes," manufacturers and purchasers of the securities have neither the time nor the inclination to create the sort of understanding our analysis has assumed. Or, to draw a normative conclusion: before you jump on a financial bullet train, make sure you know where it is going.*

19.5. Efficient Risk Sharing

Suppose we have four individuals: John, Paul, George and Ringo. Each individual has a utility function and evaluates gambles according to their expected utility. The four utility functions might be the same, but I want to think more generally about the case where they are different.

The four face a "joint lottery," described by a probability distribution over dollar prizes. This joint lottery might just be the result of some joint venture they are taking or it might be gotten as the sum of lotteries that each of the four faces individually.

The four decide to form a *risk-sharing syndicate*, where they share the proceeds from their joint lottery. That is, if the lottery gives prizes, say, $1000, $2000, $3000, and −$4000 with probabilities 0.1, 0.2, 0.3, and 0.4, then they must decide on a sharing rule for dividing the outcome among them. One possible sharing rule is equal shares. A second would be to give John twice as much as the others, except if the prize is −$4000, in which case John pays $3000 and the others pay $333.33 each.

What sort of risk-sharing rule should they settle on? Each is probably interested in getting more for himself and less for the others, so we can expect some hard bargaining among them. But, at least ideally, we might hope that the four settle on a so-called *efficient sharing rule*. A sharing rule is efficient if no other rule makes each of the four at least as well off as with the first rule and one (or more) of the four strictly better off than with the first rule.

In general, when all four parties are risk averse, finding the efficient risk-sharing rules can be quite a task. I get to the general procedure in a bit. Alternatively, in simple examples you can use Excel and Solver to solve this sort of problem (see Problem 19.7). But a special case is easier and will be important to things we do in Chapter 21, so we turn first to it.

Ringo is Risk Neutral

Suppose at least one of the parties is risk neutral, and the rest are strictly risk averse. (Someone is strictly risk averse if, for any lottery in which there is nontrivial uncertainty—in which there is positive probability of two or more different prizes—the individual's certainty equivalent for the gamble is less than the EMV of the gamble. In terms of utility functions, a strictly risk-averse utility function is strictly concave, with no linear pieces at all.) In particular, suppose Ringo is the one risk neutral party. Then *every efficient risk-sharing rule gives John, George, and Paul payoffs that are constant; that is, that don't change with the outcome. Ringo absorbs all the risk.*

In symbols, in any efficient sharing scheme, John gets some fixed amount of money y_J, Paul gets y_P, George gets y_G, and Ringo gets what is left over. In our example, Ringo gets $1000 − y_J − y_P − y_G$ with probability 0.1, $2000 − y_J − y_P − y_G$ with probability 0.2, $3000 − y_J − y_P − y_G$ with probability 0.3, and −$4000 − y_J − y_P − y_G$ with probability 0.4. The four must negotiate the amounts y_J, y_P, and y_G, but any scheme that does not give the three fixed payments and load all the risk on Ringo is inefficient. (And any sharing rule where Ringo absorbs all the risk—that is, for any values of y_J, y_P, and y_G—is efficient.)

Why is this? Take any risk-sharing rule in which John bears some risk. Change the rule as follows: Give John a payment equal to the EMV of his share, no matter what is the outcome, taking this from Ringo; and give Ringo John's old share in addition to whatever he had before, less the EMV of John's share that he gives to John. Since Ringo is risk neutral, this change does not affect his overall expected utility; he gave away the EMV of the extra risk he takes on, which to him is a net wash. George and Paul are unaffected. But John is better off, since he replaces a gamble with its EMV; since he is strictly risk averse, he strictly prefers the EMV of any gamble to taking the gamble.

To summarize (and generalize a bit), when we have risk sharing among some people, some of whom are risk averse and others of whom are risk neutral, the efficient thing to do is to load all the risk on the risk-neutral folks.

Efficient Risk Sharing in General

What if none of the parties is risk neutral? I do not try to give complete answers or explain fully the answers I give, but we can make some progress on this. (This material will prove tough for readers without strong mathematical skills. If you do not follow this, it does not matter to anything we do in the balance of this book. But having devoted so much time to bang-for-the-buck stuff in earlier chapters, it seems a shame not to harvest a result here.) Let me be a bit more general in my notation: This syndicate has I members, each of whom is a expected utility maximizer. The utility function of the ith person is written u_i. I assume that each of these individuals is risk averse, with risk neutrality included as a special case, which means that each u_i is a concave function. I also assume that each u_i is strictly increasing and differentiable and write u'_i for the derivative of u_i. Because each u_i is a concave function, this means that u'_i is a nonincreasing function. Because each u_i is strictly increasing (and concave), u'_i is strictly positive at all its arguments.

I assume that this syndicate holds a joint risky venture with total payoffs Y^1, Y^2, ..., or Y^N, with respective probabilities p^1, ..., p^N. (Note that superscripts enumerate the payoffs and subscripts enumerate the members of the syndicate. Also, make a special note that the ps are probabilities, not prices.)

A sharing rule for the syndicate in this notation is an array of numbers $\{y_i^n\}$ for $i = 1, \ldots, I$ and $n = 1, \ldots, N$, where y_i^n is the share or payoff for member i if the total payoff is Y^n. The sum of the shares should equal the total, or $\sum_{i=1}^{I} y_i^n = Y^n$ for each n.

A sharing rule $\{y_i^n\}$ is efficient if and only if, for each i and j from 1 to I and for each m and n from 1 to N,

$$\frac{u'_i(y_i^n)}{u'_i(y_i^m)} = \frac{u'_j(y_j^n)}{u'_j(y_j^m)}. \tag{$\star$}$$

Why? This is the bang-for-the-buck logic of earlier chapters at work. Fix two of the members of the syndicate, i and j. Hold fixed the sharing rules for everyone else in the syndicate and ask, If we hold j's expected utility constant (the constraint), what does it take to maximize the expected utility of i? Pick two outcomes, Y^m and Y^n. The contribution to i's expected utility of i's shares in these two states is

$$p^n u_i(y_i^n) + p^m u_i(y_i^m).$$

The contribution to j's expected utility of her shares is the same expression, but with j replacing i. So the marginal impact on i's expected utility of y_i^n is $p^n u_i'(y_i^n)$. Since a dollar more in state n for i is a dollar less for j (since everyone else's share is held fixed), the marginal impact on j's expected utility of y_i^n is $-p^n u_j'(y_j^n)$. The first marginal impact is the marginal impact on the objective (maximize i's expected utility). The second is the marginal impact on the constraint (hold j's expected utility at some fixed level). So, by bang-for-the-buck logic, the ratio of these two marginal impacts in state n should equal the ratio in state m, which, after canceling the probabilities in the numerator and denominator, is precisely the ratio condition $(\star)$.

I close with three remarks:

1. Suppose one member of the syndicate, say, number 1, is risk neutral. This means that his utility function is linear; that is, the derivative of his utility function is constant. Therefore, for any efficient sharing rule, the ratio of the derivatives of the utility function of any other member of the syndicate, evaluated at any two of her shares, must be 1. Which means, if this other member is strictly risk averse (if her utility function is strictly concave), she must get a constant amount of money no matter what is the total payoff. In other words, the special case of a risk-neutral Ringo is a corollary to the general case.

2. If you are a frustrated mathematician, here is a challenge: What is the form of efficient risk sharing when all members of the syndicate have constant risk aversion; that is, when $u_i(x) = -e^{-\lambda_i x}$ for each i? It is really not that hard if you use the equal-bangs-for-the-buck ratio condition.

3. Throughout this discussion, members of the syndicate have agreed about the probabilities of the different payoffs. Efficient risk sharing gets more complex when syndicate members disagree about the likelihood of the different outcomes. To see how this works, consult R. Wilson, "The Theory of Syndicates," *Econometrica*, 1968.

Executive Summary

- If you spread the risk of a gamble, giving a small share to each of many different risk-averse folks, since each share represents only a little risk, each share is worth nearly the expected monetary value (EMV) of the share to its holder. Thus, the value of the gamble becomes nearly the sum of the EMVs of its shares, which is just the EMV of the original gamble.

- This idea (that risk spreading promotes value) is the raison d'être for all sorts of financial and insurance markets.

- However, if the shares are correlated with the portfolio of risks other folks hold, the value of the shares depends on that correlation. If the shares are uncorrelated, their value is their EMV. If the shares have positive correlation with the portfolio of other risks, their value is less than their EMV; if the correlation is negative, their value exceeds their EMV. A fully worked-out version of this idea is the capital asset pricing model, a pillar of modern finance.

- There are good reasons why it is hard to spread thinly all risks. Two of the most important categories of reasons—and the topics to which we move in the two chapters that follow—are problems of adverse selection and moral hazard.

- The general problem of efficient risk sharing (taking a given gamble and parceling it out efficiently among a fixed set of individuals) is quite complex. But, when one of the parties is risk neutral and the others are strictly risk averse, efficient risk sharing is simple: The risk-neutral party assumes all the risk.

Problems

These problems generally require the use of Excel spreadsheets and Solver. If you find that you cannot build the required spreadsheets on your own, in several of the problems I suggest a particular sheet of a spreadsheet to consult, to get started without seeing the entire answer.

19.1 Consider the plight of Jan MBA, who owns a gamble with two equally likely prizes, \$50,000 and −\$25,000. Jan is an expected utility maximizer with utility function $u(x) = -e^{-0.0000211x}$. As we learned in the text, this gamble gives Jan a negative certainty equivalent. Suppose Jan was able to give away some percentage of this gamble. If θ is the percentage she retains, she then owns a gamble with equally likely prizes \$50,000θ and −\$25,000θ.

(a) How does Jan's certainty equivalent change as a function of θ, the fraction she retains? Create a graph of this function.

(b) What percentage retained by Jan maximizes her certainty equivalent?

(c) Write $CE(\theta)$ for the function that gives Jan's CE as a function of θ. What is the slope of the function $CE(\theta)$ at the argument $\theta = 0$?

19.2 Suppose Jan from Problem 19.1 tries to sell an α share of the gamble to a risk-averse expected-utility maximizer. No risk-averse person would pay "full EMV price," or \$12,500α, for an α share (as long as $\alpha > 0$), but if Jan sets a target of getting back 95% or 98% or some percentage less than 100% of $12,500 α for an α share, she might succeed, if α is small enough.

(a) Suppose Jan has an associate with (essentially) the same utility function as she, $-e^{-0.0000211x}$. Would this associate buy a 10% share of Jan's gamble for 95% of 10% of the full EMV? (The answer is No, and the real point of this is to get started on what comes next.)

(b) Jan is set on obtaining 95% of the EMV of the gamble, so rather than lowering the price to her associate in part a, she decides to decrease the share she will sell to him. What is the largest share α Jan can sell to her associate at a price of 95% of $12,500 α? Assume he buys as long as his CE for the full transaction is greater or equal to 0.

(c) Redo part b, if Jan decides to try for 98% of the EMV of the gamble. And find the shares needed to get either 98% or 95% of the EMV, if Jan sells to a second associate, whose utility function is $e^{-0.00001x}$. (Is this second associate more or less risk averse than the first?)

(d) (Optional, and the last part is difficult.) A third associate of Jan has utility function $u(x) = \sqrt{x + 50,000}$, where x is the associate's net from the transaction with Jan. Answer the questions of part c for this associate. Then evaluate, for this utility function u, the ratio $-u''(x)/u'(x)$ at the value $x = 0$. What does this tell you?

19.3   Suppose Jan MBA is convinced that her gamble will pay $50,000 with probability 0.7 (and lose $25,000 with probability 0.3). But everyone else in the world thinks the two probabilities are 0.5 and 0.5. Because of the latter fact, Jan can sell shares in her venture for no more than $125 per 1% (actually, she gets a bit less than this). Suppose, being very optimistic, she can get $125 per percent. What percentage share of her gamble would she wish to retain?

19.4   Jan MBA's gamble does indeed pay off $50,000 with probability 0.7 (and loses $25,000 with probability 0.3). But to sell shares in her venture, Jan has to reveal some of the details of her venture. She can sell up to 10% of her venture without compromising too many details; if she sells 10% or less, the probability of the $50,000 outcome remains 0.7. But, if she sells between 10 and 30%, the details revealed may get to her competition; her chances of getting the $50,000 payoff are only 0.65. If she sells more than 30% but no more than 50%, the probability of the $50,000 outcome falls to 0.6. And if she sells more than 50% of her venture, the probability of the $50,000 outcome falls to 0.5.

Assume that, whatever share of the venture Jan sells, she gets 95% of the appropriate EMV. That is, if she sells 25% of the venture, she gets 95% of 25% of (0.65)($50,000) + (0.35)(−$25,000). What percentage share retained by Jan maximizes her certainty equivalent?

19.5 Consider the following market in equity shares in entrepreneurial ventures:

- Each share represents a 1% share in a venture.

- Each venture will pay off either $50,000 or −$25, 000 (and there is no limited liability, so if you hold a share in a venture that loses $25,000, you must remit $250).

- Each venture (of which there are many) is controlled by an entrepreneur. Entrepreneurs are all risk-averse expected-utility maximizers and, for simplicity, all of them have the utility function $u(x) = -e^{-0.0000211x}$, where x is the proceeds to the entrepreneur from sales of shares in her venture, plus the returns from any share she retains.

- Half the ventures have probability 0.65 of being successful (returning $50,000), while the other half have probability 0.35 of success. Each entrepreneur knows the probability of success of her own venture, but she cannot directly communicate that information to investors.

- A price per 1% share in any venture is established by supply-equals-demand at p. The different ventures carry no systematic risk and so demand for shares is at the expected monetary value of each share. The supply of shares comes from entrepreneurs who, taking p as given, decide how big a fraction of their venture to sell and how big a fraction to retain.

(a) Since half the ventures have probability 0.65 of success and half have probability 0.35, a chance of a successful outcome for a randomly selected venture is 0.5. The expected payoff from a randomly selected venture is therefore $12,500. But $p = \$125$ is not an equilibrium in the share market (assuming investors are sophisticated). Why not?

(b) Is there a price p per 1% share that gives an equilibrium in this equity market? What is p?

(c) Suppose the equity market had two "tiers." If an entrepreneur retains a fraction q or greater of the shares in her venture, she will be paid $\$\overline{p}$ for the shares she does sell. But if she retains fewer than the fraction q, she is paid $\$\underline{p}$ per shares she does sell, where $\overline{p} > \underline{p}$. Can you construct an equilibrium of this sort for this equity market?

19.6 Jan, Joe, and Jess MBA each own a gamble with equally likely outcomes of $50,000 and −$25,000. Each is attempting to sell 1% shares to friends and associates. But all the friends and associates of these three already possess portfolios that have some risk.

Specifically, imagine that Jan, Joe, and Jess approach Biff, who is an expected utility maximizer with utility function $u(x) = -e^{-0.00002x}$. Biff owns a risky portfolio, the value of which will be either $2 million or $1.8 million, each with probability $1/2$. If you do the computations required, you'll find that Biff's certainty equivalent is \$1,833,873.

If Biff buys a 1% share from any of Jan, Joe, or Jess, this is added to his current risky portfolio; that is, assuming he buys only one 1% share (an assumption we maintain in this problem), the possible outcomes for him are wealth levels of \$2,000,500, \$1,999,750, \$1,800,500, and \$1,799,750.

The differences between the gambles of Jan, Joe, and Jess concern how they co-vary with Biff's initial wealth portfolio. Specifically, Jan's gamble has outcomes independent of Biff's initial portfolio. Joe's gamble is positively correlated with Biff's portfolio. And Jess's gamble is negatively correlated. Even more specifi-cally, conditional on Biff's initial portfolio being worth \$2 million, Joe's gamble pays off \$50,000 with probability 0.6, while Jess's gamble pays off \$50,000 with probability 0.4.

What is the most Biff will pay for a 1% share of Jan's gamble, Joe's gamble, Jess's gamble?

19.7   John, Paul, George, and Ringo are partners in a venture that has four possible outcomes: \$100,000 with probability 0.4, \$200,000 with probability 0.3, \$300,000 with probability 0.2, and \$400,000 with probability 0.1. The Fab Four (as they are known to their business associates) must decide how to divide the results of their venture. Up to this point, they planned to divide the money equally, so, for instance, if the outcome is \$300,000, each would walk away with \$75,000.

(a) Each of the four is an expected-utility maximizer, but they have quite different utility functions (and thus attitudes toward risk):

- John's utility function is $u_{\text{John}}(x) = \sqrt{x}$, where x is John's net proceeds from this venture (and similarly for Paul, George, and Ringo)

- Paul's utility function is $u_{\text{Paul}}(x) = \sqrt{x + 100{,}000}$.

- George's utility function is $u_{\text{George}}(x) = x^{0.3333}$.

- Ringo's utility function is $u_{\text{Ringo}}(x) = -e^{-0.00001x}$.

If we give them equal-division shares, their certainty equivalents would be, respectively, \$46,968.70, \$48,994.62, \$45,925.83, and \$47,041.85. These are com-puted via Excel; see Figure 19.1.

This does not seem efficient to Ringo, who wonders if there is not some better way to split the proceeds from the venture. Ringo wishes to know, assuming we give John, Paul, and George payoff shares that leave them, respectively, at the certainty equivalent levels \$46,968.70, \$48,994.62, and \$45,925.83, how high can we push Ringo's certainty equivalent? Answer this question for Ringo. (Warn-

		State 1	State 2	State 3	State 4
	Total	$100,000	$200,000	$300,000	$400,000
Shares	John	$25,000	$50,000	$75,000	$100,000
	Paul	$25,000	$50,000	$75,000	$100,000
	George	$25,000	$50,000	$75,000	$100,000
	Ringo	$25,000	$50,000	$75,000	$100,000
	Probabilities	0.4	0.3	0.2	0.2
Utilities	John	159.114	223.607	273.861	316.228
	Paul	353.554	387.293	418.330	447.213
	George	29.2302	36.827	42.1559	46.2981
	Ringo	-0.7789	-0.6065	-0.4724	-0.3679

	Expected utility	Certainty equivalent
John	216.7226	$46,968.70
Paul	385.9982	$48,994.62
George	35.8112	$45,925.83
Ringo	-0.6247	$47,041.85

Figure 19.1. Problem 19.7. Calculating the CE's of the Fab Four, for the equal-division sharing rule. This spreadsheet calculates expected utilities and certainty equivalents for John, Paul, George, and Ringo, assuming they split the proceeds from their venture in equal shares.

ing: I had some problems getting Solver to work on this problem. Everything worked once I asked for *Automatic Scaling* under the *Options* menu.)

(b) Suppose Ringo is risk neutral and John, Paul, and George are all as in part a of the problem. This would mean that Ringo's CE from the equal-division shares would be not $47,041.85, but instead $(0.4)(25,000) + (0.3)(50,000) + (0.2)(75,000) + (0.1)(100,000) = \$50,000$. It seems unfair that Ringo has such a large CE while John, Paul, and George all have CEs under $49,000, so the Fab Four are looking for a scheme that gives John, Paul, and George CE's of at least $50,000, while making Ringo as well off as possible. What sharing-rule scheme accomplishes this (and how well off can we make Ringo)?

20. Hidden Information: Adverse Selection, Signaling, and Screening

When one party in a potential transaction has information that affects the value of the transaction to the second party, the second party must take this into account. In the worst-case scenario, this asymmetry in information may cause the transaction to fail, despite being desirable to both parties. The term *adverse selection* is commonly used to describe this situation, especially in the context of insurance markets, but the phenomenon goes well beyond the context of insurance. Partial "solutions" include screening, where the uninformed party sets conditions that lead the informed party to reveal her information, and signaling, where the informed party takes the lead in information revelation.

In Parts II and IV of this book, we were concerned with transactions between parties where information relevant to both parties was shared. But in a wide variety of potential transactions, one party has information that is both relevant to the potential trading partner and hidden from him.

- When you contemplate buying a used car from a previous owner, the seller is likely to know a lot more about problems the car might have than do you.

- When an individual approaches an insurance company, asking for an enormous term life insurance policy, the company must worry that the individual is coming directly from her doctor's office at which she received unhappy news about her future prospects.

- When an investor is approached by an entrepreneur who is seeking individuals to invest in the entrepreneur's venture, the investor must wonder what the entrepreneur knows about the venture's prospects that is not being shared in the prospectus.

In each of these cases, the parties involved might use information revelation of one sort or another to defuse the concerns of the party who lacks the information: if you are selling a high-quality used car, you might pay for an independent inspection company (in the United States, for instance, Carfax) to prepare a report on your vehicle; the insurance company requires a physical exam; the investor is careful to do plenty of due diligence before investing. The informed party may take other actions to reassure the uninformed party; for instance, the seller of a used car may offer a six-month limited warranty. The uninformed party may structure the transaction to provide reassurance, as when an insurance company offers life insurance but with "limited benefits for the first two years."

This is a broad topic with many variations, but we can (at least) capture the main ideas here.

20.1. An Illustrative Example

To illustrate the basic ideas, we go back to Problem 19.5: Consider the following market in equity shares in entrepreneurial ventures.

- Each share represents a 1% share in a venture.

- Each venture will pay off either $50,000 or −$25, 000 (and there is no limited liability, so if you hold a share in a venture that loses $25,000, you must remit $250).

- Each venture (of which there are many) is controlled by an entrepreneur. Entrepreneurs are all risk-averse expected-utility maximizers and, for simplicity, all of them have the utility function $u(x) = -e^{-0.0000211x}$, where x is the proceeds to the entrepreneur from sales of shares in her venture, plus the returns from any share she retains.

- Half the ventures have probability 0.65 of being successful (returning $50,000), while the other half have probability 0.35 of success. Each entrepreneur knows the probability of success of her own venture, but she cannot directly communicate that information to investors.

- A price per 1% share in any venture is established by supply-equals-demand at p. The different ventures carry no systematic risk, so demand for shares is at the expected monetary value of each share. The supply of shares comes from entrepreneurs who, taking p as given, decide how big a fraction of their venture to sell and how big a fraction to retain.

Why won't a price per 1% share of $125 be an equilibrium in this market? Because while the "average venture" in this population has a success probability of 0.5 (or, more precisely, a randomly selected venture has a 50% chance of having a success probability of 0.65 and a 50% chance of having a success probability of 0.35), the "average share" in the equity market does not do that well. Suppose you are an entrepreneur with one of the good projects. What fraction of your venture do you wish to sell at a price of $125 per 1% share? Certainly not all your shares; your venture has an EMV of (0.65)($50,000) + (0.35)(−$25,000) = $23,750, so a 1% share has an EMV of $237.50. This doesn't mean that such an entrepreneur won't want to sell some of her shares. But we have to resort to Excel and Solver to find out how many.

Figure 20.1 shows an Excel spreadsheet that does this. Panel a shows the spreadsheet constructed: The probability of the success of the project (cell A3), the price per 1% share (B3), and coefficient of risk aversion of the entrepreneur (F3) are all entered as constants. The share retained by the entrepreneur (in cell

C3) is the driving variable; I begin with 50% retained. The net proceeds to the entrepreneur as a function of the price per 1% and the share she retains in the two cases are computed; they are converted to utilities, the expected utility is computed (cell I3) using the probability of the good outcome, and the expected utility is inverted (cell J3) to find the certainty equivalent. Then I ask Solver to maximize the certainty equivalent varying the share retained (C3), and Solver returned panel b: The entrepreneur chooses to retain 39.12% of her venture.

	A	B	C	D	E	F	G	H	I	J
1	prob success	price per 1% share	share retained	good outcome result	bad outcome result	coeff of risk aversion	good outcome utility	bad outcome utility	expected utility	certainty equivalent
2										
3	0.65	$125.00	50.00%	$31,250.00	-$6,250.00	0.0000211	-0.517174	-1.140966	-0.735501	$14,559.38

(a) Finding EU and CE for a given share retained

	A	B	C	D	E	F	G	H	I	J
1	prob success	price per 1% share	share retained	good outcome result	bad outcome result	coeff of risk aversion	good outcome utility	bad outcome utility	expected utility	certainty equivalent
2										
3	0.65	$125.00	39.12%	$27,169.18	-$2,169.18	0.0000211	-0.563679	-1.046833	-0.732783	$14,734.85

(b) The optimal share to retain

Figure 20.1. At a price of $125 per 1% share, how much will an entrepreneur with a good project—one with probability 0.65 of the good outcome—retain.

What about an entrepreneur with a project whose probability of success is only 0.35? We could repeat the spreadsheet analysis just done but, in fact, the answer is obvious. This entrepreneur knows that the EMV of her project is $0.65 \times$ $\$50,000 + 0.35 \times (-\$25,000) = \$1250$. Since the market (we are hypothesizing) is willing to pay, up front, $125 per 1% share, and since the entrepreneur is risk averse, this entrepreneur will of course sell 100% of her venture.

This means that the shares "in the market" are an *adverse selection* of all the shares there are. To be concrete, suppose there are 100 of these entrepreneurs, 50 of each type. For the 50 entrepreneurs with good projects, they put 61 (or so) 1% shares into the market. The 50 entrepreneurs put 100 1% shares into the market. So the total number of shares in the market is

$$(50)(61) + (50)(100) = 8050,$$

of which 5000, or roughly 62% are shares of bad ventures. If you purchase one of these shares at random, the chance you'll get a good outcome is not 50% but

$$(0.62)(0.35) + (0.38)(0.65) = 0.4635,$$

and so the EMV from a 1% share randomly bought in the market is

$$(0.4635)(500) + (0.5365)(-250) = \$97.64.$$

Paying $125 for one of these shares is too much.

Where does supply equal demand? To answer this question, we must do the following:

1. For each price p, find out what fraction of shares each type of entrepreneur will retain and what fraction they will put in the market.

2. Use the answers found in step 1 to compute the EMV of an average 1% share in the market.

3. The assumption on the demand side of the market is that there is enough investors to "soak up" all the shares provided, *if* they are priced at their EMV or less. If p is less than the EMV of the "average" share in the market, competition among investors will push the price up to that EMV. If p exceeds the EMV, investors won't buy any shares at all. So supply will equal demand at the price p where the answer to step 2 is the price p used in step 1.

Do not sail blithely by what you just read. What I'm asserting will be an equilibrium in this market is quite subtle. In particular, I'm assuming that investors, either through tremendous insight and knowledge or, more likely, through experience, understand how the price p will affect the selection of shares in the market and, therefore, the EMV of a randomly selected share. That is a big assumption; in fact, in real-life financial markets, and especially in markets in innovative financial instruments, investor expectations can probably be expected to trail reality to some extent.

But, if you buy my notion of what is an equilibrium, we can find the value of p that equilibrates supply and demand. I'm helped by the fact that there are only two types of entrepreneur and, as long as the price p is above $12.50, entrepreneurs with bad projects will want to sell 100% of their projects. So I only need to discover the share retained by entrepreneurs with good projects.

See Table 20.1. This provides data from another spreadsheet in which I replicated (in successive rows) the row of computations in Figure 20.1, varying the price per 1% share; I looked at $125, $120, $115, and so forth. Then I used Solver to find the share the good-project entrepreneurs would retain as the price per 1% share changes; in the third column of Table 20.1, I give the results of the row-by-row optimization. Note that as the price per 1% share decreases, the share retained by good entrepreneurs increases, which means (in the fourth column in Table 20.1) that the proportion of shares in the market that are from good projects decreases. This is adverse selection at work with a vengeance. Hence, the average probability of a good outcome and the EMV of a randomly selected 1% share of a venture (selected from those shares that supplied to the market) decreases. The final column of Table 20.1 shows the EMV of an average 1% share in the market. *And the equilibrium is where the EMV of an average 1% share in the market equals the price of that 1% share.* Somewhere between $p = \$85$ and $p = \$80$, and probably pretty close to $p = \$85$, the EMV of the average 1% share "catches up" to the price per share. That is our equilibrium price p.

Probability of success	Price per 1%	Share retained	Proportion of shares that are good	Average probability of a good outcome	EMV of average 1% share
0.65	$125	39.12%	0.378427	0.463528	$97.65
0.65	$120	40.80%	0.371847	0.461554	$96.17
0.65	$115	42.49%	0.365124	0.459537	$94.65
0.65	$110	44.18%	0.358251	0.457475	$93.11
0.65	$105	45.86%	0.35122	0.455366	$91.52
0.65	$100	47.56%	0.344022	0.453207	$89.90
0.65	$95	49.25%	0.33665	0.450995	$88.25
0.65	$90	50.95%	0.329093	0.448728	$86.55
0.65	$85	52.65%	0.321343	0.446403	$84.80
0.65	$80	54.36%	0.313389	0.444017	$83.01
0.65	$75	56.07%	0.30522	0.441566	$81.17
0.65	$70	57.79%	0.296822	0.439047	$79.29

Table 20.1. Finding the equilibrium price p.

Can we find a different equilibrium, where entrepreneurs are paid a higher price for their shares if they "prove" they have good projects by holding on to a fraction of their ventures? This question is inspired by the following observation: savvy investors—and it doesn't take a lot of savviness in this case—when going to buy a share in a venture, observe that shares in ventures whose entrepreneurs retain a signficant fraction of their ventures do very well, with good outcomes 65% of the time. So investors compete for shares in these ventures, bidding the price of 1% shares in such ventures to $237.50 (the EMV of a 1% share in a venture that succeeds with probability 0.65). And, at the same time, they shun shares in ventures whose entrepreneurs put 100% of their ventures on the market, since those ventures succeed only 35% of the time: the price of 1% shares in those ventures falls to $12.50.

There is, however, a problem with this: as the price of shares in ventures where the entrepreneur retains a large share of her venture rise toward $237.50 per share, the entrepreneurs want to sell off an increasing share of their ventures. When the price reaches $237.50, they want to sell off 100% of their ventures (why?), and they can no longer be distinguished from the bad-venture entrepreneurs.

So, to make this work, investors must structure their offers as follows: if an entrepreneur is willing to retain $X\%$ of her venture (for some X still to be determined), investors will pay her $237.50 per 1% share. If the entrepreneur is unwilling to retain this much, she is paid only $12.50 per 1% share.

The key to this *signaling* or *separating* equilibrium is the answer to the following question: How big must X be, so that entrepreneurs with bad projects don't want to pretend to be good entrepreneurs, in order to get the much better price for their shares? This equilibrium only works if good entrepreneurs are willing to retain $X\%$ to prove they are good, but for bad entrepreneurs, sending this signal is more costly than it is worth.

So how do we find X? Our attention shifts to the bad-project entrepreneurs. If they fail to retain $X\%$ of their ventures, they will sell 100% of their ventures at $12.50 per 1%, for a net $1250. Now look at Table 20.2.

Share retained	Expected utility	Certainty equivalent
0%	-0.6058	$23,750.00
10%	-0.6371	$21,367.23
20%	-0.6736	$18,728.56
30%	-0.7157	$15,849.78
40%	-0.7642	$12,747.99
50%	-0.8194	$9,441.00
60%	-0.8821	$5,946.81
70%	-0.9530	$2,283.21
71%	-0.9605	$1,908.20
72%	-0.9682	$1,531.69
73%	-0.9760	$1,153.69
74%	-0.9838	$774.22

Table 20.2. *Finding a fraction to retain that is "too much" for the bad-project entrepreneurs, in the separating equilibrium.* See text for explanation.

This shows the certainty equivalents for a bad-project entrepreneur as she retains an increasing fraction of her project, supposing she can sell shares at $237.50 per 1%. Table 2 does this for every 10% up to 70% and then for every 1% (beyond 70%) up to 74%. The important rows are the rows for 72% and 73% retained. Recall that a bad-project entrepreneur's certainty equivalent for selling 100% of her venture at $12.50 per 1% share is $1250. So *if*, by retaining 72%, she could get the "good price" of $237.50 per 1%, she would rather do that. But if it takes retaining 73% to get the "good price," she would rather settle for selling 100% of her venture for $12.50 per 1%.

This provides us with an alternative to the pooling equilibrium, where all shares sell for around $85. Investors are willing to pay $237.50 per 1% share to any entrepreneur who retains 73% of her venture. They are willing to pay $12.50 per share to entrepreneurs who are not willing to do this. The bad-project entrepreneurs settle for selling 100% of their ventures, while the good-project entrepreneurs are willing to retain 73%; you can compute that this gives each of the good-project entrepreneurs a certainty equivalent of $16,089.20. And since the two types *separate* themselves by their choice of how much to retain, the prices of $237.50 in one case and $12.50 in the other are market-equilibrium prices.

Which of these two market equilibria are preferred by the entrepreneurs? The bad-project entrepreneurs prefer to be *pooled*; in the pooling equilibrium they get around $85 per 1% share, for a net $8500, versus the $1250 they get in the separating equilibrium. The good-project entrepreneurs, on the other hand, prefer the separating equilibrium in which they net a certainty equivalent of $16,089.20; if all shares go for $85, a good-project entrepreneur would want to retain 52.65% of her project, for a certainty equivalent of $12,569.69. (You can find the 52.65% figure in Table 20.1, but you must do some further calculations to get the certainty-equivalent figure.)

20.2. What Drives This Model

The toy model just presented captures, in a *relatively* simple and stylized model (relative to the real world—the model is pretty subtle), the basic ideas of adverse selection and signaling/screening. A market is established in which some good changes hands or some service is provided. One side of the market—typically, the seller when the market is in a good and the buyer when a service is involved—has superior information about the quality of the good/the cost of the service. And we look first for a market price for the good or service that works for all the transactions at once—goods of all qualities and services of all cost levels are bought and sold at that single price.

From the perspective of the uninformed party, the market price must reflect the average quality or cost of the transaction. If you are buying a used car, you worry that the car you buy might be a lemon, although it could be a peach, so you are willing to pay some average of what you would pay if you knew the car's quality, an average based on the percentages of lemons and peaches that are "in the market." If you are selling life insurance, the premia you charge reflects the odds that the person buying the policy may live for a long time (good for you) or may pass on to a better place tomorrow.

The informational asymmetry—the fact that the "other" side has information—kicks in here. The owners of great used cars, unhappy at being paid a price that is appropriate for an average car, keep their car for another few years. Someone in robust good health, unhappy at paying a premium that "subsidizes" people with not much time left to live, decides not to buy insurance at all or, at least, to buy only a little. Meanwhile, the owners of bad cars—lemons—rush to the market to sell their cars, and individuals who just got bad news from their doctors call their insurance brokers.

Hence the "selection" of cars for sale and customers seeking life insurance policies is an adverse selection of the entire population. The price of used cars and life insurance adjusts to that adverse selection. This lowers the desirability of selling a good used car or the health status of someone willing to buy life insurance, so the selection of goods in the market/clients buying insurance becomes still more adverse, pushing prices further down and premia further up. An equilibria can be reached, as in our example, although in very stark examples (as in the seminal paper on this subject by George Akerlof[1]), this can cause the market to collapse almost entirely: see Problem 20.1.

Even when markets don't collapse entirely, this phenomenon leads to inefficiencies, even though markets are "competitive" in the sense that buyers and sellers are price takers. In the stylized example, efficient risk sharing would have the risk-averse entrepreneurs off-loading all the risk of their ventures onto risk-neutral investors. At the equilibrium price of $85 or so, entrepreneurs with good projects choose to hold over half their ventures.

20.3. Information

The obvious "cure" for these ills is to level the informational playing field. This is done in a variety of fashions:

Freely Available Relevant Information

Relevant information is sometimes freely available, if the uninformed party knows where to look. Demographic information is often used in this manner. For instance, age and sex are important statistical indicators of mortality rates, useful to someone selling life insurance. If you are hiring for a rurally located plant, you might avoid young women, in the belief that they are more apt to get married or have children and then quit. (Please finish reading this section before deciding I am a male chauvinist.) Banks that sell mortgages sometimes engage in redlining (refusing to make loans on houses within certain geographical districts) because the default rate for homes inside the red line has been high.

The use of demographic information in this manner is widespread, so much so that three cautions are in order.

1. The basic statistical hypothesis can be incorrect, and the nature of the decision precludes learning this. For instance, professional partnerships sometimes discriminate against younger women in both initial hiring and promotion decisions, citing higher quit rates for family reasons. But careful empirical investigation does not support this hypothesis. Organizations that discriminate against women do not learn this, however, because too

---

[1] G. Akerlof, "The Market for Lemons: Quality Uncertainty and the Market Mechanism," *Quarterly Journal of Economics*, Vol. 89, 1970, 488-500. Akerlof won the Nobel Prize in Economics in 2001 for this work.

few women are hired or promoted to test the hypothesis. Compounding this are standard cognitive biases associated with making inferences from data: An organization that promotes only a few women and then sees one quit for family reasons might well overprocess this one piece of data, relative to its true statistical value.

2. Such hypotheses can be self-generating. Take a professional partnership that chooses not to promote young women to partner because of a perception that young women are more prone to drop out for family reasons. The partnership makes this choice because, it claims, it sees this pattern of behavior among its young woman associates. But this can be a vicious cycle: Young woman associates may be more likely to drop out precisely because they (correctly) perceive that this organization is less likely to promote them. Or, in the case of redlining, if mortgage seekers inside the redlined area are forced to take loans with higher interest rates because of the perception that they are more likely to default, they may actually default more frequently because of the higher interest rates.

3. This form of discrimination raises substantial legal and ethical questions. Is it fair to judge individuals based on membership in a demographic class that they can't control? Also, in response to its pernicious social effects, laws banning this form of discrimination are often enacted.

Legally Mandated Information

Direct and relevant information is sometimes available by legal or legislative mandate. For instance, good-faith disclosure of relevant information is required in the sale of real property: the owners of houses, who presumably know a lot about the hidden defects of the property, must disclose all known defects. An extremely important example is the legal requirement for publicly traded firms to disclose relevant financial information to protect potential investors. Of course, spectacular cases such as Enron show that legal requirements to provide information do not guarantee that the information will be revealed or revealed in an informative fashion. The Financial Accounting Standards Board in the United States and the International Accounting Standards Board more generally are usually in a "catch-up" role, trying to craft informative standards for innovative business practices.

Information Required by an Independent Authority

Informed parties sometimes provide direct and relevant information to gain the certification of an independent authority. For instance, to be listed for trading on the New York Stock Exchange, firms must "voluntarily" reveal information beyond that required by government regulation. I put *voluntarily* in quotes here because the voluntary action is the decision by the firm to seek a listing on the NYSE; once that decision is made, the firm must reveal information about itself.

Information Provided (Somewhat) Voluntarily and the Unraveling Argument

The final category is information provided voluntarily. For instance, when screening prospective employees, the employer might decide that possession of a high school diploma is a good signal of the employee's longevity prospects. That is, high school dropouts are more likely to be less accepting of authority on average, more likely to give up in the face of difficulty, and so forth. You might argue that the possession of a high school diploma is similar to demographic information—indeed, education level is often classified as demographics—but while an individual cannot change race or gender, the decision to stay or drop out of high school is at least partly voluntary.

Voluntarily provided information is a big category, covering a huge variety of cases and types. We define this category broadly, to include

- *Honestly volunteered information.* Many people, asked about problems they had with a used car or a house, will volunteer the truth, simply because they are honest. Of course, to trust such information, you have to be able to judge who is honest and who might be deceptive. But some people are pretty good at sizing up another person's character, especially when it comes to nonprofessional transactions, such as the sale of a used car from one individual to another. Social norms, supported by social structure, such as a small and tight-knit community, and backed by the threat of sanctions against those discovered to have broken with the community's norms, often guarantee honesty and openness. In some instances, individuals cultivate and then have the motivation to protect a reputation for honesty as described in Chapter 4.

- *Providing the uninformed party with an opportunity to procure information.* For instance, in the U.S. used-car market, it is standard for prospective buyers to take the car to their own mechanic for a checkup, with the prospective buyer paying the cost of the inspection. This is possible only if the seller permits the prospective buyer to borrow the car. Even more prosaically, sellers of used cars "permit" prospective buyers to look under the hood and take the car out for a spin. And, on a less mundane level, when Company A is considering acquiring Company B, and Company B is not averse to the acquisition, Company B may "open its books" to Company A, to help Company A perform the required due diligence. When you are searching to fill a position in your company, you expect candidates to volunteer references whom you can then contact directly.

The title of this section includes the parenthetical *(somewhat)*, which needs explanation. The issue is, if the informed party has the ability to "volunteer" information, does it also have the incentive to do so?

This question is not entirely trivial. In the example, the entrepreneurs with bad ventures are very happy to be lumped together (the economic word is, *pooled*) with the good-venture entrepreneurs, since this raises the price they get for their 1% shares from $12.50 to $85 or so.

But if the informed party can provide useful information, it usually finds that it has the incentive to do so. In any pool—meaning a group of people with different "qualities" who are treated the same—there will be those with the "best" information: the folks with the best used cars, the customers for life insurance in the best of health. They have every incentive to break out of the pool by providing the cheap and good information about themselves. And once they are out, the folks next in line in terms of "quality" become the best folks in the pool, and they (then) have every incentive to reveal available information. And so forth: When cheap and good information is available, pools will unravel from the top. Folks at the very bottom have no incentive to reveal this information. But if someone is trying to sell you a used car and tells you that you may not take it to have a mechanic look at it and that it is being sold "as is," the inference you should make (and most used-car buyers do make) is obvious.[2]

20.4. Signaling and Screening

There are cases, however, for which providing useful information is impossible or, at least expensive. In such cases, the "good quality" folks look for ways to signal that they are of good quality.

This describes the alternate equilibrium to the one-price-for-all, $p = \$85$ equilibrium. Entrepreneurs with good-quality ventures, to distinguish themselves from entrepreneurs with low-quality ventures, hold a sizeable fraction of their ventures. This gets them a better price—in our example, a much better price per 1% share. But—the key to such arrangements—the signal must be so expensive for folks with worse quality that they don't want to send the signal, to get the high price per share. The fraction X that the good-venture entrepreneurs must hold is not determined by the characteristics of the good-venture entrepreneurs and their ventures; rather, it is the share large enough so that a bad-venture entrepreneur says, "If that's what it takes to get the good price, leave me out."

---

[2] A problem with this argument is that it presumes that the individuals in the pool know where they stand relative to the average in the pool. If they are unsure, they may not wish to reveal their quality. For instance, I once asked on a final exam the following hypothetical question: *Suppose I gave you [the student] the choice between being graded on how you did on this exam and being pooled together with everyone who doesn't take the first option. Which would you choose?* Assuming students want the best grades they can get, if students know how well they did relative to their peers, the pool should unravel from the top. That is, if I tell each student his or her individual grade and the average and let people choose, I'd expect everyone above the average to opt out of the pool. If I then computed the average of those still in the pool and gave students another chance to opt out, more would opt out, and so forth. But when I ask this question before students know how well they did, risk aversion can—and in the instance did—lead a fair number of students to choose to take the pooled grade.

Economists use the terms *signaling* and *screening* to describe arrangements of this sort, where the distinction between the two involves which party in the transaction sets the terms of the deal. If a good-venture entrepreneur, unhappy with the a price of $85 per 1% share, went to an investor and said, "Look here, I'm willing to hold 73% of my venture if you will pay me $237.50 per 1% share, which you should be willing to do because a bad-venture entrepreneur would never choose to do this," and if you as investor agree, the entrepreneur is signaling.

On the other hand, if investors say: "We'll pay $237.50 per 1% to any entrepreneur who is willing to retain 73% of her venture and we'll pay $12.50 per 1% share to anyone who does not retain at least that amount," then the investors are said to be *screening* the entrepreneurs.

Signals and screens abound:

- When a used-car dealership offers a six-month warranty on used cars it is selling, and especially when it offers a six-month warranty on some cars and not others on its lot, it is signaling: Presumably, offering a warranty on a car in good condition is a lot less expensive (in expectation) than offering the same warranty on a car that is in poor condition.

- An insurance company that offers cheap term life insurance, but with "greatly reduced benefits for the first two years," is screening, the idea being that if you know you are in poor health, the prospect of paying premiums for up to two years when you are somewhat likely to pass away sooner than that, is not attractive.

- A theory of the value of certain forms of education is that education is a signal: Suppose going to college and enduring four years is relatively painful for folks who lack certain desirable skills and, although painful, is less painful for folks who have those skills. If employers want to find (and reward) people with those skills, then going to and surviving college could be an effective signal, for those who have the desirable skills, *even if what is learned in college is of no direct value on the job.* To be clear, I don't subscribe to the italicized part of this statement. But if undertaking a course of education—or finishing high school, or serving in the military—is relatively less painful for people with certain (desirable-to-employers) characteristics than for people without those characteristics, *and if the difference in how painful is the experience is sufficient to keep the folks without the characteristics from gritting their teeth and going through with it, to get better treatment at the end,* then these can have signaling value beyond whatever extra skills are acquired.[3]

---

[3] This theory, known as job-market signaling, was first advanced by A. Michael Spence, who (1) served as dean of the Stanford Graduate School of Business for a decade—which some say has something to do with the way the GSB's curriculum is designed—and (2) won the Nobel Prize in Economics along with George Akerlof and Joseph Stiglitz in 2001, for this theory. For Spence's original work, see A. M. Spence, *Market Signaling* (Cambridge, MA: Harvard University Press, 1974).

Pooling Equilibria versus Signaling/Screening Equilibria

(You may wish to skip this section on a first reading.) In our entrepreneur example, we have two possible equilibria. The first is the *pooling equilibrium*, in which all shares have a price of $p = \$85$ (roughly), the good-venture folks retain around 52.6% of their ventures, and the bad-venture folks sell their entire ventures. This gives a good-venture entrepreneur a certainty equivalent of around $12,670. The second equilibrium is the *separating* or *signaling* or *screening equilibrium*, where the good-venture entrepreneurs retain 73% of their ventures, selling the rest at $237.50 per 1%, for a CE of $16,089.20, while the bad-venture entrepreneurs sell 100% of their ventures for $12.50 per 1%, giving them $1250 for certain. (Investors are paying the EMV of whatever shares they buy in these equilibria, so they are getting nothing out of them. In a more realistic model, we'd have to adjust what they pay so that they earn a market return on their investment, but this just complicates the story without adding anything in terms of economic insight.)

As already noted, the good-venture investors prefer the separating equilibrium, while the bad-venture investors prefer the pooling equilibrium. Is there any reason to suppose that one or the other is more likely to prevail?

Economic theory *suggests* that the separating equilibrium is likely to prevail, at least insofar as the good-venture entrepreneurs can figure all this out: Then, if the investment community is not already screening for the good ventures, the good-venture entrepreneurs have the incentive to try to signal, and the investment community should then recognize what is going on. But this is theory and somewhat controversial theory at that; in real life, we typically see a mix of some pooling and some separation.

20.5. The Winner's Curse

We conclude with the *winner's curse*, which is a variation on adverse selection. Imagine you are a general contractor who is participating in a sealed-tender auction (lowest bid wins) for a contract to undertake a very large construction project for a major corporation. Four other contractors are bidding as well. As you formulate your bid, you try to estimate what it will cost to fulfill the contract; you are simultaneously trying to estimate what your rivals will bid. You have done some construction work in the area and have connections with some subcontractors whom you expect you will hire, but there are portions of the project the costs of which are very uncertain to you. And you know that some of your rival bidders have good information—better than your information— about the costs of those portions of the contract.

In the end, you estimate that it will cost you $230 million to fulfill the contract and so, leaving yourself a margin of $20 million, you decide to bid $250 million. But $230 million is only your best guess.

Bids are submitted, and you discover that you have submitted the low bid; one rival submitted $260 million, and the three others each submitted a bid over $300 million. Should you be happy?

Perhaps not. Suppose you knew that three out of your four rivals were going to bid over $300 million. *Would that change your assessment of how much the project will cost you?* If they have information concerning how costly this project will be that you lack, and if their high bids are the result of that information telling them that costs will be high, perhaps that means costs will be high for you as well.

To be very clear, in contexts in which knowing that their cost estimates are higher than yours doesn't affect your initial cost estimate, you might regret not bidding $259 million. But the fact that the three other bidders bid over $300 million doesn't increase your regret. When, on the other hand, you suspect that your rival bidders have information about costs that you would like to have had, their bidding much higher than you should be worrisome; perhaps you underestimated what the cost of fulfilling the project will be.

This phenomenon is known as the *winner's curse*. The idea is that whoever wins an auction is, of course, the low bidder (for this sort of contract fulfillment auction; in the context of bidding to buy an object, it is the high bidder). That means the others have bid more. And, maybe, that means that the winner bid too low a price to fulfill the contract (or too high a bid to win the auction). It is called a curse because unsophisticated bidders, who don't understand this phenomenon, find that when they win the auction, they tend to lose overall— they bid too low a price relative to their costs of fulfilling the contract, or they bid too much given the value of the object at auction. Sophisticated bidders take this into account in formulating their bids: they know their bid is only relevant when they win the auction (at least, for standard winner-pays auctions), and so in determining how much to bid, they condition their assessment on what it will cost to fulfill the contract (or what is the value of the object being bid for), conditional on the fact that they are the low (high) bidder; that is, that everyone else bid more (less).

This is certainly a *hidden information* phenomenon: What is hidden from you is the information the other bidders have and you would like to have to form your assessment as to the cost of fulfilling the contract (or the value of the object at auction). But more than that, it is an *adverse selection* phenomenon, in the following sense: the auctions that you win are a *selection* of all auctions—you win when among the bidders you are most optimistic—and if your being most optimistic means you are more likely to be overly optimistic, then this is an adverse selection in terms of your assessment of the value of winning.

Executive Summary

- Problems of *hidden information* appear when one party to a transaction has access to information that other parties cannot access, if the information is relevant to the transaction.

- When items offered for sale are disproportionately drawn from the lower-quality end of the spectrum, because owners of higher-quality items are more likely to want to hold on to their items and where buyers cannot discern the quality, a problem of *adverse selection* exists.

- It is also a problem of adverse selection when, in markets for "services" such as insurance or contract fulfillment, high-cost-of-provision buyers (assumed to be better informed than the service providers about the cost of providing the service) are disproportionately represented in the population of buyers.

- In both types of adverse-selection problem, adverse selection can be a vicious cycle: Lower prices are paid because the average quality sold is low (or higher prices charged because high-cost-of-provision buyers are disproportionate in the population of buyers), which drives from the market goods of intermediate quality or clients of intermediate costs of provision, further driving the price of the goods down or the services up.

- Hidden information problems extend beyond the more obvious contexts. For instance, the *winner's curse* refers to a problem of hidden information and a form of adverse selection that occurs in auctions of various types.

- Information revelation cures problems of hidden information. Very generally, this involves information freely available that is correlated with characteristics of interest, such as demographic information; information whose provision by the informed party is compelled by law; and information voluntarily provided by the informed party or elicited voluntarily from the informed party.

- Signaling and screening is a form of (indirect) voluntarily provided information: Sellers of high-quality goods (or buyers of a service who know that fulfillment of the service for them will be of relatively low cost) take an action to indicate that their goods are of high quality (their costs will be low). The key to this "information" being useful is: Is sending this signal so costly for low-quality (high-cost) parties, that they don't want to mimic the high-quality (or low-cost) parties who send it? So, for instance, in the entrepreneur example, the share of their venture that good-venture entrepreneurs must hold to signal that they have good ventures is driven by considerations of what bad-venture entrepreneurs would (not) do.

- Signaling and screening equilibria can be *separating*, where differently informed parties take distinct actions, or *pooling*, where differently informed parties send the same signal (which may be no signal at all, in which case all the informed parties are pooled together).

- When information is voluntarily provided at the initiative of the informed party, economists call it a *signal*. When the uninformed party finds a means for eliciting this information, it is called a *screen*.

Problems

20.1 The seminal paper on the topic of adverse selection (in the literature of economics) is Akerlof's "The Market for Lemons." He describes a used-car market in which each used car that is worth X to its current owner is worth $X + 200$ to potential new owners. Current owners know the value of X for their own car; buyers have no way of telling. Suppose the distribution of X in the population of used cars is uniform between $1000 and $3000.

An equilibrium in the market is then a price p for a used car such that:

- The owner of a used car will put her car on the market if $p > X$: that is, if the price she can get for her car is more than the car is worth to her.

- The price p is the average value $\hat{X}$ of all the cars put up for sale by their current owners, plus the $200 more that any car is worth to a new owner than it is worth to its current owner.

What price(s) p give an equilibrium in this used-car market? And why did Akerlof choose the title "The Market for Lemons?"

20.2 At the Famous East Coast Business School (FECBUS), all MBA students want summer jobs working for investment banks in New York City. They want this sort of job so much that, if they are not offered a position of this sort, they refuse out of pride to do any other work. A summer job with an investment bank carries a stipend of $50,000. Therefore, a student at FECBUS who has probability p of landing such a job owns a lottery with payoffs $50,000 or $0, with probabilities p and $1 - p$. Beyond the prestige of having such a job or the shame of not having one, FECBUS students use this money to help pay for their second year of school, and being risk averse, they consider the possibility of buying insurance against the contingency of no job. Specifically, Beantown Casualty, a local insurance company, has always provided catastrophic summer income insurance to FECBUS students. Beantown offers simple policies in which the student pays a premium P and Beantown reimburses the student Q if the student fails to land a job. If a student buys this policy, the outcomes are $50,000 − P$ with probability p and $Q − P$ with probability $1 − p$.

(a) Drake Duck is a typical FECBUS first-year student. His probability of landing a summer job at an investment bank is 0.7. His utility function, used for calculating expected utility, certainty equivalents, and the like is

$$u(x) = \sqrt{x + 40{,}000},$$

where x is the proceeds from summer employment, net of any premiums paid to Beantown Casualty and net of any repayments from Beantown if Drake fails to land a job. If the alternative is to go without insurance, would Drake be willing to pay a premium of $P = \$10{,}000$ for insurance that pays back $Q = \$30{,}000$?

(b) Suppose Beantown Casualty is risk neutral. Which policies could Beantown write for Drake, assuming Beantown knows his utility function and probability of finding a job, that (1) give an expected payoff no larger than the premium, (2) give Drake a higher certainty equivalent than he gets with no insurance, and (3) are efficient in terms of risk sharing?

(c) Unhappily for Beantown, it does not know, a priori, the probability with which any individual student at FECBUS will land a summer job. But, we assume, each student knows his or her own probability. Assume that the first-year class of FECBUS consists of 500 students. For 100 students, the probability of landing a summer job is 0.9. For 100, it is 0.8. For 100 more, it is 0.7. For 100 more, it is 0.6. And for the last 100 students, the probability of landing a summer job is $p = 0.5$. To keep the problem as simple as possible, suppose that all 500 students have precisely the same utility function as does Drake.

Suppose Beantown decides to offer a single policy providing full insurance: that is, $Q = \$50{,}000$. Since the "average" student at FECBUS has probability 0.7 of getting a summer job, Beantown decides to charge a premium of $0.3 \times \$50{,}000 = \$15{,}000$. Would Beantown make or lose money with this policy? Why? (Assume that a student who does not buy insurance from Beantown goes without insurance entirely.)

(d) Suppose that Beantown is convinced that offering a single full-insurance policy is the way to go. Is there any premium Beantown could charge for full insurance that would make a positive expected profit for Beantown? Which premiums do this?

(e) In part d, you should find that the only full-insurance policies that would make a positive expected profit for Beantown involve insurance for the 100 students with a 0.5 chance of landing a job. All the rest choose not to purchase insurance. Beantown would like to insure more members of the FECBUS class, even partially, and so Beantown thinks about offering a single policy with a premium of $\$14{,}000$ and a payout of $\$30{,}000$. What would be the response to this policy? How would Beantown do in terms of expected profits?

(f) Beantown Casualty is not interested in making a huge profit writing these insurance policies—they are regulated by the insurance commissioner of the

Commonwealth of Baystateland, and in any event, the head of Beantown is an old FECBUS grad who would never try to profit at the expense of students from her old school—but it does see a value in selling some insurance to as many students of FECBUS as possible. Beantown is required by law not to offer any policy that has a negative expected profit; cross-subsidization of one policy by another is not permitted. Moreover, it is compelled to offer full insurance at terms that break even. Therefore, it is compelled, in this circumstance, to offer a full insurance policy (one that pays back $50,000) for a premium of $25,000. (See part c.)

Suppose that, in addition to this policy, Beantown offers a $10,000 insurance policy for a premium of $3500, a $2000 policy for a premium of $500, and a $200 policy for a premium of $20. What would happen? In particular, what would be Beantown's expected profit on each policy and altogether?

20.3 In a particular economy, all homeowners own identical homes worth $80,000 apiece. These homes are subject to complete loss via fire, and the Old Reliable Insurance Company (ORIC) offers policies against loss by fire. The chance of a fire at any particular home is a probability p, which is known to the homeowner but not known to ORIC. The values of p run from 0 to as high as 0.4. Homeowners have no control over the value of p; it is simply given. For instance, Peter Reece has a home on the edge of a forest, and for his house, $p = 0.1$. John Yost has a home in the suburbs, and for his house, $p = 0.03$.

ORIC is risk neutral and offers two different policies. The first is a complete insurance policy, which pays the homeowner back $80,000 in the event of a fire. The premium for this insurance policy is $11,600. The second policy offers partial insurance. It has a payback in the event of fire of $58,400, and a premium of $5900. This means that a customer who buys this policy and has no fire is out $5900. With a fire, the customer nets $58,400 − $5900 = $52,500.

All the homeowners in this society are expected utility maximizers and have the same utility function:

$$u(x) = \sqrt{x + 10,000},$$

where x is the net of this situation, including the value of the house, if there is no fire. For instance, a consumer who buys the second insurance policy and has no fire has utility $\sqrt{10,000 + 80,000 - 5900} = \sqrt{84,100} = 290$, while with a fire, the utility is $\sqrt{10,000 + 58,400 - 5900} = \sqrt{62,500} = 250$.

(a) Of the three options available (no insurance, full insurance, or partial insurance), what would be the choice of Mr. Reece? What would be the choice of Mr. Yost?

(b) For which values of p would consumers with that value of p choose no insurance? For which values of p would consumers with that value of p choose partial insurance? For which values of p would consumers with that value of p choose full insurance? You should answer so that, for any value of p between 0 and 1, we can tell what the consumer would choose. Don't worry about values of p for which there are ties.

(c) The actuaries at ORIC, based on historical experience, predict that ORIC will sell 100,000 partial insurance policies, with an average profit per policy of $1228. They predict that ORIC will sell 5000 full insurance policies, with an average *loss* per policy of $12,400. Therefore, their net profit from this business is

$$(100{,}000)(\$1228) + (5000)(-\$12{,}400) = \$60.8 \text{ million.}$$

What would be ORIC's net profit from this business if it offered only the partial insurance policy?

20.4 Among the benefits offered by corporations, at least in the United States, is health insurance. One explanation for why corporations offer such insurance is that this benefit is tax favored: Companies can compensate employees with health-insurance benefits that are treated as nontaxable income. Also, health care providers and insurers (such as Blue Shield) have historically offered better rates to employers for their employees than to individuals who ask for the same coverage. Why is this?

Some companies offer so-called flexible benefits to their employees: Employees have a certain number of pretax dollars to spend on benefits and are allowed to choose the portfolio of benefits they wish. In terms of the prices charged employers by health-care providers and insurers for their product, provided as benefits, what do you think is the effect of flexible benefit plans?

20.5 In some countries, title to an automobile includes a history of previous owners. And in those countries, the price for a particular car, holding fixed the car model and features, miles driven, and general (discernible) condition, is a decreasing function of the number of previous owners. Why is this, do you think?

20.6 In the 1980s and 1990s, a large number of first-tier firms offered no-layoff employment. These firms promised employees that, perhaps after a probationary period, an employee had a job for life; he or she would never be laid off. Some firms, such as IBM and Eastman Kodak, had made this promise for decades; in the 1980s and 1990s, this employment practice, as a piece of so-called high-commitment human resource management, became increasingly prevalent.

Such policies have substantial benefits when times are good, but they do not come for free. In particular, a firm that offers such promises and that faces economic difficulties must choose between breaking these promises and desirable reorganization. For instance, before the return of Steve Jobs to Apple Computer, Apple, which had prided itself on its no-layoff policy, found itself badly hamstrung by the policy. Apple needed to shed excess employees, but especially given its fairly young workforce, waiting for the natural process of attrition seemed much too slow.

So Apple decided to initiate a program of voluntary layoffs. It offered substantial inducements to employees to quit, including generous severance pay and excellent placement services for those who would consent to go. Apple found, to its dismay, that its program of voluntary layoffs had some bad repercussions. In particular, Apple top management, because of the voluntary layoff program, learned a lot about adverse selection. Precisely what sort of adverse selection problem did they learn about? And can you think of any way to put in place a voluntary layoff program that negates (or, at least, ameliorates) this problem of adverse selection?

20.7   In the U.S. real estate brokerage industry, brokers employed by large brokerage firms have traditionally worked for a portion of the commissions they generate. That is, if a house sale generates a 6% commission split equally between the brokers for the two sides (which is standard in many markets in the United States), the broker on one side might personally pocket 1.5% with 1.5% going to the firm for which the broker works. In return for a share in the broker's commissions, the firm provides the broker with an infrastructure, such as clerical support, phone services, and office space, and especially for new brokers, a base wage.

In comparison, RE/MAX, a national brokerage firm, permits its agents to keep 100% of the commissions they earn. The firm provides clerical services, phones, and the like, and charges its agents a fixed monthly fee for those services. RE/MAX is known for having the most aggressive agents in the business on average. If you want to find an aggressive, hard-charging agent, going to RE/MAX is usually a safe bet.

(a) Why does RE/MAX attract more aggressive agents?

(b) RE/MAX charges its agents more for the services it provides than it costs to provide those services. In fact, RE/MAX makes money by marking up the clerical and administrative services it provides to its agents. Why are aggressive agents willing to pay RE/MAX more for these services than it would cost them to procure the services independently?

(c) In addition to joining RE/MAX or a more traditional firm, realtors can go independent. How does this third option affect RE/MAX? How does it affect the more traditional firms? Put another way, would you expect a hard-charging, aggressive agent to remain with RE/MAX for the long haul? Does your answer to the question depend on aspects of the local real estate market; that is, would you give the same answer for, say, the Silicon Valley as you would for a prosperous county seat in South Carolina?

Questions about the winner's curse are generally quite difficult to pose. While very stylized, Problem 20.8 illustrates the phenomenon in about as simple a model as one can find.

20.8 Three construction firms, Ace, Base, and Case, are considering whether to declare their willingness to undertake a contruction project for the Freedonian government. The cost of fulfilling this construction project is very likely to be $100,000. But there is a chance that the cost will be $200,000. This cost does not change depending on the firm; if it is $100,000 for one firm, it is $100,000 for the other two.

The Freedonian government declared it will pay precisely $125,000 for this job. That is, the price paid to the firm doing the work is fixed in advance. The decision facing Ace, Base, and Case is whether to declare that it is willing to undertake this project. If no firm is willing to undertake the project, it will not be done. If only one of the three is willing, that firm will be awarded the job. If two firms are willing, one of the two will be chosen by a coin toss. And if all three firms declare their willingness, one of the three will be chosen at random, with each firm having a 1/3 chance of getting the job.

The three firms must each decide and then declare simultaneously and independently whether it is willing to take the job. All three are risk neutral. You are advising Ace, and the management of Ace has told you that it is willing to take the job if the expected costs of construction are less than the fixed price of $125,000.

Each of the three firms initially assessed probability 0.8 that the cost of this project will be $100,000 and 0.2 that the cost will be $200,000. But each has a 0.75 probability chance of having learned the true cost. These 0.75 probability chances are independent of one another and independent of the true cost of the facility. That is, conditional on Ace learning the true cost, the probability that Base would learn it is still 0.75, and so on. And if we condition on the true cost being $100,000, the chance that Ace would learn this is 0.75.

In fact, the management at Ace told you that it did not learn the true cost, so it still assesses 0.8 that the cost will be $100,000. And it does not know whether Base or Case knows the true cost; it assesses binominal probabilities 0.75^2 that both rivals know the true cost (whatever that is), $2 \times 0.75 \times 0.25$ that one rival knows the true cost and the other does not, and 0.25^2 that neither rival knows the true cost.

Suppose that Base and Case both use the following decision rule to determine whether they should declare their willingness to take on this project:

> If the firm in question is certain that the costs would be $100,000, then declare that it is willing to take on the contract; otherwise, do not indicate a willingness to take on the contract.

Against two rivals whose decision rules are these, should Ace, which remains uncertain about the true cost, indicate a willingness to take on this project?

21. Hidden Action: Moral Hazard and Incentives

In many transactions, one party is able to take an action that affects the value of the transaction to the second party. When the terms of the transaction specify which action will be taken, and when that provision is enforceable, there is no problem. Or, in the spirit of Chapters 3 and 4, when the action can be observed ex post and is the basis for a long-term relationship between the parties or a specific reputation of the first party, the issue may be moot. But what if the action is "hidden?" Then a so-called moral hazard exists, and it may become necessary to motivate the first party to "do the right thing" with appropriately designed incentives.

Problem 20.2 tells the story of first-year students at FECBUS, the Famous East Coast Business School, all of whom search for summer jobs with Wall Street investment banks. The students may fail to find such a summer job; those who do not, out of pride, take no summer jobs at all. Since the students are risk averse, and since a local insurance company, Beantown Casualty, is effectively risk neutral, this opens up the possibility of mutually advantageous risk-sharing arrangements: For a fair premium, Beantown Casualty will insure an individual student against the risk of failing to land a job, paying the student some compensatory amount if the student goes unemployed.

Problem 20.2 focuses on hidden information: Different students have different probabilities of landing a job. Some students have probability 0.9 of getting a job; others have (only) probability 0.5. Each student knows his or her personal probability, while Beantown cannot tell which student is which. So when Beantown Casualty offers a policy, it must worry that it will get an adverse selection of the students: Only those students who know that they have a relatively low probability of getting a job buy insurance, raising the percentage of policies on which Beantown must pay out and therefore raising the premium it must charge, which may drive even more high-probability-of-a-job students away.

In this chapter, we change this story. Suppose that the probability of landing a summer job depends not on an unchangeable (by the student) personal characteristic, but instead depends on how much effort the student expends trying to get the job. Since students are risk averse and Beantown Casualty is risk neutral, efficient risk sharing dictates that Beantown assume all the risk whether a student gets the job or not. But if Beantown promises to make students "whole" if they fail to land a job, and if students would just as soon avoid the effort needed to get a job if they could, then once fully insured, students would not put in much if any effort, lowering their chances of getting a job (to zero?) and causing Beantown to pay out on a lot of policies. Insurance by Beantown induces a moral hazard for the students.

Observe that this is an issue only if students face the risk of not getting a job, even if they try to get one. If each effort level resulted either in a job for sure or no job, then it is up to the student to determine whether the job is worth the minimum effort required to get it. There is no role for insurance or risk sharing, because there is no risk. Our story depends on there being a "noisy connection" between student effort and the outcome; students who try hard to get a job may, through no fault of their own, fail to land one.

So what does Beantown do? It offers *partial insurance*. If a student fails to land a job, the Beantown policy partially compensates the student. Some of the risk of failing to land a job is shared, but the student bears enough of the consequences of his or her actions so that she has some incentive to try to get a job. A fundamental trade-off is at work here: Less insurance means less efficient risk sharing. But less insurance means more incentive for the student to try. Striking the right balance between risk sharing and incentives is what makes for a good insurance contract, in this context.[1]

This is what this chapter is about. The issue comes up in a wide variety of contexts, for instance:

- In all forms of casualty insurance—fire, theft, even to some extent health—does the insured party have the incentive to take due care; for instance, by not keeping oily rags in the garage, locking up when leaving home, and keeping oneself in good physical condition?

- In risky entrepreneurial ventures, if the entrepreneur (in pursuit of efficient risk sharing) sells shares in her venture, does she then have the incentive to work day and night to ensure that the venture will succeed? Or do her incentives shift to using the funds raised to buy a company jet prematurely, or even to spend time surreptitiously working on her next venture?

- If the government transacts with a firm to produce some infrastructure system (e.g., an IT system) on a cost-plus basis, so that the government bears all the risk in how much work must be done to get the system to a level of acceptable performance, does the contractor then have any incentive to develop cost-effective ways of building the system? (Or, if the cost-plus contract takes the form of total cost plus a set percentage of "overhead," does the contractor have the perverse incentive to inflate costs, thereby inflating its overhead payment?)

These are contexts within which the issues of hidden action, moral hazard, and incentives—and in particular the fundamental trade-off between risk sharing and incentives—can be found. But perhaps the premier context for these issues

---

[1] Problem 21.1 presents a toy model of this story.

concerns the employee–employer relationship. So that is the context we will use for the remainder of this chapter.

21.1. Piecework Versus Wages and Safelite Glass

Safelite Glass[2] is the largest automobile-glass replacement company in the United States. Imagine that something causes your windshield to shatter or develop a crack. Perhaps you call a glass repair/replacement shop directly; more often (in the US), you call your insurance agent, who then contacts a glass repair/replacement shop. And, in the United States, the second call most often goes to Safelite. After getting the details (make and model of car, extent of damage, location of the vehicle), Safelite dispatches a panel truck or van, loaded with the appropriate tools and replacement glass if needed, driven to the vehicle's location by the *technician*, who (on the spot) does what is needed: cleans up any broken glass, removes the old windshield, and installs a new windshield; or, if the crack is small enough, applies a resin that "clarifies" and strengthens the glass. Safelite will also (as needed) replace side and back windows and mirrors.

Safelite has a variety of employees: management, of course; dispatchers and clericals who handle calls and paperwork and initiate a repair-or-replacement sequence; and warehouse workers, who load the panel trucks. But the key to the operation is the *technician*: the person who takes the loaded truck to wherever the stricken vehicle is located and does what is needed. And who, importantly, does all this on his (technicians are nearly entirely men) own.

Nowadays, with the possibility of GPS tracking, serious monitoring of even remotely located technicians is to some extent possible. But, not too long ago, a technician who left the warehouse with a loaded truck could take his time to get to the location of the vehicle, to make the repair, and to get back. Safelite paid technicians an hourly wage and, to no one's surprise, they found that their technicians took a lot of time to complete each job, more time than management at Safelite thought was necessary.

So, Safelite decided to try to motivate its technicians with a modified piece-rate system it called PPP. A piece rate was set for each type of job, and a technician would be paid each week the sum of the piece-rate payments he had earned, subject to one modification. Safelite backstopped the technicians' wages with a guaranteed minimum hourly wage: each week, each technician would be paid the larger of the sum of piece-rate payments he had earned and the guaranteed minimum hourly wage, based on the number of hours worked during the week,

---

[2] The analysis of pay-for-performance at Safelite Glass is presented in E. Lazear, "Performance, Pay, and Productivity," *American Economic Review*, Vol. 90, 2000, 1346–61; and *Performance Pay at Safelite Auto Glass (A)* and *(B)*, by Brian Hall, Edward Lazear, and Carleen Madigan, HBS Cases 9-800-291 and -292, 2001. The synopsis that is presented here is taken more or less verbatim from Chapter 2 of *The Motivation Toolkit* (New York: W. W. Norton, 2017), and is included here with the kind permission of W. W. Norton.

and as long as the technician's average hourly productivity (jobs completed per hour worked) was at least as large as the average hourly productivity of technicians prior to PPP being put in place.

To implement PPP, Safelite had to set a number of parameters, including, of course, the piece rate for each type of job. But, in addition, Safelite's management had to decide on the guaranteed minimum wage rate. Two opinions emerged about what minimum wage rate to set. Some members of top management argued that the guarantee should be less than the currently paid hourly wage. "If," they argued, "the guarantee is set, say, at the current wage rate, then no technician would make less under the new system than previously, and our labor bill can only increase."

But another group favored setting the minimum at the current wage rate, pointing out that this could, in the not-very-long-run, improve Safelite's bottom line:

1. For one thing, if the new system motivates technicians to work more quickly, customers would become more satisfied—sitting on a roadside waiting for your vehicle to be repaired is not fun—which might mean more business for Safelite.

2. And, perhaps more significantly, if the piece rates are set at levels below former unit-labor costs, then any technician who does enough to get into the piece-rate region will be working more efficiently; for the same volume of total work, Safelite can employ fewer technicians, and so its total wage bill (for the same volume of work) declines, even if the technicians who remain are paid more.

Of course, this does *not* imply that a guarantee of 100% of former wage rates is best for Safelite. They might do even better if they cut the guarantee to, say, 70% of the previous guarantee. Proponents of the 100% guarantee worried that cutting the guarantee would cause massive turnover of technicians who would feel exploited by the new system. Proponents of the 70% guarantee agreed that this might happen but that, in the long run, the lower guarantee would be better. They argued that, with the 100% guarantee, technicians would sort themselves into two groups. Some technicians—the more ambitious and hard-working—would see PPP as an opportunity to work hard and make more money; these technicians would do enough work each week so that they wouldn't need the guarantee. For these technicians, it wouldn't matter whether the guarantee was 100% or 70%.

The second group would be technicians, lazier and less inclined to work hard, who would continue to work at their previous pace, pocketing their old wages. Lowering the guarantee to 70% might induce some of these technicians to quit, and they could be replaced by harder working technicians attracted by PPP. At least some technicians who would settle for the old pace of work and their old take-home pay with a 100% guarantee would, if the guarantee were cut, pick up their pace. And any technician who settled for the 70% of the old hourly rate but with the old average hourly productivity rate would have unit-labor costs 30% lower than before. As long as the piece rate is below former unit-labor costs, this is all good for Safelite.[3]

Do Technicians Control How Much Work They Can Do Each Week?

While all these arguments are valid, they miss a second role played by the guarantee, an insurance role. The piece rate was set significantly below the old average unit-labor cost. Therefore, a technician had to do significantly more work in a week than had previously been the case, to have piece-rate-based compensation greater than what had been his old hourly-wage-rate-based compensation. An ambitious technician might set out on a given Monday morning ready to work that hard and more, but as the week went on, the technician might *through no fault of his own* find himself falling short. Perhaps the jobs he was assigned were very distant from his shop. Perhaps he found, upon getting to the job, that the warehouse workers had loaded the wrong glass into his truck. Perhaps the new windshield cracked upon being installed, not because he did anything wrong, but because of a defect in the glass. Perhaps it was simply a matter of a lack of work; business might be slow in a particular week.

And, in a given week, he might be ill or out of sorts and, for that week, want to take it easy.

People who work as Safelite technicians are semiskilled blue-collar workers. A few have modest savings, but a fair proportion of them live from paycheck to paycheck. They have rent and car payments to make; many have a family to feed. All these factors make them quite averse to week-to-week variation in their take-home pay. So a guaranteed weekly paycheck is indeed an important backstop for them. Even an ambitious technician—the sort of person Safelite wants to keep on its payroll—might see a 70% guarantee as too little insurance and look elsewhere for a job; the 100% guarantee, which is essentially a better insurance policy for the technician, might help to retain that ambitious technician.

The Fundamental Tradeoff, Again

This is the fundamental trade-off: lowering the guarantee subjects the individual technician to riskier weekly take-home pay, because the work achieved in any week, while it depends on the effort the technician exerts, also depends on factors outside the technician's control. To use the language of incentives, the outcomes (how much work is achieved) on which compensation is based are a *noisy indicator* of the efforts the employee puts in.

---

[3] Appendix 6 in the *Online Supplement* fleshes out these ideas using indifference-curve models of the choices of different types of technician.

Advocates of the 70% guarantee were correct that the lower guarantee would enhance the motivation to work hard. But when technicians are a good deal more risk averse than is Safelite, and when an individual technician—even if he tries hard—cannot guarantee that he'll hit piece-rate gold in a given week, then a lower guarantee is worse risk sharing between employer and employee. Again, this doesn't mean that a 100% guarantee gets the balance between risk sharing and incentives right. But there is a good economic reason—better risk sharing—for dialing down incentives a bit by keeping the guarantee reasonably high.

What Else Safelite Can/Should Do

As Safelite implements this modified piece-rate scheme, there are other actions it should take:

- While a wage guarantee acts as insurance, a better scheme—especially to keep technicians from being frustrated—is to remove at least to some extent the factors that adversely affect what a technician can achieve through his own efforts. The scheduling/job assignment function should be improved, so technicians are sent shorter distances to jobs. Warehouse operations should be upgraded. If glass quality is an issue, it should be improved. Safelite did at least the first two of these.

  A typical issue in piece-rate compensation is *work starvation*, where the employee working on piece rate is ready to tackle the next job, but there is no job for him to do. In the context of Safelite, job flow is hard to control. Perhaps, with centralizing dispatch, some smoothing is possible. But in other contexts, and in particular in worker-paced manufacturing, piece-rate compensation is typically accompanied by a rise in work-in-process inventory, so no employee is ever starved of work he can do.[4]

- Offering a weekly wage guarantee is one way to backstop technicians, but other and more direct methods of providing "insurance" should be considered. In particular, if work-starvation due to lack of jobs is a major issue, Safelite could offer technicians idle-time compensation: an hourly wage paid to technicians who are at the shop and ready to work, but who have no job on which to go.

- There are other aspects or dimensions to doing a "good job" as a technician besides speed. Safelite wants its drivers to take due care when driving, by obeying speed limits, stopping at stop signs, not running red lights, and so forth. On the job, Safelite wants technicians to be courteous to the customer and, for instance, to do a good job cleaning up broken glass. They cer-

---

[4] *Lincoln Electric Company* (HBS 376028-PDF-ENG), one of the most popular (and widely used) Harvard Business School cases, discusses the use of piece-rate compensation in a worker-paced manufacturing context in great detail.

tainly want technicians to be careful in installing new windshields; a poorly installed windshield, put under pressure, can crack on its own. Some technicians are "leads," responsible for training new technicians. The point is, the piece-rate system, even as modified with the weekly guarantee, motivates none of these other dimensions of good work; indeed, a technician chasing the biggest possible paycheck is *de*motivated to pay much attention to these other aspects.

So Safelite should (and did) take steps to make sure that the ambitious technician took due care of these other aspects of the job. Some of it was a "stick" approach; Safelite trucks have painted on the back "How is my driving? Report unsafe driving at [phone number]" and then a truck number. And some was a "carrot" approach with extra pay given for technicians who received favorable customer-survey numbers. (Compensation for leads was substantially modified to take account of the variety of their roles.)

The Bottom Line for Safelite

Safelite decided to go with the 100% guarantee. And, even with this high-guarantee level—advocates of the high guarantee might argue, *in part because of* the high-guarantee level—the new compensation system was a big win for Safelite. Unit labor costs decreased by around 30%. Careful empirical analysis[5] suggests that about half the decrease came from "incentive effects," where technicians who had been working slowly were (now) motivated to increase the amount of work they did. The other half came from screening effects: the new compensation system made Safelite a more attractive employer to prospective technicians who were ambitious and hard-working.

21.2. One More Time: The Fundamental Trade-Off

In a nutshell, this is the economic theory of moral hazard and incentives. Party A to some transaction takes an action that affects the value of the transaction to party B. It is for some reason impossible to make the choice of action by A contractually enforceable; typically this is because the choice of action is hidden, although it could be that B chooses *not* to monitor closely what A does.[6] And B cannot rely on either the goodwill and honesty of A to do what she promises to do, nor on her interest (if the action is observable ex post) in maintaining a long-term bilateral relationship or a general reputation for "doing the right thing."

While A's choice of action is hidden, the consequences of that choice are not:

---

[5] See Lazear, op. cit.

[6] This can be due to psychological considerations: Employees who are closely monitored sometimes take this as a license to get away with whatever they can; those who are trusted tend to be more trustworthy.

Different measures of "the outcome" can be observed and can be used as the basis for how A is compensated. Some specific outcomes are *more likely* to be observed when A chooses the action desired by B, so to motivate A to choose those actions, B offers A the promise of greater compensation if one of those outcomes is observed. In simplest form, outcomes are linearly ordered—more windshields installed in a given amount of time; more sales made; more tree-stumps pulled—each of which is more likely when A chooses to work "harder." So to motivate hard work, B tells A that he will pay her more the bigger is the outcome number.[7]

I've emphasized "more likely" to emphasize that, while A's choice of action affects the likelihood of different outcomes, it doesn't determine the outcome. Other factors, not under A's control, also influence the observed outcome. Outcomes are a *noisy signal* of A's choice of action.

So, from A's perspective, a pay-for-performance compensation scheme, where A's compensation is based on the observed outcome, is random compensation. If A is risk averse, risk sharing with B is indicated. In the extreme case where A is risk averse and B is risk netural, efficient risk sharing would remove all risk from A's compensation. But doing this reduces A's incentive to choose an action that B prefers. If A is indifferent personally among the possible action choices—if she doesn't in the least mind working hard—there is no problem. But if her compensation is guaranteed and her personal preferences over actions lead her to...loaf, then B is harmed.

And, so, the trade-off: making A's compensation more sensitive to the outcome measures dials up incentives. Making A's compensation less sensitive dials up risk sharing. Good incentives strike the right balance.

21.3. Complications and Elaborations

It is possible to build toy models that illustrate the basic trade-off; some of the problems at the end of the chapter ask you to do this, with detailed solutions given in the *Online Supplement*. But the techniques used to solve those toy problems are wholly unrealistic (they assume the designer of the compensation scheme knows, for instance, how risk averse is party A), so we won't pursue them here.

Instead, here is a list of ways in which real-life considerations and complications enter into the design of effective incentive systems.

---

[7] In the economic theory of incentives, it is typically assumed that B offers a compensation scheme to A on a take-it-or-leave-it basis. This fits best in a context where B is dealing with a number of A's at once; for instance, when B is the employer and A is one of many employees. But, of course, the compensation arrangement between A and B can be subject to negotiation between the two parties, or it can be that A takes the lead in designing the compensation scheme.

Eliminating (Or, At Least, Ameliorating) Extraneous Risk: Benchmarking and Tournaments

As a more-or-less general rule (which means it isn't quite a logical truth in all cases, but it holds in most), the less "noise" between the actions taken by the employee and the observed outcomes on which incentives are based, the closer the employer can come to having effective incentives. That is, *according to this theory*, you can have better incentives if you base the incentives on measures of employee performance that are relatively less noisy.[8]

So, if you are going to implement this sort of incentive scheme for your employees, you should think very hard about the risks they can't control but, perhaps, you can directly reduce. For instance, Safelite, when implementing PPP, improved its scheduling/dispatch function as well as its warehouse operations. In a worker-paced manufacturing process, increased work-in-process inventory can decrease the chances of work starvation.

Two techniques for "reducing" extraneous risk involve relative comparisons of performance. Suppose you operate a Honda dealership, and you wish to motivate your salesforce. The natural measures of how well each salesperson has done are the number of cars sold and the price/margin that is achieved in those sales. These measures are, of course, noisy reflections of how hard and well a particular salesperson has done in selling; for instance, he may have been unlucky in the draw of customers to whom he was assigned. The cars he may be trying to sell may be a hard sell, given some new model brought out by the competition. And when the local/national economy is doing poorly, consumers may be generally less inclined to buy new cars.

There isn't much one can do to about the luck of the draw when it comes to customers. But the local/national economy for this Honda salesperson is the same as the local/national economy for the nearby Toyota dealership. So by *benchmarking* the performance of a Honda salesperson against the overall sales of Toyotas, you can eliminate this sort of "noise," at least to some extent. By this I mean, if sales of Toyotas fall off, achieving the same level of sales of Hondas is more likely to mean a better sales job by the Honda salesperson, so his incentive reward should be higher. Or, put a bit more negatively, if you see sales of Toyotas fall off, you should be less inclined to blame a similar fall-off in the performance of your Honda salesperson on his lack of sales effort/quality, and his incentive compensation should be adjusted accordingly.

But what if Toyota introduces a new model that sells like hotcakes and, accordingly, depresses the sales of a competing Honda model? A Honda salesperson is not responsible for this decline in sales, and benchmarking against Toyota sales only compounds the "noise." The best benchmark you can find for a specific Honda salesperson is then the performance of other Honda sales-

---

[8] I emphasize *according to this theory* because competing theories of motivation based in social psychology lead to a very different conclusion. I'll get to those at the end of this section.

persons. They are selling the same vehicles, in the same economy. So maybe you want to benchmark how one of your salespersons does against the performance of Honda salespersons nationwide, or statewide, or even in your own dealership.

Indeed, when you benchmark one of your employees' performances against the performances of your other employees, and when in addition the "pot" of prizes is held fixed relative to their overall performance, you have moved from *benchmarking* to *tournament-style* compensation; for instance, where the individual who sells the most each month gets a prize, or the top 10% of salespeople do.

Benchmarking and tournament-style compensation can be very fruitfully employed to cancel noise, but there are two important caveats: First, to the extent that success by one employee can involve help (or harm) from others—if, say, one salesperson can take actions that help or harm the prospects of another for making a sale—benchmarking the first employee against the second gives the first no incentive to help and even some incentive to harm the second. The more interdependent are the efforts of the employees, the less successful benchmarking/tournaments is apt to be.

And, a very common form of benchmarking involves benchmarking the performance of an individual, or a group, against how that individual or group performed in an earlier period: "Your target for the next six months is to increase your sales by 10% over what you achieved last period." This induces the so-called *ratchet effect*, which I discuss a bit later under *Dynamics*.

Interdependence and Team-Based Incentive Schemes

When employee interdependence is very strong, it can be difficult to get good measures of how well any single employee has performed, making individual-based incentives less useful if not impossible. It is common in such circumstances to resort to team-based incentive schemes: everyone in a work team gets a bonus or some other prize if the team as a whole performs well. I'm sure that, if you have any experience with this sort of team-based compensation, you can anticipate the major difficulty: the larger the team, the greater the risk that one or more members of the team will try to free-ride on the efforts of other team members. Control of this sort of free-riding is most often accomplished (or, at least, is tried to be accomplished) through peer pressure within the team. And peer pressure can work wonders in this regard. But this raises some significant questions about team composition: since peer pressure is typically based on social rewards—that is, an underperformer is socially shunned by members of the team—do you want to form teams that are socially coherent (or, in other words, less diverse along demographic lines)? Perhaps you want to let teams form themselves. But if you do that, there is likely to be some tendency to the most able forming a team, leaving less able folks to form their own teams; how equitable is that?

Team-based compensation, used for incentive purposes—and whether you intend team-based compensation to have incentive implications or not, it will have incentive implications!—can be tricky.[9]

Dynamics

It is typical for the performance of an employee to be measured periodically, which compounds his effort choices over the full time frame of the review period. For instance, at Safelite, the review period was one work week. Insofar as the employee has a sense (at least) of how good are the results he is generating, you can get some very bad consequences for incentives near the end of the review period.

Suppose, for instance, a Safelite technician starts the week ready and willing to install enough windshields to get himself into PPP territory. Suppose that it takes twenty windshields, or four a day, to do this. And suppose that, for whatever reason, by the end of Tuesday he has managed only three. To get to twenty may take a huge effort; indeed, it may be virtually impossible. So perhaps, at this point, the technician decides to take it easy for the rest of the week and collect the guarantee. Safelite in response to this might decide to make the review period a day instead of a week. But this can exacerbate the problem: in particular, imagine a call that comes in at the end of the workday, when work has been scarce and all the technicians have decided to settle for the daily guarantee. A call to the customer with the message "We'll get to you first thing tomorrow" could conceivably result.

Tournament schemes, where the parties involved can keep track of how well they are doing relative to the "competition," can give rise to particularly perverse dynamics. Suppose the salesperson of the month—the salesperson with the most sales recorded—gets a bonus of a weekend trip to a spa or an extra 10% of total pay. Suppose, as is often the case, that to heighten the sense of competition, daily sales results are prominently posted. Then:

1. If, by the 20th of the month, one salesperson holds a sizeable lead over everyone else, everyone else may decide to slack off or even put off their best sales leads until the start of a new month. And the leader, seeing everyone else slack off, feels less pressure and does so as well.

2. Or suppose that, by the 25th of the month, it is clear that two or three salespersons are in a tight race. To win the race, what promises to customers might they make, and what deals might they cut?

The way to avoid these problems is clear: the rule that transforms results

---

[9] For a more complete discussion of the ins and outs of team-based compensation, see Baron and Kreps, *Strategic Human Resources: Frameworks for General Managers* (New York: Wiley & Sons, 1999) pages 261-8.

into compensation should be "smooth"—avoid jumps—and should rise continuously, so no matter where one is, there is always some incentive to continue to perform. In a tournament scheme, winner-take-all is a bad idea; it is better (on these grounds) to use something closer to benchmarking, where compensation is not based on who came first, second, and third, but by how much each individual beat his or her competition/comparison group.

There are no clear-cut rules about how to defeat these dynamic pathologies. But whenever you put in place an incentive compensation scheme where results are measured over some reasonably long time period, be sure to think hard about the incentives that the scheme will create as the evaluation deadline approaches.

The Ratchet Effect

The *ratchet effect* arises when the performance of individual X (or organization or team Y) is benchmarked against how she (it) performed the period before. If, near the end of a review period, X knows that she has exceeded some "performance threshold" that was set for her, she knows that improving her performance further raises the bar for herself for the next review period. Even if she is rewarded this period for further improvements, weighed against this is the contrary incentive to "ease off" and make next period less onerous for herself. Especially when rewards are discontinuous in performance relative to the previous period—for example, the employee begins to earn a sizable bonus when she beats her previous performance by, say, 5%—she may stop trying once the threshold is surpassed. Indeed, if this involves an individual X, who has a particularly outstanding (or lucky) year (or whatever is the performance period), benchmarking future performance against this outstanding performance may give her the incentive to seek employment elsewhere. She has raised the bar for herself so high, that her current job becomes quite unattractive.

Multitasking

When Safelite moved to PPP, it increased motivation for technicians to do individual jobs speedily. But, as we discussed, there are other aspects or dimensions of quality attached to the job of technician; Safelite, by motivating speed, was to some extend *demotivating* performance along those other dimensions and needed to make up for this with a mixture of carrot and stick forms of motivation.

The general issue is *multitasking*. Jobs typically involve a variety of tasks, and the performance of each task can be measured along a variety of dimensions. Moreover, the issue may not be one of motivating the employee to work hard, but instead to motivate the employee to work on the right tasks in the right way. The employee must choose how to divide his time and effort among the different tasks, and he must decide how much time and attention to give to the different dimensions of a given task. Incentive schemes in most cases do a poor job of balancing the incentives they give to employees in making these choices.

They tend to focus on a subset of the tasks and, for each task, on a subset of the dimensions of quality. And by employing the particular incentive scheme, the employer is sending the unmistakable signal that "since this is what I reward, this is what I want."

Sometimes, the issue can be dealt with by a balanced approach. You want salespersons to make new sales, but you also want them to keep established clients happy. A compensation scheme where bonus payments are based on the number of new sales made can be dysfunctional, unless there is also a reward for the percentage of old clients who "re-up" with continued sales.

Multitasking difficulties arise particularly when a job combines one or more tasks that are easily and relatively noiselessly reflected in outcome measures with one or more tasks the performance of which are hard and noisy to measure. To provide strong motivation, you sharply reward good performance on the easy to measure tasks; with relatively little noise between effort and outcome, you can do this without compromising risk sharing too badly. But then the employee is apt to direct his attention to those tasks where there is a sizeable reward available, ignoring tasks that are hard or noisy to measure.

For an example, consider the notion that teachers should be rewarded based on how their students do on some standardized test, where the "reward" can be positive (a bonus for particularly good performance) or negative (getting fired if your students do poorly). At the same time, teachers are expected to inspire their students to a lifetime of learning. The result is obvious: teachers spend their time teaching to the test, rather than trying to inspire their students.

The "solutions" in cases like this, in theory, are (1) to forgo trying to motivate the easy-to-measure, relatively-less-noisy tasks, so as not to demotivate the harder tasks, or (2) to try to prevent this conflict at the earlier stage of *job design*: Do not bundle into the job held by a single individual this range of tasks (in terms of motivation). Instead, design some jobs that comprise a portfolio of easily motivated/measured tasks, which then are motivated with strong incentive schemes, leaving the harder-to-motivate-and-measure tasks for other jobs entirely.

Subjective Evaluation Ex Post

Multitasking issues are most vicious for jobs that are complex, that require creativity and outside-the-box thinking, and for which desired actions are ambiguous ex ante. These are all, increasingly, the hallmarks of "jobs" for employees in the so-called new economy.

One typically employed fix for the difficulties these jobs present is to resort to ex post subjective reviews of performance: Rather than measure concrete outcomes and give a bonus that is determined by some formula, the boss, or some committee of bosses, looks subjectively at how each employee did ex post and decides what bonus the employee is given. In complex job situations, formulae rarely work and often are dysfunctional, so subjective ex post valuation is about the only viable alternative for administering pay for performance. But such schemes give rise to obvious problems: they motivate employees to spend a lot of time and effort in getting on the good side of the folks who will review their performance, rather than performing. And such schemes can and often do breed strong feelings of injustice on the part of employees, who (somewhat naturally) tend to believe that they did better than a more objective observer concludes.

Screening Effects

A benefit to Safelite of its incentive scheme was that it not only motivated individual technicians to work faster, but also differentially motivated different types of employee and prospective employee, thereby improving the average "quality" of the population of technicians employed by Safelite. This worked both in terms of retention—employees who took advantage of PPP were made happier by the opportunity, so were less liable to depart voluntarily—and in terms of attracting new and ambitious technicians who saw PPP as a good opportunity for themselves. As already noted, careful measurement of the impact of the incentive scheme led to the conclusion that it caused unit labor costs to fall by around 30%, and *half* of that improvement was due to an improvement in the quality of technicians employed.

The point is obvious but important: The way you compensate your employees changes the appeal of working for you differently for different types of employee, and so it changes the characteristics of those who choose to work for you and who stay on the job. This, of course, is a screening effect, very much a part of what we discussed last chapter.

While this is last-chapter material, since it interacts with economic incentives for employees, let me illustrate by answering Problem 20.7. RE/MAX is a large, national real-estate brokerage firm in the United States. Traditionally, realtors working for such agencies receive a base wage and a fraction of the commissions they generate from purchase and sale of properties, in return for which the agency provides offices, clerical assistance, and so forth. RE/MAX pioneered by turning this on its head: Agents at RE/MAX keep 100% of any commissions they generate, and they *pay* RE/MAX for the office space, clerical support, and so forth that they receive. And, in fact, they pay RE/MAX more for these things than they would have to pay if they bought equivalent services on their own.

Why do they pay this extra? Because, by doing so, they are labeled as RE/MAX agents, which is a valuable label. The compensation scheme for RE/MAX agents, relative to the traditional compensation scheme, is attractive to realtors who (a) are more certain of their abilities to make deals, and/or (b) who will work harder to make more deals. (It also is attractive, relatively, to agents who are relatively less risk averse concerning their compensation, but this factor doesn't add to the story.) If you, as a buyer or seller of a house, want a realtor who is more likely to have qualities a and b, you are more likely to find a realtor of this sort among those who work for RE/MAX than from among those who work for, say, Coldwell-Banker. Therefore, a prospective client, looking for an agent who is relatively stronger on these characteristics, looks at "working for RE/MAX" as a signal of these qualities. Since qualities a and b are desirable qualities for a realtor to have—or rather to be perceived by prospective clients as having—realtors with these characteristics are willing to "pay" for the privilege of being labeled a *RE/MAX Agent*; in particular, they are willing to overpay for the services RE/MAX provides them, since doing so gives them the label.

Of course, a *personal* reputation for characteristics a and b, if widely known, is just as good and perhaps even better, reputation-wise, as the label *RE/MAX Agent*, and it doesn't involve overpaying for office space and clerical support. So, one expects, successful RE/MAX agents, as they gain a personal reputation with a clientele, are more likely to go off on their own and establish their own agencies. And, in fact, the data support this hypothesis.

Psychological Considerations

The economic model of behavior that underpins the theory of moral hazard and, in particular, incentives to deal with moral hazards, assumes that more take-home pay or, perhaps, power, promotion, and prestige, are what the individual employee wants. So, to motivate the employee, you provide her with more of these goodies when and if the outcomes you observe indicate that she took the actions you desire.

But employment is not only an economic relationship; it is intensely social. An individual's self image—how she feels about herself—depends on the character of her employment to some extent. Some, and in some cases many, of her social relationships are formed on the job. And her feelings about the job often depend on how she is treated relative to her immediate peers (what social psychologists call *social comparisons*), whether her treatment is consistent with her perceived social status, and how others around her are treated.

Presumably, you know all about this stuff from a course you will have taken (or are taking concurrently) on organizational behavior. The point to be made is that, in designing compensation schemes in general and incentive schemes in particular, you must integrate with the economic considerations of this chapter considerations that come from a more social psychological perspective.

Since this is not a textbook in social psychology, I won't go far down this path; that is someone else's job. Ideally, you should look for a treatment of on-the-job motivation that blends these two disciplinary perspectives.[10] But two

---

[10] Because I believe that such blended treatments of motivation are best, I've written two books taking this approach. One—Baron and Kreps, *ibid.*—is an MBA-level textbook. The second—Kreps, *The Motivation Toolkit*—is a less technical account.

specific considerations are worth mentioning here:

1. Economic theories of incentives—and especially the toy models that you'll find among the problems at the end of this chapter—often stress the design of incentives for the single employee. This one-on-one incentive-design perspective can be appropriate for B2B problems of hidden information (although remember our discussion back in Chapter 5 concerning Toyota and its use of a general reputation). But when it comes to employment, you will usually be thinking about an incentive scheme that fits an entire population of not-altogether-identical employees. One of the strengths of the Safelite compensation scheme is that it provided technicians with a choice of how hard to work, accommodating both ambitious and hard-working technicians but also leaving room for some who are not so ambitious. The economic power of "give them a menu and let them choose" should not be underestimated. But, at the same time, the discussion in Chapter 4 of the "reputational spillovers" from how you treat one employee to the perceptions of other employees is on point. Specifically, a social psychologist will, at this point, warn you to beware perceptions of *procedural* and *distributive* *(in)justice,* a warning well worth heeding.

2. In the discussion of multitasking issues, I essentially asserted that, as the job becomes more complex, comprising more and different tasks, as more creativity and proaction is desired, and as the ambiguity of what is wanted increases, reliance on economic incentives for motivational purposes is decreasingly effective. Since those characteristics of a job are increasingly descriptive of key jobs for firms in the so-called new economy, this is a pretty bleak picture. While this is an economics textbook, I am constrained to point out that social psychology has some very different theories about how to motivate employees, theories that have their own dangers but that, on balance, seem to me to fit better with jobs of the sort just described. (And, with this, I refer you back to footnote 10.)

Executive Summary

- When a party to a transaction takes an action that affects the value of the transaction to the other side, a potential *moral hazard* exists: Will the action chosen by the first party be favorable or detrimental to the second party? Means for dealing with problems of moral hazard include good will and honesty on the part of the first party, contractual enforcement of an agreed-to action, observability of the action chosen ex post and a desire on the part of the first party to sustain a long-term relationship or a favorable reputation (see Chapters 3, 4, and 5), and—the topic of this chapter—direct and explicit incentives, based on some observable measure or signal of the action chosen.

- The fundamental tradeoff in incentive arises when the party taking the action influences (by her choice of action) but doesn't completely control the observed measures that determine her compensation. In such cases, and especially where the second party is much less risk averse than the first, efficient risk sharing pushes in the direction of shielding the first party from uncertainty in her compensation, while motivating her pushes in the direction of making her compensation sensitive to the observed results of her efforts.

- Beyond this basic trade-off of risk sharing (and shielding) versus motivation, incentives give rise to a host of complications and extensions. Incentive schemes should be robust to the characteristics of the individual being motivated and the situation in which motivation is being applied. Incentive schemes often screen as well as motivate. Tournament schemes and benchmarking can, if used carefully, help control the risk to which the motivated individual is subject. In some instances, group-based incentive schemes can be employed. Dynamic aspects of incentive schemes (where the choices of the first individual are taken over time) should be carefully considered. Most incentive schemes are found in situations where the individual being motivated has a multidimensional choice of "effort." The impact of a given incentive scheme on the full choice of the individual—not only how hard to work but on what tasks in particular—must be carefully considered. And explicit incentive schemes have social psychological and sociological effects that should not be ignored.

Problems

What economists (think they) know about incentive theory derives from some empirical work and, even more, from theoretical analysis of toy models. The models become quite complex as more real-world details are added, but you are in good shape for going through the "first generation" of these models. The following problems give you that opportunity, if you wish to do so.

And, if you make your way through these problems and want to go further, in the *Online Supplement* I take you through a "second-generation" problem in which there are two employees and the employer tries some benchmarking of one against the other. (Since what each employee does depends on how the employee feels the other employee will act, this brings you to issues of Nash equilibria in effort levels and a host of very interesting phenomena.)

21.1 Change the FECBUS/Beantown Casualty story of Problem 20.2 as follows. All students at FECBUS are identical in their chances of getting a job, but to land a job, they must put in an effort. They choose between two effort levels: They can try somewhat hard, which provides them with a summer job with probability 0.7; and they can try not at all, in which case they might still get a summer job, but (only) with probability 0.1.

A summer job pays a stipend of $30,000. Each student is an expected-utility maximizer, and the utility they maximize is (in this problem) a function of two variables, x and e: The variable x is their net income from a summer job (which is either $30,000 or $0), less any premium they pay for summer-income insurance, plus any reimbursement they receive from Beantown Casualty if they buy an insurance policy. The variable e reflects the level of effort they put in: $e = 30$ if they try somewhat hard, and $e = 0$ if don't try at all. The utility function (whose expectation they maximize) is then $u(x, e) = \sqrt{x + 10{,}000} - e$.

Beantown Casualty is risk neutral.

(a) If Beantown Casualty offers no insurance policies, how will students at FECBUS behave vis-à-vis summer jobs? Is it optimal for them to try somewhat hard or not at all? What is their expected utility?

(b) Suppose Beantown Casualty could write an insurance policy that specified in an enforceable manner the level of effort the student would choose. Because of the good nature of the head of Beantown Casualty, an alum of FECBUS, (or because Beantown Casualty is regulated), policies written by Beantown must be actuarially fair: The premium charged must equal the expected payout on the policy. What is the efficient policy that Beantown could write that specifies that the student doesn't try? What is the efficient policy that Beantown could write that specifies that the student tries somewhat hard? (Since Beantown writes policies that net $0 expected profit, another way to say this is: For each effort level, which actuarially fair policy written by Beantown makes the student as well off as possible?)

(c) If Beantown offers the efficient contract you found in part b for "tries somewhat hard," but cannot contractually specify the student's effort level, what happens?

(d) In an effort to provide the student with some insurance, Beantown considers partial insurance. It will collect a premium P from the student and, if the student fails to land a job, the student recovers X from Beantown, where $P = 0.3X$ if this policy induces the student to try hard and $P = 0.9X$ if the policy induces the student not to try. Looking only at integer multiples of $1000 for values of P, what value of P is best for the student?

(e) Suppose we add a third effort level: The student can try super hard, which guarantees her a job (that is, she gets a job with probability 1.0). For this effort level, $e = 55$. If this effort level is added to the mix, what is the answer to part d?

21.2 This problem takes you to the precise solution of a very standard (toy) model of incentive compensation. We imagine a salesperson whom you have employed to make one sales call. If he succeeds, you will make $60,000 in additional profit. If he fails, you will make $0. His chances of success depend on his level of effort: He can kill himself, in which case he makes the sale with probability 0.5; he can try hard, in which case there is probability 0.4 that he makes the sale; he can try, but not hard, in which case there is probability 0.25 of a sale; and he can loaf, in which case he makes the sale with probability 0.05.

You are risk neutral.

The salesperson is risk averse. He maximizes the expected value of a utility function $u(x, e) = \sqrt{x} - e$, where x is his "wage payment" from you, and e is a measure of his (dis)utility of effort: $e = 40$ if he kills himself; $e = 20$ if he tries hard; $e = 10$ if he tries, but not hard; and $e = 0$ if he loafs. To convince him to work for you, you must offer him a compensation agreement that gives him an expected utility of 100. You cannot specify contractually his level of effort: If you want him to work at any one of the levels above loafing, you must provide incentives for him to do so. So the contracts you consider are of the form: A base wage w is paid regardless of outcome and, in addition, he is paid a bonus b if he makes the sale.

Subject to the constraint that he must be willing to take the contract and to the condition that he, and not you, choose the level of effort he puts in, what contract should you offer him that makes you as well off (net of paying him) as possible?

Note: this is not an easy thing to do if you've never seen a problem like this solved. Consult the *Online Supplement* for a substantial how-to-do-it (followed by the full solution).

Problems 21.3 and 21.4 use the techniques used to solve 21.2 but in different contexts, and you should try them only after you are clear on how to solve 21.2. Since 21.3 involves casualty insurance, comparison with Problem 21.1 is natural: The major difference is that in Problem 21.1, we assume that the insurance company—either by choice or legal constraint—must write an actuarially fair policy. In Problem 21.3, the insurance company is out to make as much (expected) profit as it can, by writing and selling a specific insurance policy.

21.3   As an insurance underwriter, you have been asked to write a policy that insures a factory against loss by fire for a period of 1 year. If the factory has a fire, it will be a total loss of $8 million. The owner of the factory is an expected utility maximizer, with (gross) utility function $\sqrt{x + 1 \text{ million}}$, where x is the value of the factory at year's end; that is, $x = \$8$ million if there is no fire and $x = \$0$ if there is a fire. Your insurance company is risk neutral.

The chance of a fire depends on whether the owner of the factory takes due care. If he does not, the chance of a fire over the 1-year period is 0.05. If he does take due care, the chance of a fire over the 1-year period is 0.01. To take due care is psychologically wearing on the owner and lowers his expected utility by

50. That is, the factory owner's overall utility depends on both x and on his decision whether to take due care or not, with

$$u(x, \text{no due care}) = \sqrt{x + 1 \text{ million}} - 0 \quad \text{and}$$
$$u(x, \text{due care}) = \sqrt{x + 1 \text{ million}} - 50.$$

(a) If the factory owner cannot get insurance for the building, will he choose to take due care or not? What will be his overall expected utility?

(b) The insurance company wishes to maximize its expected profit from writing insurance for this factory owner. If it could contractually specify the level of care taken by the factory owner, what policy or contract would it write? (When the factory owner takes insurance, x in his utility function is adjusted down by the amount of any premiums he pays and up by any indemnification he receives from the insurance company in the event of fire.)

(c) Suppose the insurance company cannot contractually specify the level of care taken by the factory owner. Suppose as well that, in the pursuit of efficient risk sharing, the insurance company is determined to insure the building fully; that is, it will write a policy that pays the owner $8 million in the event of a fire. What is the best (profit-maximizing) policy of this sort the insurance company can write?

(d) The insurance company decides to investigate insurance policies with a deductible. That is, it will charge a premium P and, in the event of a fire, reimburse the factory owner $8 million less some prespecified deductible amount. What is the best (profit-maximizing) policy of this sort that the insurance company can write? Please do this by hand and not using Excel.

(e) Suppose that taking due care does not involve a "psychological cost" that lowers gross utility but instead comes at a dollar cost of, say, $100,000. That is, in the factory owner's utility function $\sqrt{x + 1 \text{ million}}$, x includes the value of the building, less any premiums paid for insurance, plus any indeminification from the insurance company in the event of fire, less $100,000 if the owner takes due care. This change in formulation makes the problem harder to solve (by hand). Why? Do not grind through the numbers unless you want practice using spreadsheets; simply redo the four previous parts of the problem with this reformulation, until you get to calculations that are too hard to do by hand.

21.4 An entrepreneur has a venture that will make either $100 million or $0. The chance that this venture will make $100 million depends on the effort level expended by the entrepreneur: If she tries hard, the chance of the $100 million outcome is 0.1. If she does not try hard, the chance of this outcome is 0.02. This entrepreneur is risk averse, with utility function

$$\sqrt{x} - \text{disutility of effort,}$$

where the disutility of effort is 0 if the entrepreneur does not try hard and 500 if she does.

(a) Assuming this entrepreneur bears all the risk of this venture, will she try hard or not? What will be her expected utility, net of the disutility of effort (if any)?

(b) A risk-neutral venture capitalist is prepared to support this venture. Specifically, the venture capitalist will pay the entrepreneur a base amount B up front, in return for which the venture capitalist will retain X out of the $100 million the venture generates, if the venture succeeds. Assuming this venture capitalist is the entrepreneur's only alternative to going it alone (doing whatever you determined the answer was in part a), and assuming the venture capitalist can make part of his contract with the entrepreneur a specification of her effort level, what is the optimal contract of this sort for the venture capitalist to write? What will be the venture capitalist's net expected monetary value with this contract?

(c) Unhappily, the venture capitalist cannot contractually specify the effort level of the entrepreneur. If the venture capitalist wishes to motivate the entrepreneur to try hard, he must do this with the terms B and X in the contract he provides. What is the best contract for the venture capitalist to offer the entrepreneur, assuming that if the entrepreneur does not accept this contract, she is stuck going it alone on this venture?

Index